Music in the Twentieth Century

GENERAL EDITOR Arnold Whittall

The twelve-note music of Anton Webern

Music in the Twentieth Century

GENERAL EDITOR Arnold Whittall

Published titles

1. Robert Orledge, *Satie the composer*

The twelve-note music of Anton Webern

Old forms in a new language

KATHRYN BAILEY

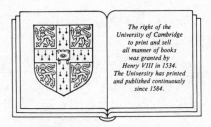

The right of the
University of Cambridge
to print and sell
all manner of books
was granted by
Henry VIII in 1534.
The University has printed
and published continuously
since 1584.

CAMBRIDGE UNIVERSITY PRESS

Cambridge

New York   Port Chester

Melbourne   Sydney

Published by the Press Syndicate of the University of Cambridge
The Pitt Building, Trumpington Street, Cambridge CB2 1RP
40 West 20th Street, New York, NY 10011, USA
10 Stamford Road, Oakleigh, Melbourne 3166, Australia

First published 1991

Printed in Great Britain at the University Press, Cambridge

British Library cataloguing in publication data
Bailey, Kathryn
  The twelve-note music of Anton Webern: old forms in a new language.
  – (Music in the twentieth century; v. 2)
  1. Austrian music. Webern, Anton – Biographies
  I. Title   II. Series
  780′.92′4

Library of Congress cataloguing in publication data
Bailey, Kathryn.
  The twelve-note music of Anton Webern: old forms in a new language
  / Kathryn Bailey.
    p.   cm. – (Music in the twentieth century: 2)
  Includes bibliographical references (p.   )
  ISBN 0 521 39088 5
  1. Webern, Anton, 1883–1945 – Criticism and interpretation.
  2. Twelve-tone system.   I. Title.
  II. Title: 12-note music of Anton Webern.   III. Series
ML410.W33834   1991
781.2′68′092 – dc20   89–70843   CIP

ISBN 0 521 39088 5

CE

to Derrick, in gratitude

Contents

Contents

Acknowledgements

As must often be the case in a book of this kind, the ideas that form the basis of the following study have evolved over a number of years of teaching. I have my students of the last twenty years – and the Universities of British Columbia and Western Ontario, which brought us all together – to thank for the discipline whose results lie in the pages ahead: had it not been necessary for me to organize and examine my own thoughts on the music of Webern very carefully in order that they should survive the scrutiny of my students, this book would almost certainly never have come to exist. I am grateful in addition for financial assistance given to me during the course of the project by the University of Western Ontario and by the Social Sciences and Humanities Research Council of Canada.

I was able to examine the first of the Webern sketchbooks on microfilm, thanks to the Pierpont Morgan Library of New York City, which owns the book. The remaining sketchbooks were made available to me for study through the generosity of Paul Sacher, who gave me a stipend enabling me to spend three months at the Paul Sacher Stiftung in Basel; I am grateful to Ingrid Westen and the librarians at the Stiftung for their help and good humour during these months, help that extended at times considerably beyond the subject of my study.

I am very much indebted to a few people who gave enormously of their time and talents in helping me to produce computer realizations of complicated and exacting illustrations – the charts of Chapter 1 and Appendix IV and the musical examples come to mind especially – and of their patience in coping with my frequent computer-generated frustration. Terence Bailey, David Lenson, Paul Merkley and Richard Parks all gave help of this sort to a degree that can only be described as saintly. The final copy was made possible through the kindness of Stephen Farmer, whose printer was commandeered for the occasion. I am grateful to Paul and Lora Merkley and to Terence Bailey for their good humour and patience during a three-week work holiday in August 1988 in which the usual pressures of running a household were simply set aside. I also thank my daughter Sara for her assumption of my domestic responsibilities as well as her cheerful acceptance of the necessity of making her own entertainment during our time together in Switzerland in 1989.

Terence Bailey read many parts of the work in its earlier stages; Arnold Whittall read the whole manuscript at various times. The thoughtful suggestions made by both, and their encouragement, were very much appreciated. Finally, I cannot adequately express my thanks to Derrick Puffett for the immense amount of time and energy he has devoted to the improvement of this project, or for the continued moral support and practical help he gave during its final stages.

Earlier versions of some of the material in the book have appeared in *Music Analysis, Tempo, Current Musicology, Journal of Musicology, Canadian Association of University Schools of Music Journal, Canada Music Book* and *Studies in Music from the University of Western Ontario.* I am grateful to the publishers of these journals for giving me an opportunity to try out some of the ideas as they developed. The music examples are reproduced by permission of Universal Edition Ltd.

Conventions in the text

It has been my wish to produce a study of Webern's twelve-note music that will be intelligible to anyone who is musically literate, not to music theorists alone. I have avoided as much as possible the very technical language of recent music theory; such theoretical terms as I have found it necessary to use appear in a glossary at the end of the book. When describing intervals I have preferred conventional terminology to the language of interval classes because I believe this is familiar to more people. In the context of twelve-note composition, which assumes equal temperament, however, the qualifying *major* and *minor* take on their literal meanings: *large* and *small*. Since the sound of an interval is not affected by its spelling, the necessity for the terms *augmented* and *diminished* disappears. Therefore, although the familiar names are used, these refer to absolute size: any interval comprising four semitones is identified as a major third, regardless of spelling, and so on. (The German manner, and therefore Webern's, of identifying intervals – *kleine Terz, große Terz* and so on – avoids the tonal/modal association of the English names.) Similarly, I make frequent references to tonic analogues, because in most of his twelve-note music Webern consciously adhered in one way or another to the requirements of the conventional tonal structures into which he moulded his work. This is clear from statements such as the following by Webern, quoted by Willi Reich in *The Path to the New Music* (p. 54): 'The original form and pitch of the row occupy a position akin to that of the "main key" in earlier music; the recapitulation will naturally return to it. We end "in the same key!" This analogy with earlier formal construction is quite consciously fostered ...' He always manages this in an abstract fashion, however; whenever I speak of a tonic analogue, or perhaps simply of a tonic, I do not intend to imply that I believe these to be tonal works. *Analogue* is the critical word; certain levels of transposition or certain combinations of rows are used in ways that are in some sense parallel to the conventional use of tonic and dominant, but tonal centres do not result.

In an attempt to reduce the visual complexity of the scores, which, as everyone knows, is considerable, I have omitted natural signs altogether whenever these are cited. In reading the musical examples, therefore, it must be understood that any note not directly preceded by an accidental is natural. This policy has necessitated the insertion of a few accidentals in the case of directly repeated coloured notes; in this situation Webern normally did not repeat the sign. I have followed his practice of omission only when the notes are tied. The sketches are reproduced as they appear, with naturals, except where otherwise indicated. To the same end all parts of all the examples are written at sounding pitch, except for the tenor part in choral works, which is notated in the usual way (one octave higher than it sounds). All transcriptions of the sketches are my own. Most letter names in the text refer either to pitch classes or to pitches that are easily identified (the only C in the bar, for example); these are in upper case. When it has seemed necessary to designate specific pitches, I have used Helmholtz notation, in which c is in the bass clef and C an octave below, middle C is represented as c^1, the note an octave higher as c^2, and so on.

Because I call the four row forms Prime, Retrograde, Inversion and Retrograde Inversion, they are represented by the letters P, R, I and RI respectively; the level of transposition of each row form is given in a subscript following the identifying letter. The untransposed Prime and Inversion begin on the same pitch; the exact retrogrades of these are the untransposed Retrograde and Retrograde Inversion. After the manner of the serialists I call this level 0 and label successive ascending semitone transpositions 1–11. To the twelve notes of the row I assign the numbers 1–12. (This is unlike the practice of the serialists, who for the most part use order numbers 0–11.)

Introduction

> The primary task of analysis is to show the functions of the individual sections: the thematic side is secondary.[1]

In the autumn of 1924, at the age of forty, Anton Webern wrote a piano piece of seventeen bars based on a twelve-note row[2] and in so doing unconsciously launched what was to become one of the most contentious movements of this century. Although Webern is not credited with the formulation of twelve-note technique, it was his style rather than Schoenberg's that the later serialists saw as suggesting the intense organization that characterized their music of the 1950s and 60s. As the result of the unsolicited but outspoken admiration of composers like Boulez and Stockhausen, Webern himself, after his death, came to be associated in the public consciousness with the most progressive aspects of integral serialism. Whether he would have welcomed this role is not clear. His comments about himself and his music, as transmitted by Willi Reich and others, show an unswerving commitment to tradition, to the idea that in contributing to the 'New Music' he was also upholding values of the past. This recognition of the essentially traditional aspect of his twelve-note music forms the basis of the present study.

The period under consideration spans the years from 1924 to 1943 and embraces both instrumental and vocal music. The accompanied solo songs (four sets in all) were written in two short periods separated by nearly a decade. Six songs composed mainly between July and the end of October of 1925 (only the first was written earlier, in the autumn of 1924), on anonymous traditional, folk and liturgical texts, became Webern's Opp. 17 and 18; another group of six, on texts by his friend Hildegard Jone, were written between February 1933 and June 1934 and designated Opp. 23 and 25.[3] (From this time onwards, Webern would set only Jone texts in his works for voices.) On both occasions the composition of solo songs was followed directly by a work for voices and instrumental ensemble, these works thereby occupying similarly spaced positions in his career: the two songs, Op. 19, on texts by Goethe, were written in 1925–6, the one-movement cantata, *Das Augenlicht* (Op. 26), in 1935. The two more ambitious works in this vein – the cantatas for solo voices, choir and orchestra, Opp. 29 and 31 – come from the last years of Webern's life: the first was written between 1 July 1938 and the end of November 1939, the second from June 1941 until November 1943. The remaining works from these years are instrumental. Only one is for a solo instrument: the Op. 27 Variations for Piano, begun in October 1935 and finished in November 1936. Four chamber works span all but the extreme ends of the twelve-note years: the Op. 20 String Trio of 1926–7; the Op. 22 Quartet for clarinet, violin, saxophone and piano, which followed immediately, in 1928–30; the Op. 24 Concerto for nine instruments, which was written intermittently and apparently with great difficulty over a period of nearly four years from January 1931 to September 1934, during which time work was interrupted periodically for the composition of the six songs, Opp. 23 and 25; and the Op. 28 String Quartet, written between November 1936 and March 1938. There are two works for orchestra, one dating from the beginning of the twelve-note period, the other from the end: the Symphony, Op. 21, composed in 1927–8 and the Variations for Orchestra, Op. 30, of 1940.

Anyone analysing unfamiliar music is predisposed to see as more significant either those features that are idiosyncratic or those that show evidence of the continuation of tradition. The analyst who concentrates on the idiosyncrasies of a work will judge it to be unconventional or even revolutionary, while one who sees familiar axioms behind the innovations will perceive the same work within a traditional context. Not all music, of course, allows both interpretations. An examination of any one of several Haydn rondos will reveal few features that make it notably different from others of the same period, while the most careful study of Boulez's *Structures* will produce little that can be explained in traditional terms. But because most Western music lends itself to both perceptions, individual bias is a significant factor in the determination of historical opinion. Ideally, a work should be seen from both perspectives. Analysis is a human activity, however, and an analyst's predisposition in this respect is surely of the same nature as a preference for gin or whisky, the chief difference being that most people are aware of their taste preferences, whereas aesthetic bias seems to be in many cases unconscious. The failure to recognize its existence leads to the too easy acceptance of one's own analysis or that of someone else with a similar bias as conclusive. In my opinion the world's view of Webern has been flawed by an accumulation of work from like-minded and mutually supportive analysts.

All the movements of Webern's twelve-note instrumental music follow traditional models. Webern was, after all, the product of a formal European musical education, and it is not surprising that the works of his mature period should be cast in those forms upon which his musical awakening had been based. His return to the forms of the eighteenth and nineteenth centuries after the aphoristic, non-traditional forms of his middle years indicates his faith in the validity of a manner of organization that some of his more radical contemporaries (though not his immediate colleagues in Vienna) were simultaneously rejecting. It is my intention to examine the ways in which he preserves these forms and their essential arguments within a system whose imperatives would seem, on the face of things, inimical in many respects to those of tradition. This aspect of his composition has been largely neglected in the literature devoted to his twelve-note music.

At first, with the discovery of Webern at Darmstadt and the subsequent extension of his techniques by Stockhausen and Boulez, analysis tended to concentrate on the nature and properties of his rows and on the perceived serial organization of parameters other than pitch. More recently, with the vastly expanded interest in analysis on both sides of the Atlantic (but especially in the United States), interest has focused on the smallest details of pitch organization, with Allen Forte's set-theoretical approach to analysis, originally conceived as a means of analysing atonal music (i.e., non-tonal music written outside the restraints of twelve-note composition), being turned to the analysis of twelve-note works by such younger writers as Martha M. Hyde and Christopher F. Hasty. I see in both these attitudes – the search for signs of integral serialism and the preoccupation with relationships of pitch – a major oversight; while I am not indifferent to Webern's originality, I consider his reinterpretation of familiar formal structures to have been one of his most significant contributions to the history of atonal music.

Webern's allure as a model for the serialists was enhanced by his asceticism, the spartan sound that seemed to match their own aspirations; Berg and Schoenberg were much less congenial to them. What excited them particularly, however (and what was probably easier to write about), was his interest in mathematics and numerical relationships, together with a pre-dilection for symmetry. (It is ironic that the only formally educated historian of the Vienna triumvirate should have been the one to whom the following generation of intensely serial – and anti-traditional – composers looked as their mentor.) The first articles on Webern were almost exclusively preoccu-pied with statistics. Conspicuous among early publications was *Die Reihe*, Vol. 2,[4] containing such articles as Armin Klammer's stultifyingly thorough statistical survey of the third movement of Op. 27 ('our investigation will not take in the thematic structure of the piece, since that is something quite foreign to serial thought, and has nothing to do with Webern's personal achievement'),[5] Herbert Eimert's study of the first movement of the Op. 28 Quartet ('one may analyse only what is in the score and manifest as sound; concepts introduced from outside help little, and are none the better for being taken from the golden treasury of fugue and sonata')[6] and Stockhausen's analysis of the second movement of the same work in terms of information and experiential time.[7]

In subsequent analyses from the 1960s and early 70s, one begins to encounter the specialized language that seems to have become more or less *de rigueur* in the world of music theorists. We are told, for example, about Op. 22 that

> The set is not symmetric in design. Interval content equivalence as a result of larger than dyadic partitioning pertains only to the first two trichords.

And that

> Multiple presentation of set forms does not rely on combinatorial relations, but in some instances set choice can be traced to particular degrees of relatedness of the forms, depending on the compositional intent.[8]

The latter is an unnecessarily periphrastic way of saying that while rows to be used together were not chosen because they are combinatorial they do not appear to have been selected at random (a fairly unremarkable observation, in spite of its apparent complexity). When reading articles that progress in this manner, one feels like a ferret burrowing after a particularly elusive rodent, which may or may not turn out to be a filling meal. Another author describes an unusual aspect of the row of Op. 30 in the following way:

> Set instances related by t_2 combine in a unique manner...The order nos. 5–11 of Pt_0 combined with order nos. 0–6 of Pt_{10} form a minimum aggregate. The order of this minimum aggregate is the set instance related by t_5.[9]

The relationship being described here is simply this: in any two rows related as P_0–P_{10}, the last two notes of the first are the first two of the second; and in rows related as P_0–P_5 the last seven notes of the first are the same as the first seven of the second ($P_0/11$–$12 = P_{10}/1$–2; $P_0/6$–$12 = P_5/1$–7).

In his love affair with jargon, the contemporary theorist often seems to ignore the parallel existence of ordinary English. This leads to results such as Brian Fennelly's unhappy reference to row elision as 'terminal coupling'[10] (copulation with the gravest consequences?). Finally, the didactic zeal of the modern writer seems to have superseded any aspirations he may have had to literary style or even basic grammar. (How often, for example, we are told about what is occurring 'on the largest level'!) The insistence on a highly specialized language and the concomitant neglect of literary style have restricted the readership of the essay in music analysis. This is particularly unfortunate in an age when the complexities of the music itself have already caused the composer and his creation to be isolated from the educated listening public. I prefer to describe the music of Webern in conventional terms, using the English equivalent of the language that was current at the end of the nineteenth century and that Webern himself used, both in his scores and sketches and in the analysis and description of his works. This is the language used by Tovey, Rosen, Cone and others who write in English about music rather than theory, and a language that most readers will find familiar.

The substance of the book is contained in Parts II and III, comprising a series of analytical chapters on specific works. These chapters cannot stand alone, however; any attempt to rationalize formal structure without a knowledge of the row and its properties and of the way in which it is used is specious, since the two aspects of any twelve-note work are interdependent. Arnold Whittall has called this one-dimensional sort of analysis 'analysis in spite of serialism', whose 'worst fault is that it completely fails to consider the music as deriving from a particular set with particular properties'.[11] Thus the need for the first two chapters of Part I, which comprise a preamble to what I consider to be the main body of the work. These deal with the rows, or sets, themselves and with what I call 'row topography': the manner in which they are combined. The third chapter of Part I is devoted to another of Webern's favourite techniques, canon. Parts II and III present the analyses. Here it seemed to me that my purpose was best served by organizing the material by topic rather than by opus, even though this resulted in the physical separation, not only of the examination of the several movements of a single work, but of the discussion of various aspects of the same movement as well. In order to minimize the difficulties arising from this fragmentation, the index at the end of the book gives the location of all references to each work. In using this format, I have tried to emphasize the continuity at the heart of Webern's use of specific formal models and to make evident the progression to be seen in his handling of certain techniques – canon, in particular.

Although the study will, I hope, be seen to be thorough within the limits I have set, it is not intended to be comprehensive. The initial limitation is that only published twelve-note works are considered; the row technique of all of these is discussed in Part I. Within this field, my purpose is to examine Webern's use of canon and his atonal adaptation of instrumental tonal structures. Obviously, some works have more to contribute than others in one or other of these respects; a few are thereby eliminated from consideration altogether. The works prior to Op. 20, and the songs Opp. 23 and 25, fall in this latter category and therefore do not reappear after Chapters 1 and 2. This is by no means intended to imply that they are in any way inferior; they simply are not organized in the same way as the instrumental music and therefore offer little insight into Webern's attitudes towards traditional forms. Their construction has much more in common with the continuously developing variation of the pre-twelve-note works than with that of their immediate neighbours. Naturally I have not attempted to deal with all the music in the same way; the nature of each movement has dictated the particular emphasis in its analysis. It is expected that the reader will have scores available; although musical examples are provided, in some cases the analysis will be properly understood only if the score of the entire movement can be consulted.

I have not recounted the circumstances surrounding the composition of the works under consideration or attempted to supply any sort of thorough chronology, because this information is already available; the reader is referred particularly to Hans and Rosaleen Moldenhauer's book, *Anton von Webern: A Chronicle of His Life and Work*,[12] and Roger Smalley's three-part article on Webern's sketches, which deals with aspects of the composition of Opp. 24, 22 and 20 respectively.[13] Neither is the present work intended as a study of the manuscripts and sketches, though I have examined these in the course of its preparation.[14] It has been my intention to present a detailed analysis of each of the twelve-note works, Opp. 20–31 (with the exception of Opp. 23 and 25, as noted earlier), with three types of structure in mind: row structure, canonic structure and formal structure. I do not know of another book with this objective.

Although there are several books in English that deal in a historical and anecdotal way with Webern's creative output – the most familiar is Kolneder[15] – none analyses the twelve-note works on anything beyond a superficial level. The most thorough of the analytical works published in German is Heinrich Deppert's *Studien zur Kompositionstechnik im instrumentalen Spätwerk Anton Weberns*,[16] but, as the title indicates, the works with voices are not included. Moreover, Deppert is not concerned with traditional structural models. The complement to Deppert's work is Dorothea Beckmann's *Sprache und Musik im Vokalwerk Anton Weberns: Die Konstruktion des Ausdrucks*,[17] but, again as the title indicates, Beckmann is more concerned with various aspects of text setting and expression than with canon and formal structure. Two quite lengthy studies – Friedhelm Döhl's *Weberns Beitrag zur Stilwende der neuen Musik*[18] and Wolfgang Martin Stroh's *Historische Legitimation als kompositorisches Problem*[19] – are, in general, of a more philosophical than analytical nature, even though Döhl, in the course of his study, presents a discussion of the nature of Webern's rows,[20] thorough analyses of selected works (Opp. 21, 22/i, 24/i, 27)[21] and an examination of specific aspects of Opp. 28/i and 30.[22] I will allow Stroh to speak for himself:

> Circumstances from Webern's life, his position toward facism [*sic*], the labor movement and Schoenberg's elite thinking together with aspects from Ortega y Gasset's theory of elites, Engel's [*sic*] historical materialism, and Freud's psychoanalysis can explain why to Webern history had to appear as a strange, uncontrollable power and why estrangement of his

professional activity has to turn into 'inner necessity'. Thus the social function of Webern's music can be seen: to feedback the ideology of the ruling class in the capitalistic system, to act as a stabilizer of the class-society, and to do all this with the assistance of musicology, which attests the quality and greatness of his music.[23]

There are monographs in German devoted to Opp. 21,[24] 27[25] and 31.[26] There are no monographs on any Webern work in English. Most of the important articles on the works under consideration will be discussed at the appropriate times.

Introduction to Part I

The stages in Webern's composition of all but one of the twelve-note works can be followed in a series of six sketchbooks. The first of these, which was begun in June 1925, includes sketches of the posthumously published *Klavierstück* and *Kinderstück*, the six songs of Opp. 17 and 18 and the first of Op. 19; this is owned by the Pierpont Morgan Library in New York City. The next book, begun in January 1926, contains the conclusion of Op. 19; this and four subsequent books, all owned by the Paul Sacher Stiftung in Basel, cover the remaining works except for the two published movements of Op. 20, sketches for which apparently do not exist. A fair copy of Op. 20, owned by a private collector in Basel and unavailable for inspection, has been described by Moldenhauer as 'an ink score of the two finished movements, in which Webern still made many alterations'.[1]

The sketches for each work begin with a statement of the row. In the songs Opp. 17–19 and in several of the works after Op. 20 – Opp. 22, 24, 26, 29 and 31 – preliminary work records the evolution of this row through a series of experiments and variations. Sketches of Opp. 21, 27 and 30 begin with a row slightly different from the one finally used; one or two alterations lead to the definitive version. In Opp. 22, 24, 26 and 29 the final version is marked *gilt* (valid, okay); in the remaining instances, the experimentation simply ceases when a satisfactory row has been achieved. The sketches of Opp. 23, 25 and 28 begin with a single statement of the row as a *fait accompli*: the preliminary work must have been done elsewhere. In every case, the statement of the row in its final form is dated. A row table, in which all the permutations are written out and numbered, bears a slightly later date. After this the compositional sketches begin. Although the row tables are separate from the sketchbooks the dates verify this sequence of events.

There are several discrepancies in the nomenclature used in Webern analyses. Since the matrix is circular, and the relationships are the same no matter which row form is understood to be the original one, the problem is essentially one of semantics. Nevertheless, it is a real problem, because disagreement about the identity of P_0 is an impediment to communication; it is difficult to follow and compare analyses that proceed from different starting points, particularly if the P–RI relationship is involved. The sketchbooks and row tables have only recently become available for examination,[2] and before the publication of the Moldenhauers' book in 1979 even their contents were not public knowledge. Until that time most analysts proceeded on the assumption that movements were written in the order in which they appeared in print; in fact, this turns out not to have been the case in all but two of the works with more than one movement: in Opp. 20, 21, 22, 23, 27, 28, 29 and 31 the movement that now stands first was not the first to be composed. Therefore, although it was Webern's habit to begin a work with the untransposed prime row, analysts working on the same premise have identified the wrong row form as P_0 as the result of having begun with the published first movement rather than with the one first written. The vocal works present a further problem. The sketchbooks make it clear that Webern was very concerned with melody. Any sketches leading to the establishment of the final form of the row, as well as those immediately following, are nearly always of melodies; in the case of songs, they are settings of portions of the text. So it is that in the works with voices, the first *sung* row of the first movement written (rather than the first row *heard*, which in every case is in the accompaniment) is the untransposed prime. Thus even analyses of Op. 25, in which the order of movements was never changed, and Op. 26, which is in one movement, have frequently proceeded from the wrong row. A third problem arises if an analysis treats the RI form of the row as the inversion of the retrograde (although this rarely happens). The row tables show unequivocally that Webern considered RI to be the retrograde of the inversion. This is an important distinction, because different transposition numbers are produced for the RI rows depending on which system is used. Many of the errors that have occurred in row orientation and numbering could have been avoided, since the prime forms of all of Webern's rows were published in the 1960s by Luigi Rognoni and Friedrich Wildgans,[3] both of whom had seen the row tables.[4] (For the benefit of latecomers, they were presented again in 1981 by Regina Busch.[5])

The Op. 24 Concerto, the only work besides the Op. 25 songs to have been composed in the order in which it now stands, presents a unique difficulty. Its row evolved through a long series of attempts to create an analogue for the two-dimensionally symmetrical Latin proverb

```
S A T O R
A R E P O
T E N E T
O P E R A
R O T A S
```

The row that was finally developed, beginning on F, generated four pages of fragments for large orchestra including piccolo, flute, oboe, clarinet, trumpet, horn, trombone, celesta, harp, glockenspiel, timpani, tutti and solo strings, and mandolin. The first of two openings of a movement for large orchestra still uses this row; in the second, it has been moved a tritone, to begin on B. The first sketch of the movement as it now stands appears subsequently, beginning on B and without reference to the instruments used in the previous sketches.[6] Two possible explanations for the tritone migration of this row come to mind, but the sketches seem to disprove both of them. In addition to the possibility that Webern simply might have changed his mind about the row in the protracted period during which he was occupied with this movement (although the row was developed and the initial sketches made in 1931, the first movement was finished only three years later), the suggestion has been put forward by Roger Smalley[7] that the row's change of tessitura coincided with the decision to dispense with a large orchestra and the extreme ranges offered by its more exotic instruments (piccolo, celesta, glockenspiel, mandolin). However, the first sketch made with the row transposed to begin on B is still for large orchestra, and the last of the sketches of the opening – of the movement as it now is – is dated 1931. (Smalley made his suggestion on the evidence of the publication of selected pages of the sketchbooks in facsimile;[8] he did not have access to the sketchbooks themselves, and the pages containing the two sketches just cited were not included in the facsimile edition. He in fact expressed his regret at not having had the opportunity to follow the compositional sequence through to its conclusion.) Whatever prompted the transposition of this row, it seems to me more realistic to assign in analysis the focal position of P_0 to the row beginning on B, since this is the version that ultimately generated the composition. This is the only instance in which I do not use Webern's *gilt* or final row as the untransposed prime.

The strange situation concerning the Op. 24 row brings into focus a casualness in Webern's row identification that I find difficult to reconcile with his carefully systematic choice of transpositions and his obvious fascination with combinations of rows that complement and interact with each other. In the row tables all the permutations are arranged in some logical order (the particular order is not regularized until Opp. 30 and 31) and assigned numbers from 1 (always P_0) to 48 (always an RI form). All the rows are labelled in the sketches. In the case of Op. 24, a new row table was not made when the sketches shifted from the row beginning on F to one beginning on B, so his numbering of the rows in the first movement begins, not with 1, which is customary, but with 21, and the entire work is accounted for in reference to the row beginning on F. The same cavalier attitude towards row designations can be observed in the sketches for works based on symmetrical rows (Opp. 21, 28, 29 and 30): the numbers used to identify row forms in the sketches are frequently not those that make clear their real relationship to each other (that one is the exact retrograde of its immediate predecessor, for example).

An important part of my thesis is that, although the twelve-note works are not tonal in any sense, the choice of transpositions to be used in important structural positions was in most cases determined by the desire to maintain (or replace) in an abstract way the traditional tonal relationships, so that the form is elucidated, in part at least, by the use of rows at a particular level of transposition (in most cases untransposed) in a position where they will fulfil the role of tonic, and by the specific distance from this tonic analogue of the transpositions chosen for other key positions. References to the 'tonic' or the 'tonic analogue' are intended only to signify that certain transpositions are used to define formal outlines, not to imply that these are perceived as or exert the pull of a tonal centre. Webern's apparent willingness to begin a movement with transposed row forms, as he did in all of Op. 24 and in subsequent movements of other works (it was his practice to orient the matrix in the same way for all movements of a single work, so that usually only that movement written first begins with P_0),[9] while not altering the validity of my argument concerning tonal analogues, *does* make these relationships difficult to see in analysis. For this reason, I have made the decision *not* to use his row designations in some cases, notably in Op. 24, but also in parts of Opp. 21, 28, 29 and 30, where I have chosen whichever of two possible row names indicates more clearly the relationship of the row in question to those surrounding it.

Although it is universal practice to analyse all movements of a work from the same matrix, the use of tonal analogues is more clearly observed if each movement is oriented towards its own zero level; to analyse all movements as proceeding from the same P_0 is equivalent to analysing all of the movements of Beethoven's Op. 106 as if they were in B♭ major: perhaps a useful way of maintaining perspective when viewing all the movements in context, but cumbersome and misleading in the analysis of the *Adagio* alone. Clearly a movable *do* is needed for the latter purpose. In the analyses referred to in the text I have used the same row designations throughout each work. Appendix III, however, includes an alternative analysis for each of the movements that do not open with P_0, in order that essential transpositional relationships at the local level can be more clearly observed.

A second aspect of the works will also be examined repeatedly: the methods used by Webern in his obsessive quest for the synthesis of horizontal and vertical, a concern that he shared with, and perhaps even learned from, Schoenberg. This continuing pursuit will be especially evident in Part II, since it often leads to the superimposition of forms; however, the particular appropriateness of twelve-note composition as a means of achieving this synthesis can be observed in the examination of row disposition and canon in Chapters 2 and 3 of Part I.

1

The rows

The twelve-note row is, as a rule, not a 'theme'.[1]

Although to equate a twelve-note row with a theme or melody is to take a simplistic view of the technique, it is nonetheless true that the construction of the row to be used as the basis for a dodecaphonic work is a process not entirely unlike the composition of the theme in a non-dodecaphonic work. It is at this point that decisions are made concerning which intervals and patterns will dominate in the ensuing work and shape its features. Webern's predilection for symmetry and logic and his preference for creating from limited material, as well as his leaning towards certain intervals, are evident in the make-up of his rows from the beginning.

That the minor second is a prominent element of most of Webern's rows will come as no surprise to anyone familiar with his earlier atonal music, in which the semitone and its permutations (the major seventh and minor ninth and the various compound intervals resulting from their enlargement by octaves) had always been favoured. Seventeen of the twenty-two rows considered in this study (including that of the unfinished Op. 32) exhibit semitone motion between adjacent notes in four or more places; in eleven of these, such motion occurs on more than five occasions.

In his earliest rows Webern seems to have been particularly concerned with limiting the number of intervals, presumably as a way of ensuring unity. This aim, in conjunction with his already well-established partiality for the semitone, produced rows that are heavily peppered with minor seconds. Considering for a moment the nine rows used in those works that were written before Op. 20 and either immediately or posthumously published, six pairs of consecutive notes are a semitone apart in one, seven pairs in five others, and eight in yet another. Of the twelve rows used in the remaining works, which display complete assurance in the use of the technique, only the first two, those of Op. 20 and Op. 21, and the penultimate, that of Op. 30, contain as many as six. (The row of Op. 30, somewhat anachronistically, contains seven.) From Op. 21 onwards, other interests seem to take precedence, and in general the later rows rely less on

13

semitones between adjacent notes as symmetry and invariance become the significant concerns.

The first row to appear in Sketchbook 1,[2] used in sketches of a setting of 'Erlösung' (the text used for the second song of Op. 18) that was later discarded, gives the impression of an experiment that had not been given sufficient thought beforehand and had consequently backfired. It consists of a series of five semitones (the last written as a major seventh) followed by a perfect fourth. It is as if the series could not be finished because the two notes left over at the end would not conform.[3]

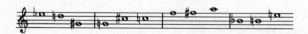

1.1

Following the initial statement of the row in the sketchbook are some experiments in layering the two hexachords and the trichords in various ways.

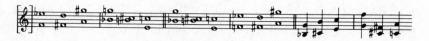

1.2

This is interesting and perhaps revealing of Webern's reliance, at this point in the development of his own twelve-note technique, on the preferences and style of Schoenberg; this was Schoenberg's preferred method of handling the row. It was not, however, to be characteristic of Webern.

The row of Op. 17/i (autumn 1924)[4] probably contains six semitones, although the exact order of the notes in the centre of the row is never made clear, since the song consists of twelve-note fields rather than linear statements (possibly another indication of Schoenberg's influence at this time).

5

1.3

The rows of Opp. 17/ii and iii (July 1925), 18/iii (October 1925) and the unpublished *Klavierstück* (summer 1925) contain seven semitones, that of the *Kinderstück* (also unpublished, composed in the autumn of 1924) eight (Example 1.4). Fourths and tritones are prominent in the song Op. 18/i (September 1925), which is built on a row containing three tritones and one fourth/fifth with the possibility of four further fourths/fifths between the

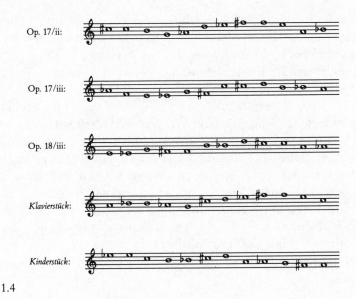

Op. 17/ii:

Op. 17/iii:

Op. 18/iii:

Klavierstück:

Kinderstück:

1.4

pairs of notes bracketed together in Example 1.5. This row contains only three semitones between adjacent notes.

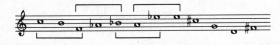

1.5

The closely related ideas of motivic derivation and symmetrical construction that produced so many of Webern's later rows (in Opp. 20, 21, 24, 28, 29 and 30) can be observed on only two occasions in the rows of published works written before 1926 (the date of composition of Op. 20). The semitone-dominated rows just examined do not also demonstrate an interest in symmetry. That of Op. 18/ii (September 1925), however, which contains only one semitone and would for this reason alone appear very different from its contemporaries, is constructed sequentially, from a series of chromaticallay descending thirds.

1.6

Like the first row in the sketchbook, this gives the impression of an idea that did not quite work. The original sequence could not be continued past the seventh note, since the eighth would have been a repetition of the first. At this point, therefore (in the middle of a sequential unit), everything suddenly moves up a minor sixth and the sequence continues, beginning the unit over again. This results in a left-over note at the end, which, as in the row from the sketchbook, does not conform to the pattern of the sequence. It is this final – it is tempting to say contrary – note that produces the only minor second in the row.

A somewhat similar experiment occurs on the third page of Sketchbook 1. Here the unit of the sequence is longer; Webern had intended to construct the two hexachords in the same way, the second beginning a perfect fourth lower than the first. This is, of course, not possible.[6] His sketch proceeds as far as the eleventh note, but notes 8–11 are crossed out (9 had already reproduced a note used earlier, and 12 would have done so again); he then experiments with a second continuation, which he carries as far as note 10; finally the idea is abandoned altogether. The technique of building a row of sequential repetitions, while not successful in this instance, is one to which Webern was to return frequently.

1.7

A similar pattern is used successfully in the Op. 18/iii row (October 1925), in which notes 6–10 are the transposition of notes 1–5 down a fourth. Here, as in Op. 18/ii, however, things seem not to come out even. In this case the final two notes of the row begin a third statement of the repeating pattern, which is of course incomplete. (The row appears in Example 1.4 above) At this point, the row of Op. 19 (1925–6) seems to represent a digression, exhibiting neither an abundance of semitones nor a sequential origin.

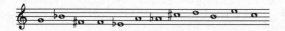

1.8

All the early experiments seem, not surprisingly, to have been leading up to the rows of Opp. 20 (1926–7) and 21 (1928). Suddenly in these two works all the ideas that had not quite gelled in earlier attempts fall into place with magnificent logic. From this time on Webern's rows give the impression of confidence and a complete mastery of the intricacies of the technique. The Op. 20 row represents a combination of the two ideas that seem to have occupied most of Webern's attention before this time. It consists of a series of six semitones separated by larger intervals; moreover, the third tetrachord is the inversion of the second.

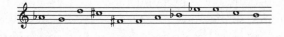

1.9

There is perhaps still the hint of imperfections not yet ironed out, inasmuch as the first tetrachord is not a permutation of the others. The formation, nevertheless, presents an interesting set of identities, and it would be presumptuous to suggest that its construction was in any sense accidental or incompletely worked out. The same series of semitones occurs in all the even-numbered transpositions of prime and retrograde and all the odd-numbered transpositions of the inversion and retrograde inversion. The same identity exists, of course, between all the odd-numbered transpositions of P and R and all the even-numbered Is and RIs.

P_0:	A♭ G	D C♯	F♯ F	A B♭	E♭ E	C B		I_1:	A B♭	E♭ E	B C	A♭ G	D C♯	F F♯
P_2:	B♭ A	E E♭	A♭ G	B C	F F♯	D C♯		I_3:	B C	F F♯	C♯ D	B♭ A	E E♭	G A♭
P_4:	C B	F♯ F	B♭ A	C♯ D	G A♭	E E♭		I_5:	C♯ D	G A♭	E♭ E	C B	F♯ F	A B♭
P_6:	D C♯	A♭ G	C B	E♭ E	A B♭	F♯ F		I_7:	E♭ E	A B♭	F F♯	D C♯	A♭ G	B C
P_8:	E E♭	B♭ A	D C♯	F F♯	B C	A♭ G		I_9:	F F♯	B C	G A♭	E E♭	B♭ A	C♯ D
P_{10}:	F♯ F	C B	E E♭	G A♭	C♯ D	B♭ A		I_{11}:	G A♭	C♯ D	A B♭	F♯ F	C B	E♭ E

P_0 and I_1 exhibit a particularly close relationship.

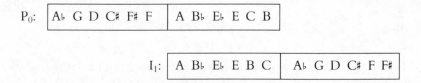

Tetrachordal identity is exhibited by rows related as I_{11} to P_0; tetrachords remain intact but occur in a different order in those related as P_6 and I_5 to P_0.

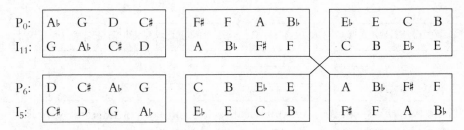

17

The music of Op. 20 employs a preponderance of two-note figures: double stops, dotted figures, single notes preceded by grace notes, two-note melodic motives isolated by rests before and after, and motives containing four or six notes of equal value perceived as pairs because of octave distribution. These pairs of notes nearly always consist of an odd-numbered followed by an even-numbered element of the row, the result being a continual bombardment of minor seconds, minor ninths and major sevenths. This emphasis on a single dissonant interval is a strongly cohesive device, giving the piece an aural unity that easily survives the strain exerted by a pointillistic style. Moreover, the focus on the minor second is particularly Webernesque, bringing this, his first major twelve-note work, clearly in line with his previous atonal compositions.

Like the row of the Op. 20 Trio, that of the Symphony, Op. 21, contains six semitones; however, at a glance the two rows look very different, partly because of the dissimilarity in the distribution of these intervals. Whereas the semitones occupy alternate positions throughout the length of the Op. 20 row, each half of the Op. 21 row contains one isolated semitone plus one chromatic run of three notes. In fact, the difference between the two rows is much more significant than the mere positioning of semitones; the later row finally achieves the permutational perfection that one feels Webern has been striving for up to this point. When the motivic sequence has been completed in this row, there are no troublesome notes left over. In addition – and the importance of this cannot be overemphasized – the result is, intervallically, a palindrome.

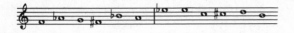

1.10

There are, in fact, two kinds of palindrome here. The more obvious of these is a simple palindrome: the second hexachord of the row reads the same as the first in reverse, though of course it is transposed. A second, more subtle (and less exact) type of palindrome is inherent in the relationship between the prime and its inversion nine semitones higher.

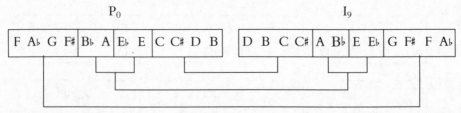

These two rows exhibit a symmetrical relationship of considerable sophistication. The most important characteristic of this relationship is that pairs of notes remain intact and operate as units. Reversal takes place on two levels. In the outer tetrachords, the units appear in reverse order in the inverted row, while the internal order of their elements is unaltered. Conversely, the order of the units within the central tetrachord is the same in both rows, while the internal order of members is reversed. At no point in the row do both kinds of reversal take place simultaneously; thus none of the tetrachords is answered by its exact retrograde. These two rows – or any two related in this way – form a closed circle, suggesting the possibility of infinite repetition.

Paradoxically, the construction of a pitch-class palindrome is not contingent on any particular quality within the row. No row can alone present an exact palindrome, as this would necessitate the repetition of the first six pitch classes; conversely, any row, even one constructed at random, is capable of producing a palindrome when combined with its own retrograde at the same level of transposition. Therefore, while the numerous pitch palindromes in Op. 21 are analogous to the construction of the row of that work, they are not the result of it. On the other hand, the less exact reversal of elements that occurs in two rows related as P_0 to I_9 is the result of the way in which this particular row is put together. It is this kind of palindrome, used in the outer sections of the first movement and at the centre of the second, that illustrates the unique properties of this row.

A symmetrical row in which the second hexachord is identical to the first in either retrograde or retrograde inversion yields only half the usual number of discrete permutations. Thus, of the forty-eight row forms appearing on the Op. 21 matrix (see Appendix II), twenty-four are redundant. Whether this limitation of resources bothered Webern at the time will probably never be known, but, for whatever reason, he abandoned this type of symmetry for several years. And, although he was to return later to the idea of rows with retrograde hexachordal identity, the Op. 21 row was to be unique; he never again used a row that was identical to its own retrograde. His next two works are built on rows possessing no symmetrical properties whatever, and when he returns once more to symmetrical organization the row he formulates, while exceedingly rich in segmental identities, is not reproduced by one of its retrograde forms and therefore generates the full complement of forty-eight rows.

The row used in Op. 22 (1929–30) has no symmetrical properties of the sort seen in Op. 21, though, as in the previous row, its first and final notes lie a tritone apart, thereby establishing a certain tonal symmetry – pairs of rows

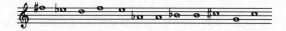

1.11

19

related as P_0 to RI_0 produce closed circular statements. The row contains five semitones. Webern's primary concern in this row seems to be invariance: the construction of a row that will produce several permutations in which the same notes occupy the same positions. This can be seen in the following set of rows, which figure importantly in the first movement.

R_7:	G	D	Ab	F#	F	E	Eb	B	C	A	Bb	C#
RI_5:	F	Bb	E	F#	G	Ab	A	C#	C	Eb	D	B
P_1:	G	E	Eb	F#	F	A	Bb	B	C	D	Ab	C#
I_{11}:	F	Ab	A	F#	G	Eb	D	C#	C	Bb	E	B

The following pair, used in the second movement, show an even greater similarity.

RI_9:	A	D	Ab	Bb	B	C	C#	F	E	G	F#	Eb
I_3:	A	C	C#	Bb	B	G	F#	F	E	D	Ab	Eb

The rows I_3 and P_9, used at the climax of the second movement (bars 169–72), are related in the same way as those above, but they exhibit invariance over larger segments as well.

I_3:	A	C	C#	(Bb)	B	G	F#	F	E	(D)	Ab	Eb
P_9:	Eb	C	B	(D)	C#	F	F#	G	Ab	(Bb)	E	A

And identical segments appear, with the contents reversed, in R_1 and RI_8, used in the same movement (bars 97–105).

R_1:	C#	Ab	D	C	B	Bb	A	F	F#	Eb	E	G
RI_8:	Ab	C#	G	A	Bb	B	C	E	Eb	F#	F	D

This interest in invariance was one that was to continue, culminating in the extraordinary similarity properties of the Op. 31 row. The works immediately following Op. 22 show a sustained interest in and exploration of this possibility.

The row of Op. 23 (1933) deserves mention as the most disjunct of all Webern's rows.

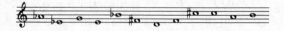

1.12

Several pairs of forms of this row exhibit strikingly similar segmental content. The following examples illustrate only a few of the possibilities used by Webern. Many others can be extrapolated from an examination of these.

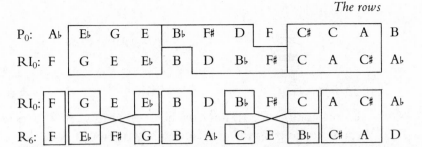

P₀:	A♭	E♭	G	E	B♭	F♯	D	F	C♯	C	A	B
RI₀:	F	G	E	E♭	B	D	B♭	F♯	C	A	C♯	A♭

RI₀:	F	G	E	E♭	B	D	B♭	F♯	C	A	C♯	A♭
R₆:	F	E♭	F♯	G	B	A♭	C	E	B♭	C♯	A	D

The row used in the Op. 24 (July 1931) Concerto for nine instruments is Webern's second masterpiece of symmetry. More sophisticated than the Op. 21 row, this series produces forty-eight discrete permutations but with a pattern of identities in some ways more reminiscent of Op. 20 than of Op. 21. These identities are the result of the row's having been constructed from a single trichord and its permutations, in the order P–RI–R–I. In the same way that all of Op. 21 was generated by a single hexachord (since the row was the statement of this hexachord followed by its repetition in retrograde), so everything in Op. 24 emanates from a three-note row consisting of a minor second followed by a major third moving in the opposite direction. The motive of a second followed by a third going in the other direction was one that Webern had favoured from the beginning. In terms of unordered content, all versions of this motive are expressions of a 014 trichord, or pitch-class set 3–3 in Allen Forte's terminology.[7]

1.13

The four trichords of P₀ appear also in R₆ (in the order 2–1–4–3), in RI₇ (in the order 3–4–1–2) and in I₁ (in the order 4–3–2–1). They appear as well, of course, backwards and in reverse order in the retrogrades of these four permutations. Webern wrote to Hildegard Jone about this row on 11 March 1931:

> I have found a 'row' (that's the 12 notes) that contains already in itself very extensive relationships (of the 12 notes amongst themselves). It is something similar to the famous old proverb:
>
> S A T O R
> A R E P O
> T E N E T
> O P E R A
> R O T A S[9]

A list of the trichordal content of the four rows with identical trichords illustrates the appositeness of this comparison.

```
1   2   3   4
2   1   4   3
3   4   1   2
4   3   2   1
```

Numerous possibilities for elision exist here, obviously. Any rows related as I_1 to P_0 present the possibility of infinite alternation if they share three notes at either end; except for the length of the shared segment, this is exactly like the situation between P_0 and I_9 of Op. 21. Any rows related as RI_7 to P_0 present the possibility of hexachordal elision; therefore two successive linear statements of either of these rows inevitably produce a statement of the other. If the complete set of eight rows with the same trichordal content is listed, other possibilities become apparent as well.

```
P0:   1   2   3   4       4   3   2   1   :R0
R6:   2   1   4   3       3   4   1   2   :P6
RI7:  3   4   1   2       2   1   4   3   :I7
I1:   4   3   2   1       1   2   3   4   :RI1
```

Naturally, if the three notes of each trichord are verticalized, P_0 and RI_1 are identical, P_0 and P_6 share a hexachord, and so on. Other, less complete, identities are also present in this matrix. For example, two notes of every trichord are identical in rows related as I_{11} to P_0

```
P0:    B   Bb  D      Eb  G   F#     Ab  E   F      C   C#  A
I11:   Bb  B   G      F#  D   Eb     C#  F   E      A   Ab  C
```

or as I_3 to P_0

```
P0:    B   Bb  D      Eb  G   F#     Ab  E   F      C   C#  A
I3:    D   Eb  B      Bb  F#  G      F   A   Ab     C#  C   E
```

A large number of rows will be found to have one note of each trichord in common with the corresponding trichord of P_0. Webern makes extensive use of all these invariance relations in the Concerto.

The extraordinary integrity exhibited by the four trichords extends also to the way in which they relate to each other. The initial notes of the four trichords of either retrograde form of the row (R or RI) produce overlapping 014 sets, as illustrated in Example 1.14. This relationship is exploited in all three movements, but is of particular importance in the second. A row with this set of possibilities is necessarily generated by hexachords containing pairs of augmented triads. In this case, the first hexachord of P_0 contains the notes of the augmented triads Eb–G–B and Bb–D–F#, the second the remaining two. This means that hexachordal content remains intact in transpositions of a major third in either direction, and that, with respect to the partitioning of the twelve notes into hexachords, all forty-eight rows conform to only four possibilities.

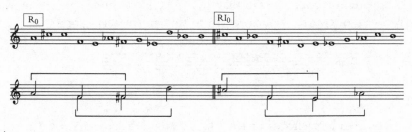

1.14

Although the row of Op. 25 (1934) is again nearly a sequence, it does not give the impression of accident that one gets from the earlier not-quite-sequential rows, probably as a result of the fact that the odd notes occur in the middle rather than at the end. This row, like that of Op. 24, divides into trichords; the intervallic content of the first, third and fourth of these is identical, a descending minor third followed by a descending minor second. The second trichord exhibits neither the same intervals nor the same contour, though it, too, is an example of a larger interval followed by one a semitone smaller – in this case a perfect fourth followed by a major third, but with a change in direction.[10] Only the minor second and minor third occur between trichords as well, and this consistent use of the same intervals gives the row a certain unity in addition to the obvious stability produced by the frequent repetition of the opening figure.

1.15

Because Webern uses only row forms at a single level of transposition in each of the Op. 25 songs, invariance between rows at different levels of transposition is irrelevant. He does, however, take advantage of similar sequences of notes in the row and its retrograde inversion.

P_0:	G E E♭	F♯	C♯	F	D	B	B♭	C	A		A♭			
RI_0:		F♯		F	D	E	E♭	C	A	C♯	A♭	B B♭ G

The next two rows, used in Op. 26 (March 1935) and Op. 27 (November 1935), are not symmetrical, in spite of the fact that both horizontal and vertical symmetry are explored extensively in the composition of the piano Variations. Although the Op. 26 row offers considerable invariant combinations, Webern does not take advantage of this property; therefore it is not significant. The Op. 26 row contains only seconds/sevenths and thirds/sixths (of both qualities in both cases): there is no perfect interval or tritone anywhere in the row. Two symmetrical formations can be seen, in notes 2–5 and in notes 7–11, but there is no overall pattern embracing the entire row. It

23

is apparently coincidental that the BACH motive appears in this row. Webern, of course, was to return to this motive very soon.

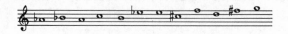

1.16

The two hexachords of the Op. 27 row are separated by a tritone; as in Op. 26, there is no possibility of a perfect fourth or fifth.

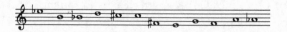

1.17

A striking set of relationships obtains between P and I of this row; these rows are combined vertically in the central movement and horizontally in both outer movements.

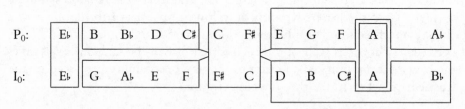

P_0:	E♭	B	B♭	D	C♯	C	F♯	E	G	F	A	A♭
I_0:	E♭	G	A♭	E	F	F♯	C	D	B	C♯	A	B♭

Webern makes use of the combinatoriality of this row only once, in the final variation of the third movement, where the fact that P_0 and I_1 are hexachordally complementary is exploited.

The row of the String Quartet, Op. 28 (January 1937), represents a further refinement and synthesis of the techniques seen in the three earlier rows of Opp. 20, 21 and 24. It is the most perfectly symmetrical of all Webern's rows. Like that of the Concerto, it is constructed from permutations of a shorter figure, but the result here is a row that is both identical with one of its own permutations, as in the case of Op. 21, and a series of six semitones, as in Op. 20. The figure that generates this row is the BACH motive, which is the initial tetrachord, beginning for some reason on C♯ rather than B♭. The second tetrachord is the inversion of this motive (or its retrograde – because of the symmetry of the motive itself, its inversion and its retrograde are identical); the third is a transposition (or the retrograde inversion) of the original. Owing to the symmetry of the generating motive (P = RI), the second hexachord of this row is also the retrograde inversion of the first; thus the row is identical to its own retrograde inversion, in this case at the ninth transposition, and twenty-four of the forty-eight rows are redundant.

24

1.18

A glance at the matrix produced by this row (see Appendix II) shows, predictably, numerous tetrachordal identities. The three tetrachords of P_0/RI_9 occur in the order 2–1–3(R) in R_5/I_5 and in the order 1(R)–3–2 in R_4/I_1. Two similar rows related as P_5 to P_0 offer the possibility of tetrachordal elision. Contiguous rows related as P_{10} to P_0 can hold two notes in common. As in the Op. 20 row, which was also a series of semitones, all even-numbered prime and retrograde rows and all odd-numbered inversions and retrograde inversions contain the same six semitones, and all odd-numbered primes and retrogrades and even-numbered inversions and retrograde inversions contain the other six.

The row of the Op. 29 Cantata (August 1938) exhibits the same type of hexachordal symmetry (P = RI), but it is much simpler: since the hexachord is not itself generated by an even shorter motive, the symmetry does not extend beyond the identity of the two hexachords.

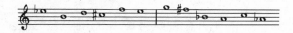

1.19

This row and the way in which it is used show Webern's continued interest in the property of invariance, an interest that was evident in Op. 24 and that would predominate in Op. 31. In any two forms of the Op. 29 row related as R_6 to P_0, the outer notes of every trichord remain the same with their positions reversed.

| P_0: | E♭ | B | D | | C♯ | F | E | | G | F♯ | B♭ | | A | C | A♭ |
| R_6: | D | F♯ | E♭ | | E | C | C♯ | | B♭ | B | G | | A♭ | F | A |

Webern seems to have liked the property P = RI; it is the only one of his symmetrical plans to which he returned a second time, and indeed a third. The row of the Op. 30 Variations for Orchestra (May 1940) is the last of these P = RI rows. Although it is not altogether like either of its predecessors, it resembles the row of Op. 28 more than that of Op. 29, since it is generated by a four-note figure and its permutations. In this case, however, the generating motive is not itself symmetrical, nor are its successive appearances self-contained as in the previous row. Instead they are elided by one note, with the result that two statements take only seven notes rather than eight. The motive consists of an ascending minor second and minor third followed by a descending minor second. The initial statement leads immediately into its retrograde inversion. The resulting seven-note figure is symmetrical: it is identical with its own retrograde inversion. Its final two notes become the initial two notes of a second statement of the same figure, resulting in a twelve-note row with the property $P_0 = RI_{11}$ (Example 1.20).

1.20

That the row is constructed from the elision of two similar seven-note figures means, of course, that two rows related as P_5 to P_0 can be elided by seven notes. A chain of rows thus elided produces an especially dense situation, more easily illustrated than described (Example 1.21). When

1.21

tetrachords are verticalized, tetrachordal elision is possible between rows related as P_7 to P_0. Webern makes considerable use of both these elisions – seven notes and four – in defining the structure of the piece.

After this prolonged interest in symmetrical row construction, it is perhaps surprising to find the Op. 31 Cantata (June 1941–November 1943) built on an asymmetrically constructed non-combinatorial row. This is not to say, however, that this row lacks arresting qualities. Its most interesting feature is its hexachordal invariance: two forms related as I_0 to R_0 hold five pitches invariant within each hexachord. The minor second and major third predominate in the Op. 31 row: there are only two other intervals, both in the first hexachord, a minor third/major sixth and a perfect fourth/fifth.

1.22

In addition to the fact that the hexachordal content of any form of this row is nearly identical to that of its inversion, several single elements retain the same position upon inversion. Since the first and final pitches are a tritone

26

apart, the extremes of P_0 and I_0 are the same. Two ordered series, one of two and one of four pitches, are retained as well: $P_0/4$–5 and $P_0/8$–11 appear, in retrograde in both cases, as $I_0/4$–5 and $I_0/8$–11 (Example 1.23).

1.23

Webern was working on what would have been his Op. 32 when his life ended in 1945. His original idea was that it should be a purely instrumental piece, a concerto, probably a chamber work similar to the earlier Op. 24.[11] By May of 1945 this original plan had been discarded in favour of a vocal work, on more of Hildegard Jone's verse.[12] The work was never finished. Seven pages of sketches do exist, however; these have been examined by R. Larry Todd in *The Musical Quarterly*.[13] Since my concern is with the published works, the unfinished Op. 32 will not be considered in later chapters. However, a few words about the evolution of the row are germane to the present discussion, since the sketches clearly show Webern's continued preoccupation with both of the concerns that have dominated his exploration of the twelve-note technique: symmetrical motivic derivation and the chromatic scale.

The first row tried is very like that of Op. 24. Both are derived rows based on a 014 set expressed as a minor second followed by a major third going in the opposite direction. It is not surprising, therefore, that the two rows exhibit similar properties and relationships. But whereas in the Op. 24 row the initial trichord is followed by its permutations in the order RI, R and I, here they appear in the order R, I and RI.

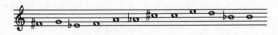

1.24

This row is altered during the course of the sketches and eventually becomes a series of chromatic segments, while maintaining its original trichordal construction. (It remains a derived row and can still be represented as P–R–I–RI, but the symmetry of the new generating motive means that, as in the Op. 28 row, only one discrete permutation is possible: P = RI and R = I.) This would seem to illustrate the tension inherent in Webern's preoccupations. The definition of a symmetrically derived row breaks down, and its usefulness as the generator of multiple but clearly perceivable permutations is lessened, as the semitone is emphasized.

1.25

Of the twenty-one rows that form the basis of Webern's published twelve-note works, thirteen are combinatorial, eight are not.[14] An examination of the hexachordal content of the rows shows all of them to have been derived from a limited number of source sets.[15] The most frequently used is Babbitt's first-order source set, in which the notes contained within each hexachord comprise six consecutive notes of the chromatic scale.[16] This is used as source material five times, to generate the rows of Opp. 17/iii, 18/ii, 21, 27 and 30. Babbitt's third-order set, in which the unordered content of each hexachord consists of minor seconds alternating with minor thirds, is used in Op. 24. Both of these source sets produce all-combinatorial rows.[17] The seven remaining combinatorial rows are only semi-combinatorial; they too, however, are all generated from only two source sets. The rows of the *Klavierstück* and of Opp. 22, 25 and 29 are all drawn from hexachords containing four semitones and a whole tone. The rows of Opp. 17/ii, 20 and 28 are derived from a similar source set, in which the whole tone has been expanded to a minor third. Several of the remaining eight, non-combinatorial rows, are also similar. The rows of the *Kinderstück* and of Opp. 18/i, 26 and 31 are drawn from the same source, as are those of Opp. 19 and 23. Only the rows of Opp. 17/i and 18/iii have unique hexachordal content.

The high incidence of combinatoriality in Webern's rows is not, I believe, the result of an interest in this phenomenon that so fascinated Schoenberg, but rather the inevitable result of Webern's preoccupation with symmetrical formations. A symmetrically constructed row is of necessity combinatorial; the reverse need not be true. (Schoenberg's rows, for example, were often combinatorial but not symmetrical.) Schoenberg's primary concern seems to have been to avoid a concentration, and thereby the possibility of the predominance, of any one pitch class. For his purposes combinatoriality was nearly indispensable. His textures were usually the result of either a series of similar rows in succession (producing secondary sets and thus keeping precipitate pitch-class repetition at bay) or a pair of complementary rows proceeding along together (resulting in a succession of aggregates and avoiding the danger of duplication). He also took advantage of the similar partitioning of combinatorial row forms and the interchangeability of hexachords that results by allowing hexachordal substitution. Neither the problem of pitch-class convergence nor the possibility of mixing and matching row forms was apparently of interest to Webern. Consequently the combinatoriality of a row seems to have been relatively unimportant as well: this property was hardly ever exploited for its own sake. Pairs of rows sounding together were chosen so as to produce exact mirror images or retrogrades or an increased incidence of particular pitches or melodic figures rather than to create aggregates or secondary sets. When the latter do occur, as at the opening of the first movement of Op. 24, it is clear that Webern was interested in a much more specific set of relationships than that of hexachords with complementary content. The first three combinatorial rows – one of these all-combinatorial, drawn from the first-order source set – are used in works built altogether from repetitions of the untransposed prime form of the row; the second use of the first-order set is in a work using only P_0, R_0, I_0 and RI_0. In this context it is obvious that the combinatoriality of these rows is of no importance.

2

Row topography

This chapter has two purposes. The more obvious – and probably the more immediately interesting – is to examine the unique treatment of the row in the individual pieces. It is these inspired realizations of the possibilities of the system that provide a measure of Webern's particular genius. Artistic creativity, however, consists of more than sheer invention: a talent for innovation is of little value without the sound basis of discipline. With this in mind, the second purpose of this chapter is to catalogue the elements of Webern's craft through an examination of his handling of mechanical details. It is those details that remain consistent from work to work that define a composer's style, and so it is that in order to understand Webern's style we must examine his treatment of the most basic elements of row technique and see how this changes from one work to the next.

Webern's understanding of the limits of the technique is very different from, say, Schoenberg's. He assiduously avoids the repetition of row segments and seldom sustains or repeats notes in such a way that their presence either precedes or outlives their mandate. He never moves backwards and forwards over a segment of the row; he does not use incomplete rows; nor does he consider hexachords with similar content to be interchangeable. After a few brief experiments in the early pieces he does not layer row segments; he almost never alters the order of notes prescribed by the row and does not return to notes already left. Nor does he ever exercise the licence to use the 'wrong' note. All these things were important features of Schoenberg's use of row technique.

In order to give a picture of the limits that Webern consistently imposed upon himself, and thereby to place the rare exceptions in perspective, the examination of the topography of each piece will, in addition to describing those aspects of the handling of the row that are peculiar to the work at hand, indicate the frequency of the following: doubling; elision (I use this term only to refer to the common use by two successive rows of a note or notes that constitute, respectively, the end and beginning of those rows – $m/12 = n/1$); overlapping (I use this term only in regard to situations where one row begins before another has finished without making use of any of the same notes); intersection (the common use of a note or notes by two rows progressing simultaneously, where the note in question is not at the extreme of both rows – m/5 = n/11, for example); repetition; segmental layering; verticalization; discrepancies in note order; omissions and extra notes.

There are essentially two ways in which music can be constructed from a row. The simplest and most direct realization of Schoenberg's stated intention to 'postpone the repetition of every tone as long as possible'[1] is through what I will refer to as block topography, in which rows are set one after the other, with all notes sounding in the order prescribed by this succession of rows, regardless of texture. Chords are produced by the verticalization of adjacent elements, and, in the case of counterpoint or imitation, the order of the notes is determined by chronological rather than linear considerations, each row encompassing the entire fabric of the music. This method seems to be the first to have been used publicly by all three of the composers of the second Viennese school. Contrasting with this is the much more sophisticated polyphonic method, which I will call linear topography, in which the fabric is the product of several rows progressing simultaneously in as many voices.

Since Webern's first published twelve-note works use block topography, it is surprising to find that the early twelve-note sketches show him experimenting almost exclusively with linear settings of the row. The first two and a half pages of Sketchbook 1 contain sketches in four parts, two in treble, one in bass, and the fourth predominantly in tenor clef. Clarinet and bass clarinet parts are labelled in a few instances. The parts are without exception examples of melodic counterpoint; although there is no doubt that the several lines of music are intended to be played together, they move independently. In all the settings, each instrumental part is a melody, in many cases considerably longer than twelve notes; each starts at a different point in the row and runs through all twelve notes in the prescribed order over and over until the end. Each melody is self-contained: the parts do not exchange rows or share notes. These pages of carefully serialized counterpoint, in conception so like the style of the major twelve-note works from Op. 20 to Op. 31, give way unexpectedly at the bottom of the third page to drafts of Op. 17/iii, in which ordering seems all but abandoned except in the voice part.

Speaking generally, the earlier twelve-note works use block topography more extensively, the incidence of linear mapping increasing until it is used exclusively in Opp. 28–31. Two early examples of quite decidedly linear presentation, Opp. 18/iii and 21, stand in sharp contrast to the surrounding works, as harbingers of what is to come. At the other end of the scale, the third movement of Op. 27 is the only late work to return to the block style of row exposition used in the early years.

In addition to the date of composition, another factor that seems to affect the topography is the apparent distinction in Webern's mind between the style and techniques appropriate to instrumental chamber music and those suitable for the solo song. It seems obvious to me that he held a traditionalist attitude to these genres: his innovations and experiments take place in the instrumental, and choral and instrumental, music; the sets of songs for solo voice are much simpler in conception. This distinction is reflected in the row topography: chamber music tends to be constructed in a linear fashion, songs are usually composed of row blocks. Of the twelve solo songs in Opp. 17, 18, 23 and 25, the already-cited anomalous third song of Op. 18 is the single example of linear mapping.

The decision to use several linear rows simultaneously rather than a single succession of rows with segments verticalized whenever necessary in order to provide all the desired parts was clearly dictated by a polyphonic conception. Almost invariably, wherever imitation occurs – and this is a technique of great importance from Op. 21 on – several rows are deployed at once, horizontally. Conversely, those movements that proceed through block topography usually do not employ canon.[2] For the most part, these latter works are simpler in conception than the others and are not the proving ground for the sort of innovative techniques that form the basis of so many of the linear pieces. The Op. 24 Concerto is an exception to this; although all three movements are set primarily in block fashion, it is surely among the most interesting and complex of Webern's twelve-note works. The distinction made between solo song and chamber music seems to arise from the basic (and traditional) concept of solo song as homophonic and chamber music as polyphonic.

Two factors, then, clearly influence the topography and nature of Webern's twelve-note works: the date of composition and the genre. The early works and the solo songs (and piano pieces) are in most cases not linear in concept; the later works and the instrumental music, generally speaking, are. Although these two opposing classifications might easily produce contradictions, this in fact does not happen very often, because as Webern's experience with the system increased, his use of the solo song as a medium decreased. Table 2.1, showing the type of topography used in all the twelve-note works, will serve to illustrate this.

The only exception to both generalizations is the previously mentioned song, Op. 18/iii – an early work, and the only solo song to use horizontal rows exclusively. Op. 21 is to some extent exceptional, inasmuch as it is not in the block style that predominates in the other early works – in this case the genre seems to take precedence over the date. The only other work that may seem to depart from the rule is the third movement of Op. 27, a late piece whose block topography may be attributed to its solo genre. (There is so little music for a solo instrument that any generalizations about Webern's attitude towards this medium would be unjustified.)

Table 2.1

Block	Combination	Linear
Klavierstück (p)		
Kinderstück (p)		
Op. 17 (s)		
Op. 18/i & ii (s)		Op. 18/iii (s)
	Op. 19 (cv)	
	Op. 20 (c)	
		Op. 21 (c)
	Op. 22/ii (c)	Op. 22/i (c)
Op. 23 (s)		
Op. 24/ii & iii (c)	Op. 24/i (c)	
Op. 25 (s)		
		Op. 26 (cv)
Op. 27/iii (p)		Op. 27/i & ii (p)
		Op. 28 (c)
		Op. 29 (cv)
		Op. 30 (o)
		Op. 31 (cv)

p = solo piano; s = solo song; c = chamber music; cv = chamber group with voices; o = orchestra

Establishing the basics: Opp. 17, 18 and 19

The first three opuses seem rather meticulously to illustrate Webern's progress in the adoption of the new technique. In this respect they call to mind the Op. 23 pieces of Schoenberg, though the latter show Schoenberg's approach to the twelve-note series through the earlier incorporation of both longer (in Op. 23/i) and shorter (in Op. 23/ii, iii and iv) series, whereas Webern's public progress begins with the twelve-note assumption.[3] We see each step – ordering, transposition, permutation, linearization, segmentation – addressed individually and then assimilated in the course of these eight pieces. Their order accurately represents their chronology, except that the third song of Op. 17 was written before the second. The latter, Op. 17/ii, is the first to adhere faithfully to the order dictated by the row. Op. 19 is the first of the sets in which the same row is used as the basis for all movements.

The first song of Op. 17 is not really constructed from a row. It presents a succession of twelve-note fields. There are nineteen of these fields, all complete but the fourth and fifth, both of which lack the note A. Repeated notes and figures are a characteristic of this piece. The first two bars plus one note of this song would appear to set the sequence of the twelve notes: one tetrachord is played horizontally, the second is verticalized, and the third is again spelled out melodically. The sequence thus established recurs only twice in the course of the piece, however, in bars 3–4 and 7–8. Odd/even pairs of notes (1–2, 3–4, etc.) tend to retain their proximity throughout, though individual notes frequently appear in reverse order and the ordering of pairs is not consistent.

The next song, Op. 17/iii, goes one step further. Here the voice reiterates a twelve-note row throughout, ending, curiously, four notes short of finishing the final (fifth) statement. (A melodic figure that follows in the clarinet does nothing to rectify this imperfection.) The instruments, in the meantime, play a succession of twelve-note fields. The ordering is irregular throughout, and the demarcation of fields is not so easily discernible as it was in the previous song.

The beginning of Op. 17/iii is puzzling. There is no question as to the identity of the row: it is given in the sketchbook[4] and is, moreover, constantly reiterated by the voice. However, the piece is begun by the instruments playing the second hexachord, and the order in the accompanying parts becomes immediately very jumbled. Throughout the song, pitch decisions in the accompaniment seem to have been made on some basis other than the series. On only two occasions do all the parts follow the order prescribed by the row (the first twelve notes in bars 1 and 2 are correctly ordered, though the starting point is note 7; and the last two voice notes in bar 7 plus all the parts in bar 8 conform to the succession 1–12), and even here the real order of notes is jumbled. In both places the row is divided into three segments – two trichords and a hexachord in the first instance, three tetrachords in the second – and these are treated as independent rows in the manner of Schoenberg. This kind of segmental layering was not used by Webern after Op. 20.

In the third of the Op. 17 songs (published as Op. 17/ii) all the parts are ordered strictly according to the series for the first time. In addition, all the parts in this song, including the voice, are derived from the same succession of twenty-two rows (all the untransposed prime) set in block topography. All the notes in the piece appear in the correct order, with the exception of the clarinet's written b^1 on the second beat of bar 14, which, as note 11, is one semiquaver early. In most cases the ends and beginnings of adjacent rows overlap (exceptions are in bars 12, 15, 16 and 19), but there is no elision.

Op. 17/i makes extensive use of repeated accompanying figures in all voices. The result is certainly not contrapuntal – the figuration is more 'harmonic' than melodic – but it is in a sense linear. It is, in fact, quite like those pages of Debussy and Stravinsky in which background spaces are filled in with layers of repetitive figures in conflicting rhythms, creating a wash of sound. Both single notes and figures of two, three or four notes are repeated; the entire background is unlike Webern's later twelve-note style. There are no chords. Long strings of repeated single notes appear in Op. 17/iii, especially in the viola part (the $c\#^2$ in bar 11 is repeated ten times, for example), but there is no repetition of figures. The two clarinets move with much more melodic independence than they do in Op. 17/i. Here again the rhythms are generally layered: dissimilar rhythmic subdivisions are played simultaneously in several parts.

The viola plays chords in bars 8, 13, 15 and 16. The notes constituting the first two of these are adjacent in the row; those in bars 15 and 16 are not. The chord that ends the piece in bar 16 is expanded by notes from the two clarinets. It contains altogether notes 2, 5, 7, 8, 9 and 12, preceded by a grace note, 6. Repeated single notes and pairs of notes appear in Op. 17/ii, though less frequently than in the previous songs. The rare chords contain adjacencies, in keeping with the strictness of order characteristic of this piece.

As in the previous opus, each of the three songs of Op. 18 is built on a different row. The topography of Op. 18/i is like that of the directly preceding Op. 17/ii: the untransposed prime is stated twenty-two times in succession, most statements overlapping to some extent but with no elision. The order is note perfect, and there is no segmental layering. The guitar, naturally, plays chords; these consist of adjacencies. Many single notes are immediately repeated; in two instances (in bars 2 and 6) two-note groups recur. There is one extra note, the c^3 in the voice in bar 7.

Op. 18/ii represents an important step in Webern's apprehension of row technique: here he uses permutation for the first time. This song comprises thirty-two successive statements of the row – seven primes followed by eight inversions, nine retrograde inversions and eight retrogrades – all untransposed. As previously, there is neither segmentation nor deviation of any sort from the prescribed order. The numerous chords are all verticalized adjacencies. Many of the rows overlap, and for the first time some notes are shared at these junctures (the held $f\sharp^3$ in bar 8, d^3 in bar 10, g in bar 11, $e\flat^1$ in bar 13, c^3 in bar 15, $b\flat^2$ in bar 16).

Op. 18/iii carries the assimilation one step further: in this song Webern uses a linear mapping for the first time publicly. Each of the three participants has his own succession of rows, which remains entirely distinct from the other two. No transpositions are used, but once again all four permutations appear; for the most part, similar row forms do not sound together. Only twice do rows overlap without sharing notes – in bars 14 and 20 – both times in the guitar, the only instrument in the ensemble that is capable of playing more than one note at a time. In other places rows are elided, holding up to three notes in common in the case of a row followed directly by its retrograde. (This happens in bars 5, 6, 7, 9, 10, 11, 16, 18, 19 and 20.) Single notes are repeated immediately (the largest number of reiterations of the same pitch is five), but there are no repeated figures or motives.

With this, the last song in Op. 18, Webern clearly has the basic technical aspects of the row well in hand. He has moved from fields of twelve unordered notes to rows of twelve ordered notes, on to permutations of this

order, and finally to the simultaneous combination of permutations. In Op.
19 all these techniques are employed, as well as limited transposition. And,
for the first time, both songs are generated by the same row.

All four permutations of the Op. 19 row are used, untransposed and at the
sixth transposition.[5] The topography is a hybrid. Blocks are formed as in
Opp. 17/ii and 18/i and ii, but here two and sometimes three are played
simultaneously. Although layering occurs already in Op. 18/iii, the technique is different there because the rows are linear. Segmentation occurs only
twice in Op. 19; elsewhere, the order is correct as prescribed by the row. In
both songs the order is perfect. Although two rows are segmented in the
three lower voices in bars 9–11, this is obscured by the non-coincidence of
segments with voices (Example 2.1). Similar-looking passages for the

order no.		1	2	3	4		1	2	3	4
voice		T	T	T	B		A	B	B	A
order no.		5	6	7	8		5	6	7	8
voice		B	B	B	T		T	T	A	B
order no.		9	10	11	12		9	10	11	12
voice		A	A	A	A		B	A	T	T

2.1   Op. 19/i, bars 9–11

chorus are produced elsewhere through the verticalization of adjacencies
(Example 2.2). The fact that, in general, row order takes precedence over
line (verticalization is preferred to segmentation) means that many melodies
are made up of a succession of notes that are not adjacent in the row.

There is considerable overlapping of rows and occasional, but not
frequent, elision. In most cases where two neighbouring rows require the
same collection of pitches, these notes are sounded twice. Immediate
repetition of notes – especially of entire chords – is a prominent feature of the
instrumental parts of Op. 19. Verticalizations are also characteristic – an
eleven-note chord occurs in bar 18 of Op. 19/i, and the same song ends with
twelve notes played at once.[6]

Perhaps one of the most interesting aspects of the Op. 19 songs is the
system of doubling in the music of the violin, clarinet and bass clarinet.

2.2   Op. 19/i

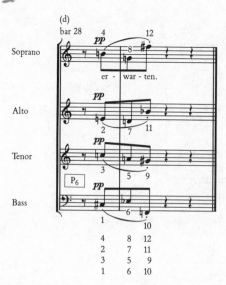

2.2   Op. 19/i

These three instruments play the bulk of the material in the introduction to each song, and they contribute to the final twelve-note chord of i. However, in the body of both songs (bar 7–29, inclusive, of i and bar 6 to the end of ii), they play only pitches that are sung at the same time, or very nearly the same time, by the voices. The single exception to this is a group of four notes in the clarinet in i/bar 22, which forms part of a statement of RI_6 and does not appear in any other voice.

Although doubling of this sort will be a characteristic of Webern's writing for this medium, used again in the much later Opp. 29/iii and 31/iii and vi, the particular technique used here is unique. While the notes played by the instruments are ordered in the same way as those in the voice parts, they are distributed quite differently, so that no single instrument of the trio consistently doubles any one of the voices. Moreover, the rhythm is changed: while most of the rhythmic differences are simply the result of rapid reiterations of the same pitch by the instruments during a note held by the voice, the voices and instruments frequently begin the same note at slightly different times, thereby producing a sort of heterophony. Three examples will serve to illustrate this (Example 2.3). Only once, in bar 6 of ii, do the celesta and guitar join in the doubling as well.

Op. 20

Op. 20 shows a mastery of row technique that far exceeds that of the preceding songs. Or, since no disapprobation of these earlier works is intended, it may be better to say that much more is attempted in Op. 20.

2.3   Op. 19/i

[All examples from Opp. 19 and 20 used in this chapter appear as published, with naturals.]

2.3 Op. 19/i

Here for the first time transpositions are used freely (forty-four of the forty-eight possible row forms appear in the course of the two movements), and their arrangement shows a kind of organization not observed in the music just preceding this. The structure of Op. 20 and of subsequent works will be discussed in Part II; for the present it will be sufficient to say that series of permutations function in a way similar to themes or formal sections, and are repeated and transposed in their entirety where the structure demands.

The treatment of the row is simpler and more straightforward in the first movement than in the second; only eighteen permutations are used, as compared with forty-two. The row is used only in successive block statements. Although these often overlap, only six notes are shared in the course of the movement: the viola's harmonic in bar 2, the violin's g^3 in bar 30, and notes 11 and 12 of both P_8 and R_5 in bar 40. There is no segmental layering in this movement; the order is straightforward throughout and is perfect with one exception: note 6 of RI₉ in bar 58 (the viola's e²) comes one semiquaver too soon. While there is frequent immediate repetition of single pitches, groups of notes are not repeated.

While the symmetry that was to become an essential of Webern's twelve-note language immediately after Op. 20 is not much in evidence here, it does, like canon, make brief, and in this case subtle, appearances. Horizontal symmetry – a palindrome – occurs in two places in the first movement, in the introduction (bars 1–3) and in the corresponding bars just prior to the return of the exposition (bars 40–3). Pitches and instrumentation are symmetrically cast in both these instances (Example 2.4). It is significant

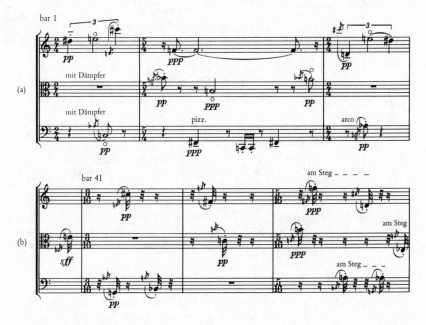

2.4   Op. 20/i, bars 1–3, bars 40–3

that, after conceiving the symmetry, Webern contrived to mask it through the use of grace notes, to the extent that it will probably be unnoticed in performance. These somewhat contradictory (complementary?) predilections – for symmetrical constructions and for concealment – coexist as essentials of Webern's twelve-note language. Friedhelm Döhl has remarked that Webern's desire to obscure details seems to be proportionally related to the complexity of the edifice he has constructed overall.[7] His most complex structures are often palindromic, and grace notes are often employed to hide the symmetry. The grace note's insistence on preceding and never following the note it enhances makes it a singularly effective tool for this purpose.[8]

The rows in the B sections (bars 10–15 and 51–6) are distributed in an unusual way. Although five different row forms are used in succession on both occasions, each pitch class is played at the same octave level and by the same instrument in all the rows concerned, each member of the trio therefore playing a very limited group of notes over and over in spite of changing row forms and transpositions. This calls to mind the technique used by bell ringers in ringing changes (Example 2.5). Although the notes are distributed differently among the instruments the second time, in bars 51–6, the same technique is applied.

2.5   Op. 20/i, bars 10–15 (pitches only)

The numerous possibilities of tetrachordal identity offered by this row were examined on p. 17. This property is exploited briefly in the introduction and coda of the second movement. The movement opens with P_0, and the return of the same music in the coda begins with I_5. Tetrachords are distributed so as to take full advantage of the similarities between these two rows. This represents the last occurrence of segmental layering in the twelve-note music of Webern:

	Introduction:				Coda:			
	P_0				I_5			
violin	Ab	G	D	C♯	C♯	D	G	G♯
viola	Gb	F	A	Bb	Gb	F	A	Bb
cello	Eb	E	C	B	Eb	E	C	B

This movement is in sonata form. The first theme, which consists of a melody in one instrument with the other two accompanying, uses the row in block form; in the polyphonic second theme, the rows are appropriately

42

linear, progressing two at a time. This apparent concordance of musical setting with row technique, while accurate in general terms, does not hold in all specific cases. Notable exceptions occur in the transition between the two themes, where an imitative passage (bars 30–2) is constructed in block fashion, and in bars 48–9, where the two accompanying voices of the second theme engage in brief imitation, both taking their notes from the same statement of I_6 (Example 2.6). Predictably, the two styles of presenting the row alternate in the development.

2.6   Op. 20/ii, bars 30–2, bars 48–9

The order is straightforward throughout this movement and is disrupted only once, in bar 186, where a grace note uses the pitch that should follow the note it precedes.[9] In bars 113–17 an E♭ harmonic that is held for five bars by the violin functions in three rows in turn, as needed. This is a more extreme example of the situation that occurred in the second bar of the first movement, and is in some way akin, as well, to the technique used in the B sections of that movement (see Example 2.5) and the transitions of this one (bars 26–30 and 131–4). The insistence on the part of each instrument on a specific pitch or pitches through a series of changing row forms seems to have been an idea in which Webern was only temporarily interested. Its only subsequent appearance is in the first movement of the Op. 28 String Quartet.

In this movement, as in the first, one row frequently begins before its predecessor has ended; however, notes are shared on only two occasions: in bars 88 ($RI_{11}/12 = I_{11}/1$) and 129 ($I_7/10 = RI_2/1$). And as before, while there is a good deal of immediate repetition of single notes (see bars 74–83 in particular), segments are not repeated.

Op. 21

The Symphony, Op. 21, makes use of a set of possibilities quite different from those explored in Op. 20. The presentation of rows is linear throughout Op. 21, in keeping with the intensely imitative nature of the work; throughout both movements rows or chains of rows operate as canonic voices. In spite of the logical association of rows and voices, however, much of the canonic imitation is difficult and some of it impossible to perceive aurally, because the orchestration throughout most of the work is pointillistic – in some places (Variations II, III and VII of the second movement, for example) extremely so, with only one or two or, infrequently, three, consecutive notes of a row played by the same instrument. A stable relationship between canonic voices and timbres, which would make imitation more easily distinguishable, is for the most part avoided.

The only sections of the work that are not entirely pointillistic are the Theme and Variations I, II, V and VI of the second movement. In the Theme, although the accompaniment is distributed among several instruments, the clarinet plays P_0 in its entirety; this is the first time in the work that an entire row has been played by one instrument. Each of the four voices in Variation I is played from start to finish by the same instrument, making this canon more easily perceived than any other in the work, though the clarity to be gained through such a careful isolation of parts is to some degree modified by the fact that all the voices are played by string instruments. Like the Theme, Variation II contains only one continuous voice. Two rows unfold simultaneously in the horn part, its notes taken alternately from I_0 and P_{11}. All the pairs of notes ($I_0/1$ and $P_{11}/1$, and so on) except for the central four, 6 and 7 of both rows, are repeated immediately.

Variation VI is topographically similar to Variation I, in that three instruments play continuously throughout. The two clarinets are in canon, while the horn plays a line formulated in the same way as the horn part in Variation II. The pattern of repetition here complements that used in the earlier variation: in this case the only notes to be repeated are the central ones, $R_{11}/7$ and $RI_0/6$. Several two–note groups are directly repeated in the clarinet parts, however: notes 7 and 8 of I_{10} and P_2 in bars 69–70 and the corresponding notes 5 and 6 of the retrograde of these rows in bars 74–5, in addition to the notes at the elision of I_{10} with RI_{10} and P_2 with R_2 (note 11, which becomes 2 after the elision, is heard four times, surrounding three occurrences of the note that effects the elision, 12/1).

Variation V is the only apparently homophonic section of the piece. Its completely static chordal texture is in fact misleading, however, as it too is a canon. It consists of melodic fragments in the harp played over eleven bars of continuously repeated four- and eight-note chords. The high and low strings are treated as two bodies, each repeating a single four-note chord throughout the length of the variation, in a denser and more insistent version of the change-ringing technique described earlier in reference to sections of Op. 20 (see Example 2.5). Rhythmically these chords are gathered into groups of five, these groups representing the verticalization of alternately the first and third tetrachords of four different row forms. The notes played by the viola and cello, for example, function successively as $I_3/1-4$, $RI_3/9-12$, $R_6/1-4$, $P_6/9-12$, $I_3/1-4$, $RI_3/9-12$, $R_6/1-4$, $P_6/9-12$, $I_3/1-4$, and $RI_3/9-12$. The two violins play the other outer tetrachords of these rows, beginning with $RI_3/1-4$, then $I_3/9-12$, $P_6/1-4$, $R_6/9-12$, and so on. The melodic line heard intermittently (and with some difficulty) in the harp provides the central tetrachords, all of which consist of the same four notes. The central note of each seven-note harp figure functions as 8 in one row and 5 in its retrograde; these are the only instances of intersection in Op. 21.

There is very little other verticalization in this work. While two or more notes are often struck together, in the overwhelming majority of cases this is the result of the momentary rhythmic coincidence of two linear voices, something quite different from the articulation of a chord as a distinct entity. (Double stops appear prominently in Variation II and occur, as well, in Variations IV, VI and VII; each of these, however, represents the congruence of two independent polyphonic lines.) Two notes are played together as a single musical element in only a few places: in the first movement, the 'tonic' tritone E♭/A is emphasized on two of its appearances (in bars 7 and 9) by occurring as a double stop; the horns play two notes at the same time on two occasions in the accompaniment of the Theme in the second movement (bars 2 and 9); and the harp plays two notes together on four occasions in both Variation VI (bars 78 and 88) and the Coda (bars 90, 93, 95 and 98). In all of these sections, however, the prevailing construction is linear. Only in Variation V are more than two notes struck together as a vertical unit.

The unique construction of the Op. 21 row has already been considered in Chapter 1.[10] The two-note elision that exploits the peculiar relationship between any two forms of this row related as P_0 and I_9 is used in all voices throughout the first and third sections (bars 1–26 and 42–66b) of the first movement and in Variations III and IV of the second. Conversely, the central section of the first movement and the remainder of the second use exact palindromes, produced by the use of forward and reverse forms of the same row in tandem. The rows in two of the voices in the central section of the first movement share their common central note; the other two do not. The only elision of this sort in the second movement is at the centre of Variation VII, where the E in the harp in bar 83 represents both $I_5/12$ and $RI_5/1$. Overlapping occurs between all the major sections of the first movement and between all the variations of the second except for the central one, Variation IV, which does not overlap with the variation on either side. Variations I and II and Variations VI and VII are elided.

At the centre of the second movement, in bar 50 (Variation IV), a bar of repeated notes seems to indicate a relaxation of the strictness that characterizes the rest of the work. This, however, turns out to be an illusion. The four rows used in the approach to this bar and the four immediately following it all converge on the nine pitches that appear here; with one exception, moreover, each of the twenty-two notes in this bar is called for and is in its correct place, so that, although the same pitches occur several times, only one of these is redundant. Each of the four rows after the centre relates to one of the four leading up to it as I_9 to P_0. Only one of these four pairs – P_8–I_5 – does not hold two notes in common at the juncture. The central B♭ in the clarinet part is an extra (repeated) note – a small thing, perhaps, but noteworthy in a context as carefully controlled as this one (Example 2.7).

2.7   Op. 21/ii, bar 50, Variation IV (pitches only)

Single elements of the row are repeated occasionally, more often in the second movement than in the first. No pitch is repeated more than once except in Variation V. Groups of notes are never repeated – again with the exception of the chords in Variation V. Note order is perfect throughout. Of the twenty-four discrete row forms produced by permutation and transposition, only three – P_9/R_3 and its reverse R_9/P_3 and I_2/RI_5 – are not used in Op. 21.

Op. 22

In Op. 21 the topography is essentially the same throughout; in contrast, the two movements of Op. 22 are very dissimilar. The row topography of the first movement is linear, as in the previous work; various types of topography occur in the second.

   Two voices proceeding in canon through the first movement are pointillistically disposed in the first and second sections and the coda (bars 1–15, 16–27 and 37b–41) and played entirely by the piano in the third (bars 28–37b). A third voice proceeds independently in these sections, both times playing two rows, elided by one note ($I_7/12 = I_1/1$). In bars 6–14 this voice is played by the saxophone; in bars 28–37 it is distributed pointillistically. Events are telescoped in bars 17–27 so that successive figures in one voice often overlap by one note, with the result that pairs of adjacent notes from the row are sounded simultaneously. These simultaneities do not function as chords, however; the scoring and registration make their linear origin perfectly clear.

Throughout the movement, the two voices of the canon use pairs of rows, prime and inverted, the sum of whose transpositions is 12; for this reason, the notes that stand first and last in P_0 – F♯ and C – occupy the same positions in both rows of each pair used in the canon. The extreme notes of the untransposed prime therefore assume particular significance as tonal axes, in spite of the fact that the untransposed prime row never occurs. With one exception, in bar 24, all rows converge literally on the same F♯, a tritone above middle C. The parallelism of the Cs is not so marked, though it is nearly as consistently treated: with two exceptions, in bars 22 and 32–3, the same two Cs are used each time – c^1 and c^2.

Rows are unusually self-contained in this movement. Overlapping occurs in bars 21 and 24 of the middle section and in bar 37b at the beginning of the coda. The only elision in the canonic voices is in bar 22, at the climax of the movement, where notes 12 of R_6 and RI_6 function also as 1 of P_6 and I_6. These two notes are the highest and lowest in the movement and are played *ff*, a dynamic that appears nowhere else. The five notes following in each row are, of course, the preceding five in retrograde; this is emphasized by their occurring at the same octave level both times.

There is no intersection in this movement, no doubling, no repetition of either notes or motives, no wrong notes and no extra notes or omissions. The order is perfect throughout. There is no verticalization of more than two notes; however, a single note followed by a major seventh or a minor ninth dyad is a characteristic motive, occurring in bars 12, 14, 25, 35, 36(a and b) and 39. A pair of dyads – a minor ninth followed by a perfect fourth – appears in both voices of the canon in bars 32 and 33. It is characteristic of Webern that, although the possibilities for movement by semitones abound in this work, hardly any semitones actually appear, this interval nearly always being expressed as a minor ninth or a major seventh.

The first movement uses a limited number of rows, chosen in most cases for their symmetrical presentation of the focal notes F♯ and C. The introduction uses only P_7 and I_5 and the coda their retrogrades; C is the fourth and F♯ the ninth note of both P_7 and I_5, and these positions are of course reversed in the coda's R_7 and RI_5. P_7 and I_5 are used in the canons of the first and third sections proper as well, along with P_1 and I_{11}, in both of which F♯ and C also occupy the fourth and ninth positions. I_7 and I_1 are used by the non-canonic voice in these sections. The middle section opens with the pair P_4 and I_8, in which F♯ stands third and C sixth, and these are followed by I_7 and P_5, probably chosen because of their inversional relationship to the opening P_7 and I_5; the remaining rows used in this section are RI_6, R_6, P_6 and I_6, in which F♯ and C are the outer notes, and RI_5 and R_7 (the retrograde of the opening rows). Thirteen row forms are used in this movement, and no row appears more than once in any section.

After the topographical simplicity and tidiness of the first movement, the second seems almost to be the work of another person, or at least to emanate from another period. It is, in fact, the first of a small group of works in which the mapping of rows is much less disciplined and logical than in those considered so far. The sort of topography first introduced in sections of this movement is used again in the songs, Opp. 23 and 25, and reaches its height in *Das Augenlicht*, Op. 26. The undisciplined row distribution in these works would seem to indicate a desire to explore a freer manner of composing with rows, but if these aberrations are to be seen as indicative of a change in attitude the chronology of the works is anomalous. The second, less strict, movement of Op. 22 was composed before the first, which adheres closely to the disciplined style of the preceding works, and it was directly followed by the conception of and initial work on Op. 24, all movements of which are topographically very neat. All of this occurred before the composition of Opp. 23, 25 and 26.

The row topography is straightforward in over two-thirds of this movement. Block successions occur in only two places – for a considerable period of time in bars 88–122 and briefly again in bars 178–84. In the rest of the movement the mapping is linear with two or three rows progressing at once. Whichever method is used, successive rows are elided by one, two or three notes in most instances. The first small departure from Webern's previous style of setting occurs in bar 51, where a grace note played by the violin is note 10 of P_4 while the note that it graces is 1 of I_9. Prior to this, grace notes and the notes they directly precede have always been consecutive members of the same row. The next hint of things to come occurs in bar 56, where $P_9/9$ in the clarinet part also functions as 10 of I_9, a row with which it does not otherwise intersect. A similar example of intersection occurs in bar 66, where $R_0/7$ functions also as $P_0/6$.

In fact, to describe these instances as intersection is not entirely accurate. They seem to be more omissions than intersections. In each of the cases just cited the note in question lies in a logical position with respect to one of the rows it serves – $P_9/9$ in bar 56 is the last note of a three–note clarinet figure that imitates in inversion a figure played by the piano in the previous bar; $R_0/7$ in bar 66 is part of a series of two–note figures in the piano outlining major sevenths and minor ninths – but is completely outside the context of the other. I_9 progresses steadily, in bars 51–6, down through the score, two notes at a time, from violin (notes 1 and 2) through clarinet (3 and 4) and saxophone (5 and 6) to piano, where all of the final hexachord is played, except for the borrowed note 10, which is played by the clarinet; the situation in bar 66 is similar. In both cases the congruence of two rows has been dealt with in reality by omitting the note in question from one of them altogether. To my knowledge English has no name for this manner of dealing with intersection, so I will refer to it by the term used by German analysts, who call the absences resulting from this treatment *Ausfälle*.[11] (An *Ausfall* is a deficiency or falling-off; in musical terms, an *Ausfall* is a note that is missing from one voice, because it is present in another at the time when it is needed.) The result of *Ausfälle* is that the row structure of one part is complete, while, for all practical purposes, that of the other – the borrower – is not, showing apparent gaps wherever an *Ausfall* occurs.[12]

The first instance of intersection on a large scale occurs in bars 61–4. The rows used here – RI_9 and I_3 – require the same pitches for notes 1, 4, 5, 8, 9 and 12. Each of these is treated as an *Ausfall* in one of the voices involved (Example 2.8).

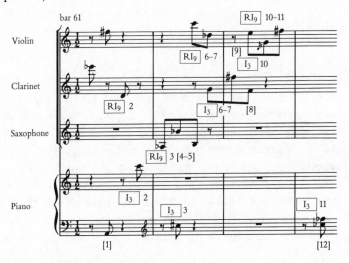

2.8   Op. 22/ii, bars 61–4 (pitches only)

The situations just noted represent two distinct types of topographical irregularity, both evidence of the dissociation of row structure from musical structure; and both appear here for the first time. The first – the isolated grace note – takes the form of a musical unit built from non-adjacent elements, which may be drawn either from the same or from different rows. The *Ausfall* constitutes an irregularity of another sort. Both types occur in the statements of P_6 and RI_6 in bars 122–5 and of RI_0 and P_0 in bars 129–31, and in considerable profusion in bars 132–79. Repeated notes are common in this movement, most often occurring in the form of a grace note that repeats the note directly preceding before going on to the next. Only one segment is repeated, by the saxophone in bar 157, and it consists of only two notes.

Despite the untidy aspect of the score and the seemingly almost random appropriation by one row of pitches belonging to another, no note that should appear in this movement is actually omitted and none comes out of order. There are, in addition, no extra notes, and none is doubled. There is one error in the score: the clarinet's grace note in bar 50 should be a G♯ rather than a G♮.[13] In contrast to the economy of the first movement, this movement uses thirty-two of the forty-eight row forms.

The same sort of nonchalance that may be observed in the attitude of the rows to each other is apparent also in their indifference to the musical structure. Although certain groups of rows clearly constitute formal sections, the precise definition of the limits of these sections is in many cases avoided through the lack of any reinforcement in the row structure. There is frequently no division between rows at the close of a musical section, as there always is in the five instrumental movements written before this one, and webs created by intersection and elision sometimes obscure structural articulations altogether.

Opp. 23 and 25

The six songs of Opp. 23 and 25 exhibit the same sort of capricious row topography as the second movement of Op. 22, with frequent communication between voices in the form of intersection, connecting elisions and even, occasionally, the exchange of parts. Each of the songs is built from two simultaneously progressing series of rows, one in the voice and one in the piano, the latter presented in block form. Both sets use a very limited number of the row forms available. Op. 23 is constructed entirely from the four untransposed rows and their tritone transpositions; Op. 25 uses only untransposed rows in the outer songs and fifth-level transpositions in the central one.

Although both sets represent the same approach to row structure, they are rather different in other ways, the songs of Op. 23 resembling the earlier ones of Opp. 17–18 with their relative expansiveness while the spare textures and reduction of means in those of Op. 25 make them seem more at home with their instrumental contemporaries. This increased concentration inevitably affects the disposition and relation of rows.

One-note elisions occur within each part wherever possible in all three songs of Op. 23. A similar elision connects the two parts in bar 21 of the first song and in bar 15 of the second. Frequently the first or last note of a piano row is not played, because the required pitch appears in the voice at the appropriate moment and is sung only. On just one occasion is the reverse true: in bar 25 of the second song the first note of the voice row, P_0, is played by the piano. On several occasions the piano finishes a row left incomplete by the voice at the end of a section of text. On three occasions, in the second and third songs, a note that is required by only one part is supplied, out of context, by the other. In the second song, the piano's $I_6/7$ is sung in bar 30; in the third song two notes of the voice rows ($RI_6/12$ in bar 17 and $R_6/12$ in bar 22) are interpolated in the piano part.

Rows intersect with great frequency in the first song, less often in the second, and only twice, in the final two bars, in the third. With one exception, in bar 15 of the first song, these shared notes are sung. Occasionally a note needed by both rows at the same time is sung twice by the voice, so that, although it is absent from the piano part, it nevertheless occurs the required number of times. The first example of this is in bars 7 and 8 of the first song (Example 2.9). The situation is more complex in the following bars (Example 2.10). In this instance, in order to maintain the correct

2.9   Op. 23/i, bars 7–8 (pitches only)

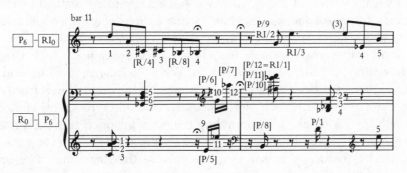

2.10   Op. 23/i, bars 11–12 (pitches only)

sequence in both rows, the first of the two $c\sharp^1$s in bar 11 must be interpreted as belonging to the piano's row and the second to the voice's, even though the first falls naturally into the row being sung. (The order of assignment of the B♭s does not matter.) The intertwining of rows is rather complex in the remainder of this bar and the beginning of bar 12. Aside from these two instances, repeated pitches, of which there are several in Op. 23, do not represent intersection.

Except for those junctures using the m/12 = n/1 elision, successive rows overlap on only a few occasions, but where they do they sometimes intersect as well. A particularly dense example of overlapping occurs in the second song; this is unusual in that it takes place in the voice rather than the accompaniment. This bar is a good illustration of the sort of confusion of parts that is characteristic of the style (Example 2.11).

2.11   Op. 23/ii, bar 14 (pitches only)

While the row structure of the first two songs is somewhat knotted and disorderly, that of the third is simple. All three songs make use of verticalization, but not all to the same extent. Three- and four-note chords are used in the first half of the first song. The texture of alternate sections of the second song, beginning with the opening seven bars, is relatively thick, dominated by chords of from three to six notes, themselves often preceded by double grace notes, which add to the density. In marked contrast to this, no verticalization of more than two pitches occurs in the third song until three-quarters of the way through, when a three-note collection makes the first of six appearances in the movement.

The row forms Webern has chosen to use exhibit a high degree of invariance (see the chart on p. 21). While in many cases he eliminates through intersection the pitch duplications that inevitably result from the use of row forms with such similar content, at other times he exploits the possibility for emphasis by sounding the pitch (or pitch class) in question in both parts either together or in close proximity. This happens with particular frequency in the first ten bars of the first song. The opening section of the second song for the most part avoids pitch reinforcements, but a strong one occurs in bar 5. Here two notes – $g\sharp^2$ and c^2 – are sung with accents and then immediately repeated (this is the only instance in all six songs of the immediate repetition of more than one note); and at the same time these notes form part of a four-note chord in the piano, in the same octave.

The Op. 25 songs are both shorter and sparer than the earlier set. Although the row treatment is essentially the same as in Op. 23, there is considerably less communication between parts here, simply as a result of the reduction of materials. And while the total number of row possibilities used in these songs is the same as in the earlier set, the number of resources drawn upon in each song has been halved: the outer songs use one set of four row forms and the central song another. The first song consists of twelve row statements, as against fifty-two in the first song of Op. 23.

Except for the first note (G) in the piano in b. 3, which is 12 of its opening RI_0 and 1 of the following P_0, there is no elision either within or between parts in the first song,[14] and communication between parts is very limited. The ends of both major sections of this song are marked by the piano's completion of a row left unfinished by the voice at the end of its couplet (P_0 in bar 5, I_0 in bar 12). There is no intersection. Both verses of text begin with the same row form in voice and in piano, thereby producing a considerable degree of pitch-class duplication. Webern emphasizes this by using the same pitches in both parts. Thus the first five notes of the voice in bars 2–3 are identical to those of the piano; the same is true of the first three in bars 5–7 (though the two parts are rhythmically different in both cases). A high proportion of the remaining pitches of the voice part also appear at the same time or very nearly so in the piano. There are ten verticalizations in this song, all consisting of four notes.

The second and third songs are much longer than the first (twenty-eight row statements over forty-two bars and twenty-three in seventy-eight bars respectively); consequently there is more sharing of pitches in these movements, though there is still considerably less, in terms of both quantity and diversity, than was observed in Op. 23. Several elisions occur within parts (six in the second song and five in the third); in addition the two parts are elided in bar 56 of the latter.[15] Intersection is frequent, especially in the third song. In all cases the *Ausfall* is in the piano part.

On three occasions in the second song both parts begin the same row form and the piano subsequently gives up at some point, allowing the voice to finish alone. This happens in bar 10, where the voice supplies the final note of I_5, which the piano has been playing in bars 9–10, but which the voice itself had apparently abandoned earlier after getting as far as note 11 in bar 8. In bar 16 the voice supplies the last three notes of P_5, which has progressed as far as note 9 in both parts just previously. And in bars 27–8 the voice similarly finishes off the two R_5s that were in progress in the preceding bars; in this instance, the piano takes up a new row while this is happening. A more complex version of the same thing can be seen in bar 20. Here both voices have played as far as note 6 of I_5; the voice sings 7 and 8 before the row moves to the piano for its completion. A complex tangle occurs in bars 52–4 of the third song. Here the piano not only finishes the voice's abandoned RI_0, but intersperses the beginning of a new R_0 among the final notes of its own I_0 as well (Example 2.12). Successive rows overlap in two

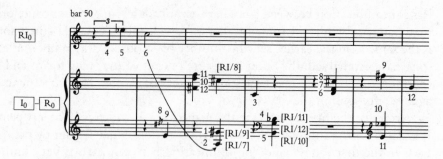

2.12   Op. 25/iii, bars 50–6 (pitches only)

instances, both in the second song – R₅ and RI₅ in bar 27 and R₅ and I₅ in bar 39.[16] Although no licence is taken with row order, there is one unexpected anomaly: an extra note, the G on the third beat of bar 33 of the second song. Since this is so uncharacteristic of Webern at any time, one suspects a misprint, though it is difficult to see what else might have been intended, as the note is logical musically at this point. Verticalizations of from two to four notes occur fairly frequently in both the second and the third songs of this opus. There is no doubling in any of the songs of either Op. 23 or Op. 25. Although there are numerous repeated notes, they are not in obvious positions. For example, the first note of a phrase is sometimes the same as the last note of the previous phrase, or a grace note may be a repetition of a note already heard. In some cases these are notes that are required by both rows at this point; at other times they are simply redundancies. Only once in all six songs is more than one note repeated at a time: the figure mentioned earlier in bar 5 of Op. 23/ii. Note order is correct, although the position of a grace note occasionally calls this into question.[17] No notes are missing altogether.

Op. 24

During the same time that he was occupied with the composition of Opp. 23 and 25, and before the inception of Op. 26, Webern was working on the Concerto for nine instruments, a work in which the handling of all elements is very disciplined and the same sort of structural questions that are raised in Op. 21, Op. 22/i and the works subsequent to Op. 26 are addressed. While Opp. 22/ii, 23, 25, and 26 seem to represent a diversion from the mainstream, Op. 24 stands inexplicably in the middle.

The only hint here of the disarray that prevails in the surrounding works is the non-alignment of rows with sections in the first movement. Here, as in Op. 22/ii, musical divisions are not always articulated by the completion of one set of rows and the beginning of new ones. The rows seem indifferent to the precise demands of structural definition – or, viewed from a different perspective, the precise demands of structural definition yield in this case to the imperatives of row technique – though the forms and transpositions, as well as the topography used, are clearly organized to reinforce the general formal outline.

Block topography is used throughout Op. 24; real linear setting, such as that used in the Symphony, does not occur, though it is suggested in the first movement, much of which consists of two successions of rows, each set in block style, progressing at the same time, rather in the manner of Opp. 23 and 25 but with no exchange of any sort between the two series. One of these is played by the piano, the other shared by the remaining eight instruments. At other places in the movement, one succession of rows encompasses all nine instruments as necessary. In most cases this results in alternating piano and orchestral rows; seven rows in the course of the movement are shared by piano and ensemble. All nine instruments contribute to the same rows throughout both the second and third movements. In all three, rows frequently overlap and are often elided, with up to three notes held in common.

This particular row offers the possibility of the elision of two row forms related as RI_7 to P_0 through an entire hexachord held in common. This elision occurs eight times in the first movement (R_7/I_2 and I_7/R_0 in bars 13–17 and again later in bars 51–5, and $R_2/I_9/R_2$ in bars 18–21 and later in bars 56–8) and twice in the second (I_4/R_9 in bars 21–4 and again on the repetition of these rows in bars 67–73). It will be noticed that the central twelve notes of two statements of the same row in succession – as, for example, the pair of R_2s in bars 18–21 and bars 56–8 – inevitably produce a third row at their centre (in the manner of a secondary set, except that here the row so produced is on the matrix), in this case I_9. Any row in which all four trichords are verticalized is capable of two interpretations. This occurs six times in the first movement (R_2/I_3 in bars 20–1 and twice more upon the return of this material in bars 56–8, P_4/RI_5 in bars 22–3, R_8/I_9 in bars 57–8 and P_6/RI_7 in the final bar) and at the end of the piece; the three rows that close the third movement are P_0/RI_1, R_0/I_1 and I_7/R_6.

The trichordal basis of the row of Op. 24 is reflected in the predominance of three-note figures, both horizontal and vertical, in the outer movements. The first theme of the first movement is expressed as a series of melodic trichords, each played entirely by one instrument, the first note of each coinciding rhythmically with the last note of the previous one. This theme comes to a cadence on three-note chords. The same sort of topography is used in the outer portions of the third movement (bars 1–13 and 56–70), which in addition use almost entirely retrograde row forms, thus exploiting also the 014 relationship of trichords discussed on pp. 21 and 22 (see example 1.14). In the second section of this movement (bars 14–27), the first three trichords of each row are verticalized and the fourth is presented melodically. In the corresponding fourth section (bars 42–55) half of the trichords

55

are verticalized and half are stated melodically. Only in the second-theme areas of the opening movement and the central section of the third is the row segmented in a way that runs counter to the inherent trichordal division.

Throughout the central movement a melody shared by six instruments (the combination but not the number changes for the middle section) is accompanied by the piano, playing dyads. In the outer sections (bars 1–28 and 59–78) this melody is a succession of the initial notes of all trichords of a series of R and RI rows, thus exploiting the 014 relationship already noted.

There is little repetition of row forms within major sections of Op. 24, but this apparent variety is abrogated by the fact that several row forms have very similar content.[18] The first movement uses fifty-four rows, of which six can be defined in two ways. Of these sixty rows, twenty-nine are redundant: thirty-one discrete row forms are used. The exposition uses twenty-one rows, of which only two are repetitions. The development contains fifteen rows, eight of which were used in the exposition; only R_7 appears twice within this section. The situation in the recapitulation and coda is the same as in the exposition. The second movement uses twenty-six rows, eleven of which are redundant; nine of these are accounted for by the return of the opening section as the last third of the piece. The third movement uses twenty-five row forms in a total of thirty-nine statements, three of these allowing alternative interpretations.

The row structure of Op. 24 is straightforward. There is no intersection or doubling and no repetition, either of single notes or of segments. The order is perfect; there are neither extra notes nor omissions. Two- and three-note segments of the row are verticalized throughout, characteristically by the piano, but also by the other instruments in the third movement. An entire hexachord is struck at once at the end of the first movement.

Op. 26

Das Augenlicht seems to represent the end of an avenue for Webern. The undisciplined handling of the row and the almost complete separation of row content from musical structure observed in this work follow naturally the directions taken in the second movement of Op. 22 and in Opp. 23 and 25; curiously, however, both tendencies disappear immediately after Op. 26.

Both elision and intersection run rampant in this work. Of some ninety-two rows stated in the course of it, only one, R_0 in the tenor in bars 8–13, is completely independent of its neighbours. Elision involves one or two notes. Intersection is ubiquitous.

The work calls for chorus and orchestra, and, although rows at times wander back and forth between the two groups, communication of this sort is limited, there being essentially vocal rows and instrumental rows. (This sets it apart from the only twelve-note work for chorus and instruments prior to this, Op. 19, in which all the parts share rows and material indiscriminately.) Since the rows show even less concern with the musical structure here than in the second movement of Op. 22, this segregation occasionally leads to a gap in the statement of a row as the result of either an orchestral or a choral section ending before its set of rows has been completed. This occurs for the first time in bars 23–37. Here the vocal rows have reached only note 5 when the choral singing is interrupted by an interlude consisting of a phrase sung by the sopranos followed by another sung by the altos, both with instrumental accompaniment. While the soprano and alto rows continue through the sung phrases, the orchestral rows are new, and those of the tenor and bass are simply halted, to be completed only upon the re-entry of the full chorus in bar 30. This reappearance of the chorus, unaccompanied, similarly interrupts the instrumental rows that began in bar 27; these are completed only in bars 31–7, after the second choral section has come to a close. Similar but less striking examples of interruption can be seen in the choral rows in bars 101–4.

The instruments routinely finish rows that have been begun by the voices and left incomplete at the end of a section of text, and occasionally the voices, on entering, take up rows already begun by the orchestra. Also, since rows are normally joined by elision in this piece, the first note of a voice row is frequently the last note of an instrumental one, and vice versa. There is a great deal of intersection between instruments and voices, as well; following the precedent of Opp. 23 and 25, the *Ausfall* is always in the instrumental row, never the voice. As a body, the voice rows are complete, though singly they intersect with each other.

The vocal music in *Das Augenlicht* is generated in a more regular fashion than its instrumental counterpart. For the most part, each section of the choir has its own row or series of rows, even though these are frequently begun or finished by the orchestra. The first intersection amongst voice parts occurs in bar 24; lateral communication occurs with increasing frequency as the piece progresses. The horizontal structuring of the vocal rows breaks down entirely only once, in bars 45–6, where R_6 is verticalized to produce the alto and tenor parts (Example 2.13).

The rows are dispersed among the instruments in an unsystematic fashion, intersecting unpredictably. As many as three rows converge on a single note in some places, and a held note sometimes serves two or more rows requiring the same pitch at different times. All the notes of a single melodic group joined by a slur are not necessarily from the same row, and, when they are, they are not always adjacent there. The same sort of discontinuity can be observed where grace notes are concerned.

The topography is essentially linear throughout, though it is a fairly frequent occurrence for two, and sometimes three, consecutive notes from a row to be played at the same time. There are only two seemingly intentional

2.13   Op. 26, bars 44–6 (pitches only)

instances of verticalization (that is, for the express purpose of creating chords): in bar 32, where the last three notes of P_{10} (the tenor row) are sung as a chord, and in the already-mentioned bar 46, where notes 7, 8 and 9 of R_6 are sounded at the same time in alto, tenor and bass. In both instances the verticalization is after the fact: a group of notes that sound together as the result of several rows progressing at the same time is commandeered by another row requiring the same notes, so that while a verticalization occurs, all the notes in question have a linear basis as well. Generally speaking, there are never fewer than two or more than four rows progressing at a time, though there are brief exceptions to this. Only one row is present for the latter half of bar 19, for a bar and a half just prior to bar 30, and again in bar 86; each of these places represents the close of an important structural division and is for instruments alone, directly preceding an unaccompanied homophonic entrance of the chorus. At one point, in bars 64–9, which Webern described as the dynamic highpoint of the movement,[19] six rows are present at the same time, four sung and two played.

Instrumental doubling is a persistent feature of Op. 26, occurring for the first time in bars 3–4 with the entry of the second voice and for the last time in bars 105 and 106, eight bars before the end. The instruments never double the voice, as they do in Op. 19 and again much later in Op. 31. Combinations vary, but those used most frequently are oboe and clarinet (with or without the flute) and viola and cello (with or without the saxophone). In the majority of cases the doubling is straightforward: two or three instruments join, always at the unison, to play a single part. The segments played in this way range from one to five notes in length, two or three being most frequent. Only in bars 58–64, a passage to be given close scrutiny presently, does a combination of instruments operate together for more than five consecutive notes.

Instrumental doubling becomes particularly complex in two places. The first of these is in bars 46–8. Here there is heavy doubling, which is quite independent of the row structure. The sketches of these bars are very simple: there are, in addition to the choral parts, the two instrumental voices (Example 2.14). As part of the process of scoring for full orchestra, these two original parts have been decomposed and their continuity obscured. Four-teen instruments are involved, playing portions of four rows, which converge briefly in two places. The instruments converge also, grouping themselves first in one way and then in another, so that no one instrument follows any of the rows. This non-alignment is illustrated in Table 2.2.[20]

This is followed after only a few bars by the section referred to earlier, bars 58–64, a passage somewhat reminiscent of Op. 19 with its ever-shifting instrumental background. In these bars the flute, oboe and clarinet support the violins; the saxophone plays with the violas and cellos throughout. The horn and trombone reinforce respectively one note only of the violin group and the cello group. The trumpet and mandolin play together, supporting first one group and then the other before turning to independent material in bar 61, in which they are joined (but not doubled) by the trombone and then the horn (Example 2.15). A much shorter example of the same sort of thing occurs in bar 71, where the glockenspiel, xylophone, trumpet and trombone each reinforce one note of the string parts, the trumpet and trombone then

2.14   Op. 26 sketch, bars 46–8 (instrumental parts only)

Table 2.2

(a) Notes required by the rows						
bars	46/3	47/1	47/2	47/3	47/4	48/1
R_6/10–12			Eb			
			E	D		
I_5(8–9, 11–12)	G#	E	Eb	D		
I_8(1–5)			E	D		
				Eb	C	C#
(b) Instrumental parts						
group 1	G#	E	Eb		C	C#
group 2			E	Eb	C	
group 3			Eb	D		
group 4					C	C#

2.15   Op. 26, bars 58–64 (reduction, pitches only)

2.16   Op. 26, bar 71 (reduction, pitches only)

diverging immediately (Example 2.16). As is customary with Webern, single notes are repeated, but not segments. These repetitions are very infrequent in the instrumental parts; they are more often to be found in the voice parts, where they are made necessary by the number of syllables in a phrase exceeding the number of row elements available.

A row analysis of this piece is difficult, as a result of the untidy behaviour of the rows and their attraction to each other. Fortunately, Webern's intentions are clear from the sketches; my analysis is his.[21] There are three instances of 'incorrect' ordering in Op. 26, all in my opinion more apparent than real, as grace notes are involved. These occur in bar 7, where the celesta has 10 then 9 of R_5; bar 102, where the violin plays $R_1/1$–3–2; and bar 84, where trombone and harp play 9–8–10 of P_4.[22] All but six of the forty-eight row forms – I_2, I_6, I_{10}, I_{11}, R_2 and P_7 – are used. There is no pattern to be discerned in the choice of row forms and transpositions, a situation that is very unusual for Webern generally, but one that is probably not unexpected in this particular work.

Op. 27

Two movements of the Variations for Piano, in which Webern seems to have shut the door firmly on his most recent style, represent a return to linear topography, something not seen since the Op. 22 Quartet. The first movement is a series of cancrizans figures in two voices; each row is accompanied by its exact retrograde, with the hands in most cases exchanging rows at the centre. On several occasions (in bars 9, 16, 31, 33, 36, 45 and 52) these rows intersect at the crossing.[23] In both of the outer sections (bars 1–18 and bars 37–54) successive cancrizans units are connected through a one-note elision in one voice only. The first large section is linked to the middle section in a similar way. A two-note elision is characteristic of the middle section, occurring in only one voice each time. This section is also joined to the next by such a connection. At two junctures in the central section, at bars 26 and 32, there is no elision. There are numerous two-note verticalizations in both voices; four adjacent notes are sounded together in bars 9, 16, 45 and 52. No note is immediately repeated; there is no doubling. The order is perfect. No note is missing. There is technically, however, one extra note, an E in bar 26; this is necessary in order to complete a symmetrical pattern begun in bar 22 as well as a sequence in bars 26–7, but it is not required by the row structure until two notes later. This movement uses eleven row forms and their retrogrades; six of these are repeated.

The second movement is a canon, so, predictably, the mapping is linear here as well. Since it is a mirror canon, each row in the *dux* is answered by its inversion in the *comes*. Four pairs of rows form two chains, RI_0–RI_5–RI_{10}–R_5 and R_0–R_7–R_2–RI_7, in which every join is accomplished through a one-note elision. These chains do not coincide exactly with the *dux* and *comes* of the canon, which read RI_0–RI_5–R_2–R_5 and R_0–R_7–RI_{10}–RI_7 respectively. Although a repeated a^1 is an important characteristic of this movement, there are no redundancies. Because the sum of the transposition numbers of each pair of rows is twelve, each pair converges on a^1, the note six semitones above the first note of P_0. The four pairs of As heard represent these meetings. There is no intersection, nor are segments repeated. Verticalizations are uniform in this movement: notes 6, 7 and 8 of every row are struck together. There are no extra notes or omissions and no doubling. The order is perfect. The topography is pointillistic with respect to register, with wide leaps necessitating rapid and extreme hand-crossing as the rows cross and recross in a highly disjunct manner.

In contrast to the preceding two movements, the third movement of Op.

27 uses block topography throughout, with a variety of elisions. The rows in Variation 1 (bars 1–12) are not joined. In Variation 2 the first two rows (P_1 and RI_0) are joined by a two–note elision; one note is held in common by the second and third rows (RI_0 and P_0) and the final two (RI_1 and RI_6); the third and fourth (P_7 and RI_1) are not joined at all; and both the fourth and fifth (RI_1 and RI_7) and the fifth and sixth (RI_7 and RI_1) are linked by an $m/12 = n/2$ intersection. Variation 3 uses a one-note elision, except in bar 30, where the note in question is repeated. The first three rows in Variation 4 are self-contained; the last two hold two notes in common, as do the last row of this variation and the first one of the next, and all those within Variation 5. The first and second and the third and fourth rows of Variation 6 are joined by four-note elision; the fourth and fifth rows are similarly joined, except that in this case the notes 9–12 of RI_1 are 1, 2, 3 and 5 (not 4) of R_0. The final two rows in the movement share one note. Since there is no overlapping without elision, there is no occasion for intersection beyond the three examples mentioned above ($12 = 2$ in Variation 2 and $12 = 5$ in Variation 6).

Verticalizations of two, three and four adjacent notes are very frequent in this movement. On one occasion, in bar 56, six notes are heard sounding at once as the result of the addition of one three-note chord to another. Repeated notes are a prominent feature of Variation 3. In some cases the notes heard twice are required by both rows; at other times they are simple repetitions. A two-note segment is repeated in bar 38 of Variation 4. The grace note in bar 18 is a repetition of the last note heard in the bar before, a technique reminiscent of the second movement of the Op. 22 Quartet.

There is no doubling in this movement, nor are there any extra notes or omissions. The note order is perfect. Twenty-two row forms are used (not the same twenty-two that were used in the first movement). A pattern emerges at one point in the movement that seems to presage the works that are to follow this one. Between bars 40 and 58 Webern uses a circular series of alternating retrograde inverted and prime rows: $RI_8–P_0–RI_{11}–P_3–RI_2–P_6–RI_5–P_9–RI_8–P_0$. This series begins in the fourth Variation, encompasses all of the fifth, and continues one row into the sixth. A circular series of this sort has not been observed since the Symphony, but such patterns are a recurring feature of the works from Op. 28 on.

Op. 28

The row topography is completely linear again in Op. 28; there are no chords, though in the first movement there is considerable telescoping of motives, with the result that two adjacent notes from a row are often struck together. Throughout most of this movement rows are segmented to produce two-, three- or four-note motives that are passed around from one instrument to another, in most cases overlapping by one note at either end. In the Theme and Variations 1 and 5, this happens irregularly, since all the motives are not the same length. Because of the make-up of this row, any odd/even pair of notes from any row played together produces a minor second, and an even/odd pair creates a third. Only one of the many simultaneities in the Theme (bars 1–15) is an odd/even pair; all the rest are consonant. Not all motives overlap in Variation 1 (bars 16–32) and in Variation 5 (bars 79–95), which Webern described as its reprise;[24] but of those that do, about half produce consonant and half produce dissonant intervals. In Variation 2 (bars 33–49), which according to Webern functions as a transition, the topography becomes more regular. For the first half of this variation, each row is divided only into hexachords, with one instrument playing notes 1–6 and a second completing the row. Notes 6 and 7 occur together. At the end of each row, the next begins in another instrument, with notes 12 of the old row and 1 of the new sounding together. All these simultaneities are thirds or sixths. In the second half of the variation, each row is divided into trichords, and as the variation progresses these begin to be telescoped, until at the end notes 3 and 4, 6 and 7, 9 and 10 and 12 and 1 are all sounded as dyads, making the number of consonances and dissonances exactly equal. The first two-thirds of Variation 6 (bars 96–112), which is the coda, also uses telescoped trichords. After bar 107 two-note motives are used; they overlap only partially, each one beginning before the last note of the previous one has stopped sounding. All the vertical intervals here are consonances. Variations 3 and 4 (bars 47–65, 66–78) are different from the surrounding ones in that the rows are divided consistently into tetrachords. This means that the simultaneities occur with exact regularity and that all are consonant.

All the variations of this movement are canonic, with rows or chains of rows in imitation. Since the overlapping of motives occurs within both *dux* and *comes*, the superposition of voices characteristic of imitation produces dense simultaneities. Throughout the first movement, only like rows are paired in canon, in all but two cases – once in Variation 2 and once in Variation 3 – prime with prime. The two rows of these pairs are in all cases separated by three semitones; since the symmetrical nature of the row is such that $P_3 = RI_0$, every row in this movement is paired with its own retrograde inversion at the same level of transposition, and therefore *dux* and *comes* are always playing opposing sets of semitones.[25]

A curious statement in Webern's own analysis of this movement is impossible to reconcile with the music. He says:

> The variations are purely *canonic* in nature! ... That is to say, the rows always run *linearly* and horizontally. At *not a single* point are notes stacked vertically from *the same row*!

While it is true that he does not build chords in this piece, which must be the sense of this statement, it is nevertheless also true that notes from the same row are stacked vertically in pairs with great frequency throughout the first movement. Perhaps the simultaneities produced by stretto segmentation, since they are the result of an essentially linear process and their precise make-up in some sense almost accidental, do not strike him as the same sort of phenomenon as those larger verticalizations that grow out of the desire for a particular sonority.

The tetrachordal invariance of this particular row (discussed on p. 24) is exploited in all three movements. In the first movement, the Theme and Variations 1, 4 and 6 are built from circular series of rows linked through tetrachordal elision. The rows used in these sections are P_6–P_2–P_{10}–P_6 and RI_6–RI_2–RI_{10}–RI_6. Each of the three sections begins at a different point in the series. Two-note elisions occur at the end of the Theme and in Variation 5; there is none in Variations 2 and 3.

In the outer sections of the second movement (a scherzo), only rows containing identical tetrachords – P_3, R_3, P_7, R_7, P_{11} and R_{11} – are used, so that the same note groups are heard, moving forwards and backwards continually, in all voices. Again, outer tetrachords are shared by successive rows. Here rows are not deployed pointillistically: each instrument states a chain of rows, which, if allowed, would continue to repeat indefinitely. This potential is recognized by the enclosure of these sections within repeat signs.

If the tetrachords of the first row (R_3) are labelled A→, B→ and C→ and the reverse of these A←, B← and C←, the content of the first eighteen bars of the piece can be represented in the following way:

$$
\begin{array}{ccccccc}
A\rightarrow & B\rightarrow & C\rightarrow & A\leftarrow & B\leftarrow & C\leftarrow & A\rightarrow \\
B\rightarrow & A\rightarrow & C\leftarrow & B\leftarrow & A\leftarrow & C\rightarrow & B\leftarrow \\
C\rightarrow & A\leftarrow & B\leftarrow & C\leftarrow & A\rightarrow & B\rightarrow & C\rightarrow \\
C\leftarrow & B\leftarrow & A\leftarrow & C\rightarrow & B\rightarrow & A\rightarrow & C\leftarrow \\
\end{array}
$$

It may be noted at this point that the structure of each voice in this section is an analogue of the structure of the row itself. In the row, the outer tetrachords are the same, while the central one is their retrograde. Similarly, each voice of the scherzo begins and ends with the same tetrachord, while its retrograde stands at the centre. All the parts are circular: each voice goes through the three tetrachords once, then a second time, playing each in retrograde, and ends with the one it opened with, in its original form.

Since the four voices are in canon at the distance of one note, and since the scherzo moves in even crotchets, the placement of tetrachords is more nearly like this:

$$
\begin{array}{ccccccccc}
A\rightarrow & B\rightarrow & C\rightarrow & A\leftarrow & B\leftarrow & C\leftarrow & A\rightarrow & & \\
& B\rightarrow & A\rightarrow & C\leftarrow & B\leftarrow & A\leftarrow & C\rightarrow & B\rightarrow & \\
& & C\rightarrow & A\leftarrow & B\leftarrow & C\leftarrow & A\rightarrow & B\rightarrow & C\rightarrow \\
& C\leftarrow & B\leftarrow & A\leftarrow & C\rightarrow & B\rightarrow & A\rightarrow & C\leftarrow & \\
\end{array}
$$

Although both direct imitation of melodic contours and cancrizans figures do occur, these are not used with consistency.[26] The effect is not of a highly organized imitative structure (though, of course, it is that) but rather of the display of many facets of the same tetrachord at once, and continuously, as if an object were being turned over and over in order that all its sides might be examined. One thinks also of Adorno's 'highly complicated machine, which remains firmly fixed in one place in spite of the dizzying movement of all its parts'.[27]

When the scherzo returns in bar 37, the same rows are used but the instruments have exchanged parts. Since the violin leads here again, as it did at the opening, the coincidence of the four parts is completely different this time. It can be represented in the following way:

$$
\begin{array}{llllllllll}
B\rightarrow & A\rightarrow & C\leftarrow & B\leftarrow & A\leftarrow & C\rightarrow & B\rightarrow & & & \\
C\rightarrow & A\leftarrow & B\leftarrow & C\leftarrow & A\rightarrow & B\rightarrow & C\rightarrow & & & \\
& & C\leftarrow & B\leftarrow & A\leftarrow & C\rightarrow & B\rightarrow & A\rightarrow & C\leftarrow & \\
& & A\rightarrow & B\rightarrow & C\rightarrow & A\leftarrow & B\leftarrow & C\leftarrow & A\rightarrow & \\
\end{array}
$$

The rows are set in a continuous manner for the first eight bars of the central section of this movement and pointillistically for the remaining eight. The rhythm of both halves of the section divides the rows into trichords and hexachords.

The central section of the third movement is likewise pointillistic, but with rows divided into tetrachords. The pattern of row distribution in the outer sections is also very similar to that in the parallel portions of the previous movement, with each instrument running through two entire rows. These eight rows can be identified as the four untransposed forms and their sixth transpositions. A list of all the possible interpretations reveals additional sets of relationships:

$$
\begin{array}{llll}
P_0 & (RI_9)- & I_0 & (R_3) \\
R_6 & (I_3)\ - & RI_0 & (P_3) \\
P_6 & (RI_3)- & I_6 & (R_9) \\
R_0 & (I_9)\ - & RI_6 & (P_9) \\
\end{array}
$$

Elision through common use of outer tetrachords is very frequent in Op. 28. Intersection also occurs in the outer sections of the second movement. In fact, this movement offers the first examples of *Ausfälle* in a canonic situation, something that is to become an important technique of the later Op. 31. The following intersections result in *Ausfälle* (the *Ausfälle* are in parentheses): $R_7/1 = (P_3/4)$ in bar 3, $P_3/5 = (P_7/4)$ in bar 4, $(P_7/8 = (P_{11}/1)$ in bar 6, $R_7/4 = (P_3/1)$ in bar 7, $R_3/2 = (P_{11}/3)$ and $P_{11}/4 = (P_7/5)$ in bar 13; and in the reprise $R_7/5 = (R_3/4)$ in bar 39, $R_3/8 = (R_{11}/1)$ in bar 41, $R_3/2 = (P_{11}/3)$ in bar 47, and $P_7/2 = (R_{11}/3)$ and $R_{11}/4 = (R_3/5)$ in bar 48. The opening section of this movement was sketched many times. In the first sketches all the notes required are present. In subsequent revisions some of the notes that were eventually excised are encircled or placed in parentheses; in yet later versions they have been removed altogether.[28] Example 2.17

(a) Sketchbook III, p. 87

2.17a

shows two early sketches of bars 1–18 and the form in which the same bars were finally published.[29]

Repeated notes are a feature of the material that Webern calls the fugue subject in bars 16ff of the third movement.[30] There are no repeated notes anywhere else in the work. The note order is perfect throughout; there are no extra notes or omissions; there is no doubling. Of the twenty-four discrete row forms available, the first movement uses fourteen, the second movement six and the third movement sixteen. In the first movement, even-numbered primes are used in succession in some sections, odd-numbered ones in others. P_{11}/RI_8 and P_0/RI_9 do not appear. Only four retrograde (or inverted) forms are used. The second movement is built entirely from three prime rows with the same tetrachordal content, and their inversions; only untransposed rows and sixth transpositions are used in the outer sections of the third movement.

Op. 29

Only linear topography is used in the first Cantata. With respect to the separation of vocal and instrumental rows and the essentially separate

(b) Sketchbook III, p. 90

2.17b

disposition of each, this work follows basically the same principles of row setting as its most recent choral predecessor, *Das Augenlicht*, but (if an appropriation of the text of the first song of the cantata may be forgiven) whereas the earlier work seems to represent *die Wolke* the cantata is certainly *der Lichtblitz*. The row structure is clear and consistent throughout; the apparently random intersection and the meandering rows that so characterize Op. 26 are not to be found here. Except for the fugal opening of the third, the outer movements are in four voices throughout, expressed by four row chains; the orchestral music of the central movement consists of four layers, also, with the solo voice adding a fifth, which does not intersect or interact with those of the orchestra. With a few exceptions at structural divisions, the row chains throughout all three movements are continuous, consisting of similar rows connected by two-note elisions.[31]

Chorus and orchestra alternate in the first movement. In the orchestral sections, rows are pointillistically distributed and operate in pairs, both rows of each pair exhibiting the same segmentation and progressing through similar successions of instruments, while in the sung portions each voice of the chorus sings one row strand in a continuous linear fashion, with no

(c) Published score

2.17c

intersection or exchange of parts. All chords are the result of the simultaneous statement of parallel elements of the four rows; in the instrumental music, only the notes of the outer trichords are sounded together in this way. There is no verticalization of row segments.

It will be remembered that the row of Op. 29 is such that in any rows related as P_0 and R_6 the first and third notes of each trichord simply exchange positions. This results in a high degree of pitch-class repetition. Webern obscures this fact in the orchestral music by changing octave, sometimes radically, when pitch classes return; in the choral music, the possibilities for exact repetition are fully exploited.

The orchestra plays groups of three chords in rhythmic unison on four occasions, in bars 1, 6, 36 and 41; these are produced by first and final trichords. In the first instance, the four rows used are R_{11}, RI_{10}, I_{11} and P_{10}. R_{11} and RI_{10} satisfy the requirements for invariance, but I_{11} and P_{10} do not. Therefore two of the four pitch classes in the first chord of both bar 1 and bar 6 recur in the third chord of the same bar; the other two do not. In both cases the repetitions are an octave away from the originals. The groups of chords occupying corresponding positions after the choral section, in bars 36 and 41, use the invariant relationship to a greater degree. The rows here are R_0 and P_6, I_3 and RI_9. Since both these pairs are separated by a tritone, all four pitch classes of the two chords in question are identical on both occasions. This identity is still understated, however, since the position of each repeated pitch class is three octaves away from its original.

The choral music is in short segments, alternating between homophony and imitation. In all the imitative segments, the voices move together rhythmically in pairs, alto with soprano and tenor with bass. They are paired in a different way melodically: the bass and tenor are mirror inversions of the soprano and alto respectively. In two cases, the 'schlug ein' and the 'bis er' segments, the alto and bass have the same material, which mirrors that of the soprano and tenor, thus creating a tighter version of the situation just described. This latter relationship – soprano and tenor in parallel motion, mirrored by alto and bass, the two voices of each pair separated by the distance of a major ninth – persists throughout all the homophonic segments. There are only three exceptions to this: the opening fragment, 'Zündender Lichtblitz', in which all four voices move in similar motion half of the time; and 'Wolke' in bar 21 and 'in Frieden' in bar 34, where in both instances the soprano and tenor intervals are expanded by an octave. As a result of these tightly controlled relationships, only six chord types occur in the homophonic choral sections, and three of these are rearrangements of the other three, so that every chord sung by the chorus is one of three basic types. All three, and their rearrangements, are symmetrical (Example 2.18).

There are no repeated notes in this movement, though frequently the same pitches and even the same chords are heard twice in close proximity as the result of the coincidence of several row forms with similar segmental content. So, for example, two concurrent rhythmic canons, one using R_2 and RI_7 and the other P_7 and I_2, produce, in bars 8–9, the motives shown in Example 2.19.

The choral section of the movement, in bars 14–35, exploits the invariant

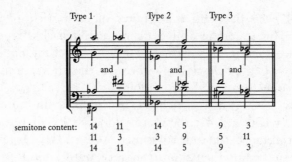

semitone content:

	Type 1		Type 2		Type 3	
	14	11	14	5	9	3
	11	3	3	9	5	11
	14	11	14	5	9	3

2.18

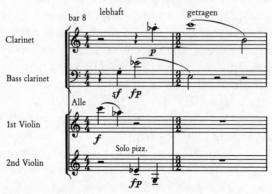

2.19   Op. 29/i, bars 8–9

properties of this row to a much greater degree, as can be seen from the following list of its content:

bars 14–19:

S	P₆:	A	F	Ab	G	B	Bb	C♯	C	E	Eb	F♯	D
A	R₀:	Ab	C	A	Bb	F♯	G	E	F	C♯	D	B	Eb
T	RI₉:	G	Eb	F♯	F	A	Ab	B	Bb	D	C♯	E	C
B	I₃:	F♯	Bb	G	Ab	E	F	D	Eb	B	C	A	C♯

bars 19–24:

S	P₃:	F♯	D	F	E	Ab	G	Bb	A	C♯	C	Eb	B
A	R₃:	B	Eb	C	C♯	A	Bb	G	Ab	E	F	D	F♯
T	RI₆:	E	C	Eb	D	F♯	F	Ab	G	B	Bb	C♯	A
B	I₆:	A	C♯	Bb	B	G	Ab	F	F♯	D	Eb	C	E

bars 23–31:

S	P₀:	Eb	B	D	C♯	F	E	G	F♯	Bb	A	C	Ab
A	R₆:	D	F♯	Eb	E	C	C♯	Bb	B	G	Ab	F	A
T	RI₃:	C♯	A	C	B	Eb	D	F	E	Ab	G	Bb	F♯
B	I₉:	C	E	C♯	D	Bb	B	Ab	A	F	F♯	Eb	G

bars 30–6:

S	P₉:	C	Ab	B	Bb	D	C♯	E	Eb	G	F♯	A	F
A	R₉:	F	A	F♯	G	Eb	E	C♯	D	Bb	B	Ab	C
T	RI₀:	Bb	F♯	A	Ab	C	B	D	C♯	F	E	G	Eb
B	I₀:	Eb	G	E	F	C♯	D	B	C	Ab	A	F♯	Bb

70

The most extreme realization of these relationships occurs in bar 21, where the second and third chords of the bar are identical except for the different disposition of parts (Example 2.20). Doubling occurs on only two

2.20   Op. 29/i, bar 21

occasions, in bars 18 and 25, which are statements of the same material and define the climactic section of the piece. Bar 18 is the only bar in the piece where chorus and orchestra appear together. Here the instruments are used only to reinforce the pitches sung by all the voices to the text 'schlug': note 3 of the four rows present here. The accentuation is extreme: both tenor and alto notes are played by four instruments, soprano and bass notes by three, all marked *sf*. When this bar returns, as bar 25, it is played by the orchestra alone, with the same number of parts as before, this time *sff*, and with percussion added. The oboe plays only two notes in the entire movement, as reinforcement in bars 18 and 25.

The pointillism of the orchestral parts in the second movement is extreme: of some 128 instrumental motives, all but 11 are two notes in length, and none is longer than four. In contrast to the previous movement, no pattern can be discerned here in the timbral distribution of these motives. The rows in the voice part are self-contained. A solo part exists throughout the movement: in the initial section it is played by the clarinet; thereafter it is sung. At the opening the clarinet plays the retrograde at the sixth transposition; this row returns at the centre of the movement, followed by its exact retrograde. Both times only four parts are present, the solo accompanied by three additional parts playing in rhythmic unison and producing three-note chords throughout. Although the appearance of these chords might suggest verticalization, this technique is not used anywhere in this movement. In the remaining sections, four instrumental voices accompany the solo, rhythmically offset so that chords do not result.

There is only limited doubling, and no notes are repeated gratuitously. Nevertheless, to an even greater degree here than in the previous movement, pitches recur in close proximity as the result of invariance. Example 2.21 shows cancrizans figures produced by the convergence of two rows in the first major section (bars 6–26). Convergence results in the repetition of single

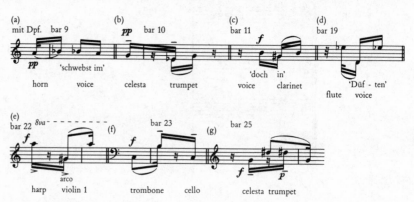

2.21   Op. 29/ii

pitches in bars 8(f^2), 16(b), 17(a^1) and 22 ($g\#^2$ – twice), and of two–note figures in bars 20–1 (d^1–$e\flat^2$, a^1–$b\flat^2$ and $b\flat^2$–$f\#^2$). The pitch-class progression B–C occurs three times in close succession in bars 15–16 (voice, flute, clarinet), but no two of these three figures are the same (Example 2.22). Single pitches are reinforced through the convergence of independent rows in bars 7(d^1), 8(b, $f\#^2$, a^1), 9($f\#^1$), 11(f^1, d^3), 12(c^1, $c\#^1$, $f\#^1$), 13(a), 14($a\flat^2$, d^2), 15(f^1), 16($e\flat^1$, a^2, $b\flat^1$, c^2), 18($c\#^2$, d^1), 19(b^1, $a\flat$), 20($f\#$, c^2, g^1), 21($e\flat^2$), 22(d^1) and 24(e^2).

2.22   Op. 29/ii

Two–note figures are played by two instruments at the same time on four occasions in this section; the first, e^1–c^1 in bar 13, represents the convergence of RI_6 (1–2 in the celesta) and R_{11} (8–9 in the voice), while the other three, all in bars 22–3, are examples of doubling, on the part of the second violin, viola and cello. This artifical augmentation, towards the end of the section, of a process of increasing density that was up to this point spontaneous begins immediately after a bar in which the concentration of legitimately reinforced pitches is particularly heavy (Example 2.23). In the return of this

2.23   Op. 29/ii

section, in bars 36–56, the situation is exaggerated. Both mandolin and glockenspiel are used to reinforce single pitches played by other instruments; indeed, the glockenspiel does nothing else. The first violin is used as a reinforcement in bars 5–6, 31 and 32, where it serves to articulate the end of the introductory section and the axis of the palindrome occurring at the centre of the expanded return of this section later in the movement. In both cases, the violin plays two notes, the f^2 of the viola followed by the harp's db^2 in bars 5–6 and bar 31, and the reverse of this in bar 32.

The third movement differs topographically from the other two in several respects. In this movement chorus and orchestra are heard together for the first time; whenever this happens (in twenty-nine bars of seventy-three) the chorus simply doubles orchestral parts, adding nothing to the pitch content of the piece. The chorus sings alone and actually contributes to the serial progress of the movement in only two bars, 66 and 70.

The movement begins with instruments alone, the chorus entering only in bar 17. No more than two parts sing at a time until the choral section beginning at bar 39, and these two double the winds only. The disposition of the voices can be represented in the following way:

bars:	17	18	19	20	21	22	23	24	25	26	27	28	29	30
$RI_3/RI_0/RI_9$:	T.	.	.	.	A.	. T.	.	.	.	B.	. T.	. A.	.	.
$RI_9/RI_6/RI_3$:		B.	.	.	.	A.	. S.	.	.	.	.	TS.	. . B.	. . .

Soprano and alto sing together for half of the following section, in bars 39–48, tenor and bass for the other half, again reinforcing the wind parts. The section in bars 49–52 is similarly divided into halves. In this case the chorus is present in only the first half, and for the first time all four voices are heard together, reinforcing the strings as well as the winds. The pitch content of these bars (49–52) is complete in both the orchestra and the chorus. The final section of this movement uses both soloist and chorus, but not at the same time. As in the second movement, the rows of the solo voice are not given instrumental reinforcement.

There are several repetitions in this movement – $I_0/11$ in bars 6–7; $RI_9/7$ and $RI_3/7$ in bars 27–9; note 10 of all four rows present in bars 50–1 plus notes 3 and 4 of the following four rows, also in bar 51; $RI_9/4$ in bar 62; and the seventh note of all four rows in bars 69–70. Verticalized dyads appear throughout, as a regular feature of one of two fugue subjects. (This fugue is discussed on pp. 292–302.) The only intervals produced in this way are major and minor sixths and major sevenths.

No notes are left out of any of the movements, nor is there any disruption in the correct order. The row is segmented for the purposes of orchestration, but segments are neither repeated nor layered.

The two-note elision used throughout all three movements results in circular series of four similar rows. Primes and retrograde inversions regress by three transpositional levels when elided in this way; retrogrades and inversions advance by the same number. Because of the symmetrical nature of the row, only six discrete chains of this type are possible, each capable of two interpretations. Webern uses five of these, only one of which cannot be interpreted as a 0–3–6–9 or 9–6–3–0 progression. (This is the series R_2–R_5–R_8–R_{11}, used in the second movement.) The only chain avoided altogether is P_{11}–P_8–P_5–P_2 (RI_4–RI_1–RI_{10}–RI_7). Alternate groups of rows in the main body of the first movement (from bar 14 on) present all four row forms and all four levels of transposition (0, 3, 6, 9) – in a sense the complete materials upon which the movement is based. In the third movement from bar 39 on, alternate groups present all four forms at the same level of transposition. Only two row forms – P_{11}/RI_4 and P_8/RI_1 – are not used at all in the course of the entire work.

Op. 30

The row topography is linear throughout Op. 30, as might be expected, since the work is imitative. Without exception, canonic voices correspond with series or chains of rows. The orchestration is pointillistic, and there is considerable doubling of parts, in the Theme and all the Variations, with the exception of the fifth. The material doubled is always melodic, never chordal. Repeated notes are a feature of Variation 1, in which melodic fragments in long note values are accompanied by chords, most of which are played as many as six or seven times. Linear groups of notes are not repeated anywhere in the work, and there is no layering of segments. Most chords are produced by the verticalization of adjacencies, although on a very few occasions in Variation 6 a chord is formed instead by the coincidence of several rows. (Often, especially in Variation 5, motivic imitation is so dense that three or four notes are struck at the same time in the course of the progress of four voices in imitation; a simultaneity of this kind does not function as a chord.) All chords of verticalized adjacencies consist of tetrachords. Since the row of this work (given as Examples 1.20 and 1.21 on p. 26 above) is symmetrical ($P_0 = RI_{11}$), there are only twenty-four discrete permutations. All of these are used.

This particular row offers the possibility of several elisions.[32] Webern uses two of these, the ordered seven-note and the unordered tetrachordal elisions. These are given structural significance: the seven-note elision is a characteristic feature of the main theme, and shared tetrachords are an intrinsic element of the transition.[33] The former is particularly interesting because of the row density it produces. Whenever the seven-note elision is used, each row from the third one on begins while two others are still being played out; the last two notes of one row function, not only as 6 and 7 of another, but also as 1 and 2 of a third. Thus the fourth and fifth notes of each row in such a chain serve a triple function; whenever two similar rows hold two notes in common a third row is inevitably present (see Example 1.20). This is a denser version of the situation in Op. 24.[34]

Each of the seven sections of this work – the Theme and six Variations – is entirely self-contained with respect to row structure, and each makes use of the row in a characteristic way. The Theme (bars 1–20) uses all four row forms, untransposed and unconnected; with a few exceptions the intervals and direction preserve the symmetry thus implied.

The apparently simple melody-and-accompaniment texture of Variation 1 (bars 21–55) belies its row structure, which consists of not two, as one would suspect, but three parallel row successions. A chain of inverted retrogrades and a chain of primes both employ the seven-note elision, and a succession of unconnected retrogrades accompanies every second row in the prime chain at the same level of transposition. Because the prime and retrograde series use the same transpositions, the central tetrachord of every retrograde is the same as that of the prime progressing at the same time; the two series converge for all these common tetrachords.

Variation 2 (bars 56–73) consists entirely of four-note chords. Two parallel row chains proceed in canon, both employing tetrachordal elision. The rows used in this Variation form interlocking arches. The first of these is a palindrome progressing up to bar 63 and then regressing as far as bar 69. The second half of this arch acts as the first half of another that does vertically what the first did horizontally. The latter consists of an I chain and a P chain, progressing to their untransposed versions in bar 69, each then regressing through the levels of transposition used by the other up to that point. The second half of this arch can be seen as the first half of yet a third, beginning in bar 69 with what would be, if continued, an I–RI chain and a P–R chain, the I(–RI) chain using the same series of transpositions as the original R–P chain, and the P(–R) chain using the set of transpositions originally appearing in the RI–I chain. This circular and therefore potentially endless progression is halted halfway through the third arch, as can be seen in the following diagram:

bar: 56   63   69   73

$$RI_0 \quad RI_7 \quad RI_2 \quad I_2 \quad I_7 \quad I_0 \quad I_5 \quad I_{10} \quad [-RI_{10} \; RI_5 \; RI_0]$$
$$R_0 \quad R_5 \quad R_{10} \quad P_{10} \quad P_5 \quad P_0 \quad P_7 \quad P_2 \quad [-R_2 \; R_7 \; R_0]$$

The seven–note elision reappears in Variation 4 (bars 110–34), where the retrograde form of the row (or the inversion) is used exclusively. The density of this variation is twice that of Variation 1, with four parallel chains rather than two. All four row chains present series of elided retrograde rows, beginning with successively higher transpositions. The result, as in Variation 2, is a small segment of an infinite circular progression. When this progression is broken at the end of the variation, the first voice is halfway through the transposition on which the second voice began, the second voice has arrived at the starting transposition of the third, and so on:

$$R_7 \; —(R_2)—R_9 \; —(R_4)—R_{11} — (R_6)—R_1—(R_8...)$$
$$R_8 \; —(R_3)—R_{10} — (R_5)—R_0 \; —(R_7)—R_2—(R_9...)$$
$$R_9 \; —(R_4)—R_{11} — (R_6)—R_1 \; —(R_8)—R_3—(R_{10}...)$$
$$R_{10}—(R_5)—R_0 \; —(R_7)—R_2 \; —(R_9)—R_4—(R_{11}...)$$

    Variation 5 (bars 135–45) is described by Webern as a restatement of material from the Theme and Variation 2.[35] Again this idea of reprise is reflected in the row structure. The melody of Variation 5 is presented by a prime followed by an inversion at the same transposition, a structure similar to the one that opened the Theme. With one exception, all other rows in the variation make use of the tetrachordal elision, which appeared in Variation 2 and has not been used since.

    In Variation 6 (bars 146–80) the texture is again dense. Both of the elisional patterns developed previously in the work are used in this variation. Four chains – three primes and one retrograde – progress simultaneously. Two of the prime chains consistently use the seven–note elision. While the remaining prime and retrograde also progress in this way until bar 167, at that point they suddenly begin to use the tetrachordal elision. This change causes them to regress through the same series of transpositions they have used up to this point and end the variation as they began it.

$$P_{10}\text{---}(P_3)\text{---}P_8\text{------}(P_1)\text{---}P_6\text{------}(P_{11})\text{---}P_4\text{------------------}$$
$$P_7\text{------}(P_0)\text{---}P_5\text{------}(P_{10})\text{---}P_3\text{------}(P_8)\text{---}P_1\text{-}$$

$$R_2\text{---}(R_9)\text{---}R_4\text{------}(R_{11})\text{---}R_6\text{---}R_{11}\text{---}R_4\text{---}R_9\text{---}R_2\text{-------}$$
$$P_9\text{------}(P_2)\text{---}P_7\text{------}(P_0)\text{------}P_5\text{------}P_0\text{------}P_7\text{---}P_2\text{---}P_9\text{-------}$$
$$\texttt{<----------------- x ----------------->}$$

There is a significant omission in Variation 5. The tetrachord that should link I_{10} and I_3 in the chain of inverted rows (B–C-A-A♭) does not occur. This creates not only a lacuna in the row structure but also a gap in a rigorous imitative framework. An examination of the orchestration shows that every section of the orchestra is represented at some point in every bar except for bar 142, in which the harp and celesta do not appear. The row structure, the imitative framework and the orchestration all demand a crotchet chord (B–C–A–A♭) in the harp or celesta on the first beat of bar 142. Several versions of this variation are sketched on p. 74 of the fourth sketchbook, and this chord is in place in all of them, including the one identified as the final one, where it is a crotchet, as expected, and is labelled 'Harfe'. Work on the next variation follows immediately. At the extreme lower right-hand corner of p. 76, surrounded by sketches of Variation 6, another version of bar 142 appears alone, one that Webern presumably found satisfactory. Completely isolated from its natural surroundings, it is numbered, and labelled *gilt* – and the chord is gone. Heinrich Deppert has adduced an elaborate explanation to cover this omission, the critical point being that Webern left out this chord because the required pitches are played by the first violin in bars 141–3.[36] I disagree with his thesis. The excision of this chord was not, I think, a negative act, performed in order to avoid reiterated pitches. (Witness, for example, the similar situation in bars 139–40, where the harp and celesta play C–C♯–B♭–A at the same time that the first violin plays B♭–A–C–C♯ in the same octave.) Rather, it was a positive one, inspired by the opportunity of using a technique that he had employed for the first time in the second movement of the Op. 28 Quartet and that was to play an almost overwhelmingly significant role in the Op. 31 Cantata, sketches for which begin just a few pages later: the use of the *Ausfall* in a canonic situation. Even though this technique was not used in Op. 30 prior to Variation 5, a version of it does occur in Variation 6, where in bars 167–77 b♭²s and b♭¹s sustained by the woodwind and a long D in the bass serve several rows in succession; it was in the midst of sketching this variation, which is different in many ways from the others, that Webern finally dropped the chord from bar 142.[37] It is as if suddenly, near the end of Op. 30, he became inspired with the new set of ideas that was to find full expression in Op. 31. Note order is perfect throughout Op. 30. The only notes missing are those constituting the *Ausfälle* in Variations 5 and 6; there is no note whose presence is not demanded by the row structure.

Op. 31

The topography is linear throughout Op. 31, although some of the movements do not give that impression because of a large number of verticalizations (in Nos. I and IV) or rhythmic unisons (in the central portion of No. V). Four row strands progress simultaneously throughout all movements except the first, in which there are only two. The movements are very different from each other and will be dealt with individually; they do, however, show certain similarities with respect to the use of the row. The inherent tendency of groups of notes to remain intact in several permutations is used to advantage in all the movements. Most contiguous rows are elided, although only in the second movement and the A sections of the third is the number of notes shared completely consistent; in this respect this cantata shows much greater diversity than the earlier one. Rows are elided at various times by one, two, three, five and six notes. Intersection and *Ausfälle* occur in all movements. In many ways the topography of Op. 31 resembles that of *Das Augenlicht* more than that of any of the intervening works, in which rows tend to be more independent and self-contained.

The texture of the six movements is quite varied. The two recitatives (Nos. I and IV), as well as the central portion of No. V, are solo and accompaniment for the most part, while other movements (the sixth and most of the third) are completely linear. The second movement is linear in conception also, but is exceedingly spare as the result of a large number of *Ausfälle*, which effectively reduce the number of voices heard, and of a pointillistic deployment of those that remain. The outer sections of the fifth movement contain chorale-like homophony. While in the second movement many redundancies are ruthlessly eliminated, all the voice parts are doubled by instruments in the refrain sections of the third movement and in all of the sixth.

I 'Schweigt auch die Welt'

The first movement of Op. 31 is the only one of the six not built from four series of rows proceeding together. In this movement there are only two, one essentially melodic, the other accompanimental. These consist of cyclic repetitions of the four row forms at the sixth transposition; the rows proceed in the same order in both parts, but the cycles are out of phase. Each part runs through its cycle three times and begins a fourth.[38] The accompanying series is in fact one row short: the final row of its second cycle, R_6, which should occur in bar 25, is missing but not missed, since the melodic series alone produces considerable congestion in this bar, resulting in the sounding of all twelve notes together. One can assume that this represents an *Ausfall* on a large scale. In the melodic series, successive rows within each cycle share one note. The cycles are elided by hexachords held in common. The elisions follow a less regular pattern in the accompanying series, where rows are not elided in most cases. The exceptions are a single note shared by the first and second rows of the second cycle and five notes held in common by the first and second and again by the third and fourth rows of the last cycle.

The high degree of invariance exhibited by this row and its inversion at the same level of transposition[39] is exploited in various ways in this movement. In any piece built on only two row forms and their untransposed retrogrades notes will appear repeatedly grouped in the same way; here, however, the frequency of recurrence of these two pitch collections is twice what would normally be expected. The four-note groups G–G♯–E–F and C♯–A–D–B♭ remain intact in all the rows used. The unusual persistence of the collection C♯–A–D–B♭ is not as apparent as it might have been because five of the eleven appearances are within verticalized hexachords. The collection G–G♯–E–F, however, is presented melodically all eleven times, using with very few exceptions some combination of the same intervals – sixths, sevenths and ninths (E–F appears as a minor second three times and E–G♯ as a major third only once) – and thereby making its ubiquity felt.

The peculiar immutability of this row is also exploited through verticalization. The sharing of verticalized hexachords in the melodic series has been noted already; every I/i–RI/ii in this series is presented as a hexad. The movement opens with the first I/i of this series played by a wind group that functions together as a choir throughout the movement: saxophone, bass clarinet, trumpet, horn, trombone and tuba. In bar 2 the strings play the first hexachord of the accompanying series, P_6/i, as a hexad. These two collections, although presented in studiously dissimilar forms here (wind instruments versus strings, closed versus open position with the attendant differences in range and degree of dissonance), hold five pitch classes in common (A, B♭, C, D and E♭) and are, therefore, very nearly the same chord. With only a few exceptions, to be discussed presently, these two hexachords, I/i and P/i (or RI/ii and R/ii), are the only ones verticalized in this movement; therefore the pitch content of all the chords in the piece is nearly identical, the only variable being the sixth note, which is sometimes B and sometimes C♯.

The voicing and orchestration of these nearly identical chords display a subtle balance of variety and stability. On the one hand, through fourteen appearances of one or the other of these collections,[40] the pitches are constantly rearranged and the spacing between voices varied so that only two of the chords (those in bars 1 and 7) are actually the same. At the same time, however, the instrumentation conforms to restrictions that I have previously likened to the practice of ringing changes, though in this case the technique is modified considerably. The wind choir plays four hexads; in all of these, the saxophone plays C♯ and the bass clarinet C. Each of the other instruments plays the same pitch in both bars 1 and 7, and a second one in bars 12 and 40. The remaining ten hexads are played by the strings. In this choir, the violas are the most stable element, always playing D and E♭. The cellos play A and B♭ in seven of ten cases; on the three occasions when they do not, these notes are played by the basses. The remaining two notes, either B and C or C and C♯, are played by the violins and basses, except in the three cases just mentioned, where they are played by the violins and cellos. These collections are disposed in various ways, with each pitch class appearing in several octaves in the course of the piece, but a kind of stability is maintained nevertheless through this fairly constant pitch-class–instrument relationship.

The verticalizations that occur within the melodic series are straightforward and serve to delineate the row structure. Those within the accompanying series are neither so straightforward nor so uniform. The two outer hexachords and the two central ones of the first cycle (P_6/i, RI_6/ii, I_6/i and R_6/ii) are all presented as hexads, thus defining the cycle. The second of these is played by the wind and is in every respect identical to the chord that opened the movement (I_6/i of the melodic series). The other three are played by the strings, the choir that predominates generally in the accompaniment. The two halves of the first cycle, so effectively framed by these four hexads, are rhythmically and texturally identical and exploit the pitch-class invariance peculiar to this row. Each half contains, between the two hexads, a symmetrical figure played by celesta and harp: a single note followed by a pentad and then the reverse of this. The first of these figures is given in Example 2.24. The two pentads in this example exhibit an unusual type of inversion in which the pitch classes, rather than the intervals, of the second when read from top to bottom are the same as those of the first read from bottom to top.

2.24   Op. 31/i

Since the rows used in the second half of the cycle are the retrograde of those in the first half, and the material is symmetrical, the pitch-class content of the events in the second half is simply that of the first half in reverse. This

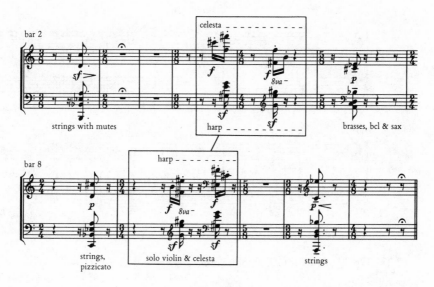

2.25   Op. 31/i, accompaniment, bars 2–12 (reduction)

relationship, however, is not emphasized. As can be seen in Example 2.25, only the hexachord I_6/ii in bar 9 is set in a way that makes its relationship to its earlier counterpart (RI_6 in bar 6) apparent. Webern has chosen to focus instead on more subtle associations. Although the strings' chord in bar 8 has the same pitch-class content as that played by the wind in the previous bar, he prefers to call attention to its similarity to the one played by the strings to open this series (P_6/i in bar 2). The four inner voices of these two chords are identical, while both the outer voices have slipped up a semitone. The similarity of the final chord of the cycle and the second, in bar 7, is pointed out in a somewhat perverse way: while these two chords have the same outer notes (albeit in different octaves), the inner make-up has changed.

Similar relationships can be seen in the remaining cycles. The accompaniment of the second cycle is truncated, partly as a result of the absence of the R_6 with which it should end (Example 2.26). The heptads defining the first half of the cycle are present here, as in the previous strophe; however, the pentads are gone from the central portion, which is now presented in a completely linear fashion by the clarinet. The initial hexad is really all that remains of the rest of this cycle, since the second hexachord of I_6 is subsumed by the giant verticalization that occurs in bar 25, marking the centre of the piece, and the row that should follow is the missing R_6. The chords have thus been reduced in number from four to three. This time the second chord, in bar 21, bears the same relationship to the first, in bar 14, that was observed in the earlier cycle between the third, in bar 8, and the first, in bar 2. (In order for the two cycles to be parallel, the chord in bar 14 should be echoed by the one in bar 23 rather than by the one in bar 21.)

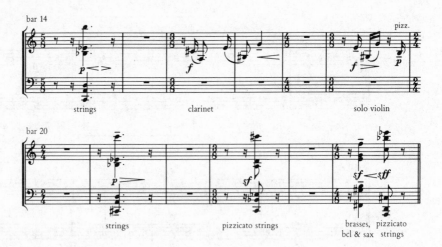

2.26 Op. 31/i, bars 14–25, accompaniment (reduction)

The accompanying material in the third cycle makes use once again, albeit in a different way, of the five-note invariance. As in the first cycle, the four pivotal hexachords are verticalized; the resulting hexads are orchestrated in reverse order this time: strings, strings, wind and strings. The five pitch classes held invariant by P_6/ii and RI_6/i are verticalized in bar 35, serving both rows at once. The unique member of the P_6/ii hexachord is taken from the voice part; that of RI_6/i is played at the same time as the five common notes, in bar 35. The corresponding figure in the second half of the cycle, consisting of the hexachords I_6/ii and R_6/i, is treated in a like fashion in bar 41. This verticalization is distinguished by its unique instrumentation: celesta, harp and solo violin. The two unshared notes are placed as before: the odd note of the hexachord I_6/ii appears in the voice part, while the odd note of R_6/i is played at the same time as the five notes held in common.

The centre of the piece, in bar 25, is marked by the verticalization of both hexachords of RI_6, the second articulated by the strings shortly after the first, which remains sounding, is played by the wind. The end of the piece is similarly marked by the sounding of all twelve notes at once, thereby presenting the total pitch material without defining any particular row form.

II 'Sehr tief verhalten'

The bass aria, 'Sehr tief verhalten', is the only movement of the six to use one system of elision consistently throughout; all successive rows hold two notes in common. Each of the four chains goes through twelve rows in the course of the movement, P and RI rows alternating in two voices, I and R in the other two, with the result that each of the forty-eight row forms is heard once.

$$I_7 \ —R_6 \ —I_9 \ —R_5 \ —I_{11} —R_{10}—I_1 \ —R_0 \ —I_3 \ —R_2 \ —I_5 \ —R_4$$
$$P_7—RI_8—P_5 \ —RI_6—P_3 \ —RI_4—P_1 \ —RI_2—P_{11} —RI_0 \ —P_9 \ —RI_{10}$$
$$I_6 \ —R_5 \ —I_8 \ —R_7 \ —I_{10} —R_9 \ —I_0 \ —R_{11}—I_2 \ —R_1 \ —I_4 \ —R_3$$
$$P_6 \ —RI_7—P_4 \ —RI_5—P_2 \ —RI_3—P_0 \ —RI_1—P_{10}—RI_{11}—P_8 \ —RI_9$$

The rows have been listed in such a way as to make their symmetry apparent: each pair of rows represents a mirror inversion, beginning at the same level of transposition and diverging at a regular rate (successive I and R rows rise by a whole tone, P and RI rows descend by the same interval), coming together again at the same level of transposition after six rows have been stated – that is, after each has traversed the distance of a tritone – and stopping just short of arrival back at the starting point. If things were to continue, an infinitely repeating closed cycle would result. To emphasize this potential, the last two notes of each chain are missing.

One row chain is sung entirely by the bass soloist. This is a straight-forward part, essentially continuous, containing two repeated notes, $I_{11}/5$ in bar 33 and $I_1/10$ in bar 40. The other three strands are distributed pointil-listically among the instruments. In the outer sections of this three-part form, the accompanying voices move quickly from one instrument to the next, playing sometimes only a single note, sometimes a group of two or three, before moving on. In one case only (the trombone in bars 60–1), four notes are played in succession before a change of timbre occurs. In the central section (bars 31–44), the pulse doubles and activity becomes more concen-trated, with groups containing as many as five notes at one point, and most frequently three. One of the instrumental chains repeats a note coincident with the first repetition in the voice: the cello repeats $P_3/5$ in bar 35.

Willam explains the large number of *Ausfälle* in this movement as the result of Webern's desire to avoid pitch repetition in a continuing quest for truly atonal music.[41] He cites Schoenberg's famous admonition (as trans-mitted by Rufer) against repeating a note until all eleven others have been heard.[42] This explanation, although bearing the unmistakable authority of the Master himself, does not seem to fit the situation in this case, however, as the score contains numerous examples of carefully contrived pitch redun-dancies.[43] (A similar situation in the outer sections of Op. 28/ii has been remarked on by Arnold Whittall, who sees Webern's admission of pitch and pitch-class repetitions and traditional chordal constructions as an essential complement to his strictly predictable linear structures.[44])

There are eight grace notes in the instrumental parts of 'Sehr tief verhalten', and none of them is produced by only that row element which properly precedes the note that follows in the same instrument. In four cases – bars 16, 41, 65 and 69 – the grace note is produced by one of the accompanying rows and the following note by another. In both bars 42 and 43 the grace note represents the intersection of those two accompanying voices that do not contain the note following. In the remaining two cases, in bars 28 and 66, the grace note again belongs to two voices, but here one of these voices contains the following note as well. This independence of grace notes, like the use of *Ausfälle*, was characteristic of *Das Augenlicht*.

There is a single anomaly in the note order, in bar 37, where notes 10–12 of RI$_4$ (all *Ausfälle*) occur in the order 11–10–12 (G, B and B♭ in the horn). An early sketch shows two additional notes in this bar, a G in the cello on the fifth beat and a B♭ in the bass clarinet on the sixth. These notes, which provide the end of RI$_4$ in the correct order, are missing in the next draft.[45] Doubling of parts occurs in only one bar in this movement: at the climax of the middle section in bar 40 the two instrumental parts are doubled, clarinet by celesta and horn by harp. There is one misprint in this movement: the viola should have a c^1 rather than the b written in bar 14.[46]

III 'Schöpfen aus Brunnen des Himmels'

Webern must have found the idea of going through his matrix using each of the possible forms of the row once an attractive one, because he repeated it in the next movement. In 'Schöpfen aus Brunnen' he achieves the same inclusiveness as in 'Sehr tief verhalten' through a diametrically opposed pattern of rows. While the material presented horizontally in each voice of the previous song was limited with respect to row forms, the sounding together of dissimilar rows produced complete vertical patterns that recurred throughout the movement. Just the opposite occurs in 'Schöpfen aus Brunnen'. Here the material is complete horizontally (the row content of all voices is identical, at different levels of transposition, each dealing with all four row forms before the end of the piece is reached), but the vertical mass is neither inclusive at any given moment nor consistent throughout. With respect to row structure, the movement is in three sections with only two row types used in each.

The central section is complete, presenting the inverted and the retrograde row at all levels of transposition. The outer sections comprise the two halves of a similar total array of the retrograde inversions and primes. Throughout, the four voices are equidistant within the octave, exhibiting the following set of symmetries.

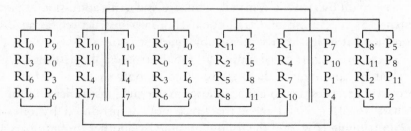

The row successions within sections will be recognized as those seen in the previous movement, the product of consistent two–note elision. This pattern of course does not hold between sections, where the row types change. Two of the voices of the first section are complete; the remaining two – those ending with RI_7 and RI_{10} – lack a final note, which is supplied by their retrogrades at the opening of the following section.[47] There is no elision at the end of the I–R constellation. The musical structure agrees with the row structure to the extent that the two outer sections match; however, the central constellation, of I and R rows, is divided further by texture into three smaller sections relating to the outer A sections as B, A and B. All the A sections are canons for three-part women's choir and orchestra; the intervening B sections are for soprano solo with an instrumental accompaniment alternating between chords and imitation. Four voices operate throughout; chords, when they occur, are produced by verticalization.

In both this movement and the sixth the voice parts are doubled by the orchestra. This is a sort of excess not encountered since the much earlier Op. 19 songs. Nearly all of the material of the three choral parts in the A sections is supported at the unison by at least one instrument and often by as many as three; even portions of the fourth voice, which is entirely orchestral, are played by two or three instruments (or sections) at once.[48] Instrumental doubling does not occur in the B sections, and the solo soprano is never supported, even when she sings briefly in the final A section (bars 52–3). The instrumental voice is not doubled in the central A section.

Even though the choral voices are continuous, their rows are segmented for the purposes of orchestral support. With few exceptions the segmentation is the same in all voices, including the orchestral one, which for the most part passes from one instrument to another without doublings. The length of segments is most extreme near the end of the movement. The first A section (bars 1–12) opens with a two-note followed by a six-note segment; thereafter groups of two or five notes predominate, with only one of four notes and one of three. The short central A section (bars 28–36) contains only four segments, of three, five, six and three notes. The final section (bars 45–59) opens with an eight-note segment followed by a single note, returning thereafter to series of from two to five.

There are few irregularities in the row structure of this movement. The row chains that begin as the alto and the instrumental voices in the final A section exchange roles in bar 54. No note occurs out of order; none is missing; and there is none that cannot be accounted for. There is no borrowing and no intersection in the A sections. The following notes in the B sections are shared: the solo soprano's three notes in bar 21 ($R_0/8$–10) double also as $R_6/3$, $R_9/6$ and $R_3/3$, in that order; in bar 22 the tuba and horn notes and the first violin's grace note ($R_3/5$, 6 and 8) function secondarily as $R_6/8$, 9 and 10; and in bar 23 the two bassoon notes ($I_0/3$ and 4) double as

$R_3/9$ and 10. Two misprints should be mentioned: the soprano's d^2 in bar 21, which should be an e^2, and the trombone's part in bar 57, which should be written in tenor clef (the latter is particularly obvious; this part should reinforce the celesta and harp).[49]

IV 'Leichteste Bürden der Bäume'

The fourth movement of Op. 31 is texturally similar to the first; both were described by Webern as recitatives[50] and consist of a melody sung by solo voice with chordal instrumental accompaniment. The fourth movement is about half the length of the first; it is in two parts, each eleven bars long. Four layers of rows can be defined. There are twelve rows in all, each of the untransposed forms occurring three times.

The melody, which begins and remains primarily in the soprano part, moving to the first violin for the last six notes of the first section (in bars 9–11) and to the horn and then the harp for the final eight notes of the song, states the four row forms in the order P–R–I–RI. The retrograde row begins on the last note of the prime; and the inversion and inverted retrograde are similarly joined. There is no elision of the retrograde and inverted rows at the centre of the song. The two rows of a second voice – R_0 and P_0 – hold one note in common, in bar 11. A third voice has three rows – RI_0 I_0 and RI_0 – with a one-note elision between RI and I in bar 5 and a tetrachordal elision between I and RI in bar 11. The R and P of an I–R–P series in the remaining voice also share one note; the inverted row that opens this series is the only row in the movement that does not join with another row at either beginning or end. Even so, this row is not entirely independent: its note 5 (the harp's E in bar 4) is also note 8 of the RI that is progressing at the same time. This is the first of a significant number of *Ausfälle*.[51]

The four rows that constitute the melody are, of course, stated in an entirely linear fashion. The other voices move between isolated single notes, triads and tetrads, all produced through verticalization. In the instrumental accompanying parts of this movement Webern uses a modified and more complex version of the change-ringing technique first observed in Op. 20 and most recently noted in connection with the first movement of Op. 31. Instrumental groupings are fixed. The four strings always play together; similarly, the flute, oboe, clarinet and bassoon, the piccolo, saxophone and bass clarinet, and the horn, trumpet and trombone always function as entities. Each of these groups plays the same row segment whenever it is called for, with the result that the repertoire of each is limited. The brass group plays the same chord three times during the course of the movement and nothing else; the piccolo, saxophone and bass clarinet repeat a single chord in the first half of the piece and its tritone transposition in the second half; and the flute, oboe, clarinet and bassoon play one chord and its inversion. The strings alone play a variety of chords, and even their scope is limited. So, although the registers of pitch classes are not fixed as they are, for example, in Op. 21/i, certain groups of pitch classes always appear in combination and are nearly always played by the same instruments.

The flute, oboe, clarinet and bassoon play only outer tetrachords: the first of a retrograde row, the last of an inversion, and the last of a prime. The piccolo, saxophone and bass clarinet play only notes 5, 6 and 7 of backward-going rows and 6, 7 and 8 of forward-going ones. The brass instruments' three notes, while always the same, are drawn from three sources: 9, 10 and 11 of RI; 2, 3 and 4 of I, which are naturally the same; and 5, 6 and 7 of P. There are no extra notes in this movement; no note is repeated or doubled; none is missing; correct order is maintained throughout.

V 'Freundselig ist das Wort'

The fifth movement consists of four identical row chains at different levels of transposition. The movement is in three sections (bars 1–16, 17–45 and 46–60). Each voice presents seventeen rows in the course of the piece: four in the opening, seven in the central and six in the final section. All contiguous rows, both within and between sections, are elided, by one, two or three notes. The elisions are the same in all voices. The outer sections (bars 1–16 and 46–60) consist of short homophonic segments for unaccompanied chorus alternating with imitative episodes for solo soprano and instruments. The central section (bars 17–45) is entirely for solo soprano with instrumental accompaniment. Thus Webern has divided his resources into two bodies: the chorus is never heard at the same time as either the solo soprano or any of the orchestra. As Willam has pointed out, this mutual exclusivity is inevitable in a piece for four-part chorus built on four simultaneously progressing row chains: whenever the chorus is singing, there are no notes left over.[52]

The association of choral voices and row chains established at the beginning is maintained throughout. The chain that supplies all the sopranos' material also provides all that of the solo soprano in those sections where the chorus is not present. In the entire piece, only one note of this chain is not sung by one of the two soprano forces: note 6 of the final row, I_6, is played by the harp in bar 58. The other three chains, while always serving the same voices in the choral sections, do not exhibit any tendency towards consistent instrumental associations in the remainder of the piece. They are all, however, segmented in the same way in those sections where their role is either imitative (in the instrumental episodes of the outer sections) or accompanying (in the central section).

Since all voices use the same series of row forms, elided in the same way, they are in theory parallel, so that, although individual chords differ to some degree whenever all four voices do not move in the same direction, all have essentially the same intervallic content. The transpositions are always related to each other as 0, 10, 7 and 6 (reading from the bass upwards). In other words, there is a major seventh, a major sixth and a minor seventh between adjacent voices from bottom to top; thus, no matter how the voices are positioned, the level of dissonance is high. In fact, there are only three chords, occurring at various levels of transposition, in all the choral segments of the movement. The first appearance of each is given in Example 2.27. As can be seen from the bar numbers in the example, the first two of these – an open and a closed version – represent the total choral material in the opening A section; the third, which is simply a version of the second in which the soprano note sounds an octave lower, makes its first appearance in the final section of the piece.

2.27

Although all the choral segments consist of reiterations of only two, or in three cases three, different chords, no two segments present the same sequence of repetition. The diagram below represents the chordal content of the A sections.

bars 1–3		bar 8	bars 10–11	bars 15–16
ababba		**bbbab**	**abbabbba**	**bbabb**
bars 46–7	bar 50	bar 52	bars 54–5	bars 59–60
bb′bba	**aabb′**	**bbaab**	**bbb′bb**	**abbbbb**

Chord **b**, being in closer position than **a**, sounds harsher; by extension, **b′** is the most strident of the three. The preceding diagram shows that chord **b** is used in the first A section with much greater frequency than **a**; the voices move even closer together upon the return of this section, in bars 46–60, with the introduction of the further-compacted version **b′**.

The accompaniment is largely chordal in the central section (the soprano aria). This portion of the movement, very different from the outer parts, is itself tripartite, with sections defined by double bars at the end of bars 24 and 31. Webern suggested in a letter to Hildegard Jone that the latter half of this aria was a loose retrograde of the first half;[53] certainly an examination of the chords used supports this.

2.28

Here again the number of discrete chordal configurations is limited. Example 2.28 shows the chords that occur in the aria.[54] Only three-note chords occur in the outer sections (bars 17–24 and 32–45); all of these, with one exception – the first of a pair of augmented triads that flank the double barline at the end of bar 24 – are versions of the same configuration. The ubiquity of this particular combination is predictable, since it results from the simultaneous sounding of three adjacent notes at any one of four places in the Op. 31 row: notes 1–3, 3–5, 7–9 and 8–10 of any forward-going row (as well as, obviously, notes 3–5, 4–6, 8–10 and 10–12 of any retrograde version). This invariance is exploited through the recurrence of the same chords, identically orchestrated, representing different segments of different rows. (See the brass chords in bars 18, 22 and 30, produced by $RI_1/4$–6, $P_{10}/3$–5 and $P_9/1$–3 respectively; the celesta chords in bars 17 and 23, which represent $RI_5/4$–6 and $P_2/3$–5; and the harp in bars 18 and 23, similarly representing $RI_4/4$–6 and $P_1/3$–5. The celesta chord is played again, an octave lower, by the strings in bar 29, where it results from $P_1/1$–3, and the harp chord recurs an octave higher in the celesta in bar 37, as $P_0/1$–3.) All the tetrads in the central section (bars 25–31) are simply this triad (on occasion inverted) with an additional note a perfect fourth above.

The chords are symmetrically arranged within each of the three sections of the aria. It follows from the row construction of this part of the movement, in which prime and inverted retrograde rows alternate regularly, that the original and inverted forms of the ubiquitous triad also alternate with regularity. If the chord as initially encountered in bar 17 is taken as the point of reference, the accompaniment of the first section of the aria consists of three original followed by three inverted and finally three more original versions. As noted above, the final (quasi-cadential) chord is an

89

augmented triad. The central section is also symmetrical, containing, after the opening augmented triad, three similar tetrads, then three versions of the characteristic triad, followed by three more tetrads. Like the final chord of the previous section, the last of these is different from its immediate predecessors, though in this case the difference is very slight. While five of the six tetrads are built from the triad in its inverted form, the cadential chord contains the original version. The triad of the soprano aria accompaniment returns near the end of the movement, twice as originally and twice inverted, in bars 57–8, following three statements in bar 56 of the inversion of the tetrad that closed the central section in bar 31. (The final instrumental chord of the piece, played by the harp in bar 58, is the result of note 6 of all four rows sounding together and is the close-position chord **b'**, elsewhere associated only with the chorus.)

The row setting of the solo soprano and choral parts is straightforward. There is one note-repetition in the choral music: all four parts repeat note 3 of a prime row at the beginning of bar 47. The soprano solo repeats pitches on four occasions, in bars 25, 28, 31, 39 and 47. There is only one anomaly, a grace note in the solo soprano part in bar 34 that does not belong to the soprano's row. The accompaniment to the soprano aria in bars 17–45 is contrapuntal in conception, though not in nature,[55] with the result that much that is heard as melodic (the figures in the piccolo in bars 25–6, the solo violin in bars 28–9, the clarinet in bars 36 and 39, the solo violin in bar 39 and the second violin, viola and cello parts in bars 29 and 36–7) is in fact a succession of parallel notes from three separate rows rather than a linear segment of the same row. There is very little intersection. With one exception, in bar 39, grace notes and the notes following are adjacent members of the same row.

The final section, which is a return to the spirit and techniques of the opening, is considerably more complex and offers concentrated examples of all the types of anomaly mentioned above: melodic figures in which successive notes belong to different rows, unattached grace notes and very free intersection.

As is customary in Webern's music for voices, the voice parts take precedence in this movement. They are all complete, while *Ausfälle* occur with considerable frequency in the instrumental parts.

The row structure of this movement is complex and does not, in general, coincide with the clearly marked – and perceived – formal structure. The seventeen sets of rows are arranged within a symmetrical framework. Although the texturally defined framework of the movement is symmetrical as well, the two structures do not match. The columns that stand fourth and fifth from the beginning in the following diagram (these are marked with asterisks) occupy a logical position in reference to the perceived ABA structure: the fourth is the last set of rows in the A section and the fifth the first set in the B section. The return of the A material at the end of the piece, however, comes earlier than the return of these two columns in retrograde as the fourth and fifth from the end of the movement (these are also marked on the chart).

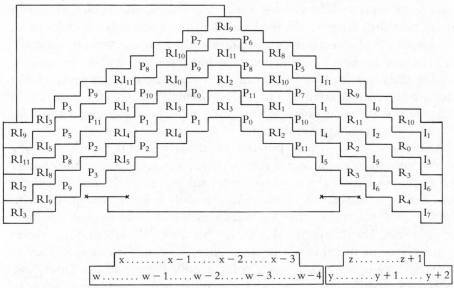

A second structure emerges from the pattern of transpositions. The first four columns of rows form a symmetrical unit. Two sets of RI rows open this section, the second set a tritone away from the first. Therefore the four rows of the second set begin with all the final notes and end with all the initial notes of the first set; in addition, the outer rows of the first column (RI_9 and RI_3) simply exchange places in the second column. These are followed by two sets of P rows using all the same transpositions but in reverse order. This four-column unit coincides with the first A section of the movement.

The fourth of these columns functions also as the first in a series of nine alternating P and RI columns in which each row is a semitone lower than the previous one of its kind in the same voice (indicated w, w − 1, x, x − 1, and so forth in the chart). This series continues until the two columns that are the retrograde of those heard fourth and fifth from the beginning are reached. Since only P and RI rows have been used up to this point, the introduction of their reverse here represents a significant alteration of the pattern. The remaining five columns of rows are alternating Is and Rs (represented on the chart by y and z), each a semitone higher than its predecessor of the same type. Thus emerges a pattern of three sections, of four, nine and five rows respectively, with the last of the four functioning also as the first of the nine. This structure divides the movement in the following way: bars 1–16/bars 12–48/bars 49–60. Only the first of these divisions makes any musical sense.

VI 'Gelockert aus dem Schoße'

There is little to be said about the row topography of 'Gelockert aus dem Schoße', perhaps Webern's most famous canon. While the combination of rows used represents numerous interrelationships, the row structure is straightforward. Each of the four voices of the choir sings through three rows; each row form appears three times in the course of the movement.[56] The first and second rows in the soprano and alto voices and the second and third in the tenors and basses are elided through one shared note; the other four junctures are effected by three-note elisions. Note 6 of the final row in each voice is repeated; there are no other repetitions, no extra notes, no omissions and no alterations in order.

A number of rests are incorporated into the subject of the canon, with the result that, although there are four voices, four notes are heard together relatively seldom. Of the seventy-three beats played in the movement, all four voices sound at the same time on only twelve, compared with thirty-four where three voices are heard together and seventeen where there are only two. The texture is reduced even further by the fact that two voices frequently come together on the same pitch. So that, for example, four of the twelve four-voice collections contain only three pitches. Three-note collections predominate before the centre of the movement; these give way in the second half to many more occasions where only two pitches are heard together.

This movement resembles the third in many ways. This is not surprising since these two pieces occupy parallel positions within the two groups of three movements that Webern conceived as units. One of the most obvious of the similarities is the extensive doubling of the choral voice parts by the orchestra, something that does not occur in the other four movements. Here all four voices of the canon are sung, unlike the canons of 'Schöpfen aus Brunnen', but all are reinforced, at the unison, by instruments. The orchestra is divided into four groups and each voice part is supported by its own unique choir: the oboe and first violin join the sopranos; the clarinet, trumpet and second violin the altos; the saxophone, horn and viola the tenors; and the bass clarinet, trombone and cello the basses. Although the row chains are sung continuously by the voices, they are segmented and passed around by the supporting instrumental parts. Also in contrast to the situation in the third song, each part is reinforced by only one instrument at a time. The parts that are divided among trios of instruments – those playing with the altos, tenors and basses – are all segmented in the same way, while the division of the voice supporting the sopranos, played by only two instruments, is unique.

Webern's treatment of rows can be seen to have changed very little during the course of twenty years. His twelve-note music, which accounts for fifteen of the thirty-one works intended for publication (and constitutes considerably more than half of his output in terms of performance time), exhibits an extraordinarily faithful adherence to the basic rules of the new system – a much stricter observance than is seen in the music of either Berg or Schoenberg. No licence is taken with the content of the row (the fact that in all the works there is only one wrong note, the G♮ in bar 50 of Op. 22/ii, surely argues against the likelihood of its being an intentional alteration). In the entire body of works from Op. 19 onwards, not a single note is missing, though an illusion of incompleteness is produced in some of the later works by the use of *Ausfälle*. The instances of inverted order are negligible: a note comes too soon on seven occasions, in Opp. 20, 26 and 31, and in three of these grace notes are involved. The prescribed order is not disrupted by chords, which are in all cases either the result of the simultaneous progression of several rows, or a verticalization of adjacent pitches from the same one. There is a single note (in bar 33 of 25/ii) whose presence cannot be explained. Although the predominantly pointillistic textures require the almost continual division of rows into segments, except for two early experiments in layering (in sections of Opp. 19 and 20) these segments never appear simultaneously. Limited repetition of single notes can be found in most of the works; however, a two-note figure is repeated on only two occasions, in bar 157 of Op. 22/ii and bar 5 of Op. 23/ii, and there is no instance of the repetition of a segment longer than this.

A fascination with logic is evident in Webern's choice and organization of row forms and transpositions. Regular patterns emerge; series of rotations are completed; the relationships between particular levels of transposition are fully explored. A row analysis shows a tight and elegant construction. Adorno gives voice to the disquiet many have felt in the face of Webern's play with numbers and logic when he speaks of 'the fetishism of the row' that 'drove [Webern] towards the cult of pure proportions'[57] and again when he laments the abdication of complementary harmony in favour of numerical accuracy.[58] This judgement might seem harsh, directed as it is towards a composer who worked painstakingly to preserve alongside the new symmetries offered by the twelve-note row the basic elements of traditional music.

3

Canon

From the outset, the twelve-note technique was perceived as an inherently polyphonic method. Schoenberg, Berg and Webern were all willing – indeed, dedicated – inheritors of the German/Austrian musical tradition, a tradition based on the study of strict counterpoint; and all three, both before and after adopting the new method, wrote music that was essentially polyphonic. Webern's realization of the contrapuntal possibilities offered by the twelve-note technique was, however, very different from his colleagues'. Whereas the counterpoint of Schoenberg and Berg seems to spring from the free development of motives characteristic of the nineteenth century, Webern looked to pre-baroque contrapuntal procedures, which he incorporated with great exactness and discipline. That he should be drawn to venerable methods may be seen as predictable, in view of his studies in musicology and especially in the music of Isaac, studies that must have left him with a more extensive knowledge of the earlier style than his colleagues possessed. However, I think one must also see this turn to late medieval procedures for inspiration as evidence of his recognition of a basic affinity between the two styles, to both of which order is central.

It is generally recognized that Webern's twelve-note music is not only polyphonic but, more specifically, canonic. George Perle remarked in 1971 on Webern's inclination to employ canon at critical points in his development.[1] His last non-dodecaphonic work, Op. 16, written in 1923–4, was a set of five canons on Latin liturgical texts for soprano, clarinet and bass clarinet. He did not return to this technique again until the fifth published work written in the new way. The songs of Opp. 17–19 show a methodical assimilation of the materials of twelve-note technique; they contain no canons. And although Op. 20 gives the impression of continual imitation, this perception is for the most part an illusion created by the frequent melodic isolation of the semitone and related intervals (major sevenths and minor ninths) as a result of the pointillistic instrumentation and the particular invariant properties of the row.[2] There are allusions to canon in bars 32–4 of the first movement and in the introduction and coda of the second movement, where the cello imitates the violin in inversion in the first

94

instance and the viola does the same in the second; in the second movement transitions (bars 26–8, 30–2, 37–8, 39); at the beginning of the closing material of the same movement (bars 59–61); and, predictably, in the development; but all these imitations are of brief duration.

When Webern finally used canon again, in Op. 21, he did it with a vengeance. Perle has called the Symphony 'one of the "classical" masterpieces of twelve-note music'.[3] Surely the most remarkable aspect of this work is the comprehensiveness of its expression of both horizontal and vertical symmetries, in canon. Having said this, one recognizes in its construction Webern's first large-scale experiment in that synthesis of the horizontal and the vertical that seemed to be an *idée fixe* and that will never be far from the surface in this study. Unlike those earlier works for which Webern had turned to canon (Perle cites, along with the Five Canons of Op. 16, the *a cappella* chorus 'Entflieht auf leichten Kähnen' of 1908), the Symphony does not stand in isolation from the works on both sides: the techniques of canon are primary formative agents in nearly all the works to follow.

Op. 21

The Symphony is, however, completely unlike anything that had come before. Roger Smalley has spoken of 'the radical evolution in Webern's style between Opus 20 and Opus 21',[4] and Perle sets Op. 21 apart from all its precedents when he says, on the one hand, that 'In the Symphony . . . the new concepts and technical devices so incoherently, if exhuberantly [*sic*] exploited in the Trio are brought under control by a return to the severe discipline of the strict canon',[5] and, on the other, that 'extrinsic resemblances between Webern's first twelve-note canon and its diatonic antecedents do not diminish the fundamental and crucial respects in which they are different'.[6] With the exception of the first eleven bars of the second movement, both movements are canons throughout; in the course of their combined 165 bars, Webern presents an anthology of canonic techniques rivalling *The Art of Fugue* in its comprehensiveness and ingenuity.

The work is, above all, an essay in symmetry, beginning, as we have seen earlier, with the construction of the row itself.[7] In the music, this symmetry is expressed vertically through mirror inversion and horizontally through the palindrome. The structure is, however, infinitely more complex than the coordination of these two dimensions would suggest, because the whole of this intricate framework of symmetries is realized in canon; therefore the mirror image, although exact, is offset, so that the result might be visualized as being lozenge-shaped rather than rectangular. While this prevents perfect vertical symmetry, complete horizontal symmetry is achieved on several occasions in the second movement as the result of the exact and immediate reversal of all the lozenges.

The first movement is in three slightly overlapping sections – bars 1–26, 25b–44 and 42–66b – with two mirror canons of considerable complexity progressing simultaneously in each. The rows and the canonic structure of the first and third sections are the same, though the music is quite different as a result of the reduction in the final section of the number of parameters treated canonically and an increased diversity in durations, range, timbral effects and so on. Both canons in the two outer sections consistently use a two-note elision and are, therefore, potentially circular.[8] This possibility is realized, however, in only one of the two. Both *dux* and *comes* of Canon I[9] come to a full close and begin anew when the section is repeated. On the other hand, the last two notes of the final row in both voices of Canon II are withheld the first time through, occurring only as the first two notes of the repetition.

Rhythm and durations are imitated exactly in both of the canons in bars 1–26, as are articulation and timbre. For the purposes of timbral imitation, Webern has constructed an orchestra of pairs of like instruments – clarinet and bass clarinet, two horns, two violins, viola and cello – and harp. Throughout this section the music played by any one of these instruments in the *dux* is imitated by its opposite number in the *comes*, the only exception being three notes (9–11 of I_9) in the second ending that are played by the bass clarinet with the viola answering. (This seems to be a sign of what is to come; the imitation of timbres is not consistent in the ensuing section, and is abandoned altogether in the recapitulation.) The harp serves both *dux* and *comes*, always answering itself. The orchestration is pointillistic, and the segmentation of the row in the two leading voices is exactly imitated. In Canon I this segmentation is regular: both rows of each voice are divided into tetrachords and the resulting groups of four, four, six, four and four notes[10] are distributed symmetrically, played by horns, clarinets, low strings, clarinets and horns respectively. Because of the peculiar relationship between the rows used, each instrument plays the same four notes upon its return. This symmetry is emphasized by the return of all notes at the same octave level. The segmentation of the rows in Canon II is neither regular nor symmetrical; it is, however, the same in both voices (Example 3.1).

The middle section of this movement (bars 25b–44) is a symmetrical *tour de force*. Like the outer sections, it consists of a pair of canons in mirror inversion. Here, however, all four voices are in agreement with respect to rhythm and segmentation, so that they join to form a single four-voice canon as well. The direction of motion is arranged so that the two prime rows mirror each other (inexactly, of course) much of the time, and the two inverted rows do the same. As the opening section exploits the type of symmetry inherent in the P_0–I_9 relationship, in which invariant groups return in reverse order, this central section exploits the other, more explicit, symmetry suggested by the peculiar structure of this row: the return of

3.1   Op. 21/i, bars 1–26 (exposition canons, voices aligned)

single elements in retrograde order. Each voice of this central section uses only two rows, the second the exact retrograde of the first. The last voice to enter, and therefore the last to finish the first set of four rows, leads in the second set, so that all the events of the first half recur in reverse order. The instruments are paired as they were in bars 1–26, except for the eight notes of I_3 and RI_3 that stand at the centre of the palindrome and are isolated by fermate.

One interpretation of the second movement of Op. 21 is as variations on

(a) Theme, as it is

canonic technique. With the exception of the Theme, each of the nine sections is a canon, and these are varied in both character and method. At least one – Variation V – is not even perceived as imitative. This movement is also a most remarkable display of symmetries, an aspect that will be dealt with in Chapter 5. Although the Theme is not a canon (Example 3.2a), it could have been (Example 3.2b): had the two rows that provide the melody (P_0) and accompaniment (R_0) exchanged roles halfway through, the result

3.2   Op. 21/ii, bars 1–11

would have been a cancrizans canon. Possible reasons for this apparent neglect of obvious potential will be discussed in Chapter 5; Webern's decision not to allow any of the first three sections of this movement to be perfectly symmetrical, though the possibility is latent in all of them, was dictated by the requirements of the structure at a higher level.

Following the deceptive simplicity of the Theme, Variation I is strikingly complex. The four voices in this variation, played entirely by the strings, comprise two canons in mirror inversion played simultaneously. The first of these is between first violin, with P_7, and cello, with I_5. The second, between second violin and viola, uses R_7 answered by RI_5. Each instrument, upon reaching the end of its first row, begins immediately to play a retrograde of everything it has just done, reversing all aspects of its forward statement (pitch, rhythm, durations, dynamics, articulation). Owing to the incestuous relationship of the four rows used at the outset, this reversal produces the same four rows again.

Webern has made the material of the second canon (between second violin and viola) shorter than that of the first, so that, although the *dux* of the second canon begins one bar later than the *dux* of the first, these two voices arrive at the centre together and begin their reversals at the same moment, thereby operating together as a non-retrogradable unit. The two *comites* behave in the same manner, arriving at their axis together half a bar later. This offers the possibility of an alternative interpretation: the *duces* of the two canons may be seen as *dux* and *comes* of a cancrizans canon between voices using the rows P_7–P_7 and R_7–R_7, exchanging parts at midpoint. The two *comites* are of course open to a similar interpretation. This alternative pairing of rows is possible because none of the symmetrical pairs of rows is elided (Example 3.3).

Although each voice taken singly – as well as each of the cancrizans pairs (the two *duces* and the two *comites*) – is a palindrome, the obvious potential for the palindromic construction of the whole variation is not realized because the leading voices do not stop at the centre of the Variation and wait for the others to finish and take over the leading roles; in other words, the vertical coincidence of parts in the second half is not the reverse of that in the first. The result is that these eleven bars are an example of a type of canon that must surely be rare: a straightforward (in the most literal, certainly not the usual, sense) double canon in mirror inversion wherein each individual part is a palindrome, while together they are not.

In the second variation, a mirror canon exists between the rows P_2–R_2 and I_{10}–RI_{10}. Again, as in Variation I, each of these voices is a palindrome in every respect, including orchestration, which in this case is extremely pointillistic, with the first two (and, therefore, the last two) notes of each voice standing as the only adjacent notes played by the same instrument in the entire variation. The combined voices of this canon form a palindrome

3.3   Op. 21/ii, bars 12–23

as well: the *comes* becomes the *dux* at the centre. Thus this canon also is open to a second interpretation: if we consider the two voices to be P_2–RI_{10} and I_{10}–R_2, this mirror canon is a cancrizans canon as well, something that was not true of either of the mirror canons in Variation I. The variation as a whole is prevented from being a palindrome by the horn part, which in the course of the eleven bars presents the forward version of two rows at once by playing alternately a note from I_0 and one from P_{11}, and then having no time to play their retrogrades. In fact, the horn nearly plays a mirror canon itself in this variation; if the first note in bar 28 were one octave lower than it is, its P_{11} would be an exact inversion of its I_0.

There are only two voices throughout Variation III, and they play a cancrizans canon. Each plays a circular series of rows using the P_0–I_9 association exploited in the first movement (I_3–P_6–I_3–P_6–I_3 and RI_3–R_6–RI_3–R_6–RI_3), with the two–note elision suggested by this relationship. Rhythm and durations are exactly imitated except for the notes at each juncture; dynamics and articulations are imitated at the outset, but this is abandoned as the variation progresses. A small, audible palindrome occurs at the centre of each pair of rows, in bars 35, 37, 39, 41 and 43. Those in bars 35 and 43 are identical, as are those in bars 37 and 41, making the overall shape abcba; ultimately the entire variation is a palindrome. It is less apparent that Variation III is a canon in inversion. The two voices cannot of course mirror each other exactly, since the *comes* answers each row of the *dux* in kind. The direction of motion is mirrored, however, producing octave complements – the tonal inversion of diatonic music rather than the mirror inversion generally encountered in twelve-note writing. It is noteworthy that this is also the technique used in the middle section of the first movement between the two rows of each like pair.

The nine sections of this movement are contrived so that taken together they form a single palindrome. Variation IV occupies the axis position and is therefore unique. It is the least exact of all the variations with respect to both imitation and symmetry. The first five bars present a rhythmic canon in four voices playing two prime and two inverted rows; however, none of the other features, including contour, is imitated. In fact, since all the voices move in the same steady triplet crotchets, the imitation is not apparent. Each of these rows is followed in the last five bars of the variation by the row with which it shares the characteristic P_0 to I_9 relationship, thereby producing another set of two inversions and two primes. The elision in all four pairs of rows occurs in the central (sixth) bar of the variation, where the rows in three of the four voices share their central two notes, while those in the voice that begins and ends the variation (I_5–P_8) do not. This bar, which is also the exact centre of the movement, is static, with single pitches or pairs of pitches repeated by the wind instruments and the harp moving together in semiquavers and quavers, and in so doing abrogating temporarily any hint of canon. Since the reversal of events in the last five bars of the variation depends on the P_0–I_9 rather than the P_0–R_0 relationship, the retrograde is necessarily less exact than the sort used elsewhere in this movement. While Webern calls attention to the correspondence of pairs of notes in the tetrachords at the end of this variation with those at the beginning by bringing them back at the same pitch level and with identical orchestration, he manipulates the notes of the central tetrachords in various ways so that the relationship of the two bars on either side of the centre is not perceivable. Thus the palindromic aspect of the variation comes into focus only in the last three bars.

From this point on, each variation has the same row structure as its earlier counterpart: V = III, VI = II, VII = I and Coda = Theme. Variation V uses the same two series of five rows as Variation III, with the slight difference that here technically they are not elided. As in the earlier variation, the centre of each pair of rows produces an easily recognized non-retrogradable figure, in this instance always played by the harp, and the entire Variation is a palindrome as well. However, the fact that it is a canon is a well-kept secret. (So well kept that most analyses of this movement – and there are many – do not recognize it.[11]) The beginning is shown in Example 3.4. The result of this most ingenious of canons is a notably uncanonic-sounding section: eleven bars that seem to be not only homophonic but entirely static as well, consisting of continual reiterations of the same chords by the strings while the harp plays short non-retrogradable figures relating to each other as ababa.

3.4 Op. 21/ii, bars 55 ff (reduction)

The canon in Variation VI is handled in the same way as the one in Variation II, except that the two voices of the mirror canon that was so pointillistically disposed in the earlier variation are played in a continuous fashion here by the clarinet and bass clarinet. The horn again plays a canon in inversion with itself, using the retrograde of its rows in the earlier variation. These two rows mirror each other exactly this time, though the rhythm and durations are not in canon.

The timbral relationship of Variation VI to Variation II is reversed in the relationship of Variation VII to Variation I. Here the long string lines of the earlier variation are replaced by extreme pointillism. The canonic structure is the same as before: two double canons reversing at midpoint to create two-dimensional symmetry. The most important difference between the two variations is that in Variation VII the four voices leave the centre in reverse order from their arrival, thereby giving this variation the overall symmetry that its earlier counterpart lacked. Although this variation is a palindrome, it cannot be said to be a cancrizans canon, since the central note in one of the voices – the note on which the piece turns – functions as an elision and is held by one instrument, thereby making a voice exchange between I_5–RI_5 and RI_5–I_5 impossible. The first half of this canon is given in Example 3.5; the second half is an exact reversal of the first.

3.5   Op. 21/ii, bars 77–83 (reduction, voices aligned)

The Coda represents a return to the simplicity of the Theme. It comprises only two rows, but here they are pointillistically orchestrated and cross at the midpoint, making this the cancrizans canon that the Theme might have been. By definition it is also a palindrome.

The imitation in Op. 21, which is almost entirely between inversionally related rows, is inclusive: not only is melodic contour exactly mirrored, but rhythm, dynamics, timbre and articulation are duplicated as well. The range of parameters imitated runs the gamut from almost total involvement in Variations I and VII to the imitation of rhythm only in Variation IV.

Op. 22

The first movement of the Op. 22 Quartet also proceeds by canon in inversion, but in spite of this technical similarity the canons of the two works – Opp. 21 and 22 – are significantly different. Pairs of identically segmented, inversionally related rows proceed in canon throughout Op. 22/i, producing a series of two- and three-note melodic figures imitated in inversion. In this case, however, although the replication of both rhythm and contour is exact, the voices are not in agreement with respect to the length of time between successive figures, even to the extent that the role of *dux* is passed from one voice to the other. This freeing of the temporal relationship of the voices produces a sort of canon in metamorphosis. (It is interesting to note that this fluid relationship between *dux* and *comes* has a precursor in the woodwind canon of 'Der Mondfleck' from *Pierrot lunaire*, a work from Schoenberg's earlier atonal period.[12])

A third voice present in the first and third sections of the movement (bars 1–15 and 28–41) does not take part in the imitation. In bars 1–15 the canon is pointillistically orchestrated, while the third voice is played entirely by the saxophone; conversely, in bars 28–41 the piano plays the canon alone, with the independent voice distributed pointillistically among the other instruments. The row structure is the same both times. In spite of the apparent thickness of texture in the middle section (bars 16–27), the result of the telescoping of events, there is in fact one less voice here: while the mirror canon carries on, the third voice disappears. The elasticity of this canon can be seen as the first step away from the precise agreement of all elements that characterized the canons of Op. 21 (see Example 3.6).

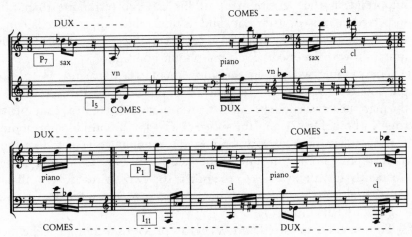

3.6   Op. 22/i, bars 1–9 canon (reduction, pitches only)

The second movement of Op. 22 is a rondo and is not canonic to the same extent as the first movement. Motives of two, three and four notes are frequently inexactly imitated, sometimes in inversion and sometimes in retrograde, now in two voices, now in three or four. Canon is sustained for a period of several bars only in the second half of the initial A section (bars 20–31) and in the first and third episodes (bars 39–63 and 153–79), where two-part imitation of a very free sort occurs. Neither individual instruments nor rows are in canon with each other; the canonic voices continually cross boundaries. Thus the canon exists independent of the row structure. Rhythms are usually (but not always – see bars 20–2, for example) imitated more or less faithfully, but the distance between voices, in both time and space, is constantly fluctuating. Similarly, although general melodic contours are maintained in imitation, the direction of imitation changes frequently, from direct to inverted and vice versa, and the size of melodic intervals is in many cases only approximated. Often additional voices join the canons briefly and then disappear, or free material is played concurrently.

Op. 24

Webern was increasingly fascinated with the idea of synthesis – specifically what he often referred to as the union of 'the two opposite modes of presentation', the horizontal and the vertical.[13] This desire to find a balance between the homophonic and the imitative methods of continuation must have influenced his subsequent movement away from the strict and inclusive imitative style of Op. 21. After Op. 22, the next, brief, appearance of canon is at the opening of the third movement of Op. 24. This passage is more important in the development of his canonic technique than might be suspected in view of its brevity and its unheralded appearance late in a work that contains no other canons: it represents the next step in the fusion of imitation with an essentially homophonic conception.

The canonic writing in this movement is a departure from Webern's previous technique in two respects. Most importantly, the two voices unfold through successive (block) rather than simultaneous (linear) statements of the row. In both Op. 21 and the much freer Op. 22 individual canonic voices correspond to discrete row strands: the mapping of rows, like the music itself, is polyphonic. (In spite of the fact that in Op. 22 the role of *dux* shifts frequently from one series to the other, the two voices are kept distinct.) In Op. 24, although a canon occurs, the row topography does not suggest polyphony (Example 3.7).

The second departure from Webern's previous technique is the inevitable result of this superposition of canon and homophonic row disposition. The product is a canon only by virtue of the rhythm: that is to say, the contour of the *comes* neither consistently duplicates nor consistently mirrors that of the

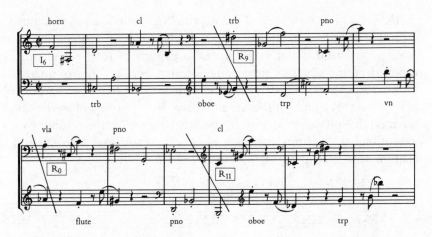

3.7   Op. 24/iii, bars 1–13 (reduction)

dux. Granted, melodic considerations are not exactly ignored: owing to the peculiar nature of this row and the fact that the canon proceeds by three-note segments, every one of these is some melodic permutation of the one it imitates, but the exact nature of the similarity, like the temporal relationship between voices in Op. 22, is constantly changing.

Op. 26

Op. 22/i and the canonic portions of Op. 24/iii represent a gradual move away from the intensive canonic technique of Op. 21, in which as many features as possible are included in the replication, towards a more subtle type of imitation, first seen in Op. 26, in which only rhythm is duplicated, and that with increasing freedom. In *Das Augenlicht* the temporal elasticity of Op. 22 is combined with the separation of pitch organization from rhythmic determination that was implicit in Op. 24. Here faithful rhythmic replication is no longer reinforced by even permutational melodic relationships.[14] The music of *Das Augenlicht* alternates between canon and homophony. Only the voices have any homophonic music: the instruments are silent for short periods in bars 20–3, 30–2, 48–51, 53–7, 87–90, 92–3 and 109–13, and in all of these bars except 48–51 and 53–7 the voices move together. The voice parts are homophonic also in bars 64–9, but here the instruments accompany them in counterpoint.

The greater share of the music for voices is canonic: two- and four-part rhythmic canons occur in bars 8–19, 37–42, 47–58, 89–91 and 96–110. The canons for the voices are regular insofar as each voice part has its own row or series of rows representing one voice of the canon. The rows of the several voices are related to each other in various ways, however, often by retrograde, with the result that they neither imitate nor mirror each other

107

melodically. The structure of the instrumental music is less straightforward. The orchestration is pointillistic, and the result is a series of fragments, ranging in length from single notes to groups of five. These imitate each other rhythmically but never melodically, though approximate melodic replicas and inversions do occur, as in bars 27–8 (trumpet and horn), bars 65–6 (trumpet and trombone) and bars 74–5 (viola and violin, oboe and clarinet). In spite of appearances, the instrumental music is, with four minor exceptions, a rhythmic canon in two voices from bar 6 to the end.[15] The canonic structure of bars 6–19 can be seen in Example 3.8.

3.8   Op. 26, bars 6–19 (reduction)

The fact that the rhythmic imitation is seldom accompanied by any sort of melodic duplication makes this a very different kind of canon from any of its predecessors, though each of the various freedoms seen here has been tried earlier. This new loosening of restrictions manifests itself also in the row structure, which, as we have seen in the previous chapter, is unsystematic and irregular. The *comes* becomes the *dux* at one point, in bar 6; and the imitation is in diminution in one instance, in bars 5–6, and in retrograde in one other, in bars 51–3. The *comes* has one less note than the *dux* in the figure in bars 65–7. Grace notes are not consistently imitated and fall in various places in both voices. While phrasing and articulation are frequently imitated, this is not done consistently. Timbre is not echoed as it was in Op. 21, though *dux* and *comes* are usually segmented in the same way. Example 3.9 (on pp. 110 and 111) is a rhythmic reduction of the orchestral music of Op. 26.

The canons of Opp. 22, 24 and 26 represent a gradual dismantling of the note-row–structure–timbre association previously maintained in imitative textures. In *Das Augenlicht* for the first time these three elements operate separately and independently, as three strands running through the musical fabric, meeting and digressing, crossing and joining, apparently at random. This work is a turning point in Webern's experimentation with the independence of parameters. Op. 27 represents a return to the inclusive style of imitation used in Op. 21, though this apparent retrenchment was to be also only a stage in his continuing reinterpretation of canon: subsequent canons depend on rhythm alone, consistent melodic replication having been permanently dispensed with after its brief return in Op. 27. The coincidence of canonic voices and rows – a correspondence abandoned in Opp. 24 and 26 and taken up again in Op. 27 – is, however, maintained thereafter.[16]

Op. 27

Symmetry is important again in the Variations for Piano: it is realized horizontally by means of cancrizans figures (canons) in the first movement, vertically through mirror canon in the second. The first movement comprises a series of palindromes reminiscent of Op. 21. Each hand plays one voice; throughout most of the piece the two voices cross at the centre, with the material exactly reversed, but in bars 11–15, and at the reprise of this phrase in bars 47–51, each hand finishes the voice that it began, and as a result the parts at the end of the palindrome appear in inverted positions and in different octaves from the beginning. Nor do the hands exchange parts in the three phrases of bars 19–29; in this case the palindrome is maintained exactly, necessitating considerable hand-crossing.

The palindromes are managed in various ways. Those in bars 1–7, 19–36 (there are six in these bars) and 37–43 are exact.[17] Those in bars 11–15 and 47–51 are maintained rhythmically, but with the inversion of parts in the second half already noted. In addition, the two dyads played by the right hand in the first half of bars 11–15 (P_8/2–3 and 4–5) and those played by the left hand in the first half of bars 47–51 (I_5/2–3 and 4–5) are inverted on their return in the second half of the phrase. In the remaining four phrases, in bars 8–10, 15–18, 44–6 and 51–4, notes 4–8 are handled in such a way that the

3.9 Op. 26, bars 6–end, instrumental parts (rhythmic reduction)

coincidence of parts is not the same going into and out of the centre. The
second and fourth of these phrases, which close, respectively, the first major
section and the movement, are rhythmically distorted in addition, the final
notes occurring after a short delay.

110

The brief second movement – the nearest in spirit (though not in style) of any in Webern's twelve-note *œuvre* to the aphorisms of his earlier, free atonal period – is a mirror canon using only prime and inverted rows. Linear contour and chords are mirrored precisely, and rhythm, duration, dynamics, articulation and grace notes are exactly imitated. The *comes* follows the *dux* at the distance of one quaver throughout. The two voices leap great distances,

111

both traversing quickly and continually the three octaves and a sixth between B and g^3. All rows converge on a^1, making this pitch the axis of symmetry for the movement. A memorable feature of this movement in performance is the rapid and frequent hand-crossing that results from the notated designation of each hand as either *dux* or *comes* for long periods at a time.[18]

The canons of both these movements are inclusive. In the second movement, rhythm, contour, dynamics, grace notes and articulation are all mirrored exactly. In the first, retrogression is precise except for those exceptions cited earlier. Here also, rhythm, contour, dynamics and articulation are imitated generally, though exceptions can be found in each of these areas.

Op. 28

In Webern's own analysis of Op. 28,[19] he refers repeatedly to the strict canons that occur in all movements. At first glance these appear to be not at all strict: melodic duplication is more the exception than the rule. In the undisputedly strict canons of Opp. 21, 22 and 27/ii, imitation involves inversionally related rows, and the inherent potential for mirroring is consistently realized. Only twice before Op. 28 do voices operating in strict canon use similar rows – in the third and fifth variations of Op. 21/ii – and the situation there is complicated by the fact that in Op. 21 similar rows are also related as retrograde to prime, so that both of these variations are cancrizans canons. It must be recalled, furthermore, that in these early instances of canon between like rows, a particular effort was made to avoid melodic replication, through the setting of the *comes* as an approximate inversion of the *dux*; forward melodic imitation is avoided.

Perhaps it is not surprising, then, that in Op. 28, where for the first time all imitation is between similar row forms, the *comes* does not take its contour from the *dux*. However, as this is also the first canon to offer the possibility of exact melodic duplication throughout, the obvious avoidance of contour replication is especially striking. Although all the motives in the Op. 28 canons are imitated by identical segments of similar rows – a regularity that had been abandoned altogether in Op. 24 and to some extent in Op. 26 – the contour of the imitation never duplicates that of the original. Webern seems to consider a rhythmic canon between voices with similar row forms to be strict, regardless of the actual melodic disposition, apparently judging the inherent sameness of like rows to be sufficiently binding. This is a significant step in the progressive abstraction from canon of those elements that make its aural recognition possible, a process that is complete in Op. 31. The disregard for contour seen in canons of this sort is the basis of Adorno's assertion that in twelve-note composition counterpoint is no longer distinguishable from the process of composition in general. He notes that with a cleverly constructed row (he uses as an example the row of Op. 24, but he might just as well have used that of Op. 28) imitation is guaranteed. In his view the result therefore does not represent a triumph of contrapuntal composition, and he concludes that the attempt to write counterpoint within this system is a 'futile struggle'.[20]

George Perle discusses the same problem from a different and more positive viewpoint. He sees the turn away from melodic imitation as a necessary corollary to the twelve-note technique. In the article cited earlier in this chapter he writes:

> The distinction between the twelve-note canon and the tonal canon is precisely analogous to the distinction between the twelve-note row as 'motive' and the tonal motive. The latter, as Babbitt has pointed out, 'assumes functional meaning within a context, and becomes, in turn, a vehicle of movement within this context; the twelve-note set, however, is the instigator of movement, and defines the functional context.' If a twelve-note canon is to be anything more than the mechanical and literal unfolding of axiomatic twelve-note operations, there must be significant criteria of association and contrast, based on special rhythmic, registral, textural, and harmonic relationships. The futility of literal surface imitation in twelve-note music was evident to Webern at once.[21]

Perle recognizes what Adorno does not: the importance of the exact imitation of parameters other than pitch in twelve-note canon. A texture in which several voices project the same row form simultaneously may be perceived as canonic or not, depending on their rhythmic and timbral similarity. It might be argued that the futility of contour imitation was perhaps not 'evident to Webern at once'; if it was, it is curious that such imitation was abandoned only in Op. 28.

In the first movement of Op. 28, which is a theme and variations, only the Theme is not a canon (recalling a parallel situation in Op. 21/ii), and, even so, these bars are imitative, presenting a series of short motives immediately repeated, in most cases in augmentation or diminution. During the canon, which begins at bar 16, the temporal distance between entries changes several times – in the middle of the first variation and at the beginning of the second, third and fourth – but it does not fluctuate either as freely or as frequently as in Opp. 22 and 26.

As in the highly controlled canons of Opp. 21, 22 and 27, each voice is expressed as a chain of rows, in this case elided, with no communication between chains. Here, however, each voice presents a series of motives, which are in most cases telescoped so that the first note of one is played at the same time as the last note of its predecessor. These motives, which are often permutations of each other, are passed from instrument to instrument, thereby giving each voice of the canon the appearance of a pair of voices in imitation. Between the voices of the canon the rhythmic imitation is exact, except that occasionally a variant is used in which the *comes* substitutes a rest for some portion of the value of the corresponding note in the *dux*. The *comes* also telescopes motives to a greater degree than the *dux* towards the end of several of the variations. (The rhythmic aspect of this movement is discussed on pp. 216ff.)

Another move in the direction of the obscurities to come in Op. 31 is seen in the presence of *Ausfälle* in the second movement of Op. 28. Although Webern had used *Ausfälle* before,[22] he had not done so in canonic situations.[23] In bars 1–18 of Op. 28/ii the four instruments move as four voices in double canon, with violin I and viola playing the same rhythm, while violin II and cello play slightly varied, less complete versions.[24] *Ausfälle* occur in both these latter parts: each lacks three notes.[25] While all the suppressed notes occur in surrounding parts, the cello's *Ausfälle* do not occur in the same position relative to the cello's played notes as do the second violin's. (So, for example, although note 4 of the cello's first row is played by the viola concurrent with note 3 in the cello, the corresponding note of the second violin's row is played by the cello while the violin rests between notes 3 and 5, and so on.) Since the borrowed notes and those played do not coincide in the same way in these two voices, the voices are in canon (as Webern has declared them to be)[26] only when the borrowed notes are omitted from consideration in the rhythmic scheme – in other words, when they are understood to be *Ausfälle*. For rhythmic purposes, every shared note occupies a legitimate position in the voice of the instrument that plays it and simply does not signify in the framework of the other.

The middle section of this movement is also canonic. The content of the first half is straightforward – a double canon in inversion, with the second violin and viola imitating the first violin and cello, respectively. The canon begun by the violins consists of one row in each voice; moving in long note values, only the first hexachord is completed by the midpoint of the section, at bar 27. At this point the canon moves to the viola and cello, who play the two remaining hexachords in bars 28–36. This canon is in mirror inversion. In addition, the first tetrachord of the *comes* is the precise retrograde of the same tetrachord of the *dux*. The second canon moves more quickly, each voice completing two rows in the course of the section. It is begun by viola and cello; the role of *dux* shifts regularly, every three notes, until bar 27, where this canon is taken up by the violins. After this point the alternation is no longer regular; the first two trichords of R_7 are heard before P_3 begins; the second, third and fourth of P_3 all occur between the third and fourth of R_7; the last two trichords of P_3 overlap; and the final one of R_7 is delayed in order to provide a close to the section in bar 36. These two voices play a mirror canon also, with only one note – 9 of the second pair of rows – not conforming. In addition, the R_3–P_3 voice is nearly a melodic palindrome. Only the first and last trichords of the P_{11}–P_7 voice attempt this.

Although the third movement is imitative throughout, there are sustained canons only in the outer sections. The greater part of the movement represents Webern's first venture into fugue. The short canons that occur as episodes in this structure are described on pp. 258–61, where the fugue is analysed. The first sixteen bars of the movement, before the fugue begins, present a complex double canon in retrograde, in which each of the four parts is played entirely by one instrument. Violin I and viola play similar rows, P_6 and P_0, the viola imitating the rhythm of the violin. At the same time, the retrograde forms of these two rows are played by violin II and cello, in canon, to the rhythmic retrograde of the violin I and viola parts. A large number of symmetrical relationships exists here. Except for minor variations, each of the four parts in the consequent phrase is the same rhythmically as one of the parts in the antecedent, in addition to the identity already noted. Rhythmically the voices are paired violin I/viola and violin II/cello throughout, which means that violin II and cello play in the antecedent phrase the rhythm that violin I and viola play in the consequent phrase, and vice versa. A structure of this sort has not been encountered since the first variation of Op. 21/ii.

Op. 29

All three movements of the Op. 29 Cantata rely on canon, the second and third extensively, and all continue the progress towards abstraction. The melodic independence enjoyed by similar row forms in the canons of Op. 28 is extended in Op. 29 to those related by inversion as well; here for the first time inversional relationships are not realized melodically. There are no *Ausfälle* in Op. 29, but the technique of independent variation that probably contributes more than anything else to the aural imperceptibility of the later canons of Op. 31 emerges here.

In the outer, instrumental, sections of the first movement, Webern almost completely obscures short canons on essentially simple material by introducing tempo changes that cut straight across all four voices, catching each at a different point in its progress. (This is almost certainly a direct response to the text of this song, in which a bolt of lightning is the central image.) The result is the nearly total obscuration of the canonic nature of the music. (These canons can be seen in Examples 9.2–9.5 on pp. 275–7.) Instrumentation is treated in this movement as it was in Op. 21: segments of the *dux* of each canon are imitated by instruments of like timbre in the *comes* – violin I/violin II, viola/cello, harp/celesta, clarinet/bass clarinet, trumpet/trombone, flute/horn. The result is an abstracted imitation in which some combination of rhythm, segmentation, articulation and timbre has moved into the role traditionally the province of, but now abandoned by, melody.

Both the second and third movements are imitative throughout. All sections of the second are canonic. The third is a complex synthesis of periodic form and fugue; while the subject is imitated continually, sustained canon does not occur.

The second movement opens with a five-bar canon that is unlike any of Webern's previous canons: although four voices are present, three of them move together in rhythmic unison, thus producing a canon in two parts. An expanded version of this canon returns at the centre of the movement (Example 3.10). Like the manipulation of tempo in the first movement, this technique – which, uncharacteristically, serves to simplify rather than to complicate – is never used again.

3.10   Op. 29/ii, bars 1–6 (reduction, pitches only, parts aligned)

Throughout the two sections that account for the major portion of this movement – bars 6–27 and 36–56 – the solo voice is accompanied by an instrumental double canon. In both cases, the four accompanying voices are set in an extremely pointillistic manner. Unexpectedly, in view of the organized treatment of timbres in the first movement, *dux* and *comes* move through the orchestra apparently at random, though parallel segmentation is maintained. The most significant aspect of these canons in the light of what was to come is the independent variation of individual voices, which results in a subtle and fluid relationship between parts that is unlike anything previously encountered. At times all four are playing the same (rhythmic) material, thereby producing a single canon in four voices. On occasion, however, they diverge in pairs and proceed as two-voiced canons, later to regroup differently, so that precise associations are not fixed throughout. Example 3.11 illustrates this mobility.

In the first sketches of both this movement and the third, the rhythm of all the voices is the same: the parts of the third movement are written in rhythmic unison, those of the second in canon.[27] In subsequent revisions of both movements various single notes have been moved to slightly earlier or later positions in one or two voices (including the solo soprano part – the *dux*

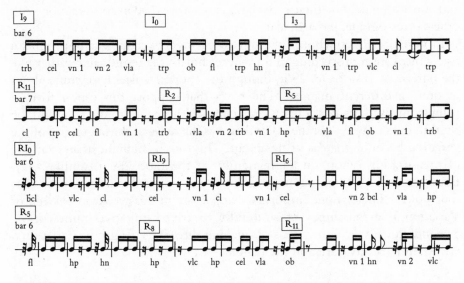

3.11   Op. 29/ii, bars 6–18 (rhythmic reduction of instrumental parts, aligned)

– in the second movement), with the result that by the final version parts that began as identical are to varying degrees dissimilar. The double canons of this movement consist of three like rows and a fourth which is the inversion of the other three, so that whenever the four voices are divided into pairs, one pair is related as prime to prime and the other as inversion to prime – in theory, one is an upright and the other an inverted canon. These relationships, however, are never realized melodically.

Op. 30

Webern continues to experiment with varied imitation in Op. 30, but not specifically with canon. Although this work is based on the variation of two four-note motives in all voices, and the work is therefore entirely imitative in conception, there is only one sustained canon, in Variation 2. As in the canons of Opp. 28 and 29, imitation focuses on the rhythmic content of the motives, ignoring their melodic contour altogether. Since both motives are four notes long and four is a factor of twelve, rows are inevitably segmented in the same way throughout, and motives are usually imitated by parallel segments; these are not, however, necessarily segments of similar rows. Exact replicas occur very seldom. The orchestration is pointillistic; although many motives are played entirely by a single instrument, at times, especially in the more complex sections of the piece, the statement of a single motive is spread over two or more instruments. Recognition becomes more difficult in this work because successive statements of the same material are altered through the use of rhythmic inversion analogues and value replacement,[28]

117

and, especially, because these types of alteration are used in combination with others – retrograde, in particular.

In Variation 2, tetrachords of two row chains are verticalized to produce a two-voice canon proceeding in four-note chords, the result being rather like the outer sections of Op. 29/ii, though the chordal voices here come about in quite a different manner. The rows that support this canon form a palindrome with its axis at bar 63; to reinforce this palindrome, although the rhythm does not reverse, the voice that was the *comes* at the beginning of the variation becomes the *dux* at this point. This canon is unique as an example of mensuration canon, an augmentation at the ratio 2:3 (Example 3.12). Elsewhere in Op. 30 only four or six notes are imitated at a time, in two or four voices. There is one important *Ausfall* late in this work, in bar 142 of Variation 5, at the climax of a carefully contrived imitative framework.[29] The individual voices of canons of two and three bars' length in Variation 6 are asymmetrically varied in the manner of Op. 29.[30]

3.12   Op. 30, bars 56–71 (reduction, pitches only)

Op. 31

Webern's last published work, the Op. 31 Cantata, represents the final stage in his progress of increasingly complex imitations. The canons of Opp. 21, 22 and 27 are intensive. The imitation in these works is clearly perceived because it involves so many parameters: intervallic contour, rhythm and durations, dynamics, articulation, timbre. It is less palpable, both in Opp. 24 and 26, where it is restricted to a replication of rhythm and durations imposed on material with unstable row associations, and in Op. 28, where, although canonic voices remain distinct and present similar row forms segmented in the same way, melodic contours are not duplicated. Imitation can still be perceived in these works, nevertheless, even in Op. 26, where the order and temporal relationship of the voices involved is constantly in flux, because the imitation of rhythms is direct and relatively simple. Thus when rhythmic replication is obscured in Opp. 29 and 30, through the divergent variation of individual voices, the end of canon as an audible technique is approached. This point is finally reached in Op. 31.

The several voices of the second cantata are varied individually, as in the earlier cantata, but whereas in Op. 29 variation took the form of simple rhythmic distortions, the voices of Op. 31 are subjected to combinations of verticalization, value replacement, augmentation and retrograde, in some cases in such a way as to obscure completely their common rhythmic basis. The fact that imitation is no longer discernible in the more complex canons of this work is evidence of a critical – but, as we have seen, by no means sudden – alteration in Webern's attitude towards, and use of, a cherished technique. It seems to me that in taking this last step he was entering finally into a realm of abstraction that was to become all too familiar in the music of the 1950s and 60s. Since music is an essentially aural art form, the validity of music in which the method of organization cannot be heard may be seen as questionable.[31]

There are six movements in the cantata: two groups of three, consisting, in both cases, of a recitative for solo voice followed by an aria for the same voice, and finally a piece for chorus. While the three pieces of each group were written in the order in which they now stand, the group that ends the work was written first. In this chapter the movements will be considered in the order of their composition.

The first movement is the only one of the six that was not conceived as a canon;[32] all the others are canons in four voices. In these latter movements, the instrumental parts are derived from the sung material, after the manner of Op. 29/ii and iii, but with much greater freedom; additional sung parts are altered very little, if at all. Thus the canonic nature of the sixth movement, the only one performed by chorus throughout, and of the choral portions of the third is clearly perceived. It is in the music for solo voice – the second and fourth movements and portions of the third and fifth – that the new abstraction is to be observed; the aural effect of these sections ranges from the only vaguely canonic to secco recitative, with in most cases no hint to the listener that the instrumental accompaniment was derived from the voice material. The sketchbooks show, nevertheless, that all of these movements were first notated in strict rhythmic canon and that they assumed their final form only through the subsequent variation of individual voices.[33]

'Leichteste Bürden der Bäume'

In writing to Willi Reich immediately following the completion of the movement that now stands fourth, Webern said:

> formally it's an introduction, a recitative! But this section is constructed in a way that perhaps none of the 'Netherlanders' ever thought up; it was probably the hardest task (in that respect) that I've ever had to fulfil!
> You see, the basis is a four-part canon of the most complicated kind.[34]

While this movement is obviously a recitative, the fact that it is a canon would almost certainly never have occurred to anyone without Webern's prompting. His remarks to Reich, however, make it apparent that canonic principles were of primary concern to him during its composition, even though to describe the result as a canon – as he has done – severely tests the limits of musical terminology. While the canonic structure of this piece was clearly to him a most crucial element in its composition, it is not in this case (as it was still in Op. 29) something that the listener can hope to – or, surely, was intended to – perceive; in Op. 31, canon has finally been abstracted to such a degree that it no longer operates for the listener on a conscious level. In view of the pleasure Webern clearly took in the concealment of carefully contrived details,[35] one can only guess at his delight in the obscurity of the Op. 31 canons. And, of course, the construction of a recitative by way of canon, however incongruous (and pointless, perhaps) this may appear on sober reflection, represents for precisely that reason a triumph in the synthesis of horizontal and vertical, as is reflected in Webern's reference to the exercise as 'probably the hardest task' he had ever had to fulfil. (The 'synthesis of horizontal and vertical' was an endeavour with which Webern was increasingly occupied in the later years of his life. His concern with synthesis will be examined in Parts II and III.)

In spite of Webern's explicit identification of this movement as a canon, none of the few theorists who have discussed the work over the years has satisfactorily explained in what way it is canonic. Leopold Spinner was the first to demonstrate the abstruse canonic nature of the movement, in an article published in 1961, in which he analyses only the first eleven bars.[36] Stroh's brief discussion of the piece, published in 1973, goes no further.[37]

120

Deppert, in his analysis of 1972, takes Spinner to task for stopping just at the point where things would have become difficult.[38] Deppert presents an impressively thorough analysis of the entire movement. His way of looking at the piece differs from Spinner's in three respects: (1) he recognizes the presence of *Ausfälle*; (2) he relates everything to an underlying twelve-element durational series, which he derives from the melody; and (3) he sees the position of all the events in the accompanying voices in terms of fields. As a result of (2) and (3), his explanation has slightly less to do with canon than one might wish. This analysis is quoted extensively but dismissed by Willam.[39] Willam's examination of Op. 31 suffers throughout from his determination to see the melodic (sung) parts of the cantata as derived from durational series; in the case of 'Leichteste Bürden', Deppert's row serves his purpose well, but he fails to recognize its generative role in the accompaniment. Spinner's description of the canonic derivation of the instrumental parts of this movement is not even mentioned.

Deppert's emerges, then, as the only analysis of the complete movement to date, but as somewhat less faithful to Webern's stated intentions than it might have been. Because of the way in which the *dux* is constructed in this movement the identification of a durational series as the basis of the events in the accompanying parts happens not to be very different from describing these same events as a rhythmic imitation of the voice part, and the results of analyses predicated on these two disparate theories do not differ significantly. However, Deppert's decision to group all events, regardless of their nature, into fields has led him to overlook some of the more specific correspondences that exist between *dux* and *comes*. The following analysis is not very different from either Spinner's or Deppert's; it bears the additional authority, however, of Webern's own sketches. The several stages of this piece occur on pp. 81–8 of Sketchbook IV.

The melody, which, according to Webern, establishes the rules for the rest of the piece,[40] is divided among soprano, solo violin, horn and harp. It comprises four rows – P, R, I and RI in that order – so that, in theory at least, each half of the song is a palindrome consisting of a forward-going row and its retrograde. The rhythm reinforces these relationships: both halves of the song are versions of the same rhythmic palindrome, creating together, inevitably, a larger palindrome analogous to, but simpler than, the inverted palindrome of the row structure.[41] The rhythm of the complete melody is given as Example 3.13. Since the voice part is itself convoluted rhythmically, the last three rows are redundant for the purposes of canonic imitation: the whole of the generating material is presented with the statement of the initial prime row. For this reason it is entirely valid to describe this piece as based on a twelve-element rhythmic series. Example 3.14 can be seen as a composite model of all the rows in the melody.[42]

Only untransposed row forms are used in this movement. The row

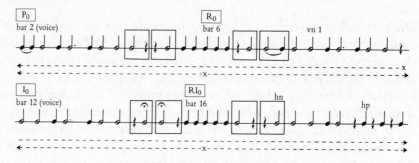

3.13   Op. 31/iv, melody (rhythm only)

3.14   Op. 31/iv, composite rhythmic model

content of the soprano voice is, as we have seen, P–R–I–RI; that of the three instrumental voices is RI–I–R–P, I–RI and R–P. (These three voices are shown in Example 3.16a below.) The forward/retrograde distinction introduced in the melody is maintained in all voices: the rhythm of P and I rows is based on the rhythm and durations of the initial prime row as it stands, while that of R and RI rows is generated by its reverse. Since the row content of each of the instrumental *comites* is different, each is unique rhythmically. The voice that begins the movement (I–RI, designated **A** in Example 3.16) is based on an imitation in augmentation, first forward, then in retrograde.[43] Voice **C**, also consisting of only two rows, R and P, is augmented as well, but, in keeping with its row content, is based on an imitation first in retrograde and then in forward fashion. Predictably, the durations are not augmented in Voice **B**, which contains four rows; this voice produces four imitations, alternately retrograde and forward-going, as the order of rows (RI, I, R and P) would suggest.

Imitation is difficult to perceive for several reasons. For one thing, intersection is fairly frequent, and most shared notes do not satisfy the rhythmic/durational requirements of all the voices they serve. *Ausfälle* are problematic here, because when rhythm is being imitated it is desirable that all voices contain the same number of notes. *Ausfälle* are ignored in the rhythmic structure, thus creating lacunae in all voices but the model. An additional difficulty is created by the fact that the orchestral voices do not proceed melodically, but rather through a combination of single notes and three- and four-note chords. In a row-for-row rhythmic imitation, verticalizations pose an obvious difficulty: rows containing simultaneities, like those with *Ausfälle*, do not offer a sufficient number of articulations to produce a rhythmic replica of the model. It is these two features of this canon – the

122

Ausfälle and the verticalizations – that make aural recognition of the imitation impossible. Webern has met these problems with an extension of his technique of value replacement.

Even the initial sketches of this movement contain some chords, though many fewer than the final version. Successive variants of one of the accompanying rows are offered below as typical. The augmented prime of Voice **C**, occupying bars 13–22, went through at least five stages of

(a) sketches for bars 13–22 (Sketchbook IV)

(b) final version of bars 13–22

3.15   Op. 31/iv, bars 13–22

evolution.[44] Example 3.15a represents the initial sketch of these bars and three successive stages in their evolution; the final version (Example 3.15b) does not appear in the sketchbook. While the first version (i) follows the rhythm of the augmented prime row of the voice part very closely, little of this model remains in the final revision (iv). One of the few things that has not changed is the length of time spanned by the statement; more specifically, events, when either moved to one side or gathered together vertically, remain within the same time span they originally occupied. This is the key to the puzzle. Each of the rows played by the orchestra is either the same length as the vocal model or, in the case of augmentations, exactly twice as long, and this period of time is divided into blocks corresponding to the rhythm of the model. In nearly all cases single notes in the published version are struck at the appropriate time. There are seven exceptions, all indicated with asterisks in Example 3.16b: notes 3, 10, 11 and 12 of the augmented I row (in Voice **A**) and 1 of the prime (in Voice **B**) do not sound at the beginning of their allotted time, but their release coincides with the end of it; notes 4 of the augmented prime (Voice **C**) and 12 of the augmented retrograde inversion (Voice **A**) fail to define either of the limits of their time slots.[45] All these slightly off-kilter notes are the result of rhythmic variation; in every case their position in the first sketches is the same as that of the corresponding note in the model.[46] In only two instances is the length of the note played the same as that in the model; one is note 5 in a forward-going row (I/5 of Voice **A** in bar 5), the other 8 in a retrograde form (R/8 of Voice **B** in bar 15) – this note is a short value in the model.[47]

When several notes from the same row are played simultaneously, their values are added together; each chord is assigned a block of time equal to the sum of the durations of all its constituent parts. So, for example, the verticalization of the last four notes of the augmented prime row of Voice **C**, played by the wind in bar 22, is apportioned a period of twelve beats, representing twice the length of the last four notes of the prime model; even though the chord occupies a very small portion of its allotted time, no other element of the row encroaches on it.

In fact, none of the chords is held for the full value dictated by the model, and, while most are played at the beginning of one of the several portions of time that they represent, as in the example just cited, it is not in all cases the first. In line with the treatment of single notes, it is occasionally the release rather than the attack of a simultaneity that plays a defining role, coinciding with the end of one of the component segments (not necessarily the first or the last). In two cases, marked with an **x** in Example 3.16b (RI/5–7 and R/5–7 of Voice **B**),[48] the position of a chord defines neither the beginning nor the end of any component of the model. It must be said further that, when rows are elided, as they are in most cases, the rhythmic succession is not maintained through the elision. (There is an extended gap between either notes 11 and 12 of the first row involved or notes 1 and 2 of the second, so that the note in question must be treated as an *Ausfall* in one of the rows.) This was not the case in the early sketches, where the note of elision was repeated as necessary. Such repetitions were only later removed.

All of this results in a distortion of the original rhythm, and, one would suppose, also in a considerable difference in pace between those sections that proceed by chords and those that move in single notes, since one chord occupies a period of time that would be filled by three or four notes played singly. Interestingly, and perhaps predictably in view of Webern's penchant for disguising structures, single notes are found most often in the two voices that proceed in augmentation (**A** and **C**), while the one moving at the original speed (**B**) is made up almost entirely of chords. Thus the voices do not display the discrepancy in pace that is one of the most basic and perceivable elements of a canon by augmentation. Instead, three orchestral voices move at a similar pace in rhythms that bear little resemblance to each other, rhythms whose relationship to the original model is completely imperceptible. In fact, since each voice changes instrumentation continually, what one hears is not a canon at all. In Example 3.16b each voice of 'Leichteste Bürden der Bäume' is compared with the model. I have used vertical lines to define durational segments (notes grouped together for purposes of verticalization and variation); these are not barlines.

'Freundselig ist das Wort'

The fifth movement of the Op. 31 Cantata was the next to be composed. In a letter to the Humpliks dated 13 August 1941[49] Webern described his next project as 'a *choral piece*' that would follow the just completed recitative (characterized as 'introductory'); later, as he neared completion of the new movement, he described it as 'an "aria" for soprano solo with chorus and orchestra'.[50] On the later occasion he goes on to say:

> In it [the fifth movement] I have managed – I believe – to achieve a *completely new* style of representation; on a purely polyphonic basis I arrive at about the most opposite sort of representation imaginable.

Again the synthesis, but this time carried further. While Webern spoke of the previous movement as a canon in describing it to Willi Reich in August 1941,[51] he did not make the same claim for this piece. Although he refers to 'Freundselig ist das Wort' as having been conceived 'on a purely polyphonic basis' (in the letter to the Humpliks) and 'on the basis of canon' (in a letter to Reich dated 31 July 1942),[52] nowhere does he say that it is a canon. This seems to me an important distinction. He speaks of the supreme significance of the soprano's line in the letter to Reich, in which the language is strikingly similar to the letter written nearly a year earlier describing the previous movement:

(a) The three accompanying voices

(b) accompanying voices barred to indicate durational segments

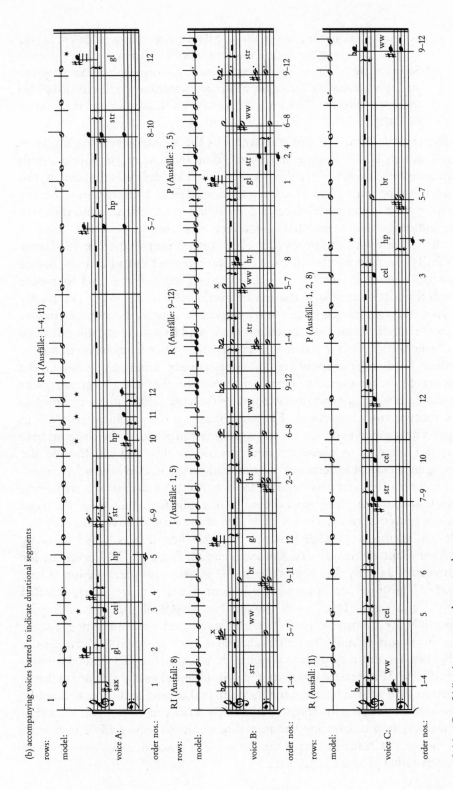

3.16 Op. 31/iv, instrumental parts only

A voice gives out the law – in this case the soprano soloist – that's to say the 'melody' – but the Greeks had the same word for that as for law: 'Nomos'. So the 'melody' has to 'lay down the law'. . . . In my case; nothing happens any more unless it's agreed on in advance according to this 'melody'! It's the law, truly the 'Nomos'! But agreed on in advance on the basis of canon![53]

The critical section of this movement is the soprano aria that lies at its centre, in bars 17–45. Here, as in the preceding movement, the soprano sings what amounts to a *dux*, since the principles used are derived from canon, but what might perhaps be more accurately described as a *cantus firmus*, and the conformation of the other voices is determined in accordance with this part. But although the variational procedures are similar to those used in 'Leichteste Bürden', the product is even further removed from its source. Ironically, the first sketches of these bars were in strict melodic canon, unlike those of 'Leichteste Bürden', which contained many three- and four-note chords from its inception. In the aria of 'Freundselig ist das Wort' as it finally evolved, the soprano sings almost continuously, accompanied by a mixture of short melodic fragments, dyads and three- and four-note chords. Since the row structure of all four voices is identical (they differ from each other only in their levels of transposition), no opportunity arises, as it did in the previous piece, for the use of either augmentation (because all voices present the same number of rows) or retrograde (because all are playing the same row form at any given time). The voice part is not convoluted as it was in the previous movement; the first row does not provide all the material here as it did there; it is therefore not possible in this case to describe the generating material in terms of a durational series. Rather, the whole voice part is the model, and it is imitated in its entirety by each of the remaining three voices, making the process used in this movement resemble the usual canonic procedure more closely than that of the earlier movement did.

It was mentioned earlier that the first sketches of bars 17–45 are very different from the music that finally emerged. Example 3.17 presents, for comparison, an early sketch (not the first)[54] and the published version of bars 17–25.[55] The three accompanying voices in this sketch are clearly labelled 'Alt', 'Tenor' and 'Bass', even though the ranges of the parts are quite impossible for human voices.[56] I think this provides an interesting insight into the reason behind the remarkable change of personality between the early sketches and the finished product. It was noted earlier that the voice parts of Op. 31 are relatively strict and not subjected to the sort of rhythmic variation that so characterizes the instrumental music, and that, as a result, those sections written for chorus are in fairly strict canon. It seems clear that the introduction of extreme variational techniques in the middle section of this movement coincided with the decision to make of it an accompanied solo aria rather than a choral piece.

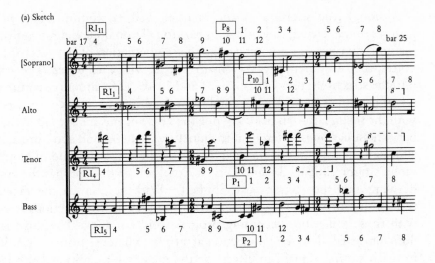

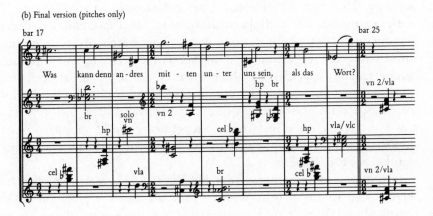

3.17   Op. 31/v, bars 17–25

The accompaniment that eventually emerged resembles that of the preceding aria, but the row segmentation is more inclusive; whereas groups of notes were gathered together in 'Leichteste Bürden' only for the purpose of isolated verticalizations, here a single segment often yields a combination of elements – single notes, dyads, chords, grace notes (with the successor sometimes belonging to another voice) and so on. The same segment is not always treated in the same way in the several voices, variants becoming increasingly divergent as the piece progresses. Rows intersect infrequently, and there are no *Ausfälle*.[57] The rules are complex, as Webern has indicated, and many specific situations receive special treatment. Nevertheless, variation of the original canon, while extreme, has not essentially altered the relative position of events or the general proportions of the piece.

Although the scansion of the text, as well as rhythmic and melodic features of the setting, cause the solo part to fall into quite definite units, these 'natural' divisions do not determine the segmentation of the accompanying voices; the latter are, however, in agreement with each other. The aria falls into three sections: bars 17–24, 25–31 and 32–45. (The imitative nature of the accompaniment causes the first and second sections to overlap: the first ends with the string chord in bar 25, while the voice begins the second in the same bar. The situation is different at the juncture of the second and third sections: although the imitation is finished by the double bar at the end of bar 31, the violin's figure in bars 32 and 33 is an extension of this and has the effect of drawing out the section just finished.) With respect to the generative relationship of solo to accompaniment, the first of these sections is simple, with those following becoming progressively complex. The third is very difficult. I shall describe one section at a time; whatever principles hold true for each section remain in effect for the next, with additional stipulations accruing. The reader is referred to the analysis in Example 3.18 (pp. 134–5).

Before proceeding with the analysis, however, I should like to digress for a moment to describe a curious detail. There are only four instances of immediate pitch repetition in this movement, three of them occurring in the central section (bars 25–31). These are all in the soprano part and are made necessary by a discrepancy between the number of syllables to be set within a given space and the number of notes made available by the predetermined row structure. On the surface these repetitions would appear to be of little importance; however, they seem to have assumed an almost perverse significance for Webern.

In response to an enquiry from Hildegard Jone concerning the shape of 'Freundselig ist das Wort', Webern told her that the piece turned on the central phrase 'Weil er am Kreuz verstummte, müssen wir ihm nach, in allen Ernst der Bitternis, ihm folget unser Hauch' ('Because he died [fell silent] on the cross, we needs must follow him, in the harshness of suffering our breath pursues him'), adding that 'What went before is now repeated backwards.' He goes on to qualify this by saying that 'all shapes are similar and *none are the same*; thus the chorus points to a secret law, to a holy riddle'.[58] This statement, somewhat imprecise to say the least, can be justified by the observation that the piece is in ABA form and by finding portions after the centre that are to varying degrees similar to corresponding portions before the centre. And perhaps the reference to a secret law, a holy riddle, was only an allusion to Goethe's essay *The Metamorphosis of Plants*, which Webern obviously found fascinating.[59] Nevertheless, he has invented a riddle of his own in these bars – perhaps not sufficiently significant to be considered holy, but certainly commendably abstruse – and it has to do with the soprano's repeated notes.

In determining the way in which the rows of the model have been segmented, it is necessary, obviously, to dispense with one of a pair of identical pitches, as they both represent the same element of the row. Normally one would suppose that the one to be thrown away is the second, it being simply an extension in time of the first. While the first repetition, in bar 25, can be treated in this way, the next, in bar 28, cannot: when the second note is dropped in this instance, the resulting segment is the only one in the entire aria in which the accompanying parts do not correspond with the model. This repetition comes *after* the word 'Kreuz', however, and the instrumental imitations of the segment to which it belongs fit into the scheme if the first of the two soprano notes is thrown away and the second considered as definitive – in other words, if the *first* note is treated as the repetition. Thus, 'what went before is now repeated backwards'. The third note-repetition, at the close of the section, in bars 30–1, can be considered in either way.

And now to return to the analysis. The following discussion refers to Example 3.18, in which the three instrumental voices of bars 17–45 are realigned so that their rhythmic similarities can be more easily seen. As in Example 3.16, the vertical lines are not barlines; they enclose matching segments in the four voices. The segmentation suggested by the rhythm of the melody in the first section (bars 17–24) is into groups of five, six and four notes respectively. For the purposes of imitation, however, the accompanying voices (bars 17–25) use the segmentation three, one, two, three, three and three, thus dividing the twenty-seven crotchet values into groups of 6, 2, 4, 5, 5 and 6. All but the second and third of these segments are expressed as three-note chords. When the four voices are aligned rhythmically (as they are in Example 3.18), it can be seen that each of the elements in the accompanying parts falls at the point where one of the components of the appropriate segment sounds in the model, with the exception of the final three-note chord in the RI_5–P_2 voice (Voice **C**). This is the chord played by the strings in bar 25 and the only element to 'hang over' into the next section. (Its lateness may possibly be accounted for by its role as a bridge figure; the opening of the second section is delayed by a crotchet rest, thereby making it necessary that this chord be late as well, if it is to function as a connective.) In the sketch of bars 17–32 (on p. 99 of Sketchbook IV) this chord is written first in the position where it is expected – on the first beat of bar 25. It is then put in parentheses and renotated where it is now (as a minim). While corresponding segments of the several accompanying voices are not identical, the events of each segment occur entirely within the unit of time determined by the model in all cases.

In the central section (bars 25–31) each voice is forty-two crotchet values in length, segmented into periods of 9, 6, 5, 7, 6 and 9 crotchets, representing groups of three, six, two, three, six and three notes respectively. While all the accompanying voices treat the second, third, fourth and final segments in similar ways, the remaining segments, the first and third, show more variation than has been observed previously. Voice **C**, which enters first, realizes the first segment as three notes played melodically; Voice **B**, entering next, plays a similar figure in which the notes have been compressed in time with the first continuing to sound through the second; further compression in the third voice (**A**) results in none of its notes sounding alone. These three variants produce a progressive increase in density. A similar textural crescendo occurs in the instrumental realizations of the fifth segment. The three notes of the final segment of this section, another bridge figure, are played singly in all voices, the only anomaly being in the second voice (**A**), where the last of the three is a grace note, which precedes a note of the model. In bars 25–31, with the exception of the curiously inverted repetition in the soprano part (the repetition of a note, whether it comes first or second, seems simply to be ignored; the repetitions in both bars 25 and 28 have been omitted in Example 3.18), these varied figures again fall within the durational confines of the appropriate segments. Here, however, in contrast to the first section, many notes and chords have been moved so that they are slightly out of kilter: they are not struck at the exact moment defined by any of their components in the model.

The third section – comprising forty-two crotchet values – is much the most complex. The segmentation here is into groups of three, one, eight, four, three, three and four notes, accounting for the equivalent of 7, 1, 12½, 6, 4½, 8 and 3 crotchets respectively. The fractional values result from a doubling of the basic pulse to the quaver in bars 39–42.[60] This section really begins with the segment already considered as the close of the previous section.[61] The similarity of segments 1 and 2 to the first two segments of bars 17–24 should be noted, as this supports the aba structure of the aria indicated by the return, at bar 32, of the tempo of bars 17–24. The presence of two later three-note segments is also reminiscent of the earlier section, though they are not verticalized here as they were there. The most extended and complex segment in the aria is the third in this section; while the material within this segment is subdivided and treated very differently in the several voices, the variants are sufficiently diverse that the segment cannot be subdivided further.

There is a certain degree of audible canonic activity within the soprano aria portion of this movement, but the obvious imitation involves very short figures, with the distance – both spatial and temporal – between fragments constantly changing, as in the canons of Opp. 22 and 26. The imitation in the first four bars of the accompaniment (bars 17–20) is easily perceived because like segments are treated similarly, with parallel instrumentation. A similar orchestrational device in bars 21–6 will almost certainly mislead the listener into hearing a canon between two voices that move from brass to celesta and harp.[62] The real imitation – that which is congruent with the row structure – will be heard briefly in bars 27–8, beginning with the grace note, and again when two voices have a similar figure in bars 30–1. In the third section, the very alert listener will hear the imitation in bars 34–7, and everyone will notice it in bar 39 and in bars 40–5, though the way bar 39 is perceived is again misleading with respect to the row structure.

Although both Spinner[63] and Stroh[64] mention the fifth movement in passing, and although it is clear that Spinner at least had identified the rhythmic procedures used,[65] to my knowledge only Willam has published an analysis of the complete movement, and here, as elsewhere, his energy is directed towards attempting to prove the validity of a durational series in the solo part. (With respect to the accompanying parts, he finds his task an unrewarding one and eventually more or less abandons it.) Curiously, he seems unconcerned by his failure to explain the meaning of Webern's remark about the relationship of these parts to the melody. He finally concludes that the temporal disposition of chords and other accompanying material here shows no relationship to the rhythm of the solo part, and that the position of the accompanying chords was determined by the desire to mask the metre and to provide a consistently varied instrumentation.[66] Again, Spinner's explanation is not referred to.

'Gelockert aus dem Schoße'

Webern described the construction of 'Gelockert aus dem Schoße' to Willi Reich and the Humpliks in similar terms. On 4 September 1942 he wrote to Reich:

> The second part (alto) sings the notes of the first (tenor) backwards, the third (soprano) has the inversion of the second, and the fourth (bass) is the inversion of the first, but moreover sings the notes of the third backwards! – So, a double interlinking, one and four, two and three (by inversion), also one and two, three and four (cancrizan).[67]

There is not a great deal more than this to be said. The construction is very tight, with, as Webern has said, interlocking sets of associations. (One thinks immediately of the first Variation in Op. 21 and the opening section of the last movement of Op. 28 as being similar. See pp. 100 and 115.) Although the concept is complex, the realization is straightforward, and in this way unlike the rest of Op. 31. It is the only movement of the six to maintain a linear four-voice canonic texture throughout, and the only one in which the temporal relationship of the voices never changes. Of all the canons in the cantata it is the most conventional.

The piece contains twelve rows, three of each type, and three in each voice, as shown in the diagram on page 136, where the voices are arranged in the order of their entry.

Row and canon

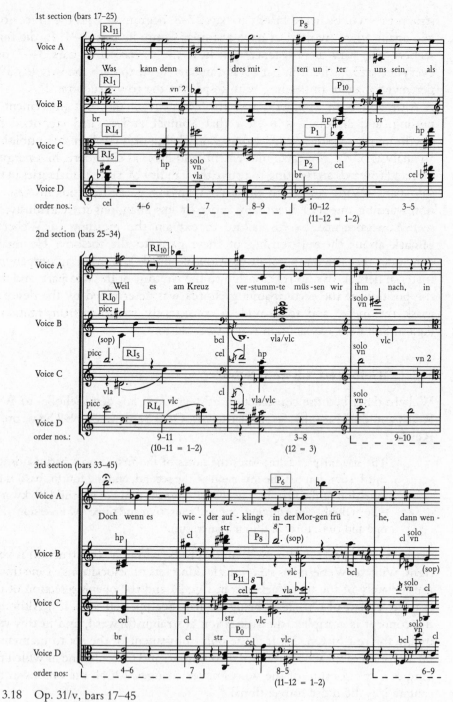

3.18   Op. 31/v, bars 17–45

135

tenor	P_8	RI_{10}	RI_4
alto	I_4	I_{10}	R_5
soprano	P_0	P_6	RI_8
bass	I_8	R_6	R_0

While the two sets of relationships outlined by Webern can be seen easily in the row structure, they are not realized melodically. In Webern's description, 'notes' must be understood to mean *pitch classes*, not *pitches*. As has been the case since Op. 27, this is a canon only insofar as all the parts are rhythmically identical.

The transpositional levels of the pairs of voices cited by Webern as being inversionally related (P_0... and I_4..., P_8... and I_8...) are such that both revolve around a D axis. However, in contrast to earlier mirror canons – Opp. 21/i, 22/i and 27/ii – neither pair of voices revolves around a particular D. Nevertheless, d^1 occupies a pivotal position of sorts. Two voices begin on this pitch and the other two on notes equidistant above and below it, and the piece closes on the same group of pitches.

'Sehr tief verhalten'

The second movement has more the appearance of a canon than either the fourth or the fifth, since it lacks the verticalizations that characterize both those movements and it contains no homophony. It is clearly a linear piece throughout, and numerous figures can be heard in imitation. Much of the time, however, its texture is more sparse than one would expect in a canon in four voices, as the result of a very large number of *Ausfälle*.

Webern spoke of this movement's canonic basis in a letter to Willi Reich written on 6 August 1943:

> I've completed another piece as part of the plan I've told you of several times; a bass aria. It's all even stricter, and for that reason it's also become still freer. That's to say, I move with complete freedom on the basis of an 'endless canon by inversion.' By variation, diminution, etc. – rather as Bach does with his theme in the 'Art of Fugue ... '[68]

The four chains are set essentially as a four-voice canon in inversion. The frequency and number of *Ausfälle* throughout this movement make it difficult to disentangle the voices and determine the extent of their rhythmic similarity. The fact that the same note often serves two or three voices at once effectively hides the exact canonic relationship of these voices, as well as exaggerating the confusion that always attends pointillistically deployed canons with respect to the number of voices operating. In the present case, Webern charted a rhythmic canon in four voices and then, seemingly (but surely not) at random, removed nearly one quarter of the notes. The canon should contain 480 notes;[69] 103 of these have been excised. The movement was sketched first as a complete canon in four voices, in which each of the accompanying voices replicated exactly the rhythm of the solo bass voice.[70] At the next stage, notes were selected for deletion and encircled. Subsequently some of the notes that remained – in both the model and the accompanying voices – were moved to positions very slightly earlier or later, with the result that the rhythmic imitation became, eventually, both incomplete and inexact. At no stage in the progress of this movement were notes gathered into chords or groups as had occurred in the variants leading to the final versions of 'Leichteste Bürden' and 'Freundselig ist das Wort'.

The singer's line was the model and is the only one of the four row chains that remained completely intact through successive variations, though even its rhythm was altered on occasion. Each of the other three chains must reach out to a neighbouring voice for notes now and again, and, when this occurs, as in 'Leichteste Bürden', the purloined note is simply absent from the rhythmic framework of the disadvantaged voice. The three accompanying rows often exhibit the same instrumental segmentation, and this makes their identities clear for a time. Frequently, however, an entire segment is missing from one voice, or even from two. Willam decides eventually that it makes no difference which of the rows a shared note is assigned to, because the exact position of individual notes in the row scheme is of no importance. He nevertheless suggests such assignments, and these are in many cases incorrect. Although he admits that the accompanying voices are imitative in the middle section of the movement, he dismisses Spinner's identification of the remainder of the movement as a canon.[71]

Example 3.19 separates the first eleven bars of the movement into the four canonic voices; the chart immediately following represents the rhythmic content of the canon. Every note in the movement is accounted for, once only, in this chart. The voices have been realigned so that their similarity can be more easily observed, and they are ordered according to their completeness: the singer's part, which lacks nothing, is given first; the row chain beginning with I_6, the instrumental voice retaining the most notes, is second; and so on. Each type-character equals the value of one crotchet; longer notes are indicated with short dashes; rests are expressed as full stops. The numerals are order numbers.[72] *Ausfälle* are omitted on the chart as they are in practice; immediate repetitions, of which there are three – in bars 33 and 40 – are also not indicated, since they are effectively prolongations. Grace notes are in bold face and are listed on either the beat they precede or the one from which their value would normally be taken – this decision was made on the basis of their position in the sketches, where they appear as ordinary notes. (Their elevation to grace was clearly late.) It should be kept in mind while reading the chart that the decision to list the entire contents of every row has resulted in redundancies: every **B** and **C** appears again immediately as 1 (**B**) or 2 (**C**) of the following row, in some cases realigned on their reappearance. The

3.19   Op. 21/ii, bars 1–11

```
I₇:   1---2-----3-4-5-6---------7-8-9-...  A-BC---
I₆:   1-..2-....3-4-..6-.........7-89-.....B-C
P₆:   1-..2-.........5-6-.........7.8.9...A-B
P₇:   1-..2-....3-4-..6-.........7-89-

R₆:   12---3-4--.5-6---7---8-9-A-.....B-C-
R₅:   1-2...3-4...5-6.......8.9.A......B.C
RI₇:  1.............4...5-6-.......9-A......B.C
RI₈:              4...5-6........8.9.A.....B.C

I₉:   1-2-3-4---5---6-7-..8-9-...A-..B-C-
I₈:   1.2.3-4---5...67....8-9-......B-C
P₄:   1.2.3.4...5...67....8-9.......B.C
P₅:   1.2.3-4...............8-9.......B-C

R₈:   1-2-3-4-5-...6--------7-8-9---..A---.....BC---
R₇:   1-2.3.4-5...6.......78-9......A......B-C-
RI₅:  1.2.3-...5...6-........8-......A.....B.C-
RI₆:  1-2.3......6-.......7-..9---.........B-.C-
```

138

```
I₁₁:   1 2 - - - 3 4 5 - . . . . 6 7 8 9 A - . BC
I₁₀:   1 - 2 - . 3 4 5 . . . . . 6 7 8 9 A . . BC
P₂:    1 . 2 - . 3 4 . . . . . . . 7 8 9 . . . BC
P₃:    1 - . 2 - . 3 4 5 - . . . . 6 7 8 9 A - . BC
```

```
R₁₀:  1 2 3 4 5 6 - 7 - 8 9 A . . BC
R₉:   1 2 3 4 5 . . 7 . 8 9 A . . . C
RI₃:  1 2 3 . 5 . 6 . . 8 9 A
RI₄:  1 2 3 4 5
```

```
I₁:   1 2 3 4 - - 5 6 7 8 9 . . . . ABC
I₀:     2 3 4 - . . 6 7 8 9 . . . . AB
P₀:       3 4 . . . . 7 8 9 . . . . . C
P₁:       3 4 - . . . 7 8 9 . . . AB
```

```
R₀:   1 2 3 . 4 5 6 7 . 8 - 9 . A - . . . . . . . . . . B - . . C - - -
R₁₁:  1 . 3 . 4 5 6 . . 8 - 9 . A - . . . . . . . . . . B - . . C -
RI₁:    2 . . 4 5 . 7 . . . 9 . . . A - . . . . . . . . . B - . . C -
RI₂:  1 . . . 4 5 6 . . . . . . . . . . . . . . . B - - - C - - -
```

```
I₃:   1 - . . 2 - - - . . 3 - 4 - 5 - 6 - - - 7 - - - 8 - - - . 9 - A - - BC - - - - - -
I₂:   1 - . . 2 - . . . . 3 - 4 - . . 6 - . . 7 - . . 8 - . . . . . 9 - A . BC -
P₁₀:  1 - . . 2 - . . . . 3 - 4 - . . 6 - . . 7 - . . . . . . . . . . 9 . . . BC -
P₁₁:  1 - - - 2 - - - . . 3 - 4 - . . . . . . . 7 - . . 8 - . . . . . 9 - A . BC -
```

```
R₂:   1 2 - - - - - - 3 4 - - 5 - - . . 6 - - - 7 - 8 - - 9 . A - BC -
R₁:   1 2 - . . . . . 3 4 . . 5 . . . 6 . . . 7 . . . 8 9 . . A . BC -
RI₁₁: 1 2 - . . . . . 3 4 . . 5 . . . . . . . . . . . . 8 - 9 A - - B
RI₀:  1 2 - . . . . . 3 4 - . 5 . . 6 - . . . . . . . . . 9 - A
```

```
I₅:   1 2 - 3 - . 4 - - - - 5 - . . 6 - 7 - . . 8 - - - - 9 . A - BC -
I₄:   1 2 - 3 - . 4 . . . 5 . . . . . 6 7 . . . . 8 - . 9 - A - . B - C
P₈:   1 . . . . . 4 . . . 5 - - . . . 6 - 7 . . . . . . . 9 A - . BC - -
P₉:                 5 - - - . . . . . . . . . 8 - . . 9 A - . B - C
```

```
R₄:   1 2 - 3 - . 4 - 5 - . . . 6 - . . 7 - - - . . 8 - - - . . 9 - A -
R₃:   1 - 2 3 . 4 - - 5 . . . . 6 - - - 7 - . . . . 8 - . . . . 9 - A -
RI₉:  1 2 - - 3 - . . . . . . . . . . . . . . . . . 8 - . . . . 9 - A -
RI₁₀: 1 - 2 3 - . 4 . 5 - . . . . . . . . . . . . . 8 - - - . . 9 - A -
```

movement is in three sections, each encompassing four sets of rows. (These divisions are represented by double lines.) At the beginning of each new section the temporal relationship of the four voices changes; since all the rows are elided, this shows up as apparent disarray in notes 11 (**B**) and 12 (**C**) of the set of rows immediately preceding the new section. In a letter to Hildegard Jone dated 18 May 1943 Webern said about 'Sehr tief verhalten':

> My work goes its way. The things I am doing in the 'Bienenkorb' [the title of the poem] will require a considerable amount of time however![73]

One can imagine that they must have.

'Schöpfen aus Brunnen des Himmels'

The third movement is in five sections, of which the first, third and fifth are essentially the same music and clearly canonic. These sections are written for three-part women's chorus and orchestra. All are rhythmic canons in four voices, three of which are sung, with orchestral support, the fourth entirely instrumental. The four voices in these three sections were rhythmically identical in the first sketches; in subsequent drafts the three choral voices have been varied slightly but the instrumental one kept as it was originally.[74] Although the choral voices are continuous, their rows are segmented for the purposes of orchestral reinforcement. With a few exceptions, for the most part in the purely orchestral voice, the segmentation is the same in all four voices.[75] The rhythms of the four parts in the first section (bars 1–13) are given in Example 3.20, realigned so that their similarity may be more easily observed. Only two notes of the voice parts have been varied from the original canon (in those bars corresponding to bars 4 and 10 in the instrumental part).

3.20   Op. 31/iii

Rhythmically, the third section (bars 29–36) is a condensed version of the first. The first soprano parts of these two sections are offered for comparison in Example 3.21. Two instances of value replacement, in the bars corresponding to bars 32 and 36 of the instrumental part, account for the only rhythmic disagreement between voices in this section (Example 3.22).

Characteristically, the fifth section (bars 45–59) is longer than either the first or third, and the parts exhibit greater freedom. It shows scant rhythmic similarity with the previous sections until the final phrase, where the dotted figure that was prominent in both the earlier sections (♪. ♪♪) returns. The identity of rows with timbral voices has been maintained throughout the first and third sections, but in bar 53 the row chain that has served the altos becomes the orchestral voice, and vice versa. There are four departures from strict rhythmic imitation (Example 3.23), and whereas previously such deviations have united the chorus against the orchestra, in this case on two occasions a single choral part is varied alone: the first soprano in bar 50 and the alto in bars 51–2. Although the alto series is also responsible for the

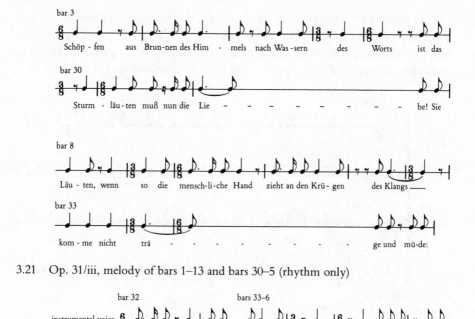

3.21   Op. 31/iii, melody of bars 1–13 and bars 30–5 (rhythm only)

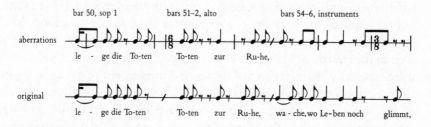

3.22   Op. 31/iii

3.23   Op. 31/iii

remaining two aberrations, in bars 54 and 55–6, these occur after this voice has moved to the orchestra.

The intervening sections (bars 13–28 and 36–44) are written for solo soprano and orchestra. In bars 13–28 the melody, sung by solo soprano, is accompanied by a quick alternation of chords and imitated melodic fragments; only the chords remain in the abbreviated reprise of this material in bars 36–44. The accompanying voices of these two sections are generated in the same way as in the fourth movement and the central section of the fifth.[76]

The chords were already in the earliest sketches. In Example 3.24 the rhythmic content of the four voices in bars 13–28 is realigned so that their general similarity can be seen; *Ausfälle* are omitted. As in previous rhythmic examples, the vertical lines are not barlines but denote segmentation.[77]

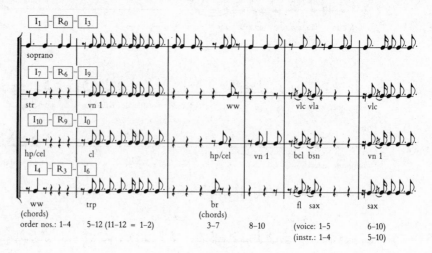

3.24   Op. 31/iii, bars 13–28 (rhythmic reduction)

It will be noted that all the accompanying voices are the same length, and that, except for the staggered chords in bars 21 and 22, they are in rhythmic agreement. That they are generated by the rhythm of the voice part is obvious. These sixteen bars seem to be a microcosm of the imitative techniques applied throughout the other movements of the cantata. The second segment (bars 16–20) is a straightforward rhythmic canon, like those of the sixth movement and the refrain sections of the third. The techniques used in the fourth and fifth movements occur in segment 1. The *Ausfälle* that were especially characteristic of the second movement reappear in segment 4: all three notes of this segment are achieved only through intersection in two of the voices and therefore have no place in the rhythmic scheme. The remaining segments – the third, fifth and sixth – display all the techniques used previously. In the last two, the rhythm of the following voices is an incomplete replication of that of the model; the number of significant notes has been reduced by the addition of grace notes. When this texture returns, in bars 36–44, the accompaniment consists only of three chords in each voice. There is no intersection. Example 3.25 shows a possible alignment of these voices, in which each conforms to the successive periods of time determined by the model.

Throughout this movement, as in the rest of Op. 31, melodic contours are not imitated. In this case, as in the aria of 'Freundselig ist das Wort', since all four voices have the same row structure, melodic imitation would have

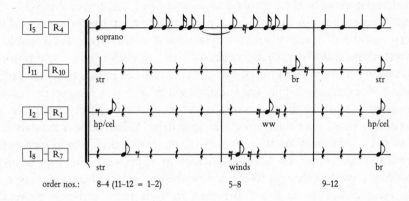

3.25   Op. 31/iii, bars 36–44 (rhythmic reduction)

produced direct replication. This happens rarely, and never involves two intervals in succession. Much of the time the voices move in pairs in opposite directions, giving the false impression of a double canon in inversion. At other times they either group themselves as three and one or proceed independently.

Because of the accident of his death, this cantata is Webern's last word on canon. One wonders whether the sort of canons for which he is remembered – those of Opp. 21, 27 and 28 – would have reappeared in subsequent works had he lived. Or perhaps he had gone irrevocably beyond this in Op. 31.

It seems appropriate at this point to quote Cesar Bresgen's reminiscence concerning Webern's activities at the end of his life.

> ... one could often see Webern in most stimulating work, which consisted of drawing with pencil and compasses on a poor quality table or on a wooden board. I well remember his system of lines, in which could be seen geometrical figures or fixed points with markings. Once – it was in the middle of August 1945 – Webern said on one of my visits that he had just finished some work which had occupied him a great deal. He had completely organized a piece, *i.e.*, he had fixed all the notes in it in respect of their pitch (sound) and also their duration in time...With this graphic plan on the table Webern regarded the real work as completed. More than once he made the assertion that he would never wish to hear his piece (played by musicians)...it was enough for him that the piece was now finished in itself...[78]

Bresgen's description of Webern's preoccupation with purely hypothetical music seems to be the dispassionate account of a neighbour's pastimes. More serious implications could be drawn from these activities, however. Adorno,

143

for instance, views Webern's apparent abdication from the realm of sounding music as the inevitable result of the twelve-note technique itself. He takes a different view of the synthesis so sought after and prized by Schoenberg and Webern: to him the integration of the horizontal and the vertical is the very essence of the twelve-note system and is therefore unavoidable. His description of Webern's late works as 'the liquidation of counterpoint'[79] is his answer to a question raised but deflected earlier in this chapter: To what extent does canon retain its validity when it is no longer perceived as imitation? Adorno raises a second question that would seem to place all of Webern's most cherished efforts in jeopardy: What achievement is represented by imitation in the absence of generally understood pre-existing vertical constraints? Is Adorno correct in supposing the significance of complex imitative designs to depend on the necessity of harmonic logic, or is the unique 'harmonic logic' inherent in each row sufficient to establish intelligible criteria for the succession of simultaneities? For Adorno it was not Webern's abstraction of canon but his attempt to use it at all that was unacceptable.

The problem of controlling imitation in twelve-note composition had been recognized by Schoenberg as well. Canon is peripheral to his style; according to his own accounts this is because he, like Adorno, found the inevitability of imitation that was built into the system disquieting. His objections seem to have arisen primarily from more specific – even mundane – considerations, however: his concern is with the avoidance of unisons and parallel octaves, and he concludes that the whole exercise is too easy to be worthy of merit.[80] Neither Schoenberg nor Adorno appears to recognize, or at least to consider seriously, the importance of rhythm as both a distinguishing feature and a control in twelve-note imitation (just as rhythm may be sufficient to establish a feeling of cadence in a twelve-note work). It was left to Webern to illustrate the possibilities inherent in rhythmic imitation, and the realization of these possibilities forms the basis of the canonic techniques that so pervade his twelve-note music. As I hope I have demonstrated, his perception of the nature and function of canon changed during the course of the years with which this study is concerned. The replication of contour and rhythm observed in the first twelve-note canons gave way in the end to complex designs in which contour was not a factor and rhythm was varied to such an extent that genealogy is effectively obscured. In Op. 31 canon was for Webern a tool, not a texture: the means by which to achieve a '*completely new* style of representation',[81] a further step in his unrelenting quest for the unity of musical space. Adorno's observation, however, that the concept of counterpoint is no longer to be found here ('his sparse sounds are precisely those remnants which the fusion of the vertical and the horizontal have left behind'[82]) strikes me as particularly acute.

In Webern's music the inclusive and the exclusive are continually held in balance. An aspiration after extremes is evident already in the make-up of his rows: because the row of Op. 24 is generated by a minimum of material – two intervals, three pitch classes – each statement of the row (or any of its permutations) provides a maximum unfolding of its possibilities. The situation is even more intense in the case of the Op. 28 row, which is in addition identical to one of its own permutations. This desire for limitation is manifest as well in the remaining symmetrical rows, which fill only half a matrix – those of Opp. 21, 29 and 30. In his choice of methods, Webern also seems to be fascinated by extremes. Consistently applied elisional procedures serve either to limit or to exhaust the matrix. Elision is restrictive in Opp. 21, 28 and 29, where potentially endless cycles of two, three and four rows respectively result. In Variation 4 of Op. 30 and in Op. 31/ii, on the other hand, the elision is comprehensive: in Op. 30 the cycle comprises all the transpositions of the retrograde, while the four voices of Op. 31/ii are managed in such a way that the entire matrix is depleted. Thus by imposing a second order (a pattern of elision) on the already ordered set of pitches, Webern geometrically increases the restrictions of a method that is already confined to start with. The fascination with limitations must also be seen as responsible for the decision to use only a small number of the available row forms in Opp. 19, 23, 25, 28/ii and iii and 31/i and iv. All of these self-imposed restrictions serve to exaggerate the discipline that was a central, and to Webern a very important, element of the twelve-note technique. Restriction of yet another sort is encountered in the change-ringing sections of Op. 20, and in an extension of this technique that occurs in parts of Op. 31, where the pitch repertoire of individual instruments is again very limited. Similar fixing of register in Op. 21 and sections of Opp. 22/i and 28 will be discussed in Part II. These limitations of *sound* (as opposed to the limitation of compositional *material*) seem to cut through the system, as if somehow taking a cross-section, or approaching a familiar problem from a 180-degree angle.

At the same time that he is following with particular obedience those precepts of the twelve-note technique that have to do with order and balance, certain habits that would seem to contradict Schoenberg's original intent emerge as characteristic of Webern's style: instrumental doubling in works for orchestra and the instrumental reinforcement of vocal parts in works for chorus and orchestra, and the deliberate manipulation of the relative importance of the twelve pitches through, on one hand, the exploitation of the possibilities for pitch-class duplication offered by invariance and, on the other, a reduction in the aural presence of certain of the twelve notes through intersection and *Ausfälle*. From his readiness to employ these techniques, one suspects that it was not the equality of the twelve notes that was of primary concern to Webern, as it was to Schoenberg, but the solving of self-imposed problems and puzzles. Indeed, all the indications are that he was a man who worked best – or at any rate felt that he did – within the confines of a very restricted system, his most original ideas resulting from an examination of the nature of the discipline and the exploration of every corner and crevice of the limited possibilities it provided.

Introduction to Part II

> So let there be no mistake: we haven't departed from the forms of the
> classical composers. What has happened since is only alteration, extension,
> abbreviation...but the forms remain the same.[1]

On the face of things it seems ironic that the forms chosen by Schoenberg
and Webern – indisputably atonal composers – should have been those
current in the classical era, of all periods of Western music the one in which
major/minor tonality occupied the most commanding position; on more
careful consideration, it was probably inevitable. The two composers were
the product of a late nineteenth-century Austrian musical education, in
which the three central disciplines of *Harmonielehre*, *Kontrapunkt* and *Formen-
lehre* were equal components. That a musician should not only study the
traditional forms but demonstrate a facility in composing with them was
understood. They represented the means through which musical expression
was accomplished, and in well over a century they had not been seriously
challenged: trouble definitely loomed on the horizon for tonal harmony, and
strict counterpoint had fallen out of fashion much earlier, but the forms of
Mozart, Haydn and Beethoven had simply been adjusted to serve succeeding
generations of composers. And as the three disciplines were treated peda-
gogically as separate, it is possible that turbulent changes in one – as had
already occurred in the case of counterpoint – might not be seen as
threatening the others.

For both Schoenberg and Webern, the return to some sort of tonal
discipline (in the form of the twelve-note technique) after some years of
composing freely atonal music was seen as a welcome opportunity also to
re-embrace the traditional homophonic forms that they felt to be so
important. In some cases this return to the old forms is indicated through
titles: suite, variations, concerto, symphony. Just as often it is apparent in the
absence of titles: here there are no rhapsodies, nocturnes or *Pieces in the Form
of a Pear*. In either case, the faithfulness to tradition is more profound than
just the use of a familiar name. However unconventional the surface of
Webern's twelve-note music may be, its adherence to the basic precepts of

traditional forms is continually reaffirmed by analysis. While his intricate counterpoint derives from the music of the remote Flemish composers whom he studied and admired, and his tonal syntax represents his own particular refinement of the new and shocking language of Schoenberg, the forms of his instrumental music are those of the late eighteenth and early nineteenth centuries: binary, ternary, rondo and, especially, sonata and variations. More specifically, like Schoenberg, he leans towards the shape these forms took in the middle works of Beethoven.

Serious difficulties were encountered in making inherently tonal structures intelligible in an atonal language. The homophonic forms of Western music originated as various expressions of a simple tonal gesture: all represented either a progressive (dramatic) or a reiterative (static) prolongation and elaboration of the cadence. Intelligibility depended on tonality. Contrast could be achieved merely by the use of a new key (frequently no other means was used – see, for instance, the monothematic sonata movements of Haydn); variations consisted essentially of recurrences of the same harmonic pattern with changes in figuration and texture; development was perceived whenever keys changed rapidly and sequentially. Only later did certain other features begin to become regularized. In his discussion of the nature of eighteenth-century sonata form in *The Classical Style*, Charles Rosen remarks that it is difficult to distinguish the defining from the acquired characteristics of a form.[2] Before the mid nineteenth century all the classical forms began to acquire characteristics that have since come to be considered definitive: a given number of contrasting themes in different keys (even the type of contrast was formalized to some extent), the association of particular treatment with specific sections (statement, development), the placing of transitions and climaxes, the use of special textures or specified changes of texture, and so on. These secondary features took on formal significance in the nineteenth century as the result of a change in the concept of what constitutes a musical idea – a change that Carl Dahlhaus attributes to the high value placed by the romantic generation on originality and inspiration.[3] Because of the romantics' insistence on the uniqueness of detail and their scorn for continuations, which were considered uninspired and superfluous, the theme diminished in scope from the expansive period of Mozart to the three- or four-note motive of, for example, Beethoven. Of necessity this reduction in the length of basic material was accompanied by an altered perception of the nature of form: Dahlhaus speaks of the transition from the balanced periodic forms of the eighteenth century to the nineteenth-century concept of 'logical' form determined by the development of musical ideas.[4] In these linear structures, essentially dramatic and melodic, the character and position of themes, as well as their treatment, played defining roles, and key relations were not always the traditional ones: the paring down of the theme and the attendant end of periodicity as the normal means of expressing ideas coincided with the decline of the tonic/dominant tonal foundations that had provided the original basis for traditional forms. This was the interpretation of musical form current with Schoenberg and his generation. Rosen says of Schoenberg:

> Form was, for Schoenberg, basically what it was for the nineteenth century: an ideal set of proportions and shapes which transcended style and language. These ideal shapes could be realized at any time in any style; they were absolute. The three great types of form were the sonata, the variation, and the *da capo* form.[5]

It is also the view of musical form that Webern would have been taught and for that reason the one I shall adopt in Part II of this study.

The nineteenth-century emphasis on secondary features meant that by the time tonality was dispensed with at the beginning of the present century the customary placement of 'acquired' features was so familiar that their retention alone was sufficient to ensure the perception of the conventional form. This excision from the fabric of musical structures of the original progenitor is, incidentally, parallel to the almost exactly contemporary elimination of natural forms from the visual arts, a process which caused an outcry of indignation and disgust similar to that aroused by the first atonal works of Schoenberg and Webern.

The abstraction of tonal forms was clearly one of the major crises faced by all atonal composers. Most, including Webern, temporarily abandoned the forms along with the tonality but later embraced them again, having come to terms with the problem in one way or another. Only the Viennese group of composers found a way to incorporate the old forms in the new atonal language; for most others, the answer involved some sort of retrenchment, as the result either of conviction about the nature of musical language (Bartók, Hindemith) or of a deliberate decision to return to traditional formal models (Stravinsky). Very few composers of this generation (only Ives and Varèse come to mind) repudiated the old forms altogether.

Webern's solution involved retention and re-emphasis: the old relationships are clearly articulated through the handling of secondary features. He took considerable care to delineate the traditional forms so that their identity could not be questioned. The conventional repeats provide signposts in Opp. 20/ii, 21/i and 22/i (all sonata movements), 27/ii (a binary form) and 28/ii (a ternary form); internal double bars define the sections in Opp. 24/ii and 28/ii (both ternary forms) and the Op. 30 Variations. The variations are numbered in Op. 21/ii. In Op. 24/i (a sonata movement) and Opp. 24/iii and 27/iii (both variations) the structure is outlined by *rit. ... .a tempo* markings. The apparent clarity thus achieved is at the same time both purposeful and deceptive. While the familiar outline acts as a guide in the listener's perception of the formal relationship of sections, upon closer inspection the content of sections thus identified frequently places these relationships in a new perspective. Webern closed the seventh lecture of the series later published as 'The Path to Twelve-Note Composition' with a reference to the tonal aspect of this re-emphasis:

> Considerations of symmetry, regularity are now to the fore, as against the emphasis formerly laid on the principal intervals – dominant, sub-dominant, mediant, etc. For this reason the middle of the octave – the diminished fifth – is now most important. For the rest, one works as before. The original form and pitch of the row occupy a position akin to that of the 'main key' in earlier music; the recapitulation will naturally return to it. We end 'in the same key!' This analogy with earlier formal construction is quite consciously fostered; here we find the path that will lead us again to extended forms.[6]

Tonal analogues vary from one work to another, but in all cases the choice of transpositions seems to have been determined by the same considerations that had guided earlier composers writing in the same forms. Although there is no question of tonality in these movements, transpositions of the row function in much the same way that keys had done previously, even (in spite of his apparent dismissal of the dominant in the lecture just cited) to the point of preserving the traditional fifth-relationship in some cases. (Many of Schoenberg's twelve-note works show a similar concern, though in his case the fifth-relationship is expressed through combinatoriality: the row form that complements the untransposed prime is the inversion a fifth above or, more often, a fifth below.)

Webern used sonata form in Opp. 20, 21, 22, 24 and 27; sonata principles are also evident in Opp. 26, 28 and 30. In all but Op. 20 the traditional first-movement form assumes its accustomed position. Each of these movements is an essay in the interpretation of a specific principle or the solution of a particular problem inherent in the atonal expression of the form, and all are different. The twelve-note instrumental music contains, in addition, five movements in variation form,[7] two rondos, three ternary forms and one binary form. There are no movements that do not conform to one of the familiar classical prototypes.[8]

One aspect of Webern's fascination with synthesis was introduced in Part I: his constantly reiterated desire to find that 'unity of musical space' to which Schoenberg made such frequent reference, that ideal of comprehensibility which the latter saw as obtainable only through a perfect integration of the horizontal and vertical aspects of a composition.[9] This ideal did not originate with Schoenberg, of course; nor was it in some way specific to the New Music, though the basic principles of the twelve-note technique, in which all dimensions of the music are determined by the same series, make it a

150

particularly appropriate vehicle. It would be difficult, for instance, to think of a better example of this kind of integration than the *Hammerklavier* sonata, with its harmonic and melodic saturation with the interval of a third.[10] The merging of horizontal and vertical makes its first appearance very early in Webern's twelve-note works, in the opening movements of Opp. 21 and 22, both of which are canonic throughout, while also answering the requirements of sonata form. A similar combination can be seen later in the inverted canon in binary form that serves as the central movement of Op. 27. Webern's concern with this sort of synthesis is repeated to the point of obsession in his references to the last four works, Opp. 28–31:

> Within the work it [the third movement of Op. 28] must be the 'crowning fulfilment,' so to speak, of the 'synthesis' of 'horizontal' and 'vertical' construction (Schoenberg!) I strove for already in the first and second movements.[11]

> It's [the third movement of Op. 29] constructed as a four-part double fugue. But the subject and counter-subject are related like antecedent and consequent (period), and elements from the other mode of presentation (horizontal) also play a part.[12]

> [Referring to Op. 30] In fact there's again the synthesis; the presentation is horizontal as to form, vertical in all other respects.[13]

> So: a style, whose material is of that kind, and whose formal construction relates the two possible types of presentation to each other [referring again to Op. 30].[14]

> ...so, once again, a very close combination of the two types of presentation [in connection with the second movement of Op. 31].[15]

> In it [the fifth movement of Op. 31] I have managed – I believe – to achieve a completely new style of presentation; on a purely polyphonic basis I arrive at about the most opposite sort of presentation imaginable.[16]

The desire for a synthesis of horizontal and vertical (of homophony and polyphony) led by extension to the search for a perfect fusion of two or more homophonic forms. The formal ramifications of Webern's fascination with structural integration will be an important theme in Part II of this study.

The first work to evince his concern with widening the scope of the 'horizontal mode of presentation' itself through the fusion of homophonic forms is the opening movement of Op. 24, which is devoted to exploring the possibilities of composite form and structural *double entendres*. It is a bithematic sonata movement which at the same time incorporates many features of baroque ritornello form. Its deviations from both of these patterns seem to result from a desire to answer also to some extent the expectations of ternary form. The first movement of Op. 27 shows a similar confusion regarding its formal identity: it is clearly an ABA form, but it also incorporates all the essentials of sonata.

The crowning works in this progress of synthesis are the opening movement of the Op. 28 Quartet and the Variations for Orchestra, Op. 30. Although described by Webern as variations, both these works are moulded also into a complex ternary superstructure that is at least as important to their total effect as the fact that they are variations. In fact, it is unlikely that Op. 30 would ever be recognized by the naïve listener as a theme and variations, even though its shape as a closed form should be easily perceived. As both works are imitative throughout, they seem to be the product of a cumulative process of amalgamation, incorporating both the synthesis of horizontal and vertical and the fusion of homophonic forms. Both are impressive essays in the homology of structures.

The progression from the classical Op. 20 to, eventually, the formal complexities of Opp. 28 and 30 – less neat and symmetrical but more profoundly integrated than anything before – recalls the career of Beethoven. The language is different, of course, but the goals and even the methods are in many ways similar. This comparison is not made lightly. Beethoven was repeatedly held up as a structural model by both Schoenberg (in the music examples of *Fundamentals*, Beethoven is the composer by default – only those examples *not* written by him are identified by composer) and Webern (in the 'Path to New Music' lectures, Beethoven is cited as composer of the 'purest' examples of sentence structure, as the final developer of classical forms, and so on), and the forms used by Beethoven seem to have served as specific models for Webern on many occasions. This is especially true in the case of sonata and rondo forms. Sometimes (in the rondo of Op. 22/ii, for example) the model is announced; at other times (as in both movements of Op. 20) it is clear although unacknowledged. Certainly the need to draw upon the resources of more than one classical form at a time seems to have been felt by both composers in their later years; both also showed a particular interest in fugue late in their careers. (Although in Beethoven's case this interest was not limited to his later years, his most ambitious and impressive efforts in this respect date from this period.) The affinity with Beethoven will be evident in the following chapters.

4

The movements in sonata form: Opp. 20/ii, 21/i, 22/i, 24/i and 27/i

Sonata occupies a position of particular pre-eminence in Western music as an acknowledged vehicle for the expression of lofty ideas. In *Fundamentals of Musical Composition* Schoenberg cites as the greatest merit of sonata form, 'which enabled it to hold a commanding position over a period of 150 years', its 'extraordinary flexibility in accommodating the widest variety of musical ideas, long or short, many or few, active or passive, in almost any combination'.[1] As regarded by the nineteenth century, the sonata is the most inherently dramatic of the homophonic forms: reduced to its essentials, the romantic sonata represents an unfolding series of events and relationships between two protagonists of contrasting keys and character. To a consider-able extent these events and relationships are stylized. Typically the first theme or group is dramatic and the second lyrical; the first is always in the tonic key (or at least begins and ends there) and the second never is; the themes are stated in succession at the beginning, prior to the section where the drama takes place, and again at the end, after it is completed, where the results of the confrontation may be seen in several ways, but most reliably in the second theme's capitulation and acceptance of the key of the first as its own; the drama is effected in the central section through the fragmentation of the themes and possibly their combination or reconstitution, perhaps imitation or inversion, without exception sequence and modulation.[2] This was the view of sonata form current at the beginning of the century and the one Webern would have learned as a student. The nineteenth century's view of the sonata as a logical dramatic gesture rather than (say) a move from tonic to dominant and its reverse resulted in a significant alteration in the proportions of the sections and their relationship to each other. What had been in the beginning a binary form was described by Schoenberg in *Fundamentals* as 'essentially a ternary structure', with as its main divisions 'the exposition, elaboration and recapitulation'.[3] Beethoven, in some of his middle-period works, already omitted the second set of repeats (thereby making it a ternary form), and in Op. 110 and other late works he dispensed with repeats altogether; this became the practice increasingly towards the end of the century.

All the sonata movements of Webern have two themes of contrasting character, distinguished from each other by rhythm, instrumentation, articulation or tempo – or a combination of these – and in most cases by different row topography. In the absence of tonality, the first of these themes to appear is tonic by definition and becomes a reference for all that ensues. The tonal relationship of the two themes is different in every piece, but in all cases great care has been taken to place the second theme in a position that will in some way balance the tonal situation of the first.

Op. 20/ii is clearly an attempt to establish a twelve-note equivalent to the classical tonal pattern. The score of this movement follows the early/middle-Beethoven format, with only the exposition repeated. As Webern's interpretation of the sonata principle became more abstract in Opp. 21 and 22 he reached further back to the earlier classical design, in which both sections are repeated. Op. 24 represents a new resolution of form and content: here the model is even earlier, and there are no repeats. They have, in fact, appeared for the last time; the remaining movements that refer to sonata form – Opp. 27/i, 28/i and 30 – are all continuous.

The first structural innovation in the sonata occurs in the opening movements of Opp. 21 and 22, in which the two themes are given their initial exposition simultaneously. Of the two, the Op. 21 movement is the more striking, because here the themes begin to unfold at the same time at the opening of the piece, whereas in Op. 22 the exposition is preceded by a relatively long introduction that resembles first theme rather more than second, thereby giving the illusion that the themes are stated in succession.

Whether the two themes are presented simultaneously or in succession seems to affect the tonal relationship of the recapitulation to the exposition of the second theme, that portion of the structure which traditionally returns in a different key. In the two works in which the themes are superimposed, the second theme returns at its original tonal level. One might be tempted to explain this as the predictable result of a contrapuntal situation; however, such an explanation would seem to be too trivial in the case of a composer who was so obviously competent in the manipulation of contrapuntal complexities. When one thinks of the awe-inspiring examples of invertible counterpoint in the music of Bach, who was working in a system in which usable vertical combinations were manifestly restricted, one really cannot suppose that Webern, whose only limitation was in fact his own discretion, would have been unable to produce similarly successful solutions had he wished to do so. More likely reasons for these unconventional tonal relationships will be discussed at the appropriate times.

On the other hand, in two of the three cases in which the themes are stated in succession, the second theme is restated at a different level, as one would expect. Only Op. 20/ii follows the conventional tonic–dominant:tonic–tonic pattern, however. In Op. 27 both themes return at new levels, and in

Op. 24/i the second theme returns at its original level of transposition while the first theme does not. These tonal 'aberrations' will be examined presently.

The outer sections of the sonata can perhaps be seen as more problematic to the twelve-note composer than the development, because tonal stability is traditionally maintained here, even though two keys are involved, and because the recapitulation is essentially repetition. The twelve-note technique offers nothing really analogous to the maintenance of one key over a period of time, except perhaps the reiteration of the same row over and over, and this is clearly too primitive to be practicable.[4] As for repetition, this was a technique to be avoided.[5] The development, on the other hand, requires a tonal atmosphere that the twelve-note composers found very congenial.

Schoenberg's elaborations follow the tonal model closely: the rows introduced in this section are ones not used in the exposition and are frequently fragmented and presented sequentially, and the musical material, which is taken from the exposition, is developed and combined in new ways. Webern also uses new rows in the development, as the equivalent of modulation, and these are frequently disposed somewhat differently from the rows in the exposition. Motives and rhythmic material from the exposition are compressed or rearranged or sometimes recombined, and treated to the usual procedures of inversion, augmentation, diminution, fragmentation and so on. He never uses incomplete rows, however. Sequences are prominent in the developments of both Opp. 22 and 27. Opp. 20 and 22 have clear preparations for the reprise: in Op. 20 the return of the first theme sneaks in rather early – a device used by Beethoven, Mahler and many others. Only Op. 21 is strikingly unconventional.

The whole of Op. 21 is concerned with various manifestations of symmetry, a conceptual rather than a musical phenomenon, and the central section of the first movement is devoted to the exaggeration and development of the types of realization used in the exposition. Only one other development, in Op. 27, approaches the degree of abstraction encountered in Op. 21, and it is no coincidence that this work, too, is devoted to exploring symmetries.

Op. 20/ii

The Op. 20 movement is, as might be predicted in view of its position as the first among the twelve-note works to be written in sonata form, the simplest and most traditional, adhering to the classical format in a literal way that would not occur again. Ironically, it has been considered one of the most difficult to follow aurally. Roger Smalley commented in 1975 that

> From the listener's point of view it is – speaking generally – easier to comprehend the structure of the works following Op. 21 than those immediately preceding it. Of all Webern's works the String Trio is, in fact,

perhaps the most difficult to grasp aurally. The degree of variation applied to the rondo theme on its several returns, and to the recapitulation of the sonata movement, is so great that it is almost impossible to perceive them as such.[6]

The movement is framed by an introduction and a coda, two statements of essentially the same material, in a slow tempo. The sonata proper comprises first and second themes separated by a transition using first-theme and then second-theme material, closing theme, development, complete recapitulation of everything up to the development, and codetta.

The classical key structure has been duplicated in as straightforward a way as possible. The first theme uses seven row forms, the second theme eight altogether different ones. Of the ten in the transition connecting the two themes, two are associated with the first theme and two with the second. The untransposed prime and retrograde function as a tonal point of reference: the introduction begins with P_0 and the coda ends with R_0. The movement proper (first theme exposition, bar 10) begins with P_0 as well, as does the recapitulation. The first theme uses both P_0 and R_0, and, perhaps because of its importance as the tonic reference, P_0 is one of the two rows from that theme to reappear in the transition. Both P_0 and R_0 are absent, significantly, from the second theme and closing material in the exposition, but R_0 appears, also significantly, in the recapitulation of the second theme.

The first theme uses the same set of rows in both exposition and recapitulation. The transition begins in the same way both times: the first four bars resemble theme I and use the same four rows on both occasions. However, at the point where the transition begins to use material anticipating the second theme (bar 30 and upbeat to bar 135) – the place where the modulation to the dominant would begin in a tonal sonata movement and therefore the point from which the recapitulation would be expected to differ tonally from the exposition – the rows used in the recapitulation do not match those of the exposition. The 'modulation' takes place in bars 135–6, where RI_6 generates the same music that was produced by P_3 in the exposition (in bars 30–2). The following row is RI_1, a fourth higher/fifth lower than the corresponding RI_8 in the exposition, and for the remainder of the recapitulation the row forms of the exposition are exactly duplicated up a fourth or down a fifth. The superficial similarity of this sequence of events to the traditional tonic–dominant–tonic motion is obvious.

This tonal analogy is rather naïve and its validity questionable; subsequent methods of compensating for the absent tonic/dominant tension basic to traditional structures are more elegant and probably more legitimate within an atonal system than is this attempt somewhat slavishly to recreate the old motions. Diatonic keys bear certain relationships to each other because they are exclusive; different permutations of a twelve-note row (or even several different twelve-note rows, though this is irrelevant in the present context) can never operate in the same way, because of the inclusive nature of the row. Although Webern's choice of transpositions is clearly analogous to the old tonic–dominant relationships, the effect is not the same, and one is tempted to say that the exercise is interesting but futile, since the validity of a tonal reference that does not manifest itself aurally is doubtful. George Perle has written in reference to this movement:

> Since the succession of row forms that is employed for each formal section does nothing, in itself, to characterize that section in any comparable manner, there is no sense in which one can attribute different tonal areas to the expository statements of the principal and subordinate themes and the same tonal area to their recapitulatory statements.[7]

While this is true, it is also true that the transposition of the second theme upon its return would normally be aurally distinguishable, because it would involve a change of register and therefore of timbre. Perle does not mention the reason that this does not happen in Op. 20: because most of the material of the second theme is inverted upon its return.

The desire for perpetual variation that lay at the foundation of the twelve-note technique seems to dictate the nature of Webern's recapitulations, which customarily repeat the original sequence of rows in a new setting, with surface details unlike those of the original. One has to suppose this practice to be based on the premise that a reprise will be heard because the series of rows is recognized.[8] However, since this assumption is open to argument, significant questions arise concerning the degree to which tonal patterns must be aurally distinguishable in order to be effective and, in consequence, the extent to which tonal metaphor can be considered valid in twelve-note music. Even if one were to grant the initial assumption, it cannot be supposed, owing to the nature of the system, that a series of rows will retain any aurally recognizable identity when transposed, especially if the setting is a linear polyphonic one in which two or more rows unfold at once. In Op. 20 Webern sets the reprise of the first (tonic) theme differently, presumably with the understanding that it will be identifiable because of its 'key'. One must suppose it is in order to make the second theme, which is transposed (in a new 'key') upon its return, recognizable as well that he writes the same music here on both occasions (though parts are distributed differently and a significant amount of the motion is inverted).

The first and second themes use dissimilar row topography. The rows appear in successive blocks in the first theme, none beginning before the previous one has finished. This kind of presentation is perhaps the best possible for establishing and maintaining row identity, as it allows the listener to hear the same series of internals over and over without the complication of extraneous intervals that are the inevitable product of two or more rows progressing simultaneously. This topography continues until

157

bar 33 of the transition, where the final note of RI_8 coincides with the first two of P_7. The following row, R_2, begins more than a bar before this P_7 has finished, and thus sets the stage for the polyphonic row presentation of the second theme. Two rows unfold simultaneously throughout the second theme until bar 57, where block topography returns. Both manners of presentation are used in the closing material and the development.

The first theme comprises two eight-bar sentences.[9] The first of these extends from bar 10 to bar 17, with the low point just before the end of the second two-bar phrase (in bar 13) and the high point in the middle of the four-bar continuation (in bar 16). It is set as melody and accompaniment and consistently exploits the superposition of duplets and triplets: without exception the accompaniment uses whichever of these subdivisions the melody is not using. The pattern alternates regularly, the melody and accompaniment exchanging rhythmic divisions every two bars; the two halves of the sentence are therefore parallel in this respect.

The second sentence, extending from bar 18 to bar 26, is both more active and more continuous than the first, a directed progression rather than a series of regularly alternating phrases. Its opening and its continuation are quite dissimilar in character and purpose, the former pushing towards the climax of the first theme and the latter representing its dénouement. The highest and lowest notes of the theme occur in bar 22. The rhythmic/metric situation of the first five bars is the same as that in the first segment of the previous sentence – duple division in the melody with triplet accompaniment – but here the melody moves more quickly, beginning with a rhythm of quavers and crotchets and becoming more active until the motion is entirely in quavers in the last bar and a half. Following this climax of activity and range, the three-bar conclusion divides into two melodic units resembling those that make up the continuation of the first sentence (bars 14–17). The structure of the first theme, therefore, is abcb', with the climax of the whole occurring near the end of c.

The series of rows through which this theme unfolds returns in another sixteen-bar section in bars 115–30. Although this is clearly the recapitulation of the first theme, the internal structure of these sixteen bars is not nearly so well defined as that of the original statement, and, in fact, aside from bar 118, which is an obvious repeat of bar 13, very little of the opening material is recognizable. Duple and triple divisions are used simultaneously throughout this section, as in the exposition, but here the three voices move independently, in contrast to the melody and accompaniment of the original appearance. The non-alignment of parts and the attendant increase in density and rhythmic diversity serve to obscure the phrase structure, which is essentially the same as in the original. Two other factors contribute to this clouding of structure: the inconspicuous beginning of the recapitulation before the development has finished (the restatement seems to come in bar

118 with the tempo change and the release of the first violin harmonic E♭) and the two internal *rit.... a tempo* markings, which did not appear in the exposition.

A discrepancy in tempo markings here further complicates this section's relationship with the opening. The tempo of the first theme in the exposition is *Zart bewegt* (♩ = ca 66), with the transition beginning *mäßiger* (♩ = ca 112) and going later to *sehr lebhaft* (♩ = ca 132). In the recapitulation the first theme is marked *mäßig* (♩ = ca 56) – the tempo of the first part of the original transition, not the tempo of the original first theme – and the transition begins *tempo, noch mäßiger* without a metronome indication, which may be understood to mean either the same speed as the earlier *mäßiger* at bar 26 (in which case the transition begins in the same tempo as the first theme in the recapitulation) or a tempo yet slower than the most recent *mäßig* in bar 118 (thus maintaining the same relationship between first theme and transition as in the exposition with everything at a slower tempo than before). The latter seems the more likely of these two interpretations. A third possibility is that the '♩ = ca 56' at bar 118 is a misprint and should read '♩ = ca 66' and that the *noch mäßiger* in bar 131 refers to the earlier *mäßiger* in bar 26, making the tempos in the recapitulation identical to those in the exposition.[10] The rest of the tempo indications are in agreement with those of the exposition until just before the end.

The material of the second theme presents the contrast to the first theme that tradition demands. There are no triplet divisions here, and as a result the rhythmic conflict that is such an essential element of the first theme is absent. The melody, played by the violin in bars 41–8, is more continuous and lyrical, and rhythmically much more straightforward, than the melodic line of the first theme. Moreover, it represents a linear statement of the row, with a second row unfolding simultaneously in the accompaniment, a different procedure from that used in the first theme. The prevailing rhythm is a dotted quaver followed by a semiquaver.

The second theme, like the first, comprises two sentences, but in this case the second of these is a varied repeat of the first, and each consists of three phrases of roughly equal length. The first phrase is five bars long (bars 40–4) and consists of just over a bar of preparation followed by three bars of violin melody; the four-bar continuation of this melody is a free variation employing diminution. Although the third phrase is also four bars long, the first of these coincides with the final bar of the violin melody so that only three bars are in fact added to the opening nine, making twelve bars altogether. These are immediately repeated without the preparatory bar, the cello playing the first three and the viola the fourth bar of the melody exactly as it appeared earlier in the violin, only an octave lower. This is noteworthy, as it is uncharacteristic for Webern to repeat in this way. The last three notes of the melody, which in the violin statement covered three bars, occur in diminution here (in the viola), taking only a single bar (bar 56). The continuation again takes three bars, this time making a total of eight.

The recapitulation of this theme, in bars 114–63, follows the exposition closely. The instrumentation is changed: essentially, the violin plays the cello's music from the exposition, the viola plays what was previously given to the violin, and the cello takes over from the viola. Thus the viola plays the melody the first time and the cello finishes for the violin the second. In addition, the contour of much of the material is inverted. The rhythmic structure, however, is exactly the same for the first twelve bars. The repetition (bars 155–63) is further varied from the original by the increasing replacement of long notes with reiterated semiquavers. The structural outlines of the second theme are the same in both exposition and recapitulation and can be best represented as aba'c.

The two themes are connected by a transition that functions in the manner of a Mozart or Beethoven transition: as I have already noted, the first portion of this is a continuation of first-theme material leading to a 'modulation' (it is clear only in retrospect exactly where this 'modulation' occurs) and the preview of second-theme material and treatment. The first-theme material used is the triplet figure, an element unique to that theme. Similarly, the second theme is represented by a characteristic figure not shared by the first theme, the semiquaver anacrusis. These two figures are combined in bars 36–7. The relationship of the two sections of the restated transition to the corresponding sections in the exposition reflects the treatment of the first and second themes from which they are derived: that is, the first (triplet) portion of the transition uses the same rows in a new setting (although very near to the original for the first full bar, it is divergent from that point on), whereas the second (dotted) portion uses a new set of rows while retaining the rhythmic structure of the exposition exactly, with an exchange of parts.[11]

The closing material (exposition, bars 60–73; recapitulation, bars 163–74) continues in the manner of the second theme, using the dotted figure introduced there. As in that theme, the series of rows used in the exposition is transposed up a fourth/down a fifth and the musical material is practically the same with many of the motions inverted. The reprise is rhythmically compressed and leads directly into a five-bar extension (bars 174–9) preceding the return of the opening material at bar 180.

Another question concerning the tempo indications arises here. In the exposition the closing material clearly begins on the last semiquaver of bar 59, and in the recapitulation in bar 163. On this latter occasion, the tempo change to *Sehr lebhaft* ($\downarrow$ = ca 66) occurs just prior to the beginning of the new section. The parallel tempo indication in the exposition comes four bars too early, in the middle of the repetition of the second theme, a position that is difficult to justify in view of the exact correspondence of the two sections in all other respects. The fact that the marking should come at the beginning of the last line on the page but comes instead, illogically, at the beginning of the line above would strongly suggest an error in printing, if there were no evidence to the contrary. Such evidence, however, seems to be provided by a letter to Schoenberg that is quoted by the Moldenhauers. In it Webern cited errors in the 1927 Universal Edition:

> Unfortunately a wrong metronome figure has remained in two places; correct: second movement, page 12, system 3 [bar 55] 'sehr lebhaft' $\quarternote = 66$ (instead of 60) and vice versa page 17, 4th system 'gemächlich' $\quarternote = 60$ (instead of 66) [bar 144].[12]

Having noted that the metronome indication was incorrect, Webern was hardly likely to have failed to observe at the same time that its placement was not as he had intended. (Or perhaps he would have – it is easy to miss one mistake while correcting another.)

A second discrepancy is more apparent than real. This concerns the *subito mäßiger* that appears at bar 65, followed by a *calando* at bar 67 and finally *ins tempo* at bar 69. There is no *mäßiger* or *calando* at this point in the recapitulation; however, a similar effect is achieved through a pair of *rit. . . . tempo* markings. The disagreement in terms is curious. Unfortunately, there would seem to be no way in which to discover the origin of these discrepancies, since sketches for the published movements of Op. 20 do not exist and the fair copy is unavailable.[13]

Predictably the development section of this first twelve-note sonata movement also conforms closely to what convention requires. It shuffles and recombines most of the significant material of the exposition in various ways. It opens in the tempo of the beginning of the transition (bars 26ff), with the rows disposed as they were in the exposition of the second theme; the material developed in this section is the repeated-note figure from the introduction. In the subsequent section (bars 84–8), still in the same tempo and using the row topography of the second theme, the metric disagreement of the first theme makes a reappearance. This is followed by development of various dotted figures from the second theme, at the first-theme tempo, and this in turn by a concentration on the pairs of semiquaver dyads that first occurred in bars 59–61, at the end of the second theme. The last large section (bars 102–17) is concerned with first-theme material, starting at the first-theme tempo but becoming progressively slower, and with the row disposition that was used in the first theme.

While the slow sections that open and close this movement look dissimilar on the score, they are, in fact, the same music. The crotchet at bar 180 is the same length as the semiquaver at the beginning; and the rhythmic content of bars 1–5 and bars 180–3 is identical (except for the first note, which becomes an acciaccatura the second time, and a few very slight differences resulting from changes of prolation in bars 181 and 182), with the viola and cello parts

161

exchanged. Melodically, also, the material is similar, though much of the motion is inverted. Two of these parts – the violin and cello in the opening, the violin and viola in the coda – are in canon for these few bars; the third plays consistently whichever rhythmic subdivision is not being used by the others. The remainder of the coda is similar to, but not a duplication of, bars 5–9 of the introduction. Here, also, both subdivisions are present at all times, thus introducing (in the first instance) and recalling (in the second) a major feature of the first theme.

The Op. 20 row is particularly suited to segmentation because of the degree of its tetrachordal invariance. So, for example, although the introduction begins with P_0 and the coda with I_5, the first four notes of both sections are the same for each instrument: violins – G♯–G–D–C♯ and C♯–D–G–G♯; viola – F♯–F–A–A♯ both times; cello – D♯–E–C–B both times. The layering of tetrachords results in a block topography of successive rows, with linear presentation of individual segments. Thus the apparently mutually exclusive row topographies of the two themes are both seen to be generated by that of the introduction.

The exposition and recapitulation are almost exactly the same length (sixty-four and sixty-five bars respectively); the development is about two-thirds this length. Although the introduction is nine bars long and the return of this material at the end takes fourteen bars, this is misleading, because after the initial four bars of the coda the tempo doubles, making the remaining ten bars equal to the parallel five in the introduction. Thus the two sections are in fact the same length. Each goes through seven rows, the introduction beginning with P_0 and the coda ending with R_0. It can be seen from Table 4.1 that the exposition and recapitulation contain the same number of rows distributed in the same way, exclusive of the closing extension; however, because some of the sections of the recapitulation overlap at the juncture, this material is run through more rapidly the second time. While the extension adds four extra rows to the reprise, in terms of time it simply fills out bars necessary in order to balance the exposition.

T_4 functions as a tonic metaphor in the first movement of Op. 20. The relationship between that transposition and the untransposed rows that act as a tonal focus in the second movement clearly corresponds to the third-relations between movements preferred increasingly by Beethoven. The influence of Beethoven's middle period can be seen in many aspects of Op. 20. The slow introduction (though not the corresponding coda) is certainly a Beethovenian touch, as is the shifting of the sonata movement to a later position in the work. Moreover, the single repeat, of the exposition only, refers to the Beethovenian and later perception of the sonata as a dramatic melodic form. (When themes are seen to dominate, the sonata becomes a three-part form: repetition of the development and recapitulation – the

Table 4.1

Section	No. of bars		No. of rows	
Introduction	9		7	
Exposition	64		38	
theme I		16		9
transition		15		11
theme II		20		10
closing		14		8
Development	45		25	
Recapitulation	65	(60 + extension)	42	(38 + extension)
theme I		16		9
transition		14		11
theme II		20		10
closing		12		8
extension		5		4
Coda	(14)		7	

conflict and its resolution – would be anticlimactic; the drama is effective only once.)

Op. 21/i

Webern reached further back in history for the format of his next work. In Op. 21 there are again only two movements, but here the sonata occupies its usual position as first movement, as well as exhibiting the binary outline of the classical form: both of its sections – exposition and development/re-capitulation – are repeated. The familiar outline is, however, deceptive: the events that unfold within this apparent rounded binary seem to represent a major reinterpretation of sonata form, in which the basic assumptions and relationships have been re-evaluated and reformulated. The result possesses a structural elegance and sophistication that are unexpected after the some-what artless approach to the form seen in Op. 20. The row structure of the entire opening section (bars 1–26) is exactly repeated from bar 42 to the end. The tonal identity of these two sections of course runs counter to the tonal motion expected in the sonata, in which traditionally the exposition ends away from the tonic and the recapitulation returns to it.

A number of other things about this movement are also problematic when it is compared with its classical precedents. The fact that the entire movement is canonic[14] immediately relates it to an earlier tradition. While canon is not unheard of in sonata form (see the *Hammerklavier* sonata, for example), it is much more likely to be associated with the development than with the statement of ideas (and with the romantic rather than with the classical form). A third departure from the classical sonata is revealed by a comparison of reprise with exposition: they are musically quite different.

Much has been written about this movement,[15] and the incongruities of its structure have been explained in various ways, one of these being that it is not a sonata movement at all. Leopold Spinner, for example, calls it a small ternary form,[16] and Friedhelm Döhl, who describes at length the handling of numerous details in relation to the expectations of sonata form, concludes that it lacks the hierarchical and discursive nature of a sonata and that its psychological shape is more accurately described as 'structural variation'.[17] Wolfgang Martin Stroh, who views the progress of events in the piece rather differently, comes to a similar conclusion: that the movement is not, finally, a sonata, even though elements of that form occur at every step of the way and the movement is susceptible to such an analysis.[18] Although my analysis agrees with both Döhl's and Stroh's in many respects, I disagree with their conclusions; I believe that Webern was experimenting with relationships within the sonata framework and that it is imperative to see this movement as a sonata in order to understand his subsequent interpretations of the same form. In *Fundamentals*, Schoenberg calls sonata a *process* rather than a *form* and cites its flexibility – its successful incorporation of diverse ideas and structures – as the reason for its long supremacy in Western music. He clearly saw sonata as a genre; I think we must assume that Webern viewed – and used – it in the same way. Analyses of the sort just cited go astray in insisting on agreement with a prototype. (Having said this, I shall nevertheless continue to speak of 'sonata form', since it is my purpose to examine Webern's formal constructions, but I do not use the term to refer to a specific historical model.)

Both of the canons in the exposition of this movement use the two-note elision peculiar to this row and its inversion nine semitones higher:[19] the *dux* of Canon I[20] goes through I_4 and P_7 and is answered by P_4 and I_1; in Canon II, P_0–I_9–P_0–I_9 is answered with I_8–P_{11}–I_8–P_{11}. The *comes* follows at the distance of two bars in both canons, and in both it exactly duplicates the rhythm, the durations, the segmentation and the sequence of timbres of the *dux*. With the exception of E♭, every pitch class occurs at only one octave level throughout these twenty-six bars. In other respects the two canons are dissimilar. Table 4.2 offers a comparison of their unique features.

Both canons continue without a break throughout the twenty-six bars, and, although they differ from each other, each is uniform from beginning to end. This constancy seems to me to make a subdivision of these bars into two theme areas difficult. Various linear divisions have been suggested, nevertheless. Spinner, who identifies the movement as a 'small ternary form', describes the material in the A section as a sentence of 24 bars, consisting of a basic four-bar phrase (Hn.2 bars 1–4) which is immediately in a slightly varied form repeated (Cln. bars 5–8), then developed by means of reduction in the following 16 bars (Vcl. bars 9–13; Cln. bars 14–16; Hn.2 bars 18–20; cadential extension bars 21–24).[21]

The motives designated as successive parts of this sentence structure comprise the entire *dux* of Canon I; the structure of the *comes* is of course the same. Spinner does not indicate how the non-alignment of the two voices in canon affects the sentence structure. (It would seem clear that canonic imitation at the distance of at least half the length of each motive must preclude a vertical division of the whole; at the same time, since the two voices of this canon are identical, I find it difficult to justify seeing either one as predominant over the other, as this analysis seems to do.) Spinner moreover makes no mention of Canon II or any of the material therein, apparently considering it to be entirely accompanimental; in fact, he sees the two voices of this canon as additional *comes* to the first ('the first movement, being throughout presented in canonic form (a 4-part canon)...'), an interpretation that is difficult to justify.

Table 4.2

Canon I	Canon II
Rows are divided consistently into tetrachords for purposes of orchestration.	Segmentation is irregular.
Orchestration is palindromic: horn–cl.–str.–cl.–horn.	Sequence of instruments used is not symmetrically organized.
Uses no harp or violins.	Uses no clarinets.
Long notes, slow tempo.	Crotchets predominate, events occur at about twice the speed of Canon I.
Stable rhythms generally support the written metre.	Variety of rhythms, do not reinforce the metre indicated.
Second pitch repeated.	No immediate pitch repetition.
Legato character: arco strings, slurs.	Diversity of colours and effects: staccato, pizzicato, mutes, grace notes, harmonics, double stops.
Canon self-contained, comes to a close before the end of the section and begins over again upon repetition.	Perpetual canon: circular, elision continues through repeat.

Stroh, whose analysis is also based on motives, views this exposition differently.[22] Table 4.3 is taken from his monograph on the Symphony.[23] He sees the opening horn motive (a) as both the generative material for the whole movement and as first theme of the exposition, which is immediately varied by the clarinets (b) and then the low strings up to bar 14. He identifies the figure containing the first acciaccatura, in bar 14 (f, the first violin figure

165

Table 4.3

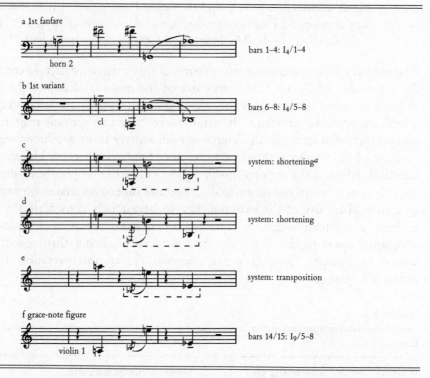

a Stroh has 'schematisch: Verkürzung' here. This is not a strict diminution, since at the second stage the quaver becomes a grace note.

in Canon II), as the contrasting second theme, which he sees as having evolved from the first through a series of transformations, both real and hypothetical (the suggested stages of this evolution appear as c, d and e in his table). The second theme continues, with string harmonics, acciaccature and *am Steg* playing on the cello (all Canon II characteristics). It cannot be denied that this sequence of events occurs, or that it follows closely the expectations of sonata form. Such an analysis, however, ignores the fact that Canon I continues to play in the same manner for eight more bars after bar 14 and that, although the events of Canon II are telescoped somewhat after that point, its material is essentially the same as it has been playing since the opening of the movement.

But perhaps more problematic is the lack of tonal differentiation between the first and second halves of this exposition. Each canon in Op. 21/i is constructed so that the last two notes are the same as the first two: the end is, literally, the beginning, and there can be no question of the section's having progressed tonally. This is a major stumbling-block for Döhl.[24]

It seems to me that Webern has rotated the exposition ninety degrees, so that the events one customarily encounters in succession in this section occur simultaneously instead, making the perception of contrast a vertical process rather than a horizontal one (and just one manifestation of the much-sought-after consolidation of horizontal and vertical). Two theme groups cohabit bars 1–26, one consisting of rather stable, memorable material with both voices beginning on the note that acts as a fixed point of reference for the entire piece, the other of more colourful but elusive material, using only transposed rows, as an analogue to the traditional second-theme key. These theme groups are, respectively, Canon I and Canon II.

The particular pair of 'keys' thus established as analogues to first and second theme is especially interesting, as the central interval of both P_0 and I_8 (the opening rows of Canon II) is the tritone A–E♭, or the extreme notes of the row at its 'tonic' level in this movement (I_4, P_4). In every appearance of P_0 and I_8 in the exposition, these central notes are played as a double stop; there are no other double stops in this section. Conversely, the central tritones of the I_4 and P_4 of Canon I are F/B and C♯/G, the outer notes of P_0 and I_8 respectively. This cross-relationship of the rows of the two canons represents a tonal complement that replaces the tonic/dominant tension traditionally existing between first and second theme.

The middle section (bars 25b–44) does not, upon initial acquaintance, seem to relate to the exposition in the way a development ordinarily does. None of the material here bears a close resemblance, melodically or rhythmically or in any other way, to material presented in bars 1–26.[25] Discounting grace notes, over 80 per cent of the notes in this section are of values that have not appeared previously. The horns, which contributed significantly to the exposition, play only four notes in the development section. The range opens out to four and a half octaves from the three octaves plus two semitones of the exposition, and registers are not frozen as they were there.

The fact that none of the musical ideas from the exposition seems to have found its way into this section is evidence, again, of a new perception of the form – a reinterpretation of its basic concepts. This section does, indeed, develop ideas that were presented in the exposition; these are not, however, ideas in the sense of musical figures, but abstract ideas expressed in musical terms. This development section explores and develops the idea postulated in the exposition – of mirror canon and palindrome as the musical realizations of horizontal and vertical symmetry.

The section is perfectly symmetrical. Like the exposition, it consists of a pair of mirror canons. In this case, however, all four voices are identical with respect to rhythm and durations and segmentation. The direction of motion is arranged so that the two prime rows mirror each other (inexactly), as do the two inverted rows. Horizontally, the whole section is a palindrome. The instruments are paired as they were in the exposition with the exception of the two bars at the centre, bars 34 and 35.

As in a traditional development the contrasting themes are played dramatically against each other, so here the technical differences that distinguished the two themes in the exposition are exaggerated and presented in new combinations. The longer note values of Canon I have been further lengthened, while the short notes characteristic of Canon II have become even shorter. The rhythms are relatively constant, as in Canon I; however, they do not conform to the written metre, a characteristic of Canon II. Rows are divided asymmetrically between instruments as they were in Canon II, but the divisions are exactly imitated. The canon that opens is elided with its continuation after the axis of the palindrome, just as the end of Canon II was joined with the beginning of its repetition; the second canon finishes completely at the axis and begins again, as did Canon I at the end of the exposition. There are numerous instrumental effects and grace notes, features associated with Canon II.[26]

The rows used at the outset of the development stand in the same relationship to each other as those at the beginning of the exposition, but here the whole complex is a perfect fifth higher. It seems fairly clear that this is Webern's version of the move to the dominant which is customary at this point.[27]

The recapitulation presents yet more problems.[28] While the row structure in bars 42–66b is identical to that in bars 1–26, the music is greatly changed. The metric stability of the first section is gone; although the same number of notes occurs over the same number of bars, the real tempo (the rate of motion, as opposed to the tempo indicated by metronome markings) seems to have sped up and the rhythm of events to have become erratic, since the increased speed of the pulse (quavers now rather than crotchets) is compensated for by spaces and prolongations that did not appear the first time around. Whereas the only values used in the first twenty-six bars were crotchets or multiples thereof, played on the beat and with very few exceptions contained within the bar, the recapitulation abounds in quavers, doubly dotted minims and syncopations of various sorts, and of the 150 notes here, only 10 are of a value that appeared in the exposition. There are three times as many grace notes here as there were in the opening section; the use of mutes and harmonics is greatly increased, making pitch recognition more difficult; and the range is expanded by a tritone, with the lowest note a tenth higher than before, placing the entire section in a more intense register. In addition, the general dynamic level is much higher.[29]

Intensifying the effect of this exaggerated diversity is the fact that timbres are no longer treated canonically: neither the segmentation nor the sequence of instruments is faithfully imitated. The replication of rhythm and durations and of intervals (in inversion) is just as exact as it was in the exposition; however, all the changes just noted conspire to produce an increased activity and the erosion of discipline, so that although the row structure of this movement is ABA it is perceived aurally as an open-ended form, a metamorphosis proceeding from stability to instability, from the regular to the irregular.

As a recapitulation, then, this third section presents two major problems: the reappearance of the rows used in the exposition of the second theme at exactly the same tonal level, and the striking differences between the music of exposition and reprise. The second of these is a necessary corollary of the first.

A transposition of the second theme would not have been practicable, owing to the fact that the two themes appear simultaneously. If both were stated at the 'tonic' level, the pitch-class content of the two canons would be the same, and repetitions and doublings would result. Webern's new interpretation of the exposition necessarily led to a new perception of the recapitulation as well. In the classical sonata the recapitulation represents a resolution of the (tonal) disagreement that characterized the exposition. In a general way, this resolution can be seen in terms of acquiescence: one of the two opposing elements – specifically, keys – gives way to the other. Because, in general, tonal opposition is not an effective tool in twelve-note music, owing to the inclusive nature of the row, and because, in this specific case, tonal resolution would have been disastrous, Webern fulfils the dramatic requirements of the recapitulation by means of dynamics, range, timbres and rhythm, all of which exhibit a great increase in activity and diversity compared with the exposition. The characteristics originally associated with Canon I yield completely, and in the reprise both canons take on the character of the exposition's Canon II.

Convention has the second theme defer to the first upon its return; here the surrender is in the opposite direction. The dramatic significance of this role reversal cannot be overestimated. It results in a basic shift of emphasis and, hence, a new perception of the form as progressive, rather than circular: a crescendo rather than an arch. The characteristics of the second-theme analogue were instability, irregularity and unpredictability. The particular forms taken by these characteristics in the exposition are magnified in the development and further exaggerated in the reprise. Since the first material to be heard in the exposition, and by far the most memorable, was the horn's opening figure – a model of stability and equilibrium – this progressive focusing of attention on those opposite qualities represented by the second canon, culminating in their complete dominance by the end of the movement, results in a gradual and inexorable increase in intensity which is aided structurally by the tension resulting from the discrepancy between what is expected and what actually happens in the recapitulation. The movement

169

ends with what Stroh has called a stretto coda.[30] Although the reprise
contains no more and no fewer rows than the exposition, Canon I finishes
earlier in relation to Canon II here, leaving Canon II to end the movement
alone, which it does in six bars of quavers, filled with grace notes and special
instrumental effects. Thus, while not a coda in the traditional sense of added
bars having no parallel in the exposition, these bars do function as a stretto
close, emphasizing the changes that have been wrought in the course of the
movement.

The perception of the form as an open one is aided by Webern's
manipulation of octave disposition and range to produce a different centre of
gravity in the recapitulation, in spite of the presence of the same row
structure as before. Pitch levels are frozen in both exposition and reprise, but
with different results. In the exposition each note of either *dux* and its
answering note in the *comes* are equidistant above and below a. In order to
maintain perfect symmetry, the note a tritone away from this point of
reference is answered by its octave, hence the single exception to the rule of
frozen registers: there must be two E♭s. The pitches used are shown in
Example 4.1. Although the same rows are used in the recapitulation, the
tessitura is considerably higher here. While it does not actually appear, e♭² is
the axis of symmetry by implication (Example 4.2). Two important

4.1   Op. 21/i, pitch content of exposition

4.2   Op. 21/i, pitch content of recapitulation

differences between the pitch resources of exposition and recapitulation have
been mentioned already. The latter section is higher-pitched generally and
the range is somewhat wider. As a result, the axis of symmetry has moved a
tritone, the greatest distance possible. Thus the progressive nature of the
movement is reinforced tonally, the overall rise in pitch paralleling the
increase in activity and intensity. And the progress of the central pitch from

A in the exposition to E♭ in the recapitulation is a macrocosmic reflection of the progress of the row that serves as tonic for the movement.

Op. 22/i

In spite of striking dissimilarities in general tenor, density, regularity, length and complexity, the first movement of the Symphony and the next work in sonata form, the opening movement of the Quartet for violin, clarinet, saxophone and piano, Op. 22, enjoy a certain consanguinity. Both movements have the classical two sets of repeats and, perhaps more importantly, canonic expositions in which two themes are presented simultaneously. Superficially the Op. 22 movement also resembles the earlier Op. 20/ii, inasmuch as it has an introduction and a coda.

In fact, first assessments are not misleading in this case: Op. 22/i differs from its predecessors much more than it resembles them. The canons that proceed from one end of this movement to the other exhibit a freedom that is diametrically opposed to the strictness observed in Op. 21,[31] and, although the outer appendages are reminiscent of the Op. 20 structure, on closer acquaintance these sections prove to function very differently in the later piece. Here both introduction and coda, which are essentially the same, are in the tempo of the main body of the movement and account for a considerably greater share of this relatively brief piece than did their counterparts in the longer Op. 20/i. Finally, whereas both the earlier works are long, complex and based on a substantial amount of material, Op. 22/i is remarkable for its brevity and its transparency, as well as for the exiguity of the figures from which it evolves.

The Op. 22 row begins on F♯ and ends a tritone away, on C. Although no untransposed row occurs in this movement, the rows of the two voices that proceed in mirror canon throughout have been chosen so that F♯ and C always occupy the same position in both voices. The F♯ above middle c is the axis of symmetry: with one exception, just after the climax, in bar 24, both voices are so arranged that they always converge literally on this pitch, and without exception corresponding notes in the two voices are equidistant from it. Thus F♯ is confirmed as the tonic analogue for the movement. Its position is established immediately, in bar 4 of the introduction, where the clarinet plays two f♯[1]'s in isolation. The climax exploits the opposite member of the 'tonic' tritone: the highest and lowest pitches of the movement, reached in bar 22, are both Cs (C and c[4]). The dominant analogue is given considerable prominence as well. The movement begins and ends on C♯ – although in both cases this is immediately balanced by a B on the other side of and equidistant from the central f♯[1], thereby reconfirming F♯ as the tonic – and C♯ is the first note of the exposition and of the reprise, as well as the final note of the development.

171

The music within the repeats is clearly intended to satisfy the demands of the bithematic classical form, in spite of the novelty of simultaneous thematic presentation. The contrast of the two themes is more marked here than it was in Op. 21. The tonic theme[32] (therefore the 'first theme' by definition, in spite of the fact that it enters very slightly later than the other one) is in mirror canon, pointillistically disposed among violin, clarinet and piano in the exposition. In contrast, the second theme is a single line played entirely by the saxophone; following convention, it begins and ends on the dominant. The fact that these two themes are exposed simultaneously is largely obscured by the tempo and nature of the introduction, which is in every way indistinguishable from the rest of the movement. At first hearing, the impression is of a canon at the outset with a lyrical theme following after five bars. Only after bar 15, when the music from bar 6 onwards is repeated, does it become apparent that the first five bars were not a part of the exposition. Upon closer examination, it is clear that the material in bars 1–5 resembles second theme as much as first.

All of the material emanates from a limited number of motives, most of which are first presented in the first five bars. For the moment I shall examine only one of these, the cadence figure in bar 5;[33] this is probably the most important motive in the piece and for this reason will be referred to as **α**. Some version of this figure appears nine times in the course of the movement. As can be seen from Example 4.3, no two appearances are identical; but the relationships are both numerous and subtle.

4.3

The canonic first theme is active, consisting entirely of semiquavers, and is notably disjunct. The two voices move continually from the piano, which provides its own answer, to the violin and clarinet, which answer each other. Each voice consists of two row statements, and these define the phrase

172

structure. Only four rhythmic figures are used; the last two of these can be seen as three-note variants of the first two, with the articulations reversed (Example 4.4). The first two phrases are built entirely from the first two

(bar 6, pno) (bar 7, vn) (bar 12, pno) (bar 15, pno)

4.4

rhythmic motives, expressed as large intervals, in the order **aba aba**. Only the three-note variants occur in the third and fourth phrases, which can be represented rhythmically as **a′b′ a′b′** (Example 4.5). Motive **b′** takes two different melodic forms here, the second of which has already been considered and identified as **α**. The first, which is subsequently of lesser significance than **α**, I shall call **β**.

4.5   Op. 22/i, first theme, bars 6–15 (reduction)

The second theme is built almost entirely from the rhythmic figure ♩♩ (**c**) and its reverse (**cr**). This theme consists of only two rows, elided by one note, and again the phrase structure is congruent with the row content. In this case two similar phrases form a closed period, beginning and ending on C♯. Following the first appearance of **cr** the antecedent phrase comes to rest on a crotchet; this is immediately followed by an extension repeating the rhythm of these three notes (**cr** plus a crotchet) with the melodic contour of the descending **α** beginning on the tonic, F♯. The consequent, after a stretto in bars 12–13, cadences with the same figure a tritone lower, now ending on

173

the dominant. The close is immediately reinforced by the first-theme cadence figure (Example 4.6). Because it is not pointillistically disposed, the saxophone line is more readily perceived as a theme than the canon. Thus the traditional predominance of the first theme is effectively abrogated here: what is heard in this exposition is a melody with pointillistic accompaniment, the first-theme cadence figure appearing to be an echo of the more substantial one played (twice) by the saxophone.

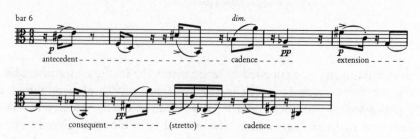

4.6   Op. 22/i, second theme, bars 6–14

The recapitulation exhibits some of the same peculiarities observed in Op. 21/i, and presumably for the same reason – because of the simultaneous statement of the two themes in the exposition. Here, as in the earlier work, the row structure of both themes is unchanged, and again the musical surface is modified, though the changes are less dramatic in the later work.

The major differences between exposition and reprise have to do with instrumentation and texture. The canonic theme, which in its first appearance was passed around by the violin, clarinet and piano, is now played by the piano alone. The voices continue to converge on f#[1], and the outer limits of the range are the same as before, though the extremes occur more often in the reprise than they did in the exposition (bringing to mind the increased range and diversity of the Op. 21/i recapitulation). A new four-note variant of motive **b** in bars 32–3 uses inverted arpeggiation, an effect that appears with considerable frequency from that point on, and the rhythm of bars 11–13 is altered in bars 33–5. Other alterations result from inverted direction, expanded intervals and altered coincidence of the two voices. In spite of the numerous alterations, the cadence is very nearly the same as before (compare figures **b** and **h** in Example 4.3). Predictably, the second theme is now divided among violin, clarinet and saxophone. Although it is rhythmically unchanged, all the motions are inverted, with the exception of the two cadential figures, in bars 32 and 35–6, which, except for a change of register, are identical to those in bars 10 and 13–14. Although the row structure has not changed, this theme recurs at a higher level generally, again reminding one of the registral transformations in the reprise of Op. 21/i.

The development section of this movement is, unlike that of Op. 21 and more definitely than that of Op. 20, devoted to the development of motives from the exposition. The dramatic demands of the traditional development are met in a conventional musical manner: intervals are expanded and as a result the range is extended in both directions. The density is increased considerably through the telescoping of events. (In spite of the increased activity and the overlapping of events, the development has in fact one less voice than the exposition, the third voice that provided the second theme statement having disappeared.)

The development consists of four units of equal length, defined, as in the exposition, by the row structure. The first three of these cadence with the α figure (Example 4.3c, d, and f); the third begins with it as well (Example 4.3e), as does the fourth (Example 4.3g). Both the third and fourth sections begin precipitately, before the preceding section has concluded; as a result, two α figures are superimposed on these occasions.

The first section begins with the characteristic rhythm of the second theme spanning an interval much larger than any used in the exposition of that theme. This is followed by development of the α motive through intervallic expansion and telescoping. The cadence (Example 4.3c) is very nearly a retrograde of that in bar 15 of the exposition (Example 4.3b). This series of events is more or less repeated at different tonal level in the next three bars, slightly altered so as to include a variant of the β figure (bar 20). This time both voices of the α cadence begin on the tonic $f\sharp^1$. Before this cadence has finished, the third section begins, with a second α figure in which both voices once again begin on the tonic axis.

Although this third section, which is the climax of the movement, is the same length as the others, its density is much greater, owing to the fact that four rows, rather than two, are gone through: all four row forms occur, at T_6, in bars 21–4. This transpositional level appears nowhere else in the movement, but it assumes an important role in the second movement, where it functions as an extension of the tonic. (This reference to the second movement at the climax of the first is another reminder of Op. 21, in which the centre of the development was a harbinger of the particular symmetry used in the variations to follow.) The climactic section, in bars 21–4, begins and ends on F$\sharp$ in both voices, with the α motive on both occasions (Example 4.3e and f). The registral extremes of the movement are reached at the end of bar 22, where two Cs representing the elision of R_6 and RI_6 with P_6 and I_6 begin a further development of the β motive. The following four bars (24–7) prepare for the recapitulation, with a slightly varied retrograde of the final phrase of the exposition of the tonic theme (bars 12–15).

These four phrases – a developmental phrase and its slightly varied sequential repetition leading to the climax, followed by a preparation for the reprise – constitute a familiar development sequence, and thus far, except for the coinciding theme statements, the form described is a more or less conventional version of the classical one.

However, sonata is not the only form referred to in this movement. While carefully retaining the most essential melodic ingredients of this form – a pair of contrasting themes and their development – Webern has also incorporated elements of a ritornello form. This becomes evident when we consider the introduction and coda. The introduction is half the length of the exposition and comprises two similar phrases. As in the earlier Op. 20 introduction, all the unique features of both themes make their initial appearance here. The first phrase introduces the motive that opens the second theme; the second phrase begins with the opening motive of the first theme. The piano supplies the cadence to both phrases – using, respectively, the β and α figures later used as first-theme cadences. The clarinet's single role is to establish F♯ as the tonic and, more specifically, f♯^{1} as the axis of symmetry. The coda is the same length as the introduction and uses the same rows in retrograde form. (There is an omission in the score here: a treble clef should precede the saxophone's last two notes, in bar 40. It has been added in Example 4.7.) That the introduction and coda should be similar in this way is, of course, not startling: this was the case also in Op. 20. Two things make the situation here different, however. The first is the relative length of these two sections and their similarity in every respect to the body of the movement. The second is the fact that the introduction/coda material makes three additional appearances during the course of the movement: in both exposition and reprise, the last four bars of the tonic theme are a variation of the introduction, and the preparation for the recapitulation in bars 24–7 is a varied retrograde, very like the coda.

Thus twenty-one of the forty-one bars of this movement are devoted to five statements of the opening material, which is in both form and character identical with the major sections of the piece. These five statements open and close the movement and separate all the interior sections, exactly in the manner of a baroque ritornello (see Example 4.7). The structure of the movement can be represented as shown in Table 4.4. Of the two forms, sonata is the more perfectly represented. The second theme, whose presence

Table 4.4

Classical form	Bars	Rows	Baroque form	Bars	Rows
Introduction	5[6]	2	Ritornello	5[6]	2
Exposition	10	6	A	6	(2)
			Ritornello	4	(2)
Development	12[15]	10	B	8½[11½]	8
			Ritornello	4	2
Recapitulation	10	6	A	6	(2)
			Ritornello	4	(2)
Coda	5	2	Ritornello	5	2

(Numbers in square brackets refer to the number of 3/8 units in sections with metre changes.)

4.7 Op. 22/i, ritornellos (reduction)

is necessary in order for this structure to be complete, is extraneous to and problematic in the ritornello form. The second-theme rows have been omitted on the right side of the table above, since the theme they produce is too long, extending through the A section and the following ritornello. In addition, the central section is more appropriate to the classical or romantic than to the baroque form: it is unquestionably a development of first- and second-theme materials together. Finally, the repeats are dictated by the classical form and are foreign to the ritornello.[34] Nevertheless, the regular return of material at the same tonal level is not a feature of the classical sonata. Much of the material of this sonata performs a dual function. The music of the piano, clarinet and violin in bars 12–15 is at once the continuation of the first-theme sentence (having been preceded by three similar two-bar phrases) and the tonic return of the ritornello that opened the movement, thus playing roles essential to both forms. The saxophone theme, on the other hand, has a place only in the classical form.

In view of Webern's obsession with synthesis, it should at least be mentioned that the sequence of events, and particularly the return of both themes of the exposition at the same tonal level, suggest also ternary and arch forms: ABA with introduction and coda, or ABCBA without. Or, somewhat less successfully, because of the repeats and the tonal identity of bars 6–15 and bars 28–37, a sonata rondo: ABA dev. ABA. There are certain discrepancies in the expression of each of these forms, and it is only in considering the requirements of all of them that one can understand the nature of the work, which represents above all the synthesis of certain elements of several in some cases rather divergent structures. (This interpretation of formal functions[35] will be recognized as something that occurs frequently in works from Beethoven's middle and later years – the choral movement of the Ninth Symphony, for example.)

We will continue to observe this desire for synthesis throughout the remainder of Webern's compositional career. The effects were first evident in Op. 21, in which material presented in the vertical manner (canon) was ordered according to the horizontal (as sonata and variations, forms understood to be homophonic). The two modes are more thoroughly integrated in Op. 22/i, where both material and structure are in some ways vertically and in others horizontally oriented. The result is neither one thing nor the other but owes something to both; whether it serves the cause of increased comprehensibility (repeatedly expressed by Webern as his primary object in all things) may be open to question. In the case of Op. 22/i, the amalgamation of forms from different historical periods leads to a certain amount of confusion of function and blurring of outlines. These difficulties, if that is what they are, increase in Op. 24.

Op. 24/i

In his first three sonata movements we have seen Webern reaching ever further backwards historically for structural models. Op. 20/ii follows the format of a sonata from Beethoven's middle period, with an introduction and coda and only the first set of repeats. Op. 21/i, with no outer appendages, follows the earlier classical model, with both repeats. Op. 22/i can be seen as another step backwards, towards the baroque: in spite of the classical repeat format, a ritornello operates alongside the two themes and development of the bithematic sonata in this movement. The next sonata, opening the Op. 24 Concerto for nine instruments, completes the historical transition: it employs a ritornello and dispenses with the repeats altogether.[36]

Webern alluded to the baroque inspiration of this movement in a letter to Emil Hertzka written on 19 September 1928: 'I have already turned to a new work; a concerto for violin, clarinet, horn, piano and string orchestra. (In the spirit of some of Bach's Brandenburg Concertos.)'[37] Although this remark does not necessarily betray a baroque-inspired structure,[38] it certainly causes musical evidence of such a form to come as no surprise. And indeed, while this movement is a further experiment in the congruity of forms, here the structural hierarchy of Op. 22/i seems to have been inverted: although we see a similar synthesis of ritornello form, sonata form, ABA ternary form and rondo, the result in this case conforms most closely to the requirements of the first of these. Altogether, the several components seem more compatible in Op. 24 than they were in Op. 22, though here, as there, the result must be seen as flawed if it is considered as representative solely of any of the contributing structures. Op. 24/i is also a study in synonym and ambiguity in which the focus on general structural similarities inevitably results in a blurring of specifics.

Since of all the forms concerned the bithematic sonata makes the most specific demands, we will examine the movement in this light first, referring to the baroque form as it is appropriate. The proportions, the transitions between sections and the nature of some of the sections themselves leave no doubt that the anatomy of the classical sonata was an important influence.

This movement begins more conventionally than any of the previous bithematic sonata movements, with two themes of markedly different character appearing in succession. The first comprises two phrases of five bars each, ending with a cadence in bars 9–10.[39] The self-contained nature (period structure) of this opening, as well as the aggressively contrapuntal texture, make it an admirable ritornello as well. Following the dictates of tradition, the second theme, in bars 13–19, is more regular and less assertive and in fact rather lacking in definition. During bars 17–19 the ensemble is gradually drawn back to the rhythms of the opening, and the section ends with some eight bars of first-theme-related material.

Perhaps the most remarkable feature of the opening theme is its extraordinary integrity, both melodic and rhythmic.[40] It consists of twenty isolated three-note groups, all except the last four presented melodically. All are expressed in the same way rhythmically, as three notes of equal value. Four durations are used to produce notated ritards (in bars 1–3 and 6–10) and acceleration (in bars 4–5). The resulting continually fluctuating tempo is made even more elastic by the addition of a series of *rit. . . .tempo* markings. The first and last of these, in bars 2–3 and 10, exaggerate anyway inevitable ritards resulting from steadily lengthening note values; the second and third, in bars 5 and 8, are puzzling, as they neutralize written accelerations. The first phrase is a rhythmic palindrome, fast–slow–fast, the second an extended ritard with the final two trichords verticalized for cadential emphasis. The dynamics are generally *forte* or *fortissimo* except at the very ends of phrases, with the cadence dropping to *pianissimo*. Seven of the nine instruments are used (only the horn and trombone are omitted), and rows are stated pointillistically in succession, each trichord played by a different instrument. Two of the five rows are played entirely by the piano.

As a result of the unusual formulation of the row itself, each of the twenty three-note groups in the first theme is some permutation of the same trichord, a minor second within a major third (a 014 set, or Forte's pc set 3–3).[41] This identity is reinforced by the use of only three shapes in the course of the theme. All eight trichords in the first phrase (bars 1–5) plus two of those in bar 6 follow the contour that I shall call **Ia**, in which a major third and a minor ninth move in opposite directions. The second phrase opens with a new shape, **Ib** (a major third and a major seventh moving in the same direction). The remaining contour, **Ic** (a minor sixth and a major seventh with a change of direction), is used exclusively for the statement of P_1 in the second phrase. The first and third of these contours (**Ia** and **Ic**) are similar, since both incorporate a change of direction. The first appearance of **Ib** is heard therefore as a departure and effectively defines the beginning of the second phrase in bar 6.

The ritornello consists of five rows – P_0, RI_1, RI_0, P_1 and I_1 – arranged so as to exploit their invariant relations. Each trichord of the second row, RI_1, is the exact pitch retrograde of the corresponding one in the initial P_0. Later, at the cadence, I_1 produces the same trichords once more, thereby establishing a close relationship between the opening phrase and the cadence.

The movement ends with a nearly complete restatement of the opening section – a predictable event in the baroque form, explainable only as a coda in the classical sonata. The five rows of the opening are apparently represented here by four: R_{11}–I_0–RI_6–P_6. In a sense, however, five rows are present here as well, since the final row is verticalized in such a way as to allow an alternative designation, RI_7. Although these are not the same five rows used in the exposition, they are extraordinarily similar, owing to the invariant properties of the row. The trichords of R_{11} have the same pitch-class content as those of RI_0, which was used to open the second phrase in bars 6–7, in reverse order; in bars 63–4 the central note of each is played at the pitch level used in the earlier statement. In bars 63–6, R_{11} is followed by I_0; these rows bear the same relationship to each other as the first and second rows of the piece. Here this identity is emphasized through instrumentation: each trichord in I_0 is played by the same instrument that played its retrograde in R_{11}. The same trichords are heard again immediately, at the same pitch level, as RI_6, which is played by the piano. This sequence of rows with the same trichordal content (R_{11}, I_0 and RI_6) is an obvious reference to the first phrase of the movement. The final hexachord of the piece is verticalized, and in this form is identical to the first hexachord of P_0, with which the movement opened.

This final section, like the opening, falls into two phrases. The first of these represents a durational inversion of the first phrase of the piece; instead of progressing from the shortest note values to the longest and back again, it does just the reverse. This is immediately followed by an abridged version of the events of the second phrase, in bars 6–10. The progression is from short to long, but since this change must be effected with twelve fewer notes this time, the two intermediate steps are omitted. As in the exposition, verticalization occurs increasingly towards the end. Contour **Ic** is used exclusively here.

The first theme/ritornello makes one other brief appearance, in bars 45–9. This reprise consists of only two rows and a hexachord (RI_2–P_5–I_6/i) and represents a distillation of the content of bars 1–10. It begins with the notated ritard from bars 1–2; the reverse of this progression, which occurred in bars 4–5, is omitted. The remainder is similar to the phrase that ends the piece, with the semiquaver movement of bars 6–10 and the two cadential chords from bar 10, the two intermediate stages having been left out. The relationships of RI_2 to the exposition's P_1 (in bars 7–8) and P_5 to I_0 and I_6/i to RI_6/ii in bars 65–8 of the coda can be seen in Example 4.8. The fourth trichord of RI_2 and the second and third of P_5 take on a contour (**Id**) not encountered in the exposition of the first theme. We shall return to this later.

This abbreviated interior appearance is easily accepted in a ritornello form. In a sonata context, where it must be the recapitulation of the first theme, it is somewhat problematic because of its incompleteness. The fact that the rows are not those used in the exposition may also appear at first to be a difficulty, but as Example 4.8 shows, the sophisticated set of tonal identities exhibited by this row allows for the restatement of pitch material without a duplication of row forms, making the apparent tonal discrepancy between exposition and reprise mythical.

As to a justification for the abridgement, a truncated recall of this particular material succeeds because the striking nature of the theme ensures

The instrumental music

4.8   Op. 24/i, bars 1–8, bars 63–8 (reduction, pitches only)

its recognition, even when not heard in its entirety. I think the reason for its abbreviation here is connected with the conception of the piece as a composite form. We shall come back to this later, but for now let it be said that a complete return of a strong first theme at this point in the piece would considerably weaken two of the structures to which this movement alludes: ternary and arch form. The real weight of restatement falls on the final section of the piece – I believe for the same reason, to strengthen the allusion to symmetrical structures – and it was no doubt felt that two returns of such consequence would interfere with the (delicate) balance of the movement.

At the conclusion of the first-theme cadence in bars 9–10 the trumpet plays a three-note segment with the contour **Ia**. This is a figure with strong first-theme associations, since this contour was used in ten of the twenty groups constituting that theme; to further emphasize this orientation, the trumpet figure in question echoes exactly a motive played by the viola in bar 6. The trumpet figure is the beginning of the transition between first and second themes, in which Webern follows convention – and his own precedent in Op. 20 – in opening with material from the first theme before proceeding to second-theme preparation. Neither second theme nor, therefore, this transition is customary in the baroque form.

The second theme is prepared by the introduction of a new rhythmic motive, ♪ ♩ ♪, stated four times in quick succession – by clarinet, piano, violin and viola. Although all these motives are inescapably versions of the ubiquitous 014 trichord, they do not conform to any of the melodic contours used in the first theme. The effect of these three bars is twofold. The introduction of new and relatively diverse material, both rhythmic and melodic, represents a relaxation of the extraordinary concentration that was paramount in the first theme; and the motion in steady quavers establishes a pulse, something that was carefully avoided in the earlier section. In addition, a denser texture is produced by a new row topography in which the piano plays its own series of rows, completely independent of the other instruments. All these things are second-theme characteristics and are in definite contrast to the first theme.

The piano and oboe begin the second theme at the change of tempo in bar 13, before the viola has finished the transition. Not only do the two sections overlap musically, but the division between transition and second theme bisects the piano's R_6 in bars 11–13. The first four notes of this row belong to the transition, the last eight to the second theme. In the recapitulation of this transition, the blurring of structural outlines is increased. Like the first theme, the transition is shortened on its return, but in the case of the transition this reduction results in its virtual disappearance. Only fragments of the characteristic rhythmic figure heard in the exposition transition are brought back.

Until now our determination of the exact location of sectional divisions has been guided by the treatment of three elements: tempo, row structure and musical features (rhythm, articulation, texture and so on). Changes in these several components have always coincided. In Op. 24 this is no longer the case. No break in the row structure reinforces the changes in tempo and rhythm at the end of the exposition transition; in the recapitulation the nonalignment of constituent elements is greatly exaggerated.

I have already shown that the row structure of the first theme is not duplicated in the reprise. This is curious. Even more curious, however, is the fact that the rows of the transition and second theme *do* return, beginning with I_6. More about this later. For the moment it is interesting to observe that, while I_6 opens the exposition transition, it occupies a slightly earlier position in the structure of the recapitulation, where the first hexachord produces the two chords that constitute the first-theme cadence – chords so parallel to those in bar 10 that there can be no doubt of their function. The following row, R_6, again serves both transition and second theme, but not in the same way as before: here the division is into three notes and nine. It is clear that the row structure does not contribute to structural definition at this point.

The confusion concerning the exact limits of the transitions is compounded by the dislocation of features. I noted earlier that the exposition transition opens with a trumpet figure recalling a tonally identical motive played by the viola in bar 6. The reverse of this situation occurs upon the return of the transition, when the viola echoes in bars 50–1 a figure played by the trumpet in bar 47. In the reprise, however, this occurs at the end of the transition, not at the beginning.

Let me consider briefly the beginning of the second theme in the exposition before continuing my examination of the incongruities of the recapitulation. R_7 (a dominant analogue), which begins in the oboe in bar 13, continues in the horn, the violin and finally the viola. The second hexachord of this row functions also as the first of I_2, which continues by restating the oboe and horn figures of bars 13–14 (Example 4.9). The parallel pair of rows in the recapitulation produces the series of three-note groups shown in Example 4.10, played by clarinet, horn, viola, trombone, clarinet and horn.

4.9   Op. 24/i, bars 13–17, first transition (reduction without piano, pitches only)

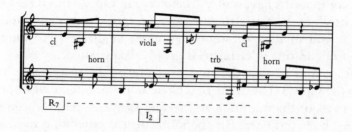

4.10   Op. 24/i, bars 51–4, second transition (reduction without piano, pitches only)

A comparison of these two series shows some interesting differences. The first trichord, which in the exposition introduced a new melodic contour, thereby helping to initiate the second theme, adopts in the restatement the familiar contour **Ic**, echoing in retrograde the figure played by the horn in bars 45–6 of the restatement of the first theme. As in the exposition, these three pitches are repeated two and a half bars later, so this first-theme connection persists. And whereas the trichord in bar 14 was presented in a new rhythm, ♩♫ , which reinforced the impression of a new theme unfolding, the corresponding figure in the horn in bars 51–2 is in the characteristic rhythm of the transition, ♪♩♪ ; this is particularly note-worthy here, since this rhythm did not occur intact in the restatement of the transition. Thus, although parallelism in the row structure would indicate that the clarinet and horn figures in bars 51–2 are the beginning of the second-theme restatement, they have been altered so as in fact to prolong the transition, which was otherwise abbreviated. Meanwhile, the piano begins its second-theme material on schedule in bar 51 with a progression practi-cally identical to the one it played at the opening of the second theme in the exposition, in bar 13.

A second inconsistency is more difficult to rationalize. The tempo change at the beginning of the second theme in the recapitulation does not correspond with the beginning of the quavers in the piano, as it did the first time. This certainly aids the cause of structural ambiguity, something that seems to be a significant feature of this movement and can perhaps be justified on that basis. Nevertheless, I find it curious. The tempo changes are less specific in the sketches than in the published score, but their positions are the same. The score has *rit. . . .sehr mäßig* (♩ = ca 50) on both occasions. An early sketch shows only *rit. . . .tempo*, without a metronome indication, in both places.[42] In a subsequent version of bars 11ff, written on the same page, *(sehr mäßig)* is added at bar 13. Thus, although Webern's intentions could have been more decisively indicated, that the discrepancy originated with him cannot be questioned.

After the striking and assertive first theme, the second theme seems rather featureless. It is primarily a piano theme, consisting of groups of two and four quavers in which single notes alternate with dyads, played quietly and mostly in a low or middle register. Above this the other instruments continue to play three-note melodic figures in the style of the first theme, except that these are now also in steady quavers and *piano*. At bar 17 the melody instruments suddenly revert to the character and rhythm of the first theme, playing at first in triplet quavers, then in triplet crotchets in bars 19–22, and finally in semiquavers at the end of bar 22. The piano continues its steady motion of dyads and chords to the beginning of bar 19, but then adapts by degrees to the activity of the other instruments, at first by abandoning its single notes and slowing its pulse from quavers to triplet crotchets in bars 19–20, and finally by thickening the latter (expressed as triplet quavers and rests) to three-note chords like those of the first theme cadence in bars 9–10. The exposition comes to a close in bars 22–3.

Bars 24–5 (with an anacrusis) are a bridge to the following section, in which the piano and three other instruments share a row for the first time since bars 7–8, and single semiquavers and a dotted rhythm – characteristics of the subsequent section – are introduced. The texture thins markedly and suddenly. This change of material and texture is characteristic of both the classical sonata and the baroque ritornello form.

The groups of three quavers played by the instruments in bars 13–17 serve a dual function. They reinforce the quaver pulse established by the piano as a feature of the second theme, but at the same time they represent a continuation of the first theme. This latter purpose becomes apparent in bar 17, but in retrospect; all the ensemble except the piano has by this time already begun an elongated repetition of the events of the opening three bars of the movement, rotated to begin with quavers rather than semiquavers, and lasting until bar 23. Throughout the piano's exposition of the second theme the rest of the ensemble continues to play the first theme, which triumphs ultimately, when the piano leaves off playing quavers in bar 19 to join in.

Two significant structural ramifications of the situation just described should be noted, with reference respectively to bithematic sonata and ritornello forms. First, while this presentation of the second theme during a continuation of the first is a retrenchment from the idea of the simultaneous exposition of two themes – the most radical aspect of Opp. 21 and 22 – it nonetheless represents a continued interest in the idea of superimposed themes and perhaps can be seen even as a refinement of that concept. Secondly, the clearly perceived return of the opening rhythm and character at bar 17 compensates for the ritornello that is otherwise missing between the section beginning in bar 13 (A) and the obviously new section in bars 26–44 (B) (see Table 4.5, p. 188). Although the melodic contours in bars 17–23 are for the most part the three used in the opening ritornello, the most-emphasized figures, in bars 19–22, rely heavily on a fourth, introduced by the violin in bar 18 (a minor sixth and a minor ninth moving in the same direction: **Id**). The relationship of this figure to the ritornello is confirmed subsequently when it forms a part of the reprise in bars 45–9 (noted earlier). Thus bars 17–23 comprise a ritornello of sorts, though this cannot be seen as the only, or even as the primary, function of these bars, since they neither show a close tonal relationship to the original ritornello nor return to the type of row topography established there. Instead, they persist with the topography introduced with the second theme.

The row structure is exactly the same in the restatement of the material of bars 11–25, thereby answering the requirement of the baroque form, in which both bars 11–17, as the A section, and bars 17–23, as a ritornello, would be expected to return at the same tonal level, but presenting a tonal anomaly in terms of the later sonata form, in which bars 13–23, as the second theme, should return at a different level. The return lasts through the RI_4 that provided the bridge to the development in bars 23–5; upon its return, however, this row is incorporated into a slightly lengthened and dramatically heightened secondary ritornello. After succumbing intitially to the triplets suggested by the rest of the parts, the piano attempts, in bars 59–60, to return to its own quaver pulse. It seems to find the virile rhythm of the ritornello/first theme too strong to resist, however, and finally submits in bars 61–2. The three-note chords that have closed each of the preceding ritornello sections do not occur here, since the final (closing) ritornello follows immediately. The end of the second-theme section in both exposition and restatement coincides with the end of RI_4 as well as with a tempo change. This reinforcement of the musical structure by both the row structure and the tempo at these two points – an unusual situation in this movement – leaves no question as to exactly where these divisions occur.

The central section of this movement begins with new material – a melody in five- and six-note segments using dotted figures, syncopations and grace notes – played exclusively by the clarinet and violin over an accompaniment in the piano, which uses its own series of rows to produce material similar to its second theme. After ten bars, additional instruments enter, and material from the first theme and transition is developed in the usual ways – diminution (trombone, bar 35, for example) and augmentation (viola, bars 35–6; bars 41–2), fragmentation (bar 37), syncopation (viola, bars 35–6). Like the new material at the beginning of this section, this development is accomplished by the other instruments while the piano continues to play its own series of rows, producing music that still resembles its second theme, but now in a new character – in a high register, mostly staccato, with sudden dynamic changes and with the dyads replaced by grace notes. All the materials of the exposition are combined in some form in these nine bars. The rows are elided – a reference to second-theme technique – but the elisions are not the same as those used earlier. The tempo is made very fluid by the imposition of a series of eight *rit. ...tempo* markings (a first-theme characteristic) on a fabric already making liberal use of syncopations, augmentations and diminutions. The section ends four notes short of the end of an R_1 row; note 9 of this row is a grace note preceding the first three-note group of the ritornello/first-theme reprise. Once again, here, the row structure does not reinforce the structural articulation indicated by musical features and tempo.

The two structures I have defined in this movement can be represented

Table 4.5

Sonata form				Ritornello form
Exposition		25 bars		
theme I	(A)	10	10	ritornello
transition		3	?	
theme II	(BA′)	11	6 + 6	A (+ ritornello)
bridge		2	?	
Development	(C)	19	19	B
Recapitulation		18		
theme I	(A)	5	5	ritornello
transition		1 +	?	
theme II	(BA′)	12	7 + 8	A (+ ritornello)
Coda	(A)	7	7	ritornello

(Discrepancies in numbers of bars are the result of overlapping sections.)

as shown in Table 4.5. Several aspects of this movement that do not conform to the expectations of either classical or romantic sonata form have already been mentioned:

(1) The A material returns twice – very abridged on the occasion where a reprise is customary, and in a sufficiently weighty manner to balance the opening only at the end, in the position of a coda.

(2) The transition and second theme occur at the same tonal level in exposition and reprise.

(3) The central section becomes a development only after ten bars of contrasting new material.[43]

None of these things presents a problem if the movement is seen as a ritornello structure. In this case, however, the following difficulties emerge:

(1) It is irregular to find a transition between the ritornello and the A section; this happens on both occasions. The bridge between A and B sections is similarly unexpected.

(2) Either there is no ritornello between sections A and B, or, if the material at bars 17 and 55 is considered as a ritornello, the preceding A sections are disproportionately brief and the B section too long.

Thus, while the structure deviates from both of these outlines in some respects, what appears as an aberration in one context represents the most characteristic feature of the other, one's requirements cancelling out the other's deficiencies. The recapitulation as I have defined it is considerably shorter than the exposition as a result of abbreviated restatements of first theme and transition. However, the outer sections of the movement are exactly balanced if the final seven bars, which I have called a coda, are considered an integral part of the return. This and the exact tonal reprise of bars 49–62 make the piece a ternary (ABA) form as well.

Although there are discrepancies in the realization of the details of each of these forms, all do apply to this movement to some extent. The result of their congruence is a composite structure with broader dimensions – or at least broader implications – than any of the components alone could have produced. As in Op. 22, a consideration of all of the contributing forms is necessary in order to make sense of the result. The structure of this movement is similar to what that of Op. 22/i would be if that movement had no repeats. In spite of their similar construction, however, the two movements make very different aural impressions, primarily because of the nature of their materials. Owing to the predominance of a few memorable first-theme/ritornello figures in all sections of Op. 22/i (the development section of that movement represents a concentration of these) and the relatively small role played by the second theme, this movement impresses with its homogeneity: one hears two similar sections separated by a third using exaggerated versions of the same materials in a more concentrated fashion. In other words, the ritornellos disappear because of their similarity to everything else. In the Op. 24 movement, on the other hand, the ritornello makes an immediate impression as the result of its distinctive rhythmic character and, since neither the piano's rather plodding second theme nor the central section bears much resemblance to it, its returns stand out in sharp relief. As the sameness of material in Op. 22 reinforces the sonata characteristics of that movement (to the extent that one hears a three-part form with a development at the centre), the contrast that is a feature of Op. 24 gives aural definition to the alternative, ritornello form.

Op. 27/i

The last sonata form is found in Webern's only twelve-note work of major proportions for a solo instrument, the Variations for Piano, Op. 27. Although the opening movement of this work is much simpler in concept than its counterpart in Op. 24, the two movements share certain structural concerns. Webern's experiments in the synthesis of homophonic structures continue in Op. 27/i.

This work seems to be a conundrum, since the designation *Variationen* clearly does not apply to the first two movements. In a letter to the Humpliks dated 18 July 1936 Webern said of the work: 'The completed part is a variations movement; the whole will be a kind of "Suite".'[44] Since the third movement was the first to be composed, this is obviously the movement referred to in the letter, and it is clearly a set of variations. The projection of the rest of the work as 'a kind of "suite"' does not suggest that the remaining movements were also to be in variation form, but rather that they would probably take on the binary and ternary forms customary in that context. And so they do: the first movement is in ABA ternary form, and

189

the second movement binary, with repeats at the centre and end. The first movement is included in this chapter because it also exhibits too many of the significant features of a sonata for the influence of that model to be ignored.[45]

Three possible interpretations of the work as a whole come, then, to mind. It can be seen as a three-movement sonata with traditional structures in all three positions – sonata, binary scherzo and variations – that is nowhere so designated by Webern; as a suite, again with movements following structures customary in that situation – ternary, binary and variations – and with the authority of Webern's own designation in private; and, finally, with the indisputable justification of Webern's official title, variations of a very peculiar sort, in which two movements of the three seem not to have anything to do with variation form. These interpretations are not mutually exclusive.

Op. 27 seems to me to be another case of Webern's fascination with structural ambiguities and double meanings. What precedent can one find for calling a work by the name of the form of its final movement? Surely the variations referred to in the title of Op. 27 are variations in the interpretation of a multi-movement structure rather than variations in the more precise sense of theme and variations. And if this is so, then all three of the interpretations offered above are to some extent valid, while none is sufficient alone. This understanding of Webern's title seems to me to be very much in keeping both with his penchant for reinterpreting the various aspects of traditional structures and with his apparent delight in subtleties and the obscuration of precise meanings, a tendency that has been glimpsed already on other occasions.

Nevertheless, writers ever since the work appeared have attempted, in the face of considerable obstacles, to rationalize all three movements as variations. This has led to the proposal of, in the words of Robert Wason, 'the most inventive and exotic meanings for the term "variations"'.[46] Perhaps the first perpetrator of exotic explanations was René Leibowitz, who in 1948 described the first movement of Op. 27 as a theme and two variations, the second as a theme with a single variation, and the third as five variations of yet another theme,[47] an analysis that has proven to be remarkably persistent. Willi Reich added considerably to the confusion with his explanation of the work, which he claimed to be Webern's own, recorded during a conversation with him. In Reich's notes the work in its entirety is described as a sonatina, in which the third movement is a small sonata form and the first a theme and two variations – just the reverse of the explanation that seems most reasonable.

Friedhelm Döhl has published the contents of Reich's notes. The first movement is outlined as follows:

First movement: Three-part Andante (at the same time theme and two
                      variations).
A   bars 1–18:   Theme.
B   bars 19–36:   quicker moving middle section, Variation 1.
A   bars 37–54:   Variation 2.

Row structure: beginning: prime row beginning on E in canon with the
                   retrograde beginning on B.[48]

Here, as in several other instances, information emanating from Reich in the
form of first-hand accounts of Webern's own thoughts and remarks is
difficult to accept at face value.[49] This interpretation of Op. 27/i is very like
Leibowitz's, which is not entirely surprising, since he and Reich were
contemporaries and both members of the Schoenberg circle. It seems
unlikely, however, that it is Webern's. It is curious, for example, that this
movement is said to begin with a prime row beginning on E and its
retrograde and that (later in the outline[50]) the row that opens the third movement is called a retrograde, since the numbering of rows throughout the
sketches shows that Webern considered this latter row to be the untransposed prime. Analyses of Op. 27 customarily proceeded on the assumption
that the first row of the first movement was the untransposed prime before
evidence from Webern's own hand showing the correct row designation
was generally known; Reich's use of the old row orientation is a detail that
causes one to wonder about the real source of his analysis.

Döhl, while apparently not questioning the authenticity of Reich's notes,
does not agree with the analysis. He suggests that, while ABA′ (first part,
contrasting section and reprise) describes the overall form, to describe it also
as a theme and two variations makes little sense. He prefers to see each of the
fourteen phrases in the movement as a variation of the prime/retrograde idea
– each a slightly different manifestation of horizontal symmetry.[51] The same
explanation was suggested in 1969 by Robert U. Nelson.[52] This interpretation of Op. 27/i brings the similarity of this movement and Op. 21/ii into
sharp focus.[53] While it is a valid description of events at the phrase level,
however, it neglects the overall structure, which is clearly of importance.[54]

The first section of this movement (bars 1–18) comprises four phrases,
each built from a forward-going row and its exact retrograde, stated at the
same time so that the second half of the phrase is the reverse of the first.
There is no question of antecedent–consequent relationships, since each of
the four phrases is palindromic and therefore complete in itself. The four
settings differ – this variation is the basis of the Nelson/Döhl interpretation –
and in only the first is the palindrome a perfect one. The structure is **aba′b′**:
a is more expansive and evenly spaced than **b**, which is precipitate both times,
becoming quite dense at the centre. The **b** phrases are identical except for a

compression of the first part the second time and a compensatory isolation of the end of the phrase in order to serve as a cadence to the A section of the piece. All four forms of the row are used, at the eighth transposition only, in the order R_8/P_8, I_8/RI_8, P_8/R_8 and I_8/RI_8. The contrasting character and row content of **a** and **b**, and their positions, suggest the repeated exposition of two themes, as tradition would have it. That bars 11–18 represent a repeat of 1–10 is indisputable; that the repetition is varied is not surprising within the twelve-note context.

This material returns in a form very like the original with hands inverted in the last eighteen bars of the movement (bars 37–54). In this reprise, however, although the musical material is structured as it was in the exposition, neither the original row forms nor their previous P–I–P–I order returns. The rows used this time are R_0/P_0, I_0/RI_0, I_5/RI_5 and P_5/R_5: the order of prime and inversion has been reversed in the final two phrases. That the phrases are transposed in pairs emphasizes the fact that **a** and **b** function as a unit, reinforcing their interpretation as first and second themes within an exposition.

In 1979 Peter Stadlen published a performance edition of Op. 27 in which he included all the comments and markings that Webern had written in the score when Stadlen was preparing to give the work its first performance.[55] Many of Webern's instructions seem to reinforce the analysis presented in the previous paragraphs. At bar 6, which is the first-theme cadence in my analysis, he has written 'Echo', and at the beginning of the second theme in bar 8, 'neu belebt' (with renewed animation). The beginning of the reprise in bar 37 is marked 'der anfängliche Tonfall (daher etwas substantieller als das Ende von Takt 36)' (in the same spirit as at the beginning – from here on, somewhat more vigorously than at the end of bar 36).

I noted earlier that the two **b** phrases (the statement and repetition of second theme) are nearly identical in the exposition, where the same rows are used for both. In spite of the fact that these two phrases do not emanate from the same pair of rows in the restatement, their tonal similarity is maintained, since I_0 and P_5 are hexachordally invariant. Nevertheless, a nagging doubt arises. When phrases are built from simultaneous statements of a row and its retrograde at the same level of transposition, what impact is made by the association of two such phrases through hexachordal invariance? None, it would seem. Of more aural significance is the fact that the end of the final two rows join to produce a triad, D–G#–C#, that was a prominent feature of both the second and fourth phrases of the exposition, where it occurred naturally as notes 5–7 of I_8. The appearance of this same chord, somewhat more artfully derived, at the end is presumably intended to give this phrase, which is 'in a new key' this time, the expected tonal identity with its counterpart in the exposition.

Two things about this return are anomalous in the context of sonata form:

the new tonal levels used throughout the restatement (and the occurrence of what amounts to a modulation), and the repetition of the entire section, without the development. The latter is surely evidence of the predominance of the requirements of ternary form over those of the sonata in this instance: the repetition is necessary in order to balance the initial A. The tonal question is not so easily explained.[56]

It is the central section that provides the strongest arguments for considering this a sonata movement, because this is truly a development. It begins with RI_1 and I_1 – the 'subdominant' level – and divides into two sections, which are elided, in bar 30.[57] Each of these comprises a sequence of three phrases, each of which is an exact palindrome.[58] Thus the most important aspect of the exposition, horizontal symmetry, is exaggerated (all palindromes were not perfect in the exposition) in a treatment reminiscent of the development of Op. 21/i. In addition, the section is based on the traditional developmental devices of sequence and modulation throughout.

The opening phrase of the first sequence lasts from bar 19 to the first note in bar 23, with the centre of the palindrome occurring in bar 21. The second phrase of this sequence is elided with the first, beginning on the B♭ near the end of bar 22 and extending as far as the B♭ in bar 26. This phrase is essentially an inversion of the first, with the axis occurring in bar 24. The second and third phrases are not elided – the third beginning on the second E in bar 26. (The first E in this bar is an extra note necessary in order to complete the symmetry of the second phrase and in terms of row structure can be explained only as an anticipation of the first note of RI_6, which properly begins with the last two notes in this bar. This is especially interesting as the earlier E in bar 22, which occasions this extra note, is itself not a member of the rows constituting the second phrase of the sequence either. It is the final note of the RI_1 that opens the first phrase and is an essential part of the characteristic three-note melodic figure that opens and closes all units of this sequence.) The third phrase extends to the E in the middle of bar 30, with its axis in bar 28, and is again upright, like the first phrase of the sequence.

This is a sequence on first-theme material. Relative to the second sequence, the events are broadly spaced: never are more than two notes heard at once, and the rhythm slows from demisemiquavers at the beginning to dotted semiquavers at the centre and moves back again. The following sequence, which begins with the final three notes of the previous one, is based, predictably, on second-theme material. It is much more dense and moves consistently in demisemiquavers. Each unit turns on a characteristic figure at its axis: these occur in bars 31, 33 and 35–6. The rows used alternate between P/R and I/RI, as in the first-theme sequence; however, the turning figure, which is built from the tritone at the centre of the row, is the same each time. The climax of the development – and of the movement – occurs in the second segment of this sequence. After the climax, the beginning of the final segment is delayed and the entire segment is played with a ritard. The end of bar 36 is a preparation for the reprise: the last four pitches of the development are heard again in retrograde order following the first dyad struck in bar 37.

With this movement Webern takes his leave of sonata form. His first five twelve-note instrumental works contain sonata movements;[59] his last two do not. Instead they explore variation form, and especially possibilities for combining variations with a closed form. In the case of the Op. 30 Variations, the closed form used is very like a sonata, but it is never so called by Webern, who refers to it sometimes as an 'andante-form', at other times as an 'adagio form'. It may be seen as curious that Webern's only late (twelve-note) string quartet, traditionally the medium for a composer's most profound reflection, does not contain as one of its movements a sonata form.

5

The movements in variation form:
Opp. 21/ii, 24/iii, 27/iii, 28/i and 30

'To develop everything else from *one* principal idea! That's the strongest unity ... But in what form? That's where art comes in! ... One form plays a special role – the *variation*.' So Webern told those attending his second-to-last 'Path to the New Music' lecture, on 3 April 1933.[1] Earlier that evening he had described the sonata as 'the most subtly worked and richest' of the classical homophonic forms.[2] It was in these two forms – sonata and variations – that he cast the major portion of his twelve-note instrumental music: five of the sixteen movements are in variation form.

Just as the sonata symbolizes the most significant and fertile development of the principle of departure and return, variation form represents linear reiteration in its most nearly pure form. Evolving as it does through constant repetitions of the same material, in ever-changing guises but always similar enough to the original for its genesis to be recognized, variation form represents the unity/variety argument (which occupied Webern's thoughts to such a degree)[3] in a straightforward way: if the repetitions are too literal, variety suffers; if, on the other hand, they are so diverse that their common basis is obscured, unity is lost. It seems to me that variation form must have been the most difficult of all the homophonic forms to adapt to the twelve-note method of composition. Variation form presupposes (in classical music and Brahms, at least) a stable element, of fixed length – traditionally a melody or bass, or a harmonic pattern – that remains recognizable through diverse treatments in the course of which its aspect changes but its most essential features do not. Since the twelve-note technique allows for neither harmonic stability nor melodic ornamentation, the traditional relationship between a theme and its variations is not a possibility. Moreover, the developing variation that Schoenberg saw as fundamental to the new technique is a continuous process that refuses to be confined or sectionalized. Nevertheless, the Viennese composers were fascinated with variation form, and both Schoenberg and Webern used it many times. Schoenberg wrote variations on atonal themes: in the 1948 essay 'Connection of Musical Ideas', he defined variation as 'changing a number of a unit's features, while preserving others',[4] and in *Fundamentals* he instructed that 'the course of events [in the theme] should not be changed [in the variations], even if the character is changed; the number and order of the segments remains the same'.[5] For him the retention of any one of many things – row forms, contour, rhythm – served as a sufficient reminder of the theme. Webern took a more radical approach. He opened his lecture of 26 February 1932 with a reference to variations:

> 'variations on a theme' – that's the primeval form, which is at the bottom of everything. Something that seems quite different is really the same. The most comprehensive unity results from this.[6]

The essential difference between the two composers' use of variation form lies in their concept of the nature of the 'something' that 'is really the same'. Schoenberg wrote variations on a theme; Webern did not.

Just as the secondary features of sonata form predominated when the underlying tonal dialogue was taken away, the most obvious surface aspects of variation form become, in the absence of a theme, the only way of distinguishing this form from any other. Thus we find movements that consist of a string of sections of equal length, each stylistically consistent within itself but contrasting with its neighbours, passing as theme and variations, even though no feature of the first section is reiterated in subsequent sections. Sections are the same length, not as the inevitable result of their treatment of material of that length, but arbitrarily, in order to give the aural impression of a theme and variations where the basic premise of the structure no longer exists. The careful clothing of a movement in the conventional attire deceives the listener into presuming the presence of the usual basic linen, an assumption which is frequently unfounded. The ease with which we are led to make this mistake demonstrates the importance of secondary features in the process of distinguishing conventional forms. Those features responsible for our perception of these movements as variations are a sham; the format exists for its own sake, the cause–effect relationship of form and content having been inverted. For this reason, Webern's use of variation form represents an irony.

There are variation movements in Opp. 21, 24, 27, 28 and 30. Three of these are given the title *Variationen*: Op. 27, Op. 30, and the second movement of Op. 21. In the course of these five movements, which span nearly Webern's entire twelve-note period, distinct changes may be observed, both in his approach to the structure and in his objectives. In the beginning he meticulously maintains the equality of sections and is careful to introduce some characteristic figure or technique into each, in the manner of the old character variations. Regular changes of colour and orchestration, register, rhythm, tempo, texture and dynamics give the illusion of variation and mask the absence of a conventional theme.

In spite of the fact that the first section of Op. 21/ii is labelled *Thema* in the score, and notwithstanding Webern's references to the opening sections of Op. 28/i and Op. 30 as the 'theme' in describing these works to friends, in point of fact none of the sets of variations has a theme that functions in the usual way. Nevertheless, the third movement of Op. 27 is the only one of the five in which subsequent 'variations' are not based in any way on material introduced at the beginning. For this reason, this set would seem to be the most abstract, and therefore the most revolutionary of all (though in my opinion neither the most complex nor the most interesting).

The several sections of the Op. 21 movement represent various realizations of the palindrome, a principle which takes on the function of a theme in this work. Op. 24/iii seems to be a preliminary excursion into territory that is to be thoroughly explored later in Opp. 28 and 30. Each of these three movements is based on a few short rhythmic figures that are stated at the outset and immediately and continuously varied thereafter. Although these figures are the source of everything that happens subsequently, they are too short and too elementary to function as a theme: they have been stated and their variation begun long before we reach the end of the section Webern has described as the theme.[7] They are motives, not themes, and, in keeping with this distinction, what happens to them in the course of the works they generate is more development than variation. They are subjected to inversion and retrograde, augmentation and diminution, imitation and octave displacement – all traditionally developmental, not variational, techniques. After Op. 21 Webern's manipulation of musical material in variation movements is developmental, not variational.

As the focus of Webern's attention turned from the invention of tonal metaphors to the synthesis of formal models, he used sonata form less frequently and variations began to predominate. Two of his last three instrumental works are titled *Variationen*; all three have a variation movement. The first of these works, Op. 27, contains Webern's last sonata movement. Perhaps because less was prescribed in variation form, it provided more fertile ground for the sort of hybrid that so fascinated him.[8] The ultimate examples of synthesis are the opening movement of the Op. 28 Quartet and the Op. 30 Variations for Orchestra, which, judging from Webern's own remarks, seem to be two very different realizations of almost exactly the same premise. In a letter written to Rudolf Kolisch on 19 April 1938 Webern said of the Op. 28 movement:

> Basically it is a variation movement, though *functionally* the individual variations correspond to the components of an *adagio form*, including *main subject, transitional secondary idea,* and *reprise* (coda); thus it is a fusion of the structural principles of a variation movement and an *adagio* form![9]

And, a year later, in an analysis of the work written for the benefit of Erwin Stein, who was writing an article about it for *Tempo*:

The first movement is a *variation movement*; however, the fact that the variations also constitute an *adagio form* is of *primary* significance. That is to say, *it* is the basis of the movement's formal structure, and the variations have come into being *in accordance* with it. Thus, the shaping of an adagio form on the basis of variations.[10]

In this letter, Webern compares his movement to the slow movement of Beethoven's Op. 135, which is a theme and variations but at the same time, and for him more importantly, a three-part song form. The analysis continues, describing the function of each variation in Op. 28/i:

the first variation is a repetition of the theme. How does it come to a repetition of the theme in an adagio? Well, because its first statement, despite its strict periodic form, still has something *introductory* about it ... The 2nd variation represents the transition to the 'second theme' that is presented in the 3rd variation, and finds its repetition in the 4th one ... With the upbeat ... to measure 81 begins the 5th variation, and therewith the reprise of the 'Adagio' ... [The] 6th variation ... represents the *coda* of the piece.

Compare this with descriptions of Op. 30 contained in letters written to Willi Reich on 3 March and 3 May 1941:

Basically my 'overture' is an 'Adagio' form ...[11]

The theme of the variations extends to the first double bar; it is conceived as a period, but has an 'introductory' character. Six variations follow (each to the next double bar). The first presents what might be called the main theme of the overture (Andante form) more fully developed; the second the transition; the third the second theme; the fourth the reprise of the main theme – for it is an andante form! – but in the manner of a development; the fifth, reverting to the manner of the introduction and transition, is followed by a coda, [which constitutes] variation six.[12]

With the exception of a few details, these two letters might be describing the same piece. Both works represent the union of two theoretically antithetical forms: variation, which is reiterative and essentially linear, and ternary form, which is circular with a reprise. In the case of Op. 30, at least, elements of sonata form are present as well. In both instances variations are used as the raw material from which to fashion an 'Adagio form', one of Webern's names for the traditional ABA slow movement form with introduction and coda. Although he describes the two movements in such similar terms, insisting that in both the adagio or andante form – he seems to use the two terms interchangeably[13] – is the 'primary consideration', the most pronounced difference between the two is in the greater aural predominance of that form in Op. 30. The Op. 28 variations are all precisely the same length – in his analysis, Webern goes to considerable pains to explain how this is so – and the aural differences between main and secondary themes are much less pronounced than in Op. 30. The variations of Op. 30 differ greatly in length, ranging from eleven to thirty-five bars, the length apparently determined by the relative importance of the various materials in the adagio form.

Webern's last variation movement is also his most ambitious attempt at synthesis, setting out to unite not only two homophonic structures based on essentially opposed principles, but two very different traditions as well: the complex rhythmic and metric procedures of the Netherlanders and the formal conventions of the nineteenth century. The quotations above provide ample evidence of the first of these intentions; the second was made clear in the same letters:

> Indeed there is again the synthesis: the presentation is 'horizontal' formally, but 'vertical' in all other respects ... it would be fundamental to say that here ... a quite different *style* is set forth ... It doesn't look like a score from pre-Wagnerian times – Beethoven, for instance – nor does it look like Bach. Should one then go back still further? Yes – but then there were no *orchestral* scores![14]

And so, with the fusion of contrasting styles as well as opposing forms, the circle would seem to close. Webern's predilection for synthesis places him directly in the Austro-German tradition that he inherited from Beethoven and Brahms. Examples of the imposition of a closed form onto a set of variations in order to provide an otherwise completely linear and therefore somewhat arbitrary structure with a dramatic contour can be found in the variation movements of the *Eroica* and Ninth Symphonies of Beethoven and the chaconne of Brahms's Fourth, to mention only a few examples.[15] Similarly, one need not look far for the appearance of contrapuntal principles – indeed, canon – in the homophonic forms of Austrian composers from Mozart to Mahler.

Op. 21/ii

Webern took considerable care in his first set of variations to retain all the outward features usually associated with the form. The movement consists of nine sections of equal length, each except for the last in a new tempo, and each consistent within itself and in contrast with its neighbours with respect to orchestration and texture, rhythm, figuration, articulation and the like: in short, a set of classical character variations. In order to remove all doubts, Webern has labelled each section – *Thema, Variations I–VII* and *Coda.*

The familiar format notwithstanding, this is no ordinary set of variations. Most notably, in spite of the title given to the first section, there is no theme.

There is nothing about the material presented in the first eleven bars that remains constant throughout the ensuing eight sections, except for the idea of horizontal symmetry, which has been already extensively explored in the first movement of the same work. As the development of themes was replaced in the earlier movement by the musical exegesis of an abstract principle, the variations in this movement provide successive interpretations of an idea that is not intrinsically musical. Nine different musical realizations of the palindrome achieve various degrees of symmetry in different ways. At the highest level, the row structure of the entire movement forms a palindrome.

The degree of saturation with respect to symmetry observed in this movement has fascinated many people. Although the work has been discussed and analysed on numerous occasions, however,[16] most of those who have scrutinized it closely have reported more or less the same findings. For this reason, reference will not be made below to others' discussions of the movement.[17] Also, the details of construction will not be described here, since this has already been done at some length in the chapters on row topography and canon. The reader is referred to pp. 43ff and 99ff. It should suffice to say that all primary decisions in the work seem to have been taken in the interests of symmetry: both the choice of rows and their disposition are evidence of this. It is intriguing, and gives a glimpse of an important facet of Webern's musical character, that the only aspect of this movement that has not been symmetrically organized is the most audible one: the surface, which includes the succession of timbres, textures, tempos and dynamics that characterize the individual variations.

The nine sections fall into three equal groups with respect to the type and completeness of symmetry exhibited. Both the Theme and Variation I are based on sets of row forms offering the possibility of complete symmetry, but in neither case is this potential realized, in the first instance because the parts do not cross at midpoint, and in the second because the *duces* do not wait for the *comites* to finish before beginning their backward motion. Variation II is symmetrical except for the horn part, which does not reverse. The first three palindromes, therefore, are for one reason or another imperfect or incomplete. The symmetrical possibilities inherent in the first three sections are, however, fully realized in the last three: the reverse of the horn's series in Variation II occurs in Variation VI, thus completing, in theory, the palindrome begun in the earlier variation, and the necessary adjustments have been made to the material of Variation I and the Theme to produce in Variation VII and the Coda the total symmetry that was lacking earlier.

The central three sections of this movement are related through the employment in all three of the P_0–I_9 symmetry used extensively in the first movement. It will be remembered that this particular relationship results in a retrogressive figure that is not precisely a palindrome.[18] True palindromes occur, nevertheless, in Variations III and V, where they result from two concurrent series of P_0–I_9-related rows, the series related to each other as P_0 and R_0. Since the two voices are similar rather than inversionally related (in this row, $P_0 = R_6$), mirror canons do not occur in any of the three central variations. Only Variation IV exhibits the sort of symmetry that characterized the first movement – the restatement of two-note cells in reverse order – without direct retrograde as well. Perhaps it is in order to provide a foil for this central, less perfectly symmetrical variation that the two flanking ones present a series of very audible palindromes (in bars 35, 37, 39, 41 and 43; and in bars 56f., 58f., 60–1, 62–3 and 65f.).

In this first set of twelve-note variations Webern was following a long tradition that would culminate for him in the structurally complex variations of Op. 30: the practice of superimposing some sort of closed form on an otherwise inherently open-ended structure. (The *Goldberg* Variations offer an early solution to this problem; examples in Beethoven have already been mentioned.) These nine variations describe an arch with Variation IV as its axis; but they also constitute a ternary form, which can be defined variously as ABA (with respect to the type of symmetrical realization) and ABC (with a view to the degree of symmetry achieved). The first two of these structures are circular and therefore in a sense diametrically opposed to the linearity of variation form.

This ingeniously constructed symmetrical edifice is to be admired only by those who examine the score and deduce the row structure, however.[19] To the listener is presented the most deceptively simple string of variations, each with its own distinctive instrumentation, rhythms, articulation and character – features that do not recur in symmetrical fashion. The naïve listener will not recognize the horn melody of Variation VI as the retrograde of the same instrument's part in Variation II because of the very different rhythmic and melodic form taken by this line on its return (though he will very likely make some connection between the two variations, since they are the only ones in which the horn plays all the time) and because of the total change in the form taken by the accompanying canon, which is highly pointillistic and uses the whole ensemble in Variation II but is continuous and played entirely by the two clarinets in Variation VI. It is doubtful that he will hear anything that would cause him to relate Variation VII to Variation I. (Here the situation is just the reverse – the material played continuously by the strings in Variation I is dispersed pointillistically throughout the orchestra on its return in Variation VII.) He will hear the numerous small symmetrical figures in Variations III and V but will certainly be unaware of their structural identity, since the third is aggressively pointillistic and the fifth completely static. Probably no section will be recognized as a palindrome until the Coda.

201

Op. 24/iii

The next appearance of variation form is in the third movement of the Op. 24 Concerto for nine instruments. Webern's concerns here are very different from those in Op. 21/ii. The Op. 21 Variations followed an abstract and intensely symmetrical first movement, and their construction was consistent with their position. Their singular features resulted from the application to variation form of the same processes that had been applied to sonata form in the preceding movement. A similar concern for consistency dictates quite a different approach to variations in the movement that completes Op. 24. A certain ambiguity of structure resulting from the fusion of several standard forms was an important characteristic of the first movement of this work (see pp. 179–89); the variations of the third movement represent another expression of this principle of formal syntheseis.

These two final movements – Opp. 21/ii and 24/iii – nevertheless display a certain family resemblance that goes beyond the generic similarity of two sets of variations. Although the Op. 24 movement is both smaller in stature and less sophisticated by far – a sort of country cousin of its illustrious predecessor – it, too, is above everything else an arch form. The symmetry of its overall construction is much less precise than that of Op. 21/ii, but at the same time almost certainly more easily perceived. Somewhat paradoxically, the same intelligibility is also responsible for making this movement recognizable as variations on a theme. Whereas in Op. 21 the most extraordinary structural uniformity was clothed in such a variety of rhythms, textures, tempos and instrumentation that the immediate impression was of continual divergence, the absence of any such monumental structural homogeneity in the Op. 24 movement is compensated for by the obvious aural similarity of four of the five sections. Whereas the Op. 21 movement seems to focus on the diversity inherent in the form, Op. 24 reminds us of its essential tautology.

One very important difference between the two movements is that the Op. 24 variations are, unlike those of Op. 21, based on specifically *musical* ideas: motives. Except for the central section, bars 28–41, the entire movement is clearly generated by the two motives introduced in the first four bars and identified in Table 5.1 as **a** and **b**. These two motives are treated as a unit; that is to say, throughout the variations they always appear together, **a** followed by **b**.

This small and relatively simple movement seems almost to be a trial sketch for the later and much more complex Op. 30 Variations for Orchestra, which is also based on the manipulation of rhythmic motives. The rhythm of the motives that generate Op. 30 mirrors ingeniously the melodic contour of the row. Here in Op. 24, as well, in a much less esoteric way, the nature of the rhythmic material seems to have been dictated by the composition of the row, inasmuch as the motives and their variant forms are

Table 5.1.

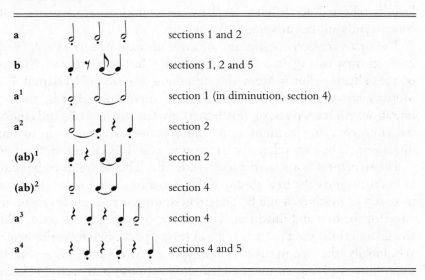

a		sections 1 and 2
b		sections 1, 2 and 5
a¹		section 1 (in diminution, section 4)
a²		section 2
(ab)¹		section 2
(ab)²		section 4
a³		section 4
a⁴		sections 4 and 5

all three notes in length. Table 5.1 lists, in the order of their appearance, the motives that occur in the course of the Op. 24 movement; several of these appear also in diminution and retrograde, as well as in various metric positions. Only the central section (bars 28–41) is not clearly based on this material. This section will be called Variation 2 in the following discussion because that describes its position in the string of variations, but its real purpose is to provide the contrasting central section required by the arch form. In basing the variations on rhythmic units of three notes' length, Webern has ensured that each of these will be some intervallic permutation of every other. Because melodic unity is inevitable, the analysis will not identify melodic relationships unless they seem particularly significant.

The Theme is a canon in two voices on a series of eight motives, **ab a¹bb abb**. All the motives except for the fourth and seventh are imitated melodically in retrograde inversion; all the rhythms are imitated exactly. The motives fall into three groups as indicated above, forming three (overlapping) similar phrases (in bars 1–4, 4–9 and 9–13), all beginning with an **a** motive and ending with **b**. The second and third of these phrases are expanded by the interpolation of an extra **b** and its imitation at the centre. (Since these two central motives are imitated differently from all the others, they, rather than the final ones, seem to be the additions.) No two of the ten **b** motives used in these thirteen bars exhibit the same melodic shape.

The preceding observations hint at the multiplicity of structures implied, even at this level. The three phrases of the Theme relate to each other simultaneously as aba by virtue of the fact that the first and third begin with motive **a** while the second begins with the variant **a¹**, abb because the second and third phrases are extended in a similar fashion, and abc because the **b** motives assume a different shape each time. This ambiguity at the phrase level is reflected at a higher level by the combination of forms sustained concurrently in the movement as a whole.

The first variation consists also of three phrases, in bars 14–19, 19–24 and 24–8, the first two again overlapping slightly. Just as canon was characteristic of the Theme, chords are a distinguishing feature of Variation 1. All **a** motives are presented by successions of three-note chords; there is no imitation. All **b** motives, of which there are ten, are melodic and conform to the same contour (a minor sixth and a major seventh going in opposite directions). They are related to each other as P–I–R–P–I–I–P–R–P–R.

The structural homonym presented by the Theme seems to be reiterated in microcosm by the first phrase of this variation. This phrase alone contains three sets of motives, **a** and **b**. The orchestration defines an aba form: it is the same for the first and third sets. The first set opens with motive **a**, while the second and third use the variant **a**^{2}; in this respect, therefore, the structure is abb. Finally, the two motives of each pair are successively closer together in time, thus implying an open-ended abc relationship as well. In the second phrase of this variation five pairs of motives, **ad**^{20} and **b**, all overlapping, produce a regular pattern that stands in contrast to the metric shifting which has been the rule up to this point. The third phrase contains only two pairs of motives, **a**^{3}–**b** and **(ab)**^{1}–**b**. The **(ab)**^{1} of the second pair is the first appearance of a variant that is not derived in a straightforward way from either of the generating motives but seems instead to demonstrate their kinship. Motive **(ab)**^{1} closely resembles **b**, since both have a trochaic beginning; however, its chordal setting and its position leave no doubt of its identification with the **a** motives, especially the immediately preceding **a**^{3}, which it is very like.

With respect to the pitch content of the chords in this variation, five of the many possibilities of spacing are used, and these are grouped in four ways (Example 5.1). The three phrases begin in the same way (with chords **a**, **b** and **c**), each a semitone lower than the preceding one. The first and third proceed in a similar way (to chords **e**, **d** and **a**); the second is unique. Thus the chordal activity in the variation reinforces two of the patterns used in the Theme, abc and aba. It is upon hearing Variation 3 after the contrasting Variation 2 that the listener first becomes aware of the arch form in which the work is cast, because this variation closely resembles the first. The most immediately apparent similarity is in texture: the single-line melodies and three-note chords that characterized the first variation return here, though the two motives have exchanged roles. The melodic units are variants of the forms of **a** that were used (chordally) in Variation 1 – **a**^{2}**r**; **a**^{4}, derived from the retrograde of **a**; and **(ab)**^{2}, an alternative version of **(ab)**^{1} – and all are imitated. The piano plays pairs of three-note chords throughout, repeating the rhythm ♩ 𝄽 ♩ at regular intervals, except in bars 52 and 53, where two chords:

	(a)	(b)	(c)	(d)	(e)
first heard in:	bar 14	bar 14	bar 15	bar 17	bar 18

groupings:

bars 14–15	a b c (motive a)	PHRASE I
bars 16–17	b a d (motive a2)
bars 18–19	e d a (motive a2)
bars 19–20	a b c (motive ad)	PHRASE II
bars 20–1	b a d (motive ad)
bars 21–2	b a d (motive ad)
bars 22–3	a b c (motive ad)
bars 23–4	e d c (motive ad)
bars 24–5	a b c (motive a3)	PHRASE III
bars 26–7	e d a (motive ab1)

5.1

additional rests occur between groups, and in bars 54 and 55, where one is omitted. While this rhythm can be thought of as either a truncated **a** or an abbreviated **b**, its use here seems more suggestive of **b**, which is otherwise absent altogether. This variation is more complex than its earlier counterpart, recalling both the events of Variation 1 and the canonic technique that characterized the Theme.

Variation 3 displays a certain ambiguity with respect to phrase structure, unlike its earlier counterpart, which divided clearly into three. In this case, the most apparent division would seem to be into two phrases, the first extending from the last note in bar 40 to the second chord in bar 48 and the second from the last note in bar 48 to bar 55. The melodic material consists of six **a** motives and their immediate imitations. The rhythm of the first two motives, a^2 in bars 41 and 42 (horn–trombone) and a^4 in bars 45 and 46 (trumpet–horn), is imitated exactly, with only a metric shift; the resulting four motives are evenly spaced and each is followed by a companion (**b**) variant. These four **a**–(**b**) pairs are heard as the first phrase (bars 42–8).

Both the third and fourth motives of the *dux*, a^1dr in bars 48 and 49 (viola) and a^1d in bars 50 and 51 (flute), are immediately imitated in retrograde (by violin and clarinet), the statement and its imitation overlapping one note. Similar telescoping occurs with the imitations of $(ab)^2$ in bars 52 and 53 and a^1dr in bar 54. The first of these is a metrically shifted direct replication like those in the first phrase; the second is in retrograde in the manner of the second phrase.

A case could be made for the existence of three phrases in this variation, in bars 41–8, 48–52 and 52–5. Aside from the obvious desirability of relating the phrase structure to that of the first variation, a rationale can be found in the distribution of imitative techniques described above. Of six **a** motives in the *dux*, the first two are imitated directly and the next two in retrograde; the last two seem to represent a summing up. This is a logical division but results in second and third phrases that are only half the length of the first. A further imbalance results from the distribution of the eight pairs of chords (**b**), four of which occur in bars 41–8, where one follows each statement of an **a** motive as well as each imitation, and four in bars 48–55, where chords come only after a statement and its imitation.

Completing the arch structure, the fourth variation is most like the Theme. It is completely static, consisting of only four trichords played over and over, sometimes as chords and sometimes melodically. The chords are arranged in three symmetrical series with respect to pitch content (bars 58–60, 63–5 and 68–70). There are here, again, three phrases – bars 56–60, 61–5 and 66–8 – and in content they are very like those of the Theme, each opening with an **a** motive, imitated and followed by **b**. All the **a**s are melodic, the **b**s chordal. The only version of **a** used is **a⁴**. Both first and second phrases are extended by the addition of a second pair of motives, **a⁴** (not imitated) and **b**. After the third phrase, two more **b**s appear, elided, and followed by a single chord, the same that opened this variation.

This final Variation stands in a peculiar sort of retrograde relationship with the Theme. The second and third phrases of the Theme were extended; the first was not. Here, if we consider the last two bars a coda, the first and second phrases are extended while the third is not.[21] Thus the abb structure of the Theme is answered with an aab in Variation 4, in line with the overall symmetry of the movement.

I have not discussed the middle section of this movement (bars 28–41) with the other variations because it does not emanate from the motives that generate the rest of the piece. Rows are elided here, and two- rather than three-note groups are emphasized. Major seventh dyads predominate in the piano part, and the other instruments play melodic fragments in which notes that are not adjacent in the row are frequently heard in succession. The rhythmic motives that are essential elements of the rest of this movement are abandoned here. It is clearly the purpose of this section to provide a contrast with the music on either side.

While there can be little doubt that this movement represents an arch form, it might be argued that it is not in variation form at all. The instrumentation (successive sections use nine, eight, seven, eight and nine instruments), the tempos (in an ABABA pattern) and even the relative lengths of sections (13, 14 + , 13 + , 14 + and 13 bars) support the arch form and, while not arguing against variation form, do nothing to further that interpretation. The most glaring impediment to variation form is, of course, the section in bars 28–41 so summarily dealt with in the preceding paragraph. However, in spite of this difficulty, the division of the Op. 24 movement into five nearly equal sections, four of which are based on clearly recognizable variants of the same material, with different but consistent treatment in each section, means that the movement is *perceived* as a theme and variations. This must surely be an important consideration.

This perception brings up a second question. The Op. 24 movement is, indeed, heard as a *theme* and variations, with the first thirteen bars functioning as the theme. This, however, is accurate in a formal sense only. The material on which the movement is based is stated in the first four bars and is subjected to variation immediately. This is true also in the Op. 30 Variations, where the germinal material is presented within the first two and a half bars, though the section that Webern has designated as Theme extends for twenty. This, of course, is in line with Schoenberg's notion of developing variation, that sort of growth and change that begins immediately and by means of which a basic idea eventually becomes a theme. Schoenberg describes the sentence, which he considers a 'higher form of construction than the period',[22] as the statement of an idea and its immediate development and variation; in his view, therefore, the traditional distinction between exposition and development (or between theme and variation) does not exist.

While the remarkable symmetrical relationships in the first movement of Op. 24 have inspired many analyses, little has been written about the less spectacular third movement.[23]

Op. 27/iii

The second of the three works that Webern entitled Variations is the Variations for Piano, Op. 27. Although numerous attempts have been made to explain this work as three sets of variations, or as a single three-movement set of variations,[24] these analyses lack credibility; it is only the third movement that seems to merit the title given the whole. This movement is unique among Webern's variation forms. Opp. 24/iii, 28/i and 30 all have themes of some sort, and even in the revolutionary Op. 21/ii the palindrome takes on this role. Only in Op. 27/iii does the opening section present nothing that is subsequently varied. There are six sections of equal length – eleven bars – in this movement, and some unique musical feature is used throughout each. Since this is exactly what we expect from a theme and variations, we are easily led to recognize this as a movement in that form.

The first section, which I will call Variation 1, since there is no real justification for calling it the Theme, comprises three phrases, in the form of three untransposed rows, P_0, I_0 and R_0. The first two rows are presented in a series of six cells separated by rests, those of the second phrase identical rhythmically to those of the first. The third phrase is continuous until the end, where the final note is delayed by a rest. The relationships and cross-references within these three row statements are numerous.[25] With the exception of the final note of R_0, in bar 12, and the two right–hand notes in bar 10, which have exchanged values, the durations (not to be confused with the rhythm) of the third phrase are those of the first (and therefore the second) in retrograde.[26] The internal structure of Variation 1 can be represented as aab. Each of the cells in these eleven bars has its own dynamic indication; there is a change after six notes of the third phrase, which perhaps justifies distinguishing two cells of six notes each here, even in the absence of an articulating rest. There are eight dynamic markings in Variation 1, which form a palindrome: *p–f–p–f–f–p–f–p*.

The texture thickens in Variation 2, where the tenuto and legato articulation and prevailing long note values of Variation 1 give way to quicker motion, predominantly staccato. Grace notes appear here for the first time, and dyads and triads occur frequently. The former are invariably major sevenths; when a third note is added, it is a major or minor third above. In keeping with the increased activity and generally higher tessitura of this variation, the dynamic range is expanded in both directions: the variation begins *pianissimo*, and the climax is *fortissimo*. The inner structure of this variation seems to bear scant resemblance to that of the one preceding. The only thing they can be said to have in common is a confusing multiplicity of sometimes contradictory relationships between constituent

5.2   Op. 27/iii

parts. The bulk of the variation consists of four units of material, shown in Example 5.2. The third appearance is truncated through the omission of the first segment, and the fourth is further shortened and compressed. On either side of this series of repetitions (in a sense a set of variations in miniature) are a related prelude and postlude. The materials shown in Example 5.3 are contained in both.

5.3   Op. 27/iii

Variation 3 is introduced in bar 23 by one of three characteristic surface features, a pair of staccato crotchets on the same pitch. This is an arresting figure in a movement in which notes have previously not been repeated. The second feature unique to this variation follows almost immediately, in bar 24: a tetrad consisting of a tritone, a perfect fourth and a minor third. This appears five times, at regular intervals, in the course of the eleven bars, always accompanied by a ritard. The almost continual tempo fluctuation resulting from these five *rits.* and the subsequent *a tempos* is the third feature that makes its first appearance in this variation. Unlike either of the previous variations, Variation 3 divides structurally into two halves, though the nature of the central six bars is such that to describe the whole as three sections is not inaccurate. The material of the first two bars, in bars 23–5, returns at a different pitch level and somewhat varied, in bars 30–2, followed by a one-bar closing that very closely resembles the events of bars 28–9. The bars in between, 25–30, contain a slightly inexact but nevertheless clearly recognizable rhythmic palindrome with the two pairs of repeated crotchets in bar 27 as the axis. This binary structure represents the third different internal arrangement seen in the movement: thus far we have encountered a bar-form in Variation 1, a highly segmented progressive form in Variation 2, and a binary form employing a palindrome in Variation 3. This succession of events suggests a new interpretation of the title: perhaps these are variations on internal structure. The range of both dynamics and pitches narrows slightly in Variation 3. Like the tempo, the dynamics are more flexible in this variation, incorporating more crescendos and decrescendos than in the earlier sections.

The fluidity that began in Variation 3 continues to the end of Variation 4. Here the tempo fluctuation results from four *molto rit....tempo* markings and, at the end of the variation, an *accelerando*. As in the preceding variation, these *molto rits* always coincide with the appearance of a tetrad, in this case consisting of a tritone, a perfect fourth and a major seventh (or, in bar 42, a perfect fourth, a tritone and a minor ninth, which is another expression of the same combination). The most characteristic feature of this variation is a melodic unit of two quavers rising or falling by at least a minor sixth, played legato. There are eighteen of these figures in the eleven bars. This variation is clearly divided into two phrases with a closing section of a bar and a half, a binary structure very like that of the previous variation. The two phrases are nearly identical palindromes: the second is a semitone lower and the hands have exchanged parts. When the two phrases are compared, the only rhythmic deviation is the omission of a crotchet rest between the last two notes in bar 38, and again in the corresponding place in bar 41; the only dynamic differences are the *fortes* that begin and end the second phrase. The closing material begins with the last four quavers of the second phrase and is a variation of the first half of the first phrase – that is to say, it recalls the first half of the palindrome. The dynamic range is expanded once again in this variation, extending from *pianissimo* to *fortissimo*. There are no graduated changes.

Variation 5 is, with a few brief exceptions, *fortissimo* throughout and presents a distinct contrast in character to the preceding two Variations, resembling, rather, the energetic activity and brusque character of Variation 2. For the most part, notes are heard one at a time here; more than two are never played simultaneously. The unique feature of this section is a syncopation that produces four beats in a 3/2 bar followed by a notated acceleration. The constant tempo fluctuations that were a feature of Variations 3 and 4 are gone; only one ritard occurs here, marking the end of the first phrase. As in Variation 2, the internal structure of Variation 5, while not complex, is somewhat complicated by cross-references and insertions. The contents are probably best described as two phrases plus a long closing extension roughly the same length as the phrase it extends. The content of the phrases is similar, each consisting of three very distinct segments, separated by rests. The first of these segments uses the sesquitertia figure quoted above; the last two move in a regular crotchet rhythm, with all the notes on afterbeats. The central segment begins both times with a heavily accented quaver on f♯⁴. The final segment of the first phrase is given in Example 5.4. The second phrase ends slightly differently (Example 5.5). The extension begins in bar 53 and consists of two slightly truncated variations of the final figure from the first phrase followed by the parallel figure from the second phrase transposed up a minor third, and, finally, three notes that seem to be a still further shortened version of the first figure (Example 5.6). The highest notes in the piece occur in this variation.

The cellular construction of Variation 1 returns in Variation 6. The rhythm is absolutely regular; notes and chords sound only on afterbeats, and, with a single exception (in bar 64), at a distance of two or four crotchets,

5.4   Op. 27/iii

5.5   Op. 27/iii

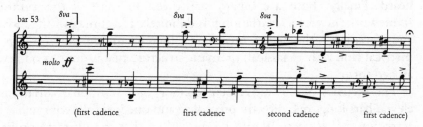

(first cadence   first cadence   second cadence   first cadence)

5.6   Op. 27/iii

resulting in a perceived 5/2 metre until the last four bars. There are more chords in this variation than in any other; triads operate here as single notes did in Variation 1. Two are used: the tritone plus perfect fourth of Variations 3 and 4, and a minor sixth plus minor third that has not appeared elsewhere.

The last variation refers to the first also in its use of imperfect palindromes. The rows are those used in Variation 1, with the addition of I_1 and RI_1. These are arranged into two phrases with identical rhythm, plus a third that is unique – exactly the situation in Variation 1 (aab). The pitches of both first and second phrases form palindromes (though the manner in which P_0 and R_0 are elided in bar 58 makes the centre of this one inexact); the durations do not. The dynamic range is narrow and the level very low, moving between *piano* and *pianissimo*, and dropping to *pianississimo* in the final bar. This is the only place in the movement where this extreme marking is found. Excluding the final bar, there are eight dynamic indications here, as there were in Variation 1, and, as there, they are arranged symmetrically: *pp–p–p–pp–pp–p–p–pp*.

The Op. 27 movement presents an unusual arch, since an even number of sections provides no axis on which to turn. Nevertheless, there can be no

211

doubt about the symmetrical relationships. The preceding description has shown that Variations 1 and 6 are similar in numerous ways, including the rows used, the prevailing note values, the cellular construction, the number and relationship of phrases and the arrangement of dynamic changes. Both Variations 2 and 5 adopt a brisk style with periods in which the motion proceeds at a steady pace quicker than that used in the outer sections, and both dynamic and tonal range are extended. Although the internal structure of the two variations is not precisely the same, both consist of a directed progression effected through the succession of several short segments, each representing a burst of energy. The central variations, 3 and 4, are likewise similar, representing above all a character that stands in contrast to the surrounding Variations 2 and 5 (*tempo, zart*) and is maintained through continual fluctuations (the rubato effect is characteristic). In addition, each of these Variations is laced with a figure that is unique (neither immediate repetition nor the quaver is used anywhere else in the movement) and easily heard. Finally, both are binary structures. In spite of this symmetrical framework, however, Variation 5 is definitely the climax of the movement and Variation 6 the dénouement/coda, thereby giving the work an asymmetrical (and rather classical) dramatic structure that is quite at odds with its arched form.

The sketches of this movement contain two additional variations, each eleven bars long, one directly preceding and one just following what is now Variation 5.[27] Robert Wason has remarked that the ultimate omission of two variations occupying these positions is curious in view of the symmetry exhibited by the work as it now stands.[28] On the other hand, the possibility that they were omitted precisely in order to create the symmetry comes to mind. With the two additional variations, which were not symmetrically placed (being numbers five and seven of eight), the work as a whole would not have displayed this quality. The relationships would have been 1 with 8, 2 with 6 and 3 with 4. The omitted sections do not show a marked specific resemblance either to each other or to any of the other variations.

This leads us to Willi Reich's notes about Op. 27, already cited in connection with the first movement. His outline of the third movement (as related by Döhl), given below,[29] is problematic. He subdivides the movement into the obvious sections, except that he lumps the last two together; he does not suggest how these come to comprise eight variations. If the two variations that were omitted in the end were included there would be eight sections, but in that case the rest of the outline would make no sense: there would be eighty-eight bars, and his analysis accounts for only the sixty-six bars in the published version. Aside from the numerical discrepancies – concerning numbers of variations and numbers of bars – the sonata outline seems contrived. In practice, the section in bars 33–43 appear to grow out of and to be of a piece with that in bars 23–33; it is not particularly developmental. Nor is the section immediately following (bars 45–55) reminiscent of the opening – surely a necessary attribute of a reprise:

> Third movement: Small sonata form (at the same time Variations 5–12).
> Main theme, bars 1–12.
> Transition, bars 12 (second half) – 23.
> Contrasting theme and codetta, bars 23 (last three crotchets) – 33.
> Development, bar 33 (last two quavers) – 42 (first two quavers).
> (Two symmetrical models, with axes at the downbeat of bar 36 and between the second and third quavers in bar 40.)
> Foreshortened reprise, bars 45–66.
>
> Row structure: begins with the retrograde starting on E♭, from bar 5 the retrograde inversion beginning on E♭.

Although there is clearly no way of knowing exactly how these peculiar notes came about, I suggest a possibility. That Webern discussed his work with Reich seems certain, and I do not question Reich's sincerity in offering notes made during or after these exchanges as Webern's own explanations. The confusion in the present set, however, makes it quite impossible to accept them as such. Nevertheless, several of the terms used suggest that the analysis did originate with Webern. Reich reports Webern's having said the following things:

(1)   that the entire piece is a 'Sonatina';

(2)   that the three movements are, respectively,
        an Andante in ABA form *and* a theme and two variations,
        a scherzo in binary form *and* two more variations, and
        a small sonata form *and* eight additional variations;

(3)   that the movements begin, respectively, with
        a prime row beginning on E,
        a prime row beginning on G♯, and
        a retrograde row beginning on E♭.

(4)   (Internal divisions are then given for all movements.)

These statements can be evaluated in the following way:

(1)   The entire piece *is* a small sonata.

(2)   The movements are, respectively,
        an ABA sonata form,
        a scherzo in binary form, and
        six variations.

(Essentially, the first and third movements are structurally the reverse of those outlined by Reich.)
The third movement originally contained eight variations.

(3)   The movements begin, respectively, with
        a retrograde row beginning on E,
        a retrograde row beginning on G♯, and
        a prime row beginning on E♭.

(4)   Reich's internal divisions are correct; the sections thus defined do not, however, relate to each other in the ways described. (Sections in the first and second movements exhibit dissimilar internal structures and therefore do not relate to each other as variations; those in the third movement do not function as elements of a sonata.)

Two layers of information emerge. On the one hand, the identification of the whole as a small sonata ('Sonatine') is accurate, and the reference to eight variations in the last movement is a true description of the piece as it existed in the sketchbook. It would seem almost certain, therefore, that these two statements originated with Webern himself in reference to the piece at some stage during its composition. I suspect that the remainder of the information was filled in by Reich upon his own examination of the score following its publication – after two variations had been excised from the last movement and the order of movements had been altered – in the light of what Webern had told him about the piece. In particular, his reference to eight variations in the third movement can only be explained as information given him by Webern that he, Reich, for that reason felt compelled to include, even though it was completely at odds with the rest of his own analysis of the later version. The errors in analysis are of the sort that would be made by someone who was working from the printed score without knowledge of the changes that had occurred.

The identification of the first row of the first movement as the untransposed prime indicates that Reich must have supposed this movement always to have been the first. If, therefore, Webern had told him, after one movement had been written, that he had completed a variation movement (as he told the Humpliks), Reich would naturally have assumed later that this was the movement to which he had referred. If Webern had also told him, later, that the piece as a whole was a 'Sonatine', then he would have felt obliged to find a sonata structure in one of the remaining movements, and no one could make a case for the second movement's following this design. Having decided where it was, he then had to subdivide it into sections corresponding to those of a sonata, difficult though that task must have been. As to the curious reference to eight variations, one can imagine Webern's mention of the content of the *third* movement at some point after he had decided upon the order but before the abridgement had taken place.

Webern's reference to variations in a movement that Reich had to suppose was also a sonata would have led naturally to his assignment of an *alter ego* to each of the movements; the designation of each as a set of variations is obviously the analysis that was current in the Vienna circle. Thus it would seem to me that a few remarks made by Webern were filled out later by his student in what he no doubt supposed to be an entirely faithful fashion. The result has confused and complicated the world's view of an already difficult work.

Although Webern was never to write a set of variations on a theme of the conventional type – a small, self-contained structure of several bars' length – he would also never write another set on no theme at all as he had in Op. 27/iii. The remaining two variation movements were to be extremely complex and impressive experiments in the consolidation of structures. In both these works, the first movement of the Op. 28 Quartet and the Op. 30 Variations for Orchestra, he abandons the arch as a superimposed structure in favour of a more complex form close to sonata form, which he referred to variously as 'Andante-form' and 'Adagio form'.

Op. 28/i

The similarity of purpose to be observed in Webern's descriptions of the variation movement of the Op. 28 Quartet and the Variations for Orchestra was remarked upon earlier. While both movements comprise a theme and six variations, the specific contribution of each of these seven sections to the superimposed closed form is not the same in the two works. Op. 30 has an introduction while Op. 28 does not; both have codas. The second theme is repeated in Op. 28 and not in Op. 30. The introduction and transition are given a reprise in Op. 30; in Op. 28 only the main theme is recalled. In both cases Webern remarks on the periodicity of the main theme.

Webern outlined the structure of the Op. 28 movement in the analysis written for Erwin Stein in 1939:[30]

```
Theme       – main subject
Variation 1 – repetition of main subject
Variation 2 – transition
Variation 3 – secondary idea
Variation 4 – repetition of secondary idea
Variation 5 – reprise of main theme
Variation 6 – coda
```

He further indicated that the movement is a ternary form, with the variations grouped in the following way: A (Theme and 1), B (2, 3 and 4), A (5 and 6).

The row structure does not reinforce the form as Webern has described it.

215

This is surprising in view of the structural importance that is usually ascribed to rows and transpositions, though the idea of tonal metaphor was largely abandoned in Op. 27 as well. The Theme uses a chain of four rows connected by tetrachordal elision – P_6–P_2–P_{10}–P_6 – plus a closing row, P_4, which is elided with P_6 by only two notes. The same circular series is used in Variation 1, beginning this time with P_2. Here this is the *comes* of a canon in which the *dux* goes through RI rows at the same transpositions. (Since $P = RI$, this latter is also a series of primes, but I prefer to use the identification that shows the transpositional identity of pairs of rows.)

The transition uses a different set of rows, with no elision; Variation 3 uses still another set, also not elided. However, Variation 4, which Webern describes as a repetition of the second theme introduced in Variation 3, returns to the tetrachordal elision of the Theme and first variation, and the *comes* uses, moreover, the same series of rows that appeared in the Theme. The *dux* plays retrograde inversions at the corresponding transpositional levels – just the reverse of the *dux–comes* relationship in Variation 1. The following variation uses only the two-note elision that occurred at the end of the Theme; the three rows of the *dux* are all rows that appeared there. Again in the coda, the rows are those that were found in the Theme and Variation 1 and are connected through tetrachordal elision. Thus the row structure is ABA, but with Variations 2 and 3 as the B section, and Variations 4, 5 and 6 constituting an expanded return of the Theme and Variation 1 – not the ABA outlined by Webern.

The structure as he describes it is supported most noticeably by the tempo and the use of mutes. The introduction (Theme) is played at ♯. = 66; the main theme (Variation 1) and its reprise (Variation 5) alternate between ♩ = 66 and ♩ = 84; the transition (Variation 2) continues at ♩ = 84; the second theme and its repetition (Variations 3 and 4) are played more slowly, at ♩ = 56; the coda (Variation 6) begins at the tempo of the first theme (♩ = 66) and finishes at the tempo of the second (♩ = 56). Mutes are used only for Variations 3 and 4 (the second theme and its repetition) and Variation 6 (the coda). This structure is defined in many other, more subtle, ways as well.

The Theme and all the variations in this movement are about sixteen bars long. Webern goes to great lengths in his analysis to explain some beginnings as upbeats and to point out that an extension at the end of the third variation is compensated for by a shortening of the fourth.[31] It was clearly very important to him that all sections should be equal in length, as had been the case in all his previous movements in variation form, in order that the customary exterior of this form should be maintained. The differences between sections, however, are more subtle here than in his previous essays in this form. There are no marked changes of range, dynamics, rhythm, texture or character here – only the already mentioned addition of mutes in Variations 3 and 4, and rather moderate tempo changes between Variations 2

216

and 3, and again between Variations 4 and 5. (The two tempos used within Variation 1 are more disparate than the basic tempos of the 'main subject' and the 'secondary idea'.) The equal length of all the sections is not, as it is in the classical form, the inevitable result of successive variations of the same sixteen-bar period (as is the case, for example, in Beethoven's variations of Diabelli's theme). The initial period is not varied in its entirety; the raw material for these variations consists of a few short rhythmic motives, and, as in the earlier Op. 24/iii and the Op. 30 that is to follow shortly, variation begins immediately.

Three rhythmic figures are introduced in bars 1–16: a pair of notes of equal value, hereafter referred to as motive **a**; three notes of equal value, referred to as **b** (I shall further distinguish between the form used here, in which the second and third notes are slurred together, and the form used later, in which all three notes are separately articulated, by calling them **b1** and **b2** respectively); and a pair of notes in trochaic rhythm, motive **c**. Webern says of the variations that they are 'purely *canonic* in nature'. Unlike the variations, in which two row chains function as *dux* and *comes*, the Theme comprises a single series of rows. Even so, motives are in nearly all cases paired so that the second of each set is perceived as an imitation of the first, in some cases direct, but more often in augmentation, diminution or retrograde.

The Theme is, as Webern points out, periodic, the antecedent extending to the end of bar 8 and the consequent to bar 16. The latter, although one bar shorter, is an expanded version of the former in terms of content. Each is in two sections – the internal divisions are at the end of bar 6 and in the middle of bar 12. Segment Ia consists of five motives – **a** and its augmentation, **b** and its diminution, and **c**. Segment Ib contains only motive **a** in diminution – staccato and legato statements, both imitated. Segment IIa comprises seven motives – the diminution of **c** and its imitation, a staccato diminution of **a** imitated directly, a double diminution of the retrograde of **b1** imitated in retrograde, and the diminution of **c**. Except for the first two **c** motives, the content of this segment is parallel to the corresponding segment of the first phrase, in diminution. Also like its earlier counterpart, segment IIb contains only motive **a**: a staccato statement in the original values and an ordinary statement, both answered in legato and diminution, and a final statement at the original speed but with tenuto crotchets and rests replacing the minims. To summarize the content of these two phrases, the first portion of each (Ia, IIa) contains all three of the basic motives, while the second (Ib, IIb) is built entirely from motive **a**. In addition, Ia, IIa and IIb all end with a single motive that is not immediately imitated – motive **c** at the centre of each phrase, and **a** at the end. These unattached final motives perform a cadential function. Register is fixed in the Theme, although not elsewhere in the movement. In addition, Webern turns again here to the change-ringing technique that I observed in the first movement of Op. 20 and alluded to elsewhere. The first violin plays only two notes – a^1 and $g\sharp^3$ – in the first fifteen bars; the second violin plays only c^2, $d\flat^1$ and $b\flat$; the viola g, $f\sharp^2$, f^2 and e^1; and the cello B, $e\flat^1$ and d^2.

The first variation, which Webern describes as 'a repetition of the theme', is, like the Theme, periodic, with a division at the end of bar 25. It opens with a new rhythmic motive, **d**, for which various derivations could be suggested: it closely resembles all three of the original generating motives, while having a metric character that is different from all of them (Example 5.7). The first phrase resembles the first phrase of the Theme insofar as it is in

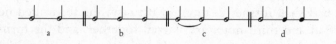

5.7

two segments, the second (in bars 22–5) using only motive **a**. Two new ideas are introduced in bars 16–21, the new motive **d** and the articulated version of **b–b2**, here in a syncopated (retrograde) form in which crotchets are preceded by crotchet rests. There are, in addition to these two figures, two statements of **b1**, in diminution and double diminution. Everything is imitated.

The second phrase also divides into two parts, between bars 30 and 31. Segment IIa contains four motives, as did the parallel segment of phrase I. The first two of these (and their imitations) are variants of motive **b2** produced through value replacement. In the first case, the second and third notes are late. (If this motive were reversed, all three notes would be articulated at the right time – see Example 5.8.) The second is further

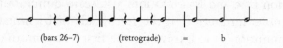

(bars 26–7)   (retrograde)   =   b

5.8

removed from the original. Only the second note appears late in this version; therefore it does not produce **b2**, either forward or in retrograde, and with it a new element – the dotted rhythm – is introduced. Because of this motive's subsequent importance, it will be called **b3** (Example 5.9). The remaining two motives are an augmentation of **d** and a diminution of **b2**. Segment IIb

b3

5.9

218

is unlike either Ib of this variation or Ib or IIb of the Theme. It contains no motive **a**, but rather a diminution of the retrograde of **b1** and a version of **d** without the slur, thus ending the variation with the motive that opened it.

The first two changes of tempo in this variation outline the phrase structure: segment Ia is in the original *Mäßig* tempo, Ib is *fließender*, and IIa is *wieder mäßig*. The position of the *wieder fließender*, however, is difficult to explain. It occurs in the middle of the third motive of phrase II, at a place where motives overlap continually. The *wieder fließender* would occur most logically at bar 31.

Variation 2, 'the transition', which carries on in the *fließender* tempo, looks quite different from the first two sections of the movement. Motives **a** and **b** are used exclusively, in six-note groups exploiting their hemiola relationship. Each voice of the canon contains four twelve-note phrases, each of these, with the exception of the last phrase of the *comes*, consisting of six crotchets followed by six minims or their equivalents, or the reverse of this, with the first note of the second group sounded at the same time as the last note of the first. The order in the four phrases of the *dux* is crotchets/minims, minims/crotchets, minims/crotchets, crotchets/minims. The *comes* duplicates this until the final phrase, which is sped up. The first phrase looks like this:

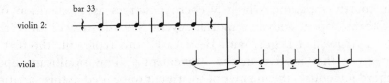

5.10

Because all the crotchets are played by the same instrument and all the minims by another, this phrase can be interpreted as the diminution of either a pair of **b2** motives or three **a** motives, followed either by the retrograde of **b1** and **b1**, both in diminution, or by three **as** – legato, articulated and legato. This ambiguity serves to point out the close relationship between motives **a** and **b**.

Although the second phrase is disposed among the instruments in a similar manner, its content is less ambiguous at the outset. It starts with three definite **a** motives, two legato and one articulated, but continues with six articulated crotchets in the ambiguous fashion of the first phrase. The manner of instrumentation changes with the third and fourth phrases. Here the rows are divided so that only three consecutive notes are played by one instrument; clearly, only **b** motives are intended. In addition to their instrumental isolation, these three-note groups are eventually telescoped, making their separation even more apparent. To add to this process of precipitation as the end of the variation approaches, the *comes* dispenses with the minim segment of the final phrase, replacing it with a continuation of the pattern of overlapping crotchet groups that opened this phrase.

The introduction of a lyrical theme in Variation 3 is obvious. Mutes are added, the tempo slows and the only one of the rhythmic motives to be used is the one that was absent from the preceding transition, the lilting trochaic. There are three phrases rather than two or four, each consisting of one row and its imitation, marked by a *poco rit.* and a rapid decrease in volume at the end. Rows are divided into tetrachords in this variation. Each is played by one instrument as a pair of **c** motives. Until the final phrase, where this variation speeds up in a manner similar to the previous one, each tetrachord presents one **c** motive in original values and one in diminution. In the final phrase, the second and third tetrachords of both voices use only the diminution. The *comes* follows the *dux* at the distance of seven crotchets in this variation. The rhythmic cells of the first phrase (o–r–r)[32] are imitated exactly; those of the second are varied (o–r–r answers r–o–r). In the imitation of the third phrase (r–d–d), the individual **c** motives of the second and third tetrachords (already in diminution) are telescoped so that the first note of each is struck at the same time as the last note of the previous one, thereby causing a breakdown of the four-note cell structure that has been sustained throughout this variation and hastening its close.

The fourth variation, which Webern describes as a repetition of the second theme, opens with an important event. The first row of this variation is RI_6, the row that begins with B–A–C–H: this represents the first clear statement of that motive in the movement.[33] This significant opening tetrachord introduces the manner of treatment to be used in this variation, as well. The third and fourth variations taken together seem to explore at another level the sort of hemiola relationship that was the subject of the transition (Variation 2). Each voice in both of these variations plays a series of nine tetrachords, the first note of each sounding with the last note of the previous one. In Variation 3 these nine tetrachords are produced by a series of three rows, one after the other, and, as a result, the variation consists of three phrases. The nine tetrachords of Variation 4, however, are produced by a series of four rows with tetrachords elided, and as a result this variation consists of two phrases rather than three. In this way Variation 4 provides a reinterpretation of the structure used in Variation 3, illustrating an alternative, essentially binary, means of generating what was previously understood to be a ternary format.

This variation also represents the union of two related techniques that have been applied only separately up to this moment. Although a circular series of rows elided through common outer tetrachords occurred in both the Theme and Variation 1, rows were actually divided into tetrachords through instrumental and rhythmic isolation only in Variation 3. The somewhat tardy marriage of these two obvious partners makes this Variation a particularly important one. It is a natural consummation; as a result, this variation seems to represent a completion of, or a climax to, what has preceded it (more the role of a reprise than a repetition of the contrasting theme, one might think). It is fitting that the BACH quotation should help to celebrate this event.

The *dux* of this variation contains only three rhythmic patterns (Example 5.11). The first of these is used for all the outer tetrachords; that is to say, all

5.11

the odd–numbered tetrachords of the nine in the series conform to this pattern. The second pattern is used for the first three central tetrachords (tetrachords 2, 4 and 6 of the variation); the third pattern occurs only once, as the central tetrachord of the final row, or the eighth in the series of nine. The *comes* imitates at a distance of only three crotchets, using variant forms on three occasions – for tetrachords 3, 6 and 9 – thereby recalling in a subtle way the ternary phrase structure of Variation 3.

Because none of the generating motives presented at the outset of this movement is four notes long, none is ready-made for use with tetrachords. Both **a** and **c** are two notes long, however, and these provide the material for the tetrachordal variations, numbers 3 and 4. As the tetrachords of Variation 3 used pairs of **c** motives exclusively, those of Variation 4 present pairs of **a** motives, staccato and legato, in both minims (including the variant ♩ ♩ ♪) and crotchets.

The mutes come off and the tempo of the opening returns for Variation 5, which Webern tells us is the reprise of the main theme. It is a greatly varied reprise. Each voice presents only three rows. All those in the *dux* – P_6, P_4 and P_2 – were used in the Theme. The tetrachordal elision that was an important feature of the Theme and Variation 1 do not occur here, however; in this order these rows are elided by only two notes at each juncture. The row structure of this variation seems, then, to be an extension of what occurred at the end of the Theme, where P_6 was followed by P_4, breaking the pattern of tetrachordal elision that had been maintained up to that point. The rhythmic motives, on the other hand, recall the opening, not the close, of the Theme. The first three, which overlap as they did at the beginning of the movement, are the same motives heard there, as well – **a** (though in diminution), the augmentation of **a**, and **b**. Following these is **b3**, which was peculiar to Variation 1, and its imitation. This latter is the beginning of a second phrase in which all the motives of the first phrase reappear in reverse order; the direction reverses again for the third phrase. Each voice consists of

221

three phrases, **aba**, where **b** is the retrograde of **a**. The *fließender* tempo from Variation 1 returns for the third phrase but is not accompanied by a recall of the *fließender* material.

This variation recalls Variation 1 – directly, in its use of two- and three-note motives, and by omission, through the absence of the tetrachords that were the outstanding feature of Variations 3 and 4. The main-theme variations show more diversity – of rhythm, tempo and motives – than the central ones; this is an important distinction. (And, it might be added, one that expresses the traditional difference between first and second themes.) The canon continues at the distance of three crotchets through Variations 5 and 6, thus reinforcing the affinity of Variations 4, 5 and 6 already established by the row structure.

The last variation, which acts as a coda, is in three phrases, the first two in the tempo of the main theme and the third in the tempo of the secondary theme. The rows are connected through tetrachordal elision. Trichords are isolated melodically in the first two phrases, which are motivically identical, each presenting a motive **d** followed by two motives **b2**, all using the sesquialtera augmentation of which Webern seems to have been increasingly fond (Example 5.12). The use of three-note groups and of the motives **b** and

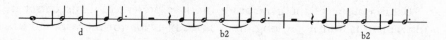

5.12

d in these two phrases recalls the main theme. The third phrase presents five motives **a** in each voice, in sesquialtera augmentation, thus recalling the closing phrase segments of the main theme as well as the secondary theme as it was expressed in Variation 4, where only motive **a** was used. Thus the coda sums up the important features of both themes, adding a new twist of its own in the form of the 2:3 augmentation.

And so the stage is set for Webern's most ambitious set of variations, the Variations for Orchestra, Op. 30.

Op. 30

The Variations for Orchestra is Webern's last instrumental essay in the synthesis of traditional structures. It is unquestionably, as its title indicates, concerned with variation, and in describing it to Willi Reich Webern labelled successive sections 'Theme', 'Variation 1', and so on. He seems to have been more interested, however, in the procedure than in the structure – in variation rather than variations. And, as always, in synthesis. The raw material of this work is very like that of Opp. 24/iii and 28/i: that is to say, the work evolves from two very short rhythmic motives stated in the first two and a half bars. The motives of Op. 30 are, however, more complex than those in the earlier works, offering the opportunity for greater diversity in variation.

As in all Webern's movements in this form, a closed structure is superimposed on the Theme and Variations. For the first time, the proportions of the several sections are dictated by the closed form. As a result individual variations are of very unequal length, ranging from eleven bars containing the equivalent of 38 quavers in Variation 5 to thirty-five bars containing the equivalent of 135 crotchets plus 11 quavers in Variation 6. This irregularity immediately sets Op. 30 apart from all the other variation movements and means that the closed form takes precedence aurally in a way that has not happened before.

Webern refers to the structure of this work at different times as an 'Adagio form' and an 'Andante-form'. To Hildegard Jone he wrote:

> this theme with its six variations finally produces, from the *formal* point of view, an edifice equivalent to that of an 'Adagio', but in *character* – in content – my piece isn't that at all – only formally. – So even though I have given the piece the title 'Variations', yet these for their part are fused into a new unit (in the sense of a different form).[34]

To Willi Reich on 3 March 1941:

> My 'overture' is basically an 'adagio'-form but the recapitulation of the first subject appears in the form of a development, so this element is also present. Beethoven's 'Prometheus' and Brahms' 'Tragic' are other overtures in adagio-forms, not sonata form![35]

His letter of 3 May 1941, quoted earlier (p. 198), goes on to outline the movement in the following way:

Theme   – introductory exposition of main theme
Variation 1 – complete unfolding of main theme
Variation 2 – transition
Variation 3 – statement of secondary theme
Variation 4 – developmental reprise of main theme
Variation 5 – reprise of introduction and transition
Variation 6 – coda

Webern's insistence on the terms 'Adagio' and 'Andante' as formal designations makes it clear that he considered the structure to be ternary, and there is no possibility of misinterpreting his remark concerning sonata form. However, as he also points out, the character is not that of a slow inner movement; what he neglects to mention is that the development that occurs in Variation 4 is not customary in this form, while it is perhaps the most distinctive feature of the sonata. His insistence that the two overtures cited as precedents are not in sonata form is curious. His assertion, through association, that his own work is not a sonata is more reasonable, since it lacks an independent development and, perhaps more important, a return of the second theme.

As in Opp. 24 and 28, that section Webern describes as the Theme is itself a continuous series of variations. Webern described the situation to Hildegard Jone in the letter of 26 May 1941:

> Imagine this: 6 notes are given . . . and what follows (in the whole length of this piece lasting about 20 minutes) is nothing other than this shape over and over again!!! Naturally in continual 'Metamorphosis' . . . First this *shape* becomes the 'theme' and then there follow six variations of this theme. But the 'theme' itself consists, as I said, of nothing but variations (metamorphoses of this first shape). Then as a *unit* it becomes the point of departure for fresh variations.[36]

And to Willi Reich on 3 May 1941:

> Now, all that occurs in the piece comes from one of the two ideas which are stated in the first and second bars (double bass and oboe)! However it can be reduced even further, as the second figure (*Gestalt*) (oboe) is already a retrograde in itself: the second two notes are the retrograde (*Krebs*) of the first two, but augmented rhythmically. These are followed in the trombone by another statement of the first figure (double bass), but in diminution! And in retrograde (*Krebs*) as far as both motives (*Motive*) and intervals are concerned.[37]

Melodically, the second two notes of the second figure are an inverted retrograde (*Krebsumkehrung*) of the first two, not a retrograde (*Krebs*) as Webern says; rhythmically, however, they do represent a retrograde, with the alteration he mentions. It seems clear, therefore, that Webern's 'Gestalt' is primarily rhythmic in nature. When he says of the third figure, 'Und im Krebs der Motive und Intervalle', 'Motive' can refer only to rhythmic disposition. These rhythmic motives are, of course, exactly analogous to the

5.13

shape of the row (Example 5.13). Succeeding statements of the rhythmic motives do not, however, consistently use the same segments of the row. This can be seen as early as the second bar of the piece, where the second voice enters with the first four notes of the row, outlining the second rhythmic motive. This means that the melodic/intervallic make-up of the generating motives is not a distinguishing feature; the significant element is the rhythm. I shall refer to the two motives that generate Op. 30 as **a** and **b**.

Value replacement is an important technique in this work; Table 5.2 shows the forms of motives **a** and **b** produced in the course of the piece.

Table 5.2.

	rhythmic notation	location
motive **a**		bars 5–6, vlc bars 139–40, vn 1
		bars 139–40, ob/bcl; trp/cl
		bars 140–1, fl/trp
		bars 132–3, cel/vlc bars 179–80, ww/vn 2; trp/vlc
		bars 130–1, vn 2 bars 144–5, cl; vn 2/vlc bars 179–80, trb/hn; vla/vn 1
		bars 13–14, hp/vla
		bars 144–5, vla
		bars 113–14, vn 2
		bars 131–2, hn/cel
		bars 115–16, hp/vlc
		bars 35–8, bass/timp/vlc
		bars 27–30, cl/bcl
		bars 51–4, vns/cl
motive **b**		bars 17–18, ob
		bars 141–2, cel/trb
		bar 166, ob
		bars 165–6, vn 1
		bars 107–9, hp
		bars 150–2, ob
		bars 150–2, hp/fl bars 175–7, trp
		bars 78–81, fl

Manipulation of replaced values occasionally leads to a further degree of variation, as, for example, in bars 40–2. The following form of the retrograde of motive **b** occurs in bars 32–4 of Variation 1.

5.14

The exact retrograde of this figure occurs in bars 40–2.

5.15

This is obviously a derivative of the forward-going **b** motive; however, it is neither the original form of that motive nor a variant that could be produced directly from it through value replacement. It can only result from a three-stage operation involving retrogression, followed by value replacement, and then a second retrogression. The extension of this principle allows variants of this sort without the prior appearance of the generative form. The following is an example.

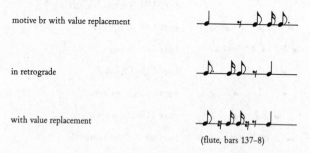

motive br with value replacement

in retrograde

with value replacement

(flute, bars 137–8)

5.16

In addition to the usual rhythmic techniques of augmentation, diminution and retrograde, each of the two generating motives is subjected to a unique type of inversion. In the case of motive **a**, the long and short values exchange positions. This occurs in Variations 4 and 5.

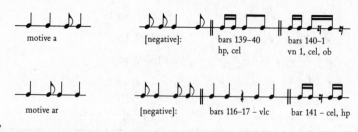

motive a   [negative]:   bars 139–40   bars 140–1
                                      hp, cel   vn 1, cel, ob

motive ar   [negative]:   bars 116–17 – vlc   bar 141 – cel, hp

5.17

This sort of inversion, combined with value replacement, leads to the following **a** variant in the first violin in bars 36–8.

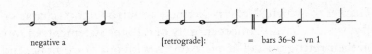

negative a   [retrograde]:   = bars 36–8 – vn 1

5.18

Since motive **b** consists of too great a variety of note values to lend itself to this process, it undergoes an inversion of its constituents whereby the halves of the motive remain intact but are rearranged. Besides the simple prime and retrograde, six other combinations are possible; Webern makes use of all of them.

Table 5.3.

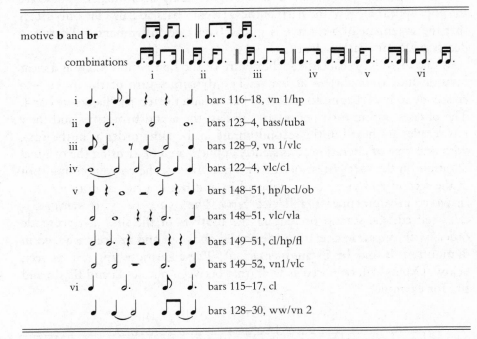

Two important derivative motives make an appearance in Variation 3. These, which I shall identify as **c** and **d**, are derived from **b** and **a** respectively and are used to produce the second theme. They are not subjected to inversion.

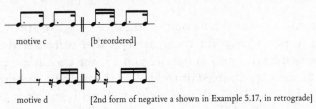

motive c   [b reordered]

motive d   [2nd form of negative a shown in Example 5.17, in retrograde]

5.19

227

The Theme, to which Webern ascribes 'an introductory character', lasts for twenty bars. It consists almost entirely of canonic statements of motives **a** and **b** and their retrogrades. The piece opens with one voice alone, and up to bar 9 the texture alternates between one and two voices. This pattern is reversed in bars 10–20, with four-note chords punctuating those sections where only one voice occurs.

This exposition of the main theme is periodic, as Webern has told us, with internal cadences at bars 8–9 and bars 13–14 marking the end of the first period and of the first phrase of the second. These cadences are similarly constructed: both are marked by a *rit.* in the *langsamer* tempo, followed by a *subito lebhaft* at the outset of the ensuing section; and both contain statements of **a** divided between the harp and one of the string instruments. (These are the only appearances of the harp in these twenty bars and also the only times that the statement of a motive is spread over two instruments.) There is a decrescendo into each cadence.

While there is no cadence at the centre of the first period, there is a clear division into two phrases at bar 4. The dynamics turn at this point – a crescendo to bar 2 begins to retreat in bar 6 – and the tempo changes at bar 4. The phrases within each period are similar; the **a** and **b** motives and their retrogrades are heard in the second phrase in the same order as in the first, with one type of alteration consistently applied: an **a** or **ar** using the original durations in the first phrase occurs in diminution at the corresponding spot in the second and vice versa, while all **b**s and **br**s in original durations are answered in augmentation and vice versa. The two periods are symmetrically related, the second presenting the motives of the first in retrograde order, with the same alterations described above (**a** and **ar** are answered in diminution, **b** and **br** in augmentation). These relationships can be seen below. Others will be noted as well (that between phrases Ia and IIa, Ib and IIb, for example):

Ia			Ib			IIa			IIb		
P_0 a	b	ard	I_0 ad	ba	ar	R_0 ard	b	a	RI_0 ar	ba	ad
RI_0	b		ad		ar	I_0 ard	chord	a	P_0 chord	ba	chord

bar 1   4   10   15

Four-note chords occur at three points in these twenty bars, providing an accompaniment in phrase two for those motives that were stated alone in phrase one. The first two times, in bars 12 and 15, the chords are played *sf* and *sff* and instruments are doubled or trebled on the melody, presumably to balance this added background, though neither chord is struck at the same time as a melody note or held for any length of time. The third occurrence of chords (there are two in this case) is at the end of the variation, after all the business is finished. These are played very quietly, with mutes. As they are identical in pitch to the group of chords that open Variation 1, they clearly act as a bridge. It will be seen as the analysis progresses that a similar preparation occurs at the end of each Variation, in which some material that is characteristic of the following one is introduced.

Variation 1, which Webern describes as the 'main theme ... more fully developed', is thirty-five bars long. Its texture – melody and accompaniment – stands in contrast to the linear polyphony of the Theme. Greatly augmented forms of **a** and **b** are accompanied by repeated crotchet chords. The melody notes are occasionally reinforced by doubling, as they were at the two points where chords occurred in the Theme. All the chords in this variation are verticalized tetrachords. Four retrograde rows (transpositions 0, 10, 8 and 6) produce twelve appearances of four discrete tetrads during the course of the variation.

This variation is in nine sections in the form of an arch, as illustrated below. The first, last and all the even-numbered sections in between are very similar. Except for the final section, each of these is three bars long and contains a single statement of **a**, **ar**, **b** or **br**. The last section is extended for two bars through the inclusion of the imitation of its motive in retrograde. This imitation, the only example in any of these six melodic sections, is this variation's preparation for the next one, in which canonic imitation is an important element. Sections 1 and 2, and 8 and 9, provide a frame for this variation. Among them all four forms of **a** and **b** are presented, with sections 6, 8 and 9 stating the retrograde forms of the motives in sections 4, 2 and 1 respectively.

Ruhig	Ruhig	Lebhaft	Ruhig	Lebhaft	Ruhig	Lebhaft	Ruhig	Ruhig
pp	*pp*	*f*	*pp*	*f*	*pp*	*f*	*pp*	*pp*
ar	b	a–ar	br	a–ar	b*	a–ar	br	a
				a–ar		a–ar		ar

bars   21–3   24–6   27–31   32–4   35–9   40–2   43–7   48–50   51–5

* This **b** is the exact rhythmic retrograde of the **br** in bars 32–4 (see Examples 5.14 and 15).

The remaining three, odd-numbered, sections are more complex and very similar to each other (Table 5.4). Section 3 contains a six-note melody, obtained by overlapping a motive **a** with its retrograde in diminution. Sections 5 and 7 both contain two such figures stated concurrently. The nine sections of this variation present a consistent alternation of the two generating motives: odd-numbered sections deal with **a**, even-numbered sections with **b**.

Variation 2, the transition, is eighteen bars long and in character quite different again from anything heard so far. There are no melodies here and the texture is consistently very thick. The entire variation proceeds in two layers of four-note chords: eight notes sometimes sound at once when these

Table 5.4.

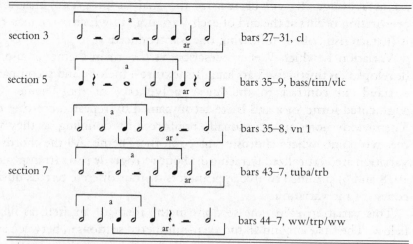

section 3   bars 27–31, cl

section 5   bars 35–9, bass/tim/vlc

                                                                    bars 35–8, vn 1

section 7   bars 43–7, tuba/trb

                                                                     bars 44–7, ww/trp/ww

* See Example 5.18

layers coincide. As in Variation 1, each of these chords is a verticalized tetrachord, but here the construction is much tighter. Only two conformations occur – reading upwards, minor third, minor sixth, minor third; and minor third, perfect fourth, minor third.

In spite of the misleading density of texture, which does not suggest a linear conception, this variation is a rhythmic canon in two voices, each proceeding in verticalized tetrachords up to bar 72. Each voice of the canon plays four statements of **a**, all augmentations based on the sesquialtera proportion (2:3). Only the second and third are exact, since the value of the third note is doubled in the others. In both voices the first two motives are elided, the last two are not. The two central motives of the *comes* are similarly joined, while those of the *dux* are separated by a rest; the result is that the *dux* becomes the *comes* at bar 63. This corresponds with a palindrome in the row structure at this point. The canon proceeds at the distance of a quaver throughout.[38] Both the rhythm as notated and the perceived rhythm are reproduced in Example 5.20. The last two bars of Variation 2 introduce, in canon, motive **c** in preparation for Variation 3.

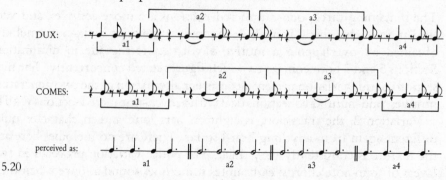

5.20

Webern's description of Variation 3 as 'secondary theme' leads us to expect a diversion at this point, and our expectations are not disappointed. The variation is thirty-six bars long – almost exactly the same length as Variation 1, in which the first theme was presented 'fully developed'. The texture offers an immediate contrast to the preceding transition – there are only two voices throughout, and no chords – and the structure is unlike that of any of the variations encountered so far. It is through-composed in four roughly symmetrical sections, each with a **c** motive in both voices at its centre. The traditional lyricism of the second theme, which implies a certain relaxation and lessening of tension relative to the dramatic opening theme, is expressed here at the structural level: whereas the first theme was complex and tightly structured, the second proceeds rather freely.

Variation 4, the 'reprise of the main theme ... in the manner of a development', is twenty-five bars long and, as Webern indicates, a complex version of Variation 1. It forms an arch exactly parallel to that of the earlier variation:

Ruhig	Ruhig	[Ruhig]	Ruhig	Lebhaft	[Lebhaft]	Lebhaft	[Lebhaft]	Ruhig
pp	*[f p f]*	*f–p*	*pp*	*f–p*	*[ff]*	*ff*	*[ff]*	*ff–pp*
★one	one	★o.s.	one	o.s.	one	o.s.	one	one

110–13 113–15 115–19 118–21 121–5 125–8 126–30 130–2 131–4
★ 'one' = a single statement; 'o.s.' = many overlapping motives.

Again, as in Variation 1, the four sections at either end of the arch – 1, 2, 8 and 9 – are similar to inner sections 4 and 6. In this case, however, each of these contains, instead of one of the four basic versions of the **a** and **b** motives (**a**, **ar**, **b** and **br**), a complete set of all four. These are for the most part unaltered and not elided.

Sections 3, 5 and 7, which were the most complex portions of Variation 1, are even more so here, presenting dense masses of elided double statements and palindromes constructed in the same manner as their Variation 1 progenitors (Table 5.5).

The similarity of corresponding sections of the arch is not so clear here as it was in Variation 1. This variation is continuous, and the sections overlap in nearly all cases. For example, section 6 comprises four statements – in cello, high woodwind, viola and violin II – the last ending only on the first note of bar 128, even though section 7 has already begun in violin I on the final beat of bar 126.

The transition, Variation 2, is played at a quick tempo throughout and is considerably shorter than the variations surrounding it, which function as thematic expositions. In consequence, Variation 5, which Webern describes as 'repeating the manner of the introduction and transition', is the shortest of

The instrumental music

Table 5.5.

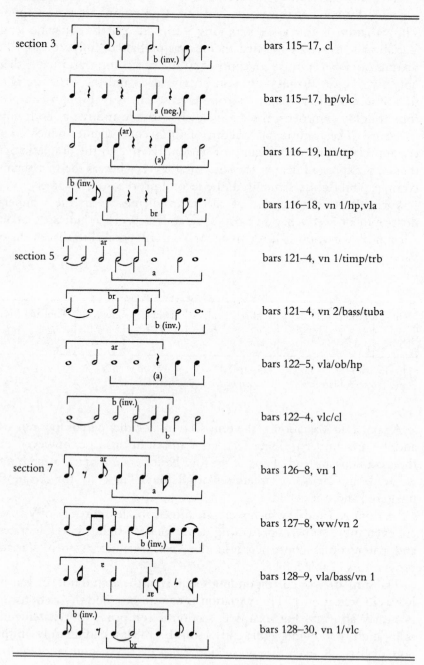

section 3	bars 115–17, cl
	bars 115–17, hp/vlc
	bars 116–19, hn/trp
	bars 116–18, vn 1/hp,vla
section 5	bars 121–4, vn 1/timp/trb
	bars 121–4, vn 2/bass/tuba
	bars 122–5, vla/ob/hp
	bars 122–4, vlc/cl
section 7	bars 126–8, vn 1
	bars 127–8, ww/vn 2
	bars 128–9, vla/bass/vn 1
	bars 128–30, vn 1/vlc

the set. It is only eleven bars long and is played relatively quickly. The first five bars are similar to the opening of the piece (the introduction), containing four statements parallel to those in bars 1–3, as shown below.

232

bars 0–1	2	2	3
a: bass *p cresc. dim. pp* Lebhaft($\flat$ = 160) A B♭ D♭ C	**b:** oboe *f* ♪=112 B D E♭ G♭	**b:** vla *f* *fp* ♪=112 B♭ B D C♯	**ar:** trombone *f cresc. dim. ....* ♪=160 F E G A♭
ar: viola *p–sf–p dim.* Lebhaft($\flat$ = 160) D E♭ G♭ F	**b:** flute *sf dim. p dim.* ♪=112 E G G♯ B	**b:** celesta, strings *p* *pp* ♪=112 [four-note chords]	**a:** violin I *f dim. p* ♪=112 B♭ A C C♯

bars 135–6	137–8	137–8	139

The similarities between parallel statements become less marked as the variation proceeds. By the fourth statement, only the note values and the row segment used remain the same as in the corresponding statement in bar 3. This gradual leavetaking of reminiscences of the introduction allows an easy entry into transition material beginning with the statement in bar 139.

The remaining seven bars of the variation (bars 139–45) have at their centre (in bar 142) the same chord exactly that formed the axis of the palindrome in Variation 2 (in bar 63). Two separate rows and two row chains proceed simultaneously throughout these seven bars, producing in bars 139–41 a flurry of **a** and **ar** motives in diminution so close together that a chord is heard on every semiquaver of the bar, recalling the textural density and quick succession of chords in the second variation. All the chords have, as well, the same conformation as those in the earlier variation, though they are not at the same levels of transposition. There are only two chord types – minor third, minor sixth, minor third; and minor third, perfect fourth, minor third. Following the central chord, the celesta, harp and strings play in four-note chords on every semiquaver of the bar a transposition of the same progression of chords that appeared at the end of Variation 2 (in bars 70–1). Motives **b** and **d** are stated once each – by the celesta and trumpet and by the first violin – and the variation ends with a four-part canon on **a** and **ar**, the **ar** being similar to that which opened the second half of the introduction in bars 10–11; here the pitches are in exact retrograde two octaves higher. The two chains in bars 139–45 – I_{10}–I_3–I_8 and R_{10}–R_3–R_8 – progress in rhythmic canon, with two exceptions. In bar 141 the harp should have ♫ instead of ♪♫ in order to preserve the rhythmic imitation; and a four-note chord containing B, C, A and A♭ has been excised from bar 142.[39]

Variation 6, the coda, is longer than any of the others. In Webern's brief description of the work he gives some indication as to the content of the preceding sections, but no clues whatever about the nature of the coda. This variation seems to be yet another version of Variation 1, representing not an even more complex rendering than occurred in Variation 4 but a completely new interpretation resulting from the application of a different set of rules. In fact, this variation is very much in the style of Op. 31. The late deletion of the chord from bar 142 is perhaps the first sign of the Op. 31 style, in which the *Ausfall* figures very importantly. The dissimilar rhythmic variation of several voices that proceed in canon is the other most significant technique used in the Cantata. Variation 6 of Op. 30 exemplifies this method of operation, which is an extension of value replacement in which each note remains within the correct time slot but may be moved to a slightly earlier or later position where it neither begins nor ends at precisely the expected time.

The variation falls into nine sections parallel to those of Variation 1. Sections 2, 4, 6, 8 and 9 are easily perceived as more complex versions of the sections occupying the same positions in the earlier variation. Sections 2, 4, 6 and 9 are four-voice canons on the motives that occupied corresponding positions there – **b**, **br** and **bri** in sections 2, 4 and 6, and **a** in section 9. In section 8 the trumpet and first violin present **b** and **br** respectively to a chordal accompaniment.[40]

In the earlier variation sections 1, 3, 5 and 7 were devoted to elided pairs of **a** and **ar** motives. Here they seem also to deal with **a** and **ar**, but in asymmetrically distorted forms. The first two bars (section 1) contain only two four-part chords played by the brasses, an immediate aural reminder of Variation 1. These chords stand in the durational relationship 5:3, thereby announcing the rule of irregular ratios that seem to govern the variation. In section 3, two of the four voices present – P_{10}/P_8 and R_2/R_4 – play in rhythmic unison what is obviously the most important melodic line. Only the length of the initial note in these two voices differs: one begins before the other, but they join at the second note. When read backwards, this melody presents a recognizable elision of **a** and **ar**, with the long notes of **a** standing in a 5:2 relationship to the short note, instead of the original 2:1 (Example 5.21). The remaining two voices play similarly distorted versions of **ar**, not

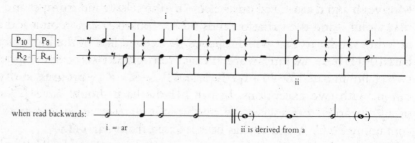

i = ar   ii is derived from a

5.21

234

apparently elided with another **a** motive, but followed by two notes that are in canon with the last two notes of the other voices, both rhythmically and melodically (Example 5.22).

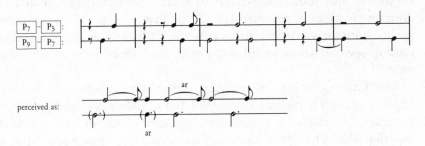

perceived as:

5.22

Section 5 opens with two more tetrads played by the brass, one note of each anticipating the other three by one beat. The four voices continue as in Example 5.23. As in section 3, these lines are asymmetrical interpretations of **a** motives. Also as in the earlier section, two voices are doubled rhythmically on a single – presumably the most important – part, while the other two accompany in canonic style. Again the last two notes of the four voices are in canon. Section 7 is very complex and unlike the rest of this variation. It is

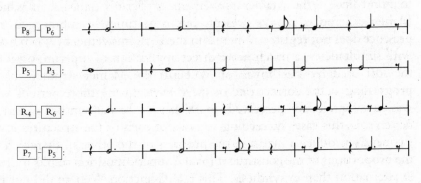

5.23

reminiscent of Variation 2: here again canonic voices are represented by successions of chords rather than by single lines. The section is framed by two tetrads played by the brass instruments; in between, the strings play series of triads while the woodwind and bass supply each of these with a fourth note, in the form of sustained notes that serve several chords in turn.[41] The chords of P_0 and R_{11} present the following rhythmic proportions: 5:2:6:8:7:8:4:5:? and 5:2:6:8:6:12:7:?.[42] The first four rhythmic units are identical in these two voices and seem to produce a distorted **ar**. The last notes do not correspond and, as in sections 3 and 5, are difficult to explain. The pedal notes produced in the woodwind and bass by P_{11} (P_4) and P_8(P_1)

235

are presented in the rhythms 10:6:11:? and 5:2:4:?, both of which can be recognized easily as asymmetrical versions of **ar**. In fact this kind of variation represents a transition from the technique used in Op. 29/ii and iii, where the rhythm of individual voices has been altered through the augmentation and diminution of only selected notes,[43] to that of Op. 31, where notes are pushed both forwards and backwards and at times even played together, thus causing several voices to fill out similar periods of time in very different ways.[44]

The final variation, in applying different techniques to the materials exposed in the Theme and Variation 1 and already developed in Variation 4, becomes, in reality, a second development. And, in spite of Webern's assertion that Op. 30 is not a sonata form, the appearance of a second development section occupying the position of coda is a phenomenon associated with that form. Specifically, it is a feature of many of the middle-period and later sonata movements of Beethoven, a model to which Webern returns again and again. Perhaps in addition a parallel of sorts could be drawn between Op. 30 – Webern's last big orchestral work – and the finale of Beethoven's last work for orchestra, which also represents the solution of the variation problem through the superimposition of closed forms. Both of these works are problematic, in part because of the occasional disappearance of the variations. An apparently unrelated comparison comes to mind here – the Mahler movement of Berio's *Sinfonia*, in which the Mahler scherzo is always present, but is at times so submerged that its presence does not register. Whereas in the Berio movement (which has to do with simultaneity, a much more direct application of superimposition than the sort used by Beethoven or Webern) the Mahler structure has been progressing at the correct rate of speed even during those periods when it was not consciously perceived, in Webern's formal syntheses (and Beethoven's, in this case) succeeding sections of each of the structures involved frequently produce a hiatus in the progress of the other(s), thereby altering the proportions of the constituent forms. Superimposition results more often in alternation than in synthesis. This is a distinction Webern did not make.

6

The movements in rondo and ternary forms: Opp. 20/i, 22/ii, 24/ii, 28/ii and 28/iii

Webern turned to rondo form on only two occasions in his twelve-note music, both during the earlier years. This may be unexpected, in view of his professed admiration for and affinity with the early and middle works of Beethoven, where this form occurs frequently. Both Webern's rondos are seven-part forms: ABA C ABA, Schoenberg's 'large Rondo form'.[1] Although this is a classical format, neither is a classical rondo. The first, in Op. 20, is a slow movement, not surprisingly calling to mind Beethoven's occasional use of rondo form for a central movement in a slow tempo.[2] (Although it now stands first, the Op. 20 rondo was originally intended as the second of three projected movements.) In keeping with the rather conventional nature of Op. 20 generally, the structural outlines of the rondo are easily identified in the score; even though the refrain is much varied upon its returns, each structural unit is distinguished by characteristic rhythmic figures, tempo and articulation. I think that the contrast of these features between refrain and episodes makes the form relatively clear aurally, as well, though I must admit some impressive opposition to this view. Stravinsky is quoted as saying of this movement: 'the music is marvelously interesting, but no one could recognize it as a rondo'.[3] Roger Smalley's concurrence with this judgement has already been noted on pp. 155–6. The second rondo, in Op. 22, is longer and more diverse, and much less clear structurally, in the score as well as to the ear. It is here that one is made aware of the difficulty inherent in composing a form that depends on repetition in a style where it is practically forbidden.

Since the original twelve-note composers earnestly avoided literal repetition, the only way left for them to implement the returns that are the basis of rondo form was the use of the same set of rows at the places where the refrain was called for. Considering that the twelve-note technique came about ostensibly as a means of ensuring that no tonal preference was established, one would suppose that if the system were used successfully the listener should not be aware of the return of a particular set of rows or of a certain level of transposition. It would seem therefore that the basic premise of the technique and the essential requirements of this form are incompatible, the real success of either resulting in, or perhaps depending upon, the failure of the other.

The type of rondo chosen by Webern – ABA C ABA – is also a ternary form. This interpretation is emphasized in both the Op. 20 and the Op. 22 movements. After Op. 22 there are no more rondos, but ABA structures continue to appear, in the form of simple ternary. Webern wrote only three three-movement works: Opp. 24, 27 and 28. ABA ternary is used for the central movement of both Op. 24 and Op. 28. The second movement of Op. 27 is in binary form. Ternary form is used also in the third movement of Op. 28, and we have already seen that the requirements of this form are an important consideration in the structure of the first movement of that work as well. This use of an ABA superstructure in a first-movement form is not new; it can be seen in the row structure of the opening movements of both Op. 21 and Op. 22 – sonata forms, in which the row content is identical in exposition and reprise, eschewing the alterations customary in the second theme group.

The central movement of Op. 24, which is the first simple ternary form, follows the same dramatic pattern as the first movement of Op. 21, though everything is on a smaller scale and the complexities of canon and palindrome are absent. In both movements the character of the reprise is considerably altered; although the same series of rows and transpositions is presented both times, the rather erratic musical setting of the reprise stands in contrast to the regularity characteristic of the exposition. While the row structure is clearly ABA, in both cases the musical format must be represented as ABC. Op. 28/ii begins and ends at a somewhat faster tempo than Op. 24/ii and increases to double this speed for the middle section. In his analysis of Op. 28, Webern refers to this movement at one point as a scherzo and later as a three-part song form.[4] He goes on to describe it in terms of a scherzo and trio, but its tempo and its position in the work would incline one more towards considering it a three-part song form. It is followed by a complex scherzo in a fast tempo. The central movement of Op. 24 is the only ternary form that is not canonic: canon is used very little in Op. 24, and not at all in this movement. In contrast, the third movement of Op. 28 not only begins and ends with complex canons but contains a fugue as well. The synthesis of horizontal and vertical in this latter movement makes it a far cry from the simplicity of the classical ABA ternary.

Op. 20/i

Although Webern's first twelve-note movement in rondo form follows a classical format – ABA C ABA – and adheres closely to the external requirements of the form, maintaining the traditional structure in the same way that sonata is preserved in the second movement of the same work, it is not a typical rondo. A departure from the classical model is seen in the return of B, which is traditionally in the tonic key after its initial appearance in the dominant but is in this case at the same tonal level on both occasions. This recurrence of the entire ABA unit in the same 'key' suggests a ternary form, and the proportions reinforce this interpretation.

Table 6.1.

Introduction		3 bars
ABA section	[A]	18 bars
A		6½ bars
B		5½ bars
A		6 bars
C section	[B]	19 bars
Introduction		3 bars
ABA section	[A]	20 bars
A		7½ bars
B		5½ bars
A		7 bars
Coda		2 bars

T_4 functions as the 'tonic' of this movement. Both the introduction (including its reappearance just before the return of the ABA section) and the coda use R_4 and P_4 exclusively. The A sections begin with I_4, use R_4, and end with I_2 and RI_8, both of which hold two tetrachords in common with I_4. No T_4s are used in the B and C sections. Although horizontal symmetries are not important elsewhere in the movement, the introduction is in the form of a palindrome, both at its initial appearance and when it returns later as a retransition at the end of the C section, though the music is different on the two occasions. Grace notes are present both times, making the palindromes more apparent visually than aurally. (Since a grace note always precedes, and never succeeds, the principal note,[5] a reversal results in the emphasis the second time of the note that was passed over quickly the first time, and vice versa.)

Each of the four A sections – in bars 4–10, 16–21, 44–51 and 57–63 – uses the same series of rows. These are expressed as a melody with an accompaniment consisting of two-note figures covering a wide range. Structurally the melody is a single phrase, extended. All appearances begin with an expansive melodic gesture; although the details of this figure are varied upon each recurrence, it is nevertheless always clearly recognizable (Example 6.1). The musical material bears less resemblance to the original with each

239

6.1   Opus 20/i

subsequent statement. The figures in bars 16–18 are similar to those in bars 4–6, and throughout the ensuing section the instrumental lines from the earlier appearance remain intact, with only slight rhythmic changes and a complete re-registration, mostly but not entirely the result of the application of invertible counterpoint. In bars 16–22 the parts are shuffled so that each instrument plays the same series of notes that another played earlier: the original violin, viola and cello parts are now played by cello, violin and viola respectively.

Both the rhythm and the integrity of figures (though they are sometimes inverted) remain unchanged or very nearly so in the two later returns of A, though the original lines do not remain intact as in bars 16–21. A pair of semiquavers on the same pitch, either preceded or followed by a third note on another pitch, or as part of a longer group, is a figure unique to and characteristic of the A sections, occurring in increasing profusion upon each return. In the third and fourth appearances of A these pairs of semiquavers are used alone as well as in their previous contexts. One other characteristic figure appearing nearly exclusively in the A sections is a pair of quavers or semiquavers outlining a major seventh or a minor ninth.

The B sections seem to be not so much the diversions one expects in a rondo as interludes. In spite of continual motion, progress is suspended, both rhythmically and tonally, rather in the manner of certain pieces by Debussy. The basic rhythmic unit is the demisemiquaver, as opposed to the semiquavers of the A sections, and, as pairs of repeated semiquavers are characteristic there, pairs of repeated demisemiquavers are a constantly recurring feature here. The two most used figures are ♪♬ and ♬♪ . The disposition of pitches in these sections was described in Chapter 2. It represents another example of the change-ringing technique already discussed. Although both B sections go through a series of five rows, the notes of each are distributed among the instruments in such a way that each instrument plays the same few notes over and over throughout the section. In bars 11–15 the violin plays only g♯, a^1 and b♭^{2}, the viola b^1, f♯^{1}, g^2, d^2 and e♭^{1}, and the cello c♯^{1}, c, E and f. (The viola has, inexplicably, two B♭s – b♭ and b♭^{2} – in bars 11 and 15, and the cello a single g♯, in bar 13.) When the B section returns in bars 51–6 the instruments have exchanged series: the violin plays the pitch classes previously given to the viola (including the two extra B♭s – both b♭ in this case – in bars 52–3); the viola takes over those played on the earlier occasion by the cello, including the g♯, which was played once by the cello in the earlier section but was really part of the violin's collection, and an extra g, in bar 55; and the cello is reduced to the only two notes remaining from the violin's set, A and b♭^{1}. Towards the end of this second B section the motion is almost entirely in demisemiquavers.

The central section of this movement (bars 22–40) consists of two statements of a seven-row series. The violin plays continuous melody throughout the first statement, which takes nine bars and divides into three equal phrases, related as antecedent–antecedent–consequent. The other two instruments accompany, mainly with two-note figures spanning large intervals and therefore reminiscent of the accompaniment in the A sections.

The second statement begins with a free inversion of the melody of the first phrase of the first statement, played by the cello and covering four bars instead of three. From this point on, the melody returns to the violin. The two remaining three-bar phrases are not similar to their counterparts in the first statement except that in both cases the rhythmic motion increases steadily. The third phrase of the second period (bars 38–40, with the upbeat) brings back the repeated demisemiquavers previously associated with the B section.

This rondo, simple as it is, hints at several structural intentions. While its tonal structure and proportions imply a ternary form, the ternary sub-division of the outer sections themselves, as well as the essential similarity of the central section to the extreme outer sections, argue against this interpretation. (If the movement is represented as ABA C ABA, then B, rather than A, offers the real contrast to C.) And this, in turn, brings to mind the sonata rondo, an interpretation which is not supported by the tonal identity of the two B sections. Thus the formal argument is seen to be in this case a circular one. As we have seen on so many occasions already, none of the implied explanations quite suffices, yet there is obviously truth in all of them.

Op. 22/ii

Webern's second essay in rondo form, the second movement of the Op. 22 Quartet, was apparently begun – conceived, at any rate – at practically the same moment the Op. 21 Symphony was finished. This is particularly interesting because these two works represent opposites in his handling of the twelve-note technique. The Symphony stands with the Op. 28 String Quartet as the most tightly organized and thoroughly controlled of all his music, while the rondo joins *Das Augenlicht* as the most amorphous. Op. 22/ii would seem to be a reaction to the meticulous order of the just-finished Op. 21: extreme has given rise to extreme.

The style of Op. 22 – particularly the rondo, which was written first – and Op. 26 would seem to indicate that in this period of Webern's compositional life he was preoccupied with applying the twelve-note technique with a certain degree of abandon; yet these works are separated by five years, during which three other works were written, one of them the Op. 24 Concerto, which is very much concerned with symmetries and permutational relationships. The exact nature of the canonic and topographical freedoms observed in Opp. 22 and 26 is discussed elsewhere.[6] The looseness in the application of the twelve-note technique to linear textures and the accompanying move away from the horizontal symmetries and tightly organized patterns that characterize most of Webern's music are evidence of an attitude that makes an impact on the structure of these works as well, causing them to be elusive and difficult to define.

Thus this second rondo presents a considerable challenge to the analyst.

The difficulties one has in sorting out and relating the events in this long and rather diffuse piece are made even greater by two references to its structure purportedly made by Webern himself. One is an outline of the projected events of the movement drafted in his sketchbook as the initial step in its composition;[7] the other is Willi Reich's assertion in the Postscript to *Path to the New Music* that Webern had remarked on the 'exact analogy' of his Op. 22 rondo to the scherzo of the second Op. 14 piano sonata of Beethoven.[8] While the existence of these two statements should make the task of analysis easier, they in fact have the opposite effect. Not only does Webern's schematic outline not agree with the order of events in the Beethoven scherzo he is supposed to have cited as a model, but the Op. 22 rondo itself does not seem to follow either pattern.

The outline is couched in the sort of picturesque terms that frequently appear in Webern's preliminary sketches:[9]

Main themes	Secondary themes	
I		Coolness of early spring (Anninger, first flora, primroses, anemones, pasque-flowers)
	I	Cosy warm sphere of the highest meadows
II		Dachstein, snow and ice, crystal–clear air
	II	Soldanella, blossoms of the highest region
III		The children on ice and snow
	I	Repetition of the first secondary theme (sphere of the alpine roses)
	II	Second secondary theme, light, sky
IV	Coda:	Outlook into the highest region

The formal scheme indicated here is not as clear as one might wish, but it can be interpreted with some assurance as ABA C ABCA. A schematic outline of the Beethoven scherzo expressed in a format similar to Webern's follows:[10]

Main themes	Secondary themes
I (bars 1–22, G major)	
	I (bars 23–38, E minor – A minor)
(transition)	
II (bars 42–64, G major)	
(transition)	
	II (bars 73–124, C major)
false reprise (bars 124–38, C major)	
III (bars 138–60, G major)	
(transition)	
start of coda (bars 174–89, F major)	
	III (bars 189–237, G major)
IV (bars 237–53, G major)	

This translates into A(B)ACADA with a false reprise anticipating the third appearance of A.[11] Both the first and third episodes are unusual. The first, B, is hardly of sufficient stature to merit the designation, since it is brief and tonally unstable, becoming in the end simply a transition leading to the second statement of A. The final episode (D) is in the tonic key and therefore functions as an extended coda rather than a diversion.

Obviously the Webern plan is so sketchy that nothing can be determined concerning his intentions with respect to such things as transitions and the false reprise. One significant discrepancy between the two outlines that can be observed, however, has to do with the content of the section(s) separating the last two appearances of the main theme. Episode D in the Beethoven scherzo cannot be interpreted as a return to material from sections B and C, and is already part of the coda.

Webern's outline	Beethoven
A	A
B	(B)
A	A
C	C
A	A
B	D(Coda)
C	
A(Coda)	A(Coda)

The Op. 22 rondo does not follow either of these plans exactly.

The first nineteen bars contain ten row statements, all untransposed. Similar clumps of untransposed rows occur at three other points in the piece – in bars 64–88, bars 129–47 and from bar 182 to the end. Untransposed rows do not appear anywhere else in the movement. Since this row ends a tritone away from its beginning, all four permutations of the row at the same level of transposition begin and end on the same two notes: in the 'tonic' position these notes are F♯ and C. The movement opens with C and F♯ and closes on a delayed and relatively sustained F♯. These tonic areas define a rondo form with four refrains, seemingly following both Webern's projected outline and his declared model. Two of these, the first and third, are followed by shorter sections using only rows transposed at the tritone, which of course also begin and end on C and F♯. In a tonal sense, then, these sections built on tritone transpositions of the row (T_6) seem to be simply extensions of the preceding tonic areas, forming a sort of complement to the tonic as it appears originally, perhaps analogous even to the customary move to the dominant at the end of a tonic exposition, and therefore structurally a part of A. Although no group of rows at T_6 appears in conjunction with either the second A section or the last, this is not entirely unprecedented.

The piece opens with minims, the basic value throughout the first nineteen bars is the crotchet, and the figure ♪♪♪♩ appears prominently twice. Although the style is linear, and there is some inexact imitation (violin–piano–saxophone in bars 9–11), this section is not canonic until the last three bars, where the piano plays a canon (a rather free one, as all the canons are in this movement) for three bars in preparation for the section that follows. The group of T_6 rows appears in bars 20–32, and here the style becomes entirely canonic. There are only two voices throughout this section, playing three relatively short canons, the first and second overlapping by one note in both voices.

The returns of the tonic section do not have a great deal in common with the initial A, or perhaps it would be more accurate to say that they seem at least as closely related to the intervening sections as to the opening. The return beginning in bar 64 is particularly difficult to apprehend, as the tonal section defined by untransposed rows does not correspond to the structure outlined by the musical content. The return of tonic rows begins at bar 64. (It actually begins with the last note in bar 63, but more about this later.) The first five bars (bars 64–8) do not more closely resemble the beginning of the piece than they do the section that has just finished; in fact they are almost certainly perceived as the end of that section. In bar 69 the tempo, dynamics, note values, figuration, texture and instrumentation change, marking the beginning of a new section that becomes (it would be impossible to say exactly where) the long episode (C) at the centre of the rondo. The untransposed rows finish in bar 88 in the middle of a quasi-symmetrical five-bar unit that seems to be already well into this episode. There is, then, no return of material that has associations with only the A section, and in fact no return of material displaying any strong connection with it at all. The return of A – and this must be considered a return if the piece is to work as a rondo – seems to depend entirely upon the use of untransposed rows and nothing else.

The second return of A presents a different set of incongruities. When the untransposed rows begin, in bar 129, the situation is similar to that at the previous return. The first three bars seem to be the end of the previous (C) section; these bars use for the last time in the piece the triplets that are unique to that section. The opening of the movement is recalled briefly here, however, making this refrain, in spite of its ensuing dissimilarities, more deserving of the name than the previous one (see Example 6.2). After a fermata, bar 132 begins with figures that resemble the first return more than the opening. Motives from both sections of the first return (bars 64–8 and 69–88) continue until the end of the untransposed rows in bar 147. At this point a complete set of tritone transpositions occurs – P, R, I and RI – in seven bars that are very similar to bars 64–8. Throughout, this section is more a return of the previous return than of the original.

The final occurrence of tonic rows, in the last ten bars, uses, finally, figures

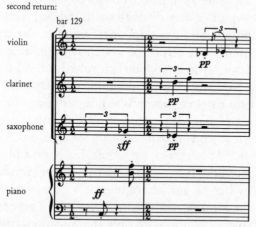

6.2   Op. 22/ii

reminiscent of the opening. This section functions as a coda, as both
Webern's schematic outline and the Beethoven model suggest that it should.

Three episodes are defined by the A sections just described: in bars 33–63,
89–129 and 153–82. The first and third of these are at the same tempo ($\downarrow$ = ca
108); the second is somewhat slower ($\downarrow$ = ca 96). All three consist of two
sections, the second at least beginning with the same series of rows as the
first. In the first case, only the opening two rows, I₉ and P₉, reappear at the
beginning of the second section. In the second episode, five rows are used
between bars 93 and 112, and the first four of these are repeated. The first
half of the final episode uses nine rows, of which six are repeated in the same
order in the second half. The music, however, changes in the second half of
each of these episodes.

Both halves of the first episode are canonic. In bars 39–51 three snippets of
material – four, two and three bars long respectively – are imitated inexactly,
more or less in inversion, by a second voice, with a third voice imitating the
two-bar fragment, two additional voices playing a three-note motive in

imitation concurrent with the third fragment, and a few free motives played without imitation. In bars 51–63 three segments – of two, three and three bars' duration – are given similar treatment: a canon in two voices with a few free notes in another voice and a third voice joining in the imitation in bar 63,[12] with an afterbeat ostinato in the piano from bar 56 to bar 62.

The treatment is very similar in the final episode (bars 153–82). Again, both halves are canonic, and in addition much of the material is reminiscent of that in bars 39–63. Here all of the first half (bars 153–69) is a single inexact canon in inversion in two voices, with other voices contributing both free material and imitation, in bars 166–9. These last three bars are very like bars 48–50, those occupying a parallel position in the first episode. On both occasions the second half of the episode is marked *nicht eilen* (in bars 51 and 169–70). The two-voice canon carries on through bars 169–79, with a good deal of additional material in other voices, some of it further imitating portions of the canon. Both the manner of treatment and the similarity of material in these two episodes make it clear that they are related, and in fact the last must be seen as a return of the first.

The central episode is very much in contrast to the rest of the movement. The first half (ca bars 93–111) is a spare, static section in which a harmonic G in the violin and a pair of dyads played by clarinet and saxophone (c^1 and b^1 moving to $b\flat$ and a^1 or the reverse) occur repeatedly at what seem to be random points during the course of three statements (each slightly varied) of a four-and-a-half-bar melodic phrase in crotchets and minims in the piano. The pitch sequence f–f#–e♭–e recurs repeatedly in various guises, accounting for most of the melody. These repetitions are made possible by the invariant properties of the row. There is no imitation here, and there are none of the quaver figures that are such a pervasive element of all other sections of the piece. This completely different sort of music begins much earlier, at bar 69, in the midst of the first return of tonic rows. The various elements that are reiterated between bars 93 and 111 make their inconspicuous appearance at different times: the violin's harmonic is first heard in bar 86, and the piano begins to play figures similar to its later melodic phrases as early as bar 73.

The second half of this episode offers contrast of another sort. After the immobility and quiet of the preceding bars, both the dynamic level and the activity increase suddenly at bar 112. The quavers return, but, more important, a completely new rhythmic element – the crotchet triplet – is introduced. These triplets are unique to this episode, disappearing at bar 132. The harmonic G in the violin disappears in this section, but the pair of dyads played by the clarinet and saxophone continue until bar 120. The speeding up of events at bar 112 means that the repetition of the first four of the five rows used in bars 89–111 takes under nine bars and has been accomplished by the middle of bar 120.

At this point there is a significant interruption. The first section of this episode used the rows I_8, R_1, RI_5, P_{11} and R_{11}; the first four of these are repeated in bars 112–20, and, although the R_{11} that should follow does not return, it is represented by its retrograde, P_{11}, but only after the insertion of a group of three rows at the sixth transposition. This interpolation is the climax of the movement.

The Beethoven scherzo said to have been identified by Webern as a model has a false reprise at this point. If Webern did, indeed, cite that movement as an analogue, the fact of its having a false reprise would surely be significant enough for us to assume that his own Op. 22 movement must have one also. If so, this group of rows, RI_6–RI_6–P_6, must be it. T_6 has been used earlier as a tonic representative, in bars 20–32. The interpretation of the early return of this portion of A as a false reprise has some validity, but the logic seems faulty. The whole point of a false reprise in tonal music is to fool the listener by serving him material he recognizes but in the wrong key. Here we are given material that we have not heard before, in the 'right' key, if we could recognize it. Since it is doubtful that anyone can perceive the return of the tritone transposition, no reprise of any sort is likely to be heard.

The structure that finally emerges is very like that of the earlier rondo in Op. 20: ABA C ABA. And, again, it is essentially a ternary form. When this structure is compared with the projected diagram (ABACABCA) and the Beethoven model (A(B)ACADA) several discrepancies become evident:

(1) The Op. 22 rondo has a much more significant B section than the Beethoven scherzo.

(2) The Op. 22 rondo lacks, for all practical purposes, a return of the refrain between episodes B and C, though the row structure would indicate the existence of one. The A section is exactly repeated at this point in the Beethoven, and a return is indicated as well in the Webern outline.

(3) The Op. 22 rondo has an analogue, although again theoretical rather than aural, to the false reprise in the Beethoven. This is not indicated in the projected outline.

.(4) The third refrain, following the central episode, is varied in Op. 22/ii and resembles the earlier (hypothetical) return more than it does the original A. This return is exact in the Beethoven.

(5) The final episode in Op. 22/ii is a variation of the first one; in Webern's projected structure it should refer to the first episode, but also to the central one as well; in the Beethoven, the final episode is new and forms a part of the coda.

(6) The final A section functions as a coda in all three of the structures in question, though in the Beethoven the coda has begun much earlier.

The fact that we have only Willi Reich's recollection and not Webern's own statement about the similarity of this movement to the Op. 14/2 scherzo casts some degree of doubt on the association, in the light of the seemingly irreconcilable differences between the two works. One is tempted to suspect a faulty recollection on Reich's part, since the scherzo of the Op. 14/1 sonata is an ABA C ABA rondo and would seem to be closer to the structure of Op. 22/ii. However, as neither movement offers an exact analogy, perhaps such speculation is not worthwhile.

The blurring of outlines is an important characteristic of this movement. In the preceding analysis, sections have been delineated on the basis of two things – row structure and changes in treatment or material – and specific bars where these sections begin and end have been suggested. In all cases, however, there is a discrepancy between the row structure and the musical structure, the most pronounced being in bars 64–88, where the music seems not to reinforce the row structure in any way. Rows stretch across sections, so that it is quite impossible to find any clean divisions in the piece. Tonic rows always begin somewhat before the place where a new section begins musically, and occasionally extend beyond where it would seem to end. Voices of canons do not necessarily follow row statements, though they sometimes do. Tempo changes rarely occur where it seems that they should.[13] In every way Webern seems to be trying to throw off the traces in this piece, and the result is, not surprisingly, difficult to come to terms with analytically.[14]

Op. 24/ii

Although the first movement of the Op. 24 Concerto is structurally unique, the other two movements seem to represent small-scale realizations of formal ideas that have been tried already. The variations/arch form of the third movement was presented in Chapter 5 as, among other things, a very much simpler expression of the general outline of the variation movement of Op. 21; the second movement bears a similar resemblance to the first movement of that same work, insofar as the row structure exhibits an ABA form while the reprise represents both a sufficiently significant accumulation of musical elements and enough variation in their disposition to produce, in dramatic terms, a progressive structure better represented as ABC than ABA. The sections of the work are defined by an internal double bar at the end of bar 28 and the return of the nine rows that open the work in bars 46–73: A(1–28) B(29–46) A(46–78). R_{10} assumes a tonic function: it opens both the outer sections and returns for the final cadence following the nine-row reprise. As tradition would have it, R_{10} is absent from the central section.

The piano plays throughout the movement, providing a steady accompaniment to the melody, which is shared pointillistically by the other instruments, each playing very little, all told. The horn is absent from the first A section, the viola from the B section. The presence of all nine instruments in the return of A gives this last section a greater timbral variety than either of the other two. The dynamic climax coincides with the return of A, as well; the eight bars of *forte* occurring here account for all but one bar played at that dynamic level in the entire movement, which otherwise ranges between *pianissimo* and *mezzo piano*, ending *pianississimo*.

This movement exploits in a concentrated way the extraordinary integrity of the row on which it is built. Two shapes are intrinsic to the Op. 24 row – the 014 set (pc set 3–3), characteristically expressed as a semitone and a major third moving in opposite directions, and the augmented triad. The first of these represents the internal content of each of the trichords as well as the relationship of notes 1, 4 and 7 and 4, 7 and 10 of any retrograde form; the row's peculiar trichordal and hexachordal symmetries are the result of its generation from interlocking augmented triads, and, as a result of this, hexachordal content is preserved through major-third transpositions in either direction (T_4 or T_8). The intrinsicality of both the 014 set and the augmented triad is most apparent in the retrograde forms of the row (see Example 1.14 on p. 23).

The A sections of the movement use only retrograde forms except at cadence points (bars 10–12 and 21–2 in the first case, bars 55–8 and 67–70 in the second), where inverted rows are introduced through elision, with the initial hexachord played entirely by the piano. It will be noted that the two hexachords of the inverted row are those of a retrograde row in reverse order; therefore the incursion of these inverted rows represents less of an interruption in the established sequence of events than might be supposed.

The opening A section is a period, comprising an antecedent and a consequent, and this is followed by a transition. This tripartite structure of the first twenty-eight bars is emphasized in several ways, perhaps most noticeably by the *calandos* in bars 10–11, 22–3 and 27–8 and by echo figures played by the piano at all these places. Even so, the precise internal structure is not as clear as might be supposed. Various disparate analyses bear witness to this. The first twenty-eight bars were analysed by Leopold Spinner in the 1955 *Die Reihe*,[15] and Christopher Wintle published an analysis of the entire movement in 1982.[16] Spinner described both antecedent and consequent as collections of very short phrases (five and six respectively). He identified the trombone's G in bar 11 as the beginning of the consequent and the same instrument's F♯ in bar 22 (but not the piano's dyad coincident with it) as the beginning of a prolongation of the consequent ('Verlängerung des Nachsatzes'). Wintle accepts this terminology, though he divides antecedent and consequent into only two units each. He agrees with Spinner's first cadence but begins the prolongation with the trumpet's e♭^{2} in bar 23. Each of these analyses is to a certain extent problematic. We shall refer to both as we proceed.

The instrumental melody of the first twenty-eight bars uses exclusively the first, fourth, seventh and tenth notes of all the retrograde forms present there. The piano supplies the remaining two notes of each trichord, in the form of dyads. Crotchet rests clearly divide the melody into segments – of 3, 5, 4, 5, 5, 4, 2, 5 and 3 notes. A three-note imbrication of this melody shows that, with one exception, all sets of three adjacent notes within these groups conform to the 014 set (pc set 3–3). The position of the only non-conforming group – the A–g♯ and e^1 played by the trombone and clarinet in bars 15–16 – helps to define the tonal structure of the A section: the e^1 of this group represents the beginning of a modulation, which is stabilized by the flute's d^2 in bar 18. We shall return to this presently.

The antecedent unfolds through a series of rows – R_{10}, RI_{10} and R_6 – whose levels of transposition outline the 'tonic' augmented triad: G–B–E♭.[17] The initial notes of the first and second trichords of each of these rows (and therefore half of the notes of the instrumental melody) also outline this triad: G and e♭ in R_{10}, B and E♭ in RI_{10}, and E♭ and B in R_6. The fourth row, I_5, which interrupts the sequence and initiates the cadence, breaks this pattern; however, for the reasons noted above, this disruption is a minor one, since the second hexachord of this row is identical to the one that opened the movement. Its appearance here in fact represents a completion, returning to the pitch classes that opened the piece: G and E♭. The relationship is emphasized by the reappearance of these notes in the same guise, as an ascending minor sixth. This event can be seen in two ways: as the tonic close of the antecedent phrase, or as the tonic opening of a parallel consequent. Both Spinner and Wintle take the second view, which at first glance also seems to take better account of the position of the *calando*. I believe that the first interpretation is more consistent with both the row structure and later events.

The series of rows begun immediately after the reiteration of the tonic hexachord (I_5/ii) are very nearly parallel to the four just finished – R_7, R_{11}, R_5 and I_4. The first is three semitones lower than the corresponding row in the previous twelve bars, the second does not correspond (this is where the modulation occurs), and the third and fourth are one semitone lower. The melody notes produced by these rows, plus the R_9 and R_3 that follow, illustrate this relationship. The consequent continues at the new tonal level until its cadence in bar 22, which is exactly parallel to that of the antecedent in bars 11–12, and a cadential extension in bars 23–4 brings (without further modulation) the return of a 'tonic' hexachord with the notes E♭ and B in the key positions, the second hexachord of R_9.

This tonic E♭–B, played by the trumpet, coincides with the *tempo* following the second *calando*, thereby occupying a position parallel to the corresponding tonic G–E♭ in bars 11–12 with respect to the tempo fluctuations, although it is later in terms of row structure. On the basis of this, I see these two pairs of tonic notes, both played by brass instruments, as the cadences of the antecedent and the consequent phrases, the consequent having been extended in order to get back to the tonic. A final modulation, which occurs with the violin's A and the clarinet's F in bars 26–8, results in a move away from this tonic, and for this reason I see bars 25–8 as a transition to the B section rather than a prolongation of A, as it is identified by both Spinner and Wintle. Neither Spinner's nor Wintle's analysis is consistent.

6.3 Op. 24/ii, bars 1–28 (reduction)

Spinner's is determined by the row structure without a concern for the *calandos*, which coincide differently with the row structure – and therefore with the cadences he has defined – on the two occasions. While Wintle's identification of the G–e♭ in bars 11–12 as the opening of the consequent and the parallel F♯–d in bar 22 as the close of the same phrase brings the *calando* into play at corresponding places in the two cadences, it seems to me illogical on both musical and serial grounds, since these two figures occupy exactly parallel positions on these two occasions.

In both bars 9–11 and the corresponding bars 20–2, the first hexachord of the inverted row is played entirely by the piano. This causes a break in its otherwise consistent pattern of pairs of dyads (in the order seventh–third–third–seventh). At each of these places a pair of sevenths occurs, with notes 4 and 5 of the inverted row as the upper notes. These notes echo exactly the previous two notes of the instrumental melody, thereby camouflaging (and, in fact, neutralizing the effect of) the presence of a row form whose notes 1 and 4 do not conform to the established pattern, as well as providing a figure with obvious cadential implications. This echo is the final gesture of both phrases in Spinner's analysis; its position is not the same on the two occasions in Wintle's view. In my analysis it occupies parallel positions in the two phrases, though it is further removed from the tonic figure the second time as a result of the extension.

Example 6.3 presents a reduction of the first twenty-eight bars of this movement in which melody and accompaniment are notated on two staves. Spinner's, Wintle's and my own divisions are indicated. It can be seen that, after the first interval, the melodic shape of my consequent closely parallels that of the antecedent. Whereas the antecedent opened and closed with an ascending minor sixth (G–E♭), the consequent opens and closes with a descending major third (E–C, E♭–B). The transition takes up this latter cadential figure, playing first C–A♭ (as a tenth) and then A–F, which is echoed by the piano in the manner adopted at both previous cadences. The note groupings and rhythm of the antecedent and consequent are similar as well.

The various structural interpretations put forward are listed below for comparison. The last line of each entry lists the number of notes in the units defined by each analyst.

Spinner	bars 1–11	bars 11–22	bars 22–8
	antecedent	consequent	prolongation
	R_{10}–RI_{10}–R_6–I_5/a	I_5/b–R_7–R_{11}–R_5–I_4/a	I_4/b–R_9–R_3–I_2/a
	3–3–2–2–2	2–3–3–2–2–2	2–2–3–1
Wintle	bars 1–11	bars 11–23	bars 23–8
	antecedent	consequent	prolongation
	R_{10}–RI_{10}–R_6–I_5/a	I_5/b–R_7–R_{11}–R_5–I_4	R_9–R_3–I_2/a
	6–8	8–8	8

Bailey	bars 1–12	bars 13–24	bars 25–8
	antecedent	extended consequent	transition
	R_{10}–RI_{10}–R_6–I_5	R_7–R_{11}–R_5–I_4–R_9	R_3–I_2/i
	3–5–4–2	3–5–4–2	4–2–2

The B section is defined by the return of the rows of the A section at the end of bar 46. There are four phrases – of five, five, four and four bars – in this central section, all very similar. Both forward-going and retrograde row forms are used here, and the exclusive use of particular row elements in the melody is abandoned. Major thirds and descending seconds – both major and minor – predominate melodically. All four begin with the rhythm ♩♪♩. In the first two and the last, the interval so played is a major third; this is expanded to a fourth at the beginning of the third phrase. All four end with a descending second played in crotchets. The last of these represents an elision with the return of A. The piano continues to play dyads throughout this section, but now all of these are major sevenths. In retrospect it can be seen that both the piano's concentration on the seventh in bar 28 and the descending major thirds in the rhythms ♩♩♩ and ♩♩ heard in the melody in bars 25–8 represented the introduction of the essential materials of the B section, thus, it would seem to me, reinforcing the view that these bars function as a transition.

The first two bars of the return – bars 46–7 – are exactly like the opening, except that the trumpet's minim g^1 is replaced by an ab^1–g^1 appoggiatura, a figure which is reiterated a semitone lower three bars later. The descending second, an important characteristic of the B section, did not occur anywhere in the original A. Its first appearance here represents the elision of the B section with the reprise; its repetition points to the divergence of reprise from original that is in most cases effected by the inversion of the sixths and sevenths used in the opening A section to give the seconds and thirds characteristically associated with B. The descending major third is introduced into the reprise in the form of a pair of tenths in the melody in bars 60–2; after this the melody capitulates completely, consisting entirely of descending major thirds (six in all) until the final interval, in bars 76–7. Thus the close of the movement provides a series of concentrated and prolonged references to the central section.

In bars 1–28 the piano's accompanying dyads are slurred together in pairs, which are separated in most instances from the pair on either side by a crotchet rest. For the first eight bars of the return the piano's dyads are grouped in pairs as they were in bars 1–28, but, whereas in the opening section each pair consisted of a seventh and a third, here like dyads are paired in most cases, recalling the practice at cadences and in the B section. The pairing itself begins to break down near the end of the antecedent, and the resulting irregularity, combined with the introduction of *tenuto* indications and minim values in place of the original slurred crotchets, causes the piano's music to resemble that of the B section increasingly. All these things conspire to create a diversity of combinations and rhythms quite unlike the carefully disciplined uniformity of material in the original A section, in spite of the fact that the two sections have precisely the same pitch-class content.

The melody of the reprise does not resume its exclusive use of notes 1, 4, 7 and 10 until bar 57. As a result, the melody of the antecedent does not outline the tonic triad in quite the same way that it did earlier, and for this reason Wintle considers the reprise to begin only at bar 57. However, a comparison of the melodies of the two antecedent phrases will show that the only 'tonic' notes to have been lost are the Bs in bars 4 and 8, and the latter has been replaced by G, another 'tonic' note. It seems to me that the exact restatement of bars 1–2 in bars 46–7 leaves no doubt that this is the beginning of the reprise. A comparison of the remainder of the melody of bars 46–73 with that of bars 1–24 given above in Example 6.3 will show that eleven of the eighteen pitch classes in the melody of the antecedent return, that all the pitch classes are the same in the melody of the consequent, and that several groups of notes recur with the same contour in both antecedent and consequent. (These are bracketed in Example 6.3.) In addition it will be noted that the groupings of notes is similar on both occasions.

The cadences occur in the same places as before, though details are treated somewhat differently. The tonic G–E♭ figure of the antecedent cadence, played this time as *tenuto* minims, is further broadened by a new marking, *sehr getragen*, the *tempo* that accompanied it the first time now coinciding with the beginning of the consequent phrase in bar 59. Since the melody instruments choose notes at random in this phrase,[18] they do not play the pair of notes that was echoed by the piano as a part of the corresponding cadence in the first A section. This echo occurs, nevertheless; the piano plays the figure both times, in bars 54–6. The tempo fluctuates twice in the consequent phrase, slowing down with the beginning of the modulation to a second *sehr getragen*, which is ended only for the 'tonic' notes b^2–g^2 in bars 66–7. The *calando* accompanying the cadence also goes to a *sehr getragen* before the tempo resumes; both the beginning and the end of this ritard are slightly offset when compared with the exposition. The echo component of this cadence takes its usual form in bars 66–8.

The transition is replaced this time by a coda, which uses only one row, the 'tonic' R_{10}. Musically it represents a combination of elements characteristic of A and B: dyads of a seventh and a third paired (A) expressed as minims (B), a pair of sevenths (A cadences, B), slurred pairs (A), three descending melodic major thirds in the rhythms ♩ 𝄾 ♩ and 𝅗𝅥 ♩ 𝅗𝅥 (B) and a melodic descending seventh (A). The trumpet plays notes of the tonic triad, g^1 and $e♭^1$: it will be recalled that the tonic notes finalizing each of the four cadences in the A sections were played by a brass instrument.[19]

The instrumental music

Op. 28/ii

The last multi-movement instrumental work, the Op. 28 Quartet, concentrates particular attention on the ternary ABA form. As we have seen, the first movement represents the superimposition of a complex three-part form onto a theme and variations. The third movement is a similarly complex scherzo in ternary form. The second movement, described by Webern as a 'scherzo in miniature',[20] is also in ternary form.

The outer (scherzo) portions of this movement exploit the tetrachordal identities inherent in the row. Only prime and retrograde rows at the third, seventh and eleventh transpositions are used: all these rows represent different combinations of the same three tetrachords. In his descriptions of this movement, Webern is insistent on the 'subject-like form' of these eighteen bars:

> The first theme is a *perpetual four-part canon*, but nevertheless structurally a 'subject' (following strictly classical principles) of eighteen measures ...[21]

> The *theme of the scherzo* is a *perpetual* four-part canon in a 'subject'-like form.[22]

Although he does not mention periodicity here, this is presumably what he is referring to when he speaks of the structure and form of a subject, because it is clear that 'subject' in this context represents a classical technique that is in opposition to the earlier linear styles whose influence is realized in the canonic nature of these eighteen bars. His objective was his usual one: the synthesis of these two historically opposed modes of presentation.

The structure of the scherzo is probably best described as a three-phrase period. The antecedent phrase is six notes long; this is answered by a six-note consequent extended by a four-note cadence. The following eight-note group seems to function as a second consequent, beginning at a faster tempo but ending in the same manner as the previous phrase, with a *poco ritard*. The last three notes are the beginning of the repeat the first time through and, with an additional note at the end, provide the closing the second time. When the scherzo returns in bar 37, the row structure is the same as in bars 1–18. Although the rhythm of each part is the same here as it was the first time, and the tempo fluctuates in the same places, the melodic contour exhibited by the tetrachords is neither followed nor inverted consistently. The repeat occurs again in this reprise, contrary to the classical custom, and a second ending is provided, in which the final tetrachord of each part is played at a very fast tempo. Webern describes this as a 'stretto-coda'.[23]

The middle section, or trio, of this movement is also canonic. It is the same length as the scherzo – eighteen bars – and is binary, with a division at bar 27. The music from that point on is, according to Webern, the 'repetition in a completely new form' of the theme that is presented in bars 19–26. There are

256

only six rows in this section. Two of these, P_7 and R_{11}, begin in the violins and move in long note values, having completed the first hexachord at bar 27, where they move to the viola and cello to finish only at the end of the section, in bar 36. Meanwhile, the two rows that begin in the viola and cello at the outset of the trio move in quavers and finish in bar 26, to be followed by two more rows played in a similar fashion by the violins. Interestingly, the rows used here are the same ones used in the scherzos: P_7, P_{11}, P_3, R_7, R_{11} and R_3. Presumably this can be seen as an analogue to a trio in the tonic key:

P_7
R_{11}
R_3 P_3
P_{11} R_7

P_7 and R_{11} are in canon, P_7 leading for the first hexachord, R_{11} for the second. This division of the row into two groups of six notes is reminiscent of the first two phrases in the scherzo. The parts of the canon are notated as shown in Example 6.4. Several things should be observed from this example. First, that the rhythm of the second half of the canon is the same as that of the first half, notated differently, and that in fact both voices move throughout the eighteen bars at a steady minim pace, which is broken only at the centre when R_{11} takes the lead. The *comes* answers the *dux* in inversion, and, in addition, its first tetrachord is the exact retrograde of the corresponding tetrachord of the *dux*. The remaining two tetrachords of these two rows have the same content also, but without a reversal in the order of notes: the second tetrachord of each row is identical to the third of the other. We have observed that while it is Webern's custom to realize inversional and retrograde relationships by writing exact mirror and cancrizans canons, he does not normally choose to emphasize the relationship of two similar groups by giving them the same contour. Nor does he here.

6.4 Op. 28/ii, bars 19–36 (two voices, pitches only)

The rows of the other two voices are divided into trichords, and the lead alternates regularly, changing parts every three notes until bar 27. Although the events become increasingly irregular after this point, the trichordal division of rows continues, in direct contrast to the practice in the scherzo, which focuses completely on division into tetrachords.

Op. 28/iii

The third movement of the Op. 28 Quartet is a more extended and complex ternary form, embodying a double fugue, and representing for Webern 'the "crowning fulfilment" ... of the "*synthesis*" of "*horizontal*" and "*vertical*" construction ... I strove for already in the first and second movements'. He continues:

> As is known, the classical cyclic forms – sonata, symphony, and so forth – evolved on the basis of the former, while 'polyphony' and its associated practices (canon, fugue, and so on) derived from the latter. And now, here I have attempted not only to comply with the principles of both styles in general, but also specifically to combine *the forms* themselves: as already through the use of '*canons*' in the preceding movements, so here in this movement through the '*fugue!*'[24]

Although confusing, in the style of many of Webern's pronouncements (he seems here to consider canon and fugue as forms – not the customary view), his description makes clear this movement's concern with synthesis. Essentially, the movement is in three parts, the third representing the reprise of the first. The middle section is, however, quite long proportionally and comprises, according to Webern, two fugal expositions alternating with two episodes, both of which are in strict four-part canon.[25]

The first scherzo, which extends to bar 16, is periodic, with an antecedent phrase of twelve notes and a consequent of the same length in each of the four voices. The four rows used in the consequent phrase are the inversions of those in the antecedent. At the same time, of course, they are also the transposed retrogrades:

$$P_0 - I_0 \quad (R_3)$$
$$R_6 - RI_0 \quad (P_3)$$
$$P_6 - I_6 \quad (R_9)$$
$$R_0 - RI_6 \quad (P_9)$$

Although I prefer to list the contents of this section in terms of prime and inverted rows in order to show clearly the limited number of transpositions used, the prime–retrograde interpretation may provide a more accurate description of the particular setting, because each of the rows in the consequent phrase offers the rhythmic retrograde of one of those in the antecedent. At the reprise of the scherzo, beginning in bar 54, the row structure is the same as in the original, but parts have been exchanged. The cello's original R_0 has moved up to the first violin, the viola's P_6 has moved to the cello, and the P_0 from the first violin has moved to the viola, while the second violin retains its R_6. This section works in the same way as the first scherzo except that the prime and retrograde rows have exchanged rhythms.

The initial exposition of the fugue subject and countersubject begins in bar 16 and extends to the viola part in bar 26. The fugue subject consists of three cells, each comprising a tetrachord, and is announced by cello/violin I/viola in bars 16–19. The answer occurs immediately in violin I/violin II/viola in bars 19–22. Traditionally this answer would be at the dominant level. Since that is not practicable here, Webern has substituted tonal alteration of a different sort. The three rhythmic cells of the answer use the same tetrachords as the corresponding ones in the subject in the same order, but the content of each tetrachord is reversed (Example 6.5). This ingenious answer is accompanied by a countersubject – this is the traditional location for the first appearance of a countersubject – containing again the same three tetrachords as the subject, in the order 2–1–3, with 3 in retrograde. The rhythm of this countersubject is that of the subject in reverse. It is at this point that the origin of the fugue subject becomes clear: its retrograde is a variant of the rhythm of the prime rows at the opening of the scherzo (Example 6.6). A subsequent entry of the subject (cello/viola/violin II in bars 22–5) is accompanied also by the countersubject (violin I/cello/viola). These three entries – of subject, answer and subject – along with the accompanying

6.5 Op. 28/iii, fugue subject and answer (pitches only)

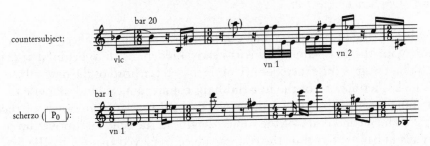

6.6 Op. 28/iii, countersubject (pitches only)

countersubject comprise the first fugal exposition. An episode in the form of a four-part rhythmic canon follows, in bars 26–37. The material of this episode is a rhythmic variant of the countersubject – (and also, therefore, of the scherzo subject [Example 6.7]).

6.7   Op. 28/iii (pitches only)

The second exposition of the fugue begins at bar 38. This is the exposition of a new subject, with entries in only two voices, both accompanied by a countersubject. The new subject is essentially an inversion of the first one; whereas the first subject was stated by prime rows, the second is presented by inversions/retrogrades. It is introduced first in the second violin; the statements of this subject, unlike those of the first, remain in one instrument. Again the countersubject, which is also presented entirely by one instrument (viola, in this case), is the rhythmic retrograde of the subject. Intervallically, of course, it is like the subject, since both use the same kind of row (Example 6.8).

6.8   Op. 28/iii (pitches only)

At bar 42 the second entry of both subject and countersubject appear in stretto with the first, though this is neatly hidden, as they begin at tonal levels that result in the exact identity of the first tetrachord of the new subject and the last tetrachord of the just-finishing countersubject, and likewise the first four notes of the new countersubject with the last four notes of the subject. The second entry of the subject begins in the cello and moves up to the viola in bar 45; this time the countersubject is played entirely by the first violin. The rhythm of the second tetrachord of this statement of the

260

countersubject (first violin in bars 44–5) is reversed so that it is the same as that of the parallel tetrachord of the subject, in order that the subject and countersubject and the two other voices, which join in bars 46 and 47, will be in strict four-part canon for the next few bars. This section, from bar 44 to bar 51, Webern calls the second episode. The two voices that join the canon late finish their last tetrachords in bars 52–3; these bars function as a retransition back to the scherzo.

According to Webern, the return of the scherzo in bar 54 is seen in a new light after the events of the middle section of the movement.[26] Since the scherzo theme and the countersubject are rhythmically identical, the retrograde voices that accompany the scherzo theme are now seen to be stating also the fugue subject; therefore this reprise functions additionally as a third exposition, in close stretto, with the fugue subject in two voices and the countersubject in two voices.

This is an ingenious construction, and one that Webern was obviously proud of. Representing the somewhat unlikely combination of an originally quite simple homophonic form (ABA ternary) with a complex polyphonic technique (fugue) it symbolized for him a significant accomplishment in the synthesis of horizontal and vertical. Perhaps its complexity saved it from the scorn of Schoenberg, who claimed that 'even the writing of whole fugues is a little too easy' using the twelve-note technique.[27] Webern would, in fact, write another fugue directly, as a part of the Op. 29 Cantata: the only two fugues of his career were double fugues written within two years of each other. Fugue and sonata have traditionally occupied similar positions of sobriety in the formal hierarchy: perhaps it is no coincidence that Webern turned to fugue after apparently abandoning (or exhausting) sonata form.

7

The movement in binary form: Op. 27/ii

The second movement of the Op. 27 Variations stands alone as the only movement in binary form in all of Webern's twelve-note music. In view of Webern's description of the entire work as 'a kind of suite',[1] and his likening it to the *Badinerie* of Bach's B minor Suite,[2] a binary structure is particularly fitting here. The movement is a mirror canon; this fact and its row structure have been discussed elsewhere.[3] The repeats divide it into two equal sections of eleven bars, each containing two rows and their inverted imitations. These two sections are defined by the appearance of identical two-note figures (bb^2–g#) at the beginning, at the centre and at the end of the movement, accentuating its balanced proportions.[4] This symmetrical simple binary structure evokes baroque associations rather than the Beethovenian ones that Webern so often alludes to in describing his own work. Indeed, the very idea of a suite suggests the eighteenth rather than the nineteenth century.

The only note values used are quavers and crotchets; with five exceptions, progress is through pairs of quavers either preceded or followed by rests of the same value, creating a perceived 3/8 metre that seems to supersede the written 2/4,[5] and that, to pursue the baroque connection, calls to mind several dance types of that period. The metrical regularity is interrupted by 2/8 units in bars 10, 12, 15, 16 and 19–20.

The texture of this movement is pointillistic and spare. There are no long notes – in the entire movement, no note in either voice is held long enough to join it to the note following in the same voice, and with the exception of bars 2, 7 and 14, where both voices have crotchets, the *dux* and *comes* never coincide. The impression is of a single, albeit an extremely athletic, voice playing a series of two-note motives with constantly changing dynamics and articulation, recalling Bach's works for unaccompanied string instruments and, even more to the point, the gigue from the first keyboard Partita.

This movement obviously revolves around a^1. The two voices of the canon converge on this pitch, so that it is heard twice in immediate succession at some point in the progress of each pair of rows, and all other pairs of corresponding notes in *dux* and *comes* are equidistant above and below it. As a result of all this centripetal activity, A assumes a tonic function. This tonal centre is a tritone distant from the initial note of the untransposed row of Op. 27. The first movement seems not to have a tonal centre, but the third movement begins and ends with groups of untransposed rows, so that the strong focus on A in the central movement may be seen as a preparation by contrast for the E♭s that seem to provide the tonal focus of the third movement.

Webern's ideal of unity (and thereby comprehensibility and perfection) through synthesis and resolution was not a very original one, in spite of his enthusiastic claims for its novelty. Just such a concern was an important part of the cultural tradition that produced him (dual-function forms are a familiar phenomenon in the nineteenth century, from Beethoven onwards), and instead of marking him as a pioneer, his constant search for synthesis simply reaffirms his place in that tradition. His answer to the problem of formal integration – the superimposition of diverse forms – achieves structural ambiguity; it might be argued that this is not the same as synthesis. In view of the widely disparate analyses and opinions his work has evoked, I think one could also question his success in increasing comprehensibility. It is nevertheless indisputable that his reassessment of formal conventions and structural components led to ingenious solutions, and that his reinterpretation of the old forms was a reviving influence at a time when they were threatened with obsolescence.

Introduction to Part III

After Op. 19 the only texts set by Webern were those written by his friend Hildegard Jone. The resulting works – the songs Opp. 23 and 25, *Das Augenlicht* and the two cantatas – were a testament to a friendship that dominated – aesthetically, at least – the later years of Webern's life. Jone's strange mystical/Christian poetry with its rapturous metaphors and allusions to nature found a kindred spirit in the naïve but intense composer who customarily outlined the movements of projected works in his sketchbooks by making associations with favourite alpine flowers and mountain retreats. His letters to the poetess are filled with exclamations of unexpected delight in having found time and again in her poetry the expression of his own thoughts. Clearly personal affection also influenced his view of her poetry and his exclusive use of it as texts for all the late works, but this is not an alternative explanation for his choice, because of course the friendship itself was a product of the close affinity of these two minds and sensibilities. It is at first surprising, nevertheless, to find a composer who for his early songs found his texts in Goethe, Rilke, Strindberg and Stefan George to turn in all his late works to a relatively unknown writer with an eccentric style. I see Webern's exclusive choice of Jone texts as significant in a wider context: Webern, whose twelve-note music has been variously described as more classical, less intense and more cerebral than that of Schoenberg and Berg, seems to have been, ironically, of the three composers the one with the least wisdom concerning the ways of the world and the least discernment with respect to the other arts. In personal and aesthetic matters, the musicologist who showed a fascination with mathematics and logic operated largely on native instinct. He recognized his own inarticulate emotions in Jone's poetry and was captivated.[1]

I suggested in Chapter 2 that Webern's most complex structures were realized in his chamber works rather than in his solo songs with piano accompaniment. There are several reasons for this, among them the more limited pitch resources and flexibility of the voice when compared with the instruments of the orchestra (as well as the timbral restrictions of the piano), but probably the most important has to do not so much with the medium as with the message. The necessity of accommodating the pre-existing structure of accents and nuances as well as the already-established expressive requirements of a text is inimical to the sort of complex manipulations of rhythm customarily practised by Webern in his instrumental music. This theory seems to be supported by the fact that, in cases where voices and orchestra alternate in the same piece, the music written for the chorus is rhythmically and structurally less complex than that given to the instruments, and that in the chamber works with voice, which in most cases do represent essays in unusual structures that are sometimes quite difficult to apprehend, the voice is set apart.

Certainly the solo songs dating from the 'mature' twelve-note period, Opp. 23 and 25, do not exhibit a concern with either structural or canonic experimentation, the two themes that can be followed generally through Webern's twelve-note career. It is, I think, significant that there are only two sets of solo songs with piano from these years and that they both date from that period when Webern seems to have been consciously turning away from the symmetrical structures that had attracted his attention earlier. This rejection of discipline was short-lived, of course, and upon his return to the drive for formal synthesis that would occupy him for the rest of his life he wrote chamber and orchestral works exclusively. Therefore, while the somewhat unfocused structures of Opp. 23 and 25 can be explained by their position in his creative output, their position is in itself no coincidence.

Das Augenlicht, the first of the works for voices and chamber orchestra, also dates from this period, and predictably shows the same abandonment of regularity and discipline. In fact, these three works together account for nearly all of the experiments in freedom. Only one other movement seems to have been composed in the same spirit: the rondo movement of Op. 22. *Das Augenlicht* is alone among the vocal chamber works in being structured along instrumental lines. The text, which is particularly abstruse, does very little to suggest a musical setting: there is no activity (as in the first movement of the Op. 29 Cantata, for instance, where a sudden violent action and its dénouement are described) and no words suggesting sound (such as the references to strings and winds in the third movement of Op. 29 or to the nightingale in the first or the bells in the third movement of Op. 31). All its metaphors are visual, not aural, ones. As a result, the music seems not to be a response to the text in any very specific way, though it is clear from a letter to Hildegard Jone that Webern fitted his musical climax to the line that he considered to be the most intense of the poem: 'O the ocean of a glance with its surf of tears!'

After *Das Augenlicht*, voices are used again only in the two cantatas, Opp. 29 and 31. In both of these works, the text exerts an influence not observed in Op. 26. Expression of the text is particularly apparent in Op. 29. As will be shown below, both the structure and the character of the instrumental music of the first cantata are determined by the text, to the extent that the choral responses to it seem superficial in comparison. This work contains one of the two fugues in Webern's twelve-note music: the only one for voices.

As we have already seen, Op. 31 is concerned particularly with invariance and the extension and abstraction of canonic techniques. The music for chorus is of two varieties: homophony, in which all four voices move in rhythmic unison, and canon of a simple and straightforward kind. All the recondite canonic goings-on occur in sections written for solo voice, and in all cases, as in the second movement of Op. 29, the voice is kept apart, providing the rhythmic model, and therefore acting in a somewhat abstract way as *dux*, but not really taking part in the proceedings. In this way the essential distinction between vocal and instrumental styles suggested above is maintained even when the two mediums are combined; while the orchestra engages in the sort of esoteric manipulations that one has come to expect in the chamber music, the voices, heard at the same time, do not. The role of the voices seems to be to present the text, that of the orchestra to respond to it.

One would not expect the works with chorus to be modelled on instrumental forms, and with the possible exception of *Das Augenlicht*, which seems to be a loose adaptation of sonata form, they are not. Their forms are determined by either the pre-existing structure of the poetry or its expressive content. Both binary and ternary forms occur, and most of the movements proceed by the alternation of two materials. Only one, Op. 29/iii, is a fugue and one, Op. 31/vi, a canon (though most contain canonic sections). Since the structure of most of these pieces is generated by poetic content rather than by conventional models, and is therefore unique, they represent in a way the greatest departure from tradition to be found in Webern's twelve-note works.

8

Das Augenlicht

Das Augenlicht is in many ways elusive and difficult to define. I have already noted a casualness in the row technique and the handling of imitation that is uncharacteristic of Webern generally. In spite of the lack of definition in many areas that Webern clearly felt to be of the greatest importance on other occasions, however, the structure of *Das Augenlicht* is by no means haphazard. On the contrary, it is interesting as an example of the expression of an intrinsically – and historically – instrumental form in a medium incorporating voices and a text. One might expect the musical organization to be determined by the text (as is true of the next of Webern's vocal works, the Op. 29 Cantata); here, however, this does not appear to be the case. The text is taken from Hildegard Jone's *Viae inviae* collection, to which Webern had already turned for the texts of the songs of Op. 23. It is among the more elusive of Jone's poetry, an unrhymed exclamation of wonder at the source of intensity in a loving glance, expressed in a series of metaphors of water and light. I offer the following translation:

> Light flows into the heart through our open eyes
>> and, as joy, streams softly out again.
>
> In a loving glance more surges up than ever entered.
> What then has happened when the eye has shone?
>
> O this is surely a miraculous vision:
>> that one man's soul has now become ablaze
>> with stars, as many as do brighten the night,
>> and with such sunlight as wakes the day.
>
> O the ocean of a glance with its surf of tears!
>
> The drops it sprays on the blades of an eyelash
>> are drenched in the light of the heart and the sun.
> And when the eyelids come like night
>> to cover softly thy flowing depths,
>> thy waters merge with those of death:

and thy deepest treasures, won by daylight,
    he takes softly with him.

And yet from its unfathomable ocean bed,
    when the daylight comes with opening eyes,
    many of its wonders arise and enter new awareness,
        and that makes it good.

Canonic imitation and homophony alternate throughout the work. The chorus presents both textures; the orchestra is only imitative. The homophonic sections – in chorale style – are sung *a cappella* with one exception, the central section designated by Webern as the dynamic highpoint of the movement (bars 64–9, to the text translated above as 'O the ocean of a glance with its surf of tears!').[1] In these climactic bars the two forces join, the orchestra accompanying the choral homophony with canonic imitation in two voices. Elsewhere in the work, whenever both voices and instruments are present, the texture is entirely polyphonic. All the instrumental music is set pointillistically.

Das Augenlicht opens with an instrumental introduction in which three parts play a free rhythmic canon[2] with melodic imitation approximated. When the first voices enter – soprano and tenor, in imitation, in bar 8 – it is over a second version of the opening instrumental canon. The choral opening is made complete by the entry of the bass and alto, also in imitation (the soprano and tenor now silent), in bar 14. The two instrumental parts continue to imitate each other, but their material is far removed from that of the opening by this time. The section is brought to a close by a series of brief figures taken from the orchestral material and played by solo instruments. Thus in the first nineteen bars all the participants are introduced, in imitative textures.

The chorale style is first heard at bar 20. The whole chorus enters together here, *pianissimo* and unaccompanied, singing two two-bar phrases, the second a variation of the first: the opening of a sentence structure as described by Schoenberg.[3] This is followed by six bars during which two phrases are sung *forte*, the first by the sopranos and the second by the altos after a bar's rest, all concurrent with a sprightly instrumental canon in two voices, played *forte* and repeated twice, *fortissimo*. At bar 30 the orchestra is silent once more and the chorus sings a three-bar continuation in chorale style, *piano* going to *pianissimo*, thereby finishing the sentence that was begun in bar 20 and interrupted (or extended) in bars 23–9. The sentence structure of the homophonic material is in marked contrast to the through-composed nature of the six-bar imitative segments sung by pairs of voices in the first section of the piece.

The first thirty-two bars of the movement constitute structurally complete and balanced statements of the two contrasting materials upon which the piece is based – imitation and chorale – and thereby function as an exposition. The order of the materials – the first in active, imitative style, the second a chorale – approximates the traditional assertive first theme and lyric second theme and, in fact, recalls the material in the first movement of Op. 22.

The reprise of the first material is broadly paced, unfolding slowly in bars 71–86. In it each voice of the chorus sings a line of text alone (in the order alto, soprano, bass, tenor); this represents another completed gesture, like that in bars 8–19, though it is much longer as a result of the spreading of the voices so that they are heard individually rather than in pairs. The orchestra continues its two-part imitation throughout, as in the corresponding section of the exposition. Only the technique, not the material itself, is the same as before.

The chorale returns in bar 87, *pianissimo* as it was earlier. Again it comprises a sentence articulated in three phrases, but this time the interruptions are more numerous and much extended. The first phrase, in bars 87–9, is followed by three bars of two-part imitation, beginning with tenor and alto and moving to the orchestra. The second chorale phrase (a variation of the first), in bars 92–3, is followed by a long and, to begin with, loud, imitative section in four voices, two vocal and two instrumental. The energy and intensity of this section are reminiscent of the central section (to be discussed presently) and its purpose seems to be a final development of material, in the fashion of many of Beethoven's codas. Unlike Beethoven's developmental codas, however, this is situated, not after the main events of the piece are completed, but just before the final phrase of the reprise: the continuation of the second-theme sentence in bars 111–13.

The middle section of the piece (bars 32–71) represents a working out of the material introduced in the first thirty-two bars. It contains a long approach to the climax and the climax itself – Webern's 'dynamischer Höhepunkt'. The approach, in bars 32–47, is contrapuntal, gradually increasing in intensity and complexity until a *forte* interruption by the sopranos in bar 42. A chordal accompaniment provided by the rest of the chorus and the orchestra in bars 45–7 accounts for the only bars of melody and accompaniment texture in the work. Bars 47–9 represent a first climax, with the sopranos continuing to sing *forte* while instrumental doubling reaches the greatest density to be found anywhere in the piece, with up to eight instruments playing the same pitch.

This first climax is followed by a relatively long rhythmic canon in four voices for chorus alone (except for four notes played rather unexpectedly by a solo cello and a muted trumpet in bars 51–3) and this, in turn, by six bars for orchestra alone, in two parts but again with a great deal of doubling, so that the entire wind and string complements are playing. The highpoint, at bar 64, is realized through the superimposition of the chorus singing in chorale style (*forte* and *fortissimo*, unlike the chorale's exposition) on the orchestra's almost frenzied imitation, also *fortissimo*. As in a double fugue – or, more to the point, a sonata development – the two materials of the exposition are combined at the climax. According to Webern, the 'largest contrast' occurs at bar 71. Here there is a sudden break, after which serenity returns. The ensuing dénouement/reprise was discussed earlier.

Das Augenlicht is an interesting solution to the problem of structuring an extended choral work: the adaptation of a traditionally instrumental form. It is a choral sonata in which the contrasting themes are represented not by specific *music* but by opposite *techniques* of making music, not accidentally polyphony and homophony. One is reminded of Opp. 21 and 27, in which a principle, rather than a theme, was the basis of development and variation. The particular version of sonata form used here – one whose coda provides the basis for a second development section – once again leads us back to the middle period of Beethoven, the source of so much of Webern's inspiration.

The remaining works for this medium, the Cantatas Opp. 29 and 31, are constructed very differently from *Das Augenlicht*. The structures of the Op. 29 songs are determined by the texts. Those of Op. 31 are for the most part the result of arcane canonic variations. None uses traditional instrumental forms in the manner of *Das Augenlicht*.

9

Cantata I

The text is expressed very directly in the Op. 29 Cantata. The shape and structure of the instrumental music are suggested by the poems; in fact, the orchestra seems to express the sense of the text in a more intrinsic way than the voices, whose responses are nearer to the surface. In the first movement orchestra and chorus alternate, and while the orchestral music displays considerable rhythmic and structural complexity the choral music does not, focusing instead on the manifold possibilities offered by invariance, a property which results, perceptually at least, in increased simplicity. In the second movement, the orchestra responds to the text through a pointillistic distribution of very short motives, at the same time engaging in canonic imitation of a mobile nature. The solo soprano, whose part could hardly have been deployed in a pointillistic fashion, remains outside this structure, providing a model for the canon that proceeds around her. The chorus and orchestra join forces only in the third movement. Here, although the structure is complex, the voices seem almost to be an afterthought: the movement is complete without them. The material is exposed by instruments alone, and when the voices join later they only reinforce instrumental parts. One cannot speak, therefore, of the structure or nature of the voice parts in this movement, because the chorus does not exist as an independent entity.

'Zündender Lichtblitz des Lebens'

The text of the first movement is presented by unaccompanied chorus in twenty-two bars at the centre, framed by thirteen bars at the beginning and twelve at the end for orchestra alone. As a result, the instrumental music that accounts for more than half of this movement never coincides with the text. Nevertheless, its particular rhythmic complexities are a musical expression of the events described therein. Hildegard Jone's poem refers to lightning as the moment of life's inception, thunder as the moment of its cessation,[1] and the eventual quiet following the thunder as the peace and tranquillity of death. The three events described are the sudden and unexpected stroke of the

272

lightning that kindles life into existence, giving substance to what was previously nebulous and obscure; the explosion of thunder – the end of life – that inevitably follows; and the gradual subsidence of all activity into a state of oblivion.

The orchestral music is, by virtue of its placement on either side of the text, in two parts. Each of these consists of two sections as well. These smaller sections, which will be identified in the following discussion as O1, O2, O3 and O4, are very similar. In some ways the whole of the orchestral close (O3–O4) is a varied return of the opening (O1–O2); in other ways these two sections represent an arch, wherein O4 answers O1, and O3 is more similar to O2. Because of the coexistence of these conflicting sets of associations, nothing ever returns just as it was; the material is in continual metamorphosis. In addition, logical divisions between contiguous sections do not occur at exactly the same place with respect to the several parameters.

The motion alternates continually between a slow tempo (a pulse of 69 is indicated) and a quicker one (with a pulse of 138). The progress from one speed to the other is automatic, since the music in the slow tempo is written entirely in minim metres and proceeds by semibreves and minims, while the faster music moves by crotchets, in crotchet metres exclusively. Absolute note values are the same in both tempos.[2] In spite of the inevitability of the changes of pulse, Webern carefully marks all of them (there are thirty-one tempo indications in forty-seven bars), the minim metres *Getragen*, those in crotchets *Lebhaft*. This is not, as it might seem to be, simply a sign of excessive meticulousness. It in fact provides the key to the rhythmic structure of the movement, which is ingenious and obscure. I shall return to this later.

Of the various patterns in the orchestral music, that produced by the distribution of tempos is probably the easiest to see. It is also the one grouping that does not conform with the others. The tempos are ordered symmetrically in section O1: the opening and closing, in the slow tempo, are separated by four bars of crotchets. This slow–fast–slow sequence recurs in section O4, beginning in bar 43. Predictably, sections O2 and O3 are symmetrical as well, and show a similar likeness to each other: the pattern is fast–slow–fast–slow–fast in both bars 8–13 and bars 36–42. The sections thus defined – bars 1–7, 8–13, 36–42 and 43–7 – are not, however, in agreement with those indicated by other means. Although the tempo structure divides at bars 7/8 and bars 42/43, sections O2 and O4 clearly begin in bars 7 and 42 respectively insofar as rhythm and texture are concerned.

One of the most striking features of this orchestral music is the simultaneities resulting from the four voices playing in rhythmic unison; these are used to define the extremities of sections. The piece opens with a group of three chords, expressed as semibreves. The return of the slow tempo at the end of section O1 brings a similar set, this time syncopated – although all the voices move at the speed of semibreves, two appear regularly on the afterbeats. Section O3, in bars 36–41, opens and closes similarly with sets of three chords played in notes of equal value. However, because the tempo structure of O3 is essentially the opposite of that of O1, the chords that frame O3 are played at four times the speed of those enclosing O1, and, while they represent a structural return, the aural effect is quite different. Sections O2 and O4 are similarly related. Both begin with a single four-note chord – in bars 7 and 42. Again, as a result of the dissimilarity of tempo sequence in the two sections, the first of these, in bar 7, is four times as long as its successor.

Each of the four sections of orchestral music consists of the statement of one row in each voice. Only outer trichords are expressed in rhythmic unison. The use of outer trichords exclusively for simultaneities, in conjunction with consistent two-note elision, results inevitably in the single-chord opening of sections O2 and O4: in both cases, only one note of the first trichord remains after the close of the previous section. These chordal openings and closings are isolated from the surrounding music by rests before and after, except at the end of O2: this directly precedes the entry of the chorus, and for that reason perhaps a cadential emphasis would be inappropriate here. The chords at the end of the movement, in bar 47, seem to sum up succinctly all the versions previously encountered: the first is in simultaneously sounded semibreves (as at the opening of both O1 and O2), the second in syncopated semibreves (as at the close of these two sections),[3] the last in crotchets (as at both ends of O3 and the opening of O4). The perception of these chords as a summation is strengthened by the orchestration: whereas in every other instance the instrumentation is the same for all three chords of the set, here each one is different.

The music in the centre of each section is imitative and pointillistic. It consists of a minimum of rhythmic material, first stated in bars 2–5 (Example 9.1). While the two figures introduced here will be referred to as **a** and **b** for the sake of clarity, they are simply two expressions of the same motive. Statements of **a** are, in bars 1–13, always divided between two instruments, the first two (slurred) notes played by one and the single note following the rest by a second. The articulation is reversed in **b**, which in these bars is always played from start to finish by the same instrument. These patterns of instrumentation are not adhered to in bars 36–47.

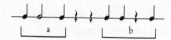

9.1

The material given in the example above (**a–b**) is played by two of the four voices in bars 2–5; the remaining two play its reverse (not its retrograde), **b–a**. Each part comprises an antecedent and a consequent, separated by two crotchet rests. Entries are regular, at the distance of a crotchet, in the order **a–b**, **b–a**, **a–b**, **b–a**. Thus at one level all four voices play in canon, since all have the same rhythm. That it is more precisely a double canon is emphasized by the fact that the two **a–b** voices are played entirely by the violins, and the **b–a** voices by the clarinets (except for one note in each of the four voices, played by celesta and harp). The rhythmic structure of section O1 is given in Example 9.2. Vertical lines in this Example separate tempo areas, not bars.

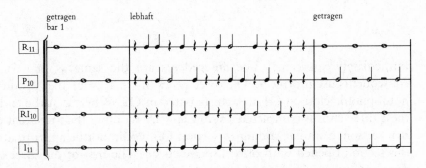

9.2   Op. 29/1, bars 1–6 (rhythm only)

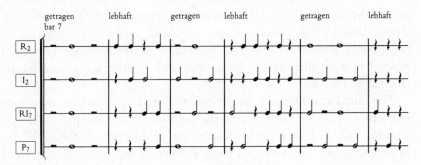

9.3   Op. 29/1, bars 7–13 (rhythm only)

The remaining three sections present variations of this material. The antecedent–consequent framework and the canonic structure are maintained in all three. The rhythmic content of section O2 is given in Example 9.3. The canonic portion of this section begins in exactly the same way as the corresponding bars of O1, but it is interrupted by the incursion of the slow tempo in bar 9. With the return of the *Lebhaft* in the following bar, another canon is apparent, this time using motive **a** in all four voices, and again interrupted before its conclusion by the return of the slow tempo.

If the slow music is rewritten with all the note values halved, this section appears as in Example 9.4. Its relationship with the preceding section is

275

The music with voices

section O2 renotated (bars 7–13)

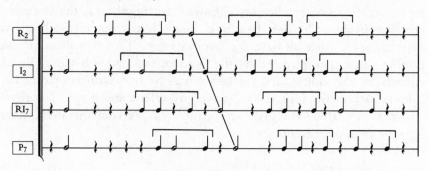

9.4

immediately apparent.[4] The antecedents are the same as in O1; all the consequents use motive **a**. The three notes of equal value that produced the homophonic close in O1 are redistributed in O2. Whereas at the end of O1 these three chords completed a symmetry by recalling the three that opened that section, a similar ending to section O2 would not be appropriate, since this section opened with only a single chord. The first of the three has this time been moved back to a position between antecedent and consequent and, like them, is in canon. The remaining two seem to retain their position at the end of the section, where they are also in canon, unlike their parallels in O1. These last several notes present a second significant structure as well, however. I shall return to this presently. When sections O3 and O4 are rewritten a similar series of events and relationships can be observed (Example 9.5).

The initial statement of the canonic material, in O1, is the only appearance that proceeds at the same tempo throughout. The subsequent variations – in sections O2, O3 and O4 – would be straightforward had Webern not imposed upon each of them a tempo structure that is not in agreement with the rhythmic structure. The result of the coincidence of these incongruous frameworks is that the tempo suddenly reduces to half in all four voices at the same time, and since the music involved is canonic each voice is wrenched into slow motion at a different point in its progress. Everything continues, exactly as it should, but at half the speed. This unexpected irruption of an outside force, producing immediate and violent change, is a vivid musical representation of the stroke of lightning that constitutes the central image of the text.

Although with respect to the sequence of tempos the two sections of the instrumental reprise recall those of the opening in reverse order, rhythmically and in every other way the reprise is a variation of the opening: O3 is most like O1, O4 like O2. The canon of O3 represents an inversion of that in O1, wherein the leading voice has the material played by the fourth voice in

276

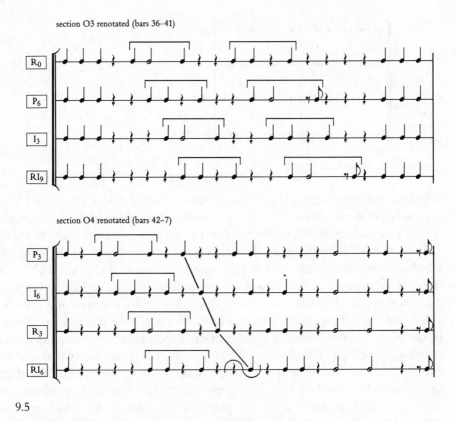

section O3 renotated (bars 36–41)

section O4 renotated (bars 42–7)

9.5

the first instance, and the other parts exchange accordingly, so that the order of entry is **b–a**, **a–b**, **b–a**, **a–b**.[5]

Similarly, the structure of O4 closely resembles that of O2, including its relationship to the section directly preceding it. O4 opens with one chord rather than three, and a second note of the same value punctuates the space between antecedent and consequent in each voice.[6] The antecedents are the same as in the immediately preceding section (as those in O2 followed the pattern set in O1), and, as in O2, there are no **b** consequents. Note 9 of I_6 – the cello's D in bar 46 – is a crotchet too late. In the final sketch this note and the rest preceding it are clearly in reverse order, the only order that is logical.[7] Assuming the printed version to be in error, all the O4 consequents begin as motive **a**, but none is completed. The first two notes of each are sounded, but then all are left hanging, except for the last, which is interrupted immediately by the return of the slow tempo. This time, unlike the parallel situation in O2, the slow tempo truly interrupts; the canon is not continued at half speed. The material that constitutes the interruption is familiar: the semibreve simultaneities opening and closing O1 that opened and would have been expected to close O2.

The interruption of simultaneities in the slow tempo here suggests a

277

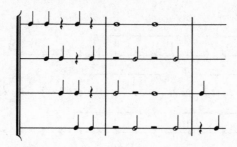

9.6   Op. 29/iii, bars 10–13

different interpretation of the end of section O2. If the slow tempo in bar 12 is seen as an interruption also, the pattern shown in Example 9.6 emerges. This is much closer to what occurred at the end of section O1 than the events as they were described earlier. Following the interpolation of the expected semibreve simultaneities (syncopated, as they were at the close of O1), the interrupted **a** motives in RI_7 and P_7 continue as if nothing had intervened. This explains the otherwise curious return to the faster tempo and crotchet values for the last two notes of the section. In the similar situation at the end of the piece the interruption is exaggerated: the first of the simultaneities is not syncopated here.[8] Following the pair of chords (there are two also at the end of O4), the final note is a crotchet in all voices. In this case none of the four voices has finished its consequent when the interruption occurs; the crotchet chord at the end of the piece can be seen as the final crotchet required for the **a** motive in each voice – an exaggeration of the delayed completion in O2.[9]

The equivocal nature of the structure extends beyond the relations between sections; the relationship between voices displays a similar set of contradictions. With the exception of the entrance of the chorus in bar 14, which represents a break with what came before, the two-note elision is used consistently throughout this movement, so that, except for the transition from bar 13 to bar 14, voices are continuous and there is no ambiguity in the succession of rows. The row structure is as follows:

bars 1–13		chorus				bars 36–47	
P_{10}	P_7	P_6	P_3	P_0	P_9	P_6	P_3
RI_{10}	RI_7	RI_9	RI_6	RI_3	RI_0	RI_9	RI_6
I_{11}	I_2	I_3	I_6	I_9	I_0	I_3	I_6
R_{11}	R_2	R_0	R_3	R_6	R_9	R_0	R_3

Since $RI = P$ and $R = I$, these four row chains represent two pairs, a prime pair and an inverted (or retrograde) pair. Throughout the whole of this movement the voices operate as pairs in other ways as well. In the instrumental music, associations are established through orchestration and

278

rhythmic organization. In the preceding examination of the latter we have found the voices to be paired in the following way:

bars 1–13: R_{11} R_2 bars 36–47: R_0 P_3
                RI_{10} RI_7 I_3 I_6

                P_{10} P_7 P_6 R_3
                I_{11} I_2 RI_9 RI_6

Clearly the rhythmic pairings do not coincide with the row structure.

A third set of associations is established by the orchestration. The chords that close section O1 in bar 6 are played by the same four instruments as those that opened that section; similarly, the last chord of the piece is orchestrated in the same way as the one that opened section O4. Therefore both the outer sections are in this respect closed. The two middle sections are not. In bars 1–6 the orchestration of the voices R_{11} and RI_{10} (which are in canon) is symmetrical, in the manner of the first movement of Op. 21. Between the two sets of chords, both played by trumpet and trombone, these voices move to the violins, to the harp and celesta, and back to the violins. The other two voices are nearly symmetrical (viola and cello to clarinets and back) but avoid absolute regularity by moving to the celesta and harp for note 9.

The orchestration is reminiscent of Op. 21 in other ways as well. In bars 1–13 the orchestra is divided into similar pairs of instruments, which answer each other. The pairs established here are:

> trumpet/trombone
> viola/cello
> violin I/violin II
> clarinet/bass clarinet
> harp/celesta
> flute/horn

These pairs are maintained until the last notes before the entry of the chorus, where 11 and 12 of R_2 are played by the horn and answered by the trombone, and the trumpet's $I_2/12$ is answered by the timpani. Gentle changes are observed in the orchestral interludes within the choral section. The four strings are shuffled so that violin I is paired with cello and violin II with viola. The continuation of the timpani's contributions after the choral section is over necessitates new associations, since this instrument did not figure in the original orchestra – in the interludes it plays with the horn and later with the trumpet – and the trombone and harp are thrown together in bars 3O–1, the only occasion in the piece where the harp is associated with an instrument other than the celesta. In bars 36–47, the timpani is answered again by the trumpet (once), the trombone and horn play together – while not the original pairing, one nevertheless established at the end of the first section – and violin II and viola are paired on one more occasion. The association of voices according to orchestration looks like this:

bars 1–13:	$R_{11}/1–12$	$R_2/3–6$	$R_2/7–10$	$R_2/11–12$
	$RI_{10}/1–12$	$RI_7/3–6$	$I_2/7–10$	$RI_7/11–12$
	$P_{10}/1–12$	$I_2/3–6$	$RI_7/7–10$	$I_2/11–12$
	$I_{11}/1–12$	$P_7/3–6$	$P_7/7–10$	$P_7/11–12$

bars 23–5:	$I_6–I_9/10–3$	bars 30–1:	$P_9/1–3$
	$P_3–P_0/10–3$		$I_0/1–3$
	$RI_6–RI_3/10–3$		$RI_0/1–3$
	$R_3–R_6/10–3$		$R_9/1–3$

bars 36–47:	$R_0/1–3$	$R_0/4–12$	$R_3/3–9$	$R_3/10$	$R_3/11–12$
	$P_6/1–3$	$I_3/4–12$	$RI_6/3–9$	$I_6/10$	$P_3/11–12$
	$I_3/1–3$	$P_6/4–12$	$P_3/3–9$	$RI_6/10$	$RI_6/11–12$
	$RI_9/1–3$	$RI_9/4–12$	$I_6/3–9$	$P_3/10$	$I_6/11–12$

The discrepancies and inconsistencies seen in these three groupings – defined by row type, rhythmic similarities and similar timbres – result in an ambiguity and blurring of structure that complement the equivocalness of the formal relationships between the four sections of orchestral music. All this is added to the considerable confusion resulting from the application of frequent and apparently arbitrarily placed tempo changes to an essentially lucid rhythmic framework. These several ambiguities combine to produce precisely that obscurity which in the text is dispelled by the bolt of lightning, and which presumably resumes once the violent but brief flash of life is over. The action that interrupts this continuing confusion and momentarily brings things into focus is performed by the chorus.

Two of the four lines in Jone's poem deal with lightning, one each with thunder and peace. The three dramatic areas (which will be identified here as C1, C2 and C3) are separated by three- and two-bar orchestral interludes; each of the lines except the second, which is all of a piece, is divided further into three small segments set apart by rests. The following pattern results:

I [Lightning] :	4 segments	(9 bars:	2–2–2–3)
	orchestral interlude	(3 bars)	
II [Thunder] :	3 segments	(4 bars:	1–2–1)
	orchestral interlude	(2 bars)	
III [Peace] :	3 segments	(4 bars:	1–1 +–1 +)

As in the instrumental portions of the piece, the texture of the choral sections alternates between homophony and imitation. The content and treatment of the ten segments are indicated below.

280

bars 14–15:	'Zündender Lichtblitz'	homophony
16–17:	'des Lebens'	imitation
18–19:	'schlug ein'	imitation
20–2:	'aus der Wolke des Wortes'	homophony
26:	'Donner'	homophony
27–8:	'der Herzschlag'	imitation
29:	'folgt nach'	homophony
32:	'bis er'	imitation
33–4:	'in Frieden'	homophony
34–5:	'verebbt'	homophony

Two row combinations recur throughout the choral sections of the piece – rows related as P_0 and R_6, in which the outer notes of each trichord exchange positions (1↔3, 4↔6, 7↔9, 10↔12), and those related as P_0 and R_0. The almost continual pitch and pitch-class repetitions through voice exchange that result from these combinations create a stasis that is important for both structure and expression.[10]

Section C1 – the 'life' music – begins with a five-note rhythmic figure played *forte* with the last two notes accented (Example 9.7). This rhythm

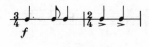

9.7

returns, *fortissimo*, at the end of this section (in bars 21–2). Since the final syllable of the text is unstressed, the penultimate chord can be seen as the goal of the musical line, as the cadential downbeat. This is a particularly dramatic chord; it is also the chord that opened the choral portion of the movement, in bar 14. Reduced to close position, its contents form a semitone cluster, F♯–G–G♯–A. It is, however, not set in close position, but is the most widespread chord sung in the entire movement: it contains both the highest notes sung by the sopranos and tenors and the lowest ones to appear in the bass and alto parts. The tenor is a major seventh above the alto; the distance between soprano and bass is over three octaves. The 'lightning' section, then, ends as it began, at maximum range and volume. Clearly its climax – the stroke of lightning ('schlug ein') in bars 18–19 – cannot, therefore, be achieved in the customary way.

In terms of range and intensity, this climax would seem to be a negative one: its imitative texture makes less impact than the homophony on either side; it exhibits the narrowest range overall of any of the four segments of C1; and, although accented, the level is generally *piano*. Yet the effect is exactly that of the unexpected dislocation described at that moment in the text. The order of entry established (in bar 16) for the imitative segments, which is maintained throughout the rest of the movement – women's voices answered by men's – is reversed here, as if the chorus had been caught off guard and as a result appears in disarray. The sense of confusion is increased by the derangement of voices: the bass and alto are a major seventh above the tenor and soprano respectively. They move closer together on the following chord, then cross in order to return to the first one once again, with the voices now in the traditional spatial relationships. These two bars are thus dominated by a single chord that bursts forth chaotically, is left briefly, and is subsequently recovered with the composure that was lacking initially. The most obvious mark of this climax is the doubling of the four 'schlug' notes by nearly all the instruments in the orchestra, the only time in the entire piece that voices and instruments sound together. The notes of the dis-ordered chord ('schlug') are doubled at the same octave; the 'corrected' return in the following bar is not instrumentally reinforced.

The events of bars 18–19 recur in an orchestral interlude in bars 24–5. The numerous relationships between the parts caused by the invariant properties

* Tenor part written at sounding pitch

9.8   Op. 29/i, bars 18–25 (pitches only)

of the row can be observed in Example 9.8.[11] Bars 24–5 (including the trombone's C♯ and the cello's C in bar 23) represent a retrograde of the pitch material that produced bars 18–19 – each of the voices in the later passage is the exact retrograde of a voice in the earlier one. The last note in each voice is doubled instrumentally, as the first one was in bar 18. Nevertheless, because the series of pitches is symmetrical and because the rhythm does not reverse along with the row structure, the later bars are at the same time a forward-going rhythmic variation of the earlier ones, in which single events occur in the same order as they did on the first occasion.

Section C2 is much shorter than C1. It opens and closes homophonically with an abbreviated reference to the rhythm at either end of the earlier section. One of the most striking similarities of these two sections is their use of the same cadence. Disregarding the final unstressed syllable of C1, which has no counterpart in C2, the two sections cadence with the same pair of chords. In most respects, C2 is remarkably like C1 without bars 14, 18–19, and 20–1.

The dramatic climax of section C2 is 'der Herzschlag' in bars 27–8. The setting of this key word is similar to that of the parallel key words of sections C1 ('des Lebens' in bars 16–17) and C3 ('in Frieden' in bars 33–4). These words express the essence of the poem: it is at least as much a poem about life and death as one about lightning and thunder. All three occur in the second segment of their respective sections. The similarity of their settings can be easily observed (Example 9.9). The first syllable of each of the significant words is set to a dotted minim, the only appearances of a note of this value anywhere in the choral music of this movement. Each is sung *piano* on the first beat of a *Getragen* bar and is preceded by a *forte* minim anacrusis in the *Lebhaft* tempo. The soprano melody is the same each time, finishing with a downward leap of a minor ninth that places it below the alto. In the first two instances – those expressing violent action – the bass mirrors the soprano, leaping above the tenor, and the alto and tenor move up and down a semitone respectively. The very fact that these two settings are imitative is of course an expression of activity. In contrast, the setting of 'in Frieden' is homophonic, and, while the same leaps occur here as in the two previous cases, they are accomplished through parallel rather than contrary motion: the tenor and soprano move downwards a ninth while the alto and bass rise a semitone. As before, this produces on the second syllable a chord with alto and tenor as the outer voices; on this occasion, the chord combines the two climactic 'schlug' dyads from bar 18. The resolution in bar 34 of all the materials that have been used previously to represent the most turbulent images seems to be a perfect expression of the peace with which the text is concerned at this point.

The rows that account for the lightning and thunder music (sections C1

9.9   Op. 29/i

and C2) offer the possibility of a palindrome. Although horizontal symmetry is neither realized through the retrogression of absolute pitches nor in any way supported by rhythm or durations, the extremes and axis of this palindrome are articulated. Strictly speaking, the symmetry continues until the first note of bar 31. However, as another set of rows has begun with the orchestral entrance in bar 30, it seems to end on the last chord sung in bar 29, which, as we have seen, is, appropriately, the same one with which the serial palindrome opened in bar 14. A less dramatic arrangement of the same four pitch classes occurs on the third beat of bar 14; these two versions of the same chord appear, in reverse order, surrounding the axis of the palindrome, in bars 21–2. Thus this chord, which as we have seen is significant for other reasons in this movement, marks the centre as well as both extremes of this otherwise unrealized palindrome (Example 9.10). The axis itself comprises the second and third chords of bar 21, chords that are identical except for voice exchanges. The soprano is below the alto in the first chord and resumes its normal position in the second; the same relationship obtains between tenor and bass. Since this axis comes nearly at the end of the 'life' section, the retrogression that follows accompanies the text concerning death. The ensuing 'peace' text is itself a smaller palindrome, containing echoes of both the 'life' and the 'death' music.

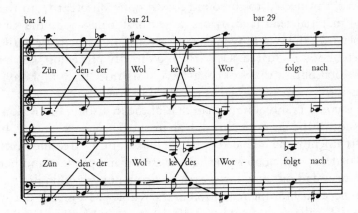

* Tenor part written at sounding pitch

9.10   Op. 29/i (pitches only)

Unlike the previous two sections, C3 begins imitatively; after the central 'in Frieden' the voices continue to sing in homophony to the end, reflecting the resolution and cessation of activity that is the subject of the text. The first four notes of the section are those that were repeated at the axis of the palindrome in sections C1 and C2. The following four notes are those that were heard on 'schlug', voiced in the 'adjusted' manner of bar 19. The section ends with a chord reminiscent of, but different from and less dramatic than, the one that opened the choral section. The outer notes are the same pitch classes as those of the first chord, but their positions are reversed, resulting in a chord that is smaller in range than the opening one. The cessation of activity has led, naturally, to a less dramatic configuration. In fact, the last line of the poem, that dealing with a static and motionless state, is set to a pitch palindrome (see Example 9.11). Only the final chord, as a reference to the opening, is not a part of this palindrome.

9.11   Op. 29/i, bars 32–5 (reduction, pitches only)

285

'Kleiner Flügel Ahornsamen'

The second song of the Op. 29 Cantata was the first of the three to be composed. It is written for solo soprano and orchestra, and Webern seems to have intended it to play a central role from the beginning, even though the work originally projected to surround it was quite different from the one that finally materialized. It provides a textural balance in the cantata, appearing between the two movements for chorus. In a schematic outline on p. 14 of Sketchbook IV (dated '11.11.30' and directly preceding sketches for 'Zündender Lichtblitz'), the work was given the title 'II. Symphony, Op. 29', and this movement was listed as the third of five.

The text is considerably longer than that of the first song, but is akin to it in its expression of the life cycle through an image taken from Nature. In this case, the instrument is the maple key, which falls from the tree and sinks into the earth in order to rise again in the light of spring and produce another tree that will in turn send out new keys, each one containing within itself all the information necessary for the repetition of the whole process. The poem is in nine lines, with a syllable content of 12, 10, 10, 9, 10, 9, 12, 10 and 9. Webern divides it into three sections of 12–10–10–9, 10–9, and 12–10–9 separated by short instrumental interludes. The opening and closing of the movement are for instruments alone as well.

It will be noted that the outer strophes begin with lines of twelve syllables and that all strophes end with lines of nine. All inner lines contain ten syllables; the central strophe is in a sense incomplete, lacking as it were the opening line. The first and third strophes open with P_0; thus the untransposed prime, or 'tonic', is used for both twelve-syllable lines of text. Tritone transpositions also occupy important positions in the melody: the piece is opened by the clarinet playing R_6 and ends with P_6 in the voice. The central strophe presents these two forms only.

Dorothea Beckmann[12] points out the centricity of the setting, in which everything points towards the middle of the second strophe, wherein the text speaks of the new tree's rising towards Heaven. Each line of text is sung to a single row; since only two of the lines contain twelve syllables, only these two coincide exactly with the rows to which they are set. The row structure of the voice part is shown in the table on the next page.

The succession R_{11}–R_2–R_5 in the first strophe and P_0–P_9–P_6 in the third will be recognized as the two–note elision used in the first movement of Op. 29 (and again in the third). As a result of this elision, the row associated with line 2 (R_{11}) runs two notes into line 3, and similarly the R_2 of that line extends beyond the beginning of the next, the overlapping in both cases pointing towards the centre of the piece. Because the first of the elided rows in the third strophe corresponds to a line of twelve syllables, the row associated with the second line (P_9) begins before that line of poetry is

syllables	row form
12	P_0
10	R_{11}
10	R_2
9	R_5
10	R_6
9	P_6
12	P_0
10	P_9
9	P_6

reached, and the same thing happens at the beginning of the third row, causing these elisions to point backwards, again to the centre of the piece. The central strophe itself is a palindrome with respect to both pitches and durations. Although the lines of poetry here contain fewer than twelve syllables, they are not elided (unlike the syllables of the Petrarch sonnet in Schoenberg's Op. 24); melismas cause these two lines to coincide exactly with the rows to which they are sung. The centre of this palindrome is the focal point of the piece. The centricity of this song is further supported by the fact that the interlude just before the middle section is the playing out of the end of the first strophe canons after the text of the strophe has finished, while the interlude following the central palindrome represents the beginning of the canon that accompanies the third strophe, whose text appears only later.

Webern wrote to Hildegard Jone:

> [Here] is the first full-score manuscript of 'Kleiner Flügel Ahornsamen' ... I am sure you will understand all from the 'drawing' that has appeared through the notes. But however freely it seems to float around ('schwebst im Winde ...') – possibly music has never before known anything so loose – it is the product of a *regular procedure more strict*, possibly, than anything that has formed the basis of a musical conception before (the *'little wings'*, 'they bear within themselves' – but really, not just figuratively – the 'whole ... form'. Just as your words have it!).[13]

Exactly what he expected her to see in the score is not clear, but it is indisputable that its visual aspect was important to him and that he considered its appearance to be an illustration of its content. He is working throughout with two- and four-note motives; with the exception of the clarinet melody at the beginning (which is functionally a logical extension of the voice rather than an instrumental part), no instrument ever plays more than four notes running, and none plays a single note except in those sections where chords are employed (and also excepting the glockenspiel, which is not used as an independent entity but only as a means of highlighting –

singly – an occasional note being played by another instrument). Of some 128 instrumental motives played in the course of the movement, all but 11 consist of two notes. As a result, the page presents a profusion of small binary objects continually whirling about from one instrument to another in no discernible order (indeed, even very careful study reveals none) as if being tossed by the wind.

The initial statement of P_0 with the first line of the text seems to be a definitive one: the two shapes given here – the returning figure in closed position and the deeply creased one that descends a minor ninth and then ascends a major seventh – are those from which the piece is constructed.[14] The shape of the whole statement is not unlike that of a maple key.

9.12   Op. 29/i, bars 32–5 (reduction, pitches only)

The movement is in four sections, relating to each other as ABAB. The two A sections are short – the second twice as long as the first – and both consist of a melody with chordal accompaniment. At the beginning of the song the melody is given by the clarinet; in the later A section it is sung. The melody in the B sections, which is sung, is accompanied by a canon in four voices.

9.13   Op. 29/ii, bars 1–5 (clarinet melody, pitches only)

The opening A section is just over five bars long. The clarinet melody is a setting of R_6 as a rhythmic palindrome. This melody is accompanied by a series of three-note chords, all of semiquaver duration. The rhythm of this series of chords is also symmetrical, and is, moreover, the same as that of the melody. Beginning one semiquaver later than the clarinet, this chordal accompaniment is the *comes* to the melody's *dux* (see Example 3.11 on p. 117). These chords are the product of three rows running parallel – P_0, P_6 and P_5 – so all contain the same intervals, a perfect fourth and a tritone, expressed in some cases as a tritone and a major seventh. They are distributed in four ways: as single chords played by the harp or the lower three strings in close position (there is one exception to this spacing, in bar 5), or as slurred pairs of notes played by three different instruments – flute/bass clarinet/trumpet, or oboe/trumpet/first violin – with varied spacing. Neither the

288

spacing nor the instrumentation of successive chords is ordered as a palindrome.

This texture returns at the centre of the piece, in bars 27–36. Here both melody and accompaniment are pitch palindromes, something that was not true of the opening section, where each part consisted of only one row statement. As if to offset this increased comprehensibility, rhythmic symmetry, which was a recognizable feature of the earlier section, is more obscure here. The rhythm of the accompaniment does not duplicate that of the melody as it did in the opening, and notes have been grouped into small units so that the retrograde portion of the palindrome consists of the reversal, not of individual durations, but of the sequence of these units. Melodically the R_6 in bars 27–35 is an inversion of its counterpart in bars 1–5; the direction of all but one of the motions is reversed (compare Examples 9.13 and 9.14). Although a greater variety of instrumental combinations is used in the accompaniment in this section, these are more tightly structured than before: the orchestration is also palindromic now. The peak of this symmetrical structure corresponds to the literal high point of the text – the tree's ascent, to be followed immediately by the descent of a new crop of seeds.

9.14   Op. 29/ii, bars 27–35 (melody, pitches only)

The two remaining sections, which account for the major portion of the piece, are in contrast to the A sections and are similar to each other. The soprano sings the first line of text in bars 6–27 in the rhythm of the clarinet melody in bars 1–6. Three more lines of text, each set to one row, follow. Each is set to a different rhythm; thus is the basic rhythmic material of the piece exposed. Each row, including the first, is given an identifying letter in Example 9.15. The accompaniment in both B sections consists of four row

9.15   Op. 29/11, bars 6–22 (melody, rhythm only)

chains playing in rhythmic canon with each other as well as with the voice, though the latter relationship is not immediately discernible. While each *comes* takes its rhythm from the voice part, the rhythm used by the clarinet in the A section (labelled **a** above) is omitted – the *comites* begin with the second unit of the soprano's line. This results in a peculiar turnabout, in which the soprano, who opens the canon, subsequently seems to be the fifth voice. Once she has finished her repetition of the rhythm that opened the piece, she falls into place after the fourth accompanying voice, imitating the instrumental material. Each of the instrumental chains comprises five rows rather than four, therefore each has two rows to accommodate after the material of the *dux* (turned *comes*) has been used up. When this occurs, the instrumental voices continue with a second **c** segment and end with an additional unit not encountered previously (**e**). The ideal *comes* – the rhythmic model that served as the basis of the three instrumental voices of bars 6–27 – is given in Example 9.16.

COMES, ideal form

* This rest is twice as long in the voice model.

9.16   Op. 29/ii, bars 6–27, instrumental canon (ideal form)

In fact, none of the *comites* has precisely this material. In the first complete sketch of bars 6–27, on pp. 5 and 8 of Sketchbook IV, this is the rhythm of all the voices except for six instances where a semiquaver has been replaced with a demisemiquaver rest and note. It seems likely that these demisemiquavers are alterations made to parts originally notated in semiquavers (dots added to rests and flags to notes); it was Webern's habit to revise rhythm in this way, and at least one of the possible additions is in a different coloured pencil from the rest of the sketch. If this was the case here, all four *comites* started life with the same rhythm: that of the model in Example 9.16. Later, numerous other variations in the rhythm were introduced, in one or two voices only, with the result that in the final version no two voices of the canon have exactly the same rhythmic material from start to finish: they work in pairs, and the specific associations change frequently. So, for example, the chain beginning with RI_0 (the leading voice, which will therefore be called 1) is imitated by the one beginning with R_5 (3) at the outset, while the R_{11} ... chain (4) imitates the I_9 ... one (2). From the thirteenth note, 4 is paired with 1, and 3

9.17   Op. 29/ii, bars 6–27, instrumental canon (rhythm only, parts aligned)

with 2; these relationships continue until the twenty-third note, at which point all four voices have the same material for a short period. And so on. The four voices join together in canon for a long stretch of eighteen notes in the second half of the section; for the last four notes they are paired as they were at the beginning (Example 9.17).[15]

The voice part of the second B section, in bars 36–56, is nearly a rhythmic retrograde of the last three rows of that in the first B section. (It will be remembered that there are only three lines of text in this strophe, as compared with four on the earlier occasion.) The first row is the retrograde of **d**, the soprano's final row in bars 6–27. This is followed by a new unit (**f**) and a forward-going **b**. The instrumental accompaniment, which begins four bars before the soprano on this occasion, does not this time take its cue from her, but begins instead by playing the last three segments of its own canon in bars 6–27 (units **d**, **c** and **e**), following this with, again, another **c**, and finally **f**, a sequence introduced by the soprano in bars 45–8. The incidence of the figure ♪♫ is considerably higher in this canon, where it replaces many of the semiquavers in the earlier one. With the exception of the penultimate note, the rhythmic content of all four voices is the same throughout this canon. In spite of the difference in the length of the text of the first and third strophes, the two B sections are exactly the same length. Each instrumental voice is seventy-one semiquavers or the equivalent in length, in both bars 6–27 and bars 36–56.[16]

'Tönen die seligen Saiten Apolls'

Although it was not Webern's original intention that the 'Chariten' movement of Op. 29 should come last,[17] it nevertheless seems particularly appropriate in that position, as it represents the combination of forces that have been heard only separately up to this point: the chorus of the first song is joined here by the soloist of the second, and the orchestra plays with both.

The handling of tempos and metres in this movement immediately brings to mind the first movement, if only because in both cases some or all of the indications seem unnecessary. In a way the situation here is the reverse of that in the earlier movement; while the carefully chronicled tempo changes there were the inevitable result of changing note values, the values here seem to change to no purpose, since their alteration is completely negated by the accompanying metronome indications.

The first thirty-eight bars are written in crotchet metres, and the motion is in crotchets and minims, with the indication ♩ = ca 104. At bar 39 the metres change to 3/8, 4/8 and 6/8 and the motion changes accordingly to crotchets and quavers. However, a tempo indication of ♪ = ca 104 makes this change a visual one only. The last two bars of this latter section (bars 47 and 48) are at a different tempo, and here again there seems to be more mechanism than necessary – a change back to crotchet metres and movement in crotchets and minims occurs as well as a tempo indication of $\int$ = ca 72, when a simple change to $\eighthnote$ = ca 72 would have brought the same result. The quaver metres ($\eighthnote$ = ca 104) are resumed in the following section (bars 49–57), which also slows in its final bar to crotchets and minims (and one semibreve) as $\int$ = ca 72. In this case an earlier increase in tempo to $\eighthnote$ = ca 144 at bar 54 has made the later indication redundant: it simply states what will in any case occur when motion in quavers is followed by motion in crotchets and minims. This is, of course, exactly the situation that existed throughout the first movement. All three tempos occur in the final section (bars 57–73).

Webern described this movement in similar terms in two letters upon its completion at the beginning of December 1939. To the Humpliks he wrote on 2 December:

> In construction it is a four-part *fugue*; but to regain all freedom of mobility within this strictness … in fact it turned into something completely different, a *scherzo form* that came about on the basis of *variations*. But still a *fugue!*[18]

And to Willi Reich one week later:

> It's constructed as a four-part double fugue. But the subject and counter-subject are related like antecedent and consequent (period), and the elements from the other mode of presentation (horizontal) also play a part. One could also speak of a scherzo, also of variations! Yet it's a strict fugue.[19]

By 'double fugue' Webern obviously means one in which two subjects are presented simultaneously at the outset, rather than one in which they are given separate expositions, with their combination reserved as a climax. It will be remembered that the only other twelve-note movement that Webern called a fugue, Op. 28/iii, was of this latter variety. In the present instance the subjects are heard together immediately, and a significant separation does not occur until bar 48, when one of them is developed alone.

The two subjects are in fact different expressions of essentially the same material, one completely melodic and vocal in origin, the other an irregular alternation of single notes and verticalized dyads in an instrumental style. For more than half of the movement, the version containing simultaneities is played only by the strings and the melodic version is the province of the winds and the voices. The subjects are first encountered in the forms shown in Example 9.18. Subject 1[20] may be seen as consisting of three parts. The first segment, containing two notes, is five beats long and is expressed at various times in the four ways shown in Example 9.19.[21] In every case this segment ends with a one-beat rest. The central portion of this subject takes fourteen beats; it consists of twelve or thirteen short notes, divided by rests into groups of 9 + 4, 9 + 1 + 2, 6 + 7 or 6 + 2 + 4 (Example 9.20).

9.18   Op. 29/iii, fugue subjects (pitches only)

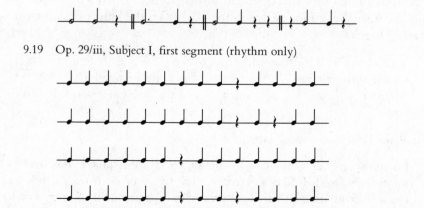

9.19   Op. 29/iii, Subject I, first segment (rhythm only)

9.20   Op. 29/iii, Subject I, central segment (rhythm only)

Subject 1 ends very much as it began, with two (longer) notes standing in a ratio of 3:2, 3:1, 2:2 or 2:1.

Subject 2 can be seen as also comprising three segments, differing in length from the corresponding part of Subject 1 but similar in content. The first segment of this subject takes the forms shown in Example 9.21. The central

9.21   Op. 29/iii, Subject II, opening segment (rhythm only)

section, like its Subject 1 progenitor, is characterized by an even rhythm; in this case there are only three events – all double stops.[22] These are separated by rests of equal value in eleven of the thirteen appearances (see Example 9.22a); the two variants are shown in Example 9.22b and c. The third segment begins with a rest and contains four events in every case. It exhibits a wide variety of forms, always including at least one double stop.

Besides the rhythmic variations noted above, the two subjects exhibit various timbral dispositions, and their contour is constantly changing.

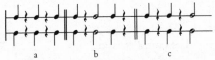

9.22   Op. 29/iii, Subject II, central segment (rhythm only)

Because of their length, a row and a half is required for the completion of either subject; therefore adjacent statements inevitably unfold through different intervallic successions and do not resemble each other melodically. Although alternate statements could exhibit the same melodic contour, these are unique as well.

The piece consists of thirty-six statements of the subjects: nineteen of Subject 1, thirteen of Subject 2, and four of a hybrid form to be examined presently. Of all these, no two are the same. The subjects are not fragmented, extended or condensed, and there is *no* other material. Obviously, then, variation is an essential process in this movement, and, since the material being varied retains its original length upon reiteration, the piece emerges as a set of variations. It exhibits, however, a density not usually encountered in connection with that form: this is a largely vertical manifestation of a form that is customarily linear. Four variations are heard simultaneously most of the time. At another level, the movement can be seen as four variations on a theme presented in bars 1–17 (or seven variations of one presented in bars 1–9). In the former case, the theme and each of the variations consists (horizontally) of a pair of subjects. (The vertical depth is the same in any case.)

Webern's reference to the antecedent–consequent relationship of the two subjects has meaning only in terms of the row structure. In the first seventeen bars the listener hears Subject 1 played twice by the wind while Subject 2 is presented twice by the strings. Only upon close scrutiny is it apparent that the two row chains that open the fugue cross after each has finished its first subject, so that their roles are reversed for the statement of the second pair; the inverted chain states Subject 1 in the wind as its antecedent, then moves to the strings for its consequent, while the inverted retrograde chain does just the opposite. Thus both voices have opened with antecedent–consequent configurations, in the course of which each subject has played both roles.

It seems reasonable to suppose that the distinction between the string and the wind/choral subjects is a reflection of the text, which makes a similar distinction between the music of Apollo's strings and the Graces. The introductory statement, in which the two subjects are pitted against each other, both vertically (as subject and countersubject) and horizontally (as mutual antecedents and consequents), thereby disguising their common derivation, would seem to parallel the opening of the text, which suggests a similar unlikelihood that Apollo and the Graces will be recognized as the origin of the music of the sunset:

> The blessed strings of Apollo sound –
> Who calls them the Graces?
> He plays his song through the darkening evening –
> Who thinks of Apollo?

The only time the string subject is heard alone is following the first section of verse, where it seems an apt reflection of the image of 'die seligen Saiten' of Apollo. This subject begins to disappear in section III (bars 39–48), during the lines

> All the former names have already faded away
>   in the sound;
> all the weaker words have already long ago died
>   in the Word.

The two statements accompanying the second of these lines of text are more pointillistically set than previous ones; characteristically the three double stops at the centre are played by a pair of string instruments, but in these two appearances this central unit has disintegrated and is played by a succession of three instruments or pairs of instruments. In section IV (bars 49–57) –

> and the fainter images melted into the seal
>   of the spectrum

– the string subject has disappeared ('melted ...') altogether. (If the other subject is seen as the prototype, was this then the 'fainter image' from the beginning?) The final set of statements corresponds with the lines

> Charis, the gift of the highest:
>   the grace of mercy shines!
> Presented in darkness to the waiting heart
>   as the dew of perfection.

Here, as we are recalled to darkness, and, by association, to Apollo, and reminded of his relationship with the Graces, and grace, the unity of purpose and the common source of the two subjects are also made apparent, their final union representing no doubt a kind of perfection.

The three formal types identified by Webern in describing this movement – fugue, variations and scherzo – are inextricably interconnected and interdependent. From his comments it would appear that, of the three, fugue was his primary consideration, or, at least, that this represented his initial intention, with the other structures accumulating around it as the movement progressed. Nevertheless, the opening eighteen bars have much less to do with fugue than with scherzo, and in fact the presence of this opening is altogether anomalous in terms of the fugue alone. The purpose of the first eighteen bars is to establish and demonstrate the antecedent–consequent nature of the subjects. It emerges as a period, the structure that nearly always opens a scherzo or variations, but one that is foreign to fugue. The fugue really begins only in bar 17, with the third subject played by the inverted retrograde chain that opened the movement. From this point on, each chain concerns itself with only one of the subjects; the antecedent–consequent arrangement is abandoned. The exposition is in stretto, with the first and third voices presenting Subject 1 and the second and fourth Subject 2. The first two voices simply continue on from their consequents of the initial period, without a break. The third voice, entering for the first time in bar 18, imitates exactly the rhythm of the first throughout the exposition. The fourth voice appears only in bar 26. Each voice presents its subject twice during the course of the exposition.

The opening period, which seems to exist for the purposes of the scherzo and variations – both essentially instrumental forms – is, appropriately, set for orchestra alone. The chorus makes its entrance when the fugue begins, doubling the two voices that are playing Subject 1. The distinction between Subject 1 as the choral subject and Subject 2 as the instrumental subject is thus made clear from the opening.

Section III, in bars 39–48, continues to combine the two subjects in the manner of the exposition. Each of the four voices states one of the subjects twice; two voices are concerned with Subject 1, the other two with Subject 2. The chorus is present, but only two voices of it at any given moment, again doubling the instruments that are playing Subject 1. All four statements of this subject are identical rhythmically. Subject 1 is confined to wind and chorus, Subject 2 played exclusively by the strings.

Section IV, in bars 48–57, is devoted entirely to Subject 1, which is presented here for the first time by full orchestra and chorus. There are still only four voices; the chorus continues to double instrumental parts, but as the entire orchestra is playing Subject 1 here, this doubling is of the string parts as well as the wind for the first time. The second set of statements is presented by instruments alone. As in each of the preceding sections, each of the four voices presents the subject twice in succession. The four first statements are rhythmically identical, the four second statements nearly so.

It is difficult to decide what to call these two sections. Structurally they occupy the space where one would expect to find fugal development. Making a decision about exactly what constitutes development as opposed to exposition is problematic in this idiom. In a tonal fugue, modulation is a sufficient reason for considering central sections developmental; in the absence of tonality, presumably inversion, stretto, augmentation or diminution should occur, but none of these is present in this case. The subjects do not, from the outset of the movement, retain recognizable melodic contours; therefore inversion is not applicable. The only stable feature to be maintained throughout is the rhythm, which would allow for augmentation and diminution, and, in fact, at first glance the latter would seem to occur in sections III and IV; but because of the tempo indications, a diminution in written values does not result in a diminution in fact. Certainly both these sections employ close stretto, but this also cannot be used to define a development in this case, since the original exposition is itself in stretto. It seems to me that the ambiguous nature of these two sections is necessary in order to allow them to service the scherzo and variations as well as the fugue. As they stand, they serve the purposes of the fugue, whether as developments or as counter-expositions, and at the same time they exhibit the periodic format required at this point by the other two structures. We shall return to this later.

The entry of the solo soprano for the first time in this movement heralds the beginning of the final section of the fugue. The soprano, singing Subject 1, is accompanied by Subject 2 in the other three voices, which are instrumental. Following this, all four voices state a new version of the subject, bringing all the resources of the movement into play in rapid alternation in a sort of fast-forward reprise: the four-part chorus doubles the orchestral parts as previously in bar 64, the chorus sings unaccompanied for the first time in bars 65–6 and again in bar 70, the solo soprano joins the orchestra without the chorus in bars 67–8 and bars 71–3, and the orchestra plays alone in bar 69. All the tempos and types of metres previously encountered return here in succession, as well. Imitation is interrupted twice by the unaccompanied chorus singing at a slow tempo in rhythmic unison. (These two bars, 65 and 70, are the only times in the movement when the chorus appears alone and does not simply double orchestral parts.) These unison figures are versions of the motive that opened both subjects throughout the movement: the pair of long notes, which in Subject 2 were followed by a short one. The first of these unison bars, bar 65, presents the figure complete, as it appeared in Subject 2. The second, in bar 70, consists of only the two long notes (with value replacement) from Subject 1. As in the first movement, the four-voice imitation seems to go on around – before and after – the four-voice homophonic interruption. The situation can be illustrated as in Example 9.23. This final version of the subject (disregarding

9.23 Op. 29/iii, bars 64–73 (rhythm only)

9.24   Op. 29/iii

the homophonic interruptions) begins with the two long notes that characteristically opened both Subject 1 and Subject 2 and ends with the group of four notes that in every case ended Subject 2 (Example 9.24). At the centre is a group of short notes of equal value surrounded on both sides by rests – looking not exactly like the centre of either subject, yet very like both. This final variant – less closely related to either subject than any of the preceding ones – seems at last to illustrate their common origin by concentrating on those figures that represent their intersection.

It may help to explain Webern's description of this movement as a scherzo if we recall his analysis of the Op. 28 Quartet. He described the second movement of that work as 'a "scherzo" in miniature' and went on to explain in the following way:

> 'Miniature' means that neither 'Scherzo' nor 'Trio' have development sections, but only a theme that is repeated . . .[23]

This makes it apparent that for Webern a scherzo had a developmental middle section, and that is certainly true of this movement, though it does not at first glance appear to have a trio, something that is usually assumed with this form.

Webern's initial demonstration of the antecedent–consequent relationship of the two subjects constitutes the opening period of the scherzo. Development begins immediately, with the fugal entries beginning in bar 17; this ends with eight bars that are in many ways very similar to the opening – one voice plays Subject 2 alone, orchestrated in the same way as the opening statement until very near the end. This acts as a shortened reprise. Sections III and IV, in bars 39–48 and 49–56, with their new metres and, in the latter section, the disappearance of the second subject, can be seen to play the role of trio. The scherzo returns with the solo soprano's entrance in bar 57 and the resumption of crotchet metres in the bars following. The final set of entries, recalling as it does features of all the previous sections, provides a satisfactory coda.

Metre and tempo changes are obviously significant in this movement, yet there are several inconsistencies I find puzzling. In general, the following arrangement holds:

> Section I (bars 1–18): crotchet metres (2/4 and 3/4) at the tempo ♩ = ca 104.
> Section II (bars 17–38): crotchet metres (2/4, 3/4, 4/4, 5/4) at ♩ = ca 104.
> Section III (bars 39–48): quaver metres (3/8, 4/8, 6/8) at ♪ = ca 104; final two bars in crotchet metres (4/4, 5/4) at ♩ = ca 72.

Section IV (bars 49–56): quaver metres (3/8, 4/8, 5/8, 6/8, 7/8, 8/8) at ♪ = ca 104; final three bars at ♪ = ca 144.

Section V/a (bars 57–63): crotchet metres (2/4, 3/4, 5/4) at ♩ = ca 104.

Section V/b (bars 64–73): alternation of quaver and crotchet metres, as well as of two tempos, ♪ = ca 104 and ♩ = ca 72.

There are a number of exceptions to this overall design; several single bars in minim metres (2/2 and 3/2) occur in those sections in which crotchet metres predominate (bars 2, 9, 17, 24, 57, 60 and 68). With two exceptions in the final section (discussed below), these metres coincide with the first or last bars of subjects – those segments containing long notes. This might imply that the longer notes at the extremities of the subjects are to be treated in some way differently than if they had been written in crotchet metres. (After all, if metre has any meaning, the effect of a note worth one beat should be slightly different from that of one worth two beats.) This seems to be overruled in this case, however, by the fact that the exact imitations of these figures fall – almost haphazardly, it would appear – in bars written in crotchet metres: 3/4, 5/4, 2/4. It is clear that the length of the crotchet is to remain constant through these metre changes (no change of tempo is indicated), and it does not seem likely that the appearance of the slower metres is to be in any way realized in performance, since their correspondence with specific portions of the subjects is only occasional.

A certain amount of ambiguity exists in connection with the tempos in the last ten bars of the movement. Metres and tempos change rapidly here, recalling all the previous events of the movement. The following indications are given:

bar 64	bar 65–6	bar 67	bar 68	bar 69	bar 70	bars 71–3
tempo	langsam	tempo I	langsam	tempo I	langsam	tempo I
♪ = ca 104	♩ = ca 72					
7/8	3/4	5/8	2/2	3/8	5/4	2,5,3/4

The beginning is clear enough: the speed of the quaver pulse is indicated in the 7/8 bar and of the crotchet pulse in the 3/4 bars. After this, however, things become more difficult. Technically, the *tempo I* indicated for bars 67 and 69 should be the tempo that opened the piece: ♩ = ca 104. However, since these are 5/8 and 3/8 bars, the tempo of bar 64 (♪ = ca 104) is clearly the one intended. The identical indication in bars 71–3, where the basic unit is the crotchet, however, obviously refers to the earlier tempo, ♩ = ca 104. This is perhaps not so surprising – one can be assumed to understand that *tempo I* indicates the application of 'ca 104' to the basic unit of whatever metre is written. A similar situation exists in connection with the *langsam* indication for bar 68, this marking having been applied previously only to bars in crotchet metres.

The inconsistency of Webern's use of *alla breve* is most apparent in a comparison of bars 60 and 68. Both these bars are in this metre, and they occupy parallel positions in statements of Subject 1 – in both cases the metre changes between the fourth and fifth notes of the long series of notes of equal value that make up the central segment of this subject. In the first instance, this series is expressed as crotchets before, after and *during* the *alla breve* bar, and all are clearly intended to be the same length, though technically the three notes that fall in the *alla breve* bar are worth only half a beat. A change in pulse or grouping here is not in agreement with any of the preceding fourteen statements of this subject. In bar 68, however, the notes in the surrounding bars, which are written in 5/8 and 3/8, are quavers (worth one beat each) and the two that fall in the *alla breve* bar are minims (one-beat notes as well, but four times the length of their neighbours). While the first instance agrees aurally, but not theoretically, with the other appearances of this subject, the second is in the spirit of its predecessors but sounds very different. The *alla breve* in bar 68 is in fact the only one in the piece that seems to have the meaning one would normally associate with it.

This latter example, in bar 68, is the technique used in the orchestral portions of the first movement: the sudden imposition of a very different tempo on four voices which, because they are in canon, are caught at different points in their statement of the same material when the change occurs. The canon continues, in slow motion for one bar, and then resumes at the previous speed.

A description of this movement using bar numbers as reference is misleading, since the third and fourth sections – bars 39–48 and 49–56 – are written in metres containing many more beats per bar than those used in the opening thirty-eight bars and the closing sixteen. A more accurate representation of balance is achieved by counting beats. This way of reckoning makes it apparent that each of these sections is of a length comparable to that of the outer two: 50, 50, 56 and 58[24] beats occur in sections I, III, IV and V respectively, in eighteen, ten, ten and sixteen bars. The second section is nearly half again as long as the opening, with seventy-four beats. This is consistent with the content: each of the five sections comprises a pair of subjects in all four voices; in the second section the fourth voice enters very late and continues long after the others. With respect to content, all five sections are exactly equal, with two statements in succession in all voices present.

Webern's first Cantata stands apart from his other works for voices in its directness of expression. The texts chosen for Op. 29 are filled with imagery of a sort not found in either Op. 26 or Op. 31, and Webern takes full advantage of the opportunities this provides. At the same time, these three pieces are carefully structured in purely musical terms, particularly the third. This was to be Webern's last fugue as well as his last scherzo. In his next –

and last – large work for voices and instruments, he is preoccupied with exploring the possibilities offered by a set of musical techniques that have not been tried before (see pp. 78ff and 119ff); neither text expression nor formal structuring plays a role of such importance here as it did in Op. 29.

10

Cantata II

The six movements of Webern's last published work were conceived and written in two groups of three pieces each. The groups are very similar in outward design, each comprising an accompanied recitative for solo voice followed by an aria for the same voice and finally a movement for chorus and orchestra. Webern thought of each of these groups of three – perhaps especially the first composed – as a cohesive unit.[1] The group that eventually became movements four, five and six was begun in the spring of 1941[2] and finished by September of the following year.[3] The other group – movements one, two and three – was begun immediately[4] thereafter and finished in November of 1943.[5] A seventh movement was begun but soon abandoned as a part of the cantata, which Webern decided was complete as it stood.[6]

'Leichteste Bürden der Bäume'

On 13 August 1941 Webern wrote to the Humpliks:

> By the same post I am sending you the first piece of my new work. It is 'Der Wind'. However unassuming and simple-seeming the result, the constructive task I set myself was an extremely difficult one! With 'the most delicate breath' this should open the new 'Cantata' – or whatever it turns out to be. *Formally*, then, it is introductory, as the heading 'Recitative' implies. It is to be followed by 'Freundselig ist das Wort' – as a *choral piece*.[7]

'Leichteste Bürden . . . ' (from the poem 'Der Wind') has the briefest text of all the movements: two lines of poetry that divide as the result of rhyming and punctuation into 8, 5 and 3, and 7, 2 and 5, syllables respectively. Webern's setting is twenty-two bars long, comprising two sections of eleven bars each. (Despite an anacrusis and constantly changing metres, the barline separating bars 11 and 12 marks the exact centre of the piece, in fact as well as appearance. There are ninety-eight crotchet values altogether, forty-nine before and forty-nine after this point.)

303

The melody, which, judging from Webern's remarks to Reich, was exemplary of the principles that guided his composition of the piece,[8] shows several layers of symmetry. The four untransposed rows that constitute the melody are arranged in such a way that, with respect to row structure, each half of the melody (bars 2–11 and 12–21) is itself a palindrome, the second the inverted retrograde of the first. Both these symmetries are preserved in a group of seven notes at the centre of each half of the song (the bracketed notes in Example 10.1); the latter is hinted at by the contour of shorter segments elsewhere (bracketed with discontinuous lines in the Example).[9] The rhythm, which has already been examined on pp. 121–2, sustains the double palindromic construction as well. The initial note of the untransposed prime functions as a tonal focus for this movement. Both halves of the melody begin and end on f♯[1]. Each is preceded by an instrumental f♯[1] as well (played by the saxophone at the opening and by the harp on the last beat of bar 11), and the glockenspiel insists on f♯[3] in the middle of the first half and twice near the end of the second (three of only four notes played by this instrument in the course of the movement).

10.1   Op. 31/v, melody (pitches only)

The accompaniment consists of five timbral groups with fixed constitution throughout, playing very limited, and therefore repetitive, material. Four of the five play chords only: the strings, the brass and two woodwind combinations, one consisting of flute, oboe, clarinet and bassoon, the other of piccolo, saxophone and bass clarinet.

Of these four groups, the brass have the most limited repertoire. They play the same chord on three occasions only: just before and just after the seven-note segment at the centre of the melody's first palindrome and at the same time as the central note of its second one. The recurrence of this chord in the manner of an intermittent pedal acts as a unifying device, underlining the sameness of the material throughout. The piccolo group plays four times in the course of the movement: an augmented triad in open position on two occasions in the first half of the piece and the same chord a tritone lower on two occasions in the second half. These four chords are evenly spaced throughout the movement and emphasize the bipartite structure, since the chord is transposed to a different level in the second half of the piece. The larger woodwind combination plays only three times in the course of the movement; its activities serve to reinforce the overall palindromic shape of the song, since the first and last chords – played near the beginning and at the very end of the piece – are the same, and the middle one, falling at the centre, is its inversion. (This inverted chord is a close aural relative of the original: the highest and lowest notes remain the same while both inner notes fall a semitone.) For ease in future reference, the chord played by this group in bar 11 will be referred to as chord **a** and its inversion, in bars 2 and 22, as chord **b**.

The strings play more diversified material than any of the three groups just discussed, and they are present a considerably greater share of the time. They act in conjunction with the larger woodwind group and the brass, commenting in some way on each chord played by these two groups. The strings' relationship with the woodwind group is the more easily perceived of its roles. It plays either chord **a** or chord **b** in response to each of the woodwind contributions. At the opening of the piece, the strings play **a** in bar 2 before the voice enters; the woodwind respond with **b** just as the soprano begins. At the centre of the movement, the soprano's re-entry with the second line of poetry is similarly framed, this time with the woodwind's **a** answered by the strings' **b**. The song finishes with two statements of **b**, played first by strings and then by woodwind, now at last in agreement. The strings play three other chords, two in the course of the first half of the piece and one near the end of the second half. These seem to be in response to those played by the brass instruments. The derivation of the second of these, in bar 8, is the clearest of the three: it is the inversion of the brass chord in bar 7. The third, in bar 18, is a transposition of the brass chord in bar 16 up a semitone, in open position with a fourth note added above. The first of the strings' responses to the brass, in bar 5, demonstrates the most tenuous relationship; it is a four-note chord like that in bar 18 and contains, besides the added note (in this case an F), a tritone transposition of all the notes played by the brass in bar 4, verticalized in a different way. In attempting to summarize the functions of the strings, it can be said that they consistently echo the flute group and brass except in the case of the first and last woodwind chords, which they anticipate.

The most variety is found in the metallic instruments – celesta and glockenspiel – and the harp, which is grouped with them. The celesta plays a variety of single notes, including the structurally significant f♯^{1} that stands at the centre of the movement, introducing the second line of poetry in the same way that the saxophone introduced the first. The glockenspiel plays a d♯^{4} in bar 2; it plays only three more times – the f♯^{3} noted above in all cases. The harp plays only in the bass clef, and very little, until bar 15, where it suddenly plays, all alone, a series of notes resulting from the intersection of several rows. This is heard somewhat indistinctly, owing to the instrument's naturally quiet timbre and the low dynamic level (*pp*), and can be seen to have an illustrative purpose, as the 'Gestalt' heard in the distance. (It accompanies the word 'fernher'.) The chord played at the end of this figure is a rearrangement of the augmented triad that was played in the first half of the song by the smaller woodwind group and abandoned by those instruments in the second half. (The top note is the same, and the lower two have exchanged positions so that the intervals are sixths now rather than thirds.)

In the course of the movement, the three most stable groups of instruments play altogether ten chords, arranged symmetrically in the order flute group–piccolo group–brass–piccolo–flute in each half. The strings' comments on the chords played by the flute and brass groups and their silence with respect to those played by the piccolo group cloud this symmetry considerably. The resulting distortion of the underlying shape of the piece – the *Gestalt* – seems to be another expression, at a deeper level than the surface events of bar 15, of the most significant idea in the text: the scarcely perceivable transmission of an essence over a long distance. The structural result is the sort of superposition of forms that we have observed frequently in the instrumental works prior to this. The melody – which is for the most part sung – and the two woodwind groups and the brass play an overall symmetrical structure consisting of two segments, while the smaller woodwind group alone, through its pitch content, emphasizes the binary rather than the circular aspect of this form. The remaining instruments – strings, harp, celesta and glockenspiel – do not contribute to this structure at all, forging instead their own, which is asymmetrical and essentially non-repetitive, climaxing in bar 15, a classical two-thirds of the way through the movement.

'Freundselig ist das Wort'

Webern described the movement following his first recitative as an aria for soprano solo with chorus and orchestra.[10] It is in three large parts, with the soprano aria occupying the central position, flanked by very similar sections in which phrases or fragments of phrases are sung alternately by unaccompanied four-part chorus and accompanied solo soprano. In the sketches, the preceding recitative, which was at that point the first movement of the work, was followed directly by the indication 'attacca no. 2'.[11]

It will be recalled that the melody of the recitative was based on a rhythmic palindrome that first occurred in bars 2–5. The entire fabric of the recitative was derived from this rhythm,[12] and it continues to play an important role in the aria following. For the purpose of examining its

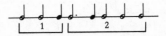

10.2 Op. 31/iv, rhythmic model, bars 2–5

presence in the latter movement, it will be useful to identify two components, marked and numbered in Example 10.2. The choral movement begins with component 1 (in diminished note values), set apart from what follows by a rest, and continues immediately with the retrograde of a truncated component 2. This large section of the piece ends with a palindromic figure based on this same version of component 2 (Example 10.3). The two relatively long and complex imitative episodes in the first A section, in bars 3–6 and 12–14, both end with a statement of component 1 in

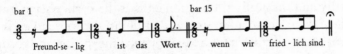

10.3 Op. 31/v, bars 1–3, 15–16 (rhythm only)

the solo violin, the first, in bar 6, inverted.[13] When the chorus returns in bar 46, its opening statement is rhythmically identical to the one in bars 1–3. This seems to be the extent of the influence of the generating rhythm on the outer sections of this movement. Its presence is felt to a much greater extent in the aria.

The aria is itself in three sections. In the first of these (bars 17–24)[14] the melody consists of three occurrences of a rhythmic ostinato consisting of components 2 and 1 elided (Example 10.4). The second section (bars 25–33)

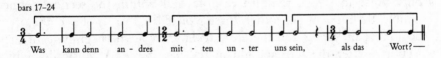

10.4 Op. 31/v, bars 17–24, melody (rhythm only)

is similarly repetitive, but the ostinato figure is longer and occurs only twice. This ostinato uses the entire rhythm as it originally appeared in bars 2–5 of the recitative; the only alteration is the subdivision of the minims at the end into crotchets (Example 10.5). It is appropriate that this, the central section and the axis of this movement, should refer more directly than any other to the recitative where the rhythmic basis of both movements was established. Component 1 operates as a motto in this section. It begins each of the statements, and it is the last thing to be sung at the end. Following this it is echoed by the solo violin in bars 32 and 33 as a bridge into the next section.

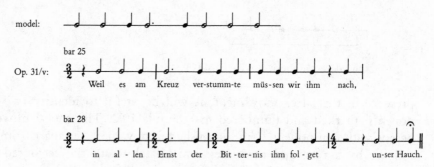

10.5 Op. 31/v, bars 25–31, melody (rhythm only)

The end of the central section provides a good example of the sort of musical/structural contradiction of which Webern seems to have been so fond. Textually and musically this section ends at the barline separating bars 31 and 32: the text comes to a full stop at that point, the soprano ends with a final statement of the rhythmic figure that opened the section and recurred in the centre at bar 28, and the final note of bar 31 is approached with a ritard and sustained with a fermata. Adding to the definition of this close is the resumption of the tempo of the first section (bars 17–24) in bar 32 and the entry alone of the solo violin, in contrast to the rather dense chordal texture of bar 31. Even the row structure (shown on p. 91) seems to indicate this as the close of a section, since the end of the soprano's P₇ corresponds exactly with the end of bar 31. It may be the row structure, nevertheless, that provides the clue to the ambiguity surrounding this barline, since the last three notes of the *dux*'s P₇ are also the first three notes of its next row, RI₉, and therefore also the opening of the following section of the aria. (A parallel row structure exists, of course, in all voices. However, the soprano is the only voice in which these three notes fall within the section defined by double barlines; in the other three voices all these notes come after the beginning of bar 32 and therefore technically at the beginning of the next section – after the fermata and in the new tempo.) Musically, while the soprano's figure bears the just-noted rhythmic associations with the material of the second section, its melodic contour is different from that of its two previous appearances, and this new contour is repeated immediately by the solo violin in its already-cited entry in bars 32–3. Therefore, this three-note group – 10–12 *cum* 1–3 – functions structurally as a bridging figure (in all voices) in spite of the fact that on the page (and to the ear) bar 31 offers one of the most apparent closures in the movement.

The third section of the aria (bars 33[32?]–45) is an extended variation of bars 17–24. Again the ostinato from these bars appears three times; each time it is further removed from the original. Value replacement is used in all three statements, and, beginning with the second, the last two minims are converted to pairs of crotchets, a technique introduced in bars 26–7 and 30 of

308

the previous section. In the third statement, this crotchet motion seems unable to stop, and as a result the figure is longer than it should be. These increasingly varied appearances lead up to a final statement which is sufficiently altered that it can no longer be identified as a variation of the ostinato, though it is a logical successor to the events leading up to it, continuing the proliferation of crotchets that began in bars 25–31 and got out of hand, as it were, in bars 39–40 (Example 10.6).

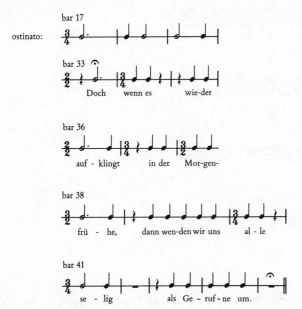

10.6   Op. 31/v, bars 32–45, melody (rhythm only)

The centre of this movement has close melodic as well as rhythmic ties with the preceding movement. The motive that provides this bond is usually four notes long and first occurs on the syllables 'Bürden der Bäu-' in the preceding recitative. It appears in its entirety four times during the course of the aria – once in each of the three sections and in the figure at the close (in bars 22–4, 29–30, 34–5 and 43–4) – and once with the first note displaced (in bar 27). These appearances are dissimilar rhythmically – two are interrupted by rests between the first and second notes (in bars 22 and 34–5). Nevertheless, the contour itself is pervasive (Example 10.7).

In the letter to Hildegard Jone dated 25 July 1942 Webern described the textual basis for casting this movement in an arch form (though in view of the frequency of his use of symmetrical structures, a textual rationale seems hardly necessary):

> at the centre are the words: 'Weil er[15] am Kreuz verstummte, müssen wir ihm nach, in allen Ernst der Bitternis, ihm folget unser Hauch.'

What went before is now repeated backwards ... '*Repeated*': 'All shapes are similar and *none are the same* ...[16]

iv, bars 4–5

Bür - den der Bäu -

v, bars 22–4

sein, als das Wort

v, bars 29–30

der Bit - ter - nis

v, bars 34–5

es wie - der auf -

v, bars 43–4

als Ge - ruf - ne

10.7 Op. 31/iv–v

As indicated, the reversal operates in very general terms only. Structurally the movement is in ABA form with a similarly tripartite B section. The symmetrical disposition of chords in the aria was thoroughly examined in Chapter 2.[17] Suffice it to say here that the accompaniment of each of the three sections of the aria is also symmetrically arranged.

	bar 17		bar 25		bar 32		bar 46	
	A				B			A
		A			B		A	
		A B A		A B A		A B A		

In addition, the orchestration of the chords in the first section of the aria (bars 17–24) is symmetrical in a way that is reminiscent of Op. 21. The ten chords in the section are clearly arranged as a double palindrome plus a cadence:

(cadence)

| celesta brass harp brass | celesta | harp brass harp celesta | strings |

The first A section (bars 1–16) consists of four homophonic choral statements separated by three imitative interjections in which the solo soprano and the solo violin figure most prominently. The text is divided into segments of 6, 10, 4, 3, 7, 7 and 5 syllables:

> Freundselig ist das Wort,
> > das uns um unsre Liebe zu sich fragt,
> 'fürchte dich nicht,
> > ich bin es,'
> tröstet durch die Dunkelheit,
> > das mitten unter uns ist,
> wenn wir friedlich sind.

This division of the poetry results in a carefully regulated dramatic shape. The first and the last three segments are of comparable length, establishing a standard for alternation. The second segment is quite extended – leisurely, even; it is followed by a very short fragment and this immediately by an even shorter one. The vivid sense of precipitation accomplished through this series of events is then dissipated by the relatively equal length of the following three segments.

Webern follows this progression of events for the first four sections, beginning with a solid choral statement in quavers that is *forte* until the final note, followed by the longest contrapuntal episode in the first section, still *forte* but rhythmically more complex and faster paced than the opening, with considerable imitation carried on by the solo violin and soprano, and culminating in a short bar of silence. The following brief choral fragment, which is suddenly *pianissimo*, begins with the quaver motion of the opening but soon changes to semiquavers. The goal of this rather breathless rush forwards – the brief statement 'ich bin es' – is executed in three demisemi-quavers, *pianissimo*, quickly imitated by all the other voices. Thus the critical and most intimate revelation of the verse is delivered in a barely perceived whisper and is over almost instantly. Webern makes this fleeting but crucial moment – the fourth of seven segments – the musical focal point of the section by setting the remaining three phrases so that musically they closely resemble the first three in reverse order, thereby making the return to normality a gradual process rather than the sudden one indicated by the poetry alone. And, incidentally, incorporating his favourite structure.

When this music returns, in bars 46–60, there are two more segments than there were the first time. This difference in numbers means that the segment that functions as the axis is now choral rather than imitative. The text is divided in the following way:

> Freundselig ist das Wort.
> > Und wenn du weißt, daß es um alles Deine weiß,
> dann kennst du es:
> > denn tut's dir weher als der Tod,
> wenn eine Wolke

> Feindseligkeit:
> der Tränen Mutter
> sich zwischen dir und ihm erweilert
> und die Kälte schafft.

The syllabic content of these segments – 6, 12, 4, 8, 5, 4, 5, 9, 5 – is not as centrally focused as in the opening section. The first and last lines contain the same number of syllables as the first and last lines of the earlier verse; however, here there is no single shortest segment, and the one occupying the central position is neither longer nor shorter than most. This problem is overcome by Webern's climax in this case encompassing the three central segments, this association producing a roughly symmetrical and certainly more pointed syllabic sequence (6, 12, 4, 17, 5, 9, 5).

The climax thus arrived at is realized in a way directly opposed to that in the opening verse, something that is, in fact, to be expected; in spite of the identical opening lines, the sentiments expressed in these two verses of poetry are very different. Whereas the opening had to do with comfort and peace ('"fürchte dich nicht"...tröstet durch die Dunkelheit...wenn wir friedlich sind'), the final verse is concerned with grief and desolation ('denn tut's dir weher als der Tod...Feindseligkeit der Tränen Mutter...die Kälte schafft'); whereas the climax of the first section, the simple statement of reassurance, was unique in its hushed simplicity, this climax, which embraces the ideas of a grief worse than death and the bitter hatred of a mother's tears – two of the most powerfully negative images one can conjure up – calls for a loud and impassioned outcry. That is precisely what occurs, in bars 51–4. These four bars contain the three central segments of the verse, the choral segment that actually stands at the centre coming as an interjection, or an interruption of the solo soprano. The music of these bars is *forte* and is the most angular of any of the soprano's material in the outer sections of the movement, containing notes both higher and lower than she is asked to sing anywhere else. The complicated feelings dealt with in this section are expressed through much more complex and disparate rhythms than those used to describe the simple peace with which the opening verse concerns itself, and urgency is felt in the compressed imitation.

In purely musical terms the similarities between the opening and closing sections are very great, but, as Webern indicates in his description to Hildegard Jone, nothing ever recurs exactly. Segments do not recur in reverse order, as one might suppose from his remarks. Perhaps the most interesting observation to be made in comparing the two sections is that their purely technical structure seems to be quite separate and distinct from the dramatic structures just outlined. This is by no means the first time that we have observed this sort of disagreement between levels or categories of structure. Just such an overlay of dissimilar plans has been, in fact, a recurring feature in the music with which this study is concerned.

The two opening choral segments are not only identical rhythmically but have similar melodic contours as well. Since they are not produced by the same row form, it is not to be expected that they should contain all the same intervals; however, the similarity of various forms of this particular row in fact does allow exactly the same ending on both occasions (Example 10.8).

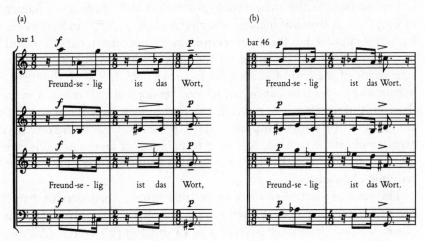

10.8   Op. 31/v, bars 1–3, 46–7

One is also struck by the similarity of the two first episodes, though it is difficult to find the recurrence of precise details. The soprano begins both times with the three descending notes of the melodic figure given above as Example 10.7. This is imitated by the solo violin on the first occasion; the second time the violin plays a counter-melody that is related only obliquely to the soprano line. Both sections contain chords, but not the same chord. The rhythm of the melody instruments is more cluttered the second time, with triplets against duplets and numerous grace notes, and the imitation is more intense.

The next three sections can best be discussed as a unit. Their surface features are not very similar, but nevertheless as a group they seem to operate in more or less the same way on both occasions. The two choral segments are short and are very similar to each other both times – that is to say that while the rhythm of bar 50 is not especially like that of its counterpart in bar 8, it *is* very similar to bar 52, as 8 is to 10. And in both cases these closely related choral segments are separated by a one-bar imitative episode moving in demisemiquavers. As a unit, therefore, bars 50–2 have a good deal in common with bars 8–10.

The similarity of the next pair of segments, in bars 12–14 and 53–4, is more obvious, though the first two bars of imitative material are missing in the later statement. The soprano's last four notes in bar 53 are very nearly a transposition of the solo violin's figure in bar 14, and there is an accompanying chord on both occasions. At this point, the parallels cease temporarily. We have come to the final choral segment of the first A section and have yet three segments remaining in the second. Upon close inspection, it becomes apparent that the two segments occupying bars 55–8 recall the aria (the central section of the movement rather than the opening). Characteristics calling the aria to mind include: the rhythm ♪ | ♩. ♪♫ in bars 54–5, which has never appeared in the outer sections but was heard in bars 25–6 and 28–30 of the aria; the first four notes of the solo soprano in bar 56, which are the retrograde of the complete melodic figure of Example 10.7; the three chords in the lower strings in bar 56, which are versions of the only tetrad found in the aria (and nowhere else); the chords in the celesta in bars 57 and 58, which are versions of the most important triad in the aria (also found nowhere else). Structurally these four bars are an interpolation of aria material just prior to the close in bars 59–60, where the parallel progress of the two A sections is resumed and finished.

The text of bars 59–60 is one syllable longer than that of bars 15–16; except for the first note, which has been added to accommodate this extra syllable, 59 and 60 are the inversion of 15 and 16 in all voices. (All the voices are parallel in the second instance; one note is displaced an octave in both tenor and bass in bars 15–16.) It should be noted that this last segment, which clearly takes its pitch content from A, is cast in a B rhythm, thereby forming a fitting summary to end the piece:

bars:	1–3	3–7	8	9	10–11	12–14			15–16
	chorus	solos	chorus	solos	chorus	solos			chorus
	homophonic	imitative	homophonic	imitative	homophonic	imitative			homophonic
			climax						

46–7	47–9	50	51	52	53–4	54–5	56–8	59–60
chorus	solos	chorus	solos	chorus	solos	chorus	solos	chorus
homophonic	imitative	homophonic	imitative	homophonic	imitative	homophonic	imitative	homophonic
			[c l	i m	a x]	[a r i a	r e c a l l e d]	

Before closing this discussion, I cite a greeting to the Humpliks dated 'Christmas 1941',[18] since it opens with a sketch of the beginning of this movement. In August of 1941 Webern had written that the first piece of his new work (the fourth movement) was completed and that he was sending them a copy in the same post. At this time he continued, 'It is to be followed by "Freundselig ist das Wort" – as a choral piece.'[19] He makes no mention at this time of the soprano solo that eventually became for him of paramount importance. The sketch of this choral piece included as part of Webern's Christmas message that year is in 4/2 metre, and the rhythm is considerably different from the final version in 3/8 and 2/8 (Example 10.9).[20]

Chorus

Freund - se - lig   ist das Wort.

10.9   Op. 31/v, sketch of opening

'Gelockert aus dem Schoße'

The piece that was to become the final movement of Op. 31 and thus his last completed work had a special personal significance for Webern. He had already announced the completion of 'Gelockert aus dem Schoße' in a letter to the Humpliks on 4 September 1942.[21] Two and a half months later he referred to it again, joyfully (joy was a scarce commodity during these years), announcing the birth of his granddaughter Liesa ('Loosed from the womb, in God's space of springtime . . . '). He included a musical quotation of the opening bars in the letter, remarking 'Thus was it written for her!'[22]

In the earlier letter he had described it as 'a sort of "chorale"' that was, however, 'not to be thought of in the *Bachian* sense'. And to Willi Reich he had written on the same day that it was 'conceived as a "chorale" . . . Long note-values but very flowing tempo.'[23] In both the September letters he describes the closely interlocking relationships of the four voices (discussed on p. 136), and he tells Reich that he thinks the 'look of the score' will 'amaze' him. Certainly it looks different from the other pieces in the collection, unlike, in fact, anything else he had written. It is the only movement of his published twelve-note music in which different metres are indicated simultaneously in different parts.[24]

It is particularly interesting to compare the notation of this piece with that of the one directly preceding it. Whereas the quaver metres and the motion in quavers, semiquavers and demisemiquavers of the outer sections of 'Freundselig ist das Wort' give the visual impression of rapid motion, and the minim metres and movement exclusively in white notes of 'Gelockert aus dem Schoße' give it the appearance of repose, the minims of the latter in fact move three times as quickly as the quavers of the former ($\flat$ = 56 in No. V, while $\downarrow$ = 168 in No. VI).[25] Beyond the fact that he thought of the latter piece as a chorale, it is difficult to imagine Webern's reason for notating either piece in the way that he did. The faithful replication in all three *comites* of the succession of metres introduced in the *dux*, in conjunction with the white notation, makes the piece look particularly archaic. Certainly 'not . . . Bachian'. A further antique device, hocket, comes to mind, particularly in the statement by all voices of their third and final rows (bar 14 onwards); to my knowledge Webern never made reference to this.

This movement is unique in Webern's œuvre by virtue of the extent to which it uses exact repetition. The three stanzas of the poem are sung to the same music, notated in the manner of a hymn (chorale), the text of each verse set directly beneath the last within a single appearance of the music. This is a significant departure for a composer who, with the exception of a few *pro forma* repeat signs in earlier sonata movements (Opp. 20, 21 and 22), had for all of his life scrupulously avoided the recurrence of musical detail in those situations where tradition expected it.

Each verse of poetry consists of five lines with an ABABA rhyming scheme. The syllabic content of the lines is 7, 6, 7, 6, 7. The rhythmic content of the setting is simple and repetitive and does not seem particularly to support the poetic relationships, beyond the fact that all poetic divisions are marked by rests. Two closely related rhythmic figures predominate, practically to the exclusion of all else. Both are five beats in length: ♩. ♩ and ♩♩♩. Each line of poetry begins with one of these figures: the movement opens with the first; thereafter all lines begin with the second. The first, third and fifth lines, which rhyme, end with the first figure as well; the second and fourth do not. The following associations result (in the diagram below, the lines of poetry are labelled A and B in accordance with the rhyme scheme, while the two rhythmic figures given above are represented as **a** and **b**):

A		B		A		B		A	
▬▬		▬▬		▬▬		▬▬		▬▬	
a	a	ba		b	a	b	(a)	b	a

The two figures combined constitute seven notes; the third and fifth lines, both of which have seven syllables, consist of one statement of **b** and one of **a** and nothing else. They are nevertheless not identical rhythmically, since **a** follows directly on the heels of **b** in line three while the two figures are separated by rests in line five. The opening line, which also has seven syllables, does not take advantage of the convenient length of **a** and **b** combined. Here the three-note figure is repeated; this necessitates the addition of an extra note, which occurs just ahead of the repetition. The second line, which, having six syllables, might have used either a pair of **a** figures or **a** and **b** overlapping, does the second, but the figures overlap by two notes rather than the required one; thus this line requires an extra note as well – in this case it comes at the end. Line four appears to contain only one **b** unit, with two minims added after a long rest, almost as an afterthought. In fact, however, the last three notes of this line can be seen as an **a** unit, either with value replacement or in retrograde.

However they are explained, these two isolated minims can perhaps be seen as an example of the difficulty that arises in setting several verses of text to the same music. The rhythm of this line works well in verse one, where the text is 'zu Stern und Mensch—und Baum', but is much less successful in the third verse with 'uns, weil ein Kind—lein spricht'. For that matter, since, as in most poetry, the rhyming words are not necessarily those at the end of grammatical phrases, the rests between lines are not very satisfactory in several cases, notably between the last phrase just quoted and the one directly preceding it. The whole effect of this kind of setting is to condemn the poem to a singsong rendition, though this is masked somewhat by the staggering of the four voices in canon.

'Schweigt auch die Welt'

Having completed what he described as the unit that was to be the first section of his new cantata,[26] Webern proceeded on to 'a *new part*' that would eventually supplant what he had just written as the opening group. Again he envisaged beginning with a recitative and aria, this time for bass voice, and both texts were chosen before he began to write.[27]

The four lines of the poem 'Strahl und Klang' comprise two rhyming couplets with the following syllabic content:

```
4   –   7   –   6
4   –   7   –   6

4   –   7   –   6
        11  –   6   –   4
```

These are set in four stanzas, of twelve, twelve, thirteen and ten bars' (44, 44, 40 and 40 beats') length, with an additional bar of four beats standing at the structural centre. The divisions are marked with double barlines, with the central bar preceding the barline that marks the end of the second section.

Interestingly, the row content does not support this structure. It is possible that this disparity between two simultaneous structures may be what Webern was referring to when he wrote to the Humpliks upon its completion:

> 'Strahl und Klang' is over and done with ... The piece took a relatively long time ... One reason, probably the main one, was the formal thing: a form emerged that must have lain dormant for a long, long time.[28]

Two series of rows progress together throughout the movement, one providing melodic material and the other accompaniment.[29] Both are cyclic, consisting of three statements of the four rows at T_6 plus an extra statement of the opening row added at the end. In both series the first two cycles correspond with the first two lines of verse; the entire second couplet is set to the remaining cycle with its additional row. The apparent discrepancy between the quantity of text presented by the first two statements of the series and that covered by the third is accounted for by the fact that the first couplet is surrounded by instrumental melody (half of each complete cycle of melodic rows is played rather than sung in this section), while in the second couplet all the melodic material is sung. The return of the melodic series to its opening row at the end results, in fact, in one more sung row in the second couplet than there was in the first. This added length is necessary in order to accommodate the final line of the poem, which is extended.

The row structure of the piece falls clearly into three strophes plus a coda, a structure that is at odds with the poetic framework of four stanzas. This structure *is*, however, supported by temporal proportions: although the four stanzas identified earlier are of nearly equal length in terms of bars and beats, the third is at a tempo twice as fast as the rest of the movement, and this, coupled with the fact that the fourth section has fewer bars than any of the other three, results in the third and fourth lines together taking only slightly longer to express than either the first or the second alone, this slight lengthening resulting from the additional syllables in the final line. In both serial and temporal terms, therefore, the movement is in three strophes. I shall henceforth refer to the poetic/musical structure of the piece in terms of *lines* and *couplets* (of which there are respectively four and two). The word *strophe* will refer only to the row structure, which consists of three strophes and coda.

The rhythmic materials used in the melody of this movement are diverse but carefully organized. The melodic material of the first strophe consists of three hexachords played – by flute, then violin, then flute – followed by three hexachords sung; this melody uses numerous durational values, involving both duple and triple divisions, and it forms a rhythmic palindrome. Its pitch classes are palindromic, also, since the row content is I_6/ii–R_6–P_6–RI_6/i, but only in the two central hexachords (R_6/ii and P_6/i) is this realized melodically (Example 10.10). The situation is reversed in the

10.10   Op. 31/i, bars 6–9, melody

second strophe, where the initial three hexachords (I_6/ii and R_6) are sung and the last three played, this time by horn and bass clarinet. The first (sung) portion of this melody is a 1:2 augmentation of the parallel (instrumental) portion of the melody of the preceding strophe, while the second half (now instrumental) is a 2:1 diminution of its (sung) predecessor (and therefore a 4:1 diminution in retrograde of the sung melody immediately preceding it in this strophe).[30] This instrumental melody is shorter than its vocal counterpart in the first strophe by six notes as the result of the verticalization of both hexachords of the RI_6 at the end of this strophe in bar 25, the structural centre of the piece.

The melody of the third strophe (the second couplet) is yet another statement of the same rhythmic palindrome, with the first half at the same tempo as the melody sung in the second strophe[31] and the second half the same as the sung portion of the first strophe, in bars 7–12. The voice begins the fourth line of text with the same music with which it opened the first couplet in bar 8. Thus the two lines of the second couplet are rhythmically identical to the two sung lines of the previous couplet, in reverse order.

As is so often the case in Webern's music, the idea of palindromic activity exists at two levels. Each strophe is a rhythmic and pitch-class palindrome: all are, in fact, variants of the same one. Only the first is rhythmically simple – both second and third employ diminution in the regression; and in none of the three are the pitch classes distributed in such a way as to create a symmetrical contour. The second strophe is also in a sense incomplete, because of the already noted verticalization of both hexachords of its final row. Since all strophes are versions of the same palindrome, it follows that, hypothetically at least, the three taken together produce a palindrome at another level (also imperfect for the reasons just mentioned). From another perspective, the second couplet mirrors the first, comprising as it does the sung portions of the earlier couplet presented in reverse order. Here again, as so often before, we see an overlay, or juxtaposition, of structures: not an ambiguity so much as a multiplicity of interpretations. The following diagram shows the way in which the binary and ternary structures of this song mesh:

		1.				2.		
		▬▬▬▬▬▬				▬▬▬▬▬▬		
couplets:	x	A	B	x		B	A		
		▬▬▬▬▬▬		▬▬▬▬▬▬			▬▬▬▬▬▬	
strophes:	a	B	A	b		A	B	[A]
	1.		2.			3.		coda

[x represents instrumental segments containing no voice part and therefore no text.]

The first and last hexachords of the melodic series in each of the three strophes are verticalized, creating a series of pillars that support and clarify the ternary row structure of the movement. In the outer strophes, these defining pillars are separated by the remaining six hexachords of the four-row cycle expressed melodically. The central strophe sacrifices one of its melodic hexachords – what would have been its final one – in order to create a double pillar at the poetic centre of the piece, in bar 25, where both hexachords of RI_6 are verticalized. Although the two hexachords are not articulated at the same moment, they subsequently sound together, resulting in the densest moment in the body of the movement. This level of density occurs only once more, in bar 48, where all twelve notes are struck simultaneously after the text has finished. These two twelve-note aggregates reinforce the binary structure of the text.

The symmetrical structure of the melody (AB BA) is suggested by the text, which in the outer lines speaks of the colours visible by day and in the central lines of the nightingale's song that supplants them when darkness falls. Several textual relationships are distinguished by identical musical settings; this is made possible by the fact that closely related words occupy parallel syllabic positions in lines 1 and 4, and in lines 2 and 3, of the poem. Because of this parallelism, repeating row cycles made it possible for Webern to set the key words of the outer lines – 'Farben (ist)' in line 1 and 'Farbige' in line 4 – in the same way, as well as those words most central to the image of lines 2 and 3 (the idea of *sound* as colour) – 'Nachtigall' and 'klingt es auf'. Later, the setting of 'Klang hervor', which acts as a short coda, reflects back to these central lines of the poem and their concern with sound rather than sight (Example 10.11). 'Farbenschimmer', in line 2, and its answering symbol in line 3, 'Aug mehr bindet', are also given the same melodic treatment (Example 10.12).

10.11   Op. 31/i

10.12

In the course of the three strophes the definition of material in the accompanying cycle seems to diminish progressively. It is reasonable to see this as a musical expression of the fading and eventual disappearance of colour that inevitably accompanies the arrival of darkness, the central image of the text.[32] This analogy would seem to be supported by the melodic cycle's shortening in the second strophe and total abandonment in the third of the instrumental melodies that are a colourful and almost iridescent (because of the changes of timbre and register) aspect of the early part of the piece.

The accompanying cycle enters in bar 2 with its first hexachord (P_6/i) verticalized. It continues with two short patterns – one note followed by five played together, and the reverse of this – in the harp and celesta.[33] These events are more or less reversed in the second half of the first strophe (the vocal portion). The rhythm and pitch classes are in retrograde, but the spacing has been changed slightly. These bars can be seen in Example 2.24 (p. 80). The accompaniment of the second strophe begins as before, with the first hexachord verticalized, but proceeds this time to a five–note melodic figure in the clarinet. An inexact retrograde inversion of this follows, as in the first strophe, and, again, a verticalized hexachord, making a palindrome of sorts. Like the melody, the accompaniment in the second half of this strophe is truncated, and therefore these events are not repeated as was the opening of the first strophe in bars 8–11.

Here, at the centre of the poetic form, the accompanying cycle gives up any melodic pretensions (just as the melodic cycle sheds its instrumental role at the same point), and for the remainder of the piece it supplies only heptads as a background for the now purely vocal melody. The entire second couplet is, in fact, nearly unaccompanied. The two rows that accompany the third line of poetry (P_6 and RI_6) are joined through a five–note elision, reducing the available notes to nineteen, eighteen of which are grouped into only three chords during the course of the thirteen bars, the first two very quiet and sustained, and the third pizzicato. The remaining note appears as a grace note in the voice part. The symmetrical double binary structure seen in the accompaniment to the first couplet has disintegrated completely. The fourth line is accompanied in the same way. The coda, consisting of only four syllables of text, set to the same contour that opened the piece, uses a single melodic row, with the first hexachord verticalized in bar 45. The final bar consists of a twelve-note verticalization that is most logically understood to be the final P_6 of the accompanying cycle, but which is, of course, really no more one row than another.

'Sehr tief verhalten'

Webern did not say as much in his letters – at least in those that have survived – about the second movement of Op. 31 as he had about the previously written ones. He sketched the first and second phrases of the song – in reverse order – at the end of a letter to the Humpliks dated 22 April 1943,[34] and mentioned the piece in a letter to Willi Reich on 6 August of the same year.[35] In this letter he calls the movement a bass aria. Part of this letter has already been quoted in Chapter 3, since it speaks of the 'Bienenkorb' movement as an 'endless canon by inversion' and makes a reference to the similarity of his exercise in variation with that of Bach in his *Art of Fugue*.[36] In this letter he goes on to say that

> formally the aria is ternary, with a c.32–bar theme of periodic structure; so, once again, a very close combination of the two types of presentation. Hymn-like character; 'Die Stille um den Bienenkorb in der Heimat.'

One notices immediately the reiteration of Webern's special preoccupation – that synthesis of the horizontal and vertical, or, more precisely, of contrapuntal conception and homophonic forms for which he was so constantly striving. Here again a canon of great complexity has been moulded into a structure that is comfortably traditional.

The poem is in three stanzas, each containing forty syllables. The first two are divided similarly into four lines of ten syllables each. The scansion of the third is different: four lines of 8, 7, 10 and 10 syllables, with a fifth line containing the five syllables remaining. This leads naturally to a periodically constructed ABA form with coda. The length of the lines also almost certainly suggested to Webern the consistent two-note elision that was used in this piece; as noted earlier, this results in, for all practical purposes, ten-note rows, which coincide with the syllabic length of the lines of poetry.

The first A section (bars 1–32) contains four phrases in two periods or a double period.[37] The row structure of the piece, in which two types of row simply alternate throughout the length of each voice, makes the existence of parallel or at least similar two-phrase periods almost inevitable in those sections of the piece where the lines are ten syllables in length. Webern takes advantage of this potential for similarity to a greater degree than one would expect, in view of his general reluctance to repeat. He humours his desire for continual variety by changing the rhythmic and metric patterns – sometimes drastically – whenever melodic contours repeat. The voice part of the first A section is given in Example 10.13 with melodic similarities bracketed. Melodically it is quite clearly an abab construction. The piece begins with a rather quixotic alteration which throws it off balance initially and delays for a considerable time the listener's recognition of the absolute regularity of the text. A rest has been placed before the final word of the first line, making it, when it comes, appear to function as the beginning of the second line. The result is two lines of nine and eleven syllables rather than ten and ten, and the rhyme scheme of the first stanza is obscured.

The pulse doubles in the middle sections (bars 32–44), and the rhythmic and metric situations continue their constant shifting; however, an examination of the voice part of the B section and a comparison of it with that of the A section (given in Example 10.13) shows that this central section is another double period, and really a variation of the first. The first and third phrases

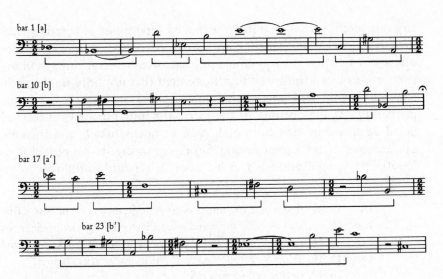

10.13   Op. 31/ii, bars 1–29, melody (pitches only)

of the B section are similar not only to each other, but to the first and third phrases of the A section, and similar relationships hold for the second and fourth phrases as well.

The third section (bars 45–74), which is clearly recognizable as a reprise by virtue of its return to the original motion in minims and semibreves and its opening, which is almost identical to the opening of the movement, is, nevertheless, different in many ways from the earlier section. Notably, it is less regular and more complex. The irregularity is built into the poem, with its first two lines of eight and seven syllables and its added line of five at the end, and is exaggerated by the imposition onto this of a musical scheme that repeats every ten units. Obviously, the very feature of this row structure that made parallel phrases almost unavoidable in the first two stanzas makes them impossible here. An examination of the material of the third section bears this out. The irregularity of the rhythmic canon within this section (discussed on pp. 136–9) also contributes to the general atmosphere of increased complexity. Possibly this change from relative clarity and perceivable regularity to obscurity is Webern's comment on the change of locale from the beehive of the first two stanzas (an external community whose highly organized activities can be clearly observed) to the interior workings of the human heart (a concealed and much less certain business).

The sparseness of the texture in this movement has already been noted in Chapter 3. It is Willam's opinion that Webern reduced the texture of this piece by removing redundancies in his quest for non-repetition of pitch classes.[38] Certainly he has decided to do away with a great deal of repetition that might have occurred; however, his motives for doing so were surely more subtle than simply a desire to avoid the temporary predominance of any one pitch, since he carefully arranged repetitions of certain pitches and groups of pitches so that they are clearly perceived. A few examples were offered in Chapter 3 of pitch classes that occur several times within a few bars. It is in fact a feature of this movement that not only single pitches but especially two- and even three-note figures are repeated within close proximity. At the opening of the piece, the initial d♭ of P₇ is immediately heard again as the first note of I₇, and c¹ opens first I₆ and then P₆. The glockenspiel offers a punctuating figure consisting of a repeated c¹ in bars 19–20, 29–30, 56–7 and 62–3. A list of other repetitions follows:

bars   4–6, d¹–e♭ in voice and viola;
bar   11, G–g♯ in voice encompasses its retrograde (a♭–G) in bass clarinet;
bars   12–14, a–c♯ in cello answered immediately by its retrograde in voice;
bars   13–15, e–c¹ in horn answered by its retrograde in glockenspiel and harp;
bars   15–16, d♯¹ in harp followed next bar by e♭¹ in bass clarinet;
bars   16–17, B–d in cello answered by its retrograde in trombone;
bars   21–2, g–B in cello followed immediately by its retrograde in voice;
bars   23–5, F♯–f in cello answered by its retrograde an octave higher in horn;
bars   23–5, f–E in cello repeated in bass clarinet;
bars   25–7, e♭ in bass clarinet followed immediately by the same pitch in voice and then harp;
bars   27–8, B♭–e♭ in harp repeated two octaves higher in viola;
bar   32, f♯–G in voice followed immediately by its retrograde in bass clarinet;
bar   34, c¹–c♯–a in voice answered in stretto by its retrograde in trombone;
bar   35, e♭¹–d² in viola repeated by clarinet;
bars   37 and 39, g–b–b♭¹ in horn and harp;
bars   37 and 39, f♯–d¹–e♭ in voice twice;
bars   39–41, c♯¹–d in cello repeated by voice;
bars   40–1, b♭¹–b in harp repeated an octave lower by voice;
bars   45–7, f–a♭ in trombone answered in stretto by its retrograde in harp;
bar   55, b♭¹ in viola and cello overlap;
bar   56, c♯ in cello followed immediately by same pitch in voice and viola (overlapping);
bars   60–1, F♯ in cello repeated immediately two octaves higher by trombone.

It will be noted that, although the repeated figure, especially in retrograde, is particularly characteristic of this movement, such repetitions cease after the opening notes of the third section, in bars 45–7. Only three single pitches are repeated after this point; in two cases, the two notes overlap so that they sound as one, and the two-octave distance between the notes in the other case makes the recognition of a pitch-class repetition much less certain than it might have been. Since repetition is the most easily perceived of all relations, giving a sense of stability, the absence of it in the third section of the movement contributes to the modulation from clarity in the first two sections to obscurity in the third.

It only remains to mention the 'hymn-like character' referred to by Webern in his letter to Reich, written in August. This aspect of the movement had apparently caused him to change the notation sometime during the period of composition since the April letter to the Humpliks cited earlier. The sketches of the first two phrases in the letter are notated in 2/4 metre, the opening phrase (sketched second, for some reason) moving in crotchets and quavers and the second (appearing first in the letter) in crotchet and quaver triplets. The score of the final version, in which the outer sections move almost entirely in white notes, makes an immediate visual impression of repose compared with these sketches.[39]

'Schöpfen aus Brunnen des Himmels'

The simplicity of 'Schöpfen aus Brunnen des Himmels . . . ' is welcome after the convolutions of 'Der Bienenkorb'.[40] Webern described it to Hildegard Jone as

> a very animated piece. Yet not so much something excited as (to express myself in Goethe's spirit) *'representing something excited'* – or so I hope at least.[41]

It moves much more quickly than the previous movement – the pulse is exactly twice as fast – and its triple metres give it a lilting quality very unlike the more introspective 'Sehr tief verhalten innerst Leben . . .'. This difference is reinforced visually through the use of quaver metres in contrast to the predominantly minim ones of the preceding movement and aurally by its generally high register; nearly all of the movement can be written in the treble clef. It is scored for three-part women's chorus, soprano solo and orchestra.

The poem is in four stanzas without rhyming. The syllabic content of all but the second stanza is (8 + 9) + (7 + 7). The first two lines of the non-conforming stanza are short, with only seven and eight syllables respectively. Webern does not follow the poetic framework in his setting; rather, he divides the third stanza into two parts and moulds the resulting five sections into an ABABA structure. As there are no orchestral interludes, the form is, uncharacteristically, asymmetrical: in terms of quavers, the sections number 63, 60, 39, 33 and 78.

A rhythmic canon in four voices runs throughout the A sections. Three of the voices are those of the women's chorus, augmented by instruments; the fourth is entirely orchestral. The segmentation of rows in the instrumental reinforcements is determined by the poetic content: while no segment is as long as a line of poetry, the beginning of a new line is always accompanied

325

by a change of instrument, and the changes within lines correspond to phrases of the text. With a few exceptions, for the most part in the purely orchestral voice, the four voices are segmented in the same way.[42] All the doubling is at the unison: since the piece is written for women's chorus, the result is a high and somewhat narrow tessitura. The orchestral voice, which is not restricted by the range of female voices, tends generally to be even higher, except in the last A section, where it dips into the bass clef briefly in order to extend the range downwards as well.

It is difficult to generalize about the use of instruments to augment the choral parts, as the combinations are very fluid, and occasional unexpected couplings prevent the sort of exclusive voice–instrument relationships that exist in 'Gelockert aus dem Schoße'. Only the following generalizations can be made. The bass clarinet, bassoon and tuba do not play in any of the A sections but are present in both the episodes. In the first episode, B1, only the oboe and English horn are absent; the second, B2, uses the entire orchestra.

The harp and celesta are treated as an orchestral choir, often playing together and nearly always playing parallel roles. Neither carries a part alone or doubles a voice line without support except in the 'murky' first half of section A3 referred to above, where each voice of the chorus is supported by one or the other of these instruments alone on the segment 'und' and the corresponding segment of the instrumental voice is played by the celesta, and the two soprano voices are doubled only by celesta (first sopranos) and harp (second sopranos) on the segment 'zur Ruhe'. Different reasons come to mind for the two brief occasions when these quiet instruments are used alone: in the first case, they are used for technical reasons, to make an unstressed word disappear, and in the second case, expressively, to represent the calm repose spoken of in the text. Elsewhere, with one exception (the orchestral voice in bar 58), whenever three instruments are heard together at least one is either the harp or celesta. One of these two instruments is also often used in combination with only one other instrument; on one occasion (in bar 57) they are used alone together in support of a voice part.

The two violins frequently play together, as do viola and cello – both logical combinations. The trumpet is present in conjunction with a high woodwind instrument in a large number of the doublings. In general terms, the flute is more consistently associated with the first sopranos, the oboe with the second sopranos and the English horn and saxophone with the altos, though each of these instruments appears with at least one of the other voices in at least one of the A sections. Similarly, the violins more often double the first sopranos and the low strings the altos, all the strings appearing at various times with the second sopranos. The orchestral fourth voice tends to move throughout the entire orchestra except in the central A section, where it consists of only woodwind and horn.

The words and phrases that Webern has chosen to stress through reinforcement by more than one instrument are either in important structural positions – the beginning or end of a stanza – or words that have to do with sound, or, in some cases, both. He triples the support for both the soprano voices on 'Schöpfen', presumably because it is the opening of the movement; the second sopranos are supported by three instruments on 'des Klangs', one supposes for programmatic reasons, though both the first sopranos and the altos sing this segment unaccompanied. The only other tripling of support comes on the word 'Sturmläuten', which fulfils both requirements – it is the initial word of a stanza, *and* it is a word that has to do with sound. Accompaniment is tripled for both the second sopranos and altos here; the first soprano part is sung for a short period by the soprano soloist, who is never supported by the orchestra. Two instruments are used as support in four places: with 'wenn so' in the first stanza, 'muß nun die Liebe!' in the third, and 'wo Leben noch glimmt' and 'zu sich' in the fourth. The last of these is the end of the piece, and the two previous are crucial phrases of the text. The reason for emphasizing 'wenn so' is less obvious. It is the beginning of the second half of the first stanza, and Webern has chosen to set it in a way that is very similar to the opening, where the first two syllables of the voice parts were augmented; it is logical that the same treatment should be given to this material on its return in order that the structural connection will be made.

The rhythm of this movement conforms with the metre to an extent that is unusual for Webern. With the exception of a few bars of 3/4 in the first B section, only 6/8 and 3/8 metres are used; hemiola and the inevitable two-against-three that results from the use of hemiola in a canonic texture are important features of all sections. The success of hemiola depends upon the prior establishment of the written metre; Webern does this with the figures shown in Example 10.14. The dotted figure (♪. ♪ ♪) that appears twice here is a prominent feature of the piece, occurring three times in section A1

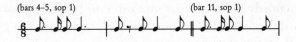

10.14 Op. 31/iii

(bars 1–12), once in a slightly varied form (♪ ⅞ ♪ ♪) in A2 (bars 29–36),[43] once near the end of A3 and in both B sections. The hemiola is expressed through the recurring figures shown in Example 10.15. The first of these is used to open the piece, with the dotted figure from Example 10.14 directly following, establishing immediately the metric argument that is basic to the movement. The melody of this figure is wide-ranging, beginning with a

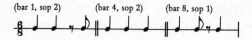

10.15   Op. 31/iii

descending minor ninth played in an accented *forte* by three instruments in addition to the sopranos. Section A2 opens with a similar figure, syncopated, and using in this case a descending major seventh (see Example 10.16).

10.16   Op. 31/iii

   The final A section, in bars 45–59, begins very differently from the two earlier ones, proceeding with essentially binary and more or less disruptive rhythms until bar 53, where the crotchet and the dotted figure that opened the piece reappear, to the text 'wo Leben noch glimmt ... ' (where life still glimmers), which represents a return to the positive atmosphere of the previous A sections. Just as the return of the opening rhythms seems to have been dictated by the text, so one can explain the murkiness and disorientation produced by the syncopations and unmetrical rhythms used in bars 45–53 as a response to the text that opens the last stanza: 'Komme durch dichtestes Dunkel und lege die Toten zur Ruhe' (Come through thickest darkness and lay the dead to rest).

   The B sections offer a contrast in several ways. The women's chorus is silent, and the text is carried by the solo soprano. Three bass instruments that do not appear in the A sections – bass clarinet, bassoon and tuba – are added. In the first B section (bars 13–28) the melody is accompanied alternately by *fortissimo* or *sforzando* chords and four-part imitation; in B2 (bars 36–44) the accompaniment is entirely chordal. The dotted figure introduced in section A1 appears in both B sections; the surrounding material is different each time, but is in both cases significant.

   B1 opens with a pair of dotted crotchets, a notation which has not occurred previously but which seems prophetic: the ubiquitous dotted figure appears slightly later sandwiched between two pairs of dotted quavers. This is of course simply an extension of the rhythmic argument set forth in the A section: it produces a hemiola at another level, dividing a bar of three into two equal parts rather than a bar of six into three. The entire phrase, with a quaver anacrusis, is imitated in stretto by the other three voices, underlining its importance. The last portion – the dotted figure followed by two dotted quavers – recurs at the end of the section, where it is again imitated directly. The dotted figure occurs in the opening phrase of B2, preceded by two crotchets outlining a descending major seventh. The whole is very like the beginning of the piece. This section ends some five bars later with a prominent set of three crotchets in a 6/8 bar, again reminiscent of section A1.

These two contrasting episodes seem to bear a sort of cross-relationship with the outer sections of the piece. The pair of dotted quavers introduced rather prominently in B1 (there are three occurrences in the 13 bars of the voice part, each imitated three times, in addition to the initial *fortissimo* announcement of the figure in a high register in augmentation) does not occur again until the end of the final A section (A3), while, as observed already, B2 refers to A1 (and A2, its smaller relative).

The movement ends with a composed ritard that ingeniously pulls together all the figures previously used, as if to provide all of them finally with a *raison d'être*. In a rather Joycean twist, the end turns out to have been the source for all that precedes it (Example 10.17[44]).

10.17   Op. 31/iii

The similarity of the first phrase of this movement to the opening of 'Freundselig ist das Wort' should be noted in passing (see Example 10.18). A

10.18

Christmas greeting from Webern to the Humpliks quoted earlier[45] begins with a notation of the opening bars of 'Freundselig ist das Wort' (with text) and continues:

> 'wenn so die menschliche Hand zieht an den Krügen des Klangs' [a quotation of the second half of the first stanza of 'Schöpfen aus Brunnen . . . ']. In the sign of the 'word' that you are referring to, dear Hildegard: may this sound be your answer to what you asked me![46]

The 'word' is an image central to both texts, but particularly so to No. V. Presumably the question (' ... what you asked me') is in 'Freundselig ist das Wort': 'Was kann denn andres mitten unter uns sein, als das Wort?'; the answer, at least partially, in 'Schöpfen aus Brunnen'. At any rate, it is clear that Webern felt the two texts to share the same concern, and it is unlikely that the musical resemblance is coincidental.

Shortly after the six movements just discussed had been finished Webern came to the decision that they constituted a logical whole and that his cantata was complete. He rearranged the two groups of pieces and wrote a letter to Hildegard Jone in which he drew parallels between the movements in their new order and the components of a Missa brevis:

> Now look at the order; isn't it basically a 'Missa brevis'?
>
> (1) 'Schweigt auch die Welt ... ' (Bass solo), isn't that a 'Kyrie'?
>
> (2) 'Sehr tief verhalten ... ' (Bass solo): the '*Gloria in excelsis deo*' of the quiet around the 'beehive at home'!
>
> (3) 'Schöpfen aus Brunnen des Himmels ... ' (female chorus with *soprano* solo). Isn't that a 'Credo'?
>
> (4) 'Leichteste Bürden der Bäume ... ' (Soprano solo)
>
> *and*
>
> (5) 'Freundselig ist das Wort' (Soprano solo and mixed chorus) a 'Benedictus, qui venit in nomine domine' and 'Sanctus'?
>
> Is not that '*blessed*' which the wind bears through the 'spaces': the 'fragrances', the 'gentle shape'? And holy, holy is 'the word' which knows of 'all that is thine'?
> 'Holy, holy': 'doch wenn es wieder aufklingt in der Morgenfrühe' ('yet when it sounds out in the dawn again') finally:
>
> (6) 'Gelockert aus dem Schoße ... ' (Chorus): 'Agnus dei' – the 'Lamb of God'.[47]

It seems safe to assume that these parallels were made solely on the basis of the text, in view of the fact that they occurred to Webern after, rather than before or during, composition. Structural or stylistic correspondences to the customary ways of setting individual sections of the Mass are not apparent in the music.

Conclusion

When, in 1924, Webern took up the twelve-note method of writing music, he became part of a compositional movement which a few decades later was to drive music analysts to invent completely new methods of dissection. The New Music's projection of tonal relationships as specific to individual situations, and the increased importance – in many cases independence – afforded rhythm, timbre and register have led to a microscopic attention to detail in an attempt to explain and understand. The unique possibilities inherent in each row are exhaustively described; pitch-class content, rhythmic details, durations, register and timbral changes are minutely examined and catalogued. The result is a great deal of information about the sound complex of each work and, if the analysis is acute, an explanation of the way in which the music derives specifically from the row that generated it. The complexion of the music dictates the approach taken; each result is unique.

Analysis can be approached either with the intention of cataloguing and defining all the events and relationships that one can perceive (aurally and/or intellectually), or with the purpose of examining and elaborating upon the composer's concept of the piece. The kind of analysis just described is of the first sort. The information it yields is an essential component of our knowledge of any piece of music, since anything that exists in the music obviously does – or may – contribute to our perception of it. It does not tell the whole story, however. In many cases works are not presented as entities, but rather as constellations of minute details, lying outside the province of historical perspective. Moreover, it seldom represents the composer's conceptions.

This is particularly true, I think, in the case of Webern, who, on close acquaintance, joins a surprising number of other artists – Bruckner comes immediately to mind – whose creativity seems, in depth and sophistication, to surpass their own understanding. Webern was naïve in many respects. His letters and opinions, together with others' reports of his reactions and behaviour, show him to have been an unsophisticated man with simple tastes and limited experience, whose knowledge and appreciation of the other arts was undeveloped. There is no indication that he thought of himself as or ever

331

wished to be a revolutionary. He was educated as a music historian, and his studies in composition included all the traditional disciplines. In his own composition he happily accepted the only forms he knew, and throughout his life he insisted on their importance in the mission to which he felt such a responsibility: the consolidation and thereby the continuation of the German musical tradition. Whenever he describes his own instrumental works, it is in reference to traditional forms; therefore, although it is by no means my contention that Webern analysis should be limited by Webern's own conceptions, I think that in order to understand his intentions we must take these forms as a point of departure.

In my introduction I quoted Arnold Whittall's caution against 'analysis in spite of serialism'. He continues with a warning against 'the dangerous belief that a satisfactory analysis of [a serial] work could be conducted solely in terms' of its reinterpretation of traditional structural elements'.[1] In my analyses I have skated perilously near the edge of this fault; I hope that I will not be seen to have succumbed. My purpose has been to present, using translations and paraphrases of his own terminology, a view of Webern's twelve-note music that is as close as possible to what I believe his own must have been. In examining the works I have tried to consider musical events and relationships in terms I think Webern would have recognized; I believe he would have found most present-day analysis of his work not only foreign to his way of thinking, but also unintelligible. I agree completely with Whittall's remark in another source that 'a little respectful scepticism about Webern's view of his own musical development might be salutary'.[2] Nevertheless, both respectful scepticism and perceptual analysis presuppose a prior attempt to give Webern's own stated intentions a sympathetic reading. It is this that I hope I have provided.

Three themes seem to have dominated Webern's thoughts and therefore to explain in large part the direction taken by his twelve-note composition: a loyalty to traditional formal principles, a particular affinity with the formal innovations of Beethoven and the desire for unity through synthesis, an end that occupied him to the point of obsession. All of these concerns were shared with Schoenberg. The latter's *Fundamentals of Musical Composition* is a manual in the use of traditional forms: sentence and periodic structures, and the large forms that result from combinations of these – the sonata, variation, rondo and ternary forms used by Webern. The great majority of Schoenberg's illustrations in *Fundamentals* are taken from Beethoven; in fact, it is only for those excerpts *not* written by Beethoven that a composer is named. Schoenberg suffered greatly at the hands of the serial composers in the 1950s, largely because of his adherence to traditional forms. In his famous criticism, 'Schoenberg is Dead', written in 1951, Boulez ascribed 'a certain weakness in most of [Schoenberg's] twelve-tone works' to his use of traditional forms:

The preclassical and classical forms ruling most of his compositions were in no way historically connected with the twelve-tone discovery; the result is that a contradiction arises between the forms dictated by tonality and a language of which the laws of organization are still only dimly perceived. It is not only that this language finds no sanction in the forms used by Schönberg, but something more negative: namely, that these forms rule out every possibility of organization implicit in the new material. The two worlds are incompatible, and he has tried to justify one by the other.

This can hardly be called a valid procedure, and it has led to a kind of twisted romantic classicism that has a forbidding mildness about it.[3]

Webern, whose sensibilities were so closely akin to Schoenberg's but who did not leave behind him an incriminating manual in composition, not only fared better than Schoenberg, but was held up as a model in opposition to him. Later in the same essay Boulez wrote:

Perhaps it would be better to dissociate Schönberg's work altogether from the phenomenon of the tone-row. The two have been confused with obvious pleasure, sometimes with unconcealed dishonesty – and a certain Webern has been only too easily forgotten ... Perhaps, like Webern, we might succeed in writing works whose form arises inevitably from the given material.[4]

Webern's spare pointillist textures and extreme distillation of material were much admired; his own remarks about the traditional basis of his music were not yet known. (In 1951 neither Reich's transcriptions of the *Weg zur neuen Musik* lectures nor Webern's letters and other writings about his own music had been published. What a disappointment it must have been for Boulez, a few years later, to find that the form of Webern's works had, after all, also been determined in the traditional ways.) It is interesting to speculate about the direction serial music might have taken had Webern not been shot dead in 1945.

Schoenberg's references to the unity of musical space and the identity of the horizontal and the vertical are probably as numerous and certainly as impassioned as Webern's frequent raptures over the effects of synthesis. Both men were idealists, continually engaged in a search for a perfect musical expression which they were convinced could be achieved. Their view of unity as essential to comprehensibility, and of comprehensibility as 'the highest law of all',[5] is one that has been central to the European musical tradition. It is only recently that the importance of unity has been questioned. In his article 'Webern and Atonality' Arnold Whittall offers an analysis of Op. 7/iii that is based on contrast; he goes on to suggest that much might be gained by analysts relinquishing their fondness for unity.[6] While this may be so in the case of perceptual analysis, any attempt at conceptual analysis – the explanation of Webern's intent with respect to the structuring

333

of his music – must be based on the assumption that all decisions were made with the desire for unity in mind.

In my analyses I have deliberately avoided one area in which questions inevitably arise concerning Webern's – or any other – twelve-note music: What degree of restraint is exercised over the vertical ('harmonic') aspect of the music? Specifically, to what extent does Webern *care* about and seek to control simultaneities? I think these questions are more easily answered in reference to the music of Berg and Schoenberg. Berg's twelve-note music rarely – and then only briefly – leaves the 'harmonic' sphere; George Perle's analysis of *Lulu*,[7] for instance, shows the opera to be anchored on several significant chords. Martha M. Hyde's work on the 'harmonic' aspect of Schoenberg's composition[8] has revealed numerous identities in horizontal and vertical collections. These latter relationships suggest the sort of two-dimensional synthesis for which Webern was always striving; a similar approach to his composition might therefore be taken. Graham H. Phipps has advanced quasi-tonal explanations for the particular simultaneities in the Op. 29 Cantata.[9] I have not discussed this problem for several reasons, among which one of the most important is that I see Webern's interests as almost entirely linear. There is a watershed between the Op. 20 Trio and the Op. 21 Symphony: whereas the texture of the Trio is homophonic, in general the music from Op. 21 onwards is linear. In the polyphonically conceived works it is difficult to determine – beyond a few basic decisions concerning consonant intervals and chords that had to be avoided – whether the vertical effect of the coincidence of parts was a matter of much concern. The sketches prove the fact of linear conception: parts are written in open score, and in subsequent revisions individual parts are often shifted horizontally or varied rhythmically so that they coincide differently. The method seems to be trial and choice; vertical collections do not appear to be a determining factor.

It was never my intention that the analyses I have presented should be exhaustive. There is a great deal yet to be said about Webern's twelve-note works. The sketchbooks give considerable insight into his working habits; now that they are accessible, it is to be hoped that in time his intentions may become clearer. I said earlier that, whereas ideally a work should be considered from both historical and idiosyncratic points of view, the weight of Webern analysis has tended to fall on the side of the idiosyncratic. I hope that the foregoing study may in some way help to strike a balance.

A comparison of row characteristics

This table lists the intervallic and combinatorial properties of all the rows used in Webern's published works. The following information is given for each row:

column 2:
the intervallic content of unordered hexachords in terms of semitones (the numbers represent the interval succession when the contents of the hexachord are arranged in ascending order, in closest position – Forte's 'best normal order', or its inversion, where this is applicable). The numbers in parentheses represent the distance between last and first notes of the hexachord. These numbers are placed at the end of hexachords that correspond directly to pitch–class sets, at the beginning of those that represent inverted pc sets. The only exception to this is those rows that consist of two completely chromatic hexachords, which have been represented as 11111(7)/(7)11111 in order to emphasize the inversional relationship of the second hexachord to the first, although in fact the two hexachords are also identical and could be just as accurately represented 11111(7)/11111(7).

column 3:
the combinatorial or symmetrical properties. The hexachordal content of all rows following the sign $\neq$ is complementary to that of P_0; row forms standing on either side of an $=$ sign are exactly identical with respect to order as well as content. Rows with no combinatorial properties are labelled 'nc'.

column 4:
the row type. Only two of the twenty-one rows are unique in terms of hexachordal content, those of Opp. 17/i and 18/iii. The others are all drawn from six types of combination, identified here with letters indicating frequency of use. The types identified are the following.

type a: Both hexachords conform to Babbitt's first-order source set, or Forte's pc set 6–1, with the interval vector [543210]. Used five times (Opp. 17/iii, 18/iii, 21, 27 and 30).

type b: Both hexachords conform to pc set 6–2, with the interval vector [443211]; one hexachord is inverted. Used four times (*Klavierstück*, Opp. 22, 25 and 29).

type c: Hexachords are pc sets 6–Z3 and 6–Z36 (one is inverted), with the interval vector [433221]. Used four times (*Kinderstück*, Opp. 18/i, 26 and 31).

type d: Both hexachords are pc set 6–5, with the interval vector [422232]; one hexachord is inverted. Used three times (Opp. 17/ii, 20 and 28).

type e: Hexachords are pc sets 6–Z10 and 6–Z39, with the interval vector [333321]. Used twice, once with both sets inverted (Opp. 19 and 23).

type f: Both hexachords conform to Babbitt's third-order source set, or pc set 6–20, with the interval vector [303630]. Used once (Op. 24).

The hexachords of the Op. 17/i row are pc sets 6–Z38 and 6–Z6, with the interval vector [421242]; those of the Op. 18/iii row are pc sets 6–Z37 and 6–Z4, with the interval vector [432321].

Klavierstück	11112(6)/(6)21111	$P_0 \neq I_7$	type b
Kinderstück	11121(6)/(5)31111	nc	type c
Op. 17/i	11141(4)/(5)11511	nc	unique
Op. 17/ii	(5)13111/11131(5)	$P_0 \neq I_3$	type d
Op. 17/iii	11111(7)/(7)11111	$P_0 \neq P_6, I_1, RI_7$	type a
Op. 18/i	(5)31111/11121(6)	nc	type c
Op. 18/ii	11111(7)/(7)11111	$P_0 \neq P_6, I_7, RI_1$	type a
Op. 18/iii	11114(4)/11211(6)	nc	unique
Op. 19	(5)21121/(4)31112	nc	type e
Op. 20	(5)13111/11131(5)	$P_0 \neq I_1$	type d
Op. 21	11111(7)/(7)11111	$P_0 \neq P_6, I_{11}, RI_5$	type a
		$P_0 = R_6$	
Op. 22	11112(6)/(6)21111	$P_0 \neq I_3$	type b
Op. 23	12112(5)/21113(4)	nc	type e
Op. 24	13131(3)/13131(3)	$P_0 \neq P_2, P_6, P_{10}$	type f
		$P_0 \neq I_1, I_5, I_9$	
		$P_0 \neq R_4, R_8$	
		$P_0 \neq RI_3, RI_7, RI_{11}$	
Op. 25	(6)21111/11112(6)	$P_0 \neq I_1$	type b
Op. 26	11113(5)/(6)12111	nc	type c
Op. 27	11111(7)/(7)11111	$P_0 \neq P_6, I_1, RI_7$	type a
Op. 28	11131(5)/(5)13111	$P_0 \neq I_9$	type d
		$P_0 = RI_9$	
Op. 29	(6)21111/11112(6)	$P_0 \neq I_5$	type b
		$P_0 = RI_5$	
Op. 30	11111(7)/(7)11111	$P_0 \neq P_6, I_{11}, RI_5$	type a
		$P_0 = RI_{11}$	
Op. 31	11121(6)/(5)31111	nc	type c

Matrices

	I0	11	6	5	10	9	1	2	7	8	4	3
P0	A^b	G	D	C$^\sharp$	F$^\sharp$	F	A	B^b	E^b	E	C	B
1	A	A^b	E^b	D	G	F$^\sharp$	B^b	B	E	F	C$^\sharp$	C
6	D	C$^\sharp$	A^b	G	C	B	E^b	E	A	B^b	F$^\sharp$	F
7	E^b	D	A	A^b	C$^\sharp$	C	E	F	B^b	B	G	F$^\sharp$
2	B^b	A	E	E^b	A^b	G	B	C	F	F$^\sharp$	D	C$^\sharp$
3	B	B^b	F	E	A	A^b	C	C$^\sharp$	F$^\sharp$	G	E^b	D
11	G	F$^\sharp$	C$^\sharp$	C	F	E	A^b	A	D	E^b	B	B^b
10	F$^\sharp$	F	C	B	E	E^b	G	A^b	C$^\sharp$	D	B^b	A
5	C$^\sharp$	C	G	F$^\sharp$	B	B^b	D	E^b	A^b	A	F	E
4	C	B	F$^\sharp$	F	B^b	A	C$^\sharp$	D	G	A^b	E	E^b
8	E	E^b	B^b	A	D	C$^\sharp$	F	F$^\sharp$	B	C	A^b	G
9	F	E	B	B^b	E^b	D	F$^\sharp$	G	C	C$^\sharp$	A	A^b

Op. 20:

Op. 21:

	I0	3	2	1	5	4	10	11	7	8	9	6
P0	F	Ab	G	F#	Bb	A	Eb	E	C	C#	D	B
9	D	F	E	Eb	G	F#	C	C#	A	Bb	B	Ab
10	Eb	F#	F	E	Ab	G	C#	D	Bb	B	C	A
11	E	G	F#	F	A	Ab	D	Eb	B	C	C#	Bb
7	C	Eb	D	C#	F	E	Bb	B	G	Ab	A	F#
8	C#	E	Eb	D	F#	F	B	C	Ab	A	Bb	G
2	G	Bb	A	Ab	C	B	F	F#	D	Eb	E	C#
1	F#	A	Ab	G	B	Bb	E	F	C#	D	Eb	C
5	Bb	C#	C	B	Eb	D	Ab	A	F	F#	G	E
4	A	C	B	Bb	D	C#	G	Ab	E	F	F#	Eb
3	Ab	B	Bb	A	C#	C	F#	G	Eb	E	F	D
6	B	D	C#	C	E	Eb	A	Bb	F#	G	Ab	F

Op. 22:

	I0	9	8	11	10	2	3	4	5	7	1	6
P0	F#	Eb	D	F	E	Ab	A	Bb	B	C#	G	C
3	A	F#	F	Ab	G	B	C	C#	D	E	Bb	Eb
4	Bb	G	F#	A	Ab	C	C#	D	Eb	F	B	E
1	G	E	Eb	F#	F	A	Bb	B	C	D	Ab	C#
2	Ab	F	E	G	F#	Bb	B	C	C#	Eb	A	D
10	E	C#	C	Eb	D	F#	G	Ab	A	B	F	Bb
9	Eb	C	B	D	C#	F	F#	G	Ab	Bb	E	A
8	D	B	Bb	C#	C	E	F	F#	G	A	Eb	Ab
7	C#	Bb	A	C	B	Eb	E	F	F#	Ab	D	G
5	B	Ab	G	Bb	A	C#	D	Eb	E	F#	C	F
11	F	D	C#	E	Eb	G	Ab	A	Bb	C	F#	B
6	C	A	Ab	B	Bb	D	Eb	E	F	G	C#	F#

Op. 23:

	I0	7	11	8	2	10	6	9	5	4	1	3
P0	Ab	Eb	G	E	Bb	F#	D	F	C#	C	A	B
5	C#	Ab	C	A	Eb	B	G	Bb	F#	F	D	E
1	A	E	Ab	F	B	G	Eb	F#	D	C#	Bb	C
4	C	G	B	Ab	D	Bb	F#	A	F	E	C#	Eb
10	F#	C#	F	D	Ab	E	C	Eb	B	Bb	G	A
2	Bb	F	A	F#	C	Ab	E	G	Eb	D	B	C#
6	D	A	C#	Bb	E	C	Ab	B	G	F#	Eb	F
3	B	F#	Bb	G	C#	A	F	Ab	E	Eb	C	D
7	Eb	Bb	D	B	F	C#	A	C	Ab	G	E	F#
8	E	B	Eb	C	F#	D	Bb	C#	A	Ab	F	G
11	G	D	F#	Eb	A	F	C#	E	C	B	Ab	Bb
9	F	C	E	C#	G	Eb	B	D	Bb	A	F#	Ab

Op. 24:

	I0	11	3	4	8	7	9	5	6	1	2	10
P0	B	Bb	D	Eb	G	F#	Ab	E	F	C	C#	A
1	C	B	Eb	E	Ab	G	A	F	F#	C#	D	Bb
9	Ab	G	B	C	E	Eb	F	C#	D	A	Bb	F#
8	G	F#	Bb	B	Eb	D	E	C	C#	Ab	A	F
4	Eb	D	F#	G	B	Bb	C	Ab	A	E	F	C#
5	E	Eb	G	Ab	C	B	C#	A	Bb	F	F#	D
3	D	C#	F	F#	Bb	A	B	G	Ab	Eb	E	C
7	F#	F	A	Bb	E	C#	Eb	B	C	G	Ab	E
6	F	E	Ab	A	C#	C	D	Bb	B	F#	G	Eb
11	Bb	A	C#	D	F#	F	G	Eb	E	B	C	Ab
10	A	Ab	C	C#	F	E	F#	D	Eb	Bb	B	G
2	C#	C	E	F	A	Ab	Bb	F#	G	D	Eb	B

Appendix II

Op. 25:

	I0	9	8	11	6	10	7	4	3	5	2	1
P0	G	E	Eb	F#	C#	F	D	B	Bb	C	A	Ab
3	Bb	G	F#	A	E	Ab	F	D	C#	Eb	C	B
4	B	Ab	G	Bb	F	A	F#	Eb	D	E	C#	C
1	Ab	F	E	G	D	F#	Eb	C	B	C#	Bb	A
6	C#	Bb	A	C	G	B	Ab	F	E	F#	Eb	D
2	A	F#	F	Ab	Eb	G	E	C#	C	D	B	Bb
5	C	A	Ab	B	F#	Bb	G	E	Eb	F	D	C#
8	Eb	C	B	D	A	C#	Bb	G	F#	Ab	F	E
9	E	C#	C	Eb	Bb	D	B	Ab	G	A	F#	F
7	D	B	Bb	C#	Ab	C	A	F#	F	G	E	Eb
10	F	D	C#	E	B	Eb	C	A	Ab	Bb	G	F#
11	F#	Eb	D	F	C	E	C#	Bb	A	B	Ab	G

Op. 26:

	I0	2	1	4	3	7	8	5	9	6	10	11
P0	Ab	Bb	A	C	B	Eb	E	C#	F	D	F#	G
10	F#	Ab	G	Bb	A	C#	D	B	Eb	C	E	F
11	G	A	Ab	B	Bb	D	Eb	C	E	C#	F	F#
8	E	F#	F	Ab	G	B	C	A	C#	Bb	D	Eb
9	F	G	F#	A	Ab	C	C#	Bb	D	B	Eb	E
5	C#	Eb	D	F	E	Ab	A	F#	Bb	G	B	C
4	C	D	C#	E	Eb	G	Ab	F	A	F#	Bb	B
7	Eb	F	E	G	F#	Bb	B	Ab	C	A	C#	D
3	B	C#	C	Eb	D	F#	G	E	Ab	F	A	Bb
6	D	E	Eb	F#	F	A	Bb	G	B	Ab	C	C#
2	Bb	C	B	D	C#	F	F#	Eb	G	E	Ab	A
1	A	B	Bb	C#	C	E	F	D	F#	Eb	G	Ab

Op. 27:

	IO	8	7	11	10	9	3	1	4	2	6	5
PO	Eb	B	Bb	D	C#	C	F#	E	G	F	A	Ab
4	G	Eb	D	F#	F	E	Bb	Ab	B	A	C#	C
5	Ab	E	Eb	G	F#	F	B	A	C	Bb	D	C#
1	E	C	B	Eb	D	C#	G	F	Ab	F#	Bb	A
2	F	C#	C	E	Eb	D	Ab	F#	A	G	B	Bb
3	F#	D	C#	F	E	Eb	A	G	Bb	Ab	C	B
9	C	Ab	G	B	Bb	A	Eb	C#	E	D	F#	F
11	D	Bb	A	C#	C	B	F	Eb	F#	E	Ab	G
8	B	G	F#	Bb	A	Ab	D	C	Eb	C#	F	E
10	C#	A	Ab	C	B	Bb	E	D	F	Eb	G	F#
6	A	F	E	Ab	G	F#	C	Bb	C#	B	Eb	D
7	Bb	F#	F	A	Ab	G	C#	B	D	C	E	Eb

Op. 28:

	IO	11	2	1	5	6	3	4	8	7	10	9
PO	C#	C	Eb	D	F#	G	E	F	A	Ab	B	Bb
1	D	C#	E	Eb	G	Ab	F	F#	Bb	A	C	B
10	B	Bb	C#	C	E	F	D	Eb	G	F#	A	Ab
11	C	B	D	C#	F	F#	Eb	E	Ab	G	Bb	A
7	Ab	G	Bb	A	C#	D	B	C	E	Eb	F#	F
6	G	F#	A	Ab	C	C#	Bb	B	Eb	D	F	E
9	Bb	A	C	B	Eb	E	C#	D	F#	F	Ab	G
8	A	Ab	B	Bb	D	Eb	C	C#	F	E	G	F#
4	F	E	G	F#	Bb	B	Ab	A	C#	C	Eb	D
5	F#	F	Ab	G	B	C	A	Bb	D	C#	E	Eb
2	Eb	D	F	E	Ab	A	F#	G	B	Bb	C#	C
3	E	Eb	F#	F	A	Bb	G	Ab	C	B	D	C#

Op. 29:

	I0	8	11	10	2	1	4	3	7	6	9	5
P0	Eb	B	D	C#	F	E	G	F#	Bb	A	C	Ab
4	G	Eb	F#	F	A	Ab	B	Bb	D	C#	E	C
1	E	C	Eb	D	F#	F	Ab	G	B	Bb	C#	A
2	F	C#	E	Eb	G	F#	A	Ab	C	B	D	Bb
10	C#	A	C	B	Eb	D	F	E	Ab	G	Bb	F#
11	D	Bb	C#	C	E	Eb	F#	F	A	Ab	B	G
8	B	G	Bb	A	C#	C	Eb	D	F#	F	Ab	E
9	C	Ab	B	Bb	D	C#	E	Eb	G	F#	A	F
5	Ab	E	G	F#	Bb	A	C	B	Eb	D	F	C#
6	A	F	Ab	G	B	Bb	C#	C	E	Eb	F#	D
3	F#	D	F	E	Ab	G	Bb	A	C#	C	Eb	B
7	Bb	F#	A	Ab	C	B	D	C#	F	E	G	Eb

Op. 30:

	I0	1	4	3	2	5	6	9	8	7	10	11
P0	A	Bb	C#	C	B	D	Eb	F#	F	E	G	Ab
11	Ab	A	C	B	Bb	C#	D	F	E	Eb	F#	G
8	F	F#	A	Ab	G	Bb	B	D	C#	C	Eb	E
9	F#	G	Bb	A	Ab	B	C	Eb	D	C#	E	F
10	G	Ab	B	Bb	A	C	C#	E	Eb	D	F	F#
7	E	F	Ab	G	F#	A	Bb	C#	C	B	D	Eb
6	Eb	E	G	F#	F	Ab	A	C	B	Bb	C#	D
3	C	C#	E	Eb	D	F	F#	A	Ab	G	Bb	B
4	C#	D	F	E	Eb	F#	G	Bb	A	Ab	B	C
5	D	Eb	F#	F	E	G	Ab	B	Bb	A	C	C#
2	B	C	Eb	D	C#	E	F	Ab	G	F#	A	Bb
1	Bb	B	D	C#	C	Eb	E	G	F#	F	Ab	A

Op. 31:

	10	3	11	10	2	9	1	5	4	8	7	6
P0	F♯	A	F	E	A♭	E♭	G	B	B♭	D	C♯	C
9	E♭	F♯	D	C♯	F	C	E	A♭	G	B	B♭	A
1	G	B♭	F♯	F	A	E	A♭	C	B	E♭	D	C♯
2	A♭	B	G	F♯	B♭	F	A	C♯	C	E	E♭	D
10	E	G	E♭	D	F♯	C♯	F	A	A♭	C	B	B♭
3	A	C	A♭	G	B	F♯	B♭	D	C♯	F	E	E♭
11	F	A♭	E	E♭	G	D	F♯	B♭	A	C♯	C	B
7	C♯	E	C	B	E♭	B♭	D	F♯	F	A	A♭	G
8	D	F	C♯	C	E	B	E♭	G	F♯	B♭	A	A♭
4	B♭	C♯	A	A♭	C	G	B	E♭	D	F♯	F	E
5	B	D	B♭	A	C♯	A♭	C	E	E♭	G	F♯	F
6	C	E♭	B	B♭	D	A	C♯	F	E	A♭	G	F♯

Row analyses (1)

This appendix and the one following are intended to be used together. They present a row analysis of each of the works from Op. 20 to Op. 31, as it were from two perspectives. Appendix III gives the row content of each movement within a formal outline; Appendix IV represents a closer view, in which the precise deployment of all the rows appearing in Appendix III is indicated. An attempt has been made to preserve structural units in the layout of the charts in Appendix IV; however, in some cases this has not been possible because of space limitations. Whereas the primary objective of the Appendix III analyses is to illustrate the way in which the rows fill out the structure, details of individual row distribution take precedence in Appendix IV.

The analyses in the text are based on a single row form for each work: with the exception of Op. 24, that form identified as the original by Webern in the sketchbooks. However, just as in tonal music all the movements of an extended work are not in the same key, so in the case of Webern's twelve-note music the several movements of a single work are not all centred tonally on the same row. In order to illustrate the tonal analogy in those movements that are as it were 'in another key', alternative analyses are provided in which the matrix has been reoriented.

In both this appendix and the one following, bar numbers identifying beginnings of sections ignore short anacruses.

Op. 20

First movement (rondo)

section			transposed:		
introduction	(1-3):	R_4 P_4	introduction	(1-3):	P_0 R_0
refrain A	(4-10):	I_4 RI_9 R_4 RI_{11} I_2 RI_8	refrain A	(4-10):	RI_6 I_{11} P_0 I_1 RI_4 I_{10}
episode B	(10-15):	R_3 R_7 I_8 P_0 P_7	episode B	(10-15):	P_{11} P_3 RI_{10} R_8 R_3
refrain A	(16-21):	I_4 RI_9 R_4 RI_{11} I_2 RI_8 R_3	refrain A	(16-21):	RI_6 I_{11} P_0 I_1 RI_4 I_{10} P_{11}
episode C	(22-30):	I_{10} P_5 RI_6 I_2 P_6 P_8 R_8	episode C	(22-30):	RI_0 R_1 I_8 RI_4 R_2 R_4 P_4
episode C	(31-40):	I_{10} P_5 RI_6 I_2 P_6 P_8 R_8	episode C	(31-40):	RI_0 R_1 I_8 RI_4 R_2 R_4 P_4
[intro]	(41-3):	R_4 P_4	[intro]	(41-3):	P_0 R_0
refrain A	(44-51):	I_4 RI_9 R_4 RI_{11} I_2 RI_8	refrain A	(44-51):	RI_6 I_{11} P_0 I_1 RI_4 I_{10}
episode B	(51-6):	R_3 R_7 I_8 P_0 P_7	episode B	(51-6):	P_{11} P_3 RI_{10} R_8 R_3
refrain A	(57-63):	I_4 RI_9 R_4 RI_{11} I_2 RI_8	refrain A	(57-63):	RI_6 I_{11} P_0 I_1 RI_4 I_{10}
coda	(64-5):	P_4	coda	(64-5):	R_0

Second movement (sonata)

introduction (1-9): $-P_0$] I_9 R_5 I_6 RI_3 P_{11} P_1

Exposition (10-73) -

theme I   (10-26): P_0 P_5 RI_2 P_1 R_8 R_8 R_0 I_7 RI_2

transition (26-40): P_6 I_{11} I_6 P_1 P_3 RI_8 P_7 R_2 RI_1 P_0 I_6

theme II   (40-59): P_9------R_7 P_{11} RI_4 I_5 I_3
RI_8 RI_8 I_6 P_9-----

closing   (60-73): RI_0 R_{10} R_2 I_1 R_2 I_{10} RI_8
R_{10}

Development (73-83): RI_1 P_8 RI_1
I_1

(84-94): RI_{11} P_{10} RI_2 RI_4
R_6 I_{11}---- R_8

(94-102): P_{10} R_5 RI_6 RI_5 RI_0 R_0
P_4

(102-18): R_{10} P_3 I_0 P_7 RI_9 I_4 I_2 [P_0-

Recapitulation (118-74) -

theme I   (118-30): P_0 P_5 RI_2 P_1 R_8 R_8 R_0 I_7 RI_2

transition (131-44): P_6 I_{11} I_6 P_1 RI_6 RI_1 P_0 R_7 RI_6 P_5 I_{11}

theme II   (144-63): P_2------ R_0 P_4 RI_9 I_{10} I_8
RI_1 RI_1 I_{11} P_2----

closing   (163-74): RI_5 R_3 R_7 I_6 R_7 I_3 RI_1
R_3

coda   (175-9): P_6 I_6 I_4
P_4 I_2

[intro]   (180-93): I_5 I_8 P_0 R_5 R_6 P_{10} R_0

Op. 21

First movement (sonata)

Exposition

theme I (1-26): I_4 P_7
                    P_4 I_1

theme II (1-26): P_0 I_9 P_0 I_9
                    I_8 P_{11} I_8 P_{11}

Development (25-44): P_{11} R_{11}
                      I_{11} RI_{11}
                      P_7 R_7
                      I_3 RI_3

Recapitulation

theme I (43-66): I_4 P_7
                    P_4 I_1

theme II (43-66): P_0 I_9 P_0 I_9
                      I_8 P_{11} I_8 P_{11}

---

transposed:

Exposition

theme I (1-26): P_0 I_3
                    I_0 P_9

theme II (1-26): I_8 P_5 I_8 P_5
                      P_4 I_7 P_4 I_7

Development (25-44): I_7 RI_7
                      P_7 R_7
                      I_3 RI_3
                      P_{11} R_{11}

Recapitulation

theme I (43-66): P_0 I_3
                    I_0 P_9

theme II (43-66): I_8 P_5 I_8 $P5$
                      P_4 I_7 P_4 I_7

Second movement (variations)

Theme (1-11): P_0
               R_0

Variation I (11-23): P_7 R_7
                      R_7 P_7
                      RI_5 I_5
                      I_5 RI_5

Variation II (23-34): I_0------
                      P_{11}-----
                      I_{10} RI_{10}
                      P_2 R_2

Variation III (34-44): I_3 P_6 I_3 P_6 I_3
                      RI_3 R_6 RI_3 R_6 RI_3

Variation IV (44-55): P_8 I_5
                      P_6 I_3
                      I_7 P_{10}
                      I_5 P_8

Variation V (55-67): I_3 P_6 I_3 P_6 I_3
                    RI_3 R_6 RI_3 R_6 RI_3

Variation VI (66-78): I_{10} RI_{10}
                    P_2 R_2
                    RI_0-----
                    R_{11}-----

Variation VII (77-89): P_7 R_7
                    R_7 P_7
                    RI_5 I_5
                    I_5 RI_5

coda (89-99): R_0
             P_0

Op. 22

First movement (sonata)

	transposed:

introduction (1-5): P_7
$\qquad\qquad\qquad\quad I_5$

Exposition (6-15) -

  theme I   (6-15): I_7 I_1

  theme II (6-15): P_1 P_7
$\qquad\qquad\qquad\qquad I_{11}$ I_5

Development (16-27): P_4 I_7 RI_6 P_6 RI_5
$\qquad\qquad\qquad\qquad I_8$ P_5 R_6 I_6 R_7

Recapitulation (28-37) -

  theme I   (28-37): I_7 I_1

  theme II (28-37): I_{11} I_5
$\qquad\qquad\qquad\qquad\quad P_1$ P_7

coda   (37-41): RI_5
$\qquad\qquad\qquad\qquad\quad R_7$

---

transposed:

introduction (1-5): P_0
$\qquad\qquad\qquad\quad I_{10}$

Exposition (6-15) -

  theme I   (6-15): I_0 I_6

  theme II (6-15): P_6 P_0
$\qquad\qquad\qquad\qquad I_4$ I_{10}

Development (16-27): P_9 I_0 RI_{11} P_{11} RI_{10}
$\qquad\qquad\qquad\qquad I_1$ P_{10} R_{11} I_{11} R_0

Recapitulation (28-37) -

  theme I   (28-37): I_0 I_6

  theme II (28-37): I_4 I_{10}
$\qquad\qquad\qquad\qquad\quad P_6$ P_0

coda   (37-41): RI_{10}
$\qquad\qquad\qquad\qquad\quad R_0$

Second movement (rondo)

refrain A (1-32) -   A1: RI_0 I_0 R_0--------
$\qquad\qquad\qquad\qquad\qquad\qquad P_0$ R_0 P_0 RI_0 I_0
$\qquad\qquad\qquad\qquad\qquad\qquad RI_0$ P_0--------

$\qquad\qquad\qquad\qquad\qquad$A2: I_6 RI_6 I_6
$\qquad\qquad\qquad\qquad\qquad\qquad P_6$ R_6 P_6

$\qquad\qquad\qquad\qquad\qquad$transition: RI_6

episode B1 (33-64) - B1/a: I_9 R_2 I_{11}--------
$\qquad\qquad\qquad\qquad\qquad\qquad\quad P_9$ R_9 P_9 RI_4 P_4

$\qquad\qquad\qquad\qquad\qquad$B1/b: I_9 R_3 RI_9
$\qquad\qquad\qquad\qquad\qquad\qquad\quad P_9$ P_2 I_3

refrain A (64-93) -   A1: P_0 RI_0 P_0 I_0
$\qquad\qquad\qquad\qquad\qquad\qquad R_0$ I_0 R_0---

$\qquad\qquad\qquad\qquad\qquad$transition: R_5 R_{11}

episode C (93-121) - C: I_8 R_1 RI_8 P_{11} R_{11}

$\qquad\qquad\qquad\qquad\qquad$C: I_8 R_1 RI_8 P_{11} - RI_6

false reprise (122-31) - A2: P_6

$\qquad\qquad\qquad\qquad\qquad$A1: RI_0
$\qquad\qquad\qquad\qquad\qquad\qquad P_0$

refrain A (132-53) - A1: I_0 R_0
$\qquad\qquad\qquad\qquad\qquad\qquad RI_0$ P_0
$\qquad\qquad\qquad\qquad\qquad\qquad R_0$ RI_0

$\qquad\qquad\qquad\qquad\qquad$A2: P_6 R_6
$\qquad\qquad\qquad\qquad\qquad\qquad I_6$ RI_6

episode B2 (153-82) - B2/a: I_3 R_8 I_5 R_{10}
$\qquad\qquad\qquad\qquad\qquad\qquad\quad P_9$ RI_4 P_7 R_7 $\qquad I_4$

$\qquad\qquad\qquad\qquad\qquad$B2/b: I_3 R_8 P_4 RI_{11} $\qquad P_2$ RI_9
$\qquad\qquad\qquad\qquad\qquad\qquad\quad P_9$ RI_4 I_5 RI_0

refrain A (182-92) -   A1: P_0 R_0----
$\qquad\qquad\qquad\qquad\qquad\qquad I_0$ R_0

$\qquad\qquad\qquad\qquad\qquad$$RI_6$ - P_{11}

347

Op. 23

'Das dunkle Herz'

```
Ia   (1-11):    RIo--------Is---------Ro----Ps
                Is Po RIs Io Rs Po RIs Rs Is Ro

Ib   (12-24):   RIo-------Is-----Ps----RIo---------Is----
                Ps RIs RIo Ro RIo Ps Is Ro Io Rs Rs Ro Po
```

```
IIa  (25-35):    Po---Ro-----Ps
                 RIs Io Is RIs RIo RIs

IIb  (36-44):    Po    Ro   Ps---
                 RIo  Ps Is Rs RIo--[Is]

IIIc (45-50):   ---Rs
                Is Ro
```

'Es stürzt aus Höhen Frische'   'Herr Jesus mein'

```
A (1-7)      B (15-19)    A (15-19)   B (20-4)    A (25-30)        A  (1-8):       Po-----Rs-----Po
                                                                                  RIs RIo Po Ro Ps Is

Rs----------|Io Ps RIs RIo |Is-----|Ro---- Io------|Po--------     B  (9-16):      Io-------------Rs----RIs--
Ro RIs Io RIs Ps|Ro Po Ps Ps  Is|Po Ro Ps|Is Io Ps RIo Po|RIs Rs Is                                Rs RIs Ps RIo Is Ps Ro Is

                                                                  A  (17-22):     RIo--Io---Rs
                                                                                  Rs Po RIo Is Rs Is

                                                                  B  (23-8):      Po----------RIs--------
                                                                                  Ps Ro RIo Ps RIo Po RIs
```

Op. 25

'Wie bin ich froh!'   'Des Herzens Purpurvogel'   'Sterne, Ihr silbernen Bienen'

```
1-6:    Po---Po/1-4┐        1-10:   Is--------              1-24:   Po-------(Po)
        RIo Po RIo  ┘5-12           Ps Ps RIs Is                    Ro RIo Po RIo (Ro)

7-12:   Io----Po Io/1-3┐    11-22:  Ps-----------Is/1-8┐    25-56:  (Po)------Ro--RIo--RIo/1-6┐
        Io Ro Ro RIo    ┘4-12       Rs RIs Ps Ps Rs   ┘9-12 Rs      (Ro) RIo Po Io Ro Io-------┘7-12 Ro

                           23-32:   Rs-----Ps------         56-78:  Io-----RIo----
                                    Is Rs RIs Rs Is                 RIo Ro Io Ro Io

                           33-42:   Is------------RIs--
                                    Is Ps RIs RIs Rs Is
```

348

Op. 24

First movement (sonata)

Exposition (1-25) -

theme I   (1-10): P_0 RI_1 RI_0 P_1

         cadence: I_1

transition (11-13): I_6--
                    (R_6)

theme II   (13-25): R_7 I_2 P_4 R_5 R_8---------
                      (R_6) I_7 R_0 R_2 (I_9) I_3/R_2 P_4/RI_5

cadence: RI_4

Development (26-44): I_0 P_2 P_1 P_0 RI_0 R_2 RI_3 R_5
                      P_7 R_7 RI_5 R_7 R_9 R_{11} R_1

Recapitulation (45-62) -

theme I   (45-9): RI_2 P_5

         cadence: (I_6)

transition (49-50):   (I_6)(R_6)

theme II   (51-62): R_7 I_2 P_4 R_5----------------R_8---
                      (R_6) I_7 R_0 I_3/R_2 (R_8/I_9) I_3/R_2 P_4

cadence: RI_4

theme I   (63-9): R_{11} I_0 RI_6 P_6/RI_7

Second movement (ternary)

A (1-24):	R_{10} RI_{10} R_6 I_5 R_7 R_{11} R_5 I_4 R_9
transition (25-8):	R_3 I_2/a
B (29-45):	I_2/b P_4 RI_0 R_2 I_1 R_5
A (46-73):	R_{10} RI_{10} R_6 I_5 R_7 R_{11} R_5 I_4 R_9
coda (74-8):	R_{10}

transposed:

A (1-24):	P_0 I_4 P_8 RI_{11} P_9 P_1 P_7 RI_{10} P_{11}
transition (25-8):	P_5 RI_8/a
B (29-45):	RI_8/b R_6 I_6 P_4 RI_7 P_7
A (46-73):	P_0 I_4 P_8 RI_{11} P_9 P_1 P_7 RI_{10} P_{11}
coda (74-8):	P_0

Third movement (variations)

Var. 1 (1-13): I_6 R_9 R_0 RI_{11}

Var. 2 (14-28): RI_8 R_9 P_{10} RI_7 R_8 R_{11} RI_{10} P_9 RI_6 P_5

Var. 3 (28-41): R_6 P_4 RI_4 P_5 RI_1 P_2 RI_{10} P_{10}

Var. 4 (41-55): P_6 I_5 P_{10} RI_4 I_8 P_2 R_{10}

Var. 5 (56-70): P_6 RI_1 R_0 RI_1 R_8 RI_1 R_0 P_6/RI_1 R_0/I_1 R_5/I_7

transposed:

Var. 1 (1-13): I_0 R_3 R_6 RI_5

Var. 2 (14-28): RI_2 R_3 P_4 RI_1 R_2 R_5 RI_4 P_3 RI_0 P_{11}

Var. 3 (28-41): R_0 P_{10} RI_{10} P_{11} RI_7 P_8 RI_4 P_4

Var. 4 (41-55): P_0 I_{11} P_4 RI_{10} I_2 P_8 R_4

Var. 5 (56-70): P_0 RI_7 R_6 RI_7 R_6 RI_7 R_6 P_6/RI_7 R_6/I_7 R_6/I_1

Appendix III

Op. 26

introduction (1-7): RI_0 / RI_6 / R_5

[Exposition] (8-32) -

A (8-19):
$$P_0 \quad I_0$$
$$R_0 \quad RI_0$$
$$I_7 \quad R_9 \quad P_9$$
$$RI_7 \quad RI_6 \quad P_6 \quad R_6$$

B (20-32):
$$RI_2\text{-----------}(RI_1)$$
$$RI_3\text{-----------}(R_4)$$
$$P_{10}\text{----------------}$$
$$P_{11}\text{----------------}$$
$$RI_5 \quad (P_5)$$
$$I_5 \quad (RI_5)$$

Development (33-71):
$$(RI_1) \quad P_3 \quad RI_0 \;|\; P_{10} \quad RI_7$$
$$(R_4) \quad R_3 \quad R_6 \;|\; P_2 \quad P_2 \quad RI_{11}$$
$$(RI_5) \quad I_3 \quad I_5 \;|\; I_1 \quad I_5 \quad R_8$$
$$(P_5) \quad R_7 \quad I_8 \;|\; P_1 \quad P_0$$

$$RI_1\text{--------}$$
$$R_6\text{--------}$$
$$R_1\text{--------}$$
$$I_1\text{--------}$$
$$RI_6 \quad R_7 \quad R_8$$
$$R_5 \quad I_7 \quad P_8$$

[Recapitulation] (72-113) -

A (72-86):
$$R_7 \quad I_9 \quad I_1 \quad R_4 \quad P_4$$
$$R_8 \quad RI_0 \quad RI_{11} \quad R_0 \quad R_1$$
$$R_9 \quad RI_7 \quad RI_1 \quad P_{11} \quad RI_8$$

B (87-113):
$$RI_6 \quad R_9 \quad R_{10} \quad RI_9 \quad R_{10} \quad I_0 \quad R_0$$
$$RI_3 \quad R_4\text{------}R_5\text{-------}RI_4 \quad R_5$$
$$RI_{10} \quad R_{11}\text{-----}RI_{10}\text{-----}I_4 \quad R_6$$
$$R_{11} \quad R_0 \quad RI_1 \quad RI_0 \quad R_1 \quad RI_0 \quad I_0$$

Op. 27

First movement (sonata)

Exposition (1-18): $R_8 \quad RI_6 \quad P_8 \quad RI_6$ / $P_8 \quad I_8 \quad R_8 \quad I_8$

Development (19-36): $RI_1 \quad P_2 \quad RI_6 \quad P_7 \quad RI_{11} \quad P_0$ / $I_1 \quad R_2 \quad I_6 \quad R_7 \quad I_{11} \quad R_0$

Recapitulation (37-54): $P_0 \quad I_0 \quad RI_5 \quad P_5$ / $R_0 \quad RI_0 \quad I_5 \quad R_5$

transposed:

Exposition (1-18): $P_0 \quad I_2 \quad R_0 \quad I_2$ / $R_0 \quad RI_2 \quad R_0 \quad RI_2$

Development (18-36): $I_7 \quad R_8 \quad I_6 \quad R_{11} \quad I_5 \quad P_4$ / $RI_7 \quad P_6 \quad RI_0 \quad P_{11} \quad RI_5 \quad R_4$

Recapitulation (37-54): $R_4 \quad RI_6 \quad I_{11} \quad R_9$ / $P_4 \quad I_6 \quad RI_{11} \quad P_9$

Second movement (binary)

A (1-11): $R_0 \quad R_7$ / $RI_0 \quad RI_5$

B (11-22): $RI_{10} \quad RI_7$ / $R_2 \quad R_5$

transposed:

A (1-11): $P_0 \quad P_5$ / $I_{10} \quad I_5$

B (11-22): $I_0 \quad P_7$ / $P_{10} \quad I_3$

Third movement (variations)

Variation 1 (1-12): $P_0 \quad I_0 \quad R_0$

Variation 2 (12-23): $P_1 \quad RI_6 \quad P_6 \quad RI_1 \quad RI_7 \quad RI_1 \quad RI_6$

Variation 3 (23-33): $RI_{11} \quad R_8 \quad R_1 \quad RI_6 \quad R_1$

Variation 4 (33-44): $I_9 \quad RI_9 \quad I_8 \quad RI_8 \quad P_0$

Variation 5 (45-55): $RI_{11} \quad P_3 \quad RI_2 \quad P_6 \quad RI_5 \quad P_9 \quad RI_8$

Variation 6 (56-66): $P_0 \quad R_0 \quad I_1 \quad RI_1 \quad R_0 \quad I_0$

350

Op. 28

First movement (variations)

Theme   (1-15): P_6 P_2 P_{10} P_6 P_4

Variation 1	(16-32):	RI_2 RI_{10} RI_6 RI_2 P_2 P_{10} P_6 P_2	Variation 4	(66-79):	RI_6 RI_2 RI_{10} RI_6 P_6 P_2 P_{10} P_6
Variation 2	(33-49):	RI_3 I_7 RI_3 RI_4 P_3 R_7 P_3 P_4	Variation 5	(80-95):	P_6 P_4 P_2 RI_6 RI_4 RI_2
Variation 3	(47-65):	RI_5 I_8 RI_5 P_5 R_8 P_5	Variation 6	(96-112):	P_{10} P_6 P_2 RI_{10} RI_6 RI_2

Second movement (ternary)

A (1-18):	R_3 R_7 R_{11} P_7 P_3 P_{11} R_7 R_{11} R_3 P_3 P_{11} P_7
B (19-36):	P_7 ---- P_{11} P_3 R_3 R_7 R_{11} ---
A (37-53):	P_7 P_3 P_{11} R_7 R_{11} R_3 P_3 P_{11} P_7 R_3 R_7 R_{11}

transposed:

A (1-19):	P_0 P_4 P_8 R_4 R_0 R_8 P_4 P_8 P_0 R_0 R_8 R_4
B (19-36):	R_8 --- R_8 R_0 P_0 R_4 P_8 ---
A (37-53):	R_4 R_0 R_8 P_4 P_8 P_0 R_0 R_8 R_4 P_0 P_4 P_8

Third movement (ternary)

A (1-15):	P_6 I_0 R_6 RI_0 P_6 I_6 R_6 RI_6

B (16-53):	(16-26)	(26-37)	(38-53)
	P_4 P_0 P_8 P_4 $\quad$ R_0 P_8	P_5 P_9 P_2 P_{10}	R_{10} R_8--P_{10} R_9--P_1 R_1

A (54-68):	R_6 RI_6 R_6 RI_0 P_0 I_0 P_6 I_6

Op. 29

'Zündender Lichtblitz des Lebens'

A (1-13)   B (14-35)   A (36-47)

A (1-13)		B (14-35)				A (36-47)	
R_{11}	R_2	P_6	P_3	P_0	P_9	P_6	P_3
I_{11}	I_2	R_0	R_3	R_6	R_9	R_0	R_3
P_{10}	P_7	RI_9	RI_6	RI_3	RI_0	RI_9	RI_6
RI_{10}	RI_7	I_3	I_6	I_9	I_0	I_3	I_6

'Tönen die seligen Saiten Apolls'

	I (1-17)			II (17-38)		
A (1-38):	RI_0	RI_9	RI_6	RI_3	RI_0	RI_9
	I_0	I_3	I_6	I_9	I_0	I_3
			.	RI_9	RI_6	RI_3
					RI_3	RI_0	RI_9

'Kleiner Flügel Ahornsamen'

A (1-6)   B (6-26)   A (27-36)   B (36-56)

A (1-6)	B (6-26)				A (27-36)		B (36-56)		
R_6	P_0	R_{11}	R_2	R_5	R_6	P_6	P_0	P_9	P_6

P_0	I_9	I_0	I_3	I_6	I_9	P_6	R_6	RI_6	RI_3	RI_0	RI_6	RI_6
P_6	RI_0	RI_3	RI_6	RI_3	RI_0	P_0	R_0	RI_0	RI_3	RI_6	RI_3	RI_0
P_5	R_5	R_6	R_{11}	R_2	R_5	P_5	R_5	R_5	R_6	R_{11}	R_2	R_5
	R_{11}	R_2	R_5	R_6	R_{11}			P_6	P_3	P_0	P_9	P_6

	III (39-48)			IV (49-57)		
B (39-57):	RI_6	RI_3	RI_0	RI_9	RI_6	RI_3
	I_6	I_9	I_0	I_3	I_6	I_9
	P_6	P_3	P_0	P_9	P_6	P_3
	R_6	R_9	R_0	R_3	R_6	R_9

	V (57-73)		
A (57-73):	RI_0	RI_9	RI_6
	I_0	I_3	I_6
	P_0	P_9	P_6
	R_0	R_3	R_6

Op. 30

Theme   (1-20): P_0 I_0 R_0 P_0
                      RI_0---I_0 RI_0

Variation 1 (21-55): RI_0-----(RI_5) RI_{10} (RI_3) RI_9-----
                      P_0 (P_5) P_{10} (P_3) P_8 (P_1) P_6
                      R_0------R_{10}-------R_8----------R_6------

Variation 2 (56-73): RI_0 RI_7 RI_2 I_2 I_7 I_0 I_5 I_{10}
                      R_0 R_5 R_{10} P_{10} P_5 P_0 P_7 P_2

Variation 3 (74-109): R_4 RI_4---P_5--------R_6
                      RI_0 R_8 P_8 RI_6 I_6 P_6 RI_4

Variation 4 (110-34): R_7 (R_2) R_9 (R_4) R_{11} (R_6) R_1
                      R_8 (R_3) R_{10} (R_5) R_0 (R_7) R_2
                      R_9 (R_4) R_{11} (R_6) R_1 (R_8) R_3
                      R_{10} (R_5) R_0 (R_7) R_2 (R_8) R_4

Variation 5 (135-45): R_7 R_0 RI_0
                      P_5------ I_5-----
                                  I_{10} (I_3) I_0
                                  RI_0 (R_3) R_8

Variation 6 (146-80): P_{10} (P_3) P_8 (P_1) P_6 (P_{11}) P_4--------
                      P_7 (P_0) P_5 (P_{10}) P_3 (P_8) P_1--------
                      R_2 (R_8) R_4 (R_{11}) R_6 R_{11} R_4 R_9 R_2
                      P_9 (P_2) P_7 (P_0) P_5 P_0 P_7 P_2 P_9

Op. 31

'Schweigt auch die Welt'

A (1-12)	A' (12-25)	A'' (25-45)	coda (45-8)
I_6 R_6 P_6 RI_6	I_6 R_6 P_6 RI_6	I_6 R_6 P_6 RI_6	I_6
P_6 RI_6 I_6 R_6	P_6 RI_6 I_6 R_6	P_6 RI_6 I_6	(P_6)

'Sehr tief verhalten innerst Leben'

A (1-32)	B (31-44)	A (45-74)
P_7 RI_8 P_5 RI_6	P_3 RI_4 P_1 RI_2	P_{11} RI_0 P_9 RI_{10}
I_7 R_6 I_9 R_8	I_{11} R_{10} I_1 R_0	I_3 R_2 I_5 R_4
I_6 R_5 I_8 R_7	I_{10} R_9 I_0 R_{11}	I_2 R_1 I_4 R_3
P_6 RI_7 P_4 RI_5	P_2 RI_3 P_0 RI_1	P_{10} RI_{11} P_8 RI_9

'Schöpfen aus Brunnen des Himmels'

A (1-13)	B (13-28)	A (29-36)	B (36-44)	A (45-59)
RI_3 P_0 RI_1	I_1 R_0 I_3	R_2 I_5---|--- R_4		P_4 RI_5 P_2
RI_5 P_6 RI_7	I_7 R_6 I_5	R_8 I_{11}--|--- R_{10}		P_{10} RI_{11} P_8
RI_0 P_9 RI_{10}	I_{10} R_9 I_0	R_{11} I_2---|--- R_1		P_1 RI_2 P_{11}
RI_6 P_3 RI_4	I_4 R_3 I_6	R_5 I_8---|--- R_7		P_7 RI_8 P_5

'Leichteste Bürden der Bäume'

A (1-11)	B (11-22)
P_0 R_0	I_0 RI_0
R_0------	P_0-------
RI_0 I_0	R_0 P_0
I_0------	RI_0------

'Freundselig ist das Wort'

A (1-16):
RI_9 RI_3 P_3 P_9
RI_{11} RI_5 P_5 P_{11}
RI_2 RI_8 P_8 P_2
RI_3 RI_9 P_9 P_3

	(17-24)	(25-31)	(32-45)
B (17-45):	RI_{11} P_0-----	----RI_{10} P_7	RI_9 P_6 RI_8
	RI_1 P_{10}-----	----RI_0 P_9	RI_{11} P_8 RI_{10}
	RI_4 P_1-----	----RI_3 P_0	RI_2 P_{11} RI_1
	RI_5 P_2-----	----RI_4 P_1	RI_3 P_0 RI_2

A (46-60):
P_5 I_{11} R_9 I_0 R_{10} I_1
P_7 I_1 R_{11} I_2 R_0 I_3
P_{10} I_4 R_2 I_5 R_3 I_6
P_{11} I_5 R_3 I_6 R_4 I_7

'Gelockert aus dem Schoße'

P_0	P_6	RI_8
I_4	I_{10}	R_8
P_8	RI_{10}	RI_4
I_8	R_6	R_0

Row analyses (2)

I decided to include the following analyses only after considerable hesitation, since the published assignment of a number to every note in all of the pieces seemed to me initially to be the sort of tedious compendium of unfiltered data that too frequently passes for analysis but is nearer to the production of telephone directories. There are too many articles that profess to offer an analysis or explanation but in fact simply list events with exhaustive thoroughness.

However, as I inspected some of the available row analyses, in formats ranging from photocopies of the author's working score containing his personally executed and often illegible pencil lines, arrows and balloons (the American way) to pages of lists of numbers followed by names of instruments, in paragraph form (the German way), I began to realize two things: that many of these people had analysed the works incorrectly and as a consequence found anomalies that do not exist, and that it was the format, not the information itself, that was responsible for my feeling that the considerable time spent wading through them was essentially time wasted. As I began to set down my own analyses in chart form I realized that if presented in some organized fashion the charts themselves can be useful, bringing repetitions, symmetries and various other relationships into focus visually. It is in the hope, then, of correcting existing errors in analysis, and in addition of providing some enlightment of a visual sort, that I offer the following charts. They do not all follow the same format, as the number of instruments involved and the way in which the row was used in individual works seemed to me to dictate different treatment in different cases. I have tried to preserve the formal outlines so that these charts can be used in conjunction with the analyses in Appendix III.

Abbreviations in the analyses

alt	alto
bcl	bass clarinet
br	brass
bsn	bassoon
cb	double bass
cel	celesta
ch	choir
cl	clarinet
eh	English horn
fl	flute
gl	glockenspiel
g + n	grace note and note following
hn	horn
hp	harp
lh	left hand
man	mandolin
mel	melody
ob	oboe
picc	piccolo
plh	piano, left hand
pno	piano
prh	piano, right hand
rh	right hand
sax	saxophone
sop	soprano
ss, ssop	solo soprano
str	strings
svn	solo violin
ten	tenor
tim	timpani
trb	trombone
trp	trumpet
vla	viola
vlc	violoncello
vn1, vn2	violin I, violin II
ww	woodwind
xyl	xylophone

Appendix IV

Op. 20/i

```
          R₄           P₄           I₄          RI₉          R₄          RI₁₁          I₂          RI₆
vn    12 56 9      4  78 BC   2  5    BC   34          234    A    34      BC     78 BC     56     C
vla      78 B    2 56        1  678      12  6 9     1  567 9 C 12  56 9A   3 6  9    2   78 B
vlc   34     A C 1 3    9A      34   9A      5 78 ABC        8 B        78      12 45     A  1 34   9A

                                          R₃           R₇          I₈          P₀          P₇
vn                             b.10   234 78 B        9A    3    9    1    78     34
vla                                              C 1234    BC     45678    23 5   9 C 12    9ABC
vlc                                   1  56 9A       5678   12      ABC    4 6   AB    5678

          I₄          RI₉          R₄          RI₁₁          I₂          RI₆          R₃
vn    1    678    12  6 9     1  567    C 12  56 9A   3  6  9A   3456      12   78
vla     34   9A      5 78 ABC       8 B       78    12 45       12    9A       56  BC
vlc   2 5     BC   34            234   9A   34     BC        78 BC       78 BC   34   9A
```

```
          I₁₀          P₅          RI₆          I₂          P₆          P₈          R₈
vn    12   678  C  34    9AB  1234  89A  1 34   9 BC   3     9    3    8  C 1 4    9A
vla    3    9A  12   78  C       7  BC       6  A  12 4  78 BC   456    B   2   78 BC
vlc      45     B       56          56      2 5 78        56   A  12    7 9A    3 56

          I₁₀          P₅          RI₆          I₂          P₆          P₈          R₈
vn       3     AB  1 4     B  45678 BC     6  A  12 45    BC 12   7 9A     5678
vla      45       2 5678   12    9A  12 5 78       67  A     56   B  234     BC
vlc   12  6789 C  3     9A C 3           34   9 BC   3   89    34  8  C 1      9A
```

356

b.41	R₄		P₄		I₄		RI₉		R₄		RI₁₁		I₂		RI₈	
vn	56 9A		34 78		2 5		12 ABC		78		34 9A		345 BC		2 78 B	
vla	12 BC		12 BC		34 9ABC		5678		234 9AB		56 BC		678		1 34 9A	
vlc	34 78		56 9A		1 678		34 9		1 56 C		12 78		12 9A		56 C	

		R₃	R₇	I₈	P₀	P₇
vn		1234 C	1234 BC	45678	3 5 9 C	12 ABC
vla	b.51	567 9A	56789	12 ABC	12 4 6 AB	45678
vlc		8 B	A	3 9	78	3 9

		I₄	RI₉	R₄	RI₁₁	I₂	RI₈	P₄
vn		34 9ABC	3 78 AB	34 78 A	34 89AB	678	3456	34 789A
vla	b.57	1 678	12 6 9	1 56 BC	2 567	345 BC	12 BC	12 56
vlc		2 5	45 C	2 9	1 C	12 9A	789A	BC

NOTE:
1) To avoid confusion, the numbers 10, 11 and 12 are represented by the letters A, B anc C respectively.
2) This chart makes no attempt to represent the temporal placement of the notes. No note in this piece appears out of order, but in many cases two notes that are adjacent in the row are played simultaneously. This is not apparent on the chart, which simply lists the notes in the order dictated by the row.
3) Notes printed in bold type are held over from the previous row.
4) Bar numbers do not take into account short anacruses.

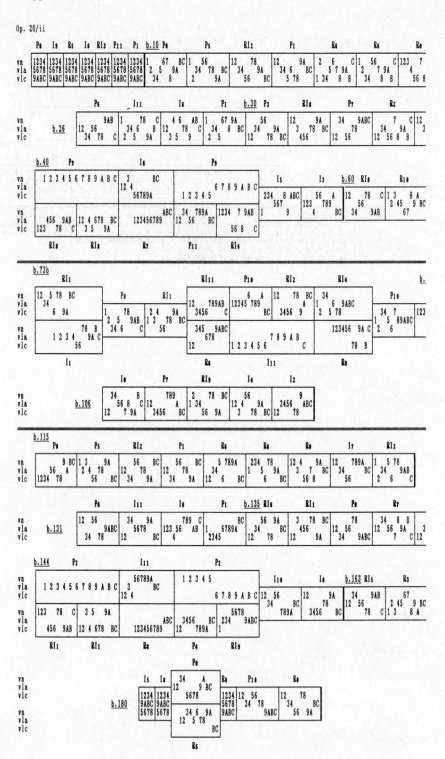

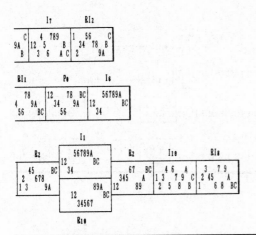

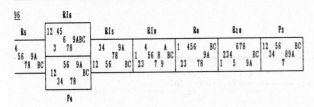

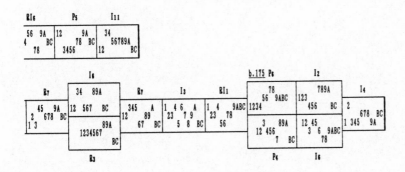

Appendix IV

Op. 21/i

<u>bs 1-26</u>

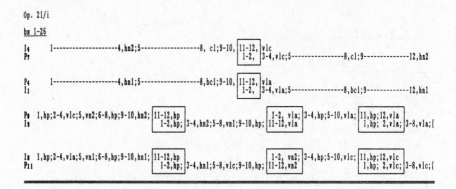

<u>bs 42-66</u>

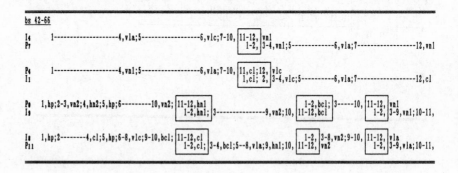

⟨9-10,hp.../9-11,bcl;12,hp⟩]

⟨9-10,hp.../9-11,vla;12,hp⟩]

```
bs 25b-44

P₁₁    1-3,cl;4,vn1;5-6,hp;7-11, |12,| vn1
R₁₁                              | 1,| 2-6,vn1;7-8,hp;9,vn1;10-12,cl

I₁₁    1-3,cl;4,vn2;5-6,hp;7-11, |12,| vn2
RI₁₁                             | 1,| 2-6,vn2;7-8,hp;9,vn2;10-12,cl

P₇/R₇  1-3,vlc;4,hn1;5-6,hp;7-------------------12,cl / 1----------------6, cl;7-8,hp;9,hn1;10-12,vlc

I₃/RI₃ 1-3,vla;4,hn2;5-6,hp;7-8,bcl;9-10,vlc;11-12,hp / 1-2,hp;3-4,vlc;5-6,bcl;7-8,hp;9,hn2;10-12,vla
```


hp;12,hn2

hp;12,vn2

Op. 21/ii

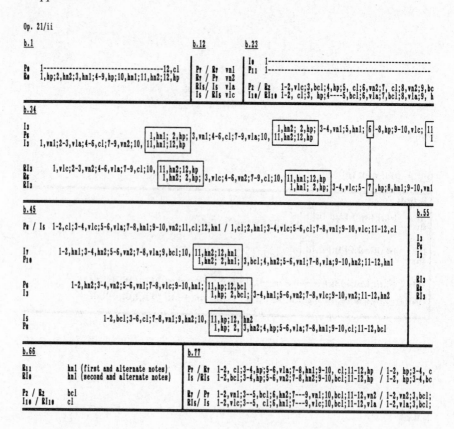

b.1

b.12

b.23

P₀ I-----------------------------------12,cl
R₀ 1,hp;2,hn2;3,hn1;4-9,hp;10,hn1;11,hn2;12,hp

P₇ / R₇ vn1
R₇ / P₇ vn2
RI₅/ I₅ vla
I₅ / RI₅ vlc

I₀ I---
P₁₁ I---

P₂ / R₂ 1-2,vlc;3,bcl;4,hp;5, cl;6,vn2;7, cl;8,vn2;9,bc
I₁₀/ RI₁₀ 1-2, cl;3, hp;4----5,bcl;6,vla;7,bcl;8,vla;9, h

---

b.34

I₃
P₆   1,hn1; 2,hp; 3,vn1;4-6,cl;7-9,vla;10, [1,hn2; 2,hp;] 3-4,vn1;5,hn1; [6] -8,hp;9-10,vlc; [11]
I₃ 1,vn1;2-3,vla;4-6,cl;7-9,vn2;10, [11,hn1;12,hp]   [11,hn2;12,hp]   1

RI₃ 1,vlc;2-3,vn2;4-6,vla;7-9,cl;10, [11,hn2;12,hp]
R₆   1,hn2; 2,hp; 3,vlc;4-6,vn2;7-9,cl;10, [11,hn1;12,hp]
RI₃   1,hn1; 2,hp; 3-4,vlc;5- [7] ,hp;8,hn1;9-10,vn1

---

b.45

b.55

P₀ / I₅ 1-2,cl;3-4,vlc;5-6,vla;7-8,hn1;9-10,vn2;11,cl;12,hn1 / 1,cl;2,hn1;3-4,vlc;5-6,cl;7-8,vn1;9-10,vlc;11-12,cl

I₇   1-2,hn1;3-4,hn2;5-6,vn2;7-8,vla;9,bcl;10, [11,hn2;12,hn1]
P₁₀   [1,hn2; 2,hn1;] 3,bcl;4,hn2;5-6,vn1;7-8,vla;9-10,hn2;11-12,hn1

I₃
P₆
I₃

P₆   1-2,hn2;3-4,vn2;5-6,vn1;7-8,vlc;9-10,hn1; [11,hp;12,bcl]
I₃   [1,hp; 2,bcl;] 3-4,hn1;5-6,vn2;7-8,vlc;9-10,vn2;11-12,hn2

RI₃
R₆
RI₃

I₅   1-2,bcl;3-6,cl;7-8,vn1;9,hn2;10, [11,hp;12,] hn2
P₆   [1,hp; 2,] 3,hn2;4,hp;5-6,vla;7-8,hn1;9-10,cl;11-12,bcl

---

b.66

b.77

R₁₁ hn1 (first and alternate notes)
RI₀ hn1 (second and alternate notes)

P₂ / R₂ cl
I₁₀ / RI₁₀ cl

P₇ / R₇ 1-2, cl;3-4,hp;5-6,vla;7-8,hn1;9-10, cl;11-12,hp / 1-2, hp;3-4, c
I₅ /RI₅ 1-2,bcl;3-4,hp;5-6,vn2;7-8,hn2;9-10,bcl;11-12,hp / 1-2, hp;3-4,bc

R₇ / P₇ 1-2,vn1;3--5,bcl;6,hn2;7---9,vn1;10,bcl;11-12,vn2 / 1-2,vn2;3,bcl;
RI₅/ I₅ 1-2,vlc;3--5, cl;6,hn1;7---9,vlc;10,bcl;11-12,vla / 1-2,vla;3,bcl;

362

```
------------------------------------------------------------------12,hn1 (downbeats)
------------------------------------------------------------------12,hn1 (afterbeats)
```

```
1;10,hp;11,bcl;12,hp / 1,hp;2,bcl;3,hp;4,bcl;5,vn2;6, cl;7,vn2;8,cl;9, hp;10-------12,bcl
p;10,cl;11, hp;12,cl / 1,cl;2, hp;3,cl;4, hp;5,vla;6,bcl;7,vla;8----9,bcl;10,hp;11-12, cl
```

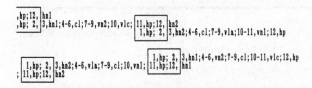

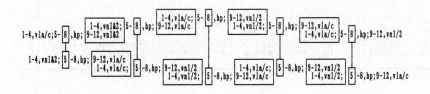

```
1;5-6,hn1;7-8,vla;9-10, hp;11-12, cl        b.89
1;5-6,hn2;7-8,vn2;9-10, hp;11-12,bcl
                                            Ro    1--3,hp;4,vn1;5-6,hp|7-9,vn1;10-11,vlc;12,hp
4---6,vn1;7,hn2;8---10,bcl;11-12,vn1
4---6,vlc;7,hn1;8---10, cl;11-12,vlc        Po    1,hp;2-3,vlc;4-6,vn1|7-8,hp;9,vn1;10---12,hp
```

363

Op. 22/i

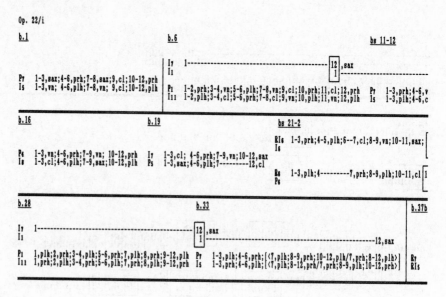

__b.1__   __b.6__   __bs 11-12__

Iᵧ   1-- 12 ,sax
I₁   1 ----------------------------

P₇ 1-3,sax;4-6,prh;7-8,sax;9,cl;10-12,prh   P₁ 1-2,prh;3-4,vn;5-6,plh;7-8,vn;9,cl;10,prh;11,cl;12,prh   P₇   1-3,prh;4-6,v
Iₛ 1-3,vn; 4-6,plh;7-8,vn; 9,cl;10-12,plh   I₁₁ 1-2,plh;3-4,cl;5-6,prh;7-8,cl;9,vn;10,plh;11,vn;12,plh   Iₛ   1-3,plh;4-6,c

__b.16__   __b.19__   __bs 21-2__

                                                                       RIₛ 1-3,prh;4-5,plh;6--7,cl;8-9,vn;10-11,sax; [
                                                                       Iₛ

P₇ 1-3,vn;4-6,prh;7-9,vn; 10-12,prh   Iᵧ 1-3,cl; 4-6,prh;7-9,vn;10-12,sax
Iₛ 1-3,cl;4-6,plh;7-9,sax;10-12,plh   Pₛ 1-3,sax;4-6,plh;7---------12,cl
                                                                       Rₛ   1-3,plh;4---------7,prh;8-9,plh;10-11,cl [1
                                                                       Pₛ

__b.28__   __b.33__   __b.37b__

Iᵧ   1-- 12 ,sax
I₁   1 --12,sax

P₁ 1,plh;2,prh;3-4,plh;5-6,prh;7,plh;8,prh;9-12,plh   P₇ 1-3,plh;4-6,prh;[<7,plh;8-9,prh;10-12,plh/7,prh;8-12,plh>]   R₇
I₁₁ 1,prh;2,plh;3-4,prh;5-6,plh;7,prh;8,plh;9-12,prh   Iₛ 1-3,prh;4-6,plh;[<7,plh;8-12,prh/7,prh;8-9,plh;10-12,prh>]   RIₛ

```
-------------12,sax
n;7-9,prh;10-12,plh
l;7-9,plh;10-12,prh
```

```
                                     b.24
12,| plh
 1,| 2-3,plh;4-6,cl;7-9,vn;10-12,plh
                                          R₇    1-3,sax;4-6,plh;7-9,vn;10-12,sax
                                          RI₅   1-3, cl;4-6,prh;7-9,sax;10-12,vn
 2,| vn
 1,| 2-3,vn;4-6,prh;7-9,sax;10-12,prh
```

```
1-3,sax;4-5,plh;6,cl;7-9,prh;10-11,sax;12,prh
1-3,vn;4-5,prh;6,cl;7-9,plh;10-11,vn;12,plh
```

Op. 22/ii

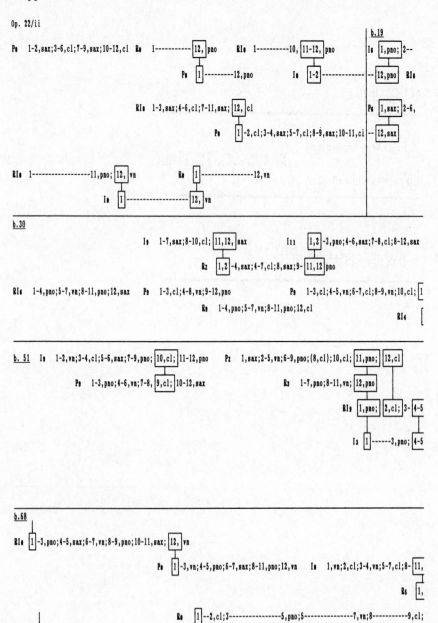

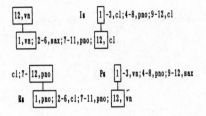

12,vn   I₆ [1]-3,cl;4-8,pno;9-12,cl

[1,vn] 2-6,sax;7-11,pno; [12,]cl

cl;7- [12,pno]   P₆ [1]-3,vn;4-8,pno;9-12,sax

R₆ [1,pno;] 2-6,cl;7-11,pno; [12,] vn

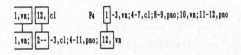

[1,vn;] [12,] cl   P₆ [1]-3,vn;4-7,cl;8-9,pno;10,vn;11-12,pno

[1,vn;] [2--]-3,cl;4-11,pno; [12,] vn

b.63

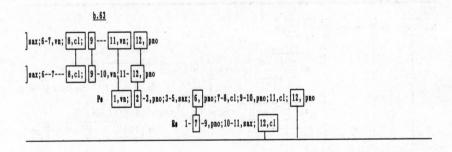

]sax;6-7,vn; [8,cl;] [9]---[11,vn;] [12,]pno

]sax;6--7---[8,cl;] [9]-10,vn;11-[12,] pno

P₆ [1,vn;] [2,]-3,pno;3-5,sax; [6,]pno;7-8,cl;9-10,pno;11,cl; [12,]pno

R₆ 1-[7]-9,pno;10-11,sax; [12,cl]

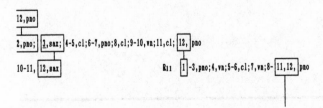

12,pno

2,pno; [3,sax;] 4-5,cl;6-7,pno;8,cl;9-10,vn;11,cl; [12,]pno

10-11, [12,sax]   R₁₁ [1]-3,pno;4,vn;5-6,cl;7,vn;8-[11,12,] pno

Appendix IV

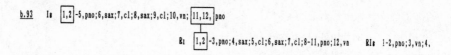

b.93   I: [1,2]-5,pno;6,sax;7,cl;8,sax;9,cl;10,vn;[11,12,]pno

                    R₁ [1,2]-3,pno;4,sax;5,cl;6,sax;7,cl;8-11,pno;12,vn   RI: 1-2,pno;3,vn;4,

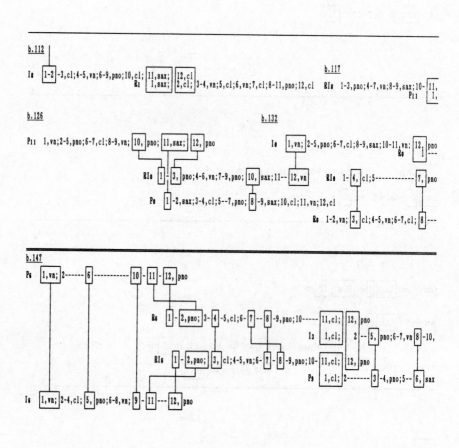

b.112

I: [1-2]-3,cl;4-5,vn;6-9,pno;10,cl; [11,sax;] [12,cl]

                  R₁ [1,sax;] [2,cl;] 3-4,vn;5,cl;6,vn;7,cl;8-11,pno;12,cl

b.117

RI: 1-3,pno;4-7,vn;8-9,sax;10-[11,
                                   P₁₁ [1,

b.126

P₁₁ 1,vn;2-5,pno;6-7,cl;8-9,vn;[10,]pno;[11,sax;][12,]pno

               RI: [1]-[3,]pno;4-6,vn;7-9,pno;[10,]sax;11--[12,vn]

            P: [1]-2,sax;3-4,cl;5--7,pno;[8]-9,sax;10,cl;11,vn;12,cl

b.132

I: [1,vn;]2-5,pno;6-7,cl;8-9,sax;10-11,vn;[12,]pno
                              R: [1]---

RI: 1-[4,]cl;5-------------[7,]pno

R: 1-2,vn;[3,]cl;4-5,vn;6-7,cl;[8]---

b.147

P: [1,vn;]2------[6]------------[10]-[11]-[12,]pno

            R: [1]-[2,]pno;3-[4]-5,cl;6-[7]--[8]-9,pno;10-----[11,cl;] [12,]pno

                      I: [1,cl;] 2--[5,]pno;6-7,vn[8]-10,

           RI: [1]-[2,]pno;[3,]cl;4-5,vn;6-[7]-[8]-9,pno;10-[11,cl;][12,]pno

                          P: [1,cl;]2-------[3]-4,pno;5--[6,]sax

I: [1,vn;]2-4,cl;[5,]pno;6-8,vn;[9]-[11]---[12,]pno

368

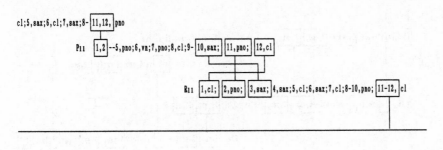

cl;5,sax;6,cl;7,sax;8- 11,12, pno

P₁₁ 1,2 --5,pno;6,vn;7,pno;8,cl;9- 10,sax; 11,pno; 12,cl

RI₁₁ 1,cl; 2,pno; 3,sax; 4,sax;5,cl;6,sax;7,cl;8-10,pno; 11-12, cl

b.122

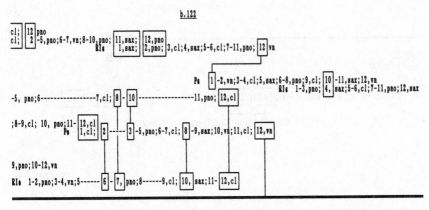

cl; 12 pno
cl; 2 -5,pno;6-7,vn;8-10,pno; 11,sax; 12,pno
RI₆ 1,sax; 2,pno; 3,cl;4,sax;5-6,cl;7-11,pno; 12 vn

P₆ 1 -2,vn;3-4,cl;5,sax;6-8,pno;9,cl; 10 -11,sax;12,vn
RI₆ 1-3,pno; 4, sax;5-6,cl;7-11,pno;12,sax

-5, pno;6----------------7,cl; 8 - 10 ----------------11,pno; 12,cl

;8-9,cl; 10, pno;11- 12,cl
P₆ 1,cl; 2 ----- 3 -5,pno;6-7,cl; 8 -9,sax;10,vn;11,cl; 12,vn

9,pno;10-12,vn
RI₆ 1-2,pno;3-4,vn;5------ 6 - 7, pno;8------9,cl; 10, sax;11- 12,cl

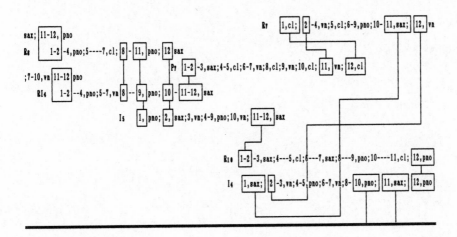

R₇ 1,cl; 2 -4,vn;5,cl;6-9,pno;10- 11,sax; 12, vn

sax; 11-12, pno
R₈ 1-2 -4,pno;5----7,cl; 8 - 11, pno; 12 sax
P₇ 1-2 -3,sax;4-5,cl;6-7,vn;8,cl;9,vn;10,cl; 11, vn; 12,cl

;7-10,vn 11-12 pno
RI₄ 1-2 --4,pno;5-7,vn 8 -- 9, pno; 10 - 11-12, sax

I₅ 1, pno; 2, sax;3,vn;4-9,pno;10,vn; 11-12, sax

R₁₀ 1-2 -3,sax;4---5,cl;6---7,sax;8---9,pno;10----11,cl; 12,pno

I₄ 1,sax; 2 -3,vn;4-5,pno;6-7,vn;8- 10,pno; 11,sax; 12,pno

369

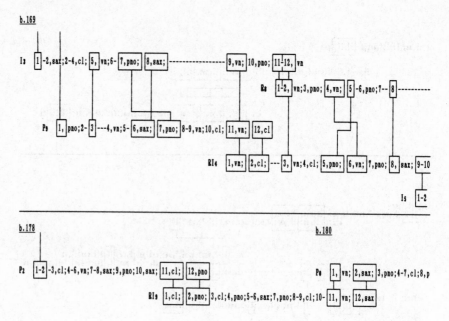

b.169

I₃ ‌1‌ -2,sax;2-4,cl; ‌5‌, vn;6- ‌7‌,pno; ‌8‌,sax; ------------------ ‌9‌,vn; 10,pno; ‌11-12‌, vn

R₈ ‌1-2‌, vn;3,pno; ‌4‌,vn; ‌5‌ -6,pno;7-- ‌8‌ ----------

P₉ ‌1‌, pno;2- ‌3‌ ---4,vn;5- ‌6‌,sax; ‌7‌,pno; 8-9,vn;10,cl; ‌11,vn‌; ‌12,cl‌

RI₄ ‌1,vn‌; ‌2,cl‌; --- ‌3‌, vn;4,cl; ‌5,pno‌; ‌6,vn‌; 7,pno; ‌8‌, sax; ‌9-10‌

I₅ ‌1-2‌

b.178

P₂ ‌1-2‌ -3,cl;4-6,vn;7-8,sax;9,pno;10,sax; ‌11,cl‌; ‌12,pno‌

RI₉ ‌1,cl‌; ‌2,pno‌; 3,cl;4,pno;5-6,sax;7,pno;8-9,cl;10- ‌11‌, vn; ‌12,sax‌

b.180

P₆ ‌1‌, vn; ‌2,sax‌; 3,pno;4-7,cl;8,p

I₆ 1,vn;2-5,pno;6-7,sax,

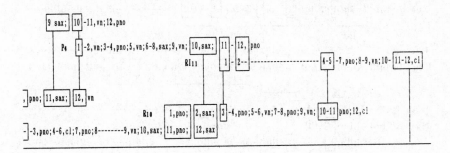

9 sax; | 10 |-11,vn;12,pno

P₄ | 1 |-2,vn;3-4,pno;5,vn;6-8,sax;9,vn;| 10,sax; | 11 |-| 12, |pno

Rl₁₁ | 1 |-| 2-- |------------------------| 4-5 |-7,pno;8-9,vn;10-| 11-12,cl |

,]pno; | 11,sax; | 12, |vn

R₁₀ | 1,pno; | 2,sax; | 3 |-4,pno;5-6,vn;7-8,pno;9,vn;| 10-11 |pno;12,cl

]-3,pno;4-6,cl;7,pno;8--------9,vn;10,sax; | 11,pno; | 12,sax

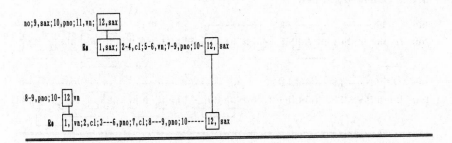

no;9,sax;10,pno;11,vn; | 12,sax

R₉ | 1,sax; |2-4,cl;5-6,vn;7-9,pno;10-| 12, |sax

8-9,pno;10-| 12 |vn

R₈ | 1, |vn;2,cl;3---6,pno;7,cl;8---9,pno;10-----| 12, |sax

Appendix IV

Op. 23/i 'Das dunkle Herz'

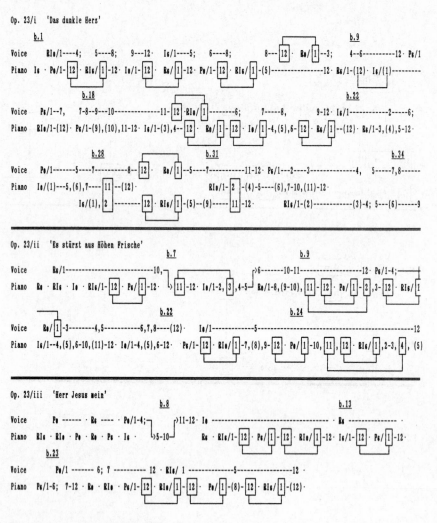

NOTE: Notes in parentheses are <u>Ausfälle</u> played by the other part.

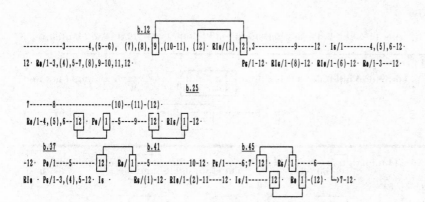

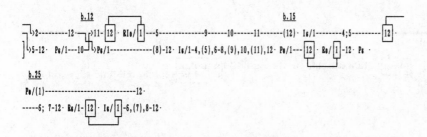

Op. 24/i

P₀   1-3,ob;4-6,fl;7-9,trp;10-12,cl   RI₁   1-3,plh;4-6,prh;7-9,plh;10-12,prh   RI₀   1-3,cl;4-6,vla;7-9,vn;10-12,ob

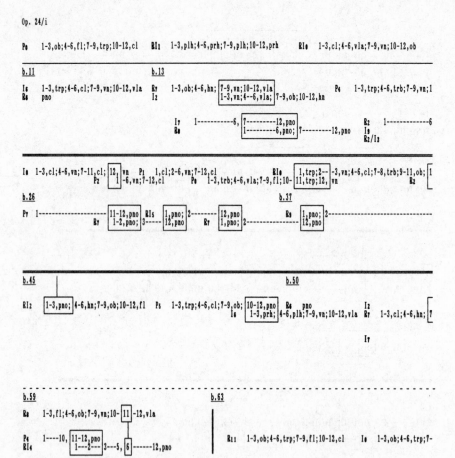

_____

b.11   b.13

I₆   1-3,trp;4-6,cl;7-9,vn;10-12,vla   R₇   1-3,ob;4-6,hn; 7-9,vn;10-12,vla   P₄   1-3,trp;4-6,trb;7-9,vn;1
R₆   pno   I₂   1-3,vn;4--6,vla; 7-9,ob;10-12,hn

                                   I₇   1-----------6, 7----------12,pno   R₂   1--------------6
                                   R₆   1---------6,pno; 7----------12,pno   I₉
                                                                                R₂/I₃

_____

I₆ 1-3,cl;4-6,vn;7-11,cl; 12 ,vn   P₁ 1,cl;2-6,vn;7-12,cl   RI₀   1,trp;2---3,vn;4-6,cl;7-8,trb;9-11,ob; 1
        P₂   1 -6,vn;7-12,cl   P₀ 1-3,trb;4-6,vla;7-9,fl;10-   11,trp;12, vn   R₂

b.26   b.37

P₇ 1------------------- 11-12,pno RI₅ 1,pno; 2-------- 12,pno   R₃ 1,pno; 2----------------
                        1-2,pno;   3----- 12,pno   R₇ 1,pno; 2   12,pno
        R₇   12,pno

_____

b.45   b.50

RI₂ 1-3,pno; 4-6,hn;7-9,ob;10-12,fl   P₅ 1-3,trp;4-6,cl;7-9,ob; 10-12,pno   R₆ pno   I₂
                                    I₆   1-3,prh; 4-6,plh;7-9,vn;10-12,vla   R₇ 1-3,cl;4-6,hn; 7

                                                                                        I₇

- -

b.59   b.63

R₃   1-3,fl;4-6,ob;7-9,vn;10- 11 -12,vla

P₄   1----10, 11-12,pno   R₁₁ 1-3,ob;4-6,trp;7-9,fl;10-12,cl   I₆ 1-3,ob;4-6,trp;7-
RI₄   1---2--- 3---5, 6 ------12,pno

_____

374

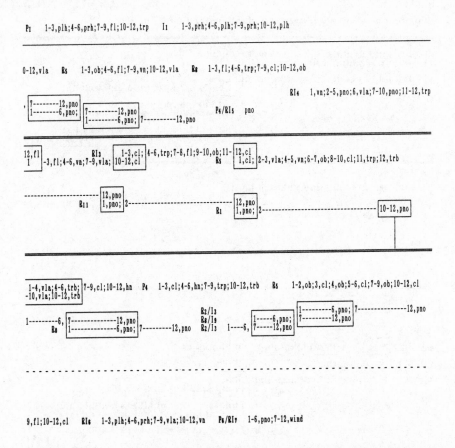

P₁   1-3,plh;4-6,prh;7-9,fl;10-12,trp   I₁   1-3,prh;4-6,plh;7-9,prh;10-12,plh

0-12,vla   R₅   1-3,ob;4-6,fl;7-9,vn;10-12,vla   R₈   1-3,fl;4-6,trp;7-9,cl;10-12,ob

RI₄   1,vn;2-5,pno;6,vla;7-10,pno;11-12,trp

, |7--------12,pno
  |1--------6,pno; |7----------12,pno
                      |1----------6,pno; |7----------12,pno   P₄/RI₅   pno

12,fl   RI₃ |1-3,cl;|4-6,trp;7-8,fl;9-10,ob;11-|12,cl
1 |-3,fl;4-6,vn;7-9,vla; |10-12,cl   R₅ |1,cl;|2-3,vla;4-5,vn;6-7,ob;8-10,cl;11,trp;12,trb

-----------------------------12,pno
              R₁₁ |1,pno;|2----------------------------|12,pno
                                                          R₁ |1,pno;|2--------------------------------|10-12,pno

1-4,vla;4-6,trb;|7-9,cl;10-12,hn   P₄   1-3,cl;4-6,hn;7-9,trp;10-12,trb   R₅   1-2,ob;3,cl;4,ob;5-6,cl;7-9,ob;10-12,cl
-10,vla;10-12,trb

1--------6,|7--------------12,pno   R₂/I₃ |1------6,pno;|7--------------12,pno
          |1--------------6,pno;   R₃/I₃   R₃/I₃ |1------6,|7-----12,pno;|7---------12,pno
R₉ |1--------------6,pno;|7---------12,pno   R₂/I₃   1----6,

9,fl;10-12,cl   RI₆   1-3,plh;4-6,prh;7-9,vla;10-12,vn   P₆/RI₇   1-6,pno;7-12,wind

375

Op. 24/ii

All the rows in this movement occur in succession, one after the other, with elision where indicated.

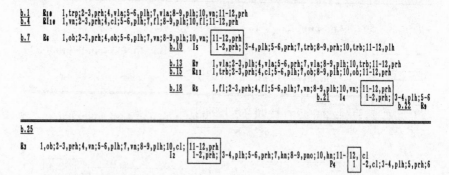

b.1 R_{10} 1,trp;2-3,prh;4,vla;5-6,plh;7,vla;8-9,plh;10,vn;11-12,prh
b.4 RI_{10} 1,vn;2-3,prh;4,cl;5-6,plh;7,fl;8-9,plh;10,fl;11-12,prh

b.7 R_8 1,ob;2-3,prh;4,ob;5-6,plh;7,vn;8-9,plh;10,vn; |11-12,prh|
    b.10 I_5 |1-2,prh;| 3-4,plh;5-6,prh;7,trb;8-9,prh;10,trb;11-12,plh

    b.13 R_7 1,vla;2-3,plh;4,vla;5-6,prh;7,vla;8-9,plh;10,trb;11-12,prh
    b.15 R_{11} 1,trb;2-3,prh;4,cl;5-6,plh;7,ob;8-9,plh;10,ob;11-12,prh

    b.18 R_8 1,fl;2-3,prh;4,fl;5-6,plh;7,vn;8-9,plh;10,vn; |11-12,prh|
       b.21 I_4 |1-2,prh;| 3-4,plh;5-6
          b.22 R_9

b.25

R_3 1,ob;2-3,prh;4,vn;5-6,plh;7,vn;8-9,plh;10,cl; |11-12,prh|
   I_2 |1-2,prh;| 3-4,plh;5-6,prh;7,hn;8-9,pno;10,hn;11- |12,| cl
     P_4 |1| -2,cl;3-4,plh;5,prh;6

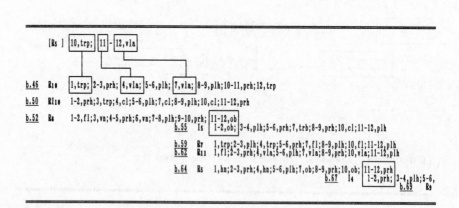

[R_8] |10,trp;| |11| - |12,vla|

b.46 R_{10} |1,trp;| 2-3,prh; |4,vla;| 5-6,plh; |7,vla;| 8-9,plh;10-11,prh;12,trp
b.50 RI_{10} 1-2,prh;3,trp;4,cl;5-6,plh;7,cl;8-9,plh;10,cl;11-12,prh
b.52 R_8 1-2,fl;3,vn;4-5,prh;6,vn;7-8,plh;9-10,prh; |11-12,ob|
    b.55 I_5 |1-2,ob;| 3-4,plh;5-6,prh;7,trb;8-9,prh;10,cl;11-12,plh

    b.59 R_7 1,trp;2-3,plh;4,trp;5-6,prh;7,fl;8-9,plh;10,fl;11-12,plh
    b.62 R_{11} 1,fl;2-3,prh;4,vla;5-6,plh;7,vla;8-9,prh;10,vla;11-12,plh

    b.64 R_8 1,hn;2-3,prh;4,hn;5-6,plh;7,ob;8-9,prh;10,ob; |11-12,prh|
       b.67 I_4 |1-2,prh;| 3-4,plh;5-6,
          b.69 R_9

,prh | 7,trb;8-9,plh;10,trb;11-12,prh
1,trb;2-3,plh; 4,trb; 5-6,prh; | 7,trp;8-9,prh;10,trp;11-12,plh

,trp;7,prh;8,trp;9,trb;10-11,pno; | 12,trb
R1₀   1,trb; | 2-3,plh;4-5,prh;6,hn;7-8,pno;9-10,hn;11- | 12,ob
R2   1,ob; | 2-3,plh;4-5,prh;6,vn;

[R2] 7-8,pno;9- | 10,vn; | 11-12,prh
I1   1-2,prh; | 3-4,plh; | 5,vn; | 6-7,fl;8-9,plh;10-11,prh; | 12,hn
R5   1,hn; | 2-3,pno;4,hn;5-6,ob;7-8,pno;9--

b.74

prh; | 7,cl;8-9,pno;10,cl;11-12,plh
1,cl;2-3,pno; 4,cl; 5-6,plh; | 7,trb;8-9,prh;10,trb;11-12,plh   R1₀   1,trp;2-3,plh;4,trp;5-6,prh;7-8,vn;9-10,prh;11-12,plh

Appendix IV

Op. 24/iii

All rows in this movement occur in succession, with the elisions indicated.

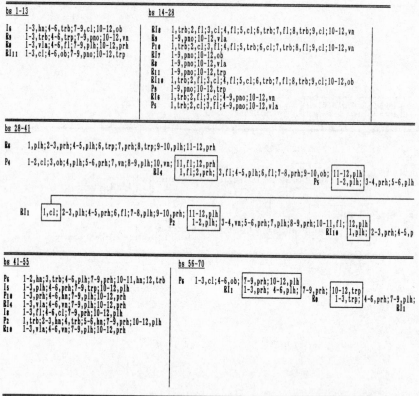

<u>bs 1-13</u>

I₆	1-3,hn;4-6,trb;7-9,cl;10-12,ob
R₃	1-3,trb;4-6,trp;7-9,pno;10-12,vn
R₀	1-3,vla;4-6,fl;7-9,plh;10-12,prh
RI₁₁	1-3,cl;4-6,ob;7-9,pno;10-12,trp

<u>bs 14-28</u>

RI₈	1,trb;2,fl;3,cl;4,fl;5,cl;6,trb;7,fl;8,trb;9,cl;10-12,vn
R₃	1-9,pno;10-12,vla
P₁₀	1,trb;2,cl;3,fl;4,fl;5,trb;6,cl;7,trb;8,fl;9,cl;10-12,vn
RI₇	1-9,pno;10-12,ob
R₂	1-9,pno;10-12,vla
RI₁₁	1-9,pno;10-12,trp
RI₁₀	1,trb;2,fl;3,cl;4,fl;5,cl;6,trb;7,fl;8,trb;9,cl;10-12,ob
P₉	1-9,pno;10-12,trp
RI₆	1,trb;2,fl;3,cl;4-9,pno;10-12,vn
P₅	1,trb;2,cl;3,fl;4-9,pno;10-12,vla

<u>bs 28-41</u>

R₆   1,plh;2-3,prh;4-5,plh;6,trp;7,prh;8,trp;9-10,plh;11-12,prh

P₄   1-2,cl;3,ob;4,plh;5-6,prh;7,vn;8-9,plh;10,vn; 11,fl;12,prh

RI₄   1,fl;2,prh; 3,fl;4-5,plh;6,fl;7-8,prh;9-10,ob; 11-12,plh

P₅   1-2,plh; 3-4,prh;5-6,plh

RI₁   1,cl; 2-3,plh;4-5,prh;6,fl;7-8,plh;9-10,prh; 11-12,plh

P₂   1-2,plh; 3-4,vn;5-6,prh;7,plh;8-9,prh;10-11,fl; 12,plh

RI₁₀   1,plh; 2-3,prh;4-5,p

<u>bs 41-55</u>

P₆	1-2,hn;3,trb;4-6,plh;7-9,prh;10-11,hn;12,trb
I₅	1-3,plh;4-6,prh;7-9,trp;10-12,plh
P₁₀	1-3,prh;4-6,hn;7-9,plh;10-12,prh
RI₄	1-3,vla;4-6,vn;7-9,plh;10-12,prh
I₈	1-3,fl;4-6,cl;7-9,prh;10-12,plh
P₂	1,trb;2-3,hn;4,trb;5-6,hn;7-9,prh;10-12,plh
RI₁₀	1-3,vla;4-6,vn;7-9,plh;10-12,prh

<u>bs 56-70</u>

P₆   1-3,cl;4-6,ob; 7-9,prh;10-12,plh

RI₁   1-3,prh; 4-6,plh; 7-9,prh; 10-12,trp

R₆   1-3,trp; 4-6,prh;7-9,plh;

RI₁

378

;7-8,vn;9,cl;10-11,prh; 12,cl

lh;6,ob;7-8,prh;9-10,plh;11- 12,vn
P₁₀ 1,vn; 2,plh;3-4,prh;5-6,plh;7,cl;8-9,prh;10-11,plh;12,cl

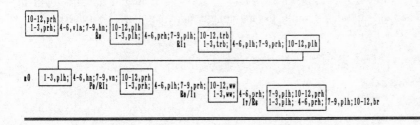

10-12,prh
1-3,prh; 4-6,vla;7-9,hn; 10-12,plh
R₀ 1-3,plh; 4-6,prh;7-9,plh; 10-12,trb
RI₁ 1-3,trb; 4-6,plh;7-9,prh; 10-12,plh

R0 1-3,plh; 4-6,hn;7-9,vn; 10-12,prh
P₀/RI₁ 1-3,prh; 4-6,plh;7-9,prh; 10-12,ww
R₀/I₁ 1-3,ww; 4-6,prh; 7-9,plh;10-12,prh
I₇/R₆ 1-3,plh; 4-6,prh; 7-9,plh;10-12,br

379

Appendix IV

Op. 25/i 'Wie bin ich froh!'

Voice   Pₒ · Pₒ/1---4;⌐   Iₒ · Pₒ · Iₒ/1---3;⌐

Piano   RIₒ/1-[12]· Pₒ/[1]-12· RIₒ ·⌐₅-12· Iₒ · Rₒ · Rₒ · RIₒ · ⌐₄-12·

Op. 25/ii 'Des Herzens Purpurvogel'

Voice   Is/1---5---6-----------------9---11;   12· Ps/1----3--------------8---------------------10-12·

Piano   Ps · Ps/1-(5)-(11)-12· RIs/1-3,(4),5-[10-12]· Is/[1-3],4-11,(12)· Rs/1--(10)-12· RIs/1-(10)-[12]· Ps/[1]---9-(10-12)

Voice   Rs/1-------[12]· Ps/[1]----7-----------------9--11;   12· Is/1---------7-------------------10- 12 · RIs/

Piano   Is/1-[12]· Rs/[1]-12· RIs · Rs/1-------(6)--[12]· Is/[1]-(2)-(6)---12· Is · Ps/1--(10)-12· RIs · RIs/1--(3)--12· Rs/1
   "   ‡

[* There is an extra note (G) in this row.]

Op. 25/iii 'Sterne, Ihr silbernen Bienen'
                                      <u>b.17</u>   <u>b.27</u>   <u>b.41</u>

Voice   Pₒ/1---2;   3-------8,9-10;   11-12· Pₒ/1------4;   5---[12]· Rₒ/[1]-12· RIₒ/1-3--------------12· RI

Piano   Rₒ · RIₒ/1-[12]· Pₒ/[1]-8,(9-10),11-12· RIₒ · Rₒ/1--8,(9),10-12· RIₒ/1-[12]· Pₒ/[1]-12· Iₒ/1--(10)-12· Rₒ/1- [12] ·

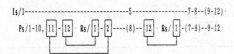

Is/1--------------------------------5-----------------7-8--(9-12)·
Ps/1-10, [11]-[12] · Rs/[1]-[2]----(8)--[12] Rs/[1]-(7-8)--9-12 ·

1--2----4-------8----------12·
--(7)--(11)-12·
        Is/1---(5)----12·

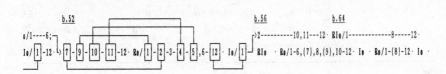

b.52   b.56   b.64
o/1----6;   2-----------10,11---12· RIo/1-------------8-----12·
Io/[1]-12·[7]-[9]-[10]-[11]-12· Ro/[1]-[2]-3-[4]-[5],6-[12]· Io/[1]· RIo · Ro/1-6,(7),8,(9),10-12· Io · Ro/1-(8)-12· Io ·

Op. 26 Das Augenlicht

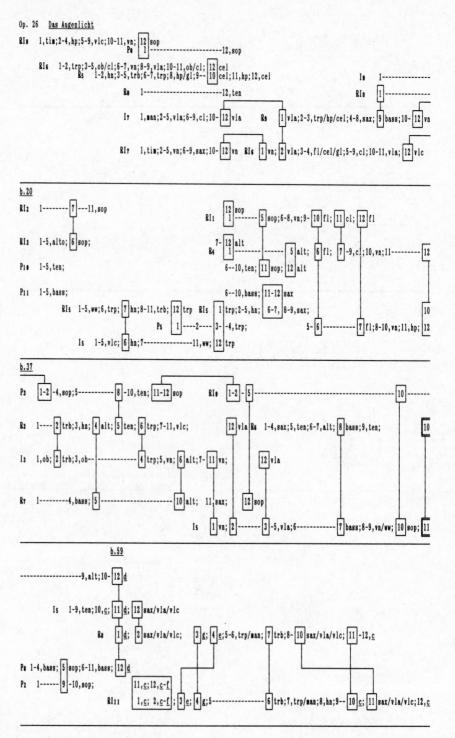

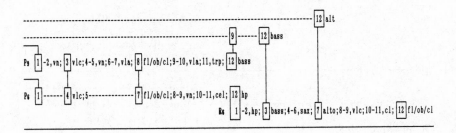

```
                                                          ┌──┐
----------------------------------------------------------│12│alt
                                          ┌─┐    ┌──┐      └──┘
------------------------------------------│9├----│12│bass
                                          └─┘    └──┘
P₉ │1│-2,vn; │3│vlc;4-5,vn;6-7,vla; │8│fl/ob/cl;9-10,vla;11,trp; │12│bass

P₆ │1├------│4│vlc;5--------------│7│fl/ob/cl;8-9,vn;10-11,cel; │12│hp
                                          R₈ │1│-2,hp; │3│bass;4-6,sax; │7│alto;8-9,vlc;10-11,cl; │12│fl/ob/cl
```

```
]cel
```

```
]cel;   │11-12│sop
]cel P₃ │1-2│------
```

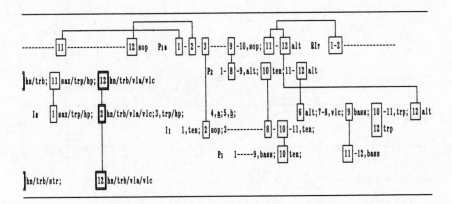

```
                ┌──┐              ┌──┐
----------------│11├--------------│12│sop  P₁₀ │1├-│2├-│3├----│9│-10,sop; │11├-│12│alt  R1₇ │1│-2│----------------
                └──┘              └──┘                         └─┘
                                               P₂ 1-│8│-9,alt; │10│ten;11-│12│alt
]hn/trb; │11│sax/trp/hp; │12│hn/trb/vla/vlc

I₈ │1│sax/trp/hp; │2│hn/trb/vla/vlc;3,trp/hp;      4,a;5,b;         │6│alt;7-8,vlc; │9│bass; │10│-11,trp; │12│alt
                       I₁ 1,ten; │2│sop;3----------│8│-│10│-11,ten;                         │12│trp
                              P₁ 1-----9,bass; │10│ten;                    │11│-12,bass

]hn/trb/str;   │12│hn/trb/vla/vlc
```

b.64

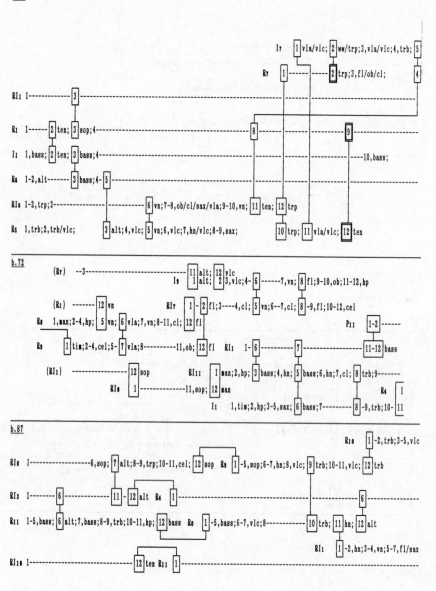

```
                                                    I₇   1 vla/vlc; 2 ww/trp;3,vla/vlc;4,trb; 5
                                              R₇    1------------2 trp;3,fl/ob/cl;              4
RI₁  1--------------3---------------------------------------------------
R₁   1------2 ten; 3 sop;4--------------------8-----------------9
I₁   1,bass; 2 ten; 3 bass;4------------------------------------------10,bass;
R₆   1-2,alt-------3 bass;4-5
RI₆  1-2,trp;3----------------------6 vn;7-8,ob/cl/sax/vla;9-10,vn; 11 ten; 12 trp
R₃   1,trb;2,trb/vlc;   3 alt;4,vlc; 5 vn;6,vlc;7,hn/vlc;8-9,sax;   10 trp; 11 vla/vlc; 12 ten
```

b.72

```
(R₇)  --3----------------------11 alt; 12 vlc
                            I₉  1 alt; 2 3,vlc;4-6------7,vn; 8 fl;9-10,ob;11-12,hp
(R₁)  -------12 vn       RI₇  1-2 fl;3----4,cl; 5 vn;6--7,cl; 8 -9,fl;10-12,cel
R₆  1,man;2-4,hp; 5 vn; 6 vla;7,vn;8-11,cl; 12 fl                    P₁₁  1-2------
R₉  1 tim;2-4,cel;5-7 vla;8----------11,ob; 12 fl  RI₁  1-6----------7------------------11-12 bass
(RI₁)  ----------------12 sop    RI₁₁  1 man;2,hp; 3 bass;4,hn; 5 bass;6,hn;7,cl; 8 trb;9------
       RI₆  1--------------11,sop; 12 man                             R₄  1
       I₁  1,tim;2,hp;3-5,sax; 6 bass;7---------8 -9,trb;10-11
```

b.87

```
                                                          R₁₀  1 -2,trb;3-5,vlc
RI₉  1------------------6,sop; 7 alt;8-9,trp;10-11,cel; 12 sop  R₃  1 -5,sop;6-7,hn;8,vlc; 9 trb;10-11,vlc; 12 trb
RI₃  1--------6---------------11 -12 alt  R₄  1------------------------------6
R₁₁  1-5,bass; 6 alt;7,bass;8-9,trb;10-11,hp; 12 bass  R₆  1 -5,bass;6-7,vlc;8-----------10 trb; 11 hn; 12 alt
                                                          RI₁  1 -2,hn;3-4,vn;5-7,fl/sax
RI₁₀  1-----------------------12 ten  R₁₁  1------------------------------
```

384

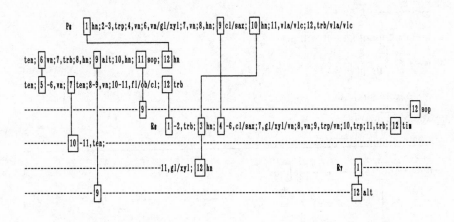

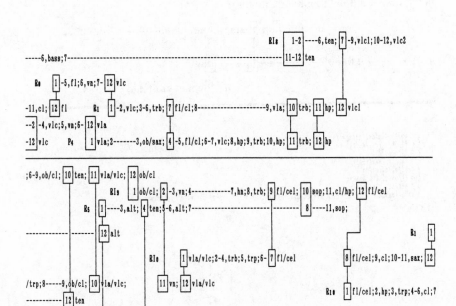

Appendix IV

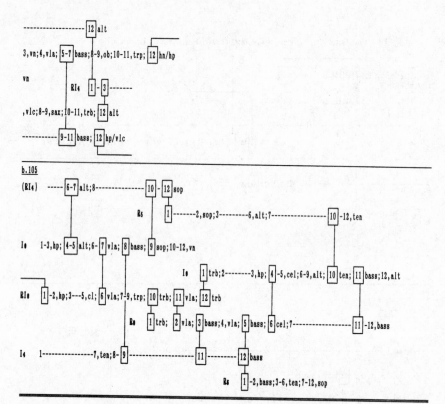

NOTE

a = ww/trp/hp/cel/gl/xyl/vn
b = fl/ob/cl/cel/gl/xyl/vn
c = fl/ob/cl/vn
d = sax/trp/man/vla/vlc
e = fl/ob/cl/hn/vn
f = fl/ob/cl/trp/man/vn
g = sax/trb/vla/vlc
A note inside a double box is played also by another voice, using different instruments.

Appendix IV

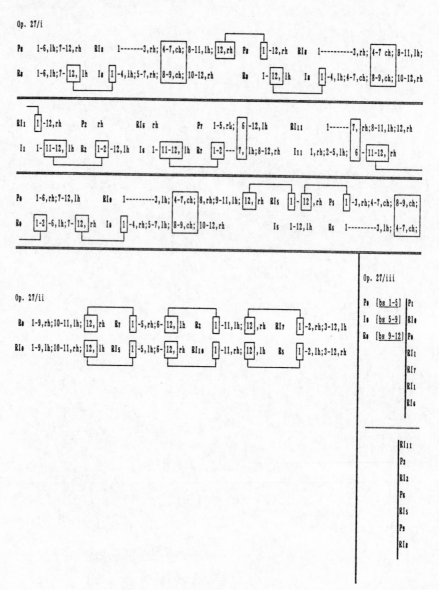

388

12, rh

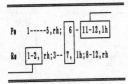

Po 1-----5,rh; 6 - 11-12,1h

Ro 1-2, rh;3-- 7, 1h;8-12,rh

10,1h;11-12,rh

8,rh;9-11,1h;12,rh

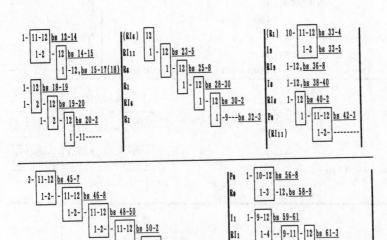

Appendix IV

Op. 28/i

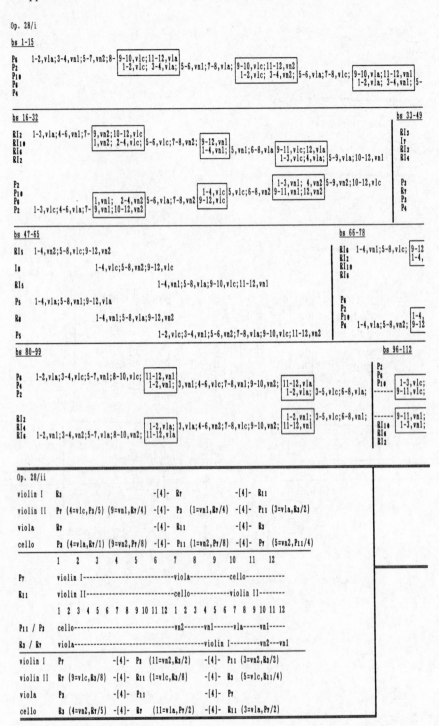

__bs 1-15__

P₆	1-2,vla;3-4,vn1;5-7,vn2;8-	9-10,vlc;11-12,vla
P₂		1-2,vlc; 3-4,vla; 5-6,vn1;7-8,vla;	9-10,vlc;11-12,vn2
P₁₀			1-2,vlc; 3-4,vn2; 5-6,vla;7-8,vlc;	9-10,vla;11-12,vn1
P₆				1-2,vla; 3-4,vn1; 5-
P₄				

__bs 16-32__   __bs 33-49__

RI₂ 1-3,vla;4-6,vn1;7- 9,vn2;10-12,vlc   RI₃
RI₁₀   1,vn2; 2-4,vlc; 5-6,vlc;7-8,vn2; 9-12,vn1   I₇
RI₆   1-4,vn1; 5,vn1;6-8,vla 9-11,vlc;12,vla RI₃
RI₂   1-3,vlc;4,vla; 5-9,vla;10-12,vn1 RI₄

P₂   1-3,vn1; 4,vn2 5-9,vn2;10-12,vlc   P₃
P₁₀   1-4,vlc 5,vlc;6-8,vn2 9-11,vn1;12,vn2   R₇
P₆   1,vn1; 2-4,vn2 5-6,vla;7-8,vn2 9-12,vlc   P₃
P₂ 1-3,vlc;4-6,vla;7- 9,vn1;10-12,vn2   P₄

__bs 47-65__   __bs 66-78__

RI₅ 1-4,vn2;5-8,vlc;9-12,vn2   RI₆ 1-4,vn1;5-8,vlc; 9-12
                                                                     RI₂   1-4,
I₆   1-4,vlc;5-8,vn2;9-12,vlc   RI₁₀
                                                                     RI₆
RI₅   1-4,vn1;5-8,vla;9-10,vlc;11-12,vn1

P₅ 1-4,vla;5-8,vn1;9-12,vla   P₆
                                                                     P₂
R₈   1-4,vn1;5-8,vla;9-12,vn2   P₁₀
                                                                     P₆ 1-4,vla;5-8,vn2; 9-12
P₅   1-2,vlc;3-4,vn1;5-6,vn2;7-8,vla;9-10,vlc;11-12,vn2

__bs 80-99__   __bs 96-112__

                                                                     P₂
                                                                     P₆
P₆ 1-2,vla;3-4,vlc;5-7,vn1;8-10,vlc; 11-12,vn1   P₁₀ 1-3,vlc;
P₄   1-2,vn1; 3,vn1;4-6,vlc;7-8,vn1;9-10,vn2; 11-12,vla   ------ 9-11,vlc;
P₂   1-2,vla; 3-5,vlc;6-8,vla;

                                                                     ------ 9-11,vn1;
RI₂   1-2,vn1; 3-5,vlc;6-8,vn1; RI₁₀ 1-3,vn1;
RI₄   1-2,vla; 3,vla;4-6,vn2;7-8,vlc;9-10,vn2; 11-12,vn1   RI₆
RI₆ 1-2,vn1;3-4,vn2;5-7,vla;8-10,vn2; 11-12,vla   RI₂

Op. 28/ii

violin I	R₃ -[4]- R₇ -[4]- R₁₁
violin II	P₇ (4=vlc,P₃/5) (9=vn1,R₇/4) -[4]- P₃ (1=vn1,R₇/4) -[4]- P₁₁ (3=vla,R₃/2)
viola	R₇ -[4]- R₁₁ -[4]- R₃
cello	P₃ (4=vla,R₇/1) (9=vn2,P₇/8) -[4]- P₁₁ (1=vn2,P₇/8) -[4]- P₇ (5=vn2,P₁₁/4)

	1	2	3	4	5	6	7	8	9	10	11	12
P₇	violin I----------------------viola------------cello------------
R₁₁	violin II----------------------cello------------violin II--------

1 2 3 4 5 6 7 8 9 10 11 12 1 2 3 4 5 6 7 8 9 10 11 12

P₁₁ / P₃	cello----------------------vn2------vn1------vla-----vn1-----
R₃ / R₇	viola----------------------------violin I---------vn2---vn1

violin I	P₇ -[4]- P₃ (11=vn2,R₃/2) -[4]- P₁₁ (3=vn2,R₃/2)
violin II	R₇ (9=vlc,R₃/8) -[4]- R₁₁ (1=vlc,R₃/8) -[4]- R₃ (5=vlc,R₁₁/4)
viola	P₃ -[4]- P₁₁ -[4]- P₇
cello	R₃ (4=vn2,R₇/5) -[4]- R₇ (11=vla,P₇/2) -[4]- R₁₁ (3=vla,P₇/2)

7,vn2;8-10,vlc; | 11-12,vla
1-2,vla; | 4,vla;5-6,vlc;7-8,vn1;9-10,vn2;11-12,vlc

1-6,vn2;7-12,vla
1-6,vlc;7-12,vn1
1-3,vn2;4-6,vn1;7-9,vn2;10-12,vn1
1-3,vn2;4-6,vn1;7-9,vn2;10-12,vn1

1-6,vn1;7-12,vn2
1-6,vla;7-12,vlc
1-3,vla;4-6,vlc;7-9,vla;10-12,vlc
1-3,vla;4-6,vlc;7-9,vla;10-12,vlc

,vn1
vn1; | 5-8,vlc; | 9-12,vn1
1-4,vn1; | 5-8,vla; | 9-12,vn2
1-4,vn2; | 5-8,vlc;9-12,vn2

1-4,vla; | 5-8,vn1;9-12,vla
1-4,vlc; | 5-6,vn1;7-8,vlc; | 9-12,vla
vla; | 5-8,vn2; | 9-12,vlc
,vla

1-2,vla; 3-4,vn1; | 5-6,vla;7-8,vn1;9-10,vla;11-12,vn1
4,vla; | 5-6,vla;7- | 1,vlc; 2-4,vla; | 5-7,vn1;8- | 9-10,vla;11-12,vn1
12,vla | 9,vlc;10-12,vla

12,vn2
4,vn2; | 5-6,vn2;7- | 9,vn1;10-12,vn2 | 5-7,vlc;8- | 9-10,vn2;11-12,vlc
1,vn1; 2-4,vn2; | 1-2,vn2; 3-4,vlc; | 5-6,vn2;7-8,vlc;9-10,vn2;11-12,vla

---

Op. 28/iii

	b.16									b.26		b.54	
vn1 P₀ I₀	P₄	1-4,vlc;5-8,vn2;	9-12,vla							P₅	R₁₀---	R₀ RI₀	
	P₆		1-4,vla;	5-8,vn1;	9-12,vn2					P₉	R₃--P₁₀-(9-12,vla)	R₀ RI₀	
vn2 R₀ RI₀	P₆			1-4,vn2;	5-8,vla;	9-12,vlc				P₂	R₃--P₁--(9-12,vn1)	P₀ I₀	
	P₄					1-4,vlc;	5-8,vla;9-12,vn2						
vla P₀ I₀					1-4,vlc;5-8,vn1;9-12,vn2					P₁₀	R₁----	P₀ I₀	
vlc R₀ RI₀ P₅	R₀						1-4,vn1;5-8,vlc;9-12,vla						

391

Op. 29/i: "Zündender Lichtblitz des Lebens"

<u>bs 1-13</u>

R₁₁   1-3,trp;4-5,vn1;6,hp;7-9,vn1;10- |11-12,trp|
R₂ |1-2,trp;| 3,fl;4-5,vn1;6,cel;7,hn;8-9,cl;10,cel;11-12,hn

RI₁₀ 1-3,trb;4-5,vn2;6,cel;7-9,vn2;10- |11-12,trb|
RI₇ |1-2,trb;| 3,hn;4-5,vn2;6,hp;7,trb;8-9,vn2;10,bcl;11-12,trb

P₁₀   1-3,vla;4-8,cl;9,cel;10- |11-12,vla|
P₇ |1-2,vla;| 3-6,cl;7,trp;8-9,vn1;10,cl;11,vla;12,tim

I₁₁   1-3,vlc;4-8,bcl;9,hp;10- |11-12,vlc|
I₂ |1-2,vlc;| 3-6,bcl;7,fl;8-9,bcl;10,hp;11,vlc;12,trp

<u>bs 14-35</u>

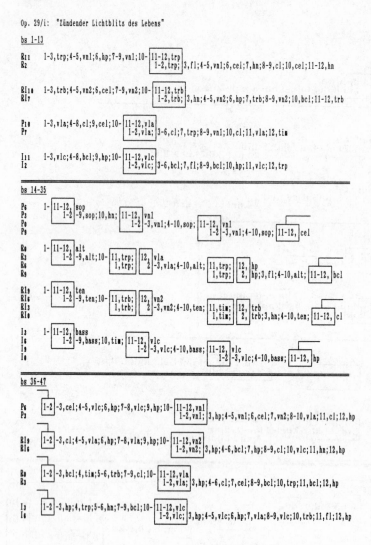

P₆   1- |11-12,| sop
P₃ |1-2| -9,sop;10,hn; |11-12,| vn1
P₀ |1-2| -3,vn1;4-10,sop; |11-12,| vn1
P₉ |1-2| -3,vn1;4-10,sop; |11-12,| cel

R₀   1- |11-12,| alt
R₃ |1-2| -9,alt;10- |11,trp;| |12,| vla
R₆ |1,trp;| |2| -3,vla;4-10,alt; |11,trp;| |12,| hp
R₃ |1,trp;| |2,| hp;3,fl;4-10,alt; |11-12,| bcl

RI₉ 1- |11-12,| ten
RI₆ |1-2| -9,ten;10- |11,trb;| |12,| vn2
RI₃ |1,trb;| |2| -3,vn2;4-10,ten; |11,tim;| |12,| trb
RI₀ |1,tim;| |2,| trb;3,hn;4-10,ten; |11-12,| cl

I₃   1- |11-12,| bass
I₆ |1-2| -9,bass;10,tim; |11-12,| vlc
I₉ |1-2| -3,vlc;4-10,bass; |11-12,| vlc
I₀ |1-2| -3,vlc;4-10,bass; |11-12,| hp

<u>bs 36-47</u>

P₆ |1-2| -3,cel;4-5,vlc;6,hp;7-8,vlc;9,hp;10- |11-12,vn1|
P₃ |1-2,vn1;| 3,hp;4-5,vn1;6,cel;7,vn2;8-10,vla;11,cl;12,hp

RI₉ |1-2| -3,cl;4-5,vla;6,hp;7-8,vla;9,hp;10- |11-12,vn2|
RI₆ |1-2,vn2;| 3,hp;4-6,bcl;7,hp;8-9,cl;10,vlc;11,hn;12,hp

R₀ |1-2| -3,bcl;4,tim;5-6,trb;7-9,cl;10- |11-12,vla|
R₃ |1-2,vla;| 3,hp;4-6,cl;7,cel;8-9,bcl;10,trp;11,bcl;12,hp

I₃ |1-2| -3,hp;4,trp;5-6,hn;7-9,bcl;10- |11-12,vlc|
I₆ |1-2,vlc;| 3,hp;4-5,vlc;6,hp;7,vla;8-9,vlc;10,trb;11,fl;12,hp

Op. 29/ii "Kleiner Flügel Ahornsamen"

bs 1-6

Rₛ   cl

Pₛ   1,hp;2-3,fl; 4,vla;5,hp;6-7,vn1;8,vla;9-10,fl; 11,vn1/vla;12,hp/vn1
Pₒ   1,hp;2-3,trp;4,vn2;5,hp;6-7,ob; 8,vn2;9-10,trp;11,vn2;   12,hp
Pₑ   1,hp;2-3,bcl;4,vlc;5,hp;6-7,trp;8,vlc;9-10,bcl;11,vlc;   12,hp

---

bs 6-26   Pₒ-R₁₁-R₂-Rₛ   voice

RIₒ   1-4,bcl;5-6,vlc;7-10,cl; |11-12,cel|
RI₉   1-2,cel; |3-4,vn1;5-8,cl;9-10,vn1; |11-12,|cel
RIₑ |1-2 |-4,cel;5-6,vn2;7-8,bcl;9-10,vla; |11-12,hp|
RI₃ |1-2,hp; |3-4,vn2;5-8,
RIₒ

Rₛ   1-4,fl;5-6,hp;7-10,hn; |11-12,hp|
Rₐ |1-2,hp; |3-4,vlc;5-6,hp;7-8,cel;9-10;vla; |11-12|ob
R₁₁ |1-2 |-4,ob;5-6,vn1;7-8,hn;9-10,vn2; |11-12,vlc|
R₂ |1-2,vlc; |3-4,vla;5
Rₛ

Iₛ   1-2,trb;3-4,cel;5-6,vn1;7-8,vn2;9-10,vla; |11-12,trp|
Iₒ |1-2,trp; |3-4,ob;5-6,fl;7-8,trp;9-10,hn; |11-12,fl|
I₃ |1-2,fl; |3-4,vn1;5-6,trp;7-8,vlc;9-10,
Iₑ
I₉

R₁₁   1-2,cl;3-4,trp;5-6,cel;7-8,fl;9-10,vn1; |11-12,trb|
R₂ |1-2,trb; |3-4,vla;5-6,vn2;7-8,trb;9-10,vn1; |11-12,hp|
Rₛ |1-2,hp; |3-4,vla;5-6,fl;7-8,ob;9-10,v
Rₐ
R₁₁

---

bs 27-36   Rₛ-Pₛ   voice

Pₛ   1,hp;2,vla;3-4,vn1;5,hp;6-7,trp;8,cel;9-10,fl; 11,vla/vn1;12,hp/vn1   Rₛ   1,hp/vn1;2,vla/vn1;3-4,fl; 5,cel;6-7,trp;8,
Pₒ   1,hp;2,vn2;3-4,trp;5,hp;6-7,trb;8,cel;9-10,cl; 11,vn2;   12,hp   Rₐ   1,hp;   2,vn2;   3-4,cl; 5,cel;6-7,trb;8,
Pₑ   1,hp;2,vlc;3-4,fl; 5,hp;6-7,hn; 8,cel;9-10,bcl;11,vlc;   12,hp   Rₛ   1,hp;   2,vlc;   3-4,bcl;5,cel;6-7,hn; 8,

---

bs 36-56   Pₒ-Pₛ-Pₑ   voice

RIₛ   1-2,trb;3-4,bcl;5-6,ob;7-8,trp;9-10,hn; |11-12,hp|
RI₃ |1-2,hp; |3-4,vla;5-8,bcl;9-10,trp; |11-12,cl|
RIₒ |1-2,cl; |3-4,man;5-6,trb;7-8,cl;9-10,vlc; |11-1|
RI₉ |1-2
RIₑ

Rₛ   1-2,ob;3-4,vlc;5-6,cl;7-8,trb;9-10,bcl; |11-12,trp|
Rₐ |1-2,trp; |3-4,vn1;5-8,cl;9-10,vn1; |11-12,bcl|
R₁₁ |1-2,bcl; |3-4,trp;5-6,vn1;7-8,bcl;9-10,vn1; |11|
R₂ |1
Rₛ

RIₒ   1-2,trp;3-4,vn1;5-6,vlc;7-8,vla;9-10,vn1; |11-12,man|
RI₉ |1-2,man; |3-4,vn2;5-6,man;7-8,ob;9-10,hn; |11-12,cel|
RIₑ |1-2,cel; |3-4,fl;5-6,hp;7-8,hn;9-10,v
RI₃
RIₒ

Pₑ   1-2,cl;3-4,fl;5-6,vn1;7-8,vn2;9-10,fl; |11-12,cel|
P₃ |1-2,cel; |3-4,vn1;5-6,fl;7-8,hp;9-10,vla; |11-12,cel|
Pₒ |1-2,cel; |3-4,ob;5-6,cel;7-8,vla;9-10,fl
Pₛ
Pₑ

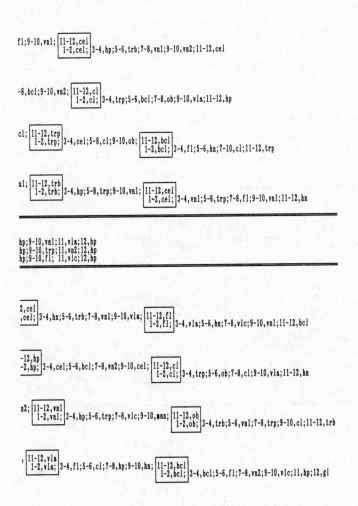

fl;9-10,vn1; | 11-12,cel
              1-2,cel; | 3-4,hp;5-6,trb;7-8,vn1;9-10,vn2;11-12,cel

-8,bcl;9-10,vn2; | 11-12,cl
                   1-2,cl; | 3-4,trp;5-6,bcl;7-8,ob;9-10,vla;11-12,hp

cl; | 11-12,trp
      1-2,trp; | 3-4,cel;5-8,cl;9-10,ob; | 11-12,bcl
                                            1-2,bcl; | 3-4,fl;5-6,hn;7-10,cl;11-12,trp

n1; | 11-12,trb
      1-2,trb; | 3-4,hp;5-8,trp;9-10,vn1; | 11-12,cel
                                             1-2,cel; | 3-4,vn1;5-6,trp;7-8,fl;9-10,vn1;11-12,hn

hp;9-10,vn1;11,vla;12,hp
hp;9-10,trp;11,vn2;12,hp
hp;9-10,fl; 11,vlc;12,hp

2,cel
,cel; | 3-4,hn;5-6,trb;7-8,vn1;9-10,vla; | 11-12,fl
                                            1-2,fl; | 3-4,vla;5-6,hn;7-8,vlc;9-10,vn1;11-12,bcl

-12,hp
-2,hp; | 3-4,cel;5-6,bcl;7-8,vn2;9-10,cel; | 11-12,cl
                                             1-2,cl; | 3-4,trp;5-6,ob;7-8,cl;9-10,vla;11-12,hn

n2; | 11-12,vn1
      1-2,vn1; | 3-4,hp;5-6,trp;7-8,vlc;9-10,man; | 11-12,ob
                                                     1-2,ob; | 3-4,trb;5-6,vn1;7-8,trp;9-10,cl;11-12,trb

, | 11-12,vla
    1-2,vla; | 3-4,fl;5-6,cl;7-8,hp;9-10,hn; | 11-12,bcl
                                               1-2,bcl; | 3-4,bcl;5-6,fl;7-8,vn2;9-10,vlc;11,hp;12,gl

Appendix IV

Op. 29/iii   "Tönen die seligen Saiten Apolls"

<u>bs 1-38</u>

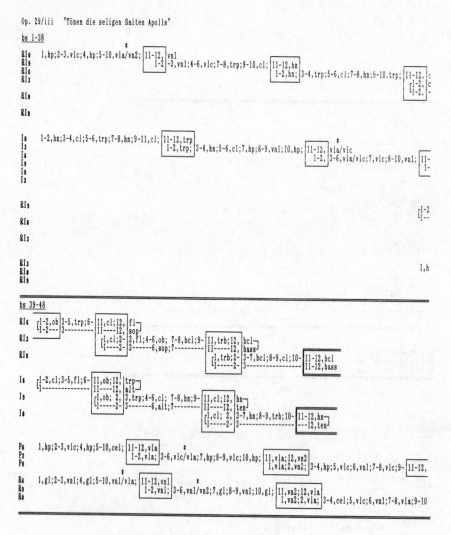

RI₀ 1,hp;2-3,vlc;4,hp;5-10,vla/vn2; [11-12, vn1]
RI₉   1-2, -3,vn1;4-6,vlc;7-8,trp;9-10,cl; [11-12,hn]
RI₆   1-2,hn; 3-4,trp;5-6,cl;7-8,hn;9-10,trp; [11-12, c]
RI₃   [1-2, c / 1-2, -]

RI₀

RI₉

I₀ 1-2,hn;3-4,cl;5-6,trp;7-8,hn;9-11,cl; [11-12,trp]
I₃   1-2,trp; 3-4,hn;5-6,cl;7,hp;8-9,vn1;10,hp; [11-12, vla/vlc]
I₆   1-2, 3-6,vla/vlc;7,vlc;8-10,vn1; [11- / 1-]
I₉
I₀
I₃

RI₉   [1-2 / --]

RI₆

RI₃

RI₃
RI₆   1,h
RI₉

<u>bs 39-48</u>

RI₆ [1-2,ob / 1-2---]3-5,trp;6- [11,cl;12, / 11----12,] [fl / sop]
RI₃   [1,cl;2- / 1---2-]3,fl;4-6,ob; 7-8,bcl;9- [11,trb;12, / 11----12,] [bcl / bass]
RI₀   [1,trb;2- / 1---2-]3-7,bcl;8-9,cl;10- [11-12,bcl / 11-12,bass]

I₆ [1-2,cl;3-5,fl;6- / 1---]11,ob;12, [trp / alt]
                       [11----12,]
I₉   [1,ob; 2, / 1---2-]3,trp;4-6,cl; 7-8,hn;9- [11,cl;12, / 11----12,] [hn / ten]
I₀   [1,cl; 2, / 1---2-]3-7,hn;8-9,trb;10- [11-12,hn / ---12,ten]

P₆ 1,hp;2-3,vlc;4,hp;5-10,cel; [11-12,vla]
P₃   1-2,vla; 3-6,vlc/vla;7,hp;8-9,vlc;10,hp; [11,vla;12,vn2]
P₀   1,vla;2,vn2; 3-4,hp;5,vlc;6,vn1;7-8,vlc;9- [11-12,]

R₆ 1,gl;2-3,vn1;4,gl;5-10,vn1/vla; [11-12,vn1]
R₉   1-2,vn1; 3-6,vn1/vn2;7,gl;8-9,vn1;10,gl; [11,vn2;12,vla]
R₀   1,vn2;2,vla; 3-4,cel;5,vlc;6,vn1;7-8,vla;9-10

396

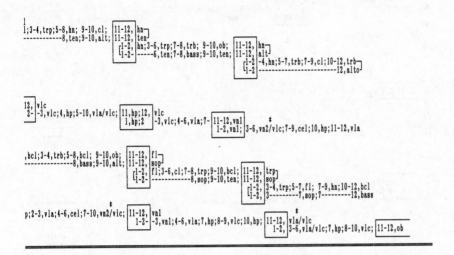

```
l
l;3-4,trp;5-8,hn; 9-10,cl; |11-12, hn⌐
-------------8,ten;9-10,alt; |11-12, ten⌐
                   ⌐1-2, hn;3-6,trp;7-8,trb; 9-10,ob; |11-12, hn⌐
                   ⌐1-2- -----6,ten;7-8,bass;9-10,ten; |11-12, alt⌐
                                         ⌐1-2 -4,hn;5-7,trb;7-9,cl;10-12,trb⌐
                                         ⌐1-2 ----------------------12,alto⌐


12, vlc
 2- -3,vlc;4,hp;5-10,vla/vlc; |11,hp;12, vlc
            1,hp;2 -3,vlc;4-6,vla;7- |11-12,vn1|   ‡
                                     1-2,vn1; 3-6,vn2/vlc;7-9,cel;10,hp;11-12,vla


,bcl;3-4,trb;5-8,bcl; 9-10,ob; |11-12, fl⌐
--------------8,bass;9-10,alt; |11-12, sop⌐
                    ⌐1-2, fl;3-6,cl;7-8,trp;9-10,bcl; |11-12, trp⌐
                    ⌐1-2- -----------8,sop;9-10,ten; |11-12, sop⌐
                                          ⌐1-2, 3-4,trp;5-7,fl; 7-9,hn;10-12,bcl
                                          ⌐1-2, 3----------7,sop;7---------12,bass

         ‡
p;2-3,vla;4-6,cel;7-10,vn2/vlc; |11-12, vn1                   ‡
                            1-2- -3,vn1;4-6,vla;7,hp;8-9,vlc;10,hp; |11-12, vla/vlc
                                                    1-2, 3-6,vla/vlc;7,hp;8-10,vlc; |11-12,ob
```

```
   ‡
vn2/vn1
```

```
,hp; |11-12,cel|
```

bs 48-73

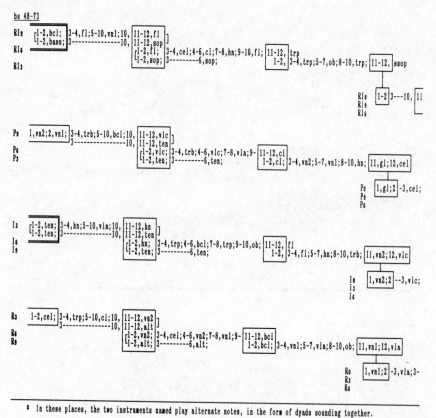

---

‡ In these places, the two instruments named play alternate notes, in the form of dyads sounding together.

Appendix IV

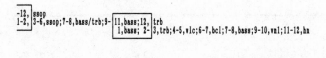

```
-12,|ssop
1-2,|3-6,ssop;7-8,bass/trb;9-|11,bass;12,|trb
                             |1,bass; 2-|3,trb;4-5,vlc;6-7,bcl;7-8,bass;9-10,vn1;11-12,hn
```

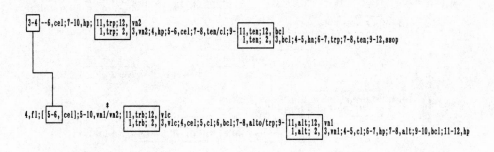

```
3-4|--6,cel;7-10,hp;|11,trp;12,|vn2
                    |1,trp; 2,|3,vn2;4,hp;5-6,cel;7-8,ten/cl;9-|11,ten;12,|bcl
                                                               |1,ten; 2,|3,bcl;4-5,hn;6-7,trp;7-8,ten;9-12,ssop
```

```
                                        ‡
4,fl;[5-6,|cel];5-10,vn1/vn2;|11,trb;12,|vlc
                             |1,trb; 2,|3,vlc;4,cel;5,cl;6,bcl;7-8,alto/trp;9-|11,alt;12,|vn1
                                                                             |1,alt; 2,|3,vn1;4-5,cl;6-7,hp;7-8,alt;9-10,bcl;11-12,hp
```

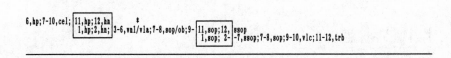

```
                             ‡
6,hp;7-10,cel;|11,hp;12,hn|3-6,vn1/vla;7-8,sop/ob;9-|11,sop;12,|ssop
              |1,hp;2,hn;|                          |1,sop; 2-|-7,ssop;7-8,sop;9-10,vlc;11-12,trb
```

399

Op. 30 Variations for orchestra

bs 1-20

P_0 1-4,cb;5-8,ob;9-12,trb
    RI_0 1-4,vla;5-8,vlc;9-10,hp;11-12,cb R_0 1-4,vlc;5-8,ww;9-12,tuba
    I_0 1-4,vn1;5-8,bcl;9-12,vn1 I_0 1-2,tuba;3-4,trb;5-8,str(ch);9-10,hp;11-12,vla

---

bs 21-55

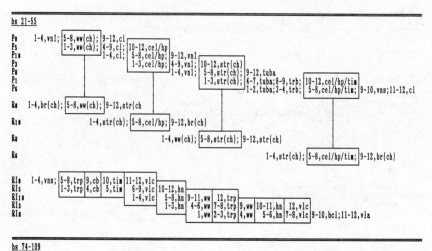

P_0 1-4,vn1; | 5-8,ww(ch); | 9-12,cl
P_5 1-3,ww(ch); | 4-9,cl; | 10-12,cel/hp
P_{10} 1-4,cl; | 5-8,cel/hp; | 9-12,vn1
P_3 1-3,cel/hp; | 4-9,vn1; | 10-12,str(ch)
P_8 1-4,vn1; | 5-8,str(ch); | 9-12,tuba
P_1 1-3,str(ch); | 4-7,tuba;8-9,trb; | 10-12,cel/hp/tim
P_6 1-2,tuba;3-4,trb; | 5-8,cel/hp/tim; | 9-10,vns;11-12,cl

R_0 1-4,br(ch); | 5-8,ww(ch); | 9-12,str(ch

RI_{10} 1-4,str(ch); | 5-8,cel/hp; | 9-12,br(ch)

R_8 1-4,ww(ch); | 5-8,str(ch); | 9-12,str(ch)

R_6 1-4,str(ch); | 5-8,cel/hp/tim; | 9-12,br(ch)

RI_0 1-4,vns; | 5-8,trp | 9,cb | 10,tim | 11-12,vlc
RI_5 1-3,trp | 4,cb | 5,tim | 6-9,vlc | 10-12,hn
RI_{10} 1-4,vlc | 5-8,hn | 9-11,ww | 12,trp
RI_3 1-3,hn | 4-6,ww | 7-8,trp | 9,ww | 10-11,hn | 12,vlc
RI_8 1,ww | 2-3,trp | 4,ww | 5-6,hn | 7-8,vlc | 9-10,bcl;11-12,vla

---

bs 74-109

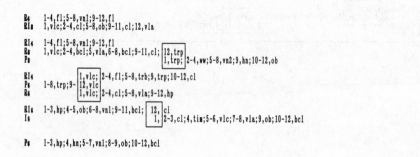

R_4 1-4,fl;5-8,vn1;9-12,fl
RI_8 1,vlc;2-4,cl;5-8,ob;9-11,cl;12,vla

RI_4 1-4,fl;5-8,vn1;9-12,fl
R_8 1,vlc;2-4,bcl;5,vla,6-8,bcl;9-11,cl; | 12,trp
P_8 | 1,trp; | 2-4,ww;5-8,vn2;9,hn;10-12,ob

RI_4 | 1,vlc; | 2-4,fl;5-8,trb;9,trp;10-12,cl
P_8 1-8,trp;9- | 12,vlc
R_8 | 1,vlc; | 2-4,cl;5-8,vla;9-12,hp

RI_8 1-3,hp;4-5,ob;6-8,vn1;9-11,bcl; | 12, | cl
I_8 | 1, | 2-3,cl;4,tim;5-6,vlc;7-8,vla;9,ob;10-12,bcl

P_8 1-3,hp;4,hn;5-7,vn1;8-9,ob;10-12,bcl

P₀   1-4,br(ch);5-8,ob;9-12,br(ch)
RI₀   1-4,vns;5-8,bcl;9-12,vnl

<u>bs 56-73</u>

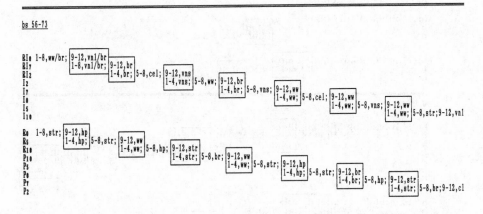

<u>bs 110-34</u>

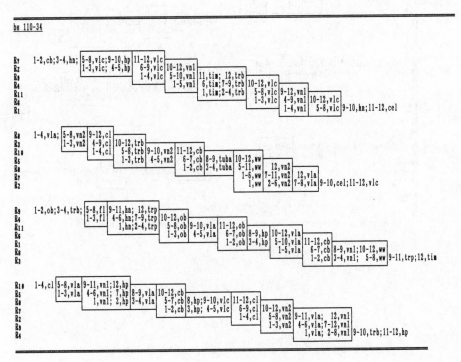

---

bs 135-45

P₅ 1-4,vla;5-8,fl;9-12,vn1

R₇ 1-4,cel;5-8,str; |9-12,cel|
R₉ |1-4,cel;| 5-8,str;9-10,hp;11-12,cel

I₅ 1-8,vn1;9-10,vn2;11-12,vla
RI₁₀ 1-2,fl;3-4,trp;5,cel;6-8,trp;9-12,vn1

I₁₀ 1-2,ob;3-4,bcl;5-6,cel;7-8,ob; |‡‡|
I₃ |‡‡| 5-8,cel; |9-12,vn2|
I₈ |1-4,vn2;| 5-8,cel;9-12,cl

RI₁₀ 1-2,trp;3-4,cl;5-6,cel;7-8,hp; |9-12,ww(ch)|
R₃ |1-4,ww(ch);| 5-8,hp; |9-12,vla|
R₆ |1-4,vla;| 5-8,hp;9-12,vla

_____

bs 146-80

P₁₀ 1-2,hn;3-4,cl;5,hp;6-8,fl;9-10,vn2; |11-12,cel|
P₃   1-3,fl; 4-5,vn2; | 6-7,cel;| 8-9,vn2;10,vn1; |11,hp;12,cel|
P₉   1-2,cel; | 3-4,vn2; 5,vn1;| 6,hp;7,cel;| 8,tuba;9-10,cb; |11-12,hp|
P₁   1,hp;2,cel;| 3,tuba; 4-5,cb;| 6-7,hp;| 8-9,vlc; |10-12,ob|─
P₆   1-2,hp;| 3-4,vlc;| 5-10,ob; |11,
P₁₁   1-5,ob;| 6,
P₄   1,

P₇ 1-2,trp;3-4,vlc;5-8,vla; |9-11,fl; 12,ob|
P₉   1-3,vla; | 4-6,fl;7-9,ob;| 10-12,vn1|
P₅   1,fl;2-4,ob;| 5-8,vn1;| 9-10,trp; |11-12,tuba|
P₁₀   1-3,vn1;| 4-5,trp;| 6-9,tuba; |10-12,fl|
P₃   1-4,tuba;| 5-8,fl;| 9,cl;10,cel; |11-12,cl|
P₆   1-3,fl;| 4,cl; 5,cel;| 6-7,cl;| 8,bcl;9,fl;10-12,vn
P₁   1-2,cl;| 3,bcl;4,fl;| 5-8,vn

R₂ 1-2,trb;3-4,vn1;5-8,vlc;9,hp;10,vla; |11-12,cel|
R₉   1-3,vlc;4,hp; 5,vla; | 6-7,cel;| 8-9,vla;10,hn; |11,hp;12,cel|
R₄   1-2,cel;| 3-4,vla; 5,hn;| 6,hp; 7,cel;| 8,hn;9-10,bcl; |11,cel; 12,vn2|
R₁₁   1,hp; 2,cel;| 3,hn; 4-5,bcl;| 6,cel;7-9,vn2; |10-12,trp|
R₆   1,cel;2-4,vn2;| 5-8,trp; |9-12,h|
R₁₁   1-4,hp
R₄
R₉
R₂

P₉ 1-2,tuba;3,hp;4,bcl;5-8,ob;9,vla; |10-12,trp|
P₂   1-3,ob;4,vla; | 5-8,trp;| 9,tuba;10,trb; |11-12,vlc|
P₇   1-3,trp;| 4,tuba; 5,trb;| 6-7,vlc;9-10,vlc; |11-12,hp|
P₆   1-2,vlc;| 3,trb; 4-5,vlc;| 6-7,hp;| 8-9,vla;10-12,vn1|
P₅   1-2,hp;| 3-4,vla; 5-8,vn1; |9-12,br|
P₆   1-4,br; |[
P₇
P₂
P₉

‡An entire tetrachord is missing at this point (see page 77). It should be 9-12 of I₁₀ and 1-4 of I₃.

```
vn1;12,cb
vn1;7,cb; 8-9,br(ch);10-12,trp
vn1;2,cb; 3-4,br(ch);  5-8,trp;9-10,vla;11-12,vn1
```

```
1
1;9-10,cl;11-12,vn2
```

```
p
; 5-7,vn2; [8-9,cl];10-12,vlc
              1,vlc;2,cl;3-4,vlc; [5,ob];6-8,cel; 9-10,vla;[11,cb];12,vla
                                                  1----------------3,vla; 4,tim;5-8,hp; 9-12,cel
                                                                                        1-4,cel; 5-8,str;9-10,trb;11-12,hn
```

```
5,ob];6-8,vla; 9-12,br
               1-4,br; 5-7,vn2;8,vn1; 9-10,vlc;[11,cb];12,vlc
                                      1----------------3,vlc; [4,tim];5-8,br; 9-12,vn2
                                                                             1-4,vn2; 5-8,hp;9-10,trp;11-12,vlc
```

Op. 31/i   "Schweigt auch die Welt"

b.1
                                                              b.12

I₆ 1-6,w(ch);7- 12,fl   RI₆

R₆   1,fl; 2-8,svn;9-11,cl; 12, bass   P₆   1, bass;2-11,h

P₆   1 -- 12, bass   R₆   1 ------- 5 -- 12, bass

RI₆   1 -6,bass 7-12,w(ch)   I₆   1-6,w(ch); 7-- 12, bass

P₆ 1-6,str(ch);7,cel;8-12,hp/cel(ch)   P₆ 1-6,str(ch);7-11,cl; 12, bass

   RI₆ 1-5,hp/cel(ch);6,cel;7-12,w(ch)   RI₆   1 - 2, bass;3-6,svn;7-12

      I₆ 1-6,str(ch);7,hp;8-12,(ch)   I₆ 1-6,str(ch);

         R₆ 1-5,(ch);6,hp;7-12,str(ch)   (R₆ missing

Op. 31/ii "Sehr tief verhalten innerst Leben"

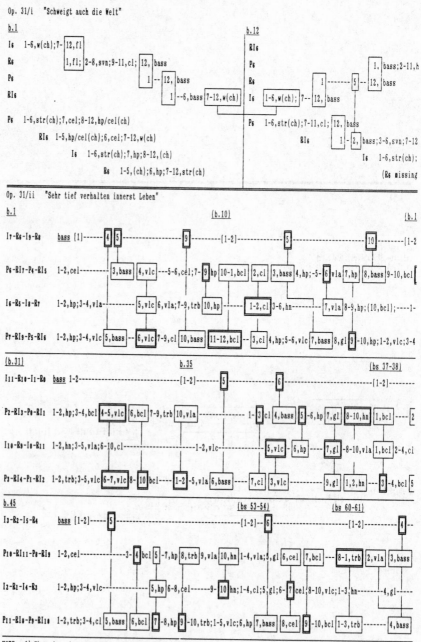

NOTE: 1) These have been treated as 10-note rows, since two-note elisions are used consistently.
      2) *Ausfälle* are indicated with connected boxes. A double box indicates voice where the note fits rhythmically; a singl-
      3) Notes in parentheses are grace notes and do not fit into the rhythmic scheme.

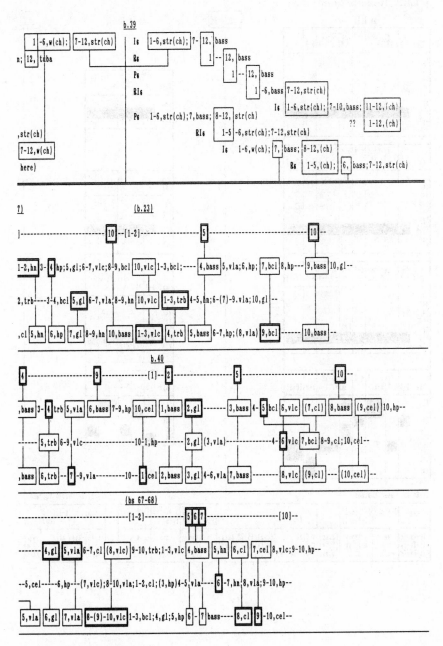

e box indicates the voice with the <u>Ausfall</u>.

Op. 31/iii "Schöpfen aus Brunnen"

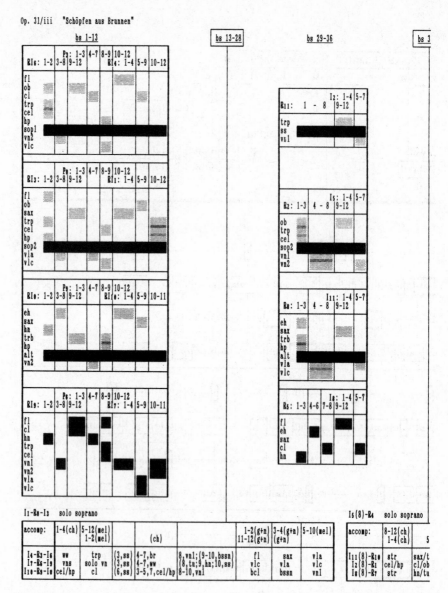

6-44

bs 45-59

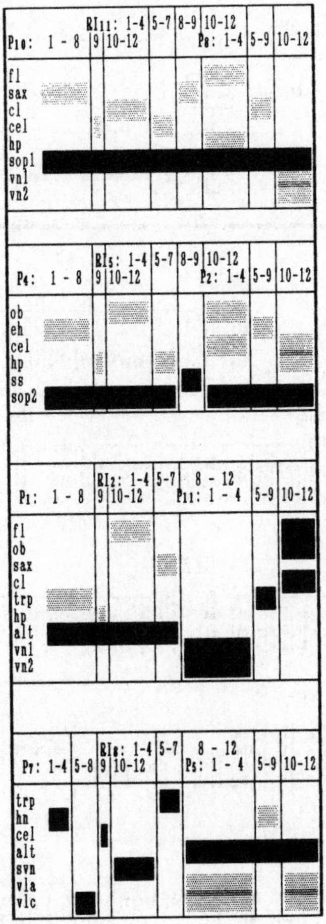

-8(ch)	9-12(ch)
rp/trb/hn /eh/sax /bssn/bcl/fl	str cel/hp br

Op. 31/iv "Leichteste Bürden der Bäume"

b.1

```
P₀   1-----------------------------------------------|12,|sop
                                              R₀   |1-|------------6,sop;7--------------------|11|-12,svn
RI₀  1-4,str(ch);5-7,ww(ch);|8,hp;|9-11,br(ch);|12,gl|
                                      I₀   |1,gl;|  2-4,br(ch);  |5,vlc;|        6-8,ww(ch);   |9-12,ww(ch)|
I₀   1,sax;2,gl;3-4,cel;  |5,hp;|    6-9,str(ch);                      10-12,hp
R₀   1-4,ww(ch);             5-6,cel;              7-|9|str(ch);       10,cel;|11|svn;|12,cel|
```

Op. 31/v "Freundselig ist das Wort"

b.1   **(bs 5-6)**

```
RI₀  ⌈7-11,sop                          RI₃ ⌈[1]------------------------------------6,sop;⌉
RI₁₁ |1-6,chorus;|[7=RI₂/12,svn];8-10,w(ch);[11=RI₃/2,sop]  RI₅ |[1]-5,         str(ch);[6=RI₂/4,svn];|7-11
RI₂  |7-11,svn                          RI₈ |[1],svn;        2-3,str(ch);   4-6,svn;|
RI₃  ⌊7-11,svn                          RI₉ ⌊[1],svn;[2=RI₂/12,svn];3-5,w(ch);[6=RI₃/2,sop];⌋
```

b.16   **(bs 21-22)**   **(b.26)**

```
RI₁₁ ⌈4-------------------10,sop    P₀ ⌈[1-2]-------------------------------9,sop  RI₁₀ ⌈[1-3]------------
RI₁  |[1-3],chorus;|4-6,br(ch);7-9,vn;10,hp(ch)  P₁₀ |[1-2], hp(ch);3-5,br(ch);6-8,str(ch);9,picc  RI₀ |[1-2]=RI₁₀/4-5,s
RI₄  |4-6,hp(ch);7-9,svn;10,cel(ch)  P₁ |[1-2],cel(ch);3-5,hp(ch);6-8,str(ch);9,picc  RI₃ |[1-2],vla;
RI₅  ⌊4-6,cel(ch);7-9,vla;10,br(ch)  P₂ ⌊[1-2], br(ch);3-5,cel(ch);6-8,str(ch);9,picc  RI₄ ⌊[1-2],vlc;
```

(bs 31-33)   **(bs 37-38)**

```
RI₉  ⌈[1-3]------------------------10,sop    P₀ ⌈[1-2]------------------------------
RI₁₁ |[[1-2=RI₉/4-5]-3],sop;    4-6,hp(ch);7,cl;8-10,str(ch)  P₈ |[1]-P₀/5,sop];[2]-3,vlc;     4-5,bcl;
RI₂  |[1-3],svn;             4-6,cel(ch);7,cl;8-10,str(ch)  P₁₁ |[1]=P₀/3,cel(ch);[[2]-3=P₀/4-5,vlc];4-5,vla;
RI₃  ⌊[1],gl;[[2-3]=RI₂/1-2,svn]];4-6, br(ch);7,cl;8-10,str(ch)  P₀ ⌊[1-2]-3,cel(ch);          [4-5=P₁₁/2
```

b.46   **(b.49)**   **b.51**

```
P₅  ⌈5-11,sop         I₁₁ ⌈[1]-5,sop;                        R₀ ⌈[1-3]--------
P₇  |[1-2]-5,chorus;|6-10,str(ch)  I₁ |[1]-5,svn;              ⌈6-9,chorus  R₁₁ |[1-2],2vn;[[
P₁₀ |6-8, str(ch);[9=P₇/11,svn];10-11,cl  I₄ |[1-2,cl;  [3=I₅/1,picc;4-5,svn;  R₂ |[1-2],vla;[[
P₁₁ ⌊6-8, str(ch); 9-11,picc  I₅ ⌊[1]-2,picc;[3=I₄/4,svn];  4-5,svn;  ⌊      R₃ ⌊[[1]=R₂/2,vla
```

b.52   **b.54**   **b.57**

```
I₀  ⌈5---------------9,sop    R₁₀ ⌈6-----------10,sop  I₁ ⌈[1-2]-5
[2  |[1-2]-4,chorus;|5-8,w(ch);[9=I₀/5,sop]  R₀ |[1-3]-5,chorus;|6-9,str(ch);10,svn  I₃ |[1-2]-5
I₅  |[5,6=I₀/6,9,sop];7-9,cel  R₃ |6-9,str(ch);10,cel(ch)  I₆ |[1-2],c
I₆  ⌊[5-6,w(ch);    7-9,hp    R₀ ⌊6-9,str(ch);10,cel(ch)  I₇ ⌊[1-2],c
```

NOTE: 1) square brackets denote elisions (indicated at beginnings of rows only) and intersections (described); elided notes o-
            top to bottom; intersections indicated only in secondary voices (voices with <u>Ausfälle</u>).]

Op. 31/vi "Gelokkert aus dem Schoße"

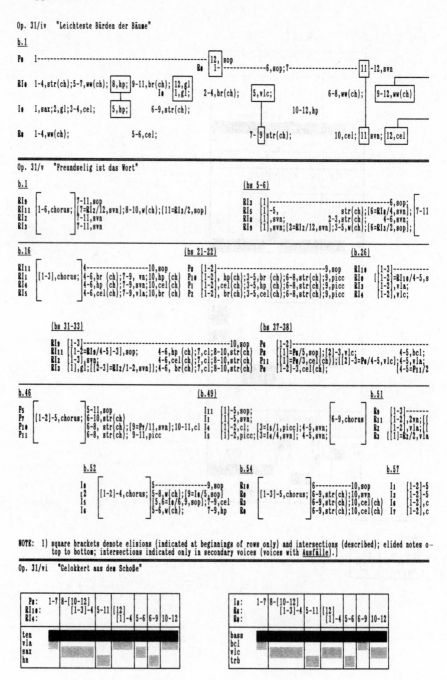

b.11

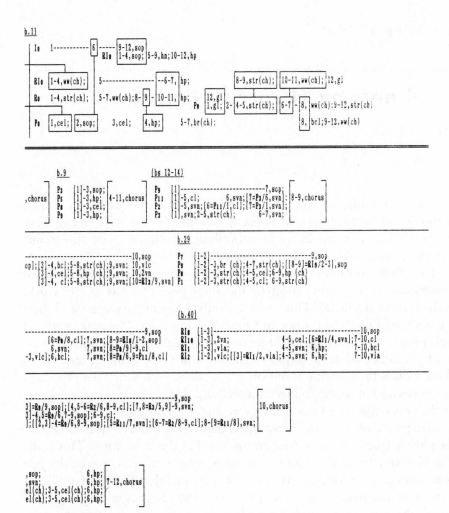

I₀   1----------- 6 ----- 9-12,sop
                   RI₉ 1-4,sop; 5-9,hn;10-12,hp

RI₀ 1-4,ww(ch);   5---------------- --6-7, hp;   8-9,str(ch); 10-11,ww(ch); 12,gl

R₀   1-4,str(ch);   5-7,ww(ch);8- 9 - 10-11, hp;   P₀ 12,gl
                                                        1,gl; 2- 4-5,str(ch); 6-7 - 8, ww(ch);9-12,str(ch)

P₀   1,cel; 2,sop;   3,cel; 4,hp;   5-7,br(ch);   8, bcl;9-12,ww(ch)

---

b.9   (bs 12-14)

,chorus   P₃ [1]-3,sop;   P₉   [1]-----------------------7,sop;
           P₅ [1]-3,hp; [4-11,chorus   P₁₁ [1]-5,cl;   6,svn;[7=P₃/6,svn]; [8-9,chorus
           P₆ [1]-3,cel;   P₂   [1]-5,svn;[6=P₁₁/1,cl];[7=P₅/1,svn];
           P₉ [1]-3,hp;   P₃   [1],svn;2-5,str(ch);   6-7,svn;

---

b.29

-----------------------------10,sop   P₇ [1-2]-----------------------9,sop
op];[3]-4,bcl;5-8,str(ch);9,svn; 10,vlc   P₉ [1-2]-3,br (ch);4-7,str(ch);[[8-9]=RI₃/2-3],sop
       [3]-4,cel;5-8,hp (ch);9,svn; 10,2vn   P₆ [1-2]-3,str(ch);4-5,cel;6-9,hp (ch)
       [3]-4, cl;5-8,str(ch);9,svn;[10=RI₃/9,svn] P₁ [1-2]-3,str(ch);4-5,cl; 6-9,str(ch)

(b.40)

-----------------------------9,sop   RI₈ [1-3]-----------------------------10,sop
  [6=P₆/8,cl];7,svn;[8-9=RI₈/1-2,sop]   RI₁₀ [1-3],2vn;   4-5,cel;[6=RI₁/4,svn];7-10,cl
       6,svn;   7,svn;[8=P₆/9]-9,cl   RI₁   [1-3],vla;   4-5,svn; 6,hp;   7-10,bcl
-3,vlc];6,bcl;   7,svn;[8=P₆/6,9=P₁₁/8,cl] RI₂ [1-2],vlc;[[3]=RI₁/2,vla];4-5,svn; 6,hp;   7-10,vla

---

-----------------------------9,sop
3]=R₃/9,sop];[4,5-6=R₂/6,8-9,cl];[7,8=R₃/5,9]-9,svn;   10,chorus
3]-4,5=R₃/6,7-9,sop];6-9,cl;
];[[2,3]-4=R₃/6,8-9,sop];[5=R₁₁/7,svn];[6-7=R₂/8-9,cl];8-[9=R₁₁/8],svn;

,sop;   6,hp;
,svn;   6,hp; 7-12,chorus
el(ch);3-5,cel(ch);6,hp;
el(ch);3-5,cel(ch);6,hp;

---

mitted from ends of rows; intersections within chords not indicated; choral parts within bracketed areas always S-A-T-B from

---

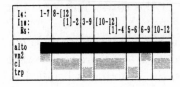

I₄:	1-7	8-[12]						
I₁₀:		[1]-2	3-9	[10-12]				
R₃:				[1]-4	5-6	6-9	10-12	
alto								
vn2								
cl								
trp								

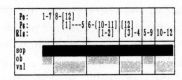

P₀:	1-7	8-[12]					
P₆:		[1]---5	6-[10-11]	[12]			
RI₈:				[1-2]	[3]-4	5-9	10-12
sop							
ob							
vn1							

A note on Webern's graces

Grace notes are one of the characteristic features of Webern's music, appearing in all the twelve-note works up to Op. 27 – in some cases, notably Opp. 20, 22, 23 and 26, in quite astonishing profusion. The directional nature of the grace note (it can only precede, never follow) and its tendency to blur rhythmic outlines meant that it was not congenial to the increased concentration on rhythmic motives and their permutations in the works directly following Op. 26. Thus there are only a few in the second and third movements of Op. 27 and none in Opp. 28, 29 and 30. The grace makes a reappearance, however, in conjunction with Webern's 'completely new style of presentation' in the Op. 31 Cantata[1] (movements II, III and V). In all these works, the notation is the same: a small quaver with a slash through the stem connected to the following note by a slur.

In the vast majority of cases, the grace and the note following it occupy successive positions in a row. Most often they occur alone: that is to say, no other pitches from the same row are sounded at the same time. This is the result either of a linear presentation of the row or of the isolation of the pair of notes within a non-linear statement. It is frequently the case that a linear statement of the row is only one of several strands progressing together: although there are other pitches sounding, perhaps even struck at the same time as the ones in question, the grace note and its successor are nevertheless isolated with respect to their own row. Thus an alteration in their exact temporal position relative to the beat, and, hence, to the other sounds heard, would not affect the correct ordering of any of the rows. This situation therefore presents no interpretative problems.

In a large number of instances, however, the main note is not isolated; very frequently it is one member of a collection of two or more pitches that are struck at the same time. In these situations, the ordering is handled in several different ways, and it is in examining these that we become aware of the subtleties of the problem.

In by far the greater number of cases involving a grace note progressing to a simultaneity, the voice with the grace proceeds to its successor in the row, and the remaining pitches sounded at the same time are those directly following. This is quite straightforward (Example V.1). A second way of handling the situation – a method used frequently, but to a much lesser

V.1   Op. 20/i, bar 13

extent than that just described – is illustrated in Example V.2. Here, as in the previous example, the grace has the pitch that, of all those used, occupies the earliest position in the row; the difference here is that this voice then skips the next element(s) of the row, proceeding directly to the last of all those notes in the collection.

V.2   Op. 20/i, bar 7

In both these examples the correct row order is maintained when the grace precedes the beat and all the notes in the collection are struck together as written. We will return to these two examples a little later.

Perhaps this is the moment to digress briefly in order to justify the emphasis placed on the precise order of pitches, as my whole argument is based on the premise that it is necessary, if possible, to perceive the grace notes in such a way as to preserve the correct position of the various elements of the row relative to each other. In the music of other composers close scrutiny of a detail such as this might seem misguided, but Webern's musical concepts exhibit such a unity of purpose that his handling of structure in the twelve-note works is inseparable from his handling of the twelve-note technique and the row itself. To disregard the system is to miss the point of a good deal that he does. His extreme fidelity to the order dictated by the row and the great care and ingenuity devoted to its maintenance are a striking aspect of his scores, leaving no doubt about his opinion of the importance of preserving the order. Details such as the arpeggios in the first movement of Op. 22 and the third song of Op. 25 with arrows indicating the direction of arpeggiation, depending on whether the row proceeds from bottom to top or vice versa, make it clear that, while it was certainly far from being Webern's only concern, fidelity to the row was of great importance to him.

And now, back to the problem. In Webern's twelve-note music there are six examples of grace notes that do not conform to any of the practices described earlier. Three of these are similar: two are to be found in the first movement of Op. 20, the third in the first song of Op. 23 (Example V.3). All of these figures appear at first glance to be anomalies in ordering: the

V.3

pitch assigned to the little note comes too early in the unfolding of the row in each instance. However, if these graces were played as appoggiature (i.e., on the beat), no anomaly would exist. It seems reasonable to suppose that this is what Webern had in mind here.

If we consider the bulk of Webern's grace notes to see how this interpretation would affect them, we find that in the case of those that are sounded in isolation, as well as those following the pattern of Example V.2, the correct order is maintained no matter which way they are realized (whether on or before the beat). The second most prevalent type, however (see Example V.1), produces an irregularity in order if the grace is played on the beat, since an appoggiatura necessarily delays the note following in the same voice, and the correct order is maintained here only if all the pitches written as simultaneities are in fact struck together.

A problem, then, emerges. We have before us at least two types of grace note, and three constructions: one (Example V.1) that apparently must be played before the beat, another (Example V.3) that cannot be played before the beat, and a third (Example V.2) that will work either way. All are notated in exactly the same manner.

There are several other situations besides that illustrated in Example V.1 that are not open to interpretation as appoggiature. If, in a figure like that shown in Example V.2, the voice playing the grace proceeds only to a later, rather than the last, pitch of the following collection, the possibilities of interpretation are limited. The small note must precede the beat; if it does not, the one following it will be out of order (Example V.4). There are other

V.4   Op. 25/iii, bar 2

examples, of double grace notes, that for the same reason cannot be treated as appoggiature (Example V.5). To discover Webern's intentions with respect to the disposition of grace notes might appear, then, to be a hopeless task, since the consistent application of either of the traditional interpretations

V.5   Op. 23/ii, bar 2

seems to be unsatisfactory. Before giving up in despair, the last three anomalous examples should be examined. The first occurs in Op. 19/i (Example V.6). Here neither of the realizations suggested above gives a satisfactory result, as the grace note in this case proceeds to a collection

V.6   Op. 19/i, bar 18

containing pitches positioned both before and after it in the row. Examples V.7a and b are very much simpler but quite as impossible. These last three instances seem to me to hold the key to Webern's attitude towards the grace note. I believe it is obvious that he considered it to be not a preamble to, but

Op. 20/ii, bars 185–6

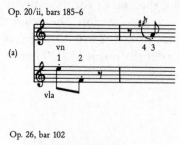

(a)

vn
1   2

4 3

vla

Op. 26, bar 102

(b)

vn

3   2

V.7

an equal part of, an entity that includes also the note or collection of notes on the following beat. This is the only interpretation that will encompass all the situations he has created. Knowing something of the precision of Webern's structures and his concern for detail, I think it more reasonable to suppose that he considered grace notes as a part of the events they appear to precede than to suppose these few anomalies to be the result of carelessness or oversight.

The fact that the notation of the grace notes is distinguished from that of the rest of the collection surely indicates that they are to be treated differently, and, more specifically, that they are to be given less importance. The desired effect would seem to be obtained by striking all the notes together and immediately letting go of the grace(s). This treatment is not new in the history of music.

A question comes to mind immediately: what of those instruments that cannot play two notes at once? There are numerous examples of graces to be sung or played by wind instruments. Interestingly, none of the seven anomalies is written for such an instrument. All are given to instruments capable of playing the two (or more) notes involved at once. All the grace notes written for wind instruments or voice can be sounded before the principal note without disturbing the order. It would seem, then, that wherever it is possible to play grace notes simultaneously with their resolutions that is probably what was intended; where it is impossible to do so, this has been accounted for in the composing, and the small note is probably meant to come before the beat.

The great majority of Webern's graces may be played before the beat, and some may be played as appoggiature. Many must be acciaccature. At least one of these interpretations will produce the notes in the correct order in each instance; analysis alone reveals the intention.

Notes

Introduction

1 Webern, recollected by Willi Reich in *The Path to the New Music*, trans. Leo Black (Bryn Mawr: Theodore Presser Co., 1963), p. 57; hereafter referred to as *Path*.

2 The *Kinderstück*, unpublished during Webern's lifetime. This work is No. 267 in Moldenhauer's Chronological Index (Hans and Rosaleen Moldenhauer, *Anton von Webern: A Chronicle of His Life and Work* (New York: Alfred A. Knopf, 1979), p. 703).

3 Most of these works seem to have required a long gestation period. In the case of Op. 23, for example, the first page of sketches bears two dates, 1.II.33 at the top and 4.IV.33 a little further down, after very little writing had been done. The first date for each work in the following list is the one found at the top of the first page of sketches, which in most cases predates the period of actual writing, sometimes by several months.

4 *Die Reihe*, Vol. 2, ed. Herbert Eimert and Karlheinz Stockhausen (Vienna: Universal Edition, 1955). Quotations are from the English edition of 1959, trans. Leo Black and Eric Smith (Bryn Mawr: Theodore Presser Co.).

5 Armin Klammer, 'Webern's Piano Variations, Op. 27, 3rd Movement', *Die Reihe*, Vol. 2, pp. 81–92. The statement quoted opens the article (p. 81).

6 Herbert Eimert, 'Interval Proportions', *Die Reihe*, Vol. 2, pp. 93–9. The quotation is from the closing sentence of the article (p. 99).

7 Karlheinz Stockhausen, 'Structure and Experiential Time', *Die Reihe*, Vol. 2, pp. 64–74.

8 Brian Fennelly, 'Structure and Process in Webern's Opus 22', *Journal of Music Theory*, Vol. 10, No. 2 (1966), pp. 300–28. The quotations are from pp. 303 and 306.

9 John W. Reid, 'Properties of the Set Explored in Webern's Variations, Op. 30', *Perspectives of New Music*, Vol. 12, No. 2 (Spring/Summer 1974), p. 346.

10 Fennelly, 'Structure and Process'.

11 Arnold Whittall, 'On Summarizing Webern', *Soundings*, No. 1 (1970), p. 54.

12 New York: Alfred A. Knopf, 1979.

13 Roger Smalley, 'Webern's Sketches', *Tempo*, Nos. 112 (March 1975), pp. 2–12; 113 (June 1975), pp. 29–40; 114 (September 1975), pp. 14–22.

416

14 Sketches for all the twelve-note works with the exception of Op. 20 are contained in six sketchbooks. The first of these is in the Pierpont Morgan Library in New York City; the remaining five are owned by the Paul Sacher Stiftung in Basel.

15 Walter Kolneder, *Anton Webern: An Introduction to His Works*, trans. Humphrey Searle (Berkeley and Los Angeles: University of California Press, 1968).

16 Heinrich Deppert, *Studien zur Kompositionstechnik im instrumentalen Spätwerk Anton Weberns* (Darmstadt: Edition Tonos, 1972).

17 Dorothea Beckmann, *Sprache und Musik im Vokalwerk Anton Weberns: Die Konstruktion des Ausdrucks*, ed. Karl Gustav Fellerer, Vol. 57 (Regensburg: Gustav Bosse Verlag, 1970).

18 Friedhelm Döhl, *Weberns Beitrag zur Stilwende der neuen Musik*, Berliner Musikwissenschaftliche Arbeiten, ed. Carl Dahlhaus and Rudolf Stephan, Vol. 12 (Munich and Salzburg: Musikverlag Emil Katzbichler, 1976).

19 Wolfgang Martin Stroh, *Historische Legitimation als kompositorisches Problem*, Göppinger Akademische Beiträge, ed. Ulrich Müller, Franz Hundsnurscher and K. Werner Jauss, No. 63 (Göppingen: Verlag Alfred Kümmerle, 1973).

20 pp. 211–19.

21 pp. 247–92, 240–2, 242–6, 293–329.

22 pp. 329–36.

23 The quotation is from the English summary that appears at the end of the book (p. 392).

24 Wolfgang Martin Stroh, *Webern: Symphonie op. 21*, Meisterwerke der Musik, ed. Ernst Ludwig Waeltner, Vol. 11 (Munich: Wilhelm Fink Verlag, 1975).

25 Written in 1952 by Dieter Schnebel; appears in *Musik-Konzepte: Sonderband Anton Webern II* (Vienna: Universal Edition, November 1984), pp. 162–217.

26 Wolfgang Willam, *Anton Weberns II. Kantate op. 31*, Beiträge zur Musikforschung, ed. Reinhold Hammerstein and Wilhelm Seidel, Vol. 8 (Munich and Salzburg: Musikverlag Emil Katzbichler, 1980).

PART I   ROW AND CANON

Introduction to Part I

1 Moldenhauer, *Anton von Webern*, p. 667, note 11.

2 The first sketchbook was purchased by the Pierpont Morgan Library in 1976. Paul Sacher acquired the remaining five as part of the Moldenhauer archives in 1984 and made them available to scholars in 1986 with the opening of the Stiftung, where Webern's row tables have resided as well since the summer of 1988.

3 Luigi Rognoni, *La scuola musicale di Vienna: Espressionismo e dodecafonia* (Turin: Giulio Einaudi, 1966), pp. 335ff; and Friedrich Wildgans, *Anton Webern: eine Studie* (Tübingen: Rainer Wunderlich Verlag, 1967), pp. 133–50.

4 Wildgans in fact owned them. The tables, which were subsequently lost for some twenty years, were brought to the Sacher Stiftung in 1988 by Regina

417

Busch, who found them in Wildgans' effects. (See the announcement of this acquisition in *Tempo*, No. 165 (June 1988), p. 58.)

5 Regina Busch, 'Über die Musik von Anton Webern', *Österreichische Musikzeit-schrift*, Vol. 36 (1981), p. 480.

6 These sketches are in the Sacher Stiftung's Sketchbook II. The Latin proverb and the preliminary work on rows is on pp. 38–9; fragments beginning on F, including an opening for large orchestra, are written out on pp. 39–42; the first one beginning on B, on p. 44, is still for large orchestra, with solo piano; the opening of the movement in the form it finally assumed first appears on p. 43; sketches of this version begin in earnest on p. 45. (This sequence illustrates Webern's habit of using the right-hand page of the blank book first, the left-hand page later.)

7 Smalley, 'Webern's Sketches (I)', p. 11.

8 *Anton von Webern: Sketches (1926–1945). Facsimile Reproductions from the Com-poser's Autograph Sketchbooks in the Moldenhauer Archive.* Commentary by Ernst Krenek, with a Foreword by Hans Moldenhauer (New York: Carl Fischer, Inc., 1968). This edition contains forty-seven plates from books that are now owned by the Sacher Stiftung and identified in their records as Sketchbooks I, II and V. (These books were not in the possession of the Sacher Stiftung at the time the facsimile edition was published.) Only pp. 38–42 of the preliminary sketches of Op. 24 were included in the facsimile edition.

9 Arnold Whittall sees Webern's willingness to shift movements so that a work begins with some row form other than P_0 as an indication of a dwindling commitment to the original prime during the process of composition. 'In other words, Webern only gradually found his "O"...' (comments made during the preparation of the present study).

1 The rows

1 Webern, in a lecture given on 2 March 1932 (*Path*, p. 55).

2 This book predates those in the Sacher Stiftung, which have been assigned roman numerals I–V. Throughout this study, I will use the Sacher Stiftung's roman numbering to identify the books in their collection and refer to the (earlier) book now in the Pierpont Morgan Library with an arabic 1. (Molden-hauer identifies the books in chronological order as One to Six.)

3 With respect to accidentals, Examples 1.1 and 1.2 appear as notated by Webern. These and all other twelve-note sketches up to the first song of Op. 19 are in Sketchbook 1.

4 Dates given for Opp. 17 and 18 are taken from Moldenhauer's worklist (*Anton von Webern*, pp. 712–13). Beginning with Op. 19 Webern constructed row tables, which are extant and can be consulted in the Sacher Stiftung. The dates given in this chapter for works from Op. 19 onwards are taken from the row tables.

5 Döhl lists the four notes at the centre of this row in the order G–E–E♭–A♭ (*Beitrag*,

p. 213). Webern's settings, however, stress the semitones. The notes of the central tetrachord appear in the following ways in the course of the song (the order used is the one suggested above in the text: $5 = \text{E}\flat$, $6 = \text{E}$, $7 = \text{A}\flat$, $8 = \text{G}$):

	b.2	b.3	b.4	b.5	b.5	b.6	b.7	b.7	b.8	b.8	b.9	b.10	b.11	b.11	b.12	b.12	b.13f	b.14f	b.15f
5	5678	78	78	65	7 5	56	65	7		567	8657	8765	6—5	8576	765	6587	7 5	8765	7856
6			56	65		78 8 6	87	7	58	8		8			78		8		8 6
7								8		6									
8																			

6 In order to produce all twelve notes of the scale with no repetitions, two similar hexachords must be separated by the interval of a tritone; any other transposition used alone (where tritone transposition does not also occur) will produce redundancies.

7 See Allen Forte, *The Structure of Atonal Music* (New Haven: Yale University Press, 1973).

8 For reasons discussed on pp. 10–11, this is the only row for which I am not using Webern's *gilt* form. In this case, I am generating the matrix from his P_6.

9 *Letters to Hildegard Jone and Josef Humplik*, ed. Josef Polnauer, trans. Cornelius Cardew (Bryn Mawr: Theodore Presser Co., 1967), No. 22, p. 17; hereafter referred to as *Letters*.

10 The first, second and fourth trichords are examples of pc set 3–3 (014); the third is set 3–4 (015).

11 See *Letters*, No. 122, p. 52.

12 See *Letters*, No. 126, p. 54.

13 R. Larry Todd, 'The Genesis of Webern's Opus 32', *The Musical Quarterly*, Vol. 66, No. 4 (October 1980), pp. 581–91.

14 The following information appears in a more concise form in Appendix I, where the specific properties of all the rows are listed for purposes of comparison.

15 I use this term to indicate any division of the twelve notes into two groups of six, regardless of whether these divisions yield rows with combinatorial possibilities.

16 Babbitt's source sets are listed and described in 'Some Aspects of Twelve-Tone Composition', *The Score and I.M.A. Magazine*, No. 12 (June 1955), pp. 53–61.

17 The terms *semi-combinatorial* and *all-combinatorial* are used to distinguish between a row amongst whose permutations *one* other row form has the same (unordered) hexachordal content as the untransposed prime and a row that upon permutation produces *at least* one I, one R and one RI form that stand in this relationship with P_0.

2 Row topography

1 Arnold Schoenberg, 'Composition with Twelve Tones (2)', in *Style and Idea*, ed. Leonard Stein, trans. Leo Black (London: Faber and Faber, 1975), p. 246.

2 The third movement of Op. 24 is an exception.

3 The serial techniques used in some of the Schoenberg pieces are discussed by John Graziano in 'Serial Procedures in Schoenberg's Opus 23', *Current Musicology*, Vol. 13 (1972), pp. 58–63, and by George Perle in *Serial Composition and Atonality* (London: Faber and Faber, 1962), pp. 42ff. See also my article 'Transitional Aspects of Schoenberg's Opus 23 No. 2', *Canadian Association of University Schools of Music Journal*, Vol. 2, No. 2 (1972), pp. 24–30. (A large portion of my article is made practically incomprehensible by an error in printing: the paragraph of text directly under Example 3 should precede Example 2.)

4 Sketchbook 1, p. 3.

5 Both Schoenberg and Berg wrote works around this time using a limited set of rows. Like Webern's Op. 19, Schoenberg's *Suite* for piano uses only the untransposed rows and their sixth transpositions, while Berg's *Lyric Suite* concentrates on these same levels of transposition plus the third and ninth. In all these cases, the final note of the row is a tritone away from its beginning. Schoenberg's subsequent works tend to concentrate on a limited number of rows as well; but this economy is the result of his interest in combinatoriality, and the transposition used is not the sixth. The Op. 33 pieces, for example, use, except in the development section of Op. 33a, only P_0, R_0, I_5 and RI_5.

6 Although a twelve-note chord obviously cannot be assigned a row designation (even though the spacing may indicate its identity), the possibilities in the case of the eleven-note chord are restricted to R_0 and RI_0.

7 Döhl, *Beitrag*, p. 200.

8 An even more striking example of this is found at the centre of the first movement of Op. 21 (bars 34–5).

9 See Appendix V for a discussion of Webern's use of grace notes in his twelve-note works.

10 See pp. 18–19.

11 So far as I can tell, the word *Ausfall* was first applied to this kind of situation by Hans Jelinek in 1958 (see Deppert, *Studien*, p. 18, note 10).

12 The deficiency may be perceived on either instrumental (as in Opp. 23 and 25) or rhythmic grounds (as in Op. 31).

13 Since Webern does not indulge in 'wrong' notes, this is clearly a mistake; it has been corrected in the Philharmonia score. A search for this note in the sketches produces unexpected results, however: it is very clearly written G in the final sketch, on p. 73 of Sketchbook I. Although it is sometimes difficult to distinguish Webern's sharps from his naturals, this is not the case here. An earlier sketch of the same bar, on p. 74, is not as clear but is still unmistakable.

14 In spite of Donald Chittum's assertion that F♯ and F are used in elisions in this song ('Some Observations on the Row Technique in Webern's Opus 25', *Current Musicology*, Vol. 12 (1971), p. 97). One could wish that he had identified the places where he supposes elision to occur, as the basis for the statement seems elusive.

15 Chittum sees an elision of RI_5 and P_5 (P_5 and RI_7 in his analysis) between parts in bar 29 of the second song ('Some Observations', p. 198), but Webern indicates

instead (and more logically) an elision within the voice part, between R_5 and P_5 in bar 28. This sketch is on p. 18 of Sketchbook III.

16 Once again Chittum is in error. In his text (p. 98) he gives bar 39 as an example of irregularity in row order; to prove his point he writes out bars 38 and 39. It is difficult to see how he could overlook the obvious: that the C in the piano left hand is $R_5/12$, while the C in the right hand is $I_5/1$ (Sketchbook III, p. 20).

17 This problem is discussed in Appendix V.

18 This is demonstrated in Chapter 1 (pp. 21–2). The influence of this invariance property on the structure of the movement is discussed in later chapters.

19 See the letter of 15 October 1935 to Hildegard Jone (*Letters*, No. 63, pp. 30–1).

20 Group 1 comprises flute, oboe, clarinet and violin; group 2 saxophone, trumpet and harp; group 3 horn, trombone, viola and cello; group 4 celesta, glockenspiel and xylophone.

21 The sketches for *Das Augenlicht* are on pp. 22–42 of Sketchbook III.

22 See Appendix V.

23 I mention at this point an early analysis of Op. 27, Howard Riley's 'A Study in Constructivist Procedures: Webern's "Variations for Piano", Op. 27, First Movement', *Music Review*, Vol. 27, No. 3 (August 1966), pp. 207–10. The article is based on an incorrect analysis: Riley claims the rows in bars 44–6 and bars 51–4 to be incomplete. It is difficult to see how he could have overlooked the similarity of these sections to the earlier sections in bars 8–10 and 15–18, in both of which he found whole rows.

24 Webern's analysis of this work, written in 1939 at the request of Erwin Stein, who wanted it for publication in *Tempo* (it was never published), has been translated by Zoltan Roman in Moldenhauer, *Anton von Webern* (pp. 751–6). The first movement is discussed on p. 752.

25 See p. 25.

26 For examples of direct imitation, see the first two B tetrachords (in bars 2–5), the two As in bars 5–8 and the B in bars 7–11; cancrizans figures occur when C and C tetrachords are elided in bars 2–4 and 6–8.

27 Theodor W. Adorno, *Philosophy of Modern Music*, trans. Anne G. Mitchell and Wesley V. Bloomster (London: Sheed and Ward, 1973), p. 89.

28 These sketches are on pp. 87–90 of Sketchbook III. Several aspects of the canon – the row content, the order in which the four instruments enter and the quaver's distance between successive entries – are set in the first sketch (on p. 88) and remain the same through subsequent revisions (on pp. 87 and 90). However, in the first sketch the voices enter in the order $R_3 \ldots, P_3 \ldots, R_7 \ldots, P_7 \ldots$; the third and fourth voices have exchanged positions in the second sketch, on p. 87, and this order is used thereafter. *All* the sketches of this section (including one marked 'Anfang 2.III' on p. 90) are written in 3/8 metre.

29 The sketches are found on pp. 88 and 87 of Sketchbook III. The published version is not in the sketchbook.

30 See his analysis of Op. 28 in Moldenhauer, *Anton von Webern*, p. 754. This movement is discussed below, pp. 258–61.

31 The chains are broken in the following places: at the beginning of the choral

section in the first movement, between bars 13 and 14; at the end of the introduction to the second movement, bars 5–6, and before and after the repeat of this material, in bars 26–7 and bars 35–6; and in the third movement at bar 39, where one voice continues but three are re-entering after a long absence.

32 See pp. 25–6.

33 Webern's description of these variations variously as an 'Adagio form' and an 'Andante-form' with a main theme, transition, second theme, reprise and coda is quoted on p. 198 below.

34 See p. 22 above.

35 Letter of 3 May 1941, in *Path*, p. 62.

36 Deppert, *Studien*, p. 209.

37 Earlier sketches of these bars, on p. 78 of Sketchbook IV, also contain complete chords in all voices throughout bars 167–77, with 'ohne b' and 'ohne h' written beside them; in later sketches the notes in question have been omitted.

38 See the analysis on p. 353.

39 Five pitch classes remain invariant in each hexachord, and when P/ii is compared with RI/i four of these five are seen to retain their original positions as well. The properties of this row are discussed on pp. 26–7.

40 While there are more than fourteen verticalizations in the movement, I exclude those in bars 5–6, 9, 25, 35, 41 and 48 from the present category. An entire row is heard at once in bars 25 and 48, and all the other examples cited above are based on five-note invariant groups rather than hexachords (even though in some cases the result is a hexad). All these cases will be discussed later.

41 Willam, *Anton Weberns II. Kantate*, p. 138.

42 This is in any case a completely specious statement which either must have been made by Schoenberg in a moment when his attention was distracted or was misunderstood after the fact. It nevertheless continues to be cited as a basic principle of the twelve-note technique, many decades after it should have been laid to rest with some embarrassment.

43 To take only a few examples from the opening pages, note the number of Fs in bars 9–12 (five), Ds in bars 15–17 (four), E♭s in bars 25–8 (four, one of which is held for eight beats), F♯s in bars 32–3 (four), and so on.

44 Arnold Whittall, 'Webern and Multiple Meaning', *Music Analysis*, Vol. 6, No. 3 (October 1987), pp. 333–53. Pitch and pitch-class redundancies in bars 1–18 are displayed on pp. 344–5.

45 The sketch containing these notes occurs on p. 9 of Sketchbook V. In a later version of this bar on the same page, these notes and many others have been enclosed in parentheses, a sign that they are to be excised. In a subsequent version, on p. 11, they are gone.

46 The only sketch of this bar occurs on p. 5 of Sketchbook V.

47 The C♯ in the alto, which is legitimately RI$_{10}$/11, is, nevertheless, the pitch needed to finish RI$_7$ and comes rhythmically at the point where RI$_7$/12 should appear.

48 Instrumental reinforcements are shown in the row analysis in Appendix IV.

49 The correct versions of these two bars are on pp. 25 and 30 of Sketchbook V.

50 In letters to both the Humpliks (*Letters*, No. 105, p. 45) and Willi Reich (*Path*, letter dated 23 August 1941, pp. 62–3).

51 In bar 8, the cello's E functions as both I/5 and R/9; the melody's R/11 (in the first violin in bar 11) is also R/11 in the accompaniment; the soprano's I/6 is also P/2 in bar 13; and several notes do double duty in bars 15 (harp), 18 (strings) and 19 (woodwind).

52 Willam, *Anton Weberns II. Kantate*, p. 54.

53 *Letters*, No. 110, pp. 46–7.

54 For the present purposes, only a group of notes articulated together and released at the same time is defined as a chord. Other notes which may still be sounding in another voice for a portion or even all of the time allotted the chord are not included. An example of this situation can be seen in bar 28, where only those notes played by the viola and cello are considered.

55 The canonic basis of this movement is discussed on pp. 128–35.

56 The row structure of this movement is illustrated on p. 353.

57 Adorno, *Philosophy*, pp. 111–12.

58 *Ibid.*, p. 83.

3   Canon

1 George Perle, 'Webern's Twelve-Tone Sketches', *The Musical Quarterly*, Vol. 57, No. 1 (January 1971), p. 6.

2 See p. 17.

3 Perle, 'Webern's Twelve-Tone Sketches', p. 6.

4 Smalley, 'Webern's Sketches (III)', p. 18.

5 Perle, 'Webern's Twelve-Tone Sketches', p. 11.

6 *Ibid.*, p. 6.

7 See pp. 18–19.

8 See the diagram on p. 18.

9 Throughout, in situations of this sort, I shall refer to the canon that begins earlier as Canon I – in this case, the one beginning in the second horn, Canon II beginning slightly later in the harp.

10 The group of six notes at the centre results from the two-note elision.

11 In spite of the identification of this canon by various writers – for example, Döhl, *Beitrag* (presented as a doctoral dissertation in 1966, published in 1976), pp. 285–6; Mark Starr, 'Webern's Palindrome', *Perspectives of New Music*, Vol. 8, No. 2 (Spring/Summer 1970), pp. 135–7; and Deppert, *Studien* (1972), pp. 66–7 – the canonic nature of Variation V has continued to elude most writers. Starr was responding to an article by Robert U. Nelson, 'Webern's Path to the Serial Variation', *Perspectives of New Music*, Vol. 7, No. 2 (Spring/Summer 1969), pp. 73–93, which offers a typical description of this variation: 'The correspondence between [Variation V] and number 3, claimed by Webern, would seem to consist in their common use of ... repetitive, retrograde figurations' (p. 80). In his monograph on the Symphony, published in 1975, Stroh gives the content of this variation as a single row, beginning on either A♭

or D, and it is further described, on p. 35, in a table where all the other variations are identified as canons of various kinds, simply as consisting of chords in semiquavers, and later (p. 40) as a setting of the row so as to realize its harmonic possibilities, with repeated chords in groups of 3 + 2 and 3 + 5 + 2. Stroh is not apparently aware of the canon in inversion that occurs here.

12 For a discussion of this aspect of the work, see pp. 94–7 of my article 'Structural Imagery in Schoenberg's *Pierrot Lunaire'*, *Studies in Music from the University of Western Ontario*, Vol. 2 (1977), pp. 93–107.

13 There are many references to this. See, for example, Webern's analysis of his Op. 28 Quartet (Moldenhauer, *Anton von Webern*, p. 753) and letters to Willi Reich (*Path*, pp. 60, 61 and 64) and Hildegard Jone (*Letters*, No. 109, p. 46).

14 It may be noted that the isolation of rhythm as an independent structural determinant is an idea that had interested Berg also. See, for example, the tavern scene in *Wozzeck*, Act III scene 3.

15 The exceptions occur in bars 3–6, 19, 33–5 and 99–100. The piece opens with two two-voice canons, one introducing the triplet and the other the duple rhythm; the alternation and contrasting of these two metric divisions form the rhythmic basis of the work. In bar 19 there is one extra note (the F in the cello). In bars 33–5 an ostinato figure is played three times, by violin, clarinet and violin, and not imitated. The canon is being sustained at this time by the saxophone and flute. The two notes played by the violins in bar 99 are imitated after four beats by the trumpet in bar 100; this imitation is superimposed on the canon, which is progressing with a time lag of one beat.

16 In most cases after Op. 26 the row structure and the canonic structure are the same. There are, however, two examples of canonic voices exchanging row chains in Op. 31: in the final section of the third movement and at the centre of the fourth.

17 There is one minor exception: the last two notes of P_7 in bar 32 are not exactly the same rhythmically as the first two of the R_7 in bar 30.

18 Relatively speaking. In absolute terms, there is no long period of time in this movement.

19 Moldenhauer, *Anton von Webern*, pp. 751–6.

20 Adorno, *Philosophy*. 'Webern realizes twelve-tone technique and thus no longer composes' (pp. 110, 95).

21 Perle, 'Webern's Twelve-Tone Sketches', p. 7. The Babbitt quotation is from a review of the fourth volume of the periodical *Polyphonie* (Paris: Edition Richard-Mass, 1949) in the *Journal of the American Musicological Society*, Vol. 3 (1950), pp. 264ff. (This volume of *Polyphonie* is entitled *Revue musicale trimestrielle* and contains, among other things, Schoenberg's 'Le Composition à douze sons'; the quotation is from Babbitt's discussion of this essay, on p. 265.)

22 See the second movement of Op. 22, the songs of Opp. 23 and 25, and *Das Augenlicht*. Particularly in sections of the first and last of these works, notes are shared by several rows with great abandon.

23 There is one example in Op. 21, for instance, in Variation V of the second movement, where the central note of each of the figures in the harp represents

the crossing of a row and its retrograde, functioning as 5 in one row and 8 in the other. A similar example exists in the first movement of Op. 27, where a row and its retrograde cross in bars 9, 16, 45 and 52, the same notes acting as 4 and 5 of one and 8 and 9 of the other. Although there is a great deal of intersection in Op. 26, the canonic structure is not affected, since the rhythmic canon is for the most part independent of the row structure.

24 The rhythm of this canon contributes to a considerable ambiguity of structure. The row content and the interval succession in bars 1–18 suggest a canon between violin I and cello (R_3–R_7–R_{11} answered by P_3–P_{11}–P_7) and a second between violin II and viola (P_7–P_3–P_{11} answered by R_7–R_{11}–R_3), though the rhythm seems to indicate a pairing of violin I with viola and violin II with cello. This multiplicity of interpretations is discussed by Arnold Whittall in 'Webern and Multiple Meaning', pp. 339–40.

25 The situation is similar in bars 37–53; here *Ausfälle* occur in all parts except the viola, which is therefore the only part to play the complete rhythmic succession from bars 1–18. See Example 2.17.

26 Moldenhauer, *Anton von Webern*, p. 753.

27 The sketches for Op. 29 are found at the beginning of Sketchbook IV.

28 I use this term to refer to the practice of inserting, in the repetition or variation of a motive, a rest as a replacement for some portion of the value of one of the notes of the original. Such a replacement changes not only the durations but possibly the rhythm as well, since the new subdivision of the original value may be expressed as either note plus rest (in which case the rhythm remains intact) or rest plus note (which for practical purposes lengthens the previous note).

29 This is discussed on p. 77.

30 These canons were also composed in the manner of those in Op. 29. All the voices were sketched first either in rhythmic unison or in canon but in rhythmic agreement; only later were individual voices varied and, if necessary, offset to form a canon. These sketches occur on pp. 75–6 of Sketchbook IV.

31 It can be argued, of course, and often has been, that the twelve-note technique itself is just such a method of organization. Certainly it is seldom possible to recognize appearances of a particular row form. It seems to me, however, that this difficulty is mitigated by the inexorable repetition of the same interval succession throughout: although the precise order of row forms is not discernible, their common basis is continually audible. The efficacy of canon, on the other hand, must rely on the recognizable imitation of either melodic contour or rhythm, and when neither of these features is replicated, the only common ground remaining between voices (the same number of notes within a fixed time span) is too abstract to be heard.

32 This is perfectly clear from the sketches, which appear at the end of Sketchbook IV.

33 The following discussion is based on the sketches for Op. 31 in Sketchbooks IV and V. These sketches represent the original working out and in most cases several successive versions, sometimes as many as six or eight. These will be referred to more specifically as the occasion arises.

34 Letter of 23 August 1941, in *Path*, p. 62.

35 This has been remarked on more than once. Siegfried Borris, in his article 'Structural Analysis of Webern's Symphony Op. 21', in *Paul A. Pisk: Essays in His Honour*, ed. John Glowacki, trans. Ursula Klein (Austin: University of Texas Press, 1966), speaks of 'Webern, who shuns auditive manifestation' (p. 233); and Döhl has observed, 'It appears that with Webern a direct proportional relationship exists between exterior simplicity and interior complexity and that that relationship is Webern's stylistic ideal' (*Beitrag*, p. 200, my translation). The centre of Op. 21/i and the fifth variation of Op. 21/ii are earlier examples of this.

36 Leopold Spinner, 'Anton Weberns Kantate Nr. 2, Opus 31: Die Formprinzipien der kanonischen Darstellung (Analyse des vierten Satzes)', *Schweizerische Musikzeitung*, Vol. 101, No. 5 (September/October 1961), pp. 303–8. To my knowledge this was the first analysis of the movement ever published.

37 Stroh, *Historische Legitimation*, pp. 1–8. The fact that Stroh's illustration goes only as far as Spinner's would seem to be evidence that it was based on Spinner's, although this is nowhere acknowledged; Spinner's work does not even appear in Stroh's bibliography.

38 This analysis appears as the introduction to Deppert's *Studien*, a work otherwise concerned with only the instrumental music (pp. 14–28). See his p. 22, note 16.

39 Willam, *Anton Weberns II. Kantate*, pp. 37–9.

40 'I read in Plato that "Nomos" (law) is also the word for "melody". Now, the melody the soprano soloist sings in my piece as the introduction (recitative) may be the *law* (Nomos) for all that follows!' (continuation of the letter to Willi Reich dated 23 August 1941, in *Path*, pp. 62–3).

41 Simpler, because Webern has not in this case (as he did in Op. 30) defined a rhythmic analogy for the melodic inversion; therefore rhythmically I is equal to P. While the contour of the second palindrome is at the same time similar to that of the first (in shape) and different from it (in direction), only the similarity survives the translation to rhythm.

42 This is the rhythmic row on which Deppert and Willam base their analyses. It appears on pp. 17 and 37 of their respective books.

43 I speak of the accompanying voices as imitations because of the voice part's role as progenitor, even though technically speaking the voice does not function as a *dux*, since it is the third of four parts to enter.

44 It is sometimes difficult to say just how many revisions occurred, since it was Webern's practice to try out several variants of the same bar, each below the previous one, in the course of a single sketch, often writing two versions of the same music in the same bar, rewriting some bars *in situ* without erasing the earlier version, and encircling notes that he had written and later decided to excise. When these space-saving revisions are made in different coloured pencils, the sequence is clear, but often this is not the case. At the next level, most passages of several bars' length (details of each already having been revised in the ways described above) appear in from two to four or five successive stages at different places in the sketches. Also, Webern's sketches are typically written in a metre two degrees distant from the one finally used. The final adjustment may

be in either direction. 'Leichteste Bürden', sketched in quaver and semiquaver metres, was later published with metres based on minims and crotchets. The four versions given in Example 3.15a are taken from pp. 87–8 of Sketchbook IV, where they occur as described above. (Because of Webern's habit of notating more than one version in the same bar, the order of the two versions of bar 15 shown as iii and iv cannot be determined with certainty.)

45 These notes are played by the celesta in bar 3 and the harp in bars 9–10; the glockenspiel in bar 17; the harp in bar 15; and the glockenspiel in bar 20 (see Example 3.23a).

46 It may be noted also in passing that all these eccentrically placed notes are played by harp and celesta, instruments that Webern customarily treats in a special way whenever he writes for them. (For example, in those movements where instruments are paired timbrally for the purposes of imitation, the harp and celesta are kept independent, each providing its own answer.)

47 In the score, these are two Es played by the harp. These are particularly important notes: E is the lowest note in the movement and makes only three appearances, in the fifth bar from the beginning, at the climax (bar 15) and in the fifth bar from the end (cello, bar 18).

48 Both these chords are played by piccolo, saxophone and bass clarinet, the first in bar 4, the second in bar 14.

49 *Letters*, No. 105, p. 45.

50 *Letters*, No. 109, p. 46.

51 Letter of 23 August 1941, in *Path*, p. 62.

52 *Path*, p. 63.

53 Letter dated 31 July 1942, in *Path*, p. 63.

54 This sketch is found on p. 100 of Sketchbook IV.

55 I have omitted natural signs, which appear in the sketch before all notes not sharpened or flattened. I have also added row designations and order numbers.

56 This seems curious at first glance, though it is possible that these voice designations refer simply to the traditional four canonic voices in the abstract. A general observation concerning the sketchbooks may also have some bearing on this particular instance. Although the rhythm has usually reached its definitive form by the latest sketchbook version, pitches typically move two or three octaves between the final sketch of a work and its publication.

57 The few shared notes fit into the rhythmic structure of both voices concerned.

58 *Letters*, No. 110, pp. 46–7. The text in the published score reads 'Weil *es* am Kreuz verstummte' and is duly translated into English as 'it', which makes not a great deal of sense (Universal Edition 12461, 12486); however, I have seen this letter quoted on two occasions, and the text reads 'er' both times. (In addition to its appearance in Polnauer's collection, it is reproduced on p. 63 of *Anton Webern: Weg und Gestalt*, ed. Willi Reich (Zurich: der Arche, 1961).)

59 The references to this are frequent and numerous, both in *Path* and in the letters. *Versuch, die Metamorphose der Pflanzen zu erklären*, published in 1790, was the first of Goethe's published writings to show an interest in scientific subjects.

60 In determining segmentation, I have purposely taken the divisions as far as

possible, defining the smallest segments that remain in place rhythmically when compared with the model and with each other. Obviously, a more balanced structure is obtained by grouping some of the resulting very small segments together. In terms of crotchet durations, for example, the three sections might be viewed in the following way: bars 17–25 as 6, 6, 5, 5 and 6; bars 25–33 as 9, 6, 12, 6 and 9; and bars 33–45 as 8, 12½, 10½ and 11. This segmentation is indicated with discontinuous brackets in Example 3.18.

61 Webern masks both the seams in this central section, in the first instance by letting the voice begin its second section before the instruments have finished the material of the first (in bar 25; see above), and in the second by isolating the cadence figure of the second section in the voice (although it occurs after a relatively long pause, it nevertheless clearly belongs to the section just ending) and begining the tempo of the new section with a sequential repetition of the same figure in the solo violin, this again, as in bar 25, overlapping with the voice's opening of the third section (bars 31–3).

62 Perhaps I should not say 'mislead', since the imitation obviously exists. However, the segments thus perceived are not parallel segments of neighbouring rows as in bars 17–20.

63 Spinner, 'Die Formprinzipien', p. 305.

64 Stroh, *Historische Legitimation*, p. 8.

65 One cannot be certain that Stroh has done the same. See note 76 below.

66 Willam, *Anton Weberns II. Kantate*, pp. 75, 81. 'No relationship, either with the solo part or the metre, can be determined for the disposition [of the individual elements of the accompanying voices]' (p. 75). 'The position of the chords in the bar is noteworthy. Notes of the accompaniment that sound together nearly always do so in unaccented positions; on only a few occasions does this happen on a beat. The accompanying voices therefore serve to stabilize the ensemble rather than the metre, which they seem to wish to conceal' (p. 81). 'The accompanying voices are subservient to the soprano and their function is determined solely by the expression of the poetry' (p. 90). (My translations.)

67 *Path*, pp. 63–4.

68 *Path*, p. 64.

69 Since every row begins on note 10 of the row that precedes it and the last two notes of the final row are missing, the piece is in reality built from forty-eight ten-note rows.

70 The sketches for this movement are at the beginning of Sketchbook V. They represent numerous revisions, with two or three successive variations often notated in the same bar. Large sections of the piece are rewritten several times, in various places, and Webern's customary system of identifying the final version breaks down at least once. The writing seems to become hasty and somewhat careless in the course of this piece, which covers many pages: natural signs, row designations and the identification of *Ausfälle*, all things that are usually meticulously indicated, are often missing here. Nevertheless, enough versions exist so that a comparison of them leaves no doubt about Webern's intentions with respect to any of these things. Willam's row analysis and identification of

428

Ausfälle (*Anton Weberns II. Kantate*, given in part on pp. 136–9, referred to subsequently on pp. 140–5) is incorrect in many particulars. Although Willam almost certainly had not seen the sketches, it must be said that an accurate analysis could have been produced, even without the aid of the sketches (as in the case of my own pre-Basel analysis), had he been looking for the canonic relationships mentioned by Webern rather than for the durational rows of his own contriving.

71 *Anton Weberns II. Kantate*, p. 157.

72 Since the system used does not allow for two-digit numbers, I have adopted the practice of using A, B and C to represent order numbers 10, 11 and 12.

73 *Letters*, No. 117, p. 50.

74 The sketches for these sections are found between pp. 19 and 31 of Sketchbook V.

75 There is only one example of a disagreement in segmentation involving the accompaniment of vocal parts. This is in bars 54–7, where the alto voice is doubled by the viola and cello for seven consecutive notes, while the parallel phrase in other voices is divided into two and five. This can be explained by the fact that the alto part has just taken over the voice which was previously the orchestral one, and both these voices – alto and orchestral – having switched parts, play long segments in order to establish their new positions. The orchestration and the manner of segmentation, as well as the nature of the exceptions, can be seen in the row analysis on pp. 406–7.

76 Stroh says that the first movement (also for solo voice and orchestra) is composed in the same way. He ends his brief look at the fourth movement with the statement that 'Webern employed this procedure not only in the first and fourth movements, but also in sections of the third and fifth movements' (*Historische Legitimation*, p. 8, my translation). However, the first movement is similar to the others mentioned only with respect to texture, and then only in a general way: while all are for solo voice and orchestra, the first contains chords of a density encountered nowhere else in the work (five, six and twelve notes). It is written in two voices, both of which are alternately melodic and chordal; neither is generated by imitation of the other. The error of Stroh's reference to the first movement in this context casts some suspicion on his implied knowledge of the third and fifth movements as well, since he does not elaborate on the nature of these latter movements. One wonders whether he has, in fact, observed the methods that operate in the third and fifth movements at first hand, or if his remark was based simply on the assumption that a similarity of texture might well be evidence of a uniformity of technique. Movements III and V are cited and six bars of the third illustrated by Spinner in his article, which Stroh must have seen, although (as noted earlier) he gives no acknowledgement of it. Willam, not surprisingly, misses the canonic basis of the third movement entirely.

77 The first six bars of this section were analysed by Spinner in his article. This construction is alluded to by Stroh; it is missed by Willam.

78 Quoted by Kolneder in *Anton Webern: An Introduction*, pp. 191–2.

79 Adorno, *Philosophy*, p. 95.
80 Schoenberg, *Style and Idea*, pp. 235, 248.
81 *Letters*, No. 109, p. 46.
82 Adorno, *Philosophy*, p. 54.

PART II   THE INSTRUMENTAL MUSIC

Introduction to Part II

 1 Anton Webern, *Der Weg zur neuen Musik*, ed. Willi Reich (Vienna: Universal Edition, 1960), p. 37 (my translation).
 2 Charles Rosen, *The Classical Style* (London: Faber and Faber, 1971), p. 30.
 3 Carl Dahlhaus, 'Issues in Composition', in *Between Romanticism and Modernism* (1974), trans. Mary Whittall (Berkeley: University of California Press, 1980), pp. 40–78.
 4 Dahlhaus, *Between Romanticism and Modernism*, p. 59.
 5 Charles Rosen, *Schoenberg* (London: Marion Boyars, 1976), p. 96. I am not sure why Rosen cites *da capo* form as the third 'great type'; I can only suppose that he includes rondo forms in this category. Schoenberg devotes the last three chapters of his *Fundamentals of Musical Composition* (ed. Gerald Strang and Leonard Stein (London: Faber and Faber, 1985)) to three extended forms: theme and variations, rondo and sonata.
 6 *Path*, p. 54 (26 February 1932). Webern's use of the future tense at the end of this statement is curious, as he had by this time already written three works in 'extended forms' – Opp. 20, 21 and 22.
 7 There is some duplication here. Although Op. 30 and the first movement of Op. 28 exhibit certain features of sonata form, both are first and foremost variations. In this study they will be considered in the chapter devoted to variation form. Since Op. 26 is for chorus and orchestra, it will be considered in Part III, even though its shape seems to have been dictated by the requirements of sonata form. This leaves, of the instrumental works, five movements in sonata form to be examined in Chapter 4.
 8 Although there is a fugue in Op. 28, it is set within the confines of ternary form.
 9 These terms as well as this notion come up frequently in Schoenberg's writings. See, for example, his essay 'Composition with Twelve Tones (1)', in *Style and Idea*, pp. 220, 225.
10 Rosen's *The Classical Style* includes a good examination of this aspect of the work (pp. 407–34).
11 From Webern's analysis of Op. 28 (Moldenhauer, *Anton von Webern*, p. 753).
12 Letter to Willi Reich dated 9 December 1939, *Path*, p. 60.
13 Letter to Reich dated 3 March 1941, *Path*, p. 60.
14 Letter to Reich dated 3 May 1941, *Path*, p. 61.
15 Letter to Reich dated 6 August 1943, *Path*, p. 64.

16 Letter to Hildegard Jone dated 3 June 1942, *Letters*, No. 109, p. 46. (Translation modified.)

4 The movements in sonata form: Opp. 20/ii, 21/i, 22/i, 24/i and 27/i

1 p. 200.

2 This is essentially the description Rosen gives in *The Classical Style* as the one current since Czerny's first definition of sonata form around 1840 (p. 30).

3 p. 200. For Schoenberg, the musical idea was a very small unit that became a theme only through growth and change which began immediately: his *developing variation*. It was because he saw development as a continual process that he objected to the use of the term to designate the central section of sonata form, in which he saw the processes to be more concerned with varied presentation than with organic growth.

4 Although both Schoenberg (in the *Walzer* of Op. 23) and Webern (in the Opp. 17 and 18 songs) did this at the beginning of their twelve-note careers.

5 Repetition generated by repeat signs in the score – a convention of structural format – is to be distinguished from the reappearance of identical material written out as a part of the basic structure. The first can be seen as optional, while the second is essential.

6 Smalley, 'Webern's Sketches (III)', p. 18.

7 Perle, 'Webern's Twelve-Tone Sketches', p. 10.

8 Indeed, Webern seemed to consider this a possibility. When he says in his *Path to the New Music* lectures, 'If an untutored ear can't always follow the course of the row, there's no harm done' (in the lecture of 26 February 1932: p. 53), he is implying that a more sophisticated ear should have no trouble. Even more: it seems clear that he *expects* this sort of recognition from the listener.

9 Schoenberg describes sentence structure on pp. 21–4 and 58–62 of *Fundamentals*. The structure he outlines consists typically of the presentation of a basic motive in a two-bar phrase, the (varied) repetition of that motive in the following two bars (the continuation) and a four-bar completion in which contrast is achieved through development or liquidation.

10 However, see Regina Busch, 'Wie Berg die richtige Reihe fand', in *Musik-Konzepte: Sonderband Anton Webern II* (Vienna: Universal Edition, November 1984), pp. 385–7, for a thorough publication history of Op. 20. She has apparently seen several of the materials relating to the various reprints of this work. The fact that Webern identified a number of errors in the metronome indications in the first printing makes it unlikely that the marking in question here could have escaped his notice.

11 Webern sent a score of Op. 20 to Berg on its completion, and Berg's analysis of it exists. It is puzzling to note that Berg marked the beginning of the transition at bar 30. This position can be justified, since both the rhythm and the tempo change here and it is from this point onwards that the rows are transposed in the

reprise. What makes his analysis curious is that in the recapitulation he saw the transition beginning in bar 131, a position corresponding not to bar 30 but to bar 26 and thereby making his analysis inconsistent. (See Busch, 'Wie Berg', p. 370.)

12 Moldenhauer, *Anton von Webern*, p. 321. The date given for this letter is 25 November 1927; unfortunately, there is no indication of its whereabouts. Some confusion attends the reference, since the Moldenhauers go on to state that the errors mentioned in the letter were not corrected in either the Philharmonia study score published in May 1928 or the 1955 reissue, and this is not in fact so.

13 See p. 9 above.

14 See pp. 96–8 for a discussion of the canonic content of this movement.

15 The following list identifies only a few of the analyses and discussions dealing with the formal structure of Op. 21/i. William Austin, 'Webern and the Tradition of the Symphony', in *Anton Webern Perspectives*, ed. Hans Moldenhauer and Demar Irvine (Seattle and London: University of Washington Press, 1966), pp. 78–85, and *Music in the Twentieth Century* (New York: Norton, 1966), pp. 357–68; Kathryn Bailey, 'Webern's Opus 21: Creativity in Tradition', *Journal of Musicology*, Vol. 2, No. 2 (Spring 1983), pp. 184–95; Borris, 'Structural Analysis', pp. 231–42; Döhl, *Beitrag*, pp. 247–69; Scott Goldthwaite, 'Historical Awareness in Anton Webern's Symphony, Op. 21', in *Essays in Musicology: In Honour of Dragan Plamenac on his 70th Birthday*, ed. Gustave Reese and R. J. Snow (Pittsburgh: University of Pittsburgh Press, 1969), pp. 65–71; Stroh, *Symphonie*.

16 Leopold Spinner, 'The Abolition of Thematicism and the Structural Meaning of the Method of Twelve-Tone Composition', *Tempo*, No. 146 (September 1983), p. 6.

17 Döhl, *Beitrag*, p. 268.

18 Stroh, *Symphonie*, p. 32.

19 See pp. 18–19.

20 The two canons occur simultaneously. My distinction of them as Canon I and Canon II is made on the basis of the order in which they make their initial appearance.

21 Spinner, 'Abolition of Thematicism', p. 6.

22 Stroh, *Symphonie*, pp. 9–26.

23 This table appears in Stroh, *Symphonie*, p. 16. The English translations are my own.

24 'Whereas [the tension created by thematic contrast in the classical sonata] leads to "development", which in its turn is resolved in a "dénouement", the canonic structure revolves "endlessly" in the same way' (my translation). Döhl, *Beitrag*, p. 252.

25 Stroh disagrees. He sees the clarinet figure that opens the development as a distortion of the first theme variant played by the cello in bars 9–10 (*Symphonie*, pp. 26–7). The following are his Examples 13 and 14:

26 Döhl, who has earlier dismissed the interpretation of the two canons of the first section as themes one and two on psychological and discursive grounds, sees no conflict or development of previous material in this middle section. He concludes that in relation to the classical sonata, this section is the 'Negativ einer "Durchführung"' (*Beitrag*, p. 263).

27 Goldthwaite describes the formal organization of the movement as AA/BABA, which he identifies as sonata form, but he more or less ignores the problems this designation evokes by saying that 'One can apply the terms Exposition, Development, and Recapitulation to the sections, but on the basis of serial rather than thematic and tonal principles.' He then states that 'even the "Development" (B) follows the procedure of using some "material" from A.' He does not elaborate as to what material it is that appears in both exposition and development, but from his previous remark one supposes he must be referring to the three row forms (P_{11}, P_7 and I_9/RI_3) that occur in both places. This seems an untenable analogy, particularly as the row forms of the development are the inevitable outcome of the single decision to begin that section in the same way as the exposition transposed up a fifth. Goldthwaite seems to accept the formal designation a priori: nowhere does he explain in what way this movement fulfils the requirements of sonata structure ('Historical Awareness', p. 68).

28 Spinner, in characteristic fashion (see the reference to his analysis of Op. 31/iv: p. 429, note 76), gives the B section very little attention, saying only 'The second part of the form is a contrasting section of ten bars (bars 25b–34) with an exact repetition in retrograde (bars 35–44)'. He neatly avoids altogether the quite considerable problems attending the third section: 'In the last two bars of this section (bars 43–4) is already introduced the entry of the theme repetition (Vla), in a rhythmically varied form, as the third part of the ternary form (bars 43–66)' ('Abolition of Thematicism', p. 6).

29 This is not to say that thematic relationships between the two sections do not exist. Stroh points out that the viola figure that introduces the reprise is a distortion of the horn fanfare at the beginning of the exposition (*Symphonie*, p. 29). This relationship is illustrated in his Example 17:

30 Stroh, *Symphonie*, pp. 31–2.

31 The Op. 22/i canon is discussed on pp. 105–6.

32 'Tonic' by virtue of its centring on f#^{1}.

33 The concept of cadence is problematic in atonal music, but the term – as well as the concept – is one I find it necessary to use in attempting to define formal structure. Most obviously, the ends of sections must, by definition, be in some way cadential. The effect is usually achieved by contour, a change in the rhythm or the real tempo (the atonal analogue of the acceleration of harmonic rhythm – Schoenberg's 'tendency of the shortest note' – or its reverse, the suspension of activity), a change of register or timbre, a ritard or a caesura, or a combination of any of these. In the present case, the figure that first occurs in bar 5 and later, at the end of the exposition, in bar 15 is a distinctive one and is reserved for the close of sections.

34 Leland Smith, in his article 'Composition and Precomposition in the Music of Webern', in *Anton von Webern Perspectives*, ed. Moldenhauer and Irvine, represents the structure of this movement in the following way (p. 98):

bars	1–5	6–15	16–24	24–7	28–37	37–44
‖ A ‖	:B	a: ‖	:'development'	A, retrograde	B a: ‖	Coda ‖
	(Sax. 'c.f.')		(A')	(recap.)	('c.f.')	(A″)

While he admits that 'this relation [to the earlier sonata form] would be even closer if Webern had included the first five bars in his first repeat', he suggests no reason for the anomalous repeats. I find his designation of the second theme as a cantus firmus difficult to justify, even though the texture is right, since the imitative parts that surround it are not derivative, but, quite the opposite, use contrasting material.

35 A term often used by the late Hans Keller, mainly in BBC radio talks. See, for instance, his series of four hour-long analytical lectures on Beethoven's Op. 130, broadcast in 1975.

36 Obviously many more influences can be seen in the musical content of these works. The preceding list refers specifically to the format: the presence or absence of introduction and coda, the scheme of repetition, and so on.

37 English translation by Eric Smith, *Die Reihe*, Vol. 2, p. 15. That Webern should turn to the Brandenburg Concertos is not surprising, since these works exploit symmetry on several levels.

38 The original, as quoted by Döhl (*Beitrag*, p. 338), reads 'im *Sinne* einiger Brandenburgischer Konzerte von Bach' (my italics).

39 In this case the cadential effect is produced by a notated deceleration (semi-quavers to triplet quavers to triplet crotchets) and progressive verticalization (single notes, then two, then three).

40 It is this aspect of the movement that has fascinated analysts. For relatively extended discussions, see Karlheinz Stockhausen, 'Weberns Konzert für 9 Instrumente Op. 24 – Analyse des ersten Satzes', *Melos*, Vol. 20, No. 12

(December 1953), pp. 343–8, and Döhl, *Beitrag*, pp. 242–6. Analyses of the movement have not dealt adequately with its formal structure.

41 The properties of this row are discussed on pp. 21–3.

42 These sketches are in Sketchbook II, those of bars 11ff on p. 48 and those of bars 49ff on the first of two leaves added at the end of the book.

43 This pair of C sections, one of them presenting new material and the other developing old, is in accordance with Schoenberg's description of the 'Great Sonata Rondo' (*Fundamentals*, pp. 190ff), except, of course, that the second A section is missing in Op. 24.

44 *Letters*, No. 68, p. 32.

45 I first suggested this analysis of the first movement in 1973, before the content of the sketches showing that the third movement was the first to be written had been made known ('The Evolution of Variation Form in the Music of Webern', *Current Musicology*, Vol. 16 (1973), p. 56). The suggestion was made simply on musical evidence. In the same year, Juri Cholopov remarked on not the structural but the dramatic/psychological resemblance of the work as a whole to a sonata, in which complex problems are concentrated in the first movement, with the remaining two movements presenting uncomplicated structures – a scherzo, and theme and variations ('Die Spiegelsymmetrie in Anton Weberns Variationen für Klavier', *Archiv für Musikwissenschaft*, Vol. 30, p. 38).

46 Robert Wason, 'Webern's Variations for Piano, Op. 27: Musical Structure and the Performance Score', *Integral: The Journal of Applied Musical Thought*, Vol. 1 (1987), pp. 57–103.

47 René Leibowitz, *Schoenberg and His School*, trans. Dika Newlin (New York: Philosophical Library, 1948), pp. 226–38.

48 Döhl, *Beitrag*, p. 294. In a footnote, Döhl says: 'Dr W. Reich kindly placed at my disposal his notes taken at that time' (my translation; I have also translated the chart).

49 Reich's inscrutable notes for the whole of Op. 27, and suggestions concerning their provenance, are discussed on pp. 212–15.

50 See p. 213.

51 Döhl, *Beitrag*, pp. 294–303. (Although this work was presented as a doctoral dissertation in 1966, it was published only ten years later.)

52 Nelson, 'Webern's Path', pp. 83–4.

53 The palindromic structure of Op. 21/ii is discussed on pp. 199–201.

54 One other opinion should be mentioned at this time. This is found in the earliest extended study of Op. 27, a monograph by Dieter Schnebel, *Die Variationen für Klavier op. 27*, written in 1952 and subsequently circulated privately, first published in a Schnebel memorial collection in 1972 and reprinted in 1984 in *Musik-Konzepte: Sonderband Anton Webern II*, pp. 162–217. In his analysis of the first movement (pp. 178–87), Schnebel says it has a lyrical quality and gives the impression of an introduction or prelude (p. 178).

55 Vienna: Universal Edition, 1979.

56 It will be argued, doubtless with vigour, that concerns of the type just expressed

are completely irrelevant to the twelve-note technique, especially as it was used by Webern, who was undeniably a composer of atonal music. In expectation of this, I quote the end of his lecture of 26 February 1932, found on p. 54 of *Path*:

> For the rest, one works as before. The original form and pitch of the row occupy a position akin to that of the 'main key' in earlier music; the recapitulation will naturally return to it. We end 'in the same key!' This analogy with earlier formal construction is quite consciously fostered ...

57 Nelson ('Webern's Path') refers to six phrases in bars 19–36, which he describes in terms of length (in bars) as 5 + 3 + 4 + 2 + 2 + 2, with no further refinements. Taken at face value, this would indicate the following divisions: bars 19–23, 24–6, 27–30, 31–2, 33–4 and 35–6, which are obviously insupportable. Assuming that Nelson was simply being cavalier about exactly what constitutes a bar, this division might conceivably represent the following: bars 19–23 (downbeat), 23 (second note)–26 (downbeat), 26 (last two notes)–30 (fourth note), 30 (last two notes)–32 (first three notes), 32 (last three notes)–34 and 35–6. This division ignores both a three-note figure in bar 26 that answers one in bars 22–3 (thereby making the second phrase exactly four bars long) and the obviously sequential relationship of the phrases.

58 There is one small exception: the E–E♭ in the left hand in bar 32 is rhythmically different from the E♭–E that it answers in bar 30, because the earlier pair is part of the elision of the two major sections and retains the shape of its own predecessor in bars 26–7.

59 *Das Augenlicht*, for instruments and chorus, also comes from this period; it is patterned after sonata form, as well. See Chapter 8.

5 The movements in variation form: Opp. 21/ii, 24/iii, 27/iii, 28/i and 30

1 *Path*, p. 35.

2 *Path*, p. 33.

3 Webern refers repeatedly to unity as the highest ideal in music. In the lectures transcribed by Reich in *Path*, for example, see pp. 18 (7 March 1933), 35 (3 April 1933), 40 (10 April 1933), 42 (15 January 1932), 52 (19 February 1932), 53 (26 February 1932) and 55 (2 March 1932).

4 In Schoenberg, *Style and Idea*, p. 287.

5 Schoenberg, *Fundamentals*, p. 168.

6 *Path*, p. 53.

7 There is no such description of the first part of Op. 24/iii, but the tempo and textural changes in bar 14 make it apparent that bars 1–13 constitute the first section. Webern defined the theme of both Op. 28 and Op. 30 in letters to friends (see below).

8 Webern was not alone in this. Similar hybrid forms were used by Mahler (in the fourth movement of the Sixth Symphony and the opening movement of the

Ninth, for example) and Schoenberg (*Pelleas und Melisande*), and can be traced back through the Liszt Sonata to Schubert's *Wanderer* Fantasy.

9 Moldenhauer, *Anton von Webern*, p. 489.

10 *Ibid.*, p. 752.

11 Webern, *Der Weg*, p. 67 (my translation).

12 *Ibid.*, p. 68 (my translation).

13 Andante form is one of those catalogued by Schoenberg in *Fundamentals* (p. 190), where it is at the top of his list of rondo forms and further characterized as 'ABA and ABAB'. To my knowledge 'adagio' form is not a term in general use, but the two letters about Op. 30 cited in the text make it clear that Webern understood it to be synonymous with 'andante-form'.

14 Webern, *Der Weg*, p. 67 (my translation).

15 The parallel with the Brahms (an obvious model for Webern's Op. 1) seems to be a particularly close one. Robert Pascall outlined a sonata form in this movement in his paper 'Genre, Genesis and Perception', delivered at the Oxford University Music Analysis Conference 1988. This structure was compared with the ternary form defined in the same movement by Michael Musgrave (*The Music of Brahms* (London: Routledge and Kegan Paul, 1985), p. 226) and the binary suggested by the return of the opening material about halfway through.

16 The following is only a partial list: Bailey, 'Creativity in Tradition'; Philip K. Bracanin, 'The Palindrome: Its Applications in the Music of Anton Webern', *Miscellanea Musicologica*, Vol. 6 (1972), pp. 38–42; Borris, 'Structural Analysis', pp. 238–42; Deppert, *Studien*, pp. 49–50, 53–60, 63–8; Döhl, *Beitrag*, pp. 273–92; Goldthwaite, 'Historical Awareness', pp. 71–81; Wilfried Gruhn, 'Reienform und Werkgestalt bei Anton Webern (Die Variationen der Sinfonie op. 21)', *Zeitschrift für Musiktheorie*, Vol. 2, No. 2 (1971), pp. 31–8; H. Wiley Hitchcock, 'A Footnote on Webern's Variations', and Mark Starr, 'Webern's Palindrome', *Perspectives of New Music*, Vol. 8, No. 2 (Spring/Summer 1970), pp. 123–6 and 127–42 respectively; Stroh, *Symphonie*, especially pp. 33–41. Nelson's article, 'Webern's Path', must be mentioned for its singular lack of perception.

17 With one exception. As in connection with the first movement of this work, I have to mention Döhl's analysis, and again for the same reason – because his and mine agree to a remarkable degree, though I was unaware of his work when doing my own. Although nearly everyone (with the notable exception of Nelson) sees the same or very similar techniques in the variations of Op. 21, Döhl is the only one who comes to exactly the same conclusions as I have about the nature of the theme (p. 273).

18 See the diagram on p. 18.

19 And not always then. I feel obliged to quote just a few remarks characteristic of Nelson's article ('Webern's Path'). Concerning the fourth variation of Op. 21, he states: 'Webern says that the variation is "the midpoint of the whole movement, after which everything goes backward"'. This seems to mean that the movement as a whole follows a forward–retrograde pattern ... and that variation 5 corresponds to variation 3, 6 to 2, 7 to 1, and coda to theme ... Such

paired relationships can indeed be found, although the evidence is at times imprecise and conjectural' (p. 80). Variation II and III form a pair and 'show little that is new'. These variations are described in terms of 'fragmentary motifs', a 'coloristic interlude in which faint two- and three-note motifs are tossed about', 'transitional, a bridge', and 'a quiet interruption of the rhythmic movement' (p. 79). Of Variation VI he says: 'its melodic lines are noticeably jagged. Its similarity to variation 2 may lie in the prominence given in both to the three instruments mentioned, and also in the likeness of their assignments: imitative figures[!] for the two clarinets, a strongly contrasting part for the horn' (p. 81). About Variation VII: 'whereas variation 1 is a double canon, variation 7 is a quadruple canon [?!]' (p. 81).

20 In my identification of motives in this and subsequent movements, a letter d, a, r or i appended to the designation already assigned indicates that the motive is in diminution, augmentation, retrograde or inversion respectively.

21 I do not consider these bars to be a coda simply in order to make this parallel work. In fact, bars 69 (last note)–70 are an addendum structurally, the symmetrical events of Variation 4 having been completed at the end of bar 69.

22 Schoenberg, *Fundamentals*, p. 58.

23 The only discussion of this movement that I have seen is Deppert's (*Studien*, pp. 85–6, 91–3 and 95–8). In general, his study is not concerned with conventional forms.

24 See pp. 190–1.

25 This movement has generated an extraordinary number of articles. The earliest was Schnebel's monograph, written in 1952 and first published in 1972. The monograph appeared subsequently in the 1984 *Musik-Konzepte: Sonderband Anton Webern II*, where this movement is analysed on pp. 193–215. Probably the first published analysis, and almost certainly the most controversial (the word 'notorious' has been used by Peter Westergaard in reference to this article and its fellows), was Klammer's 'Webern's Piano Variations', *Die Reihe*, Vol. 2, pp. 81–92. This statistical jungle elicited an examination of rhythm and metre in this movement by Westergaard – 'Some Problems in Rhythmic Theory and Analysis', *Perspectives of New Music*, Vol. 1, No. 1 (Fall/Winter 1962), pp. 180–91 – and an analysis from Philip K. Bracanin – 'Analysis of Webern's 12-Note Music: Fact and Fantasy', *Studies in Music (Australia)*, Vol. 2 (1968), pp. 103–11. The reader is also directed to Edward T. Cone, 'Analysis Today', *The Musical Quarterly*, Vol. 46, No. 2 (April 1960), pp. 172–88; James Rives Jones, 'Some Aspects of Rhythm and Meter in Webern's Opus 27', *Perspectives of New Music*, Vol. 7, No. 1 (Fall/Winter 1968), pp. 103–9; and Christopher F. Hasty, 'Rhythm in Post-Tonal Music: Preliminary Questions of Duration and Motion', *Journal of Music Theory*, Vol. 25, No. 2 (Fall 1981), pp. 183–216. This movement is also analysed by Deppert (*Studien*, pp. 101, 106–9 and 114–17) and, quite thoroughly, by Döhl (*Beitrag*, pp. 312–29).

26 The *rhythm* is not in retrograde because the rests between notes, and consequently the juxtaposition of the notes themselves, are different.

27 These sketches are found on pp. 45 and 48 of Sketchbook III.

28 Wason, 'Webern's Variations for Piano', pp. 67–8.

29 Döhl, *Beitrag*, p. 294. The translation is mine.

30 In the following paragraphs, all references to Webern's comments about this work are based on this analysis (Moldenhauer, *Anton von Webern*, pp. 751–6).

31 Moldenhauer, *Anton von Webern*, pp. 752ff.

32 o = original form; r = retrograde; d = diminution.

33 The BACH motive occurs (untransposed) as the first tetrachord of RI_6/P_9, as the second tetrachord of I_2/R_5, and as the last tetrachord of P_1/RI_{10}. Of these rows, only RI_{10} and RI_6 have been used previously in this movement. On that occasion, in Variation 1, they were elided so that the BACH tetrachord occurred only once, and it was carefully disguised through octave displacement and the intervention of two bars of music from other rows between A and C (see bars 23–6). So it is that the appearance of BACH in bars 66–8 is effectively the first.

34 *Letters*, No. 104, p. 44.

35 *Path*, p. 60.

36 *Letters*, No. 104, p. 44.

37 Webern, *Der Weg*, p. 68 (my translation).

38 Here I should like to quote again from Nelson's article ('Webern's Path'). He says of this variation that 'Webern's sonorous contrasts are manifold. We find chords that overlap, detached chords that oppose sustained chords, chains of chords that move quickly from one instrumental color to another – all projected through a wide range of dynamic and idiomatic effect' (p. 89). Which shows how easily the canonic construction can be missed altogether.

39 This omission is discussed on p. 77.

40 The first motive (bri) of section 2 and all of section 4 were initially sketched in rhythmic unison, with voices offset to form a canon later. These sketches occur on pp. 73–4 of Sketchbook IV.

41 All these chords were complete in the initial sketches: *Ausfälle* were caused by the removal of Bs and B♭s later. These early sketches are on pp. 77–8 of Sketchbook IV.

42 The question marks at the end of these sets of durations are meant to indicate that the notated length of the final note of a series is not significant, since Webern routinely shortens the duration of notes in this position. The 'real' value of a note articulated last in a series cannot be determined in the absence of the identification of a consistently applied system.

43 This technique is discussed on pp. 116–17.

44 This is discussed on pp. 122–5.

6 The movements in rondo and ternary forms: Opp. 20/i, 22/ii, 24/ii, 28/ii and 28/iii

1 Schoenberg, *Fundamentals*, p. 190.

2 See the slow movement of the *Pathétique* Sonata, Op. 13, for example.

3 Quoted in Kolneder, *Anton Webern*, p. 112.

4 Moldenhauer, *Anton von Webern*, p. 753.

5 See Appendix V for a discussion of grace notes in Webern's music.

6 On pp. 42–6 and 56–61 (topography); 105–6 and 107–9 (canon).

7 This is given by Moldenhauer (*Anton von Webern*), p. 423.

8 *Path*, p. 57.

9 This outline appears on p. 54 of Sketchbook I. I have used Moldenhauer's translation (*Anton von Webern*, p. 423).

10 The Beethoven analysis is my own.

11 Stroh sees this Beethoven movement as falling 'unambiguously' into the form ABA C ABA. He goes on to suggest that in comparing his Op. 22 rondo to this one Webern may have been referring more to a similarity of character or purpose than to specific structural similarities (*Historische Legitimation*, p. 338).

12 The last three notes in bar 63 constitute this imitation by a third voice. The last of these is the first note of P_0 referred to earlier as the note that should begin the second refrain.

13 The following table shows the discrepancies between the divisions I have suggested and those defined by major tempo changes. Parentheses in the first list indicate an internal division; those in the second list represent minor tempo indications, such as *a tempo*. Those tempo changes that coincide with structural divisions are marked with an asterisk.

Structural divisions	Tempo changes
(bars 19/20)	(bar 20)★
bars 32/3	bar 31
bars 63/4	bar 69
bars 92/3	bar 93★
(bars 111/12)	(bar 112)★
bars 121/2	bar 122★
bars 131/2	bar 132★
(bars 146/7)	(bar 150)
bars 152/3	bar 152
bars 182/3	bar 180

14 Compare, for example, the following three structural outlines suggested for this movement. The first is the one presented above. The second is Brian Fennelly's, given on p. 316 of 'Structure and Process'; the third appears on p. 99 of Leland Smith's 'Composition and Precomposition':

Bailey:	bars 1–19	20–32	32–51	51–63	64–93	93–111	112–21	122–31	132–46	147–53	153–69	170–82	183–92		
				+	+										
Fennelly:	bars 1–19	20–32	33–50	51–68	69–93	93–111	112	–	131	132	–	153	153	–	179	180–92
Smith:	bars 1	–	30	31	–	68	69–92	93–111	112–21	122–7	128	–	151	152	–	179	180–92

(I have changed the bar numbers on Fennelly's chart in two instances where they seemed to be in error; these are marked with a +. The fourth group on his chart reads 57–68, the fifth 69–96. My alterations are consistent with his text.)

15 Leopold Spinner, 'Analysis of a Period', *Die Reihe*, Vol. 2, pp. 46–50.

16 Christopher Wintle, 'Analysis and Performance: Webern's Op. 24/ii', *Music Analysis*, Vol. 1, No. 1 (March 1982), pp. 73–99.

17 See Wintle's article for a more thorough discussion of this augmented triad as the tonal basis of this movement. A few remarks about this (otherwise excellent) article should be made to anyone setting out to read it, as it contains some surprising errors. The first is Wintle's references throughout to Leopold Spinner as 'Leopold Skinner'; a second occurs on p. 85, where the sixth line of text should read 'fourth, seventh and tenth', not 'eleventh'. Finally a clarification: although Wintle identifies the retrograde row as a form of the prime (cf. the second line in his *Durchführung* table on p. 94), he does not treat the retrograde inversion in a similar way, but rather calls it RI and calculates its level of transposition from the initial note of P_0. (So, for example, what he calls RI_9 in this case I call RI_{11}.)

18 This is not to be taken literally: Webern does nothing at random. The choice of melody notes is simply much less restricted than it was in the original.

19 There is one exception to this: the second of the notes marking the cadence of the antecedent phrase in bar 58 is played by the clarinet.

20 Moldenhauer, *Anton von Webern*, pp. 752–6.

21 From a letter to Rudolf Kolisch dated 19 April 1938 and quoted by Moldenhauer, *Anton von Webern*, pp. 489–90.

22 Webern's analysis, quoted in Moldenhauer, *Anton von Webern*, pp. 752–6.

23 *Ibid.*, p. 753.

24 *Ibid.*

25 *Ibid.*, pp. 753–6.

26 *Ibid.*

27 Schoenberg, *Style and Idea*, p. 248.

7   The movement in binary form: Op. 27/ii

1 *Letters*, No. 68, p. 32.

2 Recalled by Peter Stadlen in 'Serialism Reconsidered', *The Score*, No. 22 (1958), p. 12.

3 See pp. 111–12 and 61 respectively. The details of this movement are discussed by Döhl (*Beitrag*, pp. 303–12).

4 Wilbur Ogdon has suggested a division of each of the two parts of this movement into four phrases on the basis of recurring motivic elements: see 'A Webern Analysis', *Journal of Music Theory*, Vol. 6, No. 1 (1962). Ogdon's phrase structure is refuted, only incidentally, by Peter Westergaard in 'Webern and "Total Organization": An Analysis of the Second Movement of Piano Variations, Op. 27', *Perspectives of New Music*, Vol. 1, No. 2 (Spring/Summer 1963).

5 There is considerable difference of opinion on this point. For discussions of the metric problems posed by this movement and arguments as to the reasons for the written metre, see Cone, 'Analysis Today', and David Lewin, 'A Metrical Problem in Webern's Op. 27', *Journal of Music Theory*, Vol. 6, No. 1 (1962), pp. 125–32.

PART III   THE MUSIC WITH VOICES

Introduction to Part III

1 See letter No. 63, *Letters*, pp. 30–1.

8   *Das Augenlicht*

1 'Mittelpunkt ... und ... dynamischer Höhepunkt'. All quotations and paraphrases in this chapter are from a letter to Hildegard Jone dated 15 October 1935
(*Letters*, No. 63, pp. 30–1).
2 The rhythmic canon that runs throughout this piece is shown in Example 3.9 on
pp. 110–11.
3 See Schoenberg, *Fundamentals*, pp. 20ff.

9   Cantata I

1 The crucial word in this line of the poem is *Herzschlag*, which is usually
translated as 'heartbeat'. *Herzschlag* also, however, means heart failure, and it
seems to me that this implication is critical in understanding the poem.
2 Webern changed his mind several times about the notation of this movement.
The first sketches of what is now the opening six bars are written in one bar of
3/2 followed by three of 7/4 with no change of tempo. Each voice begins and
ends with three minims, and the six notes in the centre are notated as in the
published version, so that the durational relationship between extremes and
centre is not as in the version eventually decided upon. This latter relationship is
established in the third sketch, which bears two tempo indications – *Sehr getragen*
and *Bewegt* ♪ = ♩ – and was notated first as 3/2, 4/2, 5/8, 2/8, 4/8, 3/8, 5/4 and 4/2,
then changed to 3/2, 4/2, 5/8, 3/8, 4/8, 2/8, 5/4 and 4/2 with the opening and
closing in breves and the central portion in quavers and crotchets. The *bewegt*
was changed to *lebhaft* in subsequent revisions, but these sections continued to be
notated in quavers and crotchets with the ♪ = ♩ indication. (These sketches are on
pp. 13–22 of Sketchbook IV.)
3 Both here and in bar 6 the voices that occur on the afterbeats have minims only,
preceded by rests of the same value.
4 My delight in having figured this out in 1983 was somewhat dampened by the
appearance of Robin Hartwell's article 'Duration and Mental Arithmetic: The
First Movement of Webern's First Cantata', *Perspectives of New Music*, Vol. 23,
No. 1 (Fall/Winter 1984), pp. 348–59, in which he renotates the slow portions of
this movement just as I had done. However, his conclusions are very different
from mine and seem to have more to do with arithmetic than with durations.
5 The final note of both **b** consequents (in P$_6$ and RI$_9$) is shifted so that **b** takes the
following form: ♩ ♩ ⅞ ♪. The sketches show this value replacement transpiring;
what appears in the printed score as a crotchet rest followed by a crotchet is in

both cases a minim in the final sketch (Sketchbook IV, p. 22); in RI₉, however, it has been renotated *in situ*.

6 In the fourth voice, RI₆, this note – the harp's G♯ in bar 46 – is a crotchet too late. This note is where it should be in the final sketch (Sketchbook IV, p. 21), where the rhythm of this voice and the third one, R₃, are identical.

7 Sketchbook IV, p. 21.

8 Neither is the second in the final sketch (Sketchbook IV, p. 21). In this version the last three notes in all voices are in rhythmic unison.

9 The final note in each voice was a quaver in the *lebhaft* tempo in the final sketch of this movement (Sketchbook IV, p. 21).

10 This subject has been exhaustively examined in the following articles: György Ligeti, 'Über die Harmonik in Weberns erster Kantate', *Darmstädter Beiträge zur Neuen Musik*, Vol. 3 (1960), pp.49–64; George Rochberg, 'Webern's Search for Harmonic Identity', *Journal of Music Theory*, Vol. 6, No. 1 (1962), pp. 109–22; Eberhardt Klemm, 'Symmetrien im Chorsatz von Anton Webern', *Deutsches Jahrbuch der Musikwissenschaft*, Vol. 11 (1966), pp. 107–20; David Saturen, 'Symmetrical Relationships in Webern's First Cantata', *Perspectives of New Music*, Vol. 6, No. 1 (Fall/Winter 1967), pp. 142–3; Jonathan Kramer, 'The Row as Structural Background and Audible Foreground: The First Movement of Webern's First Cantata', *Journal of Music Theory*, Vol. 15 (1971), pp. 158–81; and Graham H. Phipps, 'Tonality in Webern's Cantata I', *Music Analysis*, Vol. 3, No. 2 (July 1984), pp. 125–58 (pp. 130–41 deal with the first movement).

11 In this example the tenor part is written at the octave in which it sounds.

12 Beckmann, *Sprache und Musik im Vokalwerk Anton Weberns*, pp. 87–8.

13 *Letters*, No. 86, p. 37.

14 Phipps sees the central tetrachord of this row as germinal. 'Ahornsamen', which is undeniably the central word in the opening line of text, with respect to meaning as well as location, is set to a BACH motive (F–E–G–F♯); this BACH is embedded in a pair of what he calls false-BACH motives (D–C♯–F–E and G–F♯–Bb–A), which extend outward from the centre in both directions. He points out that the work composed just prior to this, the Op. 28 Quartet, is based on a row with the same symmetrical properties as the present one – P = RI – arising from the same starting point – BACH (Phipps, 'Tonality', pp. 141–2).

15 Throughout this comparison, I make no distinction between a quaver and a semiquaver followed by a semiquaver rest, since Webern substitutes one for the other freely. In the first sketches, all these notes were written in the same way, as quavers.

16 Phipps sees the structure of this piece as binary, with each large section displaying a ternary subdivision ('Tonality', pp. 143–4). He considers the axis of the central palindrome, the point at which the concern of the text changes from ascent (of the growing tree) to descent (of the seeds back to the earth), to be the major structural division of the movement. Although this view can be justified to some extent by a certain symmetry in the melodic rows – both outer sections of the first half of his binary form are built on R₆ and those of the second half on

P_6 – I nevertheless think that the similarity of the two canons, as well as their identical length, makes it illogical to see the first as a single section and the second as two. Phipps does not mention the presence of a canon in either of the sections that I have called B – or anywhere at all in this movement, for that matter. He describes the A sections as 'a cantus firmus line accompanied by a texture of three inverted set forms which are fragmented in different orchestral timbres' (p. 144); of the B sections he says they are 'a continuous melody in one voice accompanied by melodic fragments' (p. 145). It must be admitted, however, that his particular concern in this article is tonal focus, not rhythm or canon.

17 In a letter to the Humpliks dated 2 December 1939 (*Letters*, No. 92, p. 39), Webern says that he thinks this movement will have to be the first 'for musical reasons, but also for *textual* ones'.

18 *Letters*, No. 92, p. 39.

19 *Path*, p. 60.

20 I prefer this designation, in spite of the fact that the initial statement of what I have called Subject 1 begins slightly later than its partner. As I will show presently, the fugue proper begins in bar 17, where the four voices present the subjects in the order 1–2–1–2. Furthermore, the version of the subject played by the strings, because of its simultaneities, tends to be perceived as accompaniment, and, while the melodic subject is developed alone later in the movement, the string subject never is. Subject 2 seems to be a variant of Subject 1 in which some of the adjacent notes are played at the same time with rests inserted to make up the difference, leaving the impression that the subject played by the wind is the prototype.

21 There is some confusion about the definition of *beat* in relation to this movement (see below). For the present purposes, 'beat' refers to the shortest value used in a statement of either subject (in all cases either a crotchet or a quaver). Although only crotchet versions are given in Example 9.19, the same variants occur in quavers as well.

22 In one instance – the last appearance of Subject 2 in the exposition, beginning in bar 26 and continuing alone from 30 to 38 – the first of these three events is not a double stop.

23 See the analysis cited earlier (Moldenhauer, *Anton von Webern*, p. 753).

24 The exact number varies according to the way in which the *alla breve* and the 3/2 bars are treated.

10 Cantata II

1 In letters to both Willi Reich and the Humpliks, he calls the fourth movement an 'introduction' to the 'Freundselig' movement (*Path*, p. 62, letter of 23 August 1941; *Letters*, No. 105, dated 13 August 1941, p. 45). In a subsequent letter to Reich dated 31 July 1942 (*Path*, pp. 63–4), he says of 'Gelockert aus dem Schoße':

> Meanwhile I've completed another piece. It's to form the first part of the planned 'oratorio,' together with the preceding ones.

In a letter to the Humpliks dated 4 September 1942 (*Letters*, No. 111, p. 47) he also announces having finished 'Gelockert aus dem Schoße':

> This is for chorus and orchestra – a sort of 'chorale' which with the two preceding pieces 'Leichteste Bürden' (1) and 'Freundselig ist das Wort' (2) makes up the *first part* (within the total plan). They run as follows: 1) a *soprano solo* (like a recitative), 2) a soprano *Aria with chorus*, and 3) the Chorale (chorus).

In a much later letter to Hildegard Jone, dated 28 January 1944, when all six movements had been completed (*Letters*, No. 122, p. 52), he sets down their final order, connecting Nos. IV and V with the word 'und' and describing them as a unit.

2 According to Moldenhauer (*Anton von Webern*, p. 573), Webern announced to Josef Hueber on 20 March that he was about to begin his next work (Op. 30 having been already completed), and he informed Reich on 3 May that he was already at work on a new project. The dates of these two remarks would indicate that the piece had been begun in April. The 3 May letter to Reich (*Path*, pp. 61–2) does not contain a reference to any work besides Op. 30, so one must either assume that portions of the letter have been omitted or question Moldenhauer's accuracy. In any case, the first draft of the work (Sketchbook IV, p. 82) is dated 7 May.

3 The completion of this piece is announced in two letters dated 4 September 1942 – to Reich (*Path*, pp. 63–4) and to the Humpliks (*Letters*, No. 111, pp. 47–8).

4 Webern describes his plan for this next group of pieces in the letter of 4 September to the Humpliks and alludes to it again in a letter to them dated 19 November (*Letters*, No. 113, p. 48) in a way that sounds as if he has not yet begun to write but is about to. Completion of the first piece is announced in a letter written on 11 February 1943 (*Letters*, No. 115, p. 49).

5 In a letter to the Humpliks dated 11 October 1943 (*Letters*, No. 120, pp. 50–1) Webern says: 'my new piece should soon be finished. It is: "Schöpfen aus Brunnen des Himmels ..."'. In a letter dated 4 December (*Letters*, No. 121, p. 51) he announces that this work 'has been finished for some time' and that the score is ready.

6 The beginning of this movement is on p. 33 of Sketchbook V, dated 18 December. On 28 January Webern wrote to Hildegard Jone, 'I was already working very intensively on "Kleiner sind Götter geworden ..." – I told you recently that this was to be the next piece, the foundations were already laid – when suddenly I felt with absolute certainty ... that this work was *musically complete* in the six finished pieces!' (*Letters*, No. 122, p. 52).

7 *Letters*, No. 105, p. 45.

8 See the letter to Willi Reich quoted on p. 426, note 40.

9 The first two notes of bars 2–3 and those of bar 12, as well as bars 4 and 13, illustrate the inversional relationship of the two halves of the song; the voice part in bars 12–14 is, except for some obvious octave displacement, the retrograde inversion of the violin's melody in bars 9–11, and the horn melody in bars 18–19

bears a similar relationship to the last two notes in bar 3 and all of bar 4, thereby underlining the inverted palindrome of the whole.

10 *Letters*, No. 109, p. 46.

11 Sketchbook IV, p. 88.

12 See Example 3.15 (p. 123).

13 See pp. 226–7 for a discussion of the application of inversion to rhythm. Since this was a technique used just previously, in the Op. 30 Variations, it seems reasonable to suppose that Webern might use it again here. The parallel position of the two figures leaves no doubt as to their common origin.

14 As noted earlier (on p. 130), although this section appears to end at the double barline between bars 24 and 25, the strings' chord in bar 25 is actually the end of the previous section.

15 See note 58 on p. 427.

16 *Letters*, No. 110, pp. 46–7.

17 See pp. 88–9.

18 *Letters*, No. 107, p. 45.

19 *Letters*, No. 105, p. 45.

20 In spite of the following remark, made to them in a letter of 1 November 1942 (*Letters*, No. 112, p. 48):

> Enclosed is the line of music you asked for, in the final version – it differs from the way I wrote it in the letter in its *changed notation*, in *content* it has remained the same.

Although Webern does not identify the movement (the music referred to does not survive), Josef Polnauer has assumed it to be 'Freundselig ist das Wort', since the fragment of this piece contained in the Christmas letter of 1941 is the only musical quotation in the correspondence from the period between December 1941 and November 1942. Webern had not, in fact, written anything else during this time except 'Gelockert aus dem Schoße', which he quotes in a letter some two and a half weeks later.

21 *Letters*, No. 111, p. 47.

22 *Letters*, No. 113, p. 48.

23 *Path*, pp. 63, 64.

24 There is one other instance of this, in a movement sketched but abandoned as part of Op. 20. The sketches for this movement are in Sketchbook I, and were among those published by Moldenhauer in his facsimile collection of 1968.

25 The sketches do nothing to clarify this; on the contrary, they indicate that Webern wrestled a good deal with the problem of metre. The first sketches of the outer sections of 'Freundselig ist das Wort' (Sketchbook IV, pp. 90ff) are written in metres using minims instead of quavers. The tenor part of 'Gelockert aus dem Schoße' is written out over an entire page in the form in which it finally appeared (p. 109); on the page facing this (p. 110) all the parts are sketched in note values one quarter the length of the ones used in the original sketch (and in the final version).

26 'This ["Gelockert aus dem Schoße"] ... with the two preceding pieces "Leich-

teste Bürden" (1) and "Freundselig ist das Wort" (2) makes up the *first part* (within the total plan)' (letter to the Humpliks dated 4 September 1942, *Letters*, No. 111, p. 47).

27 *Ibid.*

28 Letter dated 11 February 1943 in *Letters*, No. 115, p. 49.

29 See pp. 78–82 for a discussion of the row structure of this movement.

30 These relationships are rhythmic ones only.

31 Although it is *written* as a further 1:2 augmentation of that version, and therefore appears to be a 1:4 augmentation of the original, this is not realized aurally because the tempo doubles at bar 26.

32 Here again Schoenberg's *Pierrot lunaire* seems to provide a precedent, though the style of the two works is altogether different. In Schoenberg's 'Nacht', the fall of darkness is represented through a similar decrease in definition (see my article 'Structural Imagery').

33 This and the following events are more thoroughly discussed on pp. 78–82.

34 *Letters*, No. 116, pp. 49–50.

35 *Path*, p. 64.

36 See p. 136.

37 The distinction between these two structures depends on the relative strength of internal cadences, and although I have, throughout this study, identified figures that I believe to function as cadences, I am not prepared to make a decision of this sort in an atonal idiom.

38 Willam, *Anton Weberns II. Kantate*, p. 137.

39 Other changes have been made as well. Although the rhythm of the second phrase is unchanged except for the lengthening of the first note, it does not in the finished version stand in triplet relationship with the preceding phrase. In addition the final note of the second phrase has been moved up an octave.

40 The canonic structure of the previous movement is extremely complex. See pp. 136–9.

41 Letter dated 2 October 1943, *Letters*, No. 120, pp. 50–1.

42 See p. 429, note 75.

43 Section A2 is a condensed version of the events of A1. See Example 3.22 on p. 141 for a comparison of these two sections.

44 The first soprano part has been quoted here, though it is not the *dux*, because the rhythm falls within the barlines more logically in this part than it does in the second soprano part, which leads.

45 See p. 314.

46 *Letters*, no. 107, pp. 107–8.

47 Letter dated 28 January 1944 in *Letters*, No. 122, p. 52.

Conclusion

1 Arnold Whittall, 'On Summarizing Webern', p. 54.

2 Whittall, 'Webern and Atonality: The Path from the Old Aesthetic', *Musical Times*, Vol. 124 (December 1983), p. 737.

3 The translation used here appeared unsigned in *The Score*, No. 6 (1952), pp. 18–22. The passage quoted is on p. 20.

4 *Ibid.*, pp. 21–2.

5 *Path*, p. 43.

6 p. 734.

7 George Perle, *The Operas of Alban Berg, Vol. 2: Lulu* (2 vols., Berkeley: University of California Press, 1985).

8 See Martha M. Hyde, *Schoenberg's Twelve-Tone Harmony: The Suite Op. 29 and the Compositional Sketches* (Ann Arbor: UMI Research Press, 1977); 'The Roots of Form in Schoenberg's Sketches', *Journal of Music Theory*, Vol. 24, No. 1 (Spring 1980), pp. 1–36; and 'The Telltale Sketches: Harmonic Structure in Schoenberg's Twelve-Tone Method', *The Musical Quarterly*, Vol. 66, No. 4 (October 1980), pp. 560–80.

9 Phipps, 'Tonality in Webern's Cantata I', pp. 125–58.

Appendix V   A note on Webern's graces

1 Webern's description in a letter to Hildegard Jone written on 3 June 1942. *Letters*, No. 109, p. 46 (translation modified).

Glossary

I include a glossary in this study, not because I expect any of the terminology to be unfamiliar to the reader, but in order to make certain that the special sense in which I employ several generally used musical terms is understood.

aggregate: a set of twelve discrete notes formed by the simultaneous progression of either the first or the second hexachords of two row forms with complementary hexachordal content.

Ausfall (plural *Ausfälle*): a deficiency caused in one voice of a polyphonic framework by its intersection with another, the common note or notes sounding only once.

combinatorial: the relationship whereby two row forms have complementary hexachordal content. A row is semi-combinatorial if it relates in this way to one of its permutations, all-combinatorial if it is complemented by three or more.

derived row: a twelve-note row that represents the combination of several permutations of a shorter set (a trichord or a tetrachord). Opp. 24 and 28 are based on derived rows.

dyad: two notes played at once (a two-note chord).

elision: the overlapping of two rows that occur in succession, so that one or more notes at the juncture are shared (are played only once to serve both rows).

heptachord: a group of seven notes.

heptad: seven notes played at once (a seven-note chord).

hexachord: six notes; half of a twelve-note row.

hexad: six notes played at once (a six-note chord).

imbrication: the systematic isolation and identification of all possible segments of a predetermined size contained in a melodic line, beginning on each note in succession.

intersection: the meeting of two (or more) rows requiring the same pitch class at the same time so that a single pitch serves both (or all) rows.

invariance: the property of a set (in the present case, a hexachord, a tetrachord or a trichord) that results in its retention of some (or in extreme cases, all) of the same pitch classes in certain transpositions or permutations.

layering: the simultaneous linear exposition of two or more materials – rows, or segments of rows.

matrix: the 12 × 12 square on which a row and all its permutations are plotted.

pc set: pitch–class set. Any group of notes, classified according to its intervallic structure when reduced to close position, and identified either with the number assigned to it by Allen Forte (see *The Structure of Atonal Music*, New Haven: Yale University Press, 1973) or with numbers matching its intervallic content measured in semitones (for example, c–c♯–e = 014).

pentachord: a group of five notes.

pentad: five notes played at once (a five–note chord).

pitch class: the set of *all* pitches having the same letter name and all their enharmonic equivalents. (For example, the pitch class C includes all Cs, B♯s, D♭♭s and so on at all octave transpositions.)

pitch: *one specific* note (for example, C, c, c¹).

retrograde inversion: the inverted row read backwards (as opposed to the retrograde of the row inverted, which gives the same result intervallically but would yield a different set of transposition numbers).

secondary set: a linear set of twelve discrete notes formed by the second hexachord of one row form and the first hexachord of another when two row forms with similar hexachordal content are heard in succession.

segmentation: the division of a row into portions – trichords, tetrachords or hexachords – either for purposes of orchestration or rhythmic grouping, or so that individual segments may be treated as independent rows.

source set: a specific division of the twelve pitch classes into two unordered hexachords; all rows generated by the same source set will exhibit similar combinatorial properties.

tetrachord: four notes; one–third of a twelve–note row.

tetrad: four notes played at once (a four–note chord).

triad: three notes played at once (a three–note chord; this term does *not* imply tertiary arrangement).

trichord: three notes; one–quarter of a twelve–note row.

value replacement: the insertion, in the repetition of a motive, of a rest as a replacement for some portion of the value of one of the notes of the original. This rest may occur either before or after the note that it shortens.

verticalization: the simultaneous occurrence of all the notes of a segment of a row, played in the manner of a chord.

Chronological worklist

The dates given below are taken from the sketchbooks. Sketches for the earlier works are dated at the beginning and at the end. Later, dates are increasingly frequent and are more precise: the date of every stage in the development of these works is carefully recorded. Conversely, although the place of composition is noted in the sketches of the early works, this practice is later abandoned. The entries below contain the dates given at the beginning and end of the sketches for each movement, the place of composition whenever that has been recorded in the sketchbooks, and the location of the sketches for each movement (roman numerals identify the books, arabic numbers the pages).

Trio, Op. 20

        begun summer 1926, finished end of June 1927
        Mödling
        (Since there are no extant sketches for Op.20, this
            information is taken from Moldenhauer, pp. 714–15.)

Symphony, Op. 21

  mvt ii: begun November 1927, finished 27 March 1928
           Mödling
           I/15–36
  mvt i: begun 11 May, finished 27 June 1928
           I/37–50

Quartet, Op. 22

  outline: 14 November 1928 (I/54)
  mvt ii: begun 30 May 1929, finished 12 April 1930
           Mödling
           I/54–II/4
  mvt i: begun 19 July, finished 13 August 1930
           II/13–26

Three Songs from *Viae inviae*, Op. 23

  no. iii: begun 1 February, finished 14 July 1933
           Maria Enzersdorf
           II/51–6

no. ii: begun 26 July, finished 18 August 1933
           II/57–62

no. i: begun 3 January, finished 15 March 1934
           II/65–70

Concerto, Op. 24

   ideas: 16 January 1931 (II/38)

   mvt i: begun 7 July 1931, finished 25 June 1934
           II/38 – added p. 2

   mvt ii: begun 31 July, finished 4 August 1934
           II/78 – inside back cover

   mvt iii: begun 27 August, finished 4 September 1934
           III/2–8

Three Songs on texts by Hildegard Jone, Op. 25

   no. i: begun 4 July, finished 16 July 1934
           Maria Enzersdorf
           II/75–6

   no. iii: begun 19 September, finished 8 October 1934
           III/9–14

   no. ii: begun 24 October, finished 15 November 1934
           III/15–20

Das Augenlicht, Op. 26

   row: 24 February 1935 (III/22)

   sketches: begun 15 June, finished 13 September 1935
           III/22–42

Variations for Piano, Op. 27

   mvt iii: begun 14 October 1935, finished 8 July 1936
           III/43–8

   mvt i: begun 22 July, finished 19 August 1936
           III/49–54

   mvt ii: begun 25 August, finished 5 November 1936
           III/53–6

String Quartet, Op. 28

   mvt iii: begun 17 November 1936, finished 20 August 1937
           III/57–72

   mvt i: begun 3 September 1937, finished 21 January 1938
           III/73–86

   mvt ii: begun 17 February, finished 26 March 1938
           III/87–94

Cantata I, Op. 29

   row: work begun on 1 July, 'gilt' on 3 August 1938 (IV/2)

   mvt ii: begun 7 September, finished 14 December 1938
           IV/2–12

mvt i: title dated 11 February
        begun 15 February, finished 25 April 1939
        IV/13–22

mvt iii: begun 3 August, finished 26 November 1939
        IV/23–46

Variations for Orchestra, Op. 30
        begun 15 April, finished 25 November 1940
        IV/27–80

Cantata II, Op. 31

mvt iv: begun 7 May, finished 31 July 1941
        IV/81–8

mvt v: begun 24 September 1941, finished 2 July 1942
        IV/89–106

mvt vi: begun August; finished 26 August 1942
        IV/107–10

mvt i: begun 16 November 1942, finished 21 January 1943
        IV/111–18

mvt ii: begun 1 April, finished 6 July 1943
        V/1–17

mvt iii: begun 16 August, finished 3 November 1943
        V/18–31

Select bibliography

PRIMARY SOURCES

Webern's twelve-note works

Zwei Lieder für gemischten Chor mit Begleitung von Celesta, Gitarre, Geige, Klarinette und Bass-klarinette, Op. 19. Vienna: Universal Edition, 1928

Trio für Geige, Bratsche und Violoncell, Op. 20. Vienna: Universal Edition, 1927

Symphonie für Klarinette, Bass-klarinette, zwei Hörner, Harfe, 1. und 2. Geige, Bratsche und Violoncell, Op. 21. Vienna: Universal Edition, 1929

Quartett für Geige, Klarinette, Tenor-saxophon und Klavier, Op. 22. Vienna: Universal Edition, 1932

Drei Gesänge aus 'Viae Inviae' von Hildegard Jone (voice and piano), Op. 23. Vienna: Universal Edition, 1936

Konzert für Flöte, Oboe, Klarinette, Horn, Trompete, Posaune, Geige, Bratsche und Klavier, Op. 24. Vienna: Universal Edition, 1948

Drei Lieder nach Gedichten von Hildegard Jone (voice and piano), Op. 25. Vienna: Universal Edition, 1956

Das Augenlicht für gemischten Chor und Orchester, Op. 26. Vienna: Universal Edition, 1956

Variationen für Klavier, Op. 27. Vienna: Universal Edition, 1937

Streichquartett, Op. 28. Vienna: Universal Edition, 1939

I. Kantate für Sopran-Solo, gemischten Chor und Orchester, Op. 29. Vienna: Universal Edition, 1957

Variationen für Orchester, Op. 30. Vienna: Universal Edition, 1956

II. Kantate für Sopran- und Bass-Solo, gemischten Chor und Orchester, Op. 31. Vienna: Universal Edition, 1956

Webern's writings

Der Weg zur neuen Musik, ed. Willi Reich. Vienna: Universal Edition, 1960

The Path to the New Music, ed. Willi Reich, trans. Leo Black. Bryn Mawr: Theodore Presser Co., 1963 [a translation of the above]

Letters to Hildegard Jone and Josef Humplik, ed. Josef Polnauer, trans. Cornelius Cardew. Bryn Mawr: Theodore Presser Co., 1967

Sketches, facsimiles, etc.

Anton von Webern: Sketches (1926–1945). Facsimile Reproductions from the Composer's Autograph Sketchbooks in the Moldenhauer Archive. Commentary by Ernst Krenek, with a Foreword by Hans Moldenhauer. New York: Carl Fischer, Inc., 1968

Sketchbook. Pierpont Morgan Library, New York (Moldenhauer's 'Sketchbook I'; referred to as 'Sketchbook 1' above)

Sketchbooks I–V. Paul Sacher Stiftung, Basel (Moldenhauer's 'Sketchbooks II–VI'; referred to as 'Sketchbooks I–V' above)

Webern's Row Tables. Paul Sacher Stiftung, Basel

SECONDARY SOURCES

Adorno, Theodor W. *Philosophy of Modern Music*, trans. Anne G. Mitchell and Wesley V. Bloomster. London: Sheed and Ward, 1973

Austin, William W. 'Webern and the Tradition of the Symphony'. In *Anton Webern Perspectives*, ed. Hans Moldenhauer and Demar Irvine. Seattle and London: University of Washington Press, 1966

Music in the Twentieth Century. New York: Norton, 1966

Babbitt, Milton. 'Some Aspects of Twelve-Tone Composition'. *The Score and I.M.A. Magazine*, No. 12 (June 1955)

Beckmann, Dorothea. *Sprache und Musik im Vokalwerk Anton Weberns: Die Konstruktion des Ausdrucks*. Kölner Beiträge zur Musikforschung, ed. Karl Gustav Fellerer, Vol. 57. Regensburg: Gustav Bosse Verlag, 1970

Borris, Siegfried. 'Structural Analysis of Webern's Symphony Op. 21'. In *Paul A. Pisk: Essays in His Honour*, ed. John Glowacki, trans. Ursula Klein. Austin: University of Texas Press, 1966

Bracanin, Philip K. 'Analysis of Webern's 12–Note Music: Fact and Fantasy'. *Studies in Music (Australia)*, Vol. 2 (1968)

'The Palindrome: Its Applications in the Music of Anton Webern'. *Miscellanea Musicologica*, Vol. 6 (1972)

Busch, Regina. 'Über die Musik von Anton Webern'. *Österreichische Musikzeitschrift*, Vol. 36 (1981)

'Wie Berg die richtige Reihe fand'. In *Musik-Konzepte: Sonderband Anton Webern II*. Vienna: Universal Edition, November 1984

Chittum, Donald. 'Some Observations on the Row Technique in Webern's Opus 25'. *Current Musicology*, No. 12 (1971)

Cholopov, Juri. 'Die Spiegelsymmetrie in Anton Weberns Variationen für Klavier'. *Archiv für Musikwissenschaft*, Vol. 30 (1973)

Cone, Edward T. 'Analysis Today'. *The Musical Quarterly*, Vol. 46, No. 2 (April 1960)

Deppert, Heinrich. *Studien zur Kompositionstechnik im instrumentalen Spätwerk Anton Weberns*. Darmstadt: Edition Tonos, 1972

Döhl, Friedhelm. *Weberns Beitrag zur Stilwende der Neuen Musik*. Berliner Musikwissenschaftliche Arbeiten, ed. Carl Dahlhaus and Rudolf Stephan, Vol. 12. Munich and Salzburg: Musikverlag Emil Katzbichler, 1976

Eimert, Herbert. 'Interval Proportions'. *Die Reihe*, Vol. 2 [for full reference see *Die Reihe*]

Fennelly, Brian. 'Structure and Process in Webern's Opus 22'. *Journal of Music Theory*, Vol. 10, No. 2 (Fall 1966)

Forte, Allen. *The Structure of Atonal Music*. New Haven: Yale University Press, 1973

Goldthwaite, Scott. 'Historical Awareness in Anton Webern's *Symphony*, Op. 21'. In *Essays in Musicology – In Honour of Dragan Plamenac on his 70th Birthday*, ed. Gustave Reese and R. J. Snow. Pittsburgh: University of Pittsburgh Press, 1969

Graziano, John. 'Serial Procedures in Schoenberg's Opus 23'. *Current Musicology*, No. 13 (1972)

Gruhn, Wilfried. 'Reienform und Werkgestalt bei Anton Webern (Die Variationen der Sinfonie op. 21)'. *Zeitschrift für Musiktheorie*, Vol. 2, No. 2 (1971)

Hartwell, Robin. 'Duration and Mental Arithmetic: The First Movement of Webern's First Cantata'. *Perspectives of New Music*, Vol. 23, No. 1 (Fall/Winter 1984)

Hasty, Christopher F. 'Rhythm in Post-Tonal Music: Preliminary Questions of Duration and Motion'. *Journal of Music Theory*, Vol. 25, No. 2 (Fall 1981)
  'Composition and Context in Twelve-Note Music of Anton Webern'. *Music Analysis*, Vol. 7, No. 3 (October 1988)

Hitchcock, H. Wiley. 'A Footnote on Webern's Variations'. *Perspectives of New Music*, Vol. 8, No. 2 (Spring/Summer 1970)

Jones, James Rives. 'Some Aspects of Rhythm and Meter in Webern's Opus 27'. *Perspectives of New Music*, Vol. 7, No. 1 (Fall/Winter 1968)

Klammer, Armin. 'Webern's Piano Variations, Op. 27, 3rd Movement'. *Die Reihe*, Vol. 2 [for full reference see *Die Reihe*]

Klemm, Eberhardt. 'Symmetrien im Chorsatz von Anton Webern'. *Deutsches Jahrbuch der Musikwissenschaft*, Vol. 11 (1966)

Kolneder, Walter. *Anton Webern: An Introduction to His Works*, trans. Humphrey Searle. Berkeley and Los Angeles: University of California Press, 1968

Kramer, Jonathan. 'The Row as Structural Background and Audible Foreground: The First Movement of Webern's First Cantata'. *Journal of Music Theory*, Vol. 15 (1971)

Leibowitz, René. *Schoenberg and His School*, trans. Dika Newlin. New York: Philosophical Library, 1948

Lewin, David. 'A Metrical Problem in Webern's Op. 27'. *Journal of Music Theory*, Vol. 6, No. 1 (1962)

Ligeti, György. 'Über die Harmonik in Weberns erster Kantate', *Darmstädter Beiträge zur Neuen Musik*, Vol. 3 (1960)

Moldenhauer, Hans and Rosaleen. *Anton von Webern: A Chronicle of His Life and Work*. New York: Alfred A. Knopf, 1979

Nelson, Robert U. 'Webern's Path to the Serial Variation', *Perspectives of New Music*, Vol. 7, No. 2 (Spring/Summer 1969)

456

Ogdon, Wilbur. 'A Webern Analysis'. *Journal of Music Theory*, Vol. 6, No. 1 (1962)

Perle, George. *Serial Composition and Atonality*. London: Faber and Faber, 1962
  'Webern's Twelve-Tone Sketches'. *The Musical Quarterly*, Vol. 57, No. 1 (January 1971)

Phipps, Graham H. 'Tonality in Webern's Cantata I'. *Music Analysis*, Vol. 3, No. 2 (July 1984)

Reich, Willi, ed. *Anton Webern: Weg und Gestalt*. Zurich: der Arche, 1961

Reid, John W. 'Properties of the Set Explored in Webern's Variations, Op. 30'. *Perspectives of New Music*, Vol. 12, No. 2 (Spring/Summer 1974)

Die Reihe, Vol. 2 [Webern issue], ed. Herbert Eimert and Karlheinz Stockhausen. Vienna: Universal Edition, 1955. English edn, trans. Leo Black and Eric Smith. Bryn Mawr: Theodore Presser Co., 1959

Riley, Howard. 'A Study in Constructivist Procedures: Webern's "Variations for Piano", Op. 27, First Movement'. *Music Review*, Vol. 27, No. 3 (August 1966)

Rochberg, George. 'Webern's Search for Harmonic Identity'. *Journal of Music Theory*, Vol. 6, No. 1 (1962)

Rognoni, Luigi. *La scuola musicale di Vienna: Espressionismo e dodecafonio*. Turin: Giulio Einaudi, 1966. English edn, *The Second Vienna School: Expressionism and Dodecaphony*, trans. Robert W. Mann. London: John Calder, 1977

Saturen, David. 'Symmetrical Relationships in Webern's First Cantata'. *Perspectives of New Music*, Vol. 6, No. 1 (Fall/Winter 1967)

Schnebel, Dieter. *Die Variationen für Klavier op. 27*. 1952; first published 1972. Reprinted in *Musik-Konzepte: Sonderband Anton Webern II*. Vienna: Universal Edition, November 1984

Schoenberg, Arnold. 'Composition with Twelve Tones (2)'. In *Style and Idea*, ed. Leonard Stein, trans. Leo Black. London: Faber and Faber, 1975

Smalley, Roger. 'Webern's Sketches'. *Tempo*, Nos. 112–14 (March, June, September 1975)

Smith, Leland. 'Composition and Precomposition in the Music of Webern'. In *Anton von Webern Perspectives*, ed. Hans Moldenhauer and Demar Irvine. Seattle and London: University of Washington Press, 1966

Spinner, Leopold. 'The Abolition of Thematicism and the Structural Meaning of the Method of Twelve-Tone Composition'. *Tempo*, No. 146 (September 1983)
  'Analysis of a Period: Concerto for 9 Instruments, Op. 24, Second Movement'. *Die Reihe*, Vol. 2 [for full reference see *Die Reihe*]
  'Anton Weberns Kantate Nr. 2, Opus 31: Die Formprinzipien der kanonischen Darstellung (Analyse des vierten Satzes)'. *Schweizerische Musikzeitung*, Vol. 101, No. 5 (September/October 1961)

Stadlen, Peter. 'Serialism Reconsidered'. *The Score*, No. 22 (February 1958)

Starr, Mark. 'Webern's Palindrome'. *Perspectives of New Music*, Vol. 8, No. 2 (Spring/Summer 1970)

Stockhausen, Karlheinz. 'Weberns Konzert für 9 Instrumente Op. 24 – Analyse des ersten Satzes'. *Melos*, Vol. 20, No. 12 (December 1953)
  'Structure and Experiential Time'. *Die Reihe*, Vol. 2 [for full reference see *Die Reihe*]

Stroh, Wolfgang Martin. *Historische Legitimation als kompositorisches Problem.* Göppinger Akademische Beiträge, ed. Ulrich Müller, Franz Hundsnurscher and K. Werner Jauss, No. 63. Göppingen: Verlag Alfred Kümmerle, 1973

    Webern: Symphonie op. 21. Meisterwerke der Musik, ed. Ernst Ludwig Waeltner, Vol. 11. Munich: Wilhelm Fink Verlag, 1975

Todd, R. Larry. 'The Genesis of Webern's Opus 32'. *The Musical Quarterly*, Vol. 64, No. 4 (October 1980)

Wason, Robert. 'Webern's *Variations for Piano*, Op. 27: Musical Structure and the Performance Score.' *Integral: The Journal of Applied Musical Thought*, Vol. 1 (1987)

Westergaard, Peter. 'Some Problems in Rhythmic Theory and Analysis'. *Perspectives in New Music*, Vol. 1, No. 1 (Fall/Winter 1962)

    'Webern and "Total Organization": An Analysis of the Second Movement of Piano Variations, Op. 27'. *Perspectives of New Music*, Vol. 1, No. 2 (Spring 1963)

Whittall, Arnold. 'On Summarizing Webern'. *Soundings*, No. 1 (1970).

    'Webern and Atonality: The Path from the Old Aesthetic'. *Musical Times*, Vol. 124 (December 1983)

    'Webern and Multiple Meaning'. *Music Analysis*, Vol. 6, No. 3 (October 1987)

Wildgans, Friedrich. *Anton Webern: eine Studie.* Tübingen: Rainer Wunderlich Verlag, 1967

Willam, Wolfgang. *Anton Weberns II. Kantate op. 31.* Beiträge zur Musikforschung, ed. Reinhold Hammerstein and Wilhelm Seidel, Vol. 8. Munich and Salzburg: Musikverlag Emil Katzbichler, 1980

Wintle, Christopher. 'Analysis and Performance: Webern's Op. 24/ii'. *Music Analysis*, Vol. 1, No. 1 (March 1982)

Index

459

Index